THE UNIVERSITY OF
WINCHESTER

Martial Rose Library
Tel: 01962 827306

To be returned on or before the day marked above, subject to recall.

Software Modeling and Design

This book provides all you need to know for modeling and design of software applications, from use cases to software architectures in UML. It shows you how to apply the COMET UML-based modeling and design method to real-world problems. The author describes architectural patterns for various architectures, such as broker, discovery, and transaction patterns for service-oriented architectures, and layered patterns for software product line architectures, and addresses software quality attributes, including maintainability, modifiability, testability, traceability, scalability, reusability, performance, availability, and security.

Complete case studies illustrate design issues for different software architectures: a banking system for client/server architectures, an online shopping system for service-oriented architectures, an emergency monitoring system for component-based software architectures, and an automated guided vehicle system for real-time software architectures.

Organized as an introduction followed by several self-contained chapters, the book is perfect for senior undergraduate or graduate courses in software engineering and for experienced software engineers who want a quick reference at each stage of the analysis, design, and development of large-scale software systems.

Hassan Gomaa is Professor of Computer Science and Software Engineering at George Mason University. Gomaa has more than thirty years' experience in software engineering, in both industry and academia. He has published more than 170 technical papers and is the author of three books: *Designing Software Product Lines with UML; Designing Concurrent, Distributed, and Real-Time Applications with UML*; and *Software Design Methods for Concurrent and Real-Time Systems*.

SOFTWARE MODELING AND DESIGN

UML, Use Cases, Patterns, and Software Architectures

Hassan Gomaa

George Mason University, Fairfax, Virginia

CAMBRIDGE
UNIVERSITY PRESS

CAMBRIDGE UNIVERSITY PRESS
Cambridge, New York, Melbourne, Madrid, Cape Town,
Singapore, São Paulo, Delhi, Tokyo, Mexico City

Cambridge University Press
32 Avenue of the Americas, New York, NY 10013-2473, USA

www.cambridge.org
Information on this title: www.cambridge.org/9780521764148

First published 2011

Printed in the United States of America

A catalog record for this publication is available from the British Library.

Library of Congress Cataloging in Publication data

Gomaa, Hassan.
Software modeling and design : UML, use cases, patterns, and software architectures /
Hassan Gomaa.
   p.   cm.
Includes bibliographical references and index.
ISBN 978-0-521-76414-8 (hardback)
1. Computer software – Development.   2. Software architecture.   3. Computer simulation.   I. Title.
QA76.76.D47G6522   2011
003′.3–dc22   2010049584

ISBN 978-0-521-76414-8 Hardback

To Gill, William and Neela, Alex,
Amanda and Neil, and Edward

Contents

Preface

OVERVIEW

This book describes a use case–driven UML-based method for the modeling and design of software architectures, including object-oriented software architectures, client/server software architectures, service-oriented architectures, component-based software architectures, concurrent and real-time software architectures, and software product line architectures. The book provides a unified approach to designing software architectures and describes the special considerations for each category of software architecture. In addition, there are four case studies, a client/server banking system, a service-oriented architecture for an online shopping system, a distributed component-based emergency monitoring system, and a real-time automated guided vehicle system.

This book describes a UML-based software modeling and design method called COMET (Collaborative Object Modeling and Architectural Design Method). COMET is a highly iterative object-oriented software development method that addresses the requirements, analysis, and design modeling phases of the object-oriented development life cycle.

The book is intended to appeal to readers who wish to design software architectures using a systematic UML-based method that starts from requirements modeling with use cases, through static and dynamic modeling, to software design based on architectural design patterns.

WHAT THIS BOOK PROVIDES

Various textbooks on the market describe object-oriented analysis and design concepts and methods. This book addresses the specific needs of designing software architectures. It addresses UML-based design of software architectures, starting with use cases for requirements modeling, static modeling with class diagrams, and dynamic modeling with object interaction analysis and state machine modeling, through software design with architectural design patterns. All examples are described using the UML 2 notation, the latest version of the standard. In particular, this book:

- Provides a comprehensive treatment of the application of the UML-based object-oriented concepts to requirements modeling, analysis modeling, and design modeling. Requirements modeling addresses use case modeling to describe functional requirements with extensions to describe nonfunctional requirements. Analysis modeling addresses static modeling and dynamic modeling (both interaction and state machine modeling). Design modeling addresses important architectural issues, including a systematic approach for integrating use case–based interaction diagrams into an initial software architecture and applying architectural and design patterns for designing software architectures.
- Provides a common approach for requirements and analysis modeling and then addresses specific design issues (in a separate chapter for each category of software architecture) for designing the software architecture for object-oriented software systems, client/server systems, service-oriented systems, component-based systems, real-time systems, and software product lines.
- Describes how software architectures are designed by first considering software architectural patterns relevant for that category of software architecture, such as client/service patterns for client/server and component-based software architecture; brokering, discovery, and transaction patterns for service-oriented architectures; real-time control patterns for real-time software architecture; and layered patterns for software product line architectures.
- Describes software quality attributes, which can have a profound effect on the quality of a software product. Many of these attributes can be addressed and evaluated at the time the software architecture is developed. The software quality attributes covered include maintainability, modifiability, testability, traceability, scalability, reusability, performance, availability, and security.
- Presents four detailed case studies. Case studies are presented by software architecture area, including a banking system for client/server architectures, an online shopping system for service-oriented architecture, an emergency monitoring system for component-based software architecture, and an automated guided vehicle system for the real-time software architecture.
- Appendices include a glossary, a bibliography, and a catalog of architectural design patterns. There is also be an appendix on teaching considerations for teaching academic and industrial courses based on this book. Exercises follow most chapters.

INTENDED AUDIENCE

This book is intended for both academic and professional audiences. The academic audience includes senior undergraduate- and graduate-level students in computer science and software engineering, as well as researchers in the field. The professional audience includes analysts, software architects, software designers, programmers, project leaders, technical managers, program managers, and quality-assurance specialists who are involved in the analysis, design, and development of large-scale software systems in industry and government.

WAYS TO READ THIS BOOK

This book may be read in various ways. It can be read in the order in which it is presented, in which case Chapters 1 through 4 provide introductory concepts; Chapter 5 provides an overview of the COMET/UML software modeling and design method; Chapters 6 through 20 provide an in-depth treatment of software modeling and design; and Chapters 21 through 24 provide detailed case studies.

Alternatively, some readers may wish to skip some chapters, depending on their level of familiarity with the topics discussed. Chapters 1 through 4 are introductory and may be skipped by experienced readers. Readers familiar with software design concepts may skip Chapter 4. Readers particularly interested in software modeling and design can proceed directly to the description of COMET/UML, starting in Chapter 5. Readers who are not familiar with UML, or who are interested in finding out about the changes introduced by UML 2, can read Chapter 2 in conjunction with Chapters 5 through 20.

Experienced software designers may also use this book as a reference, referring to various chapters as their projects reach a particular stage of the requirements, analysis, or design process. Each chapter is relatively self-contained. For example, at different times one might refer to Chapter 6 for a description of use cases, to Chapter 7 for a discussion of static modeling, and to Chapter 9 for a description of dynamic interaction modeling. Chapter 10 can be referenced for designing state machines; Chapter 12 and Appendix A for software architectural patterns; Chapter 14 for object-oriented software architectures; and Chapter 15 for designing a relational database from a static model. Chapter 16 can be consulted for service-oriented architectures; Chapter 17 for distributed component-based software design; Chapter 18 for real-time design; and Chapter 19 for software product line design. One can also improve one's understanding of how to use the COMET/UML method by reading the case studies, because each case study explains the decisions made at each step of the requirements, analysis, and design modeling processes in the design of a real-world application.

Hassan Gomaa
George Mason University
December 2010
Email: hgomaa@gmu.edu
Web: http://mason.gmu.edu/~hgomaa

Annotated Table of Contents

Chapter 5: Overview of Software Modeling and Design Method

This chapter provides an overview of the software modeling and design method, including requirements modeling, analysis modeling, and design modeling. An overview of the different kinds of software architectures addressed in this textbook is given.

PART II: SOFTWARE MODELING

Chapter 6: Use Case Modeling

This chapter starts with an overview of requirements analysis and specification. It then goes on to describe the use case modeling approach to developing requirements. This is followed by an approach for developing use cases. The chapter covers use cases, actors, identifying use cases, documenting use cases, and use case relationships. An introduction is given to activity diagrams for precise modeling of individual use cases. Use cases are extended to document nonfunctional requirements.

Chapter 7: Static Modeling

This chapter describes static modeling concepts, including associations, whole/part relationships (composition and aggregation), and generalization/specialization relationships. Special topics include modeling the boundary of the system and modeling entity classes, which are information-intensive classes.

Chapter 8: Object and Class Structuring

This chapter describes the categorization of application classes, or the role the class plays in the application. The major categories covered are boundary objects, entity objects, control objects, and application logic objects. This chapter also describes the corresponding behavior pattern for each category of object.

Chapter 9: Dynamic Interaction Modeling

This chapter describes dynamic interaction modeling concepts. Interaction (sequence or communication) diagrams are developed for each use case, including the main scenario and alternative scenarios. It also describes how to develop an interaction model starting from the use case.

Chapter 10: Finite State Machines

This chapter describes finite state machine modeling concepts. In particular, a state-dependent control class needs to be modeled with a finite state machine and depicted as a statechart. This chapter covers events, states, conditions, actions, entry and exit actions, composite states, and sequential and orthogonal states.

Chapter 11: State-Dependent Dynamic Interaction Modeling

This chapter describes dynamic interaction modeling for state-dependent object interactions. It describes how state machines and interaction diagrams relate to each other and how to make them consistent with each other.

PART III: ARCHITECTURAL DESIGN

Chapter 12: Overview of Software Architectures

This chapter introduces software architecture concepts. Multiple views of a software architecture and an overview of software architectural patterns (architectural structure and communication patterns) are presented. A template for software architectural patterns is provided, and interface design is introduced and discussed.

Chapter 13: Software Subsystem Architectural Design

This chapter presents issues in software architectural design, including the transition from analysis to architectural design, separation of concerns in subsystem design, subsystem structuring criteria, and the design of subsystem message communication interfaces.

Chapter 14: Designing Object-Oriented Software Architectures

This chapter describes object-oriented design of sequential software architectures, particularly design using the concepts of information hiding, classes, and inheritance. In class interface design, the designer of the class needs to decide what information should be hidden and what information should be revealed in the class interface, which consists of the operations provided by the class. This chapter also discusses design by contract and sequential class design, which includes the design of data abstraction classes, state machine classes, graphical user interface classes, and business logic classes. Detailed design of classes is also considered.

Chapter 15: Designing Client/Server Software Architectures

The design of clients and servers is described in this chapter. It also includes a discussion of client/service patterns (structural and behavioral), sequential and concurrent services, and mapping a static model to a relational database, which includes the design of database wrappers and logical relational database design.

Chapter 16: Designing Service-Oriented Architectures

This chapter describes the characteristics of service-oriented architectures. It discusses Web services and service patterns, including registration, brokering, and discovery patterns. It then describes transaction patterns and transaction design, including atomic transactions, two-phase commit protocol, compound transactions, and long-living transactions. This chapter also presents information on how to design services for reuse, how to build applications that reuse services, and service coordination.

Chapter 17: Designing Component-Based Software Architectures

This chapter describes distributed component-based software architectural design. The design of component interfaces (provided and required) is described. The chapter also discusses how component-based software architectures can be depicted with the structured class and composite structure diagram notation introduced in UML 2, which allows components, ports, connectors, and provided and required interfaces to be depicted.

Chapter 18: Designing Concurrent and Real-Time Software Architectures

This chapter considers the characteristics of embedded real-time systems. It discusses concurrency and control; control patterns for real-time systems; concurrent task structuring, including event-driven tasks, periodic tasks, and demand-driven tasks; and design of task interfaces, including message communication, event synchronization, and communication through passive objects.

Chapter 19: Designing Software Product Line Architectures

This chapter presents characteristics of software product lines – modeling commonality and variability for a family of systems. Also discussed are feature modeling, variability modeling, software product line architectures, and application engineering. Variability modeling in use cases, static and dynamic models, and software architectures is also considered.

Chapter 20: Software Quality Attributes

This chapter describes software quality attributes and how they are used to evaluate the quality of the software architecture. Software quality attributes include maintainability, modifiability, traceability, usability, reusability, testability, performance, and security. The chapter also presents a discussion of how the architectural design method supports the software quality attributes.

PART IV: CASE STUDIES

Each case study provides a detailed description of how to apply the concepts and methods described so far to the design of different kinds of software architecture: client/server software architecture, service-oriented architecture, component-based software architecture, and real-time software architecture. In each case study, the rationale for the modeling and design decisions is discussed.

Chapter 21: Client/Server Software Architecture Case Study: Banking System

This chapter describes how the software modeling and design method is applied to the design of a client/server system that consists of a bank server and several ATM clients. The design of the ATM client is also an example of concurrent software design. The design of the banking service is an example of a sequential object-oriented design.

Chapter 22: Service-Oriented Architecture Case Study: Online Shopping System

This chapter describes how the software modeling and design method is applied to the design of a service-oriented architecture for an online shopping system, which consists of multiple services invoked by multiple clients and needs brokering, discovery, and service coordination.

Chapter 23: Component-Based Software Architecture Case Study: Emergency Monitoring System

This chapter describes how the software modeling and design method is applied to the design of a component-based software architecture, an emergency monitoring system, in which software components can be assigned to the hardware configuration at deployment time.

Chapter 24: Real-Time Software Architecture Case Study: Automated Guided Vehicle System

This chapter describes how the software modeling and design method is applied to the design of a real-time automated guided vehicle system (consisting of several concurrent tasks), which is part of a factory automation system of systems.

Appendix A: Catalog of Software Architectural Patterns

The software architectural structure, communication, and transaction patterns used in this textbook are documented alphabetically in a common template for easy reference.

Appendix B: Teaching Considerations

This appendix describes approaches for teaching academic and industrial courses based on this textbook.

Acknowledgments

I gratefully acknowledge the reviewers of earlier drafts of the manuscript for their constructive comments, including Rob Pettit, Kevin Mills, Bran Selic, and the anonymous reviewers. I am very grateful to the students in my software design and reusable software architecture courses at George Mason University for their enthusiasm, dedication, and valuable feedback. Many thanks are also due to Koji Hashimoto, Erika Olimpiew, Mohammad Abu-Matar, Upsorn Praphamontripong, and Sylvia Henshaw for their hard work and careful attention producing the figures. I am also very grateful to the Cambridge University Press editorial and production staff, including Heather Bergman, Lauren Cowles, David Jou, Diane Lamsback, and the production staff at Aptara, without whom this book would not have seen the light of day.

I gratefully acknowledge the permission given to me by Pearson Education, Inc., to use material from my earlier textbooks, *Designing Concurrent, Distributed, and Real-Time Applications with UML*, © 2000 Hassan Gomaa, Reproduced by permission of Pearson Education, Inc., and *Designing Software Product Lines with UML*, © 2005 Hassan Gomaa, Reproduced by permission of Pearson Education, Inc.

Last, but not least, I would like to thank my wife, Gill, for her encouragement, understanding, and support.

PART I

Overview

1

Introduction

1.1 SOFTWARE MODELING

Modeling is used in many walks of life, going back to early civilizations such as Ancient Egypt, Rome, and Greece, where modeling was used to provide small-scale plans in art and architecture (Figure 1.1). Modeling is widely used in science and engineering to provide abstractions of a system at some level of precision and detail. The model is then analyzed in order to obtain a better understanding of the system being developed. According to the Object Modeling Group (OMG), "modeling is the designing of software applications before coding."

In model-based software design and development, software modeling is used as an essential part of the software development process. Models are built and analyzed prior to the implementation of the system, and are used to direct the subsequent implementation.

A better understanding of a system can be obtained by considering it from different perspectives (also referred to as multiple views) (Gomaa 2006; Gomaa and Shin 2004), such as requirements models, static models, and dynamic models of the software system. A graphical modeling language such as UML helps in developing, understanding, and communicating the different views.

This chapter introduces object-oriented methods and notations, an overview of software modeling and architectural design, and an introduction to model-driven architecture and UML. The chapter then briefly describes the evolution of software design methods, object-oriented analysis and design methods, and concurrent, distributed, and real-time design methods.

1.2 OBJECT-ORIENTED METHODS AND THE UNIFIED MODELING LANGUAGE

Object-oriented concepts are crucial in software analysis and design because they address fundamental issues of software modifiability, adaptation, and evolution. Object-oriented methods are based on the concepts of information hiding, classes, and inheritance. Information hiding can lead to systems that are more self-contained

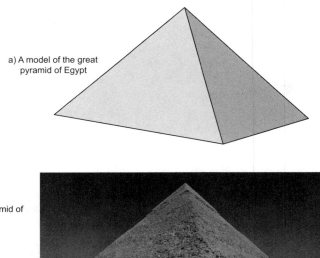

a) A model of the great
pyramid of Egypt

b) The great pyramid of
Egypt

Figure 1.1. Example of modeling and architecture

and hence are more modifiable and maintainable. Inheritance provides an approach for adapting a class in a systematic way.

With the proliferation of notations and methods for the object-oriented analysis and design of software applications, the Unified Modeling Language (UML) was developed to provide a standardized graphical language and notation for describing object-oriented models. However, because UML is methodology-independent, it needs to be used together with an object-oriented analysis and design method. Because the UML is now the standardized graphical language and notation for describing object-oriented models, this book uses the UML notation throughout.

Modern object-oriented analysis and design methods are model-based and use a combination of use case modeling, static modeling, state machine modeling, and object interaction modeling. Almost all modern object-oriented methods use the UML notation for describing software requirements, analysis, and design models (Booch, Rumbaugh, and Jacobson 2005; Fowler 2004; Rumbaugh, Booch, and Jacobson 2005).

In **use case modeling**, the functional requirements of the system are defined in terms of use cases and actors. **Static modeling** provides a structural view of the system. Classes are defined in terms of their attributes, as well as their relationships with other classes. **Dynamic modeling** provides a behavioral view of the system. The use cases are realized to show the interaction among participating objects. Object interaction diagrams are developed to show how objects communicate with each other to realize the use case. The state-dependent aspects of the system are defined with statecharts.

1.3 SOFTWARE ARCHITECTURAL DESIGN

A **software architecture** (Bass, Clements, and Kazman 2003; Shaw and Garlan 1996) separates the overall structure of the system, in terms of components and their interconnections, from the internal details of the individual components. The emphasis on components and their interconnections is sometimes referred to as *programming-in-the-large*, and the detailed design of individual components is referred to as *programming-in-the-small*.

A software architecture can be described at different levels of detail. At a high level, it can describe the decomposition of the software system into subsystems. At a lower level, it can describe the decomposition of subsystems into modules or components. In each case, the emphasis is on the external view of the subsystem/component – that is, the interfaces it provides and requires – and its interconnections with other subsystems/components.

The software quality attributes of a system should be considered when developing the software architecture. These attributes relate to how the architecture addresses important nonfunctional requirements, such as performance, security, and maintainability.

The software architecture is sometimes referred to as a high-level design. A software architecture can be described from different views, as described in Section 1.7. It is important to ensure that the architecture fulfills the software requirements, both functional (what the software has to do) and nonfunctional (how well it should do it). It is also the starting point for the detailed design and implementation, when typically the development team becomes much larger.

1.4 METHOD AND NOTATION

This section defines important terms for software design.

A **software design notation** is a means of describing a software design either graphically or textually, or both. For example, class diagrams are a graphical design notation, and pseudocode is a textual design notation. UML is a graphical notation for object-oriented software applications. A design notation suggests a particular approach for performing a design; however, it does not provide a systematic approach for producing a design.

A **software design concept** is a fundamental idea that can be applied to designing a system. For example, information hiding is a software design concept.

A **software design strategy** is an overall plan and direction for developing a design. For example, object-oriented decomposition is a software design strategy.

Software structuring criteria are heuristics or guidelines used to help a designer in structuring a software system into its components. For example, object structuring criteria provide guidelines for decomposing the system into objects.

A **software design method** is a systematic approach that describes the sequence of steps to follow in order to create a design, given the software requirements of the application. It helps a designer or design team identify the design decisions to be made, the order in which to make them, and the structuring criteria to use in making them. A design method is based on a set of design concepts, employs one or more design strategies, and documents the resulting design, using a design notation.

During a given design step, the method might provide a set of structuring criteria to help the designer in decomposing the system into its components.

The Collaborative Object Modeling and Design Method, or COMET, uses the UML notation to describe the design. COMET is based on the design concepts of information hiding, classes, inheritance, and concurrent tasks. It uses a design strategy of concurrent object design, which addresses the structuring of a software system into active and passive objects and defines the interfaces between them. It provides structuring criteria to help structure the system into objects during analysis, and additional criteria to determine the subsystems and concurrent tasks during design.

1.5 COMET: A UML-BASED SOFTWARE MODELING AND DESIGN METHOD FOR SOFTWARE APPLICATIONS

This book describes a UML-based software modeling and architectural design method called COMET. COMET is an iterative use case driven and object-oriented software development method that addresses the requirements, analysis, and design modeling phases of the software development life cycle. The functional requirements of the system are defined in terms of actors and use cases. Each use case defines a sequence of interactions between one or more actors and the system. A use case can be viewed at various levels of detail. In a *requirements* model, the functional requirements of the system are defined in terms of actors and use cases. In an *analysis* model, the use case is realized to describe the objects that participate in the use case and their interactions. In the *design* model, the software architecture is developed, addressing issues of distribution, concurrency, and information hiding.

1.6 UML AS A STANDARD

This section briefly reviews the evolution of UML into a standard modeling language and notation for describing object-oriented designs. The evolution of UML is described in detail by Kobryn (1999). UML 0.9 unified the modeling notations of Booch, Jacobson (1992), and Rumbaugh et al. (1991). This version formed the basis of a standardization effort, with the additional involvement of a diverse mix of vendors and system integrators. The standardization effort culminated in submission of the initial UML 1.0 proposal to the OMG in January 1997. After some revisions, the final UML 1.1 proposal was submitted later that year and adopted as an object modeling standard in November 1997.

The OMG maintains UML as a standard. The first adopted version of the standard was UML 1.3. There were minor revisions with UML 1.4 and 1.5. A major revision to the notation was made in 2003 with UML 2.0. The latest books on UML conform to UML 2.0, including the revised editions of Booch, Rumbaugh, and Jacobson (2005), Rumbaugh, Booch, and Jacobson (2005), Fowler (2004), Eriksson et al. (2004), and Douglass (2004). There have been minor revisions since then. The current version of the standard is referred to as UML 2.

1.6.1 Model-Driven Architecture with UML

In the OMG's view, "modeling is the designing of software applications before coding." The OMG promotes model-driven architecture as the approach in which UML models of the software architecture are developed prior to implementation. According to the OMG, UML is methodology-independent; UML is a notation for describing the results of an object-oriented analysis and design developed via the methodology of choice.

A UML model can be either a platform-independent model (PIM) or a platform-specific model (PSM). The PIM is a precise model of the software architecture before a commitment is made to a specific platform. Developing the PIM first is particularly useful because the same PIM can be mapped to different middleware platforms, such as COM, CORBA, .NET, J2EE, Web Services, or another Web platform. The approach in this book is to use the concept of model-driven architecture to develop a component-based software architecture, which is expressed as a UML platform–independent model.

1.7 MULTIPLE VIEWS OF SOFTWARE ARCHITECTURE

A software architecture can be considered from different perspectives, which are referred to as different views. Kruchten (Kruchten 1995) introduced the 4+1 view model of software architecture, in which he advocated a multiple-view modeling approach for software architectures, in which the use case view is the unifying view (the 1 view of the 4+1 views). The views are the logical view, which is a static modeling view; the process view, which is a concurrent process or task view; and the development view, which is a subsystem and component design view. Hofmeister et al. (2000) describe an industrial perspective on applied software architecture consisting of four views: a conceptual view, which describes the main design elements and the relationships between them; a code view, which consists of the source code organized into object code, libraries, and directories; a module view, which consists of subsystems and modules; and an execution view, which is a concurrent and distributed execution perspective.

In this book, we will describe and depict the different modeling views of the software architecture in UML. The views are as follows:

- **Use case view.** This view is a functional requirements view, which is an input to develop the software architecture. Each use case describes the sequence of interactions between one or more actors (external users) and the system.
- **Static view.** The architecture is depicted in terms of classes and relationships, which can be associations, whole/part relationships (compositions or aggregations), or generalization/specialization relationships. Depicted on UML class diagrams.
- **Dynamic interaction view.** This view describes the architecture in terms of objects as well as the message communication between them. This view can also be used to depict the execution sequence of specific scenarios. Depicted on UML communication diagrams.

- **Dynamic state machine view.** The internal control and sequencing of a control component can be depicted using a state machine. Depicted on UML statechart diagrams.
- **Structural component view.** The software architecture is depicted in terms of components, which are interconnected through their ports, which in turn support provided and required interfaces. Depicted on UML structured class diagrams.
- **Dynamic concurrent view.** The software architecture is viewed as concurrent components, executing on distributed nodes, and communicating by messages. Depicted on UML concurrent communication diagrams.
- **Deployment view.** This depicts a specific configuration of the distributed architecture with components assigned to hardware nodes. Depicted on UML deployment diagrams.

1.8 EVOLUTION OF SOFTWARE MODELING AND DESIGN METHODS

In the 1960s, programs were often implemented with little or no systematic requirements analysis and design. Graphical notations – in particular, flowcharts – were often used, either as a documentation tool or as a design tool for planning a detailed design prior to coding. Subroutines were originally created as a means of allowing a block of code to be shared by calling it from different parts of a program. They were soon recognized as a means of constructing modular systems and were adopted as a project management tool. A program could be divided up into modules, where each module could be developed by a separate person and implemented as a subroutine or function.

With the growth of structured programming in the early seventies, the ideas of top-down design and stepwise refinement (Dahl 1972) gained prominence as program design methods, with the goal of providing a systematic approach for structured program design. Dijkstra developed one of the first software design methods with the design of the T.H.E. operating system (Dijkstra 1968), which used a hierarchical architecture. This was the first design method to address the design of a concurrent system, namely, an operating system.

In the mid- to late 1970s, two different software design strategies gained prominence: data flow–oriented design and data structured design. The data flow oriented–design approach as used in Structured Design (see Budgen [2003] for an overview) was one of the first comprehensive and well-documented design methods to emerge. The idea was that a better understanding of the functions of the system could be obtained by considering the flow of data through the system. It provided a systematic approach for developing data flow diagrams for a system and then mapping them to structure charts. Structured Design introduced the coupling and cohesion criteria for evaluating the quality of a design. This approach emphasized functional decomposition into modules and the definition of module interfaces. The first part of Structured Design, based on data flow diagram development, was refined and extended to become a comprehensive analysis method, namely, Structured Analysis (see Budgen [2003] for an overview).

An alternative software design approach was that of data structured design. This view was that a full understanding of the problem structure is best obtained from consideration of the data structures. Thus, the emphasis is on first designing the data structures and then designing the program structures based on the data structures. The two principal design methods to use this strategy were Jackson Structured Programming (Jackson 1983) and the Warnier/Orr method.

In the database world, the concept of separating logical and physical data was key to the development of database management systems. Various approaches were advocated for the logical design of databases, including the introduction of entity-relationship modeling by Chen.

Parnas (1972) made a great contribution to software design with his advocacy of information hiding. A major problem with early systems, even in many of those designed to be modular, resulted from the widespread use of global data, which made these systems prone to error and difficult to change. Information hiding provided an approach for greatly reducing, if not eliminating, global data.

A major contribution for the design of concurrent and real-time systems came in the late 1970s with the introduction of the MASCOT notation and later the MASCOT design method. Based on a data flow approach, MASCOT formalized the way tasks communicate with each other, either through channels for message communication or through pools (information-hiding modules that encapsulate shared data structures). The data maintained by a channel or pool are accessed by a task only indirectly by calling access procedures provided by the channel or pool. The access procedures also synchronize access to the data, typically using semaphores, so that all synchronization issues are hidden from the calling task.

There was a general maturation of software design methods in the 1980s, and several system design methods were introduced. Parnas's work with the Naval Research Lab (NRL), in which he explored the use of information hiding in large-scale software design, led to the development of the Naval Research Lab Software Cost Reduction Method (Parnas, Clements, and Weiss 1984). Work on applying Structured Analysis and Structured Design to concurrent and real-time systems led to the development of Real-Time Structured Analysis and Design (RTSAD) (see Gomaa [1993] for an overview) and the Design Approach for Real-Time Systems (DARTS) (Gomaa 1984) methods.

Another software development method to emerge in the early 1980s was Jackson System Development (JSD) (Jackson 1983). JSD views a design as being a simulation of the real world and emphasizes modeling entities in the problem domain by using concurrent tasks. JSD was one of the first methods to advocate that the design should model reality first and, in this respect, predated the object-oriented analysis methods. The system is considered a simulation of the real world and is designed as a network of concurrent tasks, in which each real-world entity is modeled by means of a concurrent task. JSD also defied the then-conventional thinking of top-down design by advocating a middle-out behavioral approach to software design. This approach was a precursor of object interaction modeling, an essential aspect of modern object-oriented development.

1.9 EVOLUTION OF OBJECT-ORIENTED ANALYSIS AND DESIGN METHODS

In the mid- to late 1980s, the popularity and success of object-oriented programming led to the emergence of several object-oriented design methods, including

Booch, Wirfs-Brock, Wilkerson, and Wiener (1990), Rumbaugh et al. (1991), Shlaer and Mellor (1988, 1992), and Coad and Yourdon (1991, 1992). The emphasis in these methods was on modeling the problem domain, information hiding, and inheritance.

Parnas advocated using information hiding as a way to design modules that were more self-contained and therefore could be changed with little or no impact on other modules. Booch introduced object-oriented concepts into design initially with information hiding, in the **object-based design** of Ada-based systems and later extended this to using information hiding, classes, and inheritance in **object-oriented design**. Shlaer and Mellor (1988), Coad and Yourdon (1991), and others introduced object-oriented concepts into analysis. It is generally considered that the object-oriented approach provides a smoother transition from analysis to design than the functional approach.

Object-oriented analysis methods apply object-oriented concepts to the analysis phase of the software life cycle. The emphasis is on identifying real-world objects in the problem domain and mapping them to software objects. The initial attempt at object modeling was a static modeling approach that had its origins in information modeling, in particular, entity-relationship (E-R) modeling or, more generally, semantic data modeling, as used in logical database design. Entities in E-R modeling are information-intensive objects in the problem domain. The entities, the attributes of each entity, and relationships among the entities, are determined and depicted on E-R diagrams; the emphasis is entirely on data modeling. During design, the E-R model is mapped to a database, usually relational. In object-oriented analysis, objects in the problem domain are identified and modeled as software classes, and the attributes of each class, as well as the relationships among classes, are determined (Coad 1991; Rumbaugh et al. 1991; Shlaer and Mellor 1988).

The main difference between *classes* in static object-oriented modeling and *entity types* in E-R modeling is that classes have operations but entity types do not have operations. In addition, whereas information modeling only models persistent entities that are to be stored in a database, other problem domain classes are also modeled in static object modeling. The advanced information modeling concepts of aggregation and generalization/specialization are also used. The most widely used notation for static object modeling before UML was the Object Modeling Technique (OMT) (Rumbaugh et al. 1991).

Static object modeling was also referred to as *class modeling* and *object modeling* because it involves determining the classes to which objects belong and depicting classes and their relationships on class diagrams. The term *domain modeling* is also used to refer to static modeling of the problem domain (Rosenberg and Scott 1999; Shlaer and Mellor 1992).

The early object-oriented analysis and design methods emphasized the structural aspects of software development through information hiding and inheritance but neglected the dynamic aspects. A major contribution by the OMT (Rumbaugh et al. 1991) was to clearly demonstrate that dynamic modeling was equally important. In addition to introducing the static modeling notation for the object diagrams, OMT showed how dynamic modeling could be performed with statecharts for showing the state-dependent behavior of active objects and with sequence diagrams to show the sequence of interactions between objects. Rumbaugh et al. (1991) used statecharts, which are hierarchical state transition diagrams originally conceived by Harel (1988, 1998), for modeling active objects. Shlaer and Mellor (1992) also used state transition diagrams for modeling active objects. Booch initially used object diagrams to show the instance-level interactions among objects and later sequentially numbered the interactions to more clearly depict the communication among objects.

Jacobson (1992) introduced the use case concept for modeling the system's functional requirements. Jacobson also used the sequence diagram to describe the sequence of interactions between the objects that participate in a use case. The use case concept was fundamental to all phases of Jacobson's object-oriented software engineering life cycle. The use case concept has had a profound impact on modern object-oriented software development.

Prior to UML, there were earlier attempts to unify the various object-oriented methods and notations, including Fusion (Coleman et al. 1993) and the work of Texel and Williams (1997). The UML notation was originally developed by Booch, Jacobson, and Rumbaugh to integrate the notations for use case modeling, static modeling, and dynamic modeling (using statecharts and object interaction modeling), as described in Chapter 2. Other methodologists also contributed to the development of UML. An interesting discussion of how UML has evolved and how it is likely to evolve in the future is given in Cobryn [1999] and Selic (1999).

1.10 SURVEY OF CONCURRENT, DISTRIBUTED, AND REAL-TIME DESIGN METHODS

The Concurrent Design Approach for Real-Time Systems (CODARTS) method (Gomaa 1993) built on the strengths of earlier concurrent design, real-time design, and early object-oriented design methods by emphasizing both information-hiding module structuring and concurrent task structuring.

Octopus (Awad, Kuusela, and Ziegler 1996) is a real-time design method based on use cases, static modeling, object interactions, and statecharts. For real-time systems, ROOM (Selic, Gullekson, and Ward 1994) is an object-oriented real-time design method that is closely tied in with a **CASE** (Computer-Assisted Software Engineering) tool called ObjecTime. ROOM is based around actors, which are active objects that are modeled using a variation on statecharts called ROOMcharts. A ROOM model is capable of being executed and thus could be used as an early prototype of the system.

Buhr (1996) introduced an interesting concept called the use case map (based on the use case concept) to address the issue of dynamic modeling of large-scale systems.

For UML-based real-time software development, Douglass (2004, 1999) has provided a comprehensive description of how UML can be applied to real-time systems.

An earlier version of the COMET method for designing concurrent, real-time, and distributed applications, which is based on UML 1.3, is described in Gomaa (2000). This new textbook expands on the COMET method by basing it on UML 2, increasing the emphasis on software architecture, and addressing a wide range of software applications, including object-oriented software architectures, client/server software architectures, service-oriented architectures, component-based software architectures, concurrent and real-time software architectures, and software product line architectures.

1.11 SUMMARY

This chapter introduced object-oriented methods and notations, software architectural design, and UML. The chapter briefly described the evolution of software design methods, object-oriented analysis and design methods, and concurrent, distributed, and real-time design methods. Chapter 2 provides an overview of the UML notation. Chapter 3 describes software life cycles and methods. Chapter 4 describes software design and architecture concepts. Chapter 5 describes the use case–based software life cycle for the COMET method.

EXERCISES

Multiple-choice questions: For each question, choose one of the answers.

1. What is software modeling?
   (a) Developing models of software.
   (b) Designing software applications before coding.
   (c) Developing software diagrams.
   (d) Developing software prototypes.

2. What is the Unified Modeling Language?
   (a) A programming language for describing object-oriented models.
   (b) A diagramming tool for drawing object-oriented models.
   (c) A graphical language for describing object-oriented models.
   (d) A standardized graphical language and notation for describing object-oriented models.

3. What is a software architecture?
   (a) The software inside a building.
   (b) The structure of a client/server system.
   (c) The overall structure of a software system.
   (d) The software classes and their relationships.

4. What is a software design notation?
   (a) Notes about the software design.
   (b) A graphical or textual description of the software.
   (c) Documentation of the software.
   (d) A systematic approach for producing a design.

5. What is a software design concept?
   (a) A graphical or textual description of the software.
   (b) Documentation of the software.
   (c) A fundamental idea that can be applied to designing a system.
   (d) A systematic approach for producing a design.

6. What is a software design strategy?
   (a) A graphical or textual description of the software.
   (b) A fundamental idea that can be applied to designing a system.
   (c) A systematic approach for producing a design.
   (d) An overall plan and direction for developing a design.

7. What are software structuring criteria?
   (a) Fundamental ideas that can be applied to designing a system.
   (b) Systematic approaches for producing a design.
   (c) Guidelines used to help in structuring a software system into its components.
   (d) Overall plans for developing a design.

8. What is a software design method?
   (a) A systematic approach for producing a design.
   (b) Guidelines used to help in structuring a software system into its components.
   (c) An overall plan for developing a design.

(d) A graphical or textual description of the software.

9. What is a platform-independent model (PIM)?
   (a) A software platform before a commitment is made to a specific hardware platform.
   (b) A precise model of the software architecture before a commitment is made to a specific platform.
   (c) A precise model of the software architecture mapped to a specific platform.
   (d) A graphical or textual description of the software.

10. What is a platform-specific model (PSM)?
    (a) A specific hardware platform.
    (b) A precise model of the software architecture before a commitment is made to a specific platform.
    (c) A precise model of the software architecture mapped to a specific platform.
    (d) A graphical or textual description of the software.

2

Overview of the UML Notation

The notation used for the COMET method is the Unified Modeling Language (UML). This chapter provides a brief overview of the UML notation. The UML notation has evolved since it was first adopted as a standard in 1997. A major revision to the standard was made in 2003, so the current version of the standard is UML 2. The previous versions of the standard are referred to as UML 1.x.

The UML notation has grown substantially over the years, and it supports many diagrams. The approach taken in this book is the same as Fowler's (2004), which is to use only those parts of the UML notation that provide a distinct benefit. This chapter describes the main features of the UML notation that are particularly suited to the COMET method. The purpose of this chapter is not to be a full exposition of UML, because several detailed books exist on this topic, but rather to provide a brief overview. The main features of each of the UML diagrams used in this book are briefly described, but lesser-used features are omitted. The differences between UML 2 notation and UML 1.x notation are also briefly explained.

2.1 UML DIAGRAMS

The UML notation supports the following diagrams for application development:

- **Use case diagram**, briefly described in Section 2.2.
- **Class diagram**, briefly described in Section 2.4.
- **Object diagram** (an instance version of the class diagram), which is not used by COMET.
- **Communication diagram**, which in UML 1.x was called the *collaboration diagram*, briefly described in Section 2.5.1.
- **Sequence diagram**, briefly described in Section 2.5.2.
- **State Machine diagram**, briefly described in Section 2.6.
- **Activity diagram**, which is not used extensively by COMET, is described briefly in Chapter 6.

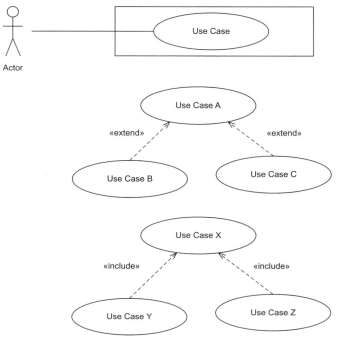

Figure 2.1. UML notation for a use case diagram

- **Composite structure diagram**, a new diagram introduced in UML 2 that is actually better suited for modeling distributed components in a UML platform–independent model. The composite structure diagram is described in Chapter 17.
- **Deployment diagram**, briefly described in Section 2.9.

Chapters 6 through 19 describe how these UML diagrams are used by the COMET method.

2.2 USE CASE DIAGRAMS

An **actor** initiates a use case. A **use case** defines a sequence of interactions between the actor and the system. An actor is depicted as a stick figure on a use case diagram. The system is depicted as a box. A use case is depicted as an ellipse inside the box. Communication associations connect actors with the use cases in which they participate. Relationships among use cases are defined by means of *include* and *extend* relationships. The notation is depicted in Figure 2.1.

2.3 CLASSES AND OBJECTS

Classes and objects are depicted as boxes in the UML notation, as shown in Figure 2.2. The class box always holds the class name. Optionally, the attributes and operations of a class may also be depicted. When all three are depicted, the top

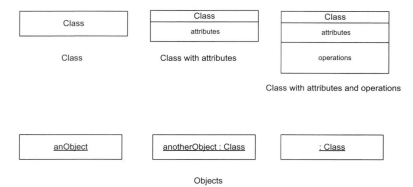

Figure 2.2. UML notation for objects and classes

compartment of the box holds the class name, the middle compartment holds the attributes, and the bottom compartment holds the operations.

To distinguish between a class (the type) and an object (an instance of the type), an object name is shown underlined. An object can be depicted in full with the object name separated by a colon from the class name – for example, anObject : Class. Optionally, the colon and class name may be omitted, leaving just the object name – for example, anObject. Another option is to omit the object name and depict just the class name after the colon, as in : Class. Classes and objects are depicted on various UML diagrams, as described in Section 2.4.

2.4 CLASS DIAGRAMS

In a **class diagram**, classes are depicted as boxes, and the static (i.e., permanent) relationships between them are depicted as lines connecting the boxes. The following three main types of relationships between classes are supported: associations, whole/part relationships, and generalization/specialization relationships, as shown in Figure 2.3. A fourth relationship, the dependency relationship, is often used to show how packages are related, as described in Section 2.7.

2.4.1 Associations

An **association** is a static, structural relationship between two or more classes. An association between two classes, which is referred to as a *binary association*, is depicted as a line joining the two class boxes, such as the line connecting the ClassA box to the ClassB box in Figure 2.3a. An association has a name and optionally a small black arrowhead to depict the direction in which the association name should be read. On each end of the association line joining the classes is the multiplicity of the association, which indicates how many instances of one class are related to an instance of the other class. Optionally, a stick arrow may also be used to depict the direction of navigability.

The **multiplicity** of an association specifies how many instances of one class may relate to a single instance of another class (see Figure 2.3a, right). The multiplicity

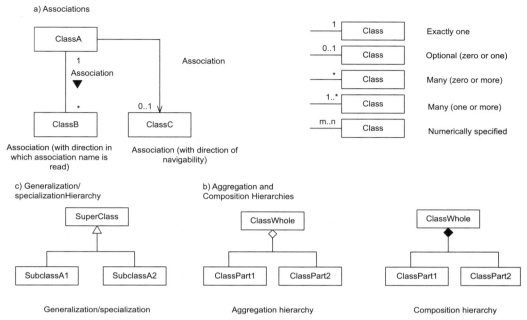

Figure 2.3. UML notation for relationships on a class diagram

of an association can be exactly one (1), optional (0..1), zero or more (*), one or more (1..*), or numerically specified (m..n), where *m* and *n* have numeric values.

2.4.2 Aggregation and Composition Hierarchies

Aggregation and composition hierarchies are **whole/part** relationships. The composition relationship (shown by a black diamond) is a stronger form of whole/part relationship than the aggregation relationship (shown by a hollow diamond). The diamond touches the aggregate or composite (Class Whole) class box (see Figure 2.3*b*).

2.4.3 Generalization/Specialization Hierarchy

A generalization/specialization hierarchy is an **inheritance** relationship. A generalization is depicted as an arrow joining the subclass (child) to the superclass (parent), with the arrowhead touching the superclass box (see Figure 2.3*c*).

2.4.4 Visibility

Visibility refers to whether an element of the class is visible from outside the class, as depicted in Figure 2.4. Depicting visibility is optional on a class diagram. **Public visibility**, denoted with a + symbol, means that the element is visible from outside the class. **Private visibility**, denoted with a – symbol, means that the element is visible only from within the class that defines it and is thus hidden from other classes. **Protected visibility**, denoted with a # symbol, means that the element is visible from within the class that defines it and within all subclasses of the class.

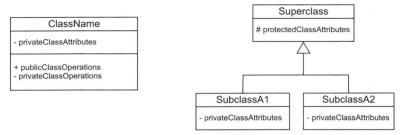

Figure 2.4. UML notation for visibility on a class diagram

2.5 INTERACTION DIAGRAMS

UML has two main kinds of interaction diagrams, which depict how objects interact: the communication diagram and the sequence diagram. On these interaction diagrams, objects are depicted in rectangular boxes. However, object names are not underlined. The main features of these diagrams are described in Sections 2.5.1 and 2.5.2.

2.5.1 Communication Diagrams

A **communication diagram**, which was called a *collaboration diagram* in UML 1.x, shows how cooperating objects dynamically interact with each other by sending and receiving messages. The diagram depicts the structural organization of the objects that interact. Objects are shown as boxes, and lines joining boxes represent object interconnection. Labeled arrows adjacent to the arcs indicate the name and direction of message transmission between objects. The sequence of messages passed between the objects is numbered. The notation for communication diagrams is illustrated in Figure 2.5. An optional iteration is indicated by an asterisk (*), which means that a message is sent more than once. An optional condition means that the message is sent only if the condition is true.

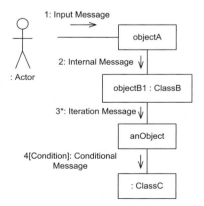

Figure 2.5. UML notation for a communication diagram

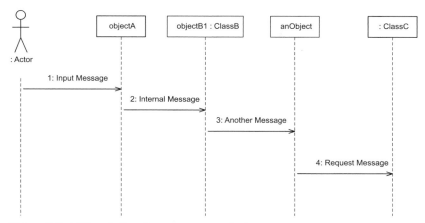

Figure 2.6. UML notation for a sequence diagram

2.5.2 Sequence Diagrams

A different way of illustrating the interaction among objects is to show them on a sequence diagram, which depicts object interaction arranged in time sequence, as shown in Figure 2.6. A **sequence diagram** is a two-dimensional diagram in which the objects participating in the interaction are depicted horizontally and the vertical dimension represents time. Starting at each object box is a vertical dashed line, referred to as a *lifeline*. Optionally, each lifeline has an activation bar (not shown), depicted as a double solid line, which shows when the object is executing.

The actor is usually shown at the extreme left of the page. Labeled horizontal arrows represent messages. Only the source and destination of the arrow are relevant. The message is sent from the source object to the destination object. Time increases from the top of the page to the bottom. The spacing between messages is not relevant.

UML 2 has substantially extended the notation for sequence diagrams to allow for loops and conditionals, as described in Chapters 9 and 11.

2.6 STATE MACHINE DIAGRAMS

In the UML notation, a state transition diagram is referred to as a **state machine diagram**. In this book, the shorter term **statechart** is generally used. In the UML notation, states are represented by rounded boxes, and transitions are represented by arcs that connect the rounded boxes, as shown in Figure 2.7. The initial state of the statechart is depicted by an arc originating from a small black circle. Optionally, a final state may be depicted by a small black circle inside a larger white circle, sometimes referred to as a *bull's-eye*. A statechart may be hierarchically decomposed such that a composite state is broken down into substates.

On the arc representing the state transition, the notation *Event [condition]/ Action* is used. The **event** causes the state transition. The optional Boolean **condition** must be true, when the event occurs, for the transition to take place. The

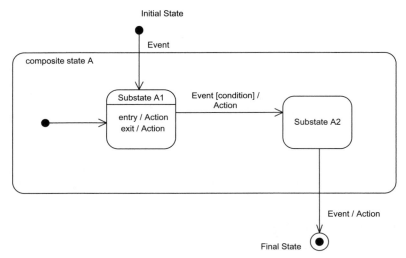

Figure 2.7. UML notation for a state machine: composite state with sequential substates

optional **action** is performed as a result of the transition. Optionally, a state may have any of the following:

- An **entry action**, performed when the state is entered
- An **exit action**, performed on exit from the state

Figure 2.7 depicts a composite state A decomposed into sequential substates A1 and A2. In this case, the statechart is in only one substate at a time; that is, first substate A1 is entered and then substate A2. Figure 2.8 depicts a composite B decomposed into orthogonal regions BC and BD. In this case, the statechart is in each of the orthogonal regions, BC and BD, at the same time. Each orthogonal

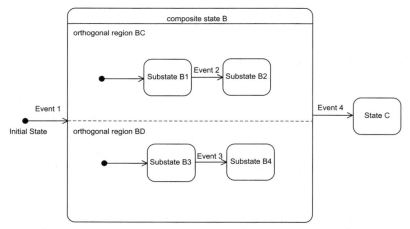

Figure 2.8. UML notation for a state machine: composite state with orthogonal substates

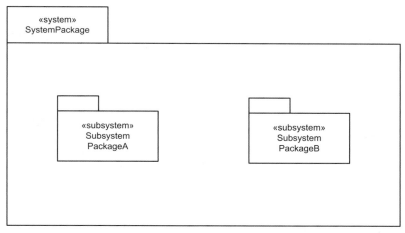

Figure 2.9. UML notation for packages

substate is further decomposed into sequential substates. Thus, when the composite B is initially entered, each of the substates B1 and B3 is also entered.

2.7 PACKAGES

In UML, a **package** is a grouping of model elements – for example, to represent a system or subsystem. A package is depicted by a folder icon, a large rectangle with a small rectangle attached on one corner, as shown in Figure 2.9. Packages may also be nested within other packages. Possible relationships between packages are dependency (shown in Figure 2.9) and generalization/specialization relationships. Packages may be used to contain classes, objects, or use cases.

2.8 CONCURRENT COMMUNICATION DIAGRAMS

In the UML notation, an active object can be used to depict a *concurrent object*, *process*, *thread*, or *task*, and is depicted by a rectangular box with two vertical parallel lines on the left- and right-hand sides. An **active object** has its own thread of control and executes concurrently with other objects. By contrast, a **passive object** has no thread of control. A passive object executes only when another object (active or passive) invokes one of its operations.

Active objects are depicted on **concurrent communication diagrams**, which depict the concurrency viewpoint of the system (Douglass 2004). On a concurrent communication diagram, a UML 2 active object is depicted as a rectangular box with two vertical parallel lines on the left- and right-hand sides; a passive object is depicted as a regular rectangular box. The UML 1.x notation for active objects – rectangular boxes with thick black lines – is no longer used. An example is given in Figure 2.10, which also shows the notation for multiobjects (useful UML 1.x notation although no longer used in UML 2), used when more than one object is instantiated from the same class.

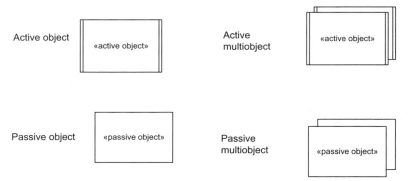

Figure 2.10. UML notation for active and passive objects

2.8.1 Message Communication on Concurrent Communication Diagrams

Message interfaces between tasks on concurrent communication diagrams are either **asynchronous** (loosely coupled) or **synchronous** (tightly coupled).

The UML notation for message communication is summarized in Figure 2.11. Figure 2.12 depicts a concurrent communication diagram, a version of the communication diagram that shows active objects (concurrent objects, processes, tasks, or threads) and the various kinds of message communication between them. For synchronous message communication, two possibilities exist: (1) synchronous message communication with reply (arrow with black arrowhead for request and dashed arrow with stick arrowhead for reply) and (2) synchronous message communication without reply (arrow with black arrowhead for request). Note that from UML 1.4 onwards, the UML notation for asynchronous communication has changed from an arrow with a half arrowhead to an arrow with a stick arrowhead. Note also that showing a simple message as an arrow with a stick arrowhead is a convention used in UML 1.3 and earlier. It is useful, however, to use simple messages during analysis modeling when no decision has yet been made about the type of message communication.

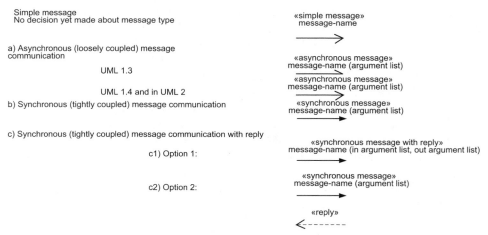

Figure 2.11. UML notation for messages

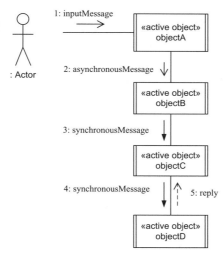

Figure 2.12. UML notation for a concurrent communication diagram

2.9 DEPLOYMENT DIAGRAMS

A **deployment diagram** shows the physical configuration of the system in terms of physical nodes and physical connections between the nodes, such as network connections. A node is shown as a cube, and the connection is shown as a line joining the nodes. A deployment diagram is essentially a class diagram that focuses on the system's nodes (Booch, Rumbaugh, and Jacobson 2005).

In this book, a node usually represents a computer node, with a constraint (see Section 2.10.3) describing how many instances of this node may exist. The physical connection has a stereotype (see Section 2.10.1) to indicate the type of connection, such as «local area network» or «wide area network». Figure 2.13 shows two examples of deployment diagrams. In the first example, nodes are connected via a wide area network (WAN); in the second, they are connected via a local area network (LAN). In the first example, the ATM Client node (which has one node for each ATM) is connected to a Bank Server that has one node. Optionally, the objects that reside at the node may be depicted in the node cube. In the second example, the network is shown as a node cube. This form of the notation is used when more than two computer nodes are connected by a network.

2.10 UML EXTENSION MECHANISMS

UML provides three mechanisms to allow the language to be extended (Booch, Rumbaugh, and Jacobson 2005; Rumbaugh, Booch, and Jacobson 2005). These are stereotypes, tagged values, and constraints.

2.10.1 Stereotypes

A **stereotype** defines a new building block that is derived from an existing UML modeling element but tailored to the modeler's problem (Booch,

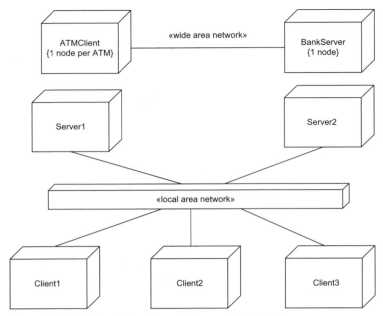

Figure 2.13. UML notation for a deployment diagram

Rumbaugh, and Jacobson 2005). This book makes extensive use of stereotypes. Several standard stereotypes are defined in UML. In addition, a modeler may define new stereotypes. This chapter includes several examples of stereotypes, both standard and COMET-specific. Stereotypes are indicated by guillemets (« »).

Figure 2.9 shows the stereotypes «system» and «subsystem» to distinguish between two different kinds of packages. Figure 2.11 uses stereotypes to distinguish among different kinds of messages.

In UML 1.3, a UML modeling element could be depicted only with one stereotype. However, UML 1.4 onward extended the stereotype concept to allow a modeling element to be depicted by more than one stereotype. Therefore, different, possibly orthogonal, characteristics of a modeling element can now be depicted with different stereotypes. The COMET method takes advantage of this additional functionality.

The UML stereotype notation allows a modeler to tailor a UML modeling element to a specific problem. In UML, stereotypes are enclosed in guillemets usually within the modeling element (e.g., class or object), as depicted in Figure 2.14a. However, UML also allows stereotypes to be depicted as symbols. One of the most common such representations was introduced by Jacobson (1992) and is used in the Unified Software Development Process (USDP) (Jacobson, Booch, and Rumbaugh 1999). Stereotypes are used to represent «entity» classes, «boundary» classes, and «control» classes. Figure 2.14b depicts the Process Plan «entity» class, the Elevator Control «control» class, and the Sensor Interface «boundary» class using the USDP's stereotype symbols.

Alternative a (standard UML notation for depicting stereotypes):

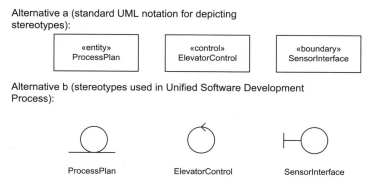

Alternative b (stereotypes used in Unified Software Development Process):

Figure 2.14. Alternative notations for UML stereotypes

2.10.2 Tagged Values

A **tagged value** extends the properties of a UML building block (Booch, Rumbaugh, and Jacobson 2005), thereby adding new information. A tagged value is enclosed in braces in the form {tag = value}. Commas separate additional tagged values. For example, a class may be depicted with the tagged values {version = 1.0, author = Gill}, as shown in Figure 2.15.

2.10.3 Constraints

A **constraint** specifies a condition that must be true. In UML, a constraint is an extension of the semantics of a UML element to allow the addition of new rules or modifications to existing rules (Booch, Rumbaugh, and Jacobson 2005). For example, for the Account class depicted in Figure 2.15, the constraint on the attribute balance is that the balance can never be negative, depicted as {balance >=0}. Optionally, UML provides the Object Constraint Language (Warmer and Kleppe 1999) for expressing constraints.

2.11 CONVENTIONS USED IN THIS BOOK

For improved readability, the conventions used for depicting names of classes, objects, and so on in the figures are sometimes different from the conventions used for the same names in the text. In the figures, examples are shown in Times Roman

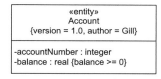

Figure 2.15. UML notation for tagged values and constraints

font. In the body of the text, however, examples are shown in a different font to distinguish them from the regular Times Roman font. Some specific additional conventions used in the book vary depending on the phase of the project. For example, the conventions for capitalization are different in the analysis model (which is less formal) than in the design model (which is more formal).

2.11.1 Requirements Modeling

In both figures and text, use cases are shown with an uppercase initial letter and spaces in multiword names – for example, Withdraw Funds.

2.11.2 Analysis Modeling

The naming conventions for the analysis model are as follows.

Classes

Classes are shown with an uppercase initial letter. In the figures, there are no spaces in multiword names – for example, CheckingAccount. In the text, however, spacing is introduced to improve the readability – for example, Checking Account.

Attributes are shown with a lowercase initial letter – for example, balance. For multiword attributes, there are no spaces between the words in figures, but spaces are introduced in the text. The first word of the multiword name has an initial lowercase letter; subsequent words have an initial uppercase letter – for example, accountNumber in figures, and account Number in text.

The type of the attribute has an initial uppercase letter – for example, Boolean, Integer, or Real.

Objects

Objects may be depicted in various ways, as described next:

- **An individual named object.** In this case, the first letter of the first word is lowercase, and subsequent words have an uppercase first letter. In figures, the objects appear as, for example, aCheckingAccount and anotherCheckingAccount. In the text, these objects appear as a Checking Account and another Checking Account.
- **An individual unnamed object.** Some objects are shown in the figures as class instances without a given object name – for example, : CheckingAccount. In the text, this object is referred to as Checking Account. For improved readability, the colon is removed, and a space is introduced between the individual words of a multiword name.

This means that, depending on how the object is depicted in a figure, it will appear in the text sometimes with a first word in which the initial letter is uppercase and sometimes with a first word in which the initial letter is lowercase.

Messages

In the analysis model, messages are always depicted as simple messages (see Figure 2.11 and Section 2.8.1) because no decision has yet been made about the message type. Messages are depicted with an uppercase initial letter. Multiword messages are shown with spaces in both figures and text – for example, Simple Message Name.

Statecharts

In both figures and text, states, events, conditions, actions, and activities are all shown with initial letter uppercase and spaces in multiword names – for example, the state Waiting for PIN, the event Cash Dispensed, and the action Dispense Cash.

2.11.3 Design Modeling

The naming conventions for the design model are as follows.

Active and Passive Classes

The naming conventions for active classes (concurrent classes) and passive classes are the same as for classes in the analysis model (see Section 2.11.2).

Active and Passive Objects

The naming conventions for active objects (concurrent objects) and passive objects are the same as for objects in the analysis model (see Section 2.11.2).

Messages

In the design model, the first letter of the first word of the message is lowercase, and subsequent words have an uppercase first letter. In both the figures and text, there is no space between words, as in alarmMessage.

Message parameters are shown with a lowercase initial letter – for example, speed. For multiword attributes, there are no spaces between the words in both the figures and text. The first word of the multiword name has a lowercase initial letter, and subsequent words have an uppercase initial letter – for example, cumulativeDistance– in both figures and text.

Operations

The naming conventions for operations (also known as methods) follow the conventions for messages in both figures and text. Thus, the first letter of the first word of both the operation and the parameter is lowercase, and subsequent words have an uppercase first letter. There is no space between words – for example, validatePassword (userPassword).

2.12 SUMMARY

This chapter briefly described the main features of the UML notation and the main characteristics of the UML diagrams used in this book.

For further reading on UML 2 notation, Fowler (2004) and Ambler (2005) provide introductory material. More detailed information can be found in Booch,

Rumbaugh, and Jacobson (2005) and Eriksson et al. (2004). A comprehensive and detailed reference to UML is Rumbaugh, Booch, and Jacobson (2005).

EXERCISES

Multiple-choice questions: For each question, choose one of the answers.

1. How is an actor depicted on a use case diagram?
   (a) An oval
   (b) A stick figure
   (c) A box
   (d) A dashed line

2. How is a use case depicted on a use case diagram?
   (a) An oval
   (b) A stick figure
   (c) A box
   (d) A dashed line

3. How is a class depicted on a class diagram?
   (a) A box with one compartment
   (b) A box with one or two compartments
   (c) A box with one, two, or three compartments
   (d) An oval

4. How is an association depicted on a class diagram?
   (a) A solid line joining two class boxes
   (b) A dashed line joining two class boxes
   (c) A diamond touching the upper class box
   (d) An arrowhead touching the upper class box

5. How is public visibility depicted for a class element on a class diagram?
   (a) + sign
   (b) − sign
   (c) # sign
   (d) *sign

6. What are the two kinds of UML interaction diagrams?
   (a) Class diagram and sequence diagram
   (b) Sequence diagram and communication diagram
   (c) Class diagram and communication diagram
   (d) Statechart and communication diagram

7. What does an interaction diagram depict?
   (a) Objects and links
   (b) Classes and relationships
   (c) Objects and messages
   (d) States and events

8. What does a statechart diagram depict?
   (a) Objects and links
   (b) Classes and relationships
   (c) Objects and messages
   (d) States and events

9. What is a UML package?
   (a) A box
   (b) A grouping of classes
   (c) A grouping of use cases
   (d) A grouping of model elements

10. What does a deployment diagram depict?
   (a) The physical configuration of the system in terms of physical classes and physical connections between the classes
   (b) The physical configuration of the system in terms of physical objects and physical connections between the objects
   (c) The physical configuration of the system in terms of physical nodes and physical connections between the nodes
   (d) The physical configuration of the system in terms of physical computers and physical networks between the computers

3

Software Life Cycle Models and Processes

A software life cycle is a phased approach to developing software, with specific deliverables and milestones within each phase. A software life cycle model is an abstraction of the software development process, which is convenient to use for planning purposes. This chapter takes a software life cycle perspective on software development. Different software life cycle models (also referred to as software process models), including the spiral model and the Unified Software Development Process, are briefly described and compared. The roles of design verification and validation and of software testing are discussed.

3.1 SOFTWARE LIFE CYCLE MODELS

The waterfall model was the earliest software life cycle model to be widely used. This section starts with an overview of the waterfall model. It then outlines alternative software life cycle models that have since been developed to overcome some of the limitations of the waterfall model. These are the throwaway prototyping life cycle model, the incremental development life cycle model (also referred to as evolutionary prototyping), the spiral model, and the Unified Software Development Process.

3.1.1 Waterfall Life Cycle Model

Since the 1960s, the cost of developing software has grown steadily and the cost of developing and purchasing hardware has rapidly decreased. Furthermore, software now typically costs eighty percent of a total project's budget, whereas in the early days of software development, the hardware was by far the largest project cost (Boehm 2006).

The problems involved in developing software were not clearly understood in the 1960s. In the late sixties, it was realized that a software crisis existed. The term *software engineering* was coined to refer to the management and technical methods, procedures, and tools required to effectively develop a large-scale software system. With the application of software engineering concepts, many large-scale software systems have been developed using a software life cycle. The first widely used software life cycle model, often referred to as the waterfall model, is shown in Figure 3.1. It is generally considered the conventional or "classical" software life cycle. The waterfall model is an idealized process model in which each phase is completed before the next phase is started, and a project moves from one phase to the next without iteration or overlap.

3.1.2 Limitations of the Waterfall Model

The waterfall model is a major improvement over the undisciplined approach used on early software projects and has been used successfully on many projects. In practice, however, some overlap is often necessary between successive phases of the life cycle, as well as some iteration between phases when errors are detected (Figure 3.2). Moreover, for some software development projects, the waterfall model presents the following significant problems:

- Software requirements, a key factor in any software development project, are not properly tested until a working system is available to demonstrate to the end-users. In fact, several studies have shown that errors in the requirements specification are usually the last to be detected (often not until system or acceptance testing) and the most costly to correct.
- A working system becomes available only late in the life cycle. Thus, a major design or performance problem might go undetected until the system is almost operational, at which time it is usually too late to take effective action.

For software development projects with a significant risk factor – for example, due to requirements that are not clearly understood or are expected to change – variations or alternatives to the waterfall model have been proposed.

Two different software prototyping approaches have been used to overcome some of the limitations of the waterfall model: throwaway prototypes and evolutionary prototypes. Throwaway prototypes can help resolve the first problem of the waterfall model, which was described in the preceding list, and evolutionary prototypes can help resolve the second problem.

3.1.3 Throwaway Prototyping

Throwaway prototypes can be used to help clarify user requirements. This approach is particularly useful for getting feedback on the user interface and can be used for systems that have a complex user interface.

A throwaway prototype may be developed after a preliminary requirements specification (Figure 3.3). By giving users the capability of exercising the prototype, much valuable feedback can be obtained that is otherwise frequently difficult to get. Based on this feedback, a revised requirements specification can be prepared. Subsequent development proceeds, following the conventional software life cycle.

Throwaway prototyping, particularly of the user interface, has been shown to be an effective solution to the problem of specifying requirements for interactive information systems. Gomaa (1990) described how a throwaway prototype was used to help clarify the requirements of a highly interactive manufacturing application.

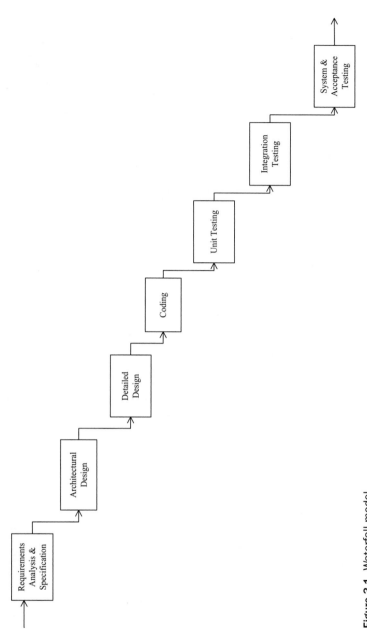

Figure 3.1. Waterfall model

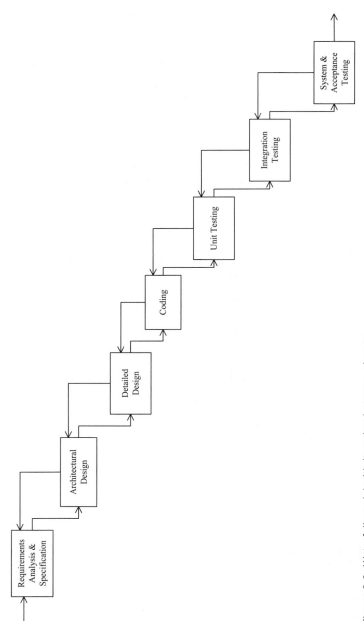

Figure 3.2. Waterfall model with iteration between phases

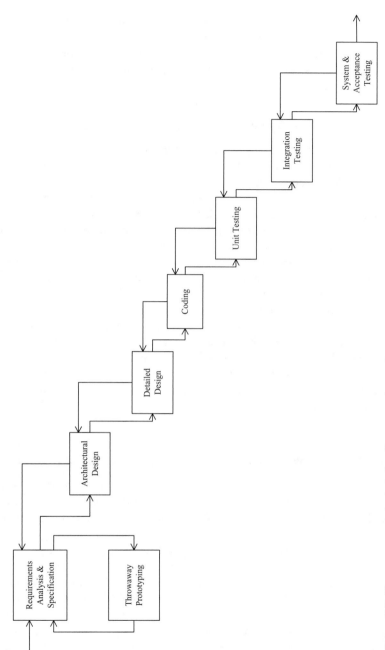

Figure 3.3. Throwaway prototyping of software requirements

The biggest problem it helped overcome was the communications barrier that existed between the users and the developers.

Throwaway prototypes can also be used for experimental prototyping of the design (Figure 3.4). This can be used to determine if certain algorithms are logically correct or to determine if they meet their performance goals.

3.1.4 Evolutionary Prototyping by Incremental Development

The evolutionary prototyping approach is a form of incremental development in which the prototype evolves through several intermediate operational systems (Figure 3.5) into the delivered system. This approach can help in determining whether the system meets its performance goals and in testing critical components of the design. It also reduces development risk by spreading the implementation over a longer time frame. Use cases and scenario-based communication diagrams can be used to assist in selecting system subsets for each increment.

One objective of the evolutionary prototyping approach is to have a subset of the system working early, which is then gradually built on. It is advantageous if the first incremental version of the system tests a complete path through the system from external input to external output.

An example of evolutionary prototyping by means of incremental development is described in Gomaa (1990). Using this approach on a real-time robot controller system (Gomaa 1986) resulted in availability of an early operational version of the system, providing a big morale boost for both the development team and management. It also had the important benefits of verifying the system design, establishing whether certain key algorithms met their performance goals, and spreading system integration over time.

3.1.5 Combining Throwaway Prototyping and Incremental Development

With the incremental development life cycle model approach, a working system in the form of an evolutionary prototype is available significantly earlier than with the conventional waterfall life cycle. Nevertheless, much greater care needs to be taken in developing this kind of prototype than with a throwaway prototype because it forms the basis of the finished product; thus, software quality has to be built into the system from the start and cannot be added as an afterthought. In particular, the software architecture needs to be carefully designed and all interfaces specified.

The conventional waterfall life cycle is impacted significantly by the introduction of throwaway prototyping or incremental development. It is also possible to combine the two approaches, as shown in Figure 3.6. A throwaway prototyping exercise is carried out to clarify the requirements. After the requirements are understood and a specification is developed, an incremental development life cycle is pursued. After subsequent increments, further changes in requirements might be necessary owing to changes in the user environment.

3.1.6 Spiral Model

The **spiral model** is a risk-driven process model originally developed by Boehm (1988) to address known problems with earlier process models of the software life

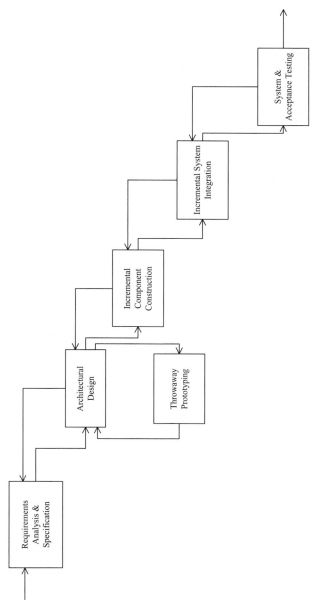

Figure 3.4. Throwaway prototyping of architectural design

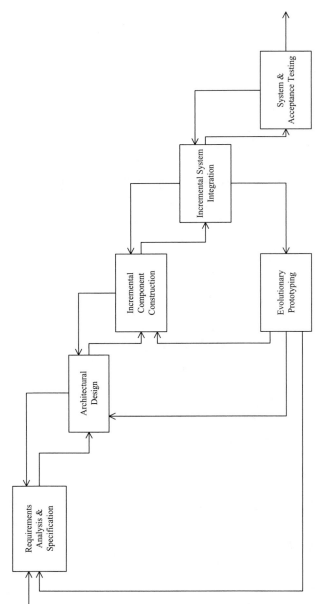

Figure 3.5. Incremental development software life cycle

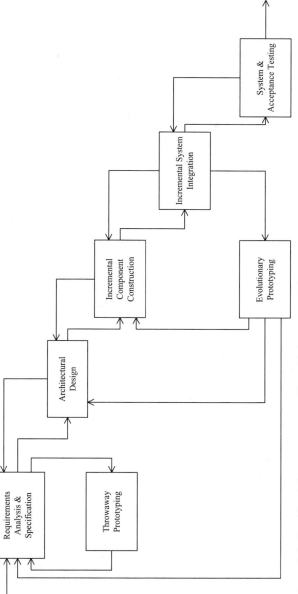

Figure 3.6. Combined throwaway prototyping with incremental development software life cycle model

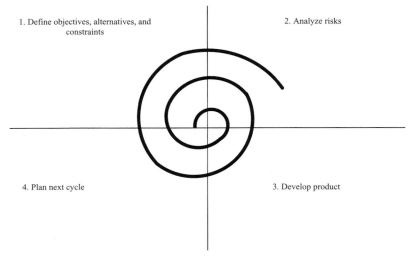

1. Define objectives, alternatives, and
constraints

2. Analyze risks

4. Plan next cycle

3. Develop product

Figure 3.7. Spiral process model

cycle – in particular, the waterfall model. The spiral model is intended to encompass other life cycle models, such as the waterfall model, the incremental development model, and the throwaway prototyping model.

In the spiral model, the radial coordinate represents cost, and the angular coordinate represents progress in completion of a cycle of the model. The spiral model consists of the following four quadrants, as shown in Figure 3.7:

1. **Define objectives, alternatives, and constraints.** Detailed planning for this cycle: identify goals and alternative approaches to achieving them.
2. **Analyze risks.** Detailed assessment of current project risks; plan activities to be performed to alleviate these risks.
3. **Develop product.** Work on developing product, such as requirements analysis, design, or coding.
4. **Plan next cycle.** Assess progress made on this cycle and start planning for next cycle.

Each cycle of the spiral model iterates through these four quadrants, although the number of cycles is project-specific. The descriptions of the activities in each quadrant are intended to be general enough that they can be included in any cycle.

The goal of the spiral model is to be risk-driven, so the risks in a given cycle are determined in the "analyze risks" quadrant. To manage these risks, certain additional project-specific activities may be planned to address the risks, such as requirements prototyping if the risk analysis indicates that the software requirements are not clearly understood. These project-specific risks are termed *process drivers*. For any process driver, one or more project-specific activities need to be performed to manage the risk (Boehm and Belz 1990).

An example of identifying a project-specific risk is to determine that the initial software requirements are not well understood. A project-specific activity performed to manage the risk is to develop a throwaway prototype, with the goal of getting feedback from the users in order to help clarify the requirements.

Phases

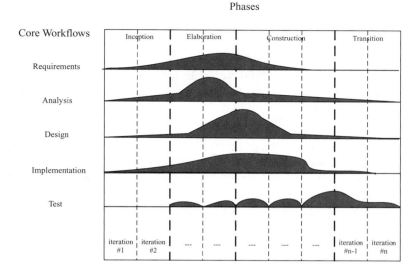

Iterations

Figure 3.8. Unified Software Development Process
(Jacobson et al, THE UNIFIED SOFTWARE DEVELOPMENT PROCESS, Figure 1.5
"Unified Software Development Process" p. 11, © 1999 Pearson Educa-
tion, Inc. Reproduced by permission of Pearson Education, Inc.)

3.1.7 Unified Software Development Process

The Unified Software Development Process (USDP), as described in Jacobson
et al. (1999), is a use case–driven software process that uses the UML notation. The
USDP is also known as the Rational Unified Process (RUP) (Kroll and Kruchten
2003; Kruchten 2003). USDP/RUP is a popular process for UML-based software
development. This section describes how the PLUS method can be used with the
USDP/RUP process.

The USDP consists of five core workflows and four phases and is iterative, as
shown in Figure 3.8. An **artifact** is defined as a piece of information that is produced,
modified, or used by a process (Kruchten 2003). A **workflow** is defined as a sequence
of activities that produces a result of observable value (Kruchten 2003). A **phase** is
defined as the time between two major milestones during which a well-defined set
of objectives is met, artifacts are completed, and decisions about whether to move
on to the next phase are made (Kruchten 2003). There is usually more than one
iteration in a phase; thus, a phase iteration in USDP corresponds to a cycle in the
spiral model.

Each cycle goes through all four phases and addresses the development of a core
workflow. The workflows and products of each workflow are as follows:

1. **Requirements.** The product of the requirements workflow is the use case
   model.
2. **Analysis.** The product of the analysis workflow is the analysis model.
3. **Design.** The products of the design workflow are the design model and the
   deployment model.

4. **Implementation.** The product of the implementation workflow is the implementation model.
5. **Test.** The product of the test workflow is the test model.

Like the spiral model, the USDP is a risk-driven process. The life cycle phases of the USDP are as follows (Jacobson, Booch, and Rumbaugh 1999; Kruchten 2003):

1. **Inception.** During the inception phase, the seed idea is developed to a sufficient level to justify entering the elaboration phase.
2. **Elaboration.** During the elaboration phase, the software architecture is defined.
3. **Construction.** During the construction phase, the software is built to the point at which it is ready for release to the user community.
4. **Transition.** During the transition phase, the software is turned over to the user community.

3.2 DESIGN VERIFICATION AND VALIDATION

Boehm (1981) differentiates between *software validation* and *software verification*. The goal of software validation is to ensure that the software development team "builds the right system," that is, to ensure that the system conforms to the user's needs. The goal of software verification is to ensure that the software development team "builds the system right," that is, to ensure that each phase of the software system is built according to the specification defined in the previous phase.

Topics discussed briefly in this section are software quality assurance and performance analysis of software designs. Another important activity is testing the fully integrated system against the software requirements, which is carried out during system testing, as described in Section 3.3 on software testing.

3.2.1 Software Quality Assurance

Software quality assurance is a name given to a set of activities whose goal is to ensure the quality of the software product. Software verification and validation are important goals of software quality assurance.

Throwaway prototyping can be used for validation of the system (before it is developed) against the user requirements, to help ensure that the team "builds the right system," that is, a system that actually conforms to the user's requirements. Throwaway prototypes can also be used for experimental prototyping of the design.

Software technical reviews can help considerably with software verification and validation. In software verification, it is important to ensure that the design conforms to the software requirements specification. Requirements tracing and technical reviews of the software design help with this activity.

3.2.2 Performance Analysis of Software Designs

Analyzing the performance of a software design before implementation is necessary to estimate whether the design will meet its performance goals. If potential performance problems can be detected early in the life cycle, steps can be taken to overcome them.

Approaches for evaluating software designs use queuing models (Menascé, Almeida, and Dowdy 2004; Menascé, Gomaa, and Kerschberg 1995; Menascé and Gomaa 2000) and simulation models (Smith 1990). For concurrent systems, Petri nets (David 1994; Jensen 1997; Pettit and Gomaa 2006; Stansifer 1994) can be used for modeling and analyzing concurrent designs. An approach described in (Gomaa 2000) is to analyze the performance of real-time designs by using real-time scheduling theory.

3.3 SOFTWARE LIFE CYCLE ACTIVITIES

Whichever software life cycle is adopted, the software engineering activities briefly described in the following sections will need to be carried out.

3.3.1 Requirements Analysis and Specification

In this phase, the user's requirements are identified and analyzed. The requirements of the system to be developed are specified in a Software Requirements Specification (SRS). The SRS is an external specification of the software. Its goal is to provide a complete description of *what* the system's external behavior is without describing *how* the system works internally. The issues of what constitutes a SRS are described lucidly in Davis (1993).

With some systems, such as embedded systems, in which the software is part of a larger hardware/software system, it is likely that a systems requirements analysis and specification phase precedes the software requirements analysis and specification. With this approach, system functional requirements are allocated to software and hardware before software requirements analysis begins (Davis 1993).

3.3.2 Architectural Design

A software architecture (Bass, Clements, and Kazman 2003; Shaw and Garlan 1996) separates the overall structure of the system, in terms of components and their interconnections, from the internal details of the individual components. The emphasis on components and their interconnections is sometimes referred to as programming-in-the-large, and detailed design of individual components is referred to as programming-in-the-small. During this phase, the system is structured into its constituent components and the interfaces between these components are defined.

3.3.3 Detailed Design

During the detailed design phase, the algorithmic details of each system component are defined. This is often achieved using a Program Design Language (PDL) notation, also referred to as Structured English or pseudocode. Internal data structures are also designed.

3.3.4 Coding

During the coding phase, each component is coded in the programming language selected for the project. Usually a set of coding and documentation standards have to be adhered to.

3.4 SOFTWARE TESTING

Because of the difficulty of detecting errors and then locating and correcting the detected errors, software systems are usually tested in several stages (Ammann and Offutt 2008). Unit and integration testing are "white box" testing approaches, requiring knowledge of the internals of the software; system testing is a "black box" testing approach based on the software requirements specification, without knowledge of the software internals.

3.4.1 Unit Testing

In unit testing, an individual component is tested before it is combined with other components. Unit testing approaches use test-coverage criteria. Frequently used test-coverage criteria are statement coverage and branch coverage. *Statement coverage* requires that each statement should be executed at least once. *Branch coverage* requires that every possible outcome of each branch should be tested at least once.

3.4.2 Integration Testing

Integration testing involves combining tested components into progressively more complex groupings of components and then testing these groupings until the whole software system has been put together and the interfaces tested.

3.4.3 System Testing

System testing is the process of testing an integrated hardware and software system to verify that the system meets its specified requirements (IEEE 1990). The whole system or major subsystems are tested to determine conformance with the requirements specification. To achieve greater objectivity, it is preferable to have system testing performed by an independent test team.

During system testing, several features of the software system need to be tested (Beizer 1995). These include the following:

- **Functional testing.** To determine that the system performs the functions described in the requirements specification.
- **Load (stress) testing.** To determine whether the system can handle the large and varied workload it is expected to handle when operational.

■ **Performance testing.** To test that the system meets its response time requirements.

3.4.4 Acceptance Testing

The user organization or its representative usually carries out acceptance testing, typically at the user installation, prior to acceptance of the system. Most of the issues relating to system testing also apply to acceptance testing.

3.5 SUMMARY

This chapter has taken a software life cycle perspective on software development. Various software life cycle models, also referred to as software process models (including the spiral model and the Unified Software Development Process) were briefly described and compared. The roles of design verification and validation and of software testing were discussed. Chapter 5 describes the use case–based software life cycle for the COMET method.

EXERCISES

Multiple-choice questions: For each question, choose one of the answers.

1. What is a software life cycle?
   (a) The life of the software
   (b) A cyclic approach to developing software
   (c) A phased approach to developing software
   (d) The life of software developed in cycles

2. What is the waterfall life cycle model?
   (a) Software developed under a waterfall
   (b) A process model in which each phase is completed before the next phase is started
   (c) A process model in which phases are overlapped
   (d) A process model in which phases are cyclic

3. Which of the following is a limitation of the waterfall life cycle model?
   (a) Software is developed in phases.
   (b) Each phase is completed before the next phase is started.
   (c) Software development is cyclic.
   (d) Software requirements are not properly tested until a working system is available.

4. Which of the following approaches can overcome the limitation in the previous question?
   (a) Phased software development
   (b) Throwaway prototyping
   (c) Evolutionary prototyping
   (d) Incremental development

5. What is evolutionary prototyping?
   (a) Phased software development
   (b) Throwaway prototyping
   (c) Risk-driven development
   (d) Incremental development

6. What approach does the spiral model emphasize?
   (a) Phased software development
   (b) Throwaway prototyping
   (c) Risk-driven development
   (d) Incremental development

7. What is the goal of software validation?
   (a) Building the system
   (b) Building the right system
   (c) Building the system right
   (d) Testing the system

8. What is the goal of software verification?
   (a) Building the system
   (b) Building the right system
   (c) Building the system right
   (d) Testing the system

9. What is "white box" testing?
   (a) Unit testing
   (b) Integration testing
   (c) Testing with knowledge of the system internals
   (d) Testing without knowledge of the software internals

10. What is "black box" testing?
   (a) System testing
   (b) Integration testing
   (c) Testing with knowledge of the system internals
   (d) Testing without knowledge of the software internals

4

Software Design and Architecture Concepts

This chapter describes key software design concepts that have shown their value over the years for the design of software architectures. First, object-oriented concepts are introduced, and objects and classes are described. Then there is a discussion of the role of information hiding in object-oriented design and an introduction to the concept of inheritance. Next, the concurrent processing concept and the concept of concurrent objects in concurrent applications are introduced. This is followed by an overview of software design patterns, software architecture, and the main characteristics of component-based systems. Finally, the concept of software quality attributes is discussed. Examples in this chapter are described in UML. An overview of the UML notation is given in Chapter 2.

Section 4.1 provides an overview of object-oriented concepts. Section 4.2 describes information hiding. Section 4.3 describes inheritance and generalization/specialization relationships. Section 4.4 provides an overview of concurrent processing. Section 4.5 gives an overview of software design patterns, with the actual patterns described in subsequent chapters. Section 4.6 provides an overview of software architecture and the main characteristics of component-based systems. Finally, Section 4.7 gives an introduction to software quality attributes.

4.1 OBJECT-ORIENTED CONCEPTS

The term *object-oriented* was first introduced in connection to object-oriented programming and Smalltalk, although the object-oriented concepts of information hiding and inheritance have earlier origins. Information hiding and its use in software design date back to Parnas (1972), who advocated using information hiding as a way to design modules that were more self-contained and, hence, could be changed with little or no impact on other modules. The concepts of classes and inheritance were first used in Simula 67 (Dahl and Hoare 1972), but only with the introduction of Smalltalk did they start gaining widespread acceptance.

Object-oriented concepts are considered important in software development because they address fundamental issues of adaptation and evolution. Because the object-oriented model of software development is considered especially conducive to evolution and change, the software modeling approach takes an object-oriented perspective. This section describes object-oriented concepts at the problem (analysis) level and the solution (design) level.

4.1.1 Objects and Classes

An **object** is a real-world physical or conceptual entity that provides an understanding of the real world and, hence, forms the basis for a software solution. A real-world object can have physical properties (they can be seen or touched); examples are a door, motor, or lamp. A conceptual object is a more abstract concept, such as an account or transaction.

Object-oriented applications consist of objects. From a design perspective, an object groups both data and procedures that operate on the data. The procedures are usually called operations or methods. Some approaches, including the UML notation, refer to the operation as the specification of a function performed by an object and the method as the implementation of the function (Rumbaugh et al. 2005). In this book, the term *operation* refers to both the specification and the implementation, in common with Gamma et al. (1995), Meyer (2000), and others.

The **signature** of an operation specifies the operation's name, the operation's parameters, and the operation's return value. An object's **interface** is the set of operations it provides, as defined by the signatures of the operations. An object's type is defined by its interface. An object's implementation is defined by its class. Thus, Meyer refers to a class as an implementation of an **abstract data type** (Meyer 2000).

An object (also referred to as an *object instance*) is a single "thing" – for example, John's car or Mary's account. A **class** (also referred to as an *object class*) is a collection of objects with the same characteristics; for example, Account, Employee, Car, or Customer. Figure 4.1 depicts a class Customer and two objects a Customer and another Customer that are instances of the class Customer. The objects an Account and another Account are instances of the class Account.

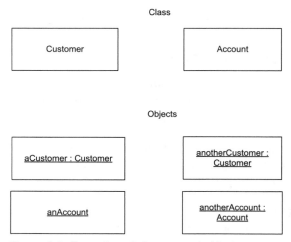

Figure 4.1. Examples of classes and objects

Class with attributes

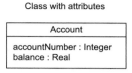

Objects with values

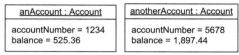

Figure 4.2. Example of a class with attributes

An **attribute** is a data value held by an object in a class. Each object has a specific value of an attribute. Figure 4.2 shows a class with attributes. The class Account has two attributes: account Number and balance. Two objects of the Account class are shown: an Account and another Account. Each account has specific values of the attributes. For example, the value of account Number of the object an Account is 1234, and the value of account Number of the object another Account is 5678. The value of balance of the former object is $525.36, and the value of balance of the latter is $1,897.44. An attribute name is unique within a class, although different classes may have the same attribute name; for example, both the Customer and Employee classes have attributes name and address.

An **operation** is the specification of a function performed by an object. An object has one or more operations. The operations manipulate the values of the attributes maintained by the object. Operations may have input and output parameters. All objects in the same class have the same operations. For example, the class Account has the operations read Balance, credit, debit, open, and close. Figure 4.3 shows the Account class with its operations.

An object is an instance of a class. Individual objects are instantiated as required at execution time. Each object has a unique identity, which is the characteristic that distinguishes it from other objects. In some cases, this identity may be an attribute (e.g., an account number or a customer name), but it does not need to be an attribute. Consider two blue balls: they are identical in every respect; however, they have different identities.

```
                    Account
        accountNumber : Integer
        balance : Real
        readBalance () : Real
        credit (amount : Real)
        debit (amount : Real)
        open (accountNumber : Integer)
        close ()
```

Figure 4.3. Example of class with attributes and operations

4.2 INFORMATION HIDING

Information hiding is a fundamental software design concept relevant to the design of all software systems. Early systems were frequently error-prone and difficult to modify because they made widespread use of global data. Parnas (1972, 1979) showed that by using information hiding, developers could design software systems to be substantially more modifiable by greatly reducing or – ideally – eliminating global data. Parnas advocated information hiding as a criterion for decomposing a software system into modules. Each information hiding module should hide a design decision that is considered likely to change. Each changeable decision is called the *secret* of the module. With this approach, the goal of *design for change* could be achieved.

4.2.1 Information Hiding in Object-Oriented Design

Information hiding is a basic concept of object-oriented design. Information hiding is used in designing the object, in particular when deciding what information should be visible and what information should be hidden. Those parts of an object that need not be visible to other objects are hidden; therefore, if the internals of the object change, only this object is affected. The term *encapsulation* is also used to describe information hiding by an object.

With information hiding, the information that could potentially change is encapsulated (i.e., hidden) inside an object. The information can be externally accessed only indirectly by the invocation of operations – access procedures or functions – that are also part of the object. Only these operations can access the information directly; thus, the hidden information and the operations that access it are bound together to form an **information hiding object**. The specification of the operations (i.e., the name and the parameters of the operations) is called the *interface* of the object. The object's interface is also referred to as the *abstract interface*, *virtual interface*, or *external interface*. The interface represents the visible part of the object – that is, the part that is revealed to users of the object. Other objects call the operations provided by the object.

A potential problem in application software development is that an important data structure, one that is accessed by several objects, might need to be changed. Without information hiding, any change to the data structure is likely to require changes to all the objects that access that data structure. Information hiding can be used to hide the design decision concerning the data structure, its internal linkage, and the details of the operations that manipulate it. The information hiding solution is to encapsulate the data structure in an object. The data structure is accessed only directly by the operations provided by the object.

Other objects may only indirectly access the encapsulated data structure by calling the operations of the object. Thus, if the data structure changes, the only object affected is the one containing the data structure. The external interface supported by the object does not change; hence, the objects that indirectly access the data structure are not affected by the change. This form of information hiding is called **data abstraction**.

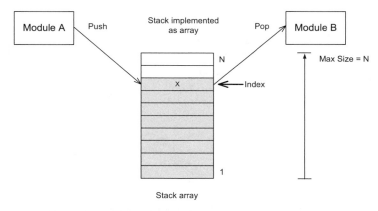

Note: This diagram does not conform to the UML notation.

Figure 4.4. Example of global access to stack array

4.2.2 Example of Information Hiding

An example of information hiding in software design is given next and compared with the functional approach, which does not use information hiding. To illustrate the benefits of information hiding, consider the functional and information hiding solutions to the following problem. A stack is accessed by several modules; the modules are procedures or functions in the functional solution and objects in the information hiding solution. In the functional solution, the stack is a global data structure. With this approach, each module accesses the stack directly, so each module needs to know the representation of the table (array or linked list) in order to manipulate it (Figure 4.4).

The information hiding solution is to hide the representation of the stack – for example, an array – from the objects needing to access it. An information hiding object – the stack object – is designed as follows (Figure 4.5):

- A set of operations is defined to manipulate the data structure. In the case of the stack, typical operations are push, pop, full, and empty.

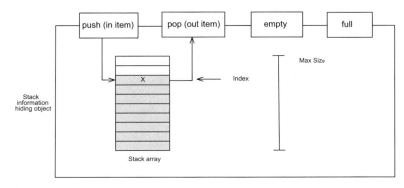

Note: This diagram does not conform to the UML notation.

Figure 4.5. Example of a stack information hiding object implemented as an array

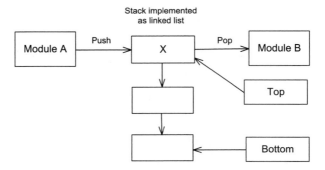

Note: This diagram does not conform to the UML notation.

Figure 4.6. Example of global access to a stack linked list

- The data structure is defined. In the case of the stack, for example, a one-dimensional array is defined. A variable is defined to refer to the top of the stack, and another variable has the value of the size of the array.
- Other objects are not permitted to access the data structure. They can call the object's operations to push an item onto the stack or pop an item off the stack.

Now assume that the design of the stack is changed from an array to a linked list. Consider its impact on the functional and information hiding solutions. In both cases, the data structure for the stack has to change. However, in the functional solution, the stack is implemented as a global data structure, so every module that accesses the stack also has to change because it operates directly on the data structure. Instead of manipulating array indexes, the module has to manipulate the pointers of the linked list (Figure 4.6).

In the information hiding solution, in addition to the internal stack data structure changing drastically, the internals of the information hiding object's operations have to change because they now access a linked list instead of an array (Figure 4.7). However, the external interface of the object, which is what is visible to the other

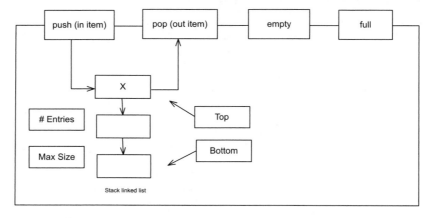

Note: This diagram does not conform to the UML notation.

Figure 4.7. Example of a stack information hiding object implemented as a linked list

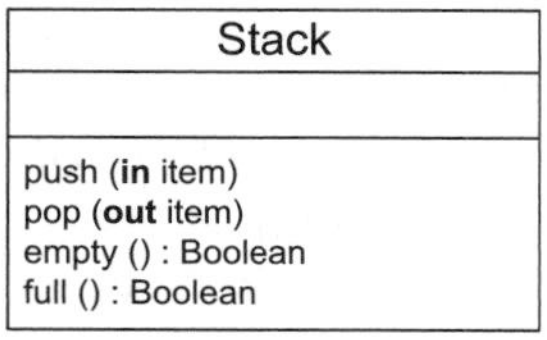

```
┌─────────────────────────────────┐
│             Stack               │
├─────────────────────────────────┤
│                                 │
├─────────────────────────────────┤
│ push (in item)                  │
│ pop (out item)                  │
│ empty () : Boolean              │
│ full () : Boolean               │
└─────────────────────────────────┘
```

Figure 4.8. Example of a stack information hiding class

objects, does not change. Thus, the objects that use the stack are not affected by the change; they continue to call the object's operations without even needing to be aware of the change.

The same concepts can be applied to designing a stack class, which is a template for creating stack objects. A stack class is defined, which hides the data structure to be used for the stack and specifies the operations that manipulate it, as shown in Figure 4.8. Individual stack objects are instantiated as required by the application. Each stack object has its own identity. It also has its own local copy of the stack data structure, as well as a local copy of any other instance variables required by the stack's operations.

4.2.3 Designing Information Hiding Objects

The main purpose of the previous two examples is to illustrate the benefits of information hiding. It is important to realize that encapsulation raises the level of abstraction by abstracting away the internal complexity of the object. This increases the size of granularity. It is only necessary to consider the interface, not the internal complexity; thus, in the stack example, we do not need to initially consider the internal details of the stack. In fact, we should start the design of an information hiding object by considering what interface the object should provide. For the design of the stack, for example, the interface needs to provide push, pop, empty, and full operations. For a message queue, there should be operations to enqueue and dequeue a message; the actual data structure for the queue can be decided later. In applying information hiding to the design of the I/O device interface, the crucial issue is the specification of the operations that constitute the virtual device interface, and not the details of how to interface to the real-world device.

Thus, the design of an object (or class) is a two-step process – first to design the interface, which is the external view, and then to design the internals. The first step is part of the high-level design, and the second step is part of the detailed design. This is likely to be an iterative process because there are usually tradeoffs to consider in deciding what should be externally visible and what should not. It is generally not a good idea to reveal all the variables encapsulated in an object – for example, through get and set operations – because that means that little information is hidden.

4.3 INHERITANCE AND GENERALIZATION/SPECIALIZATION

Inheritance is a useful abstraction mechanism in analysis and design. Inheritance naturally models objects that are similar in some, but not all, respects; thus, the objects have some common properties as well as unique properties that distinguish them. Inheritance is a classification mechanism that has been widely used in other fields. An example is the taxonomy of the animal kingdom, in which animals are classified as mammals, fish, reptiles, and so on. Cats and dogs have common properties that are generalized into the properties of mammals. However, they also have unique properties (e.g., a dog barks and a cat mews).

Inheritance is a mechanism for sharing and reusing code between classes. A child class inherits the properties (encapsulated data and operations) of a parent class. It can then adapt the structure (i.e., encapsulated data) and behavior (i.e., operations) of its parent class. The parent class is referred to as a **superclass** or *base class*. The child class is referred to as a **subclass** or *derived class*. The adaptation of a parent class to form a child class is referred to as *specialization*. Child classes may be further specialized, allowing the creation of class hierarchies, also referred to as **generalization/specialization** hierarchies.

Class inheritance is a mechanism for extending an application's functionality by reusing the functionality specified in parent classes. Thus, a new class can be incrementally defined in terms of an existing class. A child class can adapt the encapsulated data (referred to as instance variables) and operations of its parent class. It adapts the encapsulated data by adding new instance variables. It adapts the operations by adding new operations or by redefining existing operations. It is also possible for a child class to suppress an operation of the parent; however, such suppression is not recommended, because in that case the subclass no longer shares the interface of the superclass.

Consider the example of bank accounts given in Figure 4.9. Checking accounts and savings accounts have some attributes in common and others that are different. The attributes that are common to all accounts – namely, account Number and balance – are made attributes of an Account superclass. Attributes specific to a savings account, such as cumulative Interest (in this bank, checking accounts do not accumulate any interest), are made attributes of the subclass Savings Account. Attributes specific to a checking account, such as last Deposit Amount, are made attributes of the subclass Checking Account.

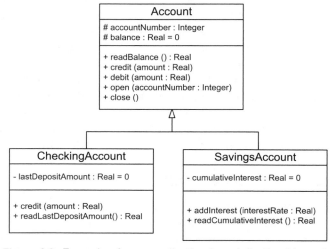

Figure 4.9. Example of a generalization/specialization hierarchy

For each of the subclasses, new operations are added. For the Savings Account subclass, the new operations are read Cumulative Interest to read cumulative Interest, and add Interest to add the daily interest. For the Checking Account subclass, the new operation is read Last Deposit Amount. This example is treated in more detail in Chapter 14.

4.4 CONCURRENT PROCESSING

An object may be active or passive. Whereas objects are often passive – that is, they wait for another object to invoke an operation and never initiate any actions – some object-oriented methods and languages, such as Ada and Java, support active objects. Active objects, also referred to as concurrent objects, execute independently of other active objects.

4.4.1 Sequential and Concurrent Applications

A **sequential application** is a sequential program that consists of passive objects and has only one thread of control. When an object invokes an operation in another object, control is passed from the calling operation to the called operation. When the called operation finishes executing, control is passed back to the calling operation. In a sequential application, only synchronous message communication (procedure call or method invocation) is supported.

In a **concurrent application**, there are typically several concurrent objects, each with its own thread of control. Asynchronous message communication is supported, so a concurrent source object can send an asynchronous message to a concurrent destination object and then continue executing, regardless of when the destination object receives the message. If the destination object is busy when the message arrives, the message is buffered for the object.

4.4.2 Concurrent Objects

Concurrent objects are also referred to as *active objects*, *concurrent processes, concurrent tasks*, or *threads* (Gomaa 2000). A **concurrent object** (**active object**) has its own thread of control and can execute independently of other objects. **Passive objects** have operations that are invoked by concurrent objects. Passive objects can invoke operations in other passive objects. A passive object has no thread of control; thus, passive objects are instances of passive classes. An operation of a passive object, once invoked by a concurrent object, executes within the thread of control of the concurrent object.

A concurrent object represents the execution of a sequential program or a sequential component in a concurrent program. Each concurrent object deals with one sequential thread of execution; thus, no concurrency is allowed within a concurrent object. However, overall system concurrency is achieved by the execution of multiple concurrent objects in parallel. Concurrent objects often execute asynchronously (i.e., at different speeds) and are relatively independent of each other for significant periods of time. From time to time, concurrent objects need to communicate with each other and synchronize their actions.

4.4.3 Cooperation between Concurrent Objects

In the design of concurrent systems, several problems need to be considered that do not arise in the design of sequential systems. In most concurrent applications, concurrent objects must cooperate with each other in order to perform the services required by the application. The following three problems commonly arise when concurrent objects cooperate with each other:

1. The **mutual exclusion problem** occurs when concurrent objects need to have exclusive access to a resource, such as shared data or a physical device. A variation on this problem, in which the mutual exclusion constraint can sometimes be relaxed, is the *multiple readers and writers* problem.
2. The **synchronization problem** occurs when two concurrent objects need to synchronize their operations with each other.
3. The **producer/consumer problem** occurs when concurrent objects need to communicate with each other in order to pass data from one concurrent object to another. Communication between concurrent objects is often referred to as interprocess communication (IPC).

4.4.4 Synchronization Problem

Event synchronization is used when two tasks need to synchronize their operations without communicating data between the tasks. The source task executes a *signal (event)* operation, which signals that an event has taken place. Event synchronization is asynchronous. In the UML, the two tasks are depicted as active objects with an asynchronous event signal sent from the sender task to the receiver task. The destination task executes a *wait (event)* operation, which suspends the task until the source task has signaled the event. If the event has already been signaled, the destination task is not suspended. An example is given next.

Example of Synchronization between Concurrent Objects
Consider an example of event synchronization from concurrent robot systems. Each robot system is designed as a concurrent object and controls a moving robot arm. A pick-and-place robot brings a part to the work location so that a drilling robot can drill four holes in the part. On completion of the drilling operation, the pick-and-place robot moves the part away.

Several synchronization problems need to be solved here. First, there is a collision zone where the pick-and-place and drilling robot arms could potentially collide. Second, the pick-and-place robot must deposit the part before the drilling robot can start drilling the holes. Third, the drilling robot must finish drilling before the pick-and-place robot can remove the part. The solution is to use event synchronization, as described next.

The pick-and-place robot moves the part to the work location, moves out of the collision zone, and then signals the event part Ready. This signal awakens the drilling robot, which moves to the work location and drills the holes. After completing the drilling operation, the drilling robot moves out of the collision zone and then signals a second event, part Completed, which the pick-and-place robot is waiting to receive.

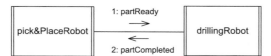

Figure 4.10. Example of synchronization between concurrent objects

After being awakened, the pick-and-place robot removes the part. Each robot executes a loop, because the robots repetitively perform their operations. The solution is as follows (see also Figure 4.10):

Pick-and-Place Robot

```
while workAvailable do
    Pick up part
    Move part to work location
    Release part
    Move robot arm to safe position
    signal (partReady)
    wait (partCompleted)
    Pick up part
    Remove part from work location
    Place part
end while;
```

Drilling Robot

```
while workAvailable do
    wait (partReady)
    Move robot arm to work location
    Drill four holes
    Move robot arm to safe position
    signal (partCompleted)
end while;
```

4.4.5 Producer/Consumer Problem

A common problem in concurrent systems is that of producer and consumer concurrent objects. The producer concurrent object produces information, which is then consumed by the consumer concurrent object. In a concurrent system, each concurrent object has its own thread of control and the concurrent objects execute asynchronously. It is therefore necessary for the concurrent objects to synchronize their operations when they wish to exchange data. Thus, the producer must produce the data before the consumer can consume it. If the consumer is ready to receive the data but the producer has not yet produced it, then the consumer must wait for the producer. If the producer has produced the data before the consumer is ready to receive it, then either the producer has to be held up or the data needs to be buffered for the consumer, thereby allowing the producer to continue.

A common solution to this problem is to use message communication between the producer and consumer concurrent objects. Message communication between concurrent objects serves two purposes:

1. Transfer of data from a producer (source) concurrent object to a consumer (destination) concurrent object.
2. Synchronization between producer and consumer. If no message is available, the consumer has to wait for the message to arrive from the producer. In some cases, the producer waits for a reply from the consumer.

Message communication between concurrent objects may be asynchronous or synchronous. The concurrent objects may reside on the same node or be distributed over several nodes in a distributed application. With asynchronous message communication, the producer sends a message to the consumer and continues without waiting for a response. With synchronous message communication, the producer sends a message to the consumer and then immediately waits for a response.

4.4.6 Asynchronous Message Communication

With **asynchronous message communication**, also referred to as **loosely coupled message communication**, the producer sends a message to the consumer and either does not need a response or has other functions to perform before receiving a response. Thus, the producer sends a message and continues without waiting for a response. The consumer receives the message. As the producer and consumer concurrent objects proceed at different speeds, a first-in-first-out (FIFO) message queue can build up between producer and consumer. If there is no message available when the consumer requests one, the consumer is suspended.

An example of asynchronous message communication is given in Figure 4.11, in which the producer concurrent object sends messages to the consumer concurrent object. A FIFO message queue can exist between the producer and the consumer.

4.4.7 Synchronous Message Communication with Reply

In the case of **synchronous message communication with reply**, also referred to as **tightly coupled message communication with reply**, the producer sends a message to the consumer and then waits for a reply. When the message arrives, the consumer accepts the message, processes it, generates a reply, and then sends

Figure 4.11. Asynchronous (loosely coupled) message communication

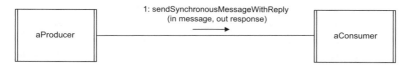

Figure 4.12. Synchronous (tightly coupled) message communication with reply

the reply. The producer and consumer then both continue. The consumer is suspended if no message is available. For a given producer/consumer pair, no message queue develops between the producer and the consumer. It is also possible to have **synchronous message communication without replydesing pattern** as described in Chapter 12.

An example of synchronous message communication with reply is given in Figure 4.12 in which the producer sends a message to the consumer; after receiving the message, the consumer sends a reply to the producer.

4.5 DESIGN PATTERNS

In software design, one frequently encounters a problem that one has solved before on a different project. Often the context of the problem is different; it might be a different application, a different platform, or a different programming language. Because of the different context, one usually ends up redesigning and reimplementing the solution, thereby falling into the "reinventing the wheel" trap. The field of software patterns, including architectural and design patterns, is helping developers avoid unnecessary redesign and reimplementation.

The concept of a pattern was first developed by Christopher Alexander in the architecture of buildings and described in his book *The Timeless Way of Building* (Alexander 1979). In software, the field of design patterns was popularized by Gamma, Helms, Johnson, and Vlissides in their book *Design Patterns* (1995), in which they described 23 design patterns. Later, Buschmann et al. (1996) described patterns that span different levels of abstraction, from high-level architectural patterns through design patterns to low-level idioms.

A **design pattern** describes a recurring design problem to be solved, a solution to the problem, and the context in which that solution works (Buschmann et al. 1996; Gamma et al. 1995). The description specifies objects and classes that are customized to solve a general design problem in a particular context. A design pattern is a larger-grained form of reuse than a class because it involves more than one class and the interconnection among objects from different classes. A design pattern is sometimes referred to as a *microarchitecture*.

After the original success of the design pattern concept, other kinds of patterns were developed. The main kinds of reusable patterns are as follows:

- **Design patterns.** In a widely cited book (Gamma et al. 1995), design patterns were described by four software designers – Erich Gamma, Richard Helm, Ralph Johnson, and John Vlissides – who were named in some quarters as the "gang of four." A design pattern is a small group of collaborating objects.

- **Architectural patterns.** This work was described by Buschmann et al. (1996) at Siemens. Architectural patterns are larger-grained than design patterns, addressing the structure of major subsystems of a system.
- **Analysis patterns.** Analysis patterns were described by Fowler (2002), who found similarities during analysis of different application domains. He described recurring patterns found in object-oriented analysis and described them with static models, expressed in class diagrams.
- **Product line–specific patterns**. These are patterns used in specific application areas, such as factory automation (Gomaa 2005) or electronic commerce. By concentrating on a specific application domain, design patterns can provide more tailored domain-specific solutions.
- **Idioms.** Idioms are low-level patterns that are specific to a given programming language and describe implementation solutions to a problem that use the features of the language – for example, Java or C++. These patterns are closest to code, but they can be used only by applications that are coded in the same programming language.

4.6 SOFTWARE ARCHITECTURE AND COMPONENTS

A **software architecture** (Bass et al. 2003; Shaw and Garlan 1996) separates the overall structure of the system, in terms of components and their interconnections, from the internal details of the individual components. This section describes the design of component interfaces, an important issue in software architecture. It describes how interfaces are specified before describing provided and required interfaces, and connectors that interconnect components.

4.6.1 Components and Component Interfaces

The term *component* is used in different ways. It is often used in a general sense to mean modular systems, in which the modules could be developed in different ways depending on the particular platform the software architecture.

A **component** is a self-contained, usually concurrent, object with a well-defined interface that is capable of being used in applications different from that for which it was originally designed. To fully specify a component, it is necessary to define it in terms of the operations it *provides* and the operations it *requires* (Magee et al. 1994; Shaw and Garlan 1996). Such a definition is in contrast to conventional object-oriented approaches, which describe an object only in terms of the operations it provides. However, if a preexisting component is to be integrated into a component-based system, it is just as important to understand – and therefore to represent explicitly – both the operations that the component requires and those that it provides.

4.6.2 Connectors

In addition to defining the components, a software architecture must define the connectors that join the components. A **connector** encapsulates the interconnection protocol between two or more components. Different kinds of message communication between components include **asynchronous** (loosely coupled) and **synchronous** (tightly coupled). The interaction protocols for each of these types of communication can be encapsulated in a connector. For example, although asynchronous message communication between components on the same node is logically the same as between components on different nodes, different connectors would be used in the two cases. In the former case, the connector could use a shared memory buffer; the latter case would use a different connector that sends messages over a network.

4.7 SOFTWARE QUALITY ATTRIBUTES

Software quality attributes (Bass, Clements, and Kazman 2003) refer to the quality requirements of the software, which are often referred to as nonfunctional requirements. Each of the nonfunctional requirements needs to be explicitly considered in the design of the software architecture. The quality attributes are addressed and evaluated at the time the software architecture is developed, and can have a profound effect on the quality of a software product. The quality attributes include the following:

- **Maintainability.** The extent to which software is capable of being changed after deployment.
- **Modifiability.** The extent to which software is capable of being modified during and after initial development.
- **Testability.** The extent to which software is capable of being tested.
- **Traceability.** The extent to which products of each phase can be traced back to products of previous phases.
- **Scalability.** The extent to which the system is capable growing after its initial deployment.
- **Reusability.** The extent to which software is capable of being reused.
- **Performance.** The extent to which the system meets its performance goals, such as throughput and response times.
- **Security.** The extent to which the system is resistant to security threats.
- **Availability.** The extent to which the system is capable of addressing system failure.

4.8 SUMMARY

This chapter described key concepts in software design and important concepts for developing component-based software architectures. The object-oriented concepts introduced here form the basis of several of the forthcoming chapters. Chapter 7 describes how static modeling is applied to modeling software systems. Chapters 9, 10, and 11 describe how dynamic modeling is applied to modeling software systems. Chapters 9 and 11 describe dynamic modeling between objects using object interaction modeling, and Chapter 10 focuses on dynamic modeling within an object using finite state machines.

This chapter introduced nonfunctional requirements in terms of software quality attributes. Specifying nonfunctional requirements is described in Chapter 6, whereas Chapter 20 describes how the software quality attributes are addressed in the software architecture. Design patterns are described in more detail in Chapter 12.

This chapter also described the concepts of component-based software architectures, emphasizing component fundamentals rather than technologies, which tend to change frequently. The development of component-based software architectures is described further in Chapter 17.

EXERCISES

Multiple-choice questions: For each question, choose one of the answers.

1. Which of the following are object-oriented concepts?
   (a) Modules and interfaces
   (b) Modules and information hiding
   (c) Classes, information hiding, and inheritance
   (d) Concurrency and information hiding

2. Which of the following is a characteristic of an object?
   (a) A function or subroutine
   (b) A module
   (c) Groups data and procedures that operate on the data
   (d) Groups a function and an algorithm

3. What is a class?
   (a) An object instance
   (b) The implementation of the object
   (c) A collection of objects with the same characteristics
   (d) A collection of objects with different characteristics

4. What is an operation (also known as method) of a class?
   (a) Specification and the implementation of a function performed by a class
   (b) Specification and the implementation of a subroutine provided by a class
   (c) Specification and the implementation of a function or procedure provided by a class
   (d) Specification and the implementation of an interface provided by a class

5. What is the signature of an operation?
   (a) The operation's name
   (b) The operation's function or subroutine
   (c) The operation's name, parameters, and return value
   (d) The object's interface

6. What is the interface of a class?
   (a) The signature of a class
   (b) The specification of operations provided by the class
   (c) The internals of the class
   (d) The implementation of the class

7. What is an attribute?
   (a) A description of a class
   (b) An internal property of a class
   (c) A data item held by a class
   (d) A parameter of a class

8. What is information hiding in software design?
   (a) Hiding information so that it cannot be found
   (b) Hiding a design decision that is considered likely to change
   (c) Hiding information to make it secure
   (d) Encapsulating data in a class

9. What is data abstraction?
   (a) Another name for information hiding
   (b) Encapsulating data so that its structure is hidden
   (c) Storing data in a database
   (d) Storing data in a data structure

10. What is inheritance?
   (a) A mechanism for inheriting characteristics from a parent
   (b) A mechanism for sharing and re-using code between classes
   (c) A mechanism for sharing data between classes
   (d) A mechanism for hiding information between classes

5

Overview of Software Modeling and Design Method

The software modeling and design method described in this book is called COMET (Collaborative Object Modeling and Architectural Design Method), which uses the UML notation. COMET is an iterative use case–driven and object-oriented method that specifically addresses the requirements, analysis, and design modeling phases of the software development life cycle. This chapter considers the COMET method from a software life cycle perspective. The development process for the COMET method is a use case–based software process, which is compatible with the Unified Software Development Process (USDP) (Jacobson, Booch, and Rumbaugh 1999) and the spiral model (Boehm 1988). This chapter presents the COMET use case–based software life cycle and describes how the COMET method may be used with the USDP or the spiral model. It then outlines the main activities of the COMET method and concludes with a description of the steps in using COMET.

Section 5.1 describes the COMET use case–based software life cycle, and Section 5.2 compares COMET with other software processes. Section 5.3 gives an overview of the requirements, analysis, and design modeling activities in COMET. Section 5.4 gives an overview of the design of different kinds of software architectures covered in this textbook.

5.1 COMET USE CASE–BASED SOFTWARE LIFE CYCLE

The COMET use case–based software life cycle model is a highly iterative software development process based around the **use case** concept. In the requirements model, the functional requirements of the system are described in terms of actors and use cases. Each use case defines a sequence of interactions between one or more actors and the system. In the analysis model, the use case is realized to describe the objects that participate in the use case and their interactions. In the design model, the software architecture is developed, describing components and their interfaces. The full COMET use case–based software life cycle model is illustrated in Figure 5.1 and described next. The COMET life cycle is highly iterative. The COMET method ties in the three phases of requirements, analysis, and design modeling by means of a use case–based approach, as outlined next.

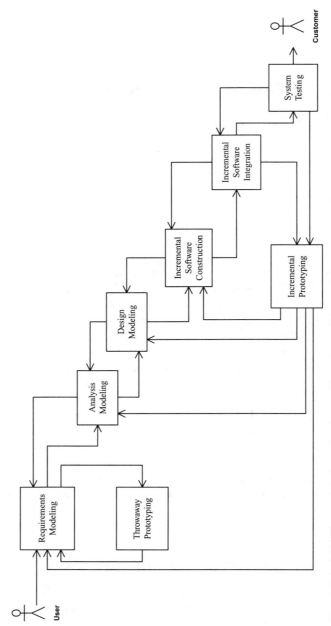

Figure 5.1. COMET use case–based software life cycle model

5.1.1 Requirements Modeling

During the **requirements modeling** phase, a requirements model is developed in which the functional requirements of the system are described in terms of actors and use cases. A narrative description of each use case is developed. User inputs and active participation are essential to this effort. If the requirements are not well understood, a throwaway prototype can be developed to help clarify the requirements, as described in Chapter 2.

5.1.2 Analysis Modeling

In the **analysis modeling** phase, static and dynamic models of the system are developed. The static model defines the structural relationships among problem domain classes. The classes and their relationships are depicted on class diagrams. Object structuring criteria are used to determine the objects to be considered for the analysis model. A dynamic model is then developed in which the use cases from the requirements model are realized to show the objects that participate in each use case and how they interact with each other. Objects and their interactions are depicted on either communication diagrams or sequence diagrams. In the dynamic model, state-dependent objects are defined using statecharts.

5.1.3 Design Modeling

In the **design modeling** phase, the software architecture of the system is designed, in which the analysis model is mapped to an operational environment. The analysis model, with its emphasis on the problem domain, is mapped to the design model, with its emphasis on the solution domain. Subsystem structuring criteria are provided to structure the system into subsystems, which are considered as aggregate or composite objects. Special consideration is given to designing distributed subsystems as configurable components that communicate with each other using messages. Each subsystem is then designed. For sequential systems, the emphasis is on the object-oriented concepts of information hiding, classes, and inheritance. For the design of concurrent systems, such as real-time, client/server, and distributed applications, it is necessary to consider concurrent tasking concepts in addition to object-oriented concepts.

5.1.4 Incremental Software Construction

After completion of the software architectural design, an *incremental software construction* approach is taken. This approach is based on selecting a subset of the system to be constructed for each increment. The subset is determined by choosing the use cases to be included in this increment and the objects that participate in these use cases. Incremental software construction consists of the detailed design, coding, and unit testing of the classes in the subset. This is a phased approach by which the software is gradually constructed and integrated until the whole system is built.

5.1.5 Incremental Software Integration

During *incremental software integration*, the integration testing of each software increment is performed. The integration test for the increment is based on the use cases selected for the increment. Integration test cases are developed for each use case. Integration testing is a form of white box testing, in which the interfaces between the objects that participate in each use case are tested.

Each software increment forms an *incremental prototype*. After the software increment is judged to be satisfactory, the next increment is constructed and integrated by iterating through the incremental software construction and incremental software integration phases. However, if significant problems are detected in the software increment, iteration through the requirements modeling, analysis modeling, and design modeling phases might be necessary.

5.1.6 System Testing

System testing includes the functional testing of the system – namely, testing the system against its functional requirements. This testing is black box testing and is based on the black box use cases. Thus, functional test cases are built for each black box use case. Any software increment released to the customer needs to go through the system testing phase.

5.2 COMPARISON OF THE COMET LIFE CYCLE WITH OTHER SOFTWARE PROCESSES

This section briefly compares the COMET life cycle with the Unified Software Development Process (USDP) and the spiral model. The COMET method can be used in conjunction with either the USDP or the spiral model.

5.2.1 Comparison of the COMET Life Cycle with Unified Software Development Process

The USDP, as described in Jacobson, Booch, and Rumbaugh (1999) and briefly described in Chapter 3, emphasizes process and – to a lesser extent – method. The USDP provides considerable detail about the life cycle aspects and some detail about the method to be used. The COMET method is compatible with USDP. The workflows of the USDP are the requirements, analysis, design, implementation, and test workflows.

Each phase of the COMET life cycle corresponds to a workflow of the USDP. The first three phases of COMET have the same names as the first three workflows of the USDP – not surprising, because the COMET life cycle was strongly influenced by Jacobson's earlier work (Jacobson 1992). The COMET incremental software construction activity corresponds to the USDP implementation workflow. The incremental software integration and system test phases of COMET map to the test workflow of USDP. COMET separates these activities because integration testing is viewed as a development team activity, whereas a separate test team should carry out system testing.

5.2.2 Comparison of the COMET Life Cycle with the Spiral Model

The COMET method can also be used with the spiral model (Boehm 1988). During the project planning for a given cycle of the spiral model, the project manager decides what specific technical activity should be performed in the third quadrant, which is the product development quadrant. The selected technical activity, such as requirements modeling, analysis modeling, or design modeling, is then performed in the third quadrant. The risk analysis activity, performed in the second quadrant, and cycle planning, performed in the fourth quadrant, determine how many iterations are required through each of the technical activities.

5.3 REQUIREMENTS, ANALYSIS, AND DESIGN MODELING

The UML notation supports requirements, analysis, and design concepts. The COMET method described in this book separates requirements activities, analysis activities, and design activities. It should be emphasized that the UML models need to be supplemented with additional information to fully describe the software architecture.

Requirements modeling addresses developing the functional and nonfunctional requirements of the system. COMET differentiates analysis from design as follows: *analysis* is breaking down or decomposing the problem so it is understood better; *design* is synthesizing or composing (putting together) the solution. These activities are described in more detail in the next sections.

5.3.1 Activities in Requirements Modeling

In the requirements model, the system is considered as a black box. The use case model is developed.

- **Use case modeling.** Define actors and black box use cases. The functional requirements of the system are described in terms of use cases and actors. The use case descriptions are a behavioral view; the relationships among the use cases give a structural view. Use case modeling is described in Chapter 6.
- Addressing nonfunctional requirements is also important at the requirements phase. The UML notation does not address this. However, the use case modeling approach can be supplemented to address nonfunctional requirements, as described in Chapter 6.

5.3.2 Activities in Analysis Modeling

In the analysis model, the emphasis is on understanding the problem; hence, the emphasis is on identifying the problem domain objects and the information passed between them. Issues such as whether the object is active or passive, whether the message sent is asynchronous or synchronous, and what operation is invoked at the receiving object are deferred until design time.

In the analysis model, the analysis of the problem domain is considered. The activities are as follows:

- **Static modeling.** Define problem-specific static model. This is a structural view of the information provided in the system. Classes are defined in terms of their attributes, as well as their relationship with other classes. Operations are defined in the design model. For information-intensive systems, this view is of great importance. The emphasis is on the information modeling of real-world classes in the problem domain. Static modeling is described in Chapter 7.
- **Object structuring.** Determine the objects that participate in each use case. Object structuring criteria are provided to help determine the software objects in the system, which can be entity objects, boundary objects, control objects, and application logic objects. Object structuring is described in Chapter 8. After the objects have been determined, the dynamic interactions between objects are depicted in the dynamic model.
- **Dynamic interaction modeling.** The use cases are realized to show the interaction among the objects participating in each use case. Communication diagrams or sequence diagrams are developed to show how objects communicate with each other to execute the use case. Chapter 9 describes stateless dynamic modeling, including the dynamic interaction modeling approach, which is used to help determine how objects interact with each other to support the use cases. Chapter 11 describes state-dependent dynamic interaction modeling, in which the interaction among the state-dependent control objects and the statecharts they execute is explicitly modeled.
- **Dynamic state machine modeling.** The state-dependent view of the system is defined using hierarchical statecharts. Each state-dependent object is defined in terms of its constituent statechart. Designing finite state machines and statecharts is described in Chapter 10.

5.3.3 Activities in Design Modeling

In the design model, the solution domain is considered. During this phase, the analysis model is mapped to a concurrent design model. For designing software architectures, the following activities are performed:

- Integrate the object communication model. Develop integrated object communication diagram(s). This is described in Chapter 13.
- Make decisions about subsystem structure and interfaces. Develop the overall software architecture. Structure the application into subsystems. This is described in Chapter 13.
- Make decisions about what software architectural and design patterns to use in the software architecture. Software architectural patterns are described in Chapters 12, 15, 16, 17, and 18.
- Make decisions about class interfaces, in particular for sequential software architectures. For each subsystem, design the information hiding classes (passive

classes). Design the operations of each class and the parameters of each operation. This is described in Chapter 14.

■ Make decisions about how to structure the distributed application into distributed subsystems, in which subsystems are designed as configurable components, and define the message communication interfaces between the components. This is described in Chapters 13, 15, 16, and 17.

■ Make decisions about the characteristics of objects, particularly whether they are active or passive. For each subsystem, structure the system into concurrent tasks (active objects). During task structuring, tasks are structured using the task-structuring criteria, and task interfaces are defined. This is described in Chapter 18.

■ Make decisions about the characteristics of messages, particularly whether they are asynchronous or synchronous (with or without reply). Architectural communication patterns are described in Chapters 12, 13, 15, 16, 17, and 18.

COMET emphasizes the use of structuring criteria at certain stages in the analysis and design process. Object structuring criteria are used to help determine the objects in the system, subsystem structuring criteria are used to help determine the subsystems, and concurrent object structuring criteria are used to help determine the concurrent (active) objects in the system. UML stereotypes are used throughout to clearly show the use of the structuring criteria.

5.4 DESIGNING SOFTWARE ARCHITECTURES

During software design modeling, design decisions are made relating to the characteristics of the software architecture. The chapters in the design modeling section of this textbook describe the design of different kinds of software architectures:

■ **Object-Oriented Software Architectures.** Chapter 14 describes object-oriented design using the concepts of information hiding, classes, and inheritance.

■ **Client/Server Software Architectures.** Chapter 15 describes the design of client/server software architectures. A typical design consists of one server and multiple clients.

■ **Service-Oriented Architectures.** Chapter 16 describes the design of service-oriented architectures, which typically consist of multiple distributed autonomous services that can be composed into distributed software applications.

■ **Distributed Component-Based Software Architectures.** Chapter 17 describes the design of component-based software architectures, which can be deployed to execute on distributed platforms in a distributed configuration.

■ **Real-Time Software Architectures.** Chapter 18 describes the design of real-time software architectures, which are concurrent architectures usually having to deal with multiple streams of input events. They are typically state-dependent, with either centralized or decentralized control.

■ **Software Product Line Architectures.** Chapter 19 describes the design of software product line architectures, which are architectures for families of products that need to capture both the commonality and variability in the family.

5.5 SUMMARY

This chapter described the COMET use case–based software life cycle for the development of UML-based object-oriented software applications. It compared the COMET life cycle with the USDP and the spiral model, and described how the COMET method can be used with either the USDP or the spiral model. The chapter then described the main activities of the COMET method and concluded with a description of the steps in using COMET. Each of the steps in the COMET method is described in more detail in the subsequent chapters of this textbook.

For software intensive systems, in which the software is one component of a larger hardware/software system, systems modeling can be carried out before software modeling. A dialect of UML called SysML is a general purpose modeling language for systems engineering applications (Friedenthal et al 2009).

EXERCISES

The following questions relate to the software modeling and design method (COMET) described in this book.

Multiple-choice questions: For each question, choose one of the answers.

1. What is carried out during requirements modeling?
   (a) Functional requirements of the system are described in terms of functions, inputs, and outputs.
   (b) Functional requirements of the system are described in terms of actors and use cases.
   (c) Functional requirements of the system are described textually.
   (d) Functional requirements of the system are determined by interviewing users.

2. What is carried out during analysis modeling?
   (a) Developing use case models
   (b) Developing data flow and entity-relationship diagrams
   (c) Developing static and dynamic models
   (d) Developing software architectures

3. What is carried out during design modeling?
   (a) Developing use case models
   (b) Developing data flow and entity-relationship diagrams
   (c) Developing static and dynamic models
   (d) Developing software architectures

4. What is carried out during incremental software construction?
   (a) Detailed design and coding of the classes in a subset of the system
   (b) Detailed design, coding, and unit testing of the classes in a subset of the system
   (c) Coding and unit testing of the classes in a subset of the system
   (d) Unit and integration testing of the classes in a subset of the system

5. What is carried out during incremental software integration?
   (a) Implementation of the classes in each software increment
   (b) Unit testing of the classes in each software increment
   (c) Integration testing of the classes in each software increment
   (d) System testing of the classes in each software increment

6. What is carried out during system testing?
   (a) White box testing
   (b) Black box testing
   (c) Unit testing
   (d) Integration testing

PART II

Software Modeling

6

Use Case Modeling

The requirements of a system describe what the user expects from the system – in other words, what the system will do for the user. When defining the requirements of a system, the system should be viewed as a black box, so that only the external characteristics of the system are considered. Both functional and nonfunctional requirements need to be considered. Requirements modeling consists of requirements analysis and requirements specification.

Use case modeling is an approach for describing the functional requirements of the system, as described in this chapter. The system's data requirements in terms of the information that needs to be stored by the system are determined using static modeling, as described in Chapter 7. The inputs to the system and the outputs from the system are described initially in the use case models and then specified in more detail during static modeling.

This chapter gives an overview of software requirements analysis and specification in Section 6.1. It then goes on to describe the use case approach to defining functional requirements, as well as how to extend use cases to describe nonfunctional requirements. This chapter describes the concepts of **actors** and **use cases**, and then goes on to describe use case relationships, in particular, the *include* and *extend* relationships. Section 6.2 gives an overview of use case modeling followed by an example of a simple use case. Section 6.3 then describes actors and their role in use case modeling. The important topic of how to identify use cases is covered in Section 6.4. Section 6.5 describes how to document use cases. Section 6.6 gives some examples of use case descriptions. Section 6.7 then describes use case relationships. Modeling with the *include* relationship is described in Section 6.8; modeling with the *extend* relationship is described in Section 6.9. Use case guidelines are described in Section 6.10, specifying nonfunctional requirements is described in Section 6.11, use case packages are described in Section 6.12, and how to describe use cases more precisely using activity diagrams is described in Section 6.13.

6.1 REQUIREMENTS MODELING

There are two main reasons for developing a new software system: either to replace a manual system or to replace an existing software system. In the first case, the new system is developed to replace a manual system, in which records might be kept on paper documents and stored in filing cabinets. Alternatively, the new system might be developed to replace an existing software system that has become seriously outdated, for example, because it runs on obsolete hardware (such as a centralized mainframe system) or because it was developed using an obsolete language such as Cobol and/or because the system has little or no documentation. Whether developing a new system or replacing an existing system, it is very important to specify the requirements of the new system precisely and unambiguously. There are frequently many users of the system; in a large company, these might be engineers, marketing and sales staff, managers, IT staff, administrative staff, etc. The requirements of each group of users, often referred to as stakeholders, must be understood and specified.

6.1.1 Requirements Analysis

The software requirements describe the functionality that the system must provide for the users. Requirements analysis involves analyzing the requirements – for example, by interviewing users – and analyzing the existing system(s), manual or automated. Questions to ask users include the following: What is your role in the current system (manual or automated)? How do you use the current system? What are the advantages and limitations of the current system? What features should the new system provide for you? Analyzing an existing manual system involves understanding and documenting the current system, determining which features of the current system should be automated and which should remain manual, and discussing with users what functions could be done differently when the system is automated. Analyzing an existing software system necessitates extracting the software requirements, separating functional requirements from functions that result from design or implementation decisions, identifying nonfunctional requirements, deciding what functions should be done differently, and what new functions should be added.

6.1.2 Requirements Specification

After the analysis, the requirements need to be specified. The requirements specification is the document that needs to be agreed on by the requirements analysts and the users. It is the starting point for the subsequent design and development, so it must also be understood by the developers. Both functional requirements and nonfunctional requirements need to be specified.

A functional requirement describes the functionality the system must be capable of providing in order to fulfill the purpose of the system. In defining a functional requirement, it is necessary to describe what functionality the system needs to provide, what information needs to be input to the system from the external environment (such as external users, external systems, or external devices), what the system needs to output to the external environment, and what stored information the system reads or updates. For example, for a functional requirement to view the balance of a bank account, the user would need to input the account number, and the system would need to read the balance from the customer account and output the balance.

A nonfunctional requirement, sometimes referred to as a quality attribute, refers to a quality-of-service goal that the system must fulfill. Examples of nonfunctional requirements are a performance requirement specifying a system response time of 2 seconds, an availability requirement specifying a system must be operational for 99% of the time, or a security requirement, such as protection from system penetration.

6.1.3 Quality Attributes of Software Requirements Specification

The following attributes are considered desirable for a well-written Software Requirements Specification (SRS):

- **Correct.** Each requirement is an accurate interpretation of the user's needs.
- **Complete.** The SRS includes every significant requirement. In addition, the SRS needs to define the system's response to every possible input, whether it is correct or incorrect. Finally, there should not be any "TBDs".
- **Unambiguous.** This means that every stated requirement has only one interpretation. Vague statements must be replaced.
- **Consistent.** This refers to ensuring that individual requirements do not conflict. There might be conflicting terms, such as two terms that refer to the same concept. There might be conflicting requirements, such as one requirement making an incorrect assumption about a requirement upon which it depends. There might also be problems when a new requirement is added at a later stage that conflicts with an existing requirement.
- **Verifiable.** The requirements specification is, in effect, a contract between the developer and the customer organization. Software acceptance criteria are developed from the requirements specification. It is therefore necessary that every requirement can be tested to determine that system meets requirement.
- **Understandable by non-computer specialists.** Because the users of the system are likely to be non-computer specialists, it is important that the requirements specification be written in a narrative text that is easily understood.
- **Modifiable.** Because the requirements specification is likely to go through several iterations and needs to evolve after the system has been deployed, it is necessary for the requirements specification to be modifiable. To assist with this goal, the requirements specification needs to have a table of contents, an index, and cross-references. Each requirement should only be stated in one place; otherwise, inconsistencies could creep into the specification.
- **Traceable.** The requirements specification needs to be traceable backwards to the system level requirements and to the user needs. It also needs to be traceable forwards to the design component(s) that satisfy each requirement and to the code components that implement each requirement.

Frequently, dilemmas arise in the process of developing a requirements specification because some of these goals are conflicting. For example, to make the requirements specification understandable might conflict with the goals of making it consistent and unambiguous. User involvement is required at all stages of the requirements specification process to ensure that user needs are incorporated into the requirements specification. Ideally, users should be on the requirements specification team. Several reviews need to be held with users. Developing a throwaway prototype can be helpful to clarify user requirements, as described in Chapter 3. Prototyping is especially useful for automating a manual system when users might have little idea of what an automated system would be like. An overview of quality attributes is given in Chapter 4, and a detailed description is presented in Chapter 20.

6.2 USE CASES

In the use case modeling approach, functional requirements are described in terms of actors, which are users of the system, and use cases. A **use case** defines a sequence of interactions between one or more actors and the system. In the requirements phase, the use case model considers the system as a black box and describes the interactions between the actor(s) and the system in a narrative form consisting of user inputs and system responses. The **use case model** describes the functional requirements of the system in terms of the actors and use cases. The system is treated as a black box – that is, dealing with **what** the system does in response to the actor's inputs, not the internals of **how** it does it. During subsequent analysis modeling (see Chapter 8), the objects that participate in each use case are determined.

A use case always starts with input from an actor. A use case typically consists of a sequence of interactions between the actor and the system. Each interaction consists of an input from the actor followed by a response from the system. Thus, an actor provides inputs to the system and the system provides responses to the actor. The system is always considered as a black box, so that its internals are not revealed. Whereas a simple use case might involve only one interaction between an actor and the system, a more typical use case will consist of several interactions between the actor and the system. More complex use cases might also involve more than one actor.

Consider a simple banking example in which an automated teller machine (ATM) allows customers to withdraw cash from their bank accounts. There is one actor, the ATM Customer, and one use case, Withdraw Funds, as shown in Figure 6.1. The Withdraw Funds use case describes the sequence of interactions between the

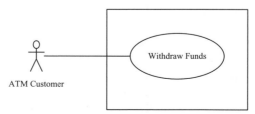

Figure 6.1. Example of actor and use case

customer and the system; the use case starts when the customer inserts an ATM card into the card reader, then responds to the system's prompt for the PIN, and eventually receives the cash dispensed by the ATM machine.

6.2.1 A Simple Use Case

As an example of a very simple use case, consider View Alarms from the Emergency Monitoring System. There is one actor, the Monitoring Operator, who can request to view the status of all alarms. The essentials of the use case description consist of the following:

- The name of the use case, View Alarms.
- The name of the actor, Monitoring Operator.
- A one-sentence use case summary, which provides a brief description.
- The description of the main sequence of events. For this use case, the first step is the operator request and the second step is the system response.
- The description of any alternative to the main sequence. For this use case, there could be an alternative at step 2, which would be executed if there is a monitoring emergency.

Use case name: View Alarms
Summary: The monitoring operator views outstanding alarms.
Actor: Monitoring Operator
Main sequence:
  1. The monitoring operator requests to view the outstanding alarms.
  2. The system displays the outstanding alarms. For each alarm, the system displays the name of the alarm, alarm description, location of alarm, and severity of alarm (high, medium, low).
Alternative sequences:
Step 2: Emergency situation. System displays emergency warning message to operator.

A more comprehensive approach to documenting a use case description is given in Section 6.5, and a more detailed example is presented in Section 6.6.

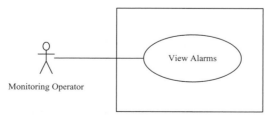

Figure 6.2. Example of simple use case

6.3 ACTORS

An **actor** characterizes an external user (i.e., outside the system) that interacts with the system (Rumbaugh et al. 2005). In the use case model, actors are the only external entities that interact with the system; in other words, actors are outside the system and not part of it.

6.3.1 Actors, Roles, and Users

An actor represents a role played in the application domain, typically by a human user. A user is an individual, whereas an actor represents the role played by all users of the same type. For example, there are several customers in the Banking System, who are all represented by the ATM Customer actor. Thus, ATM Customer actor models a user type, and individual customers are instances of the actor.

An actor is very often a human user. For this reason, in UML, an actor is depicted using a stick figure. In many information systems, humans are the only actors. In other systems, however, there are other types of actors in addition to or in place of human actors. Thus, it is possible for an actor to be an external system that interfaces to the system. In some applications, an actor can also be an external I/O device or a timer. External I/O device and timer actors are particularly prevalent in real-time embedded systems, in which the system interacts with the external environment through sensors and actuators.

6.3.2 Primary and Secondary Actors

A **primary actor** initiates a use case. Thus, the use case starts with an input from the primary actor to which the system has to respond. Other actors, referred to as **secondary actors**, can participate in the use case. A primary actor in one use case can be a secondary actor in another use case. At least one actor must gain value from the use case; usually, this is the primary actor.

An example of primary and secondary actors is shown in Figure 6.3. The Remote System actor initiates the Generate Monitoring Data use case, in which the remote system sends monitoring data that is displayed to monitoring operators. In this use case, the Remote System is the primary actor that initiates the use case, and the Monitoring Operator is a secondary actor who receives the monitoring data and, hence, gains value from the use case.

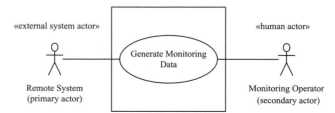

Figure 6.3. Example of primary and secondary actors, as well as external system actor

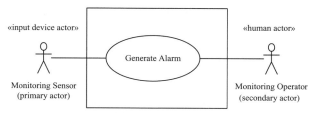

Figure 6.4. Example of input device actor

6.3.3 Modeling Actors

A **human actor** typically uses various I/O devices to physically interact with the system. Frequently, a human actor interacts with the system via standard I/O devices, such as a keyboard, display, or mouse. In some cases, however, a human actor might interact with the system via nonstandard I/O devices, such as various sensors. In all these cases, the human is the actor and the I/O devices are not actors. Thus, the actor is an end-user.

Consider some examples of human actors. In the Emergency Response System, an example of an actor is the Monitoring Operator who interacts with the system via standard I/O devices, as shown in Figure 6.2. Another example of a human actor is an ATM customer (Figure 6.1) who interacts with the Banking System by using several I/O devices, including a card reader, cash dispenser, and receipt printer, in addition to a keyboard and display.

An actor can also be an **external system actor** that either initiates (as primary actor) or participates (as secondary actor) in the use case. An example of an external system actor is the Remote System in the Emergency Monitoring System. The Remote System initiates the Generate Monitoring Data use case, as shown in Figure 6.3. The remote system sends monitoring data that is displayed to monitoring operators.

In some case, an actor can be an **input device actor** or an **input/output device actor**. This can happen when there is no human involvement with the use case and the actor providing external input to the system is an input device or I/O device. Typically, the input device actor interacts with the system via a sensor. An example of an input device actor is Monitoring Sensor, which provides sensor input to the Generate Alarm use case shown in Figure 6.4. The Monitoring Operator is also a secondary actor in this use case.

An actor can also be a **timer actor** that periodically sends timer events to the system. Periodic use cases are needed when certain information needs to be output by the system on a regular basis. An example of a timer actor is given in Figure 6.5.

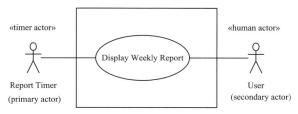

Figure 6.5. Example of timer actor

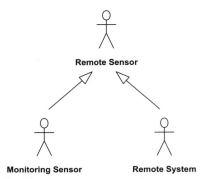

Figure 6.6. Generalization and specialization of actors

The Report Timer actor initiates the Display Daily Report use case, which periodically (e.g., at noon every day) prepares a daily report and displays it to the user. In this example, the timer is the primary actor and the user is the secondary actor. In use cases in which a timer is the primary actor, it is usually the secondary actor (the user in this example) who gains value from the use case.

If it is possible for a human user to play two or more independent roles, this is represented by a different actor for each role. For example, the same user might play, at different times, both an ATM Operator role (when replenishing the ATM cash dispenser with cash) and an ATM Customer role (when withdrawing cash) and thus be modeled by two actors.

In some systems, different actors might have some roles in common but other roles that are different. In this situation, the actors can be generalized, so that the common part of their roles is captured as a generalized actor and the different parts by specialized actors. As an example, consider the Emergency Response System (Chapter 23), in which two actors, a Monitoring Sensor actor and a Remote System actor, behave in a similar way by monitoring remote sensors and sending sensor data and alarms to the system. This similar behavior can be modeled by a generalized actor, Remote Sensor, which represents the common role (i.e., the behavior that is common to both the specialized actors), as shown in Figure 6.6.

6.3.4 Who Is the Actor?

Sometimes it is not clear who the actor is. In fact, the first assessment may not be correct. For example, in the use case Report Stolen Card, in which a user actor phones the bank to inform them that the ATM card has been stolen, it would seem obvious that the customer is the actor. However, if the customer in fact talks over the phone to a bank clerk, who actually enters the information into the system, then it is the clerk who is the actor.

6.4 IDENTIFYING USE CASES

To determine the use cases in the system, it is useful to start by considering the actors and the interactions they have with the system. Each use case describes a sequence

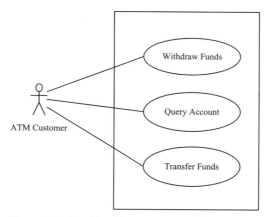

Figure 6.7. Banking System actor and use cases

of interactions between the actor and the system. In this way, the functional requirements of the system are described in terms of the use cases, which constitute a functional specification of a system. However, when developing use cases, it is important to avoid a functional decomposition in which several small use cases describe small individual functions of the system rather than describe a sequence of events that provides a useful result to the actor.

Let us consider the banking example again. In addition to withdrawing cash from the ATM, the ATM Customer actor is also allowed to query an account or transfer funds between two accounts. Because these are distinct functions initiated by the customer with different useful results, the query and transfer functions should be modeled as separate use cases, rather than being part of the original use case. Thus, the customer can initiate three use cases, as shown in Figure 6.7: Withdraw Funds, Query Account, and Transfer Funds.

The main sequence of the use case describes the most common sequence of interactions between the actor and the system. There may also be branches off the main sequence of the use case that describe less frequent interactions between the actor and the system. These alternative sequences are deviations from the main sequence that are executed only under certain circumstances – for example, if the actor makes an incorrect input to the system. Depending on the application requirements, an alternative sequence through the use case can sometimes join up later with the main sequence. The alternative sequences are also described in the use case.

In the Withdraw Funds use case, the main sequence is the sequence of steps for successfully achieving a withdrawal. Alternative sequences are used to address various error cases, such as when the customer enters the wrong PIN and must be reprompted, when an ATM card is not recognized or has been reported stolen, and so on.

Each sequence through the use case is called a **scenario**. A use case usually describes several scenarios, one main sequence and a number of alternative sequences. Note that a scenario is a complete sequence through the use case, so a scenario could start out executing the main sequence and then follow an alternative branch at the decision point. For example, one of the Withdraw Funds scenarios starts with the main sequence of the customer inserting the ATM card into the card reader, entering the PIN number in response to the prompt but then receiving an error message because the PIN was incorrect, and then entering the correct PIN.

6.5 DOCUMENTING USE CASES IN THE USE CASE MODEL

Each use case in the use case model is documented in a use case description, as follows:

Use case name: Each use case is given a name.

Summary: A brief description of the use case, typically one or two sentences.

Dependency: This optional section describes whether the use case depends on other use cases – that is, whether it includes or extends another use case.

Actors: This section names the actors in the use case. There is always a primary actor that initiates the use case. In addition, there may be secondary actors that also participate in the use case. For example in the Withdraw Funds use case, the ATM Customer is the only actor.

Preconditions: One or more conditions that must be true at the start of use case, from the perspective of this use case; for example, the ATM machine is idle, displaying a "Welcome" message.

Description of main sequence: The bulk of the use case is a narrative description of the main sequence of the use case, which is the most usual sequence of interactions between the actor and the system. The description is in the form of the input from the actor, followed by the response of the system.

Description of alternative sequences: Narrative description of alternative branches off the main sequence. There may be several alternative branches from the main sequence. For example, if the customer's account has insufficient funds, display apology and eject card. The step in the use case at which the alternative sequence branches off from the main sequence is identified as well as a description of the alternative.

Nonfunctional requirements: Narrative description of nonfunctional requirements, such as performance and security requirements.

Postcondition: Condition that is always true at the end of the use case (from the perspective of this use case) if the main sequence has been followed; for example, customer's funds have been withdrawn.

Outstanding questions: During development, questions about the use case are documented for discussions with users.

6.6 EXAMPLE OF USE CASE DESCRIPTION

An example of a use case is given in this section for Make Order Request, which is one of the use cases from the Online Shopping System. Figure 6.8 shows a use case

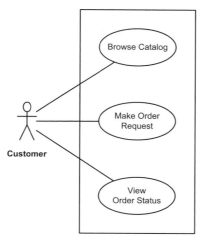

Figure 6.8. Online Shopping System actor and use cases

diagram for the customer-initiated use cases in the Online Shopping System. There is one actor – namely, the Customer, who browses a catalog and requests to purchase items – and three use cases that are the major functions initiated by the actor, which are Browse Catalog, to browse the catalog and select items, Make Order Request, to provide the account and credit card information for the purchase, and View Order, to view the status of the order. In the main sequence of the Make Order Request use case, the customer makes an order request to purchase items from an online catalog and has sufficient credit to pay for the items. The alternative sequences deal with other situations, which occur less frequently: the customer has no account and has to create one, or the customer has an invalid credit card.

Use case name: Make Order Request
Summary: Customer enters an order request to purchase items from the online shopping system. The customer's credit card is checked for sufficient credit to pay for the requested catalog items.
Actor: Customer
Precondition: The customer has selected one or more catalog items.
Main sequence:
1. Customer provides order request and customer account Id to pay for purchase.
2. System retrieves customer account information, including the customer's credit card details.
3. System checks the customer's credit card for the purchase amount and, if approved, creates a credit card purchase authorization number.
4. System creates a delivery order containing order details, customer Id, and credit card authorization number.
5. System confirms approval of purchase and displays order information to customer.

Alternative sequences:
Step 2: If customer does not have account, the system creates an account.
Step 3: If the customer's credit card request is denied, the system prompts the customer to enter a different credit card number. The customer can either enter a different credit card number or cancel the order.
Postcondition: System has created a delivery order for the customer.

6.7 USE CASE RELATIONSHIPS

When use cases get too complex, dependencies between use cases can be defined by using the *include* and *extend* relationships. The objective is to maximize extensibility and reuse of use cases. *Inclusion use cases* are determined to identify common sequences of interactions in several use cases, which can then be extracted and reused.

Another use case relationship provided by the UML is the use case generalization. *Use case generalization* is similar to the extend relationship because it is also used for addressing variations. However, users often find the concept of use case generalization confusing, so in the COMET method, the concept of generalization is confined to classes. Use case variations can be adequately handled by the *extend* relationship.

6.8 THE INCLUDE RELATIONSHIP

After the use cases for an application are initially developed, common sequences of interactions between the actor and the system can sometimes be determined that span several use cases. These common sequences of interactions reflect functionality that is common to more than one use case. A common sequence of interactions can be extracted from several of the original use cases and made into a new use case, which is called an **inclusion use case**. An inclusion use case is usually abstract; that is, it cannot be executed on its own. An abstract use case must be executed as part of a concrete – that is, executable – use case.

When this common functionality is separated into an inclusion use case, this use case can now be reused by other use cases. It is then possible to define a more concise version of the old use case, with the common interaction sequence removed. This concise version of the old use case is referred to as a **base use case** (or concrete use case), which includes the inclusion use case.

Inclusion use cases always reflect functionality that is common to more than one use case. When this common functionality is separated into an inclusion use case, the inclusion use case can be reused by several base (executable) use cases. Inclusion use cases can often be developed only after an initial iteration in which several use cases have been developed. Only then can repeated sequences of interactions be observed that form the basis for the inclusion use cases.

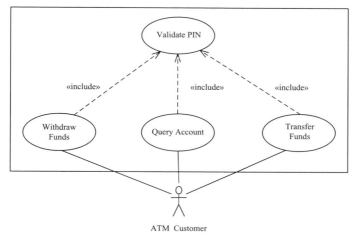

Figure 6.9. Example of an inclusion use case and include relationships

An inclusion use case is executed in conjunction with a base use case, which includes and, hence, executes the inclusion use case. In programming terms, an inclusion use case is analogous to a library routine, and a base use case is analogous to a program that calls the library routine.

An inclusion use case might not have a specific actor. The actor is, in fact, the actor of the base use case that includes the inclusion use case. Because different base use cases use the inclusion use case, it is possible for the inclusion use case to be used by different actors.

6.8.1 Example of Include Relationship and Inclusion Use Cases

As an example of an inclusion use case, consider a Banking System (see Banking System case study described in Chapter 21). There is one actor, the ATM Customer. Initial analysis of the system identifies three use cases, which are the major functions initiated by the actor – the Withdraw Funds, Query Account, and Transfer Funds use cases. In the Withdraw Funds use case, the main sequence involves reading the ATM card, validating the customer's PIN, checking that the customer has enough funds in the requested account, and then – providing the validation is successful – dispensing cash, printing a receipt, and ejecting the card. Further analysis of these three use cases reveals that the first part of each use case – namely, reading the ATM card and validating the customer's PIN – is identical. There is no advantage to repeating this sequence in each use case, so instead, the PIN validation sequence is split off into a separate inclusion use case called Validate PIN, which is used by the (revised) Withdraw Funds, Query Account, and Transfer Funds use cases. The use case diagram for this example is shown in Figure 6.9. The relationship between the two types of use cases is an *include* relationship; the Withdraw Funds, Query Account, and Transfer Funds use cases *include* the Validate PIN use case.

The main parts of the use case descriptions are given for the inclusion use case, Validate PIN, and a base use case, Withdraw Funds, that includes the Validate PIN use case:

Validate PIN Inclusion Use Case

Use case name: Validate PIN
Summary: System validates customer PIN.
Actor: ATM Customer
Precondition: ATM is idle, displaying a "Welcome" message.
Main sequence:
  1. Customer inserts the ATM card into the card reader.
  2. If system recognizes the card, it reads the card number.
  3. System prompts customer for PIN.
  4. Customer enters PIN.
  5. System checks the card's expiration date and whether the card has been reported as lost or stolen.
  6. If card is valid, system then checks whether the user-entered PIN matches the card PIN maintained by the system.
  7. If PIN numbers match, system checks what accounts are accessible with the ATM card.
  8. System displays customer accounts and prompts customer for transaction type: withdrawal, query, or transfer.

Alternative sequences: (Description of alternatives as given in Chapter 21.)

Withdraw Funds Base Use Case

Use case name: Withdraw Funds
Summary: Customer withdraws a specific amount of funds from a valid bank account.
Actor: ATM Customer
Dependency: Include Validate PIN use case.
Precondition: ATM is idle, displaying a "Welcome" message.
Main sequence:
  1. Include Validate PIN use case.
  2. Customer selects **Withdrawal**.
  3. (Continue with withdrawal description as given in Chapter 21.)

6.8.2 Structuring a Lengthy Use Case

The *include* relationship can also be used to structure a lengthy use case. The base use case provides the high-level sequence of interactions between actor(s) and system. Inclusion use cases provide lower-level sequences of interactions between

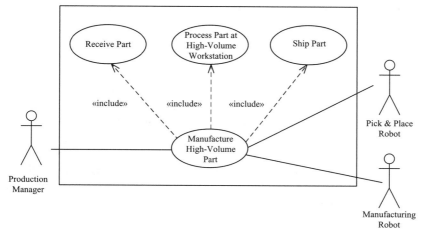

Figure 6.10. Example of multiple inclusion use cases and include relationships

actor(s) and system. An example of this is the Manufacture High-Volume Part use case (Figure 6.10), which describes the sequence of interactions in manufacturing a part. This process involves receiving the raw material for the part to be manufactured (described in the Receive Part use case), executing a manufacturing step at each factory workstation (described in the Process Part at High-Volume Workstation use case), and shipping the manufactured part (described in the Ship Part use case).

6.9 THE EXTEND RELATIONSHIP

In certain situations, a use case can get very complex, with many alternative branches. The extend relationship is used to model alternative paths that a use case might take. A use case can become too complex if it has too many alternative, optional, and exceptional sequences of interactions. A solution to this problem is to split off an alternative or optional sequence of interactions into a separate use case. The purpose of this new use case is to extend the old use case, if the appropriate condition holds. The use case that is extended is referred to as the **base use case**, and the use case that does the extending is referred to as the **extension use case**.

Under certain conditions, a base use case can be extended by a description given in the extension use case. A base use case can be extended in different ways, depending on which condition is true. The extend relationship can be used as follows:

- To show a conditional part of the base use case that is executed only under certain circumstances
- To model complex or alternative paths.

It is important to note that the base use case does not depend on the extension use case. The extension use case, on the other hand, depends on the base use case and executes only if the condition in the base use case that causes it to execute is true. Although an extension use case usually extends only one base use case, it is possible for it to extend more than one. A base use case can be extended by more than one extension use case.

6.9.1 Extension Points

Extension points are used to specify the precise locations in the base use case at which extensions can be added. An extension use case may extend the base use case only at these extension points (Fowler 2004; Rumbaugh et al. 2005).

Each extension point is given a name. The extension use case has one insertion segment for the extension point. This segment is inserted at the location of its extension point in the base use case. The extend relationship can be conditional, meaning that a condition is defined that must be true for the extension use case to be invoked. Thus, it is possible to have more than one extension use case for the same extension point, but with each extension use case satisfying a different condition.

A segment defines a behavior sequence to be executed when the extension point is reached. When an instance of the use case is executed and reaches the extension point in the base use case, if the condition is satisfied, then execution of the use case is transferred to the corresponding segment in the extension use case. Execution transfers back to the base use case after completion of the segment.

An extension point with multiple extension use cases can be used to model several alternatives in which each extension use case specifies a different alternative. The extension conditions are designed such that only one condition can be true and, hence, only one extension use case selected, for any given situation.

The value of the extension condition is set during runtime execution of the use case because, at any one time, one extension use case could be chosen and, at a different time, an alternative extension use case could be chosen. In other words, the extension condition is set and changes during runtime of the use case.

Although it is possible for an extension use case to extend a use case at more than one extension point, this approach is only recommended if the extension points are extended in the identical way by the extension use case. In particular, use of multiple insertion segments within one extension use case is tricky and, therefore, considered error-prone.

6.9.2 Example of Extension Point and Extension Use Cases

Consider the following example for a supermarket system (Figure 6.11). An extension point called payment is declared in a base use case called Checkout Customer. The base use case deals with checking out a customer purchase. Three extension use cases deal with the type of payment made: Pay by Cash, Pay by Credit Card, and Pay by Debit Card. A selection condition is provided for each extension use case. The extend relationship is annotated with the extension point name and the selection condition – for example, «extend» (payment) [cash payment], as depicted in Figure 6.11. The mutually exclusive selection conditions are [cash payment], [credit card payment], and [debit card payment], respectively. During execution of the use case, depending on how the customer chooses to pay, the appropriate selection condition is set to true.

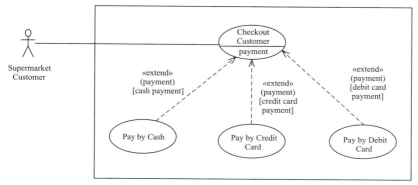

Figure 6.11. Example of an extend relationship and extension use cases

Checkout Customer Base Use Case

Use case name: Checkout Customer
Summary: System checks out customer.
Actor: Customer
Precondition: Checkout station is idle, displaying a "Welcome" message.
Main sequence:
    1. Customer scans selected item.
    2. System displays the item name, price, and cumulative total.
    3. Customer repeats steps 1 and 2 for each item being purchased.
    4. Customer selects payment.
    5. System prompts for payment by cash, credit card, or debit card.
    6. «payment»
    7. System displays thank-you screen.

In this base use case description, at step 6 «payment» is a placeholder that identifies the location at which the appropriate extension use case is executed. For the Pay by Cash extension use case, the extension condition is a selection condition called [cash payment]. This extension use case is executed if the condition [cash payment] is true.

Pay by Cash Extension Use Case

Use case name: Pay by Cash
Summary: Customer pays by cash for items purchased.
Actor: Customer
Dependency: Extends Checkout Customer.
Precondition: Customer has scanned items but not yet paid for them.
Description of insertion segment:
    1. Customer selects payment by cash.
    2. System prompts customer to deposit cash in bills and/or coins.
    3. Customer enters cash amount.

4. System computes change.
5. System displays total amount due, cash payment, and change.
6. System prints total amount due, cash payment, and change on receipt.

For the Pay by Credit Card extension use case, the selection condition is called [credit card payment] (see Figure 6.11). This extension use case is executed if the [credit card payment] condition is true, meaning that the user chose to pay by credit card. Of course, if the user chose instead to pay by cash, then the Pay by Cash use case would be executed instead.

Pay by Credit Card Extension Use Case

Use case name: Pay by Credit Card
Summary: Customer pays by credit card for items purchased.
Actor: Customer
Dependency: Extends Checkout Customer.
Precondition: Customer has scanned items but not yet paid for them.
Description of of insertion segment:
1. Customer selects payment by credit card.
2. System prompts customer to swipe card.
3. Customer swipes card.
4. System reads card ID and expiration date.
5. System sends transaction to authorization center containing card ID, expiration date, and payment amount.
6. If transaction is approved, authorization center returns positive confirmation.
7. System displays payment amount and confirmation.
8. System prints payment amount and confirmation on receipt.

The use case description for the Pay by Debit Card extension use case is handled in a similar way, except that the customer also needs to enter a PIN. Pay by Cash has a selection condition called [debit card payment].

6.10 USE CASE STRUCTURING GUIDELINES

Careful application of use case relationships can help with the overall organization of the use case model; however, use case relationships should be employed judiciously. It should be noted that small inclusion use cases corresponding to individual functions (such as Dispense Cash, Print Receipt, and Eject Card) should not be considered. These functions are too small, and making them separate use cases would result in a functional decomposition with fragmented use cases in which the use case descriptions would be only a sentence each and not a description of a sequence of interactions. The result would be a use case model that is overly complex and difficult to understand – in other words, a problem of not being able to see the forest (the overall sequence of interactions) for the trees (the individual functions)!

6.11 SPECIFYING NONFUNCTIONAL REQUIREMENTS

Nonfunctional requirements can be specified in a separate section of the use case description, in much the same way that alternative sequences are specified. For example, for the Validate PIN use case, there could be a security requirement that the card number and PIN must be encrypted. There could also be a performance requirement that the system must respond to the actor inputs within 5 seconds. If the nonfunctional requirements apply to a group of related use cases, then they can be documented as such, as described in the next section.

The nonfunctional requirements can be specified in a separate section of the use case. For the Validate PIN use case, they would be described as follows:

Security requirement: System shall encrypt ATM card number and PIN.
Performance requirement: System shall respond to actor inputs within 5 seconds.

6.12 USE CASE PACKAGES

For large systems, having to deal with a large number of use cases in the use case model often gets unwieldy. A good way to handle this scale-up issue is to introduce a **use case package** that groups together related use cases. In this way, use case packages can represent high-level requirements that address major subsets of the functionality of the system. Because actors often initiate and participate in related use cases, use cases can also be grouped into packages based on the major actors that use them. Nonfunctional requirements that apply to a group of related use cases could be assigned to the use case package that contains those use cases.

For example, in the Emergency Monitoring System, the major actors of the system are the Remote Sensor, Monitoring Operator, and Emergency Manager, each of whom initiates and participates in several use cases. Figure 6.12 shows an example of a use case package for the Emergency Monitoring System – namely, the Emergency Monitoring Use Case Package, which encompasses four use cases. The Monitoring Operator is the primary actor of the View Alarms and View Monitoring Data use cases and a secondary actor of the other use cases. The Remote Sensor is the primary actor of the Generate Alarm and Generate Monitoring Data use cases.

6.13 ACTIVITY DIAGRAMS

An activity diagram is a UML diagram depicting the flow of control and sequencing among activities. An activity diagram shows the sequence of activities, decision nodes, loops, and even concurrent activities. Activity diagrams are widely used in workflow modeling – for example, for service-oriented applications.

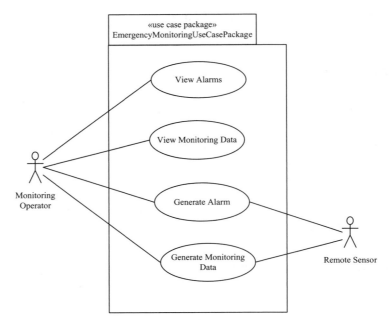

Figure 6.12. Example of use case package

A use case model can also be described using an activity diagram. However, to depict a use case, a subset of the activity diagram capabilities is sufficient. In particular, it is not necessary to model concurrent activities for use cases.

An activity diagram can be used to represent the sequential steps of a use case, including the main sequence and all the alternative sequences. An activity diagram can therefore be used to provide a more precise description of the use case, because it shows exactly where in the sequence and what the condition is for an alternative sequence to diverge from the main sequence. An activity node can be used to represent one or more sequential steps of the use case. A high-level activity node can be used to represent a use case, which can then be decomposed into a separate activity diagram. Activity diagrams can also be used to depict sequencing among use cases.

For depicting a use case, an activity diagram uses activity nodes, decision nodes, arcs to join sequential activity nodes, and loops. An activity node is used to depict one or more steps in the use case description. A decision node is used to depict a situation in which, based on the result of the decision, an alternative sequence could branch off from the main sequence. Depending on the use case, the alternative sequence could rejoin the main sequence – for example, by looping back to a previous activity node or rejoining the main sequence further down.

Activity nodes can be aggregate nodes that are hierarchically decomposed to give a lower-level activity diagram. This concept can be used to depict inclusion and extension use cases. Thus, an activity node in a base use case can be used to

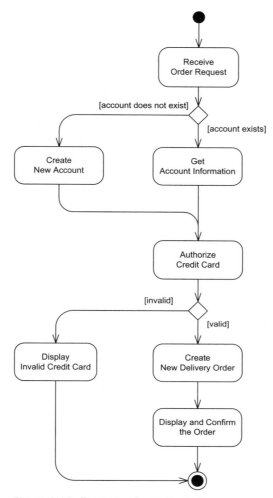

Figure 6.13. Example of activity diagram

represent a link to an inclusion (or extension) use case, which is then depicted on a separate lower-level activity diagram.

An example of an activity diagram is given in Figure 6.13 for the Make Order Request use case of the Online Shopping System (see Section 6.6). This use case consists of a main sequence in which the customer makes an order request to purchase items from an online catalog and has sufficient credit to pay for the items. The alternative sequences are for creating a new customer account and for an invalid credit card. Each decision point that results in an alternative scenario is explicitly depicted. In the example, the customer enters the order request information, system gets account information (with an alternative sequence to create a new account), and requests credit card authorization. If the credit card is valid, the system creates a new delivery order and displays the order. If the credit card is invalid, the system displays an invalid credit card prompt.

6.14 SUMMARY

This chapter provided an overview of requirements analysis and specification and described the use case approach to defining the functional requirements of the system. It described the concepts of actor and use cases. It also described use case relationships, particularly the extend and include relationships.

The use case model has a strong influence on subsequent software development; thus, use cases are realized in the analysis model during dynamic interaction modeling, as described in Chapters 9 and 11. For each use case, the objects that participate in the use case are determined by using the object structuring criteria described in Chapter 8, and the sequence of interactions between the objects is defined. Software can be incrementally developed by selecting the use cases to be developed in each phase of the project, as described in Chapter 5. Integration and system test cases should also be based on use cases. Statecharts can also be used to depict the states and transitions for a state-dependent use case, as described in Chapter 10.

EXERCISES

Multiple-choice questions: For each question, choose one of the answers.

1. What is a use case?
   (a) A case study involving users
   (b) A sequence of interactions between the user and the system
   (c) A sequence of interactions between the user and the objects in the system
   (d) A sequence of user inputs to the system

2. What is an actor in a use case?
   (a) An object inside the system
   (b) A person who performs on stage
   (c) An external entity that interacts with the system
   (d) The customer to whom the system will be delivered

3. What is a primary actor?
   (a) The actor who goes on stage first
   (b) The actor that starts the use case
   (c) An actor that participates in the use case
   (d) An object inside the system

4. What is a secondary actor?
   (a) The actor who goes on stage second
   (b) The actor that starts the use case
   (c) An actor that participates in the use case
   (d) An object inside the system

5. What is an alternative sequence in a use case?

(a) A sequence that describes an error case
(b) A sequence that is different from the main sequence
(c) A sequence that describes interactions with a secondary actor
(d) A sequence that describes interactions with a primary actor

6. What can an inclusion use case be used for?
   (a) To describe an inclusive use case
   (b) To describe a lengthy interaction with an actor
   (c) To describe functionality that is common to more than one use case
   (d) To describe a use case that includes other use cases

7. What can an extension use case be used for?
   (a) To describe a lengthy interaction with an actor
   (b) To describe functionality that is common to more than one use case
   (c) To describe the functionality of a use case that is extended by another use case(s)
   (d) To describe a conditional part of a different use case that is only executed under certain circumstances

8. What can an activity diagram be used for in use case modeling?
   (a) To depict the sequence of activities executed by all the use cases in the system

(b) To depict the sequence of external activities that the use case interacts with

(c) To depict the sequence of active objects in a use case

(d) To depict the activities in the main and alternative sequences of a use case

9. How can a nonfunctional requirement be described in a use case model?

(a) In a separate section of the use case description

(b) As a use case precondition

(c) As a use case postcondition

(d) In a separate document

10. What is a use case package?

(a) A package describing the actors in the system

(b) A package describing the use cases in the system

(c) A group of related use cases

(d) The package of objects that participate in the use case

7

Static Modeling

The static model addresses the static structural view of a problem, which does not vary with time. A static model describes the static structure of the system being modeled, which is considered less likely to change than the functions of the system. In particular, a static model defines the classes in the system, the attributes of the classes, the relationships between classes, and the operations of each class. In this chapter, **static modeling** refers to the modeling process and the UML **class diagram** notation is used to depict the static model.

The concepts of objects, classes, and class attributes are described in Chapter 4. This chapter describes the relationships between classes. Three types of relationships are described: **associations**, whole/part (**composition** and **aggregation)** relationships, and **generalization/specialization (inheritance)** relationships. In addition, this chapter addresses special considerations in static modeling of the problem domain, including static modeling of the total system context and software system context, as well as static modeling of entity classes. Design of class operations is deferred to the design phase, and is addressed during class design, as described in Chapter 14.

Static models are depicted on class diagrams, as described in this chapter. Section 7.1 describes the different kinds of associations between classes. Section 7.2 describes whole/part relationships, particularly composition and aggregation hierarchies. Section 7.3 describes generalization/specialization hierarchies. Section 7.4 provides an overview of constraints. Section 7.5 describes static modeling with UML, in which the initial emphasis is on modeling the physical classes and entity classes. The next topic, covered in Section 7.6, is static modeling of the scope of the total system (hardware and software) and the scope of the software system in order to determine the border between the total system and the external environment, and then the border between the software system and the external environment. Section 7.7 describes the categorization of classes using UML stereotypes, and Section 7.8 describes how UML stereotypes can be applied to modeling external classes. Static modeling of the entity classes, which are data-intensive classes, is described in Section 7.9.

7.1 ASSOCIATIONS BETWEEN CLASSES

An **association** defines a relationship between two or more classes, denoting a static, structural relationship between classes. For example, Employee *Works in* Department, where Employee and Department are classes and *Works in* is an association. The classes are nouns, whereas the association is usually a verb or verb phrase.

A *link* is a connection between instances of the classes (objects) and represents an instance of an association between classes. For example, Jane *Works in* Manufacturing, where Jane is an instance of Employee and Manufacturing is an instance of Department. A link can exist between two objects if, and only if, there is an association between their corresponding classes.

Associations are inherently bidirectional. The name of the association is in the forward direction: Employee *Works in* Department. There is also an implied opposite direction of the association (which is often not explicitly stated): Department *Employs* Employee. Associations are most often binary – that is, representing a relationship between two classes. However, they can also be unary (self-associations), ternary, or higher order.

7.1.1 Depicting Associations on Class Diagrams

On class diagrams, an association is shown as an arc joining the two class boxes, with the name of the association next to the arc. An example is given in Figure 7.1 of the association Company *Is led by* CEO.

In class diagrams, association names usually read from left to right and top to bottom. However, on a large class diagram with many classes, classes are usually in different positions relative to each other. To avoid ambiguity when reading UML class diagrams, COMET uses the UML arrowhead notation to point in the direction in which the association name should be read, as shown in Figure 7.1.

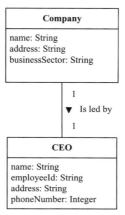

Figure 7.1. Example of one-to-one association

7.1.2 Multiplicity of Associations

The *multiplicity* of an association specifies how many instances of one class can relate to a single instance of another class. The multiplicity of an association can be as follows:

- **One-to-one association.** In a one-to-one association between two classes, the association is one-to-one in both directions. Thus, an object of either class has a link to only one object of the other class. For example, in the association Company *Is led by* CEO (i.e., Chief Executive Officer), a particular company has only one CEO, and a CEO is leader of only one company. An example is the company Apple with its CEO Steve Jobs. The static modeling notation for a one-to-one association is illustrated in Figure 7.1.
- **One-to-many association.** In a one-to-many association, there is a one-to-many association in one direction between the two classes and a one-to-one association between them in the opposite direction. For example, in the association, Bank *Administers* Account, an individual bank administers many accounts, but an individual account is administered by only one bank. The static modeling notation for a one-to-many association is illustrated in Figure 7.2.
- **Numerically specified association.** A numerically specified association is an association that refers to a specific number. For example, in the association Car *Is entered through* Door, one car has two doors or four doors (depicted as 2, 4) but never one, three, or five doors. The association in the opposite direction is still one-to-one – that is, a door belongs to only one car. Note that a particular car manufacturer makes the decision of how many doors a car can have; another manufacturer might make a different decision. A numerically specified association is illustrated in Figure 7.3.
- **Optional association.** In an optional association, there might not always be a link from an object in one class to an object in the other class. For example, in the association Customer *owns* Debit Card, customers can choose whether or not they have a debit card. The optional (zero or one) association is shown in Figure 7.4. It is also possible to have a zero, one, or more association. For example, in the association Customer *Owns* Credit Card, a customer could have no credit

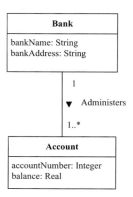

Figure 7.2. Example of one-to-many association

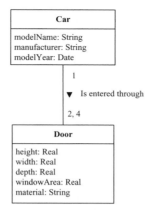

Figure 7.3. Numerically specified association

cards, one credit card, or many credit cards, as shown in Figure 7.5. Note that in both these examples, the association in the opposite direction is one-to-one (e.g., Credit Card *Owned by* Customer).

■ **Many-to-many association.** A many-to-many association is an association between two classes with a one-to-many association in each direction. For example, in the association Course *Is attended by* Student, Student *Enrolls in* Course, there is a one-to-many association between a course and the students who attend it, because a course is attended by many students. There is also a one-to-many association in the opposite direction, because a student could enroll in many courses. This is illustrated in Figure 7.6, which shows the association in each direction.

An example of classes and their associations in a banking application is given in Figure 7.7. The Bank class has a one-to-many association with the Customer class and with the Debit Card class. Thus, a bank provides a service for many customers

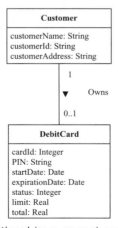

Figure 7.4. Optional (zero or one) association

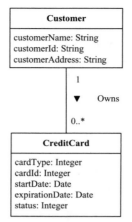

Figure 7.5. Optional (zero, one, or many) association

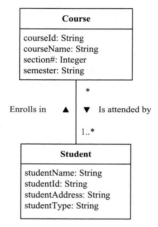

Figure 7.6. Many-to-many association

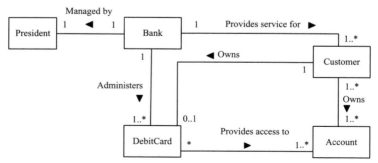

Figure 7.7. Example of associations on a class diagram

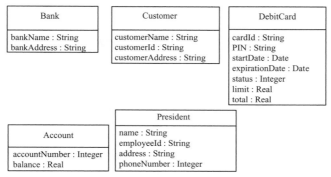

Figure 7.8. Example of class attributes

and administers many debit cards. Customer has a many-to-many association with Account, so a customer might own more than one account, and an account could be a joint account belonging to more than one customer. Customer has an optional association with Debit Card, so a given customer might or might not own a debit card, but a debit card must belong to a customer. Bank has a one-to-one association with President, so a bank can have only one president, and a president can be president of only one bank. The attributes of these classes are shown in Figure 7.8.

7.1.3 Ternary Associations

A ternary association is a three-way association among classes. An example of a ternary association is among the classes Buyer, Seller, and Agent. The association is that the Buyer negotiates a price with the Seller through an Agent. This is illustrated in Figure 7.9. The ternary association is shown as a diamond joining the three classes. A higher-order association, which is an association among more than three classes, is quite rare.

7.1.4 Unary Associations

A unary association, also referred to as a self-association, is an association between an object of one class and another object in the same class. Examples are Person

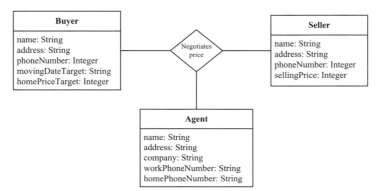

Figure 7.9. Example of ternary association

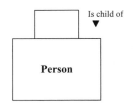

Figure 7.10. Example of unary association

Is child of Person (Figure 7.10), Person *Is married to* Person, and Employee *Is boss of* Employee.

7.1.5 Association Classes

An *association class* is a class that models an association between two or more classes. The attributes of the association class are the attributes of the association. In a complex association between two or more classes, it is possible for an association to have attributes. This happens most often in many-to-many associations, where an attribute does not belong to any of the classes but belongs to the association.

For an example of an association class, consider the many-to-many association between Project and Employee classes. In this association, a project is staffed by many employees and an employee can work on many projects:

Project *Is staffed by* Employee
Employee *Works on* Project

Figure 7.11 illustrates the two classes, Employee and Project, as well as an association class called Hours, whose attribute is hours Worked. The attribute hours Worked is not an attribute of either the Employee or Project classes. It is an attribute of the association between Employee and Project because it represents the hours worked by a specific employee (of which there are many) on a specific project (an employee works on many projects).

7.2 COMPOSITION AND AGGREGATION HIERARCHIES

Both composition and aggregation hierarchies address a class that is made up of other classes. Composition and aggregations are special forms of a relationship in which classes are connected by the *whole/part* relationship. In both cases, the relationship between the parts and the whole is an *Is part of* relationship.

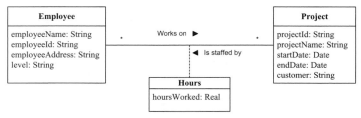

Figure 7.11. Example of association class

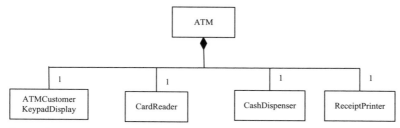

Figure 7.12. Example of composition hierarchy

A composition is a stronger relationship than an aggregation, and an aggregation is a stronger relationship than an association. In particular, a composition relationship is a stronger relationship between the parts and the whole than an aggregation relationship. A composition is also a relationship among instances. Thus, the part objects are created, live, and die together with the whole. The part object can belong to only one whole.

A composite class often involves a physical relationship between the whole and the parts. Thus, the ATM is a composite class consisting of four parts: a Card Reader, a Cash Dispenser, a Receipt Printer, and the ATM Customer Keypad Display classes (as shown in Figure 7.12). The ATM composite class has a one-to-one association with each of its four part classes.

The aggregation hierarchy is a weaker form of whole/part relationship. In an aggregation, part instances can be added to and removed from the aggregate whole. For this reason, aggregations are likely to be used to model conceptual classes rather than physical classes. In addition, a part could belong to more than one aggregation. An example of an aggregation hierarchy is a College in a university (Figure 7.13), whose parts are an Admin Office, several Departments, and several Research Centers. New departments can be created, and old departments are occasionally removed or merged with other departments. Research centers can also be created, removed, or merged.

In both composition and aggregation, attributes are propagated from the whole to the part. Thus, each ATM has an ATM Id that also identifies the specific card

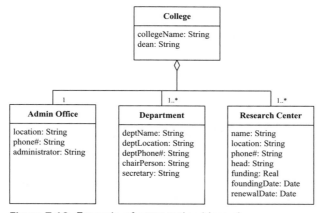

Figure 7.13. Example of aggregation hierarchy

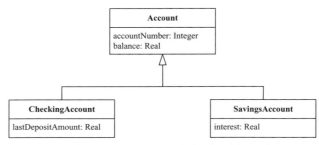

Figure 7.14. Generalization/specialization hierarchy

reader, cash dispenser, and customer keypad/display, which are part of the ATM composite class.

7.3 GENERALIZATION/SPECIALIZATION HIERARCHY

Some classes are similar but not identical. They have some attributes in common and others that are different. In a **generalization/specialization hierarchy**, common attributes are abstracted into a generalized class, which is referred to as a *superclass*. The different attributes are properties of the specialized class, which is referred to as a *subclass*. There is an *Is a* relationship between the subclass and the superclass. The superclass is also referred to as a parent class or ancestor class. The subclass is also referred to as a child class or descendent class.

Each subclass inherits the properties of the superclass but then extends these properties in different ways. The properties of a class are its attributes or operations. Inheritance allows the adaptation of the superclass to form the subclass. The subclass inherits the attributes and the operations from the superclass. The subclass could then add attributes, add operations, or redefine operations. Each subclass could itself also be a superclass, which is specialized further to develop other subclasses. Designing superclass and subclass operations is described in Chapter 14.

Consider the example of bank accounts given in Figure 7.14. Checking accounts and savings accounts have some attributes in common and others that are different. The attributes that are common to all accounts – namely, account Number and balance – are made the attributes of an Account superclass. Attributes specific to a savings account, such as the interest accumulated (in this bank, checking accounts do not accumulate any interest), are made the attributes of the subclass Savings Account. Attributes specific to a checking account, such as the last Deposit Amount, are made the attributes of the subclass Checking Account.

Savings Account *Is a* Account
Checking Account *Is a* Account

A *discriminator* is an attribute that indicates which property of the object is being abstracted by the generalization relationship. For example, the *discriminator* in the Account generalization just given, account Type, discriminates between Checking Account and Savings Account, as shown in Figure 7.15. The discriminator does not need to be an attribute of the generalized or specialized classes. Thus, it is not an attribute of the Account superclass or the two subclasses.

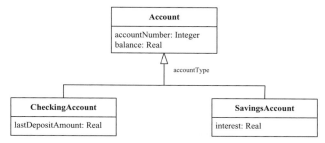

Figure 7.15. Discriminator in generalization/specialization

7.4 CONSTRAINTS

A *constraint* specifies a condition or restriction that must be true (Rumbaugh, Booch, and Jacobson 2005). A constraint is expressed in any textual language. The UML also provides a constraint language, the Object Constraint Language (OCL) (Warmer and Kleppe 1999), which can optionally be used.

One kind of constraint is a restriction on the possible values of an attribute. Consider the following: in the banking example, it might be stipulated that accounts are not allowed to have a negative balance. This can be expressed as a constraint on the attribute balance of the Account class to state that the balance is not allowed to be negative, {balance >= 0}. On a class diagram, the constraint on the attribute is shown next to the attribute to which it applies, as illustrated in Figure 7.16.

Another kind of constraint is a restriction on an association link. Usually objects on the "many" side of an association have no order. However, in some cases, objects in the problem domain might have an explicit order that is desirable to model. Consider, for example, the one-to-many association Account *Modified by* ATM Transaction. In this association, ATM transactions are ordered by time; hence, the constraint can be expressed as {ordered by time}. This constraint can be depicted on a class diagram, as shown in Figure 7.17.

7.5 STATIC MODELING AND THE UML

The approach used in COMET is to have a conceptual static model early in the analysis phase that is used to model and help understand the problem domain. The goal is to focus on those parts of the problem domain that benefit most from static modeling, particularly the physical classes and the data-intensive classes, which are called entity classes. This section describes the initial conceptual static modeling carried out during analysis; the more detailed static modeling carried out during design is described in Chapter 14.

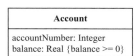

Figure 7.16. Example of constraints on objects

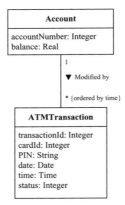

Figure 7.17. Example of ordering in an association

7.5.1 Static Modeling of the Problem Domain

In static modeling of the problem domain, the initial emphasis is on modeling physical classes and entity classes. **Physical classes** are classes that have physical characteristics – that is, they can be seen and touched. Such classes include physical devices (which are often part of the problem domain in embedded applications), users, external systems, and timers. **Entity classes** are conceptual data-intensive classes that are often persistent – that is, long-living. Entity classes are particularly prevalent in information systems (e.g., in a banking application, examples include accounts and transactions).

In embedded systems, in which there are several physical devices such as sensors and actuators, class diagrams can help with modeling these real-world devices. For example, in the Banking System, in which the ATM is an embedded subsystem, it is useful to model real-world devices, their associations, and the multiplicity of the associations. Composite classes are often used to show how a real-world class is composed of other classes (e.g., the ATM depicted in Figure 7.18).

Consider the static model of the problem domain for the banking application. A bank provides a service for several ATMs, as shown on Figure 7.18. Each ATM is a composite class consisting of a Card Reader, a Cash Dispenser, a Receipt Printer, and an ATM Customer Keypad Display. The ATM Customer actor inserts the card into the Card Reader and interacts though the ATM Customer Keypad Display. The Cash Dispenser dispenses cash to the ATM Customer actor. The Receipt Printer prints a receipt for the ATM Customer actor. The physical entities represent classes in the problem domain for which there will need to be a conceptual representation in the software system. These decisions are made during object and class structuring, as described in Chapter 8. In addition, the Operator actor is a user whose job is to maintain the ATM.

7.6 STATIC MODELING OF THE SYSTEM CONTEXT

It is very important to understand the scope of a computer system – in particular, what is to be included inside the system and what is to be left outside the system.

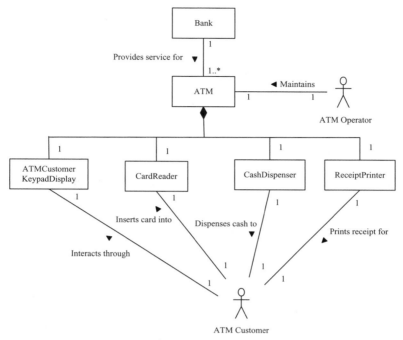

Figure 7.18. Conceptual static model for Banking System

Context modeling explicitly identifies what is inside the system and what is outside. Context modeling can be done at the total system (hardware and software) level or at the software system (software only) level. A diagram that explicitly shows the border between the system (hardware and software), which is treated as a black box, and the external environment is called a **system context diagram**. A diagram that explicitly shows the border between the software system, also treated as a black box, and the external environment (which now includes the hardware) is called a **software system context diagram**. These views of the border around the system are more detailed than those usually provided by a use case diagram.

In developing the system context diagram, it is helpful to consider the context of the total hardware/software system (i.e., both hardware and software) before considering the context of the software system. This is particularly useful in situations in which hardware/software tradeoffs need to be made. In considering the total hardware/software system, only users (i.e., human actors) and external systems are outside the system. I/O devices are part of the hardware of the system and therefore appear inside the total system.

As an example, consider the total hardware/software system for the Banking System. From a total hardware/software system perspective, the ATM Customer and ATM Operator actors, shown in Figure 7.18, are outside the system, as shown in Figure 7.19. All the others entities shown in Figure 7.18, in particular the I/O devices, which include the card reader, cash dispenser, receipt printer, and the ATM Customer keypad/display, are part of the total hardware/software system (Figure 7.19).

From the total system perspective – that is, both hardware and software – the ATM Customer and ATM Operator actors are external to the system, as shown in

Figure 7.19. Banking hardware/software system context class diagram

Figure 7.19. The ATM Operator interacts with the system via a keypad and display. The ATM Customer actor interacts with the system via four I/O devices, which are the card reader, cash dispenser, receipt printer, and ATM Customer keypad/display. From a total hardware/software system perspective, these I/O devices are part of the system. From a software perspective, the I/O devices are external to the software system. On the software system context class diagram, the I/O devices are modeled as external classes, as shown on Figure 7.20.

The software system context class diagram can be determined by static modeling of the external classes that connect to the system. In particular, the physical classes described in the previous section are often I/O devices that are external classes to the software system. Alternatively, the software system context class diagram can be determined from the use cases by considering the actors and what devices they use to interface to the system. Both approaches are described in Section 7.8.

7.7 CATEGORIZATION OF CLASSES USING UML STEREOTYPES

The dictionary definition of *category* is "a specifically defined division in a system of classification." In class structuring, the COMET method advocates categorizing classes in order to group together classes with similar characteristics. Whereas classification based on inheritance is an objective of object-oriented modeling, it is

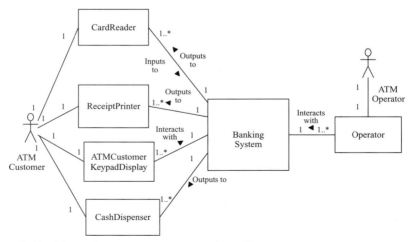

Figure 7.20. Banking software system context class diagram

Figure 7.21. Example of UML classes and their stereotypes

essentially tactical in nature. Thus, classifying the Account class into a Checking Account and a Savings Account is a good idea because Checking Account and Savings Account have some attributes and operations in common and others that differ. Categorization, however, is a strategic classification – a decision to organize classes into certain groups because most software systems have these kinds of classes and because categorizing classes in this way helps to better understand the system being developed.

In UML, stereotypes are used to distinguish among the various kinds of classes. A **stereotype** is a subclass of an existing modeling element (e.g., an application or external class) that is used to represent a usage distinction (e.g., the kind of application or external class). In the UML notation, a stereotype is enclosed by guillemets, like this: «entity». In software applications, a class is categorized by the role it plays in the application. Application classes are categorized according to their role in the application, such as «entity» class or «boundary» class, as will be described in Chapter 8. External classes are categorized on the basis of their characteristics in the external environment, such as «external system» or «external user», as will be described in Section 7.8.

Examples shown in Figure 7.21 from the Banking System are the external I/O device Card Reader, the external output devices Cash Dispenser and Receipt Printer, and the entity classes Account and Customer.

7.8 MODELING EXTERNAL CLASSES

Using the UML notation for the static model, the system context is depicted showing the hardware/software system as an aggregate class with the stereotype «system», and the external environment is depicted as external classes to which the system has to interface, as shown in Figure 7.19. In the case of a software system, the context is depicted showing the software system as an aggregate class with the stereotype «software system», and the external environment is depicted as external classes to which the software system has to interface, as shown in Figure 7.20.

Figure 7.22 shows the classification of external classes, which are categorized by stereotype (see Section 7.7); thus, stereotypes are used to distinguish among the various kinds of external classes. In Figure 7.22, each box represents a different category of external class, and the relationships between them are inheritance relationships. Thus, an external class is classified as an «external user» class, an «external device» class, an «external system» class, or an «external timer» class. Only external users and external systems are actually external to the total system. Hardware devices and timers are part of the total system but are external to the software

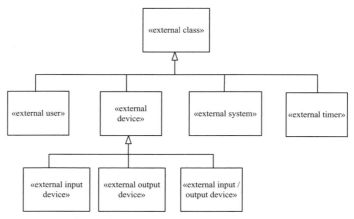

Figure 7.22. Classification of external classes by stereotype

system; thus, Figure 7.22 classifies external classes from the perspective of the software system.

As depicted in Figure 7.22, an external device is classified further as follows:

- **External input device.** A device that only provides input to the system – for example, a sensor
- **External output device.** A device that only receives output from the system – for example, an actuator
- **External I/O device.** A device that both provides input to the system and receives output from the system – for example, an ATM card reader

A human user often interacts with the software system by means of standard I/O devices such as a keyboard/display and mouse. The characteristics of these standard I/O devices are of no interest because they are handled by the operating system. The interface to the user is of much greater interest in terms of what information is being output to the user and what information is being input by the user. For this reason, an external user interacting with the software system via standard I/O devices is depicted as an «external user».

A general guideline is that a human user should be represented as an external user class only if the user interacts with the system via standard I/O devices. On the other hand, if the user interacts with the software system via application-specific I/O devices, these I/O devices should be represented as external device I/O classes.

For a real-time embedded system, it is desirable to identify low-level external classes that correspond to the physical I/O devices to which the software system must interface. These external classes are depicted with the stereotype «external I/O device». Examples are the Arrival Sensor external input device and the Motor external output device in the Automated Guided Vehicle System.

An «external system» class is needed when the system interfaces to other systems, to either send data or receive data. Thus, in the Automated Guided Vehicle System, the software system interfaces to two external systems: the Supervisory System and the Display System.

An «external timer» class is used if the application needs to keep track of time and/or if it needs external timer events to initiate certain actions in the system. External timer classes are most frequently needed in real-time systems. An example from the Automated Guided Vehicle System is the Clock. It is needed because the software system needs external timer events to initiate various periodic activities. Sometimes the need for periodic activities only becomes apparent during design.

The associations between the software system aggregate class and the external classes are depicted on the software system context class diagram, showing in particular the multiplicity of the associations. The standard association names on software system context class diagrams are *Inputs to*, *Outputs to*, *Communicates with*, *Interacts with*, and *Signals*. These associations are used as follows:

external input device» *Inputs to* « software system»
«software system» *Outputs to* «external output device»
«external user» *Interacts with* « software system»
«external system» *Communicates with* « software system»
«external timer» *Signals* « software system»

Examples of associations on software system context class diagrams are as follows:

Card Reader *Inputs to* Banking System
Banking System *Outputs to* Cash Dispenser
Operator *Interacts with* Banking System
Supervisory System *Communicates with* Automated Guided Vehicle System
Clock *Signals* Automated Guided Vehicle System

7.8.1 Examples of Developing a Software System Context Class Diagram from External Classes

An example of a software system context class diagram is shown in Figure 7.20, which shows the external classes to which the Banking System has to interface. The external classes are determined directly from the static model of the problem domain as described previously. Furthermore, the external classes are categorized by stereotype, as described next.

In this example, three of these I/O devices are categorized as external device classes: the Card Reader, the Receipt Printer, and the Cash Dispenser. The ATM Customer Keypad/Display external class is categorized as an external user class because it is a standard I/O device. The Operator external class is also categorized as an external user class for the same reason. Because there is one instance of each of these external classes for each ATM and there are many ATMs, there is a one-to-many association between each external class and the Banking System. The software system context class diagram in which external classes are depicted using stereotypes is shown in Figure 7.23. Depicting the external class stereotype explicitly on the software system context class diagram visually describes the role played by each external class of the system. Thus, it is immediately obvious which classes represent external output devices and which classes represent external users.

Another example of a software system context class diagram is given for the Automated Guided Vehicle System, which is shown in Figure 7.24. This software

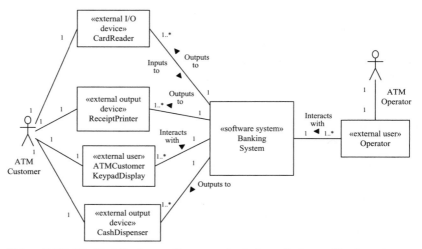

Figure 7.23. Banking System software context class diagram with stereotypes

system has six external classes: there are two external systems (Supervisory System and Display System), one external input device (Arrival Sensor), two external output devices (Robot Arm and Motor), and one external timer (Clock).

7.8.2 Actors and External Classes

Consider next how to derive the software system context class diagram by analyzing the actors that interact with the system. Actors are a more abstract concept than external classes. The relationship between actors and external classes is as follows:

- An **I/O device actor** is equivalent to an external I/O device class. This means the I/O device actor interfaces to the system via an external I/O device class.
- An **external system actor** is equivalent to an external system class.

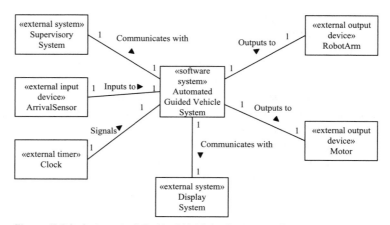

Figure 7.24. Automated Guided Vehicle System software system context class diagram with external class stereotypes

- A **timer actor** interfaces to the system via an external timer class, which provides timer events to the system.
- A **human user actor** has the most flexibility. In the simplest case, the user actor interfaces to the system via standard user I/O devices, such as keyboard, visual display, and mouse. The external class is given the name of its user actor because what is of interest is the logical information coming from the user. However, in more complex use cases, it is possible for a human actor to interface with the system through a variety of external classes. An example of this is the customer actor in the Banking System, in which the actor interfaces with the system via several external I/O devices, as described in Section 7.8.3.

7.8.3 Example of Developing a Software System Context Class Diagram from Actors

In order to determine the external classes from the actors, it is necessary to understand the characteristics of each actor and how each actor interacts with the system, as described in the use cases. Consider a situation in which all the actors are human users. In the Banking System, there are two actors, both of whom are human users: the ATM Customer and the ATM Operator, as shown in the system context class diagram of Figure 7.19.

Figure 7.23 shows the software system context class diagram for the Banking System, with the Banking System as one aggregate class and external classes that interface to it. The ATM operator actor interfaces to the system via a standard user I/O device and so is depicted as an «external user» class called Operator, because in this case the user's characteristics are more important than those of the I/O devices. However, the customer actor actually interfaces to the system via one standard user I/O device representing the keyboard/display and three application-specific I/O devices. The application-specific I/O devices are an «external I/O device», the Card Reader, and two «external output devices», the Receipt Printer and the Cash Dispenser. These five external classes all have one-to-many associations with the Banking System.

7.9 STATIC MODELING OF ENTITY CLASSES

Entity classes are conceptual data-intensive classes – that is, their main purpose is to store data and provide access to this data. In many cases, entity classes are persistent, meaning that the data is long-living and would need to be stored in a file or database. Whereas some approaches advocate static modeling of all software classes during analysis, the COMET approach emphasizes static modeling of entity classes, in order to take advantage of the strengths of the static modeling notation for expressing classes, attributes, and relationships among classes. Entity classes are particularly prevalent in information systems; however, many real-time and distributed systems have significant data-intensive classes. Concentrating on modeling entity classes is similar to modeling a logical database schema. Entity classes are often mapped to a database in the design phase, as described in Chapter 15.

The main difference between object-oriented static modeling and entity-relationship modeling, which is frequently used for logical database design, is that whereas both approaches model classes, attributes of each class, and relationships

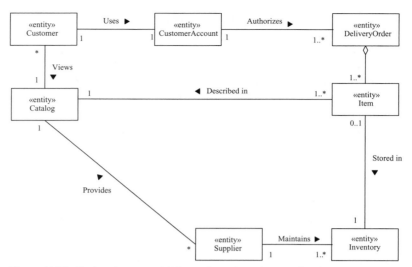

Figure 7.25. Entity class model for online shopping application

among classes, object-oriented static modeling also allows class operations to be specified. During static modeling of the problem domain, the COMET emphasis is on determining the entity classes that are defined in the problem, their attributes, and their relationships. Specifying operations is deferred until design modeling, as described in Chapter 14. Static modeling of entity classes is referred to as entity class modeling.

One example of entity class modeling comes from an online shopping application, in which customers, accounts, and catalogs are all mentioned in the problem description. Each of these real-world conceptual entities is modeled as an entity class and depicted with the stereotype «entity». The attributes of each entity class are determined, and the relationships among the entity classes are defined.

The example of an entity class model for the online shopping application is shown in Figure 7.25. Because this static model depicts only entity classes, all the classes have the «entity» stereotype to depict the role they play in the application. Figure 7.25 shows the Customer entity class, which has a one-to-one association with the Customer Account class, which in turn has a one-to-many association with the Delivery Order class. The latter class is an aggregation of the Item class, which in turn has a many-to-one association with the Catalog class (in which the item is described) and an optional association with Inventory (in which the item is stored; the zero is because the inventory may be out of a specific item). This example is described in more detail in the Online Shopping System case study (Chapter 22).

7.9.1 Modeling Class Attributes

An important consideration in modeling entity classes is to define the attributes of each entity class. An entity class is data-intensive, meaning that it has several attributes. If an entity class appears to have only one attribute, then it is questionable whether it really is an entity class. Instead, it is more likely that this doubtful entity should be modeled as an attribute of a different class.

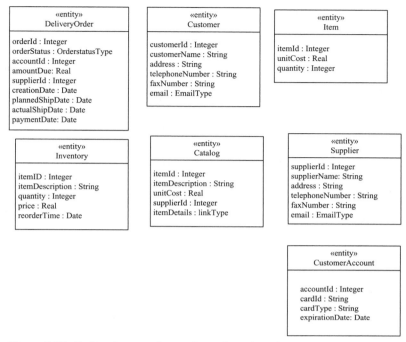

Figure 7.26. Entity class attributes for online shopping application

Consider the attributes of the entity classes that are shown in Figure 7.26. Each class has several attributes that provide information that distinguishes this class from other classes. Furthermore, each instance of the class has specific values of these attributes to differentiate it from other instances of the class. Thus, the Customer class is characterized by attributes that describe the information needed to identify an individual customer, including a customer Id, the customer's name, address, telephone number, fax number, and email address. On the other hand, the Customer Account class contains attributes that provide details of the account.

7.10 SUMMARY

This chapter described some of the basic concepts of static modeling, including the relationships between classes. Three types of relationships have been described: **associations**, **composition/aggregation** relationships, and **generalization/ specialization** relationships. In addition, this chapter described how static modeling is used to model the structural views of the problem domain. This consists of static modeling of the total system context, which depicts the classes external to the total hardware/software system; static modeling of the software system context, which depicts the classes external to the software system; and static modeling of the entity classes, which are conceptual data-intensive classes.

Static modeling of the solution domain is deferred to the design phase. Although static modeling also includes defining the operations of each class, it is easier to determine the operations of a class after dynamic modeling. Because of this, determining the operations of a class is deferred to class design, as described in Chapter 14.

EXERCISES

Multiple-choice questions: For each question, choose one of the answers.

1. What is a class?
    (a) A course
    (b) An object instance
    (c) A client or server in the system
    (d) A collection of objects with the same characteristics

2. What is an attribute?
    (a) A relationship between two classes
    (b) A parameter of an operation or method
    (c) A data value held by an object in a class
    (d) The return value from an operation

3. What is an association?
    (a) A relationship between two classes
    (b) A relationship between two objects
    (c) A link between two classes
    (d) A link between two objects

4. What is meant by the multiplicity of an association?
    (a) The number of associations in a class
    (b) The number of associations between two classes
    (c) How many instances of one class relate to how many instances of another class
    (d) How many instances of one class relate to a single instance of another class.

5. What is an association class?
    (a) A class with multiple associations
    (b) A class with one association
    (c) A class that models an association between two or more classes
    (d) A class that models an association between two or more objects

6. What is a generalization/specialization hierarchy?
    (a) A whole/part relationship
    (b) An inheritance relationship
    (c) An association between a generalized class and a specialized class
    (d) A layered hierarchy

7. What is a composition hierarchy?
    (a) A weak form of a generalization/specialization hierarchy
    (b) A strong form of a generalization/specialization hierarchy
    (c) A weak form of a whole/part relationship
    (d) A strong form of a whole/part relationship

8. What is an aggregation hierarchy?
    (a) A weak form of a generalization/specialization hierarchy
    (b) A strong form of a generalization/specialization hierarchy
    (c) A weak form of a whole/part relationship
    (d) A strong form of a whole/part relationship

9. What does the system context class diagram define?
    (a) The entity classes in the system
    (b) How the system interfaces to other systems
    (c) The boundary between the system and the external environment
    (d) The context classes in the system

10. What is an entity class?
    (a) A class on an entity/relationship diagram
    (b) A class that stores data
    (c) A class that interfaces to an external entity
    (d) An external class

8

Object and Class Structuring

After defining the use cases and developing a static model of the problem domain, the next step is to determine the software objects in the system. At this stage, the emphasis is on software objects that model real-world objects in the problem domain.

Software objects are determined from the use cases and from the static model of the problem domain. This chapter provides guidelines on how to determine the objects in the system. Object structuring criteria are provided, and the objects are categorized by using stereotypes. The emphasis is on problem domain objects to be found in the real world and not on solution domain objects, which are determined at design time.

The static modeling described in Chapter 7 was used to determine the external classes, which were then depicted on a software system context class diagram. These external classes are used to help determine the software boundary classes, which are the software classes that interface to and communicate with the external environment. The entity classes and their relationships were also determined during static modeling. In this chapter, the objects and classes needed in the software system are determined and categorized. In particular, the focus is on the additional software objects and classes that were not determined during the static modeling of the problem domain.

The static relationship between classes is considered in the **static model**, as described in the previous chapter, and the dynamic relationship between the objects is considered in the **dynamic model**, as described in Chapters 9, 10, and 11.

Section 8.1 gives an overview of object and class structuring, and Section 8.2 describes modeling application classes and objects. Section 8.3 presents an overview of object and class structuring categories. Section 8.4 describes external classes (first introduced in Chapter 7) and their relationship to software boundary classes, whereas Section 8.5 describes the different kinds of boundary classes and objects. Section 8.6 describes entity classes and objects, which were first introduced in Chapter 7. Section 8.7 describes the different kinds of control classes and objects. Section 8.8 describes application logic classes and objects.

8.1 OBJECT AND CLASS STRUCTURING CRITERIA

There is no one unique way to decompose a system into objects, because the decisions made are based on the judgment of the analyst and the characteristics of the problem. Whether objects are in the same class or in a different class depends on the nature of the problem. For example, in an automobile catalog, cars, vans, and trucks might all be objects of the same class. For a vehicle manufacturer, however, cars, vans, and trucks might all be objects of different classes. The reason for this might be that for an automobile catalog, the same type of information is needed for each vehicle, whereas for the vehicle manufacturer, more detailed information is needed, which is different for the different types of vehicles.

Object and class structuring criteria are provided to assist the designer in structuring a system into objects. The approach used for identifying objects is to look for real-world objects in the problem domain and then design corresponding software objects that model the real world. After the objects have been identified, the interactions among objects are depicted in the dynamic model on **communication diagrams** or **sequence diagrams,** as described in Chapters 9 and 11.

8.2 MODELING APPLICATION CLASSES AND OBJECTS

Section 7.9 described static modeling of entity classes, which benefit most from static modeling in the analysis phase because they are information-intensive. Entity classes, however, are only one kind of software class within the system. Before dynamic modeling can be undertaken, as described in Chapters 9, 10, and 11, it is necessary to determine what software classes and objects are needed to realize each use case. Identification of software objects and classes can be greatly assisted by applying object and class structuring criteria, which provide guidance on structuring an application into objects. This approach categorizes software classes and objects by the roles they play in the application.

In this step, classes are categorized in order to group together classes with similar characteristics. Figure 8.1 shows the categorization of application classes. Stereotypes (see Section 7.7) are used to distinguish among the various kinds of application

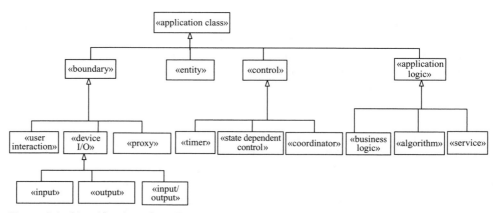

Figure 8.1. Classification of application classes by stereotype

classes. Because an object is an instance of a class, an object has the same stereotype as the class from which it is instantiated. Thus, the categorization described in this section applies equally to classes and objects.

In Figure 8.1, each box represents a different category of application class, and the relationships between them are inheritance relationships. Therefore, an application class is classified as an entity class, a boundary class, a control class, or an application logic class. These stereotypes are classified further, as shown in Figure 8.1 and described here.

This classification process is analogous to classifying books in a library, with major classes such as fiction and nonfiction, and further classification of fiction into classics, mysteries, adventure, and so on, and nonfiction into biography, autobiography, travel, cooking, history, and other categories. It is also analogous to the taxonomy of the animal kingdom, which is divided into major categories (mammal, bird, fish, reptile, and so on) that are further divided into subclasses (e.g., cat, dog, and monkey are subclasses of mammal).

8.3 OBJECT AND CLASS STRUCTURING CATEGORIES

Objects and classes are categorized according to the roles they play in the application. There are four main object and class structuring categories, as shown in Figure 8.1: boundary objects, entity objects, control objects, and application logic objects. Most applications will have objects from each of the four categories. However, different types of applications will have a greater number of classes in one or other category. Thus, information-intensive systems will have several entity classes, which is why static modeling is so vital for these systems. On the other hand, real-time systems are likely to have several device I/O boundary classes to interface to the various sensors and actuators. They are also likely to have complex state-dependent control classes because these systems are highly state-dependent. These object structuring categories are summarized in the following list and described in detail in Sections 8.4 through 8.7.

The four main object and class structuring categories (Figure 8.1) are as follows:

1. **Entity object.** A software object, in many cases persistent, which encapsulates information and provides access to the information it stores. In some case, an entity object could be accessed via a service object.
2. **Boundary object.** Software object that interfaces to and communicates with the external environment. Boundary objects are further categorized as:
   - **User interaction object.** Software object that interacts with and interfaces to a human user.
   - **Proxy object.** Software object that interfaces to and communicates with an external system or subsystem.
   - **Device I/O boundary object.** Software object that receives input from and/or outputs to a hardware I/O device.
3. **Control object.** Software object that provides the overall coordination for a collection of objects. Control objects may be **coordinator objects, state-dependent control objects,** or **timer objects**.

4. **Application logic object.** Software object that contains the details of the application logic. Needed when it is desirable to hide the application logic separately from the data being manipulated because it is considered likely that the application logic could change independently of the data. For information systems, application logic objects are usually **business logic objects,** whereas for real-time, scientific, or engineering applications, they are usually **algorithm objects**. Another category is **service objects**, which provide services for client objects, typically in service-oriented architectures and applications.

In most cases, what category an object fits into is usually obvious. However, in some cases, it is possible for an object to satisfy more than one of the aforementioned criteria. For example, an object could have characteristics of both an entity object, in that it encapsulates some data, and an algorithm object, in that it executes a significant algorithm. In such cases, allocate the object to the category it seems to fit best. Note that it is more important to determine all the objects in the system than to be unduly concerned about how to categorize a few borderline cases.

For each object structuring criterion, there is an object behavioral pattern, which describes how the object interacts with its neighboring objects. It is useful to understand the object's typical pattern of behavior, because when this category of object is used in an application, it is likely to interact with the same kinds of neighboring objects in a similar way. Each behavioral pattern is depicted on a UML communication diagram.

8.4 EXTERNAL CLASSES AND SOFTWARE BOUNDARY CLASSES

As described in Section 7.8, external classes are classes that are outside the software system and that interface to the system. Boundary classes are classes inside the system that interface to and communicate with the external classes. To help determine the boundary classes in the system, it is necessary to consider the external classes to which they are connected.

Identifying the external classes that communicate with and interface to the system helps identify some of the classes in the system itself, namely, the boundary classes. Each of the external classes communicates with a boundary class in the system. There is usually a one-to-one association between the external class (assuming it has been identified correctly) and the internal boundary class with which it communicates. External classes interface to software boundary classes as follows:

- An **external user class** interfaces to and interacts with a **user interaction class**.
- An **external system class** interfaces to and communicates with a **proxy class**.
- An **external device class** provides input to and/or receives output from a **device I/O boundary class**. Continuing with this classification:
  - An **external input device class** provides input to an **input class.**
  - An **external output device class** receives output from an **output class.**
  - An **external I/O device class** provides input to and receives output from an **I/O class.**
- An **external timer class** signals to a **software timer class.**

An external device class represents an I/O device type. An external I/O device object represents a specific I/O device, that is, an instance of the device type. In the next section, we consider the internal objects that interface to and communicate with the external objects.

8.5 BOUNDARY CLASSES AND OBJECTS

This section describes the characteristics of the three different kinds of boundary objects: user interaction objects, proxy objects, and device I/O boundary objects. In each case, an example is given of a boundary class, followed by an example of a behavioral pattern in which an instance of the boundary class, that is, a boundary object, communicates with neighboring objects in a typical interaction sequence.

8.5.1 User Interaction Objects

A **user interaction object** communicates directly with the human user, receiving input from the user and providing output to the user via standard I/O devices such as the keyboard, visual display, and mouse. Depending on the user interface technology, the user interface could be very simple (such as a command line interface) or it could be more complex (such as a graphical user interface [GUI] object). A user interaction object may be a composite object composed of several simpler user interaction objects. This means that the user interacts with the system via several user interaction objects. Such objects are depicted with the «user interaction» stereotype.

An example of a simple user interaction class called Operator Interaction is depicted in Figure 8.2a. An instance of this class is the Operator Interaction object (see Figure 8.2b), which is depicted in a typical behavioral pattern for user interaction objects. The object accepts operator commands from the operator actor; requests sensor data from an entity object, Sensor Data Repository; and displays the data it receives to the operator. More complex user interaction objects are also possible. For example, the Operator Interaction object could be a composite user interaction object composed of several simpler user interaction objects. This would allow the operator to receive dynamic updates of workstation status in one window, receive dynamic updates of alarm status in another window, and conduct an interactive dialog with the system in a third window. Each window is composed of several GUI widgets, such as menus, buttons, and simpler windows.

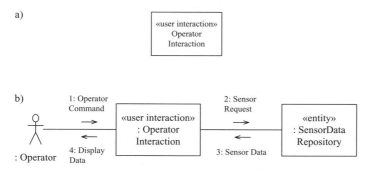

Figure 8.2. Example of user interaction class and object

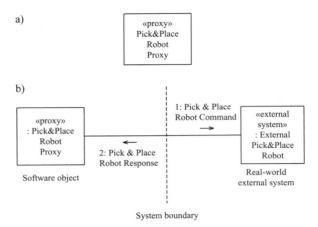

(Note: the dashed line for the system boundary is for illustrative purpose only and does not conform to the UML notation.)

Figure 8.3. Example of proxy class and object

8.5.2 Proxy Objects

A **proxy object** interfaces to and communicates with an external system. The proxy object is the local representative of the external system and hides the details of "how" to communicate with the external system.

An example of a proxy class is a Pick & Place Robot Proxy class. An example of a behavioral pattern for a proxy object is given in Figure 8.3, which depicts a Pick & Place Robot Proxy object that interfaces to and communicates with the External Pick & Place Robot. The Pick & Place Robot Proxy object sends pick and place robot commands to the External Pick & Place Robot. The real-world robot responds to the commands.

Each proxy object hides the details of how to interface to and communicate with the particular external system. A proxy object is more likely to communicate by means of messages to an external, computer-controlled system, such as the robot in the preceding example, rather than through sensors and actuator, as is the case with device I/O boundary objects. However, these issues are not addressed until the design phase.

8.5.3 Device I/O Boundary Objects

A **device I/O boundary object** provides the software interface to a hardware I/O device. Device I/O boundary objects are needed for nonstandard application-specific I/O devices, which are more prevalent in real-time systems, although they are often needed in other systems as well. Standard I/O devices are typically handled by the operating system, so special-purpose device I/O boundary objects do not need to be developed as part of the application.

A physical object in the application domain is a real-world object that has some physical characteristics – for example, it can be seen and touched. For every real-world physical object that is relevant to the problem, there should be a corresponding software object in the system. In the Automated Guided Vehicle System, for example, the vehicle motor and arm are relevant real-world physical objects,

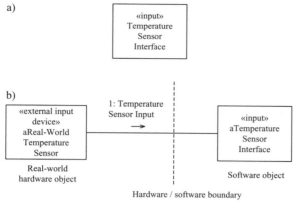

Figure 8.4. Example of input class and object

because they interact with the software system. On the other hand, the vehicle chassis and wheels are not relevant real-world objects, because they do not interact with the software system. In the software system, the relevant real-world physical objects are modeled by means of software objects, such as the vehicle motor and arm software objects.

Real-world physical objects usually interface to the system via sensors and actuators. These real-world objects provide inputs to the system via sensors or receive outputs from the system via actuators. Thus, to the software system, the real-world objects are actually I/O devices that provide inputs to and receive outputs from the system. Because the real-world objects correspond to I/O devices, the software objects that interface to them are referred to as device I/O boundary objects.

For example, in the Automated Guided Vehicle System, the station arrival indicator is a real-world object that has a sensor (input devices) that provides inputs to the system. The motor and arm are real-world objects that are controlled by means of actuators (output devices) that receive outputs from the system.

An **input object** is a device I/O boundary object that receives input from an external input device. Figure 8.4 shows an example of an input class Temperature Sensor Interface and an instance of this class, an input object, on a communication diagram. An input object, a Temperature Sensor Interface object, receives temperature sensor input from an external real-world hardware object, a Real-World Temperature Sensor input device. Figure 8.4 also shows the hardware/software boundary, as well as the stereotypes for the hardware «external input device» and the software «input» objects. Thus, the input object provides the software system interface to the external hardware input device.

An **output object** is a device I/O boundary object that sends output to an external output device. Figure 8.5 shows an example of an output class called Red Light Interface, as well as an instance of this class, the Red Light Interface object, which sends outputs to an external real-world object, the Red Light Actuator external output device. The Red Light Interface software object sends On and Off Light commands to the hardware Red Light Actuator. Figure 8.5 also shows the hardware/software boundary.

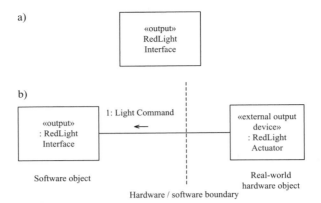

(Note: the dashed line for the hardware/software boundary is for illustrative purpose only and does not conform to the UML notation.)

Figure 8.5. Example of output class and object

A hardware I/O device can also be a device that both sends inputs to the system and receives outputs from the system. The corresponding software class is an I/O class, and a software object that is instantiated from this class is an I/O object. An **input/output (I/O) object** is a device I/O boundary object that receives input from and sends output to an external I/O device. This is the case with the ATM Card Reader Interface class shown in Figure 8.6*a* and its instance, the ATM Card Reader Interface object (see Figure 8.6*b*), which receives ATM card input from the external I/O device, the ATM Card Reader. In addition, ATM Card Reader Interface sends eject and confiscate output commands to the card reader.

In some applications, there are many real-world objects of the same type. These are modeled by means of one device I/O object for each real-world object, in which all the objects are instances of the same class. For example, the Factory Automation System, which controls many automated guided vehicles, has many vehicle motors of the same type and many robotic arms of the same type. There is one instance of the Motor Interface class and one instance of the Arm Interface class for each automated guided vehicle.

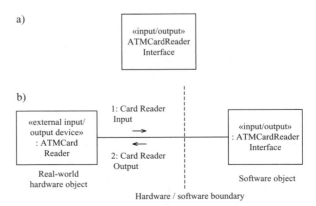

(Note: the dashed line for the hardware/software boundary is for illustrative purpose only and does not conform to the UML notation.)

Figure 8.6. Example of I/O class and object

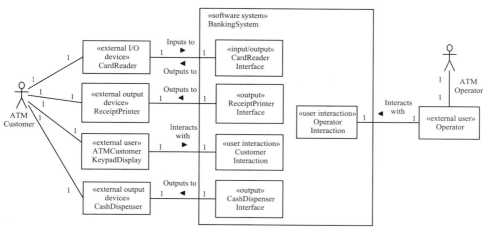

Figure 8.7. Banking System external classes and boundary classes

8.5.4 Depicting External Classes and Boundary Classes

Chapter 7 discussed how to determine the scope of the system and how to develop a **software system context class diagram**, which shows all the external classes that interface to and communicate with the system. It is useful to expand this diagram to show the boundary classes that communicate with the external classes. The boundary classes are software classes inside the system that are at the boundary between the system and the external environment. The system is shown as an aggregate class, and the boundary classes, which are part of the system, are shown inside the aggregate class. Each external class, which is external to the system, has a one-to-one association with a boundary class. Thus, starting with the external classes, as depicted on the software system context class diagram, helps determine the boundary classes.

Starting with the software system context class diagram for the Banking System, we determine that each external class communicates with a boundary class (Figure 8.7). The software system is depicted as an aggregate class, which contains the boundary classes that interface to the external classes. In this application, there are three device I/O boundary classes and two user interaction classes. The device I/O boundary classes are the Card Reader Interface, through which ATM cards are read, the Cash Dispenser Interface, which dispenses cash, and the Receipt Printer Interface, which prints receipts. The Customer Interaction class is a user interaction class, which displays textual messages and prompts to the customer and receives the customer's inputs. The Operator Interaction class provides the user interface to the ATM operator, who replenishes the ATM machine with cash. There is one instance of each of these boundary classes for each ATM.

8.6 ENTITY CLASSES AND OBJECTS

An **entity object** is a software object that stores information. Entity objects are instances of entity classes, whose attributes and relationships with other entity classes are determined during static modeling, as described in Chapter 7. Entity objects store data and provide limited access to that data via the operations they provide. In some cases, an entity object might need to access other entity objects in order to update the information it encapsulates.

Figure 8.8. Example of entity class and object

In many information system applications, the information encapsulated by entity objects is stored in a file or database. In these cases, the entity object is persistent, meaning that the information it contains is preserved when the system is shut down and then later powered up. In some applications, such as real-time systems, entity objects are often stored in main memory. These issues are addressed during the design phase, as described in Chapter 14.

An example of an entity class from the banking application is the Account class (Figure 8.8). The stereotype «entity» is shown to clearly identify what kind of class it is. Instances of the Account class are entity objects (as shown in Figure 8.8), which are also identified by the stereotype «entity». The attributes of Account are account Number and balance. The object an Account is a persistent (long-living) object that is accessed by several objects that realize various use cases. These use cases include customer use cases for account withdrawals, inquiries, and transfers at various ATM machines, as well as human teller use cases to open and close the account and to credit and debit the account. The account is also accessed by objects that realize a use case that prepares and prints monthly statements for customers.

An example of an entity class from a sensor monitoring example is the Sensor Data class (Figure 8.9). This class stores information about analog sensors. The attributes are sensor Name, sensor Value, upper Limit, lower Limit, and alarm Status. An example of an instance of this class is the temperature Sensor Data object.

8.7 CONTROL CLASSES AND OBJECTS

A **control object** provides the overall coordination of the objects that realize a use case. Simple use cases do not need control objects. However, in a more complex use case, a control object is usually needed. A control object is analogous to the conductor of an orchestra, who orchestrates (controls) the behavior of the other objects that participate in the use case, notifying each object when and what it should perform. Depending on the characteristics of the use case, the control object may be state-dependent. There are several kinds of control objects, which are described in the sections that follow.

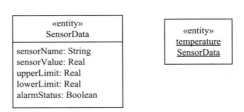

Figure 8.9. Example of entity class and object

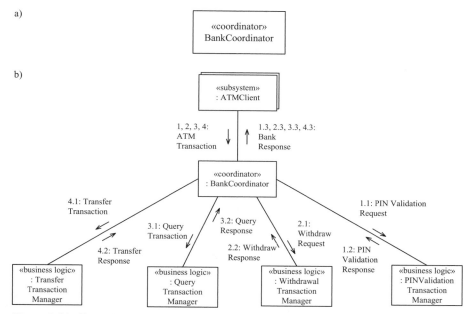

Figure 8.10. Example of coordinator class and object

8.7.1 Coordinator Objects

A **coordinator object** is an overall decision-making object that determines the over-all sequencing for a collection of related objects. A coordinator object is often required to provide the overall sequencing for execution of a use case. It makes the overall decisions and decides when, and in what order, other objects partici-pate in the use case. A coordinator object makes its decision based on the input it receives and is not state-dependent. Thus, an action initiated by a coordinator object depends only on the information contained in the incoming message and not on what previously happened in the system.

An example of a coordinator class is the Bank Coordinator, which is depicted in Figure 8.10*a*. The instance of this class, the Bank Coordinator object receives ATM transactions from a client ATM. Depending on the transaction type, the Bank Coor-dinator directs the transaction to the appropriate transaction-processing object to execute the transaction. In the Banking System, these are a Withdrawal Transaction Manager object, a Transfer Transaction Manager object, a Query Transaction Manager object, or a PIN Validation Transaction Manager object (see Figure 8.10*b*).

Another kind of coordinator is a coordinator object in a service-oriented appli-cation, which coordinates the interaction between a user interaction object and one or more service objects. An example of this is described in Section 8.8.3.

8.7.2 State-Dependent Control Objects

A **state-dependent control object** is a control object whose behavior varies in each of its states. A finite state machine is used to define a state-dependent control object and is depicted by using a statechart. Statecharts, which were originally conceived by Harel (1988, 1998), can be either flat (nonhierarchical) or hierarchical, as described

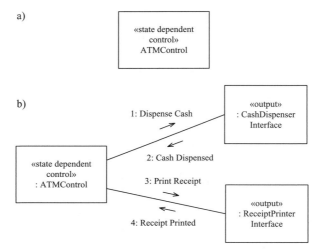

Figure 8.11. Example of state-dependent control class and object

in Chapter 10. This section gives only a brief overview of state-dependent control objects, which are described in much more detail in Chapters 10 and 11.

A state-dependent control object receives incoming events that cause state transitions and generates output events that control other objects. The output event generated by a state-dependent control object depends not only on the input received by the object but also on the current state of the object. An example of a state-dependent control object is the ATM Control object (Figure 8.11), which is defined by means of the ATM Control statechart. In the example, ATM Control is shown controlling two other output boundary objects, Receipt Printer Interface and Cash Dispenser Interface.

In a control system, there are usually one or more state-dependent control objects. It is also possible to have multiple state-dependent control objects of the same type. Each object executes an instance of the same finite state machine (depicted as a statechart), although each object is likely to be in a different state. An example of this is the Banking System, which has several ATMs, where each ATM has an instance of the state-dependent control class, ATM Control, which is also shown in Figure 8.11. Each ATM Control object executes its own instance of the ATM Control statechart and keeps track of the state of the local ATM. Another example is from the Automated Guided Vehicle System, in which the control and sequencing of the vehicle is modeled by means of a state-dependent control object, Vehicle Control, and defined by means of a statechart. Consequently, each vehicle has a vehicle control object. More information about state-dependent control objects is given in Chapter 11.

8.7.3 Timer Objects

A **timer object** is a control object that is activated by an external timer – for example, a real-time clock or operating system clock. The timer object either performs some action itself or activates another object to perform the desired action.

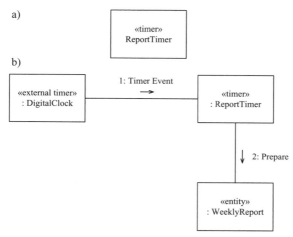

Figure 8.12. Example of a timer class and object

An example of a timer class, Report Timer, is given in Figure 8.12. An instance of this class, the timer object Report Timer, is activated by a timer event from an external timer, the Digital Clock. The timer object then sends a Prepare message to the Weekly Report object.

8.8 APPLICATION LOGIC CLASSES AND OBJECTS

This section describes the three kinds of application logic objects, namely, business logic objects, algorithm objects, and service objects. As with control objects, application logic objects are more likely to be considered when the dynamic model, not the initial conceptual static model, is being developed.

8.8.1 Business Logic Objects

A **business logic object** defines the business-specific application logic for processing a client request. The goal is to encapsulate (hide) business rules that could change independently of each other into separate business logic objects. Another goal is to separate the business rules from the entity data that they operate on, because the business rules can change independently of the entity data. Usually a business logic object accesses various entity objects during its execution.

Business logic objects are only needed in certain situations. Sometimes, there is a choice between encapsulating the business logic in a separate business logic object or, if the business logic is sufficiently simple, having it as an operation of an entity object. The guideline is that if the business rule can be executed only by accessing two or more entity objects, there should be a separate business logic object. On the other hand, if accessing one entity object is sufficient to execute the business rule, it could be provided by an operation of that object.

An example of a business logic class is the Withdrawal Transaction Manager class, which is shown in Figure 8.13. An instance of this class, the Withdrawal Transaction Manager business logic object, services withdrawal requests from ATM customers.

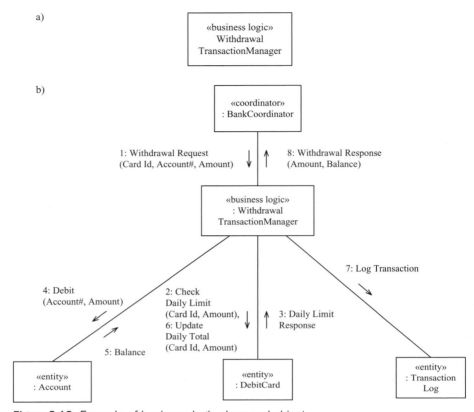

a)

b)

Figure 8.13. Example of business logic class and object

It encapsulates the business rules for processing an ATM withdrawal request. For example, the first business rule is that the customer must have a minimum balance of $50 after the withdrawal takes place; the second business rule is that the customer is not allowed to withdraw more than $250 per day with a debit card. The Withdrawal Transaction Manager object accesses an Account object to determine if the first business rule will be satisfied. It accesses the Debit Card object, which maintains a running total of the amount withdrawn by an ATM customer on this day, to determine if the second business rule will be satisfied. If either business rule is not satisfied, the withdrawal request is rejected.

A business logic object usually has to interact with entity objects in order to execute its business rules. In this way, it resembles a coordinator object. However, unlike a coordinator object, whose main responsibility is to supervise other objects, the prime responsibility of a business logic object is to encapsulate and execute the business rules.

8.8.2 Algorithm Objects

An **algorithm object** encapsulates an algorithm used in the problem domain. This kind of object is more prevalent in real-time, scientific, and engineering domains. Algorithm objects are used when there is a substantial algorithm used in the problem domain that can change independently of the other objects. Simple algorithms

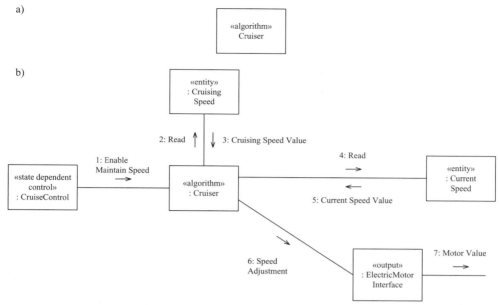

Figure 8.14. Example of algorithm class and object

are usually operations of an entity object that operate on the data encapsulated in the entity. In many scientific and engineering domains, algorithms are refined iteratively because they are improved independently of the data they manipulate (e.g., for improved performance or accuracy).

An example from a Train Control System is the Cruiser algorithm class. An instance of this class, the Cruiser object, calculates what adjustments to the speed should be made by comparing the current speed of the train with the desired cruising speed (Figure 8.14). The algorithm is complex because it must provide gradual accelerations or decelerations of the train when they are needed, so as to have minimal effect on the passengers.

An algorithm object frequently encapsulates data it needs for computing its algorithm. These data may be initialization data, intermediate result data, or threshold data, such as maximum or minimum values.

An algorithm object frequently has to interact with other objects in order to execute its algorithm (e.g., Cruiser). In this way, it resembles a coordinator object. Unlike a coordinator object, however, whose main responsibility is to supervise other objects, the prime responsibility of an algorithm object is to encapsulate and execute the algorithm.

8.8.3 Service Objects

A **service object** is an object that provides a service for other objects. They are usually provided in service-oriented architectures and applications, as described in Chapter 16. Client objects can request a service from the service object, which the service object will respond to. A service object never initiates a request; however, in response to a service request it might seek the assistance of other service objects. Service objects play an important role in service-oriented architectures, although

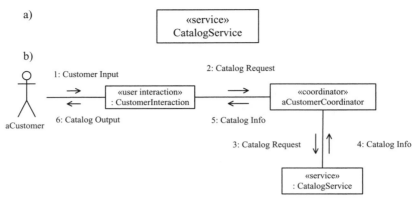

Figure 8.15. Example of service class and object

they are used in other architectures as well, such as client/server architectures and component-based software architectures. A service object might encapsulate the data it needs to service client requests or access another entity object(s) that encapsulate the data.

An example of a service class is the Catalog Service class given in Figure 8.15a. An example of executing an instance of this class, the Catalog Service object, is shown in Figure 8.15b. The Catalog Service object provides support for viewing various catalog items from the supplier's catalog and selecting items from the catalog. The Customer Coordinator assists the Customer Interaction object in finding a supplier catalog, provided by the Catalog Service object, and making selections from the catalog. In addition to service classes and objects, coordinator classes and objects are also frequently used in service-oriented architectures and applications, as described in Chapter 16.

8.9 SUMMARY

This chapter described how to determine the software objects and classes in the system. Object and class structuring criteria were provided, and the objects and classes were categorized by using stereotypes. The emphasis is on problem domain objects and classes, which are to be found in the real world, and not on solution domain objects, which are determined at design time. The object and structuring criteria are usually applied to each use case in turn during dynamic interaction modeling, as described in Chapters 9 and 11, to determine the objects that participate in each use case. The sequence of interaction among the objects is then determined. Subsystem structuring criteria are described in Chapter 13. The design of the operations provided by each class is described in Chapter 14.

EXERCISES

Multiple-choice questions: For each question, choose one of the answers.

1. What is a boundary object?
   (a) An external object
   (b) An object that stores data
   (c) An object that communicates with an external object
   (d) An object that controls other objects

2. What is a control object?

(a) An object that depends on other objects

(b) An object that communicates with an external object

(c) An object that controls other objects

(d) An object that is controlled by other objects

3. What is a state-dependent control object?

   (a) An object that depends on a state machine

   (b) An object that communicates with a state machine

   (c) An object that controls a state machine

   (d) An object that executes a state machine

4. What is a coordinator object?

   (a) A manager object

   (b) An object that makes decisions based on a state machine

   (c) A decision-making object

   (d) An object that decides which entity object to interact with

5. How would you determine a boundary class from the context diagram?

   (a) By looking at it

   (b) By selecting the external classes on the context diagram

   (c) By determining the software classes that communicate with the external classes

   (d) By drawing the boundary between the hardware and software classes

6. What is a timer object?

   (a) An external clock

(b) An internal clock

(c) An object that is awakened by an external timer

(d) An object that interacts with a clock

7. What do class structuring criteria help with?

   (a) Structuring an application into classes

   (b) Defining the attributes of a class

   (c) Defining the associations of a class

   (d) Defining the operations of a class

8. What is the classification process for application classes analogous to?

   (a) Categorizing books in a library

   (b) Deciding how many copies of a book are needed

   (c) Finding the classrooms in a school

   (d) Identifying what labs the school has

9. What is the purpose of a stereotype in class structuring?

   (a) To label a class according to its class structuring criterion

   (b) To identify the objects that belong to the same class

   (c) To distinguish between external objects and software objects

   (d) To identify the association between two classes

10. What is a business logic object?

    (a) An object used in business applications

    (b) An object that defines business-specific application logic

    (c) The internal logic of an object

    (d) A business object that determines whether a client request is logical

9

Dynamic Interaction Modeling

Dynamic modeling provides a view of a system in which control and sequencing are considered, either within an object (by means of a finite state machine) or between objects (by analysis of object interactions). This chapter addresses dynamic interaction between objects.

Dynamic interaction modeling is based on the realization of the use cases developed during use case modeling. For each use case, it is necessary to determine how the objects that participate in the use case dynamically interact with each other. The object structuring criteria described in Chapter 8 are applied to determine the objects that participate in each use case. This chapter describes how, for each use case, an interaction diagram is developed to depict the objects that participate in the use case and the sequence of messages passed between them. The interaction is depicted on either a communication diagram or a sequence diagram. A narrative description of the object interaction is also provided in a message sequence description. Please note that all references to *system* in this chapter are to the *software system*.

This chapter first describes object interaction modeling using communication diagrams and sequence diagrams before describing how they are used in dynamic interaction modeling. It then describes the details of the dynamic interaction modeling approach for determining how objects collaborate with each other. This chapter describes stateless dynamic interaction modeling, also referred to as basic dynamic interaction modeling. Chapter 11 describes state-dependent dynamic interaction modeling, which, unlike stateless dynamic interaction modeling, involves state-dependent communication controlled by a statechart.

Section 9.1 presents an overview of object interaction modeling and describes the two kinds of interaction diagrams, communication and sequence diagrams. Section 9.2 describes message sequence numbering on interaction diagrams. Section 9.3 introduces dynamic interaction modeling, and Section 9.4 describes stateless dynamic interaction modeling. Section 9.5 provides two examples of stateless dynamic interaction modeling.

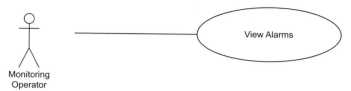

Figure 9.1. Use case diagram for the View Alarms use case

9.1 OBJECT INTERACTION MODELING

For each use case, the objects that realize the use case dynamically cooperate with each other and are depicted on either a UML communication diagram or a UML sequence diagram, as described in this section.

9.1.1 Communication Diagrams

A **communication diagram** is a UML interaction diagram that depicts a dynamic view of a group of objects interacting with each other by showing the sequence of messages passed among them. During analysis modeling, a communication diagram is developed for each use case; only objects that participate in the use case are depicted. On a communication diagram, the sequence in which the objects participate in each use case is depicted by means of message sequence numbers. The message sequencing on the communication diagram should correspond to the sequence of interactions between the actor and the system already described in the use case.

As an example of using a communication diagram to depict the objects that participate in a use case, consider the View Alarms use case from the Emergency Monitoring System case study (Figure 9.1), in which a Monitoring Operator views outstanding alarms. The communication diagram (Figure 9.2) for this simple use case

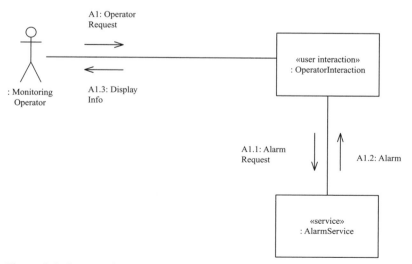

Figure 9.2. Communication diagram for the View Alarms use case

consists of only two objects: a user interaction object and a service object. The user interaction object is called Operator Interaction. The service object is called Alarm Service.

The communication diagram for this use case depicts the user interaction object, Operator Interaction, making a request to the service object, Alarm Service and receiving a response (see Figure 9.2).

9.1.2 Sequence Diagrams

The interaction among objects can also be shown on a sequence diagram, which shows object interactions arranged in time sequence. A **sequence diagram** shows the objects participating in the interaction and the sequence in which messages are sent. Sequence diagrams can also depict loops and iterations. Sequence diagrams and communication diagrams depict similar (although not necessarily identical) information, but in different ways. Usually either communication diagrams or sequence diagrams are used to describe a dynamic view of a system, but not both.

Because the sequence diagram shows the order of messages sent sequentially from the top to the bottom of the diagram, numbering the messages is not essential. In the following example, however, the messages on the sequence diagram are numbered to show their correspondence to the communication diagram.

An example of a sequence diagram for the View Alarms use case is shown in Figure 9.3. This sequence diagram conveys the same information as the communication diagram shown in Figure 9.2.

9.1.3 Analysis and Design Decisions in Object Interaction Modeling

In the analysis model, messages represent the information passed between objects. Interaction diagrams (communication diagrams or sequence diagrams) help in determining the operations of the objects because the arrival of a message at an object usually invokes an operation. In COMET, however, the emphasis during

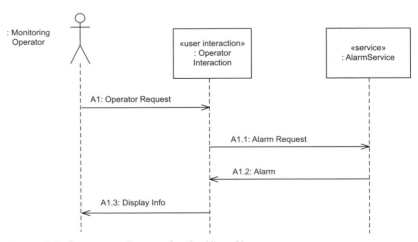

Figure 9.3. Sequence diagram for the View Alarms use case

analysis modeling is on capturing the information passed between objects, rather than on the operations invoked. During design, we might decide that two different messages arriving at an object invoke different operations or, alternatively, the same operation, with the message name being a parameter of the operation. However, these decisions should be postponed to the design phase. The kind of message passed between objects – synchronous or asynchronous – is a design decision that is also postponed to the design phase. At the analysis stage, all messages passed between objects are shown as simple messages.

In the analysis phase, no decision is made about whether an object is active or passive; this decision is also deferred to the design phase.

9.1.4 Sequence Diagram versus Communication Diagram

Either a sequence diagram or a communication diagram can be used to depict the object interaction and sequence of messages passed among objects. In its sequential form, the sequence diagram clearly shows the order in which messages are passed between objects, but seeing how the objects are connected to each other is more difficult. However, using iterations (such as do-while) and decision statements (if-then-else) can obscure the sequence of object interactions.

The communication diagram shows the layout of the objects, particularly how the objects are connected to each other. The message sequence is shown on both diagrams. Because the message sequence depicted on the communication diagram is less readily visible than on the sequence diagram, the message sequence is numbered. However, even with the message numbering on the communication diagram, it sometimes takes longer to see the sequence of messages. On the other hand, if an interaction involves many objects, a sequence diagram can become difficult to read. The diagram might have to be shrunk to fit on a page, or it might span several pages.

The COMET preference is to use communication diagrams rather than sequence diagrams, because an important step in the transition to design is the integration of the communication diagrams to create the initial software architecture of the system, as described in Chapter 13. This integration is much easier with communication diagrams than with sequence diagrams. If the analysis started with sequence diagrams, it would be necessary to convert each sequence diagram to a communication diagram before the integration could be done. Sometimes, however, the sequence diagram is very helpful, in particularly for very complex and lengthy interactions.

9.1.5 Use Cases and Scenarios

A **scenario** is one specific path through a use case. Thus, a particular message sequence depicted on an interaction diagram actually depicts a scenario and not a use case. To show all the alternatives through a use case, development of more than one interaction diagram is often necessary.

By using conditions, it is possible to depict alternatives on an interaction diagram and, hence, to depict the whole use case on a single interaction diagram. However, such comprehensive interaction diagrams are usually more difficult to read. In practice, depicting an individual scenario on an interaction diagram is usually clearer.

By using a sequence diagram with loops and branches, it is also possible to depict the interaction sequence of the whole use case consisting of the main sequence and all the alternative sequences. This is described in more detail in Section 9.5.

9.1.6 Generic and Instance Forms of Interaction Diagrams

The two forms of an interaction (sequence or communication) diagram are the generic form and the instance form. The **instance form** describes a specific scenario in detail, depicting one possible sequence of interactions among object instances. The **generic form** describes all possible interactions in which the objects might participate, and so can include loops, branches, and conditions. The generic form of an interaction diagram can be used to describe both the main sequence and the alternatives of a use case. The instance form is used to depict a specific scenario, which is one instance of the use case. Using the instance form might require several interaction diagrams to depict a given use case, depending on how many alternatives are described in the use case. Examples of instance and generic forms of interaction diagrams, both communication diagrams and sequence diagrams, are given in the examples in Section 9.5.

For all but the simplest use cases, an interaction diagram is usually much clearer when it depicts an instance form rather than a generic form of interaction. It can rapidly become too complicated if several alternatives are depicted on the same diagram. In the instance form of the sequence diagram, time moves down the page, so that it is easy to follow the message sequence. However, in the generic form – with loops, branches, and conditions – this is no longer the case, making the message sequence more difficult to follow.

9.2 MESSAGE SEQUENCE NUMBERING ON INTERACTION DIAGRAMS

Messages on a communication diagram or sequence diagram are given message sequence numbers. This section provides some guidelines for numbering message sequences. These guidelines follow the general UML conventions; however, they have been extended to better address concurrency, alternatives, and large message sequences. These conventions are followed in the examples given in this chapter (see Section 9.5 for more examples) and in the case studies in Chapters 20 through 24.

9.2.1 Message Labels on Interaction Diagrams

A message label on a communication or sequence diagram has the following syntax (only those parts of the message label that are relevant in the analysis phase are described here):

[sequence expression]: Message Name (argument list)

where the sequence expression consists of the message sequence number and an indicator of recurrence.

- **Message sequence number.** The message sequence number is described as follows: The first message sequence number represents the event that initiates the message sequence depicted on the communication diagram. Typical message sequences are 1, 2, 3, ... ; A1, A2, A3, ...

A more elaborate message sequence can be depicted with the Dewey classification system, such that A1.1 precedes A1.1.1, which in turn precedes A1.2. In the Dewey system, a typical message numbering sequence would be A1, A1.1, A1.1.1, A1.2.

- **Recurrence.** The recurrence term is optional and represents conditional or iterative execution. The recurrence term represents zero or more messages that are sent, depending on the conditions being met.
  1. *** [iteration-clause].** An asterisk (*) is added after the message sequence number to indicate that more than one message is sent. The optional iteration clause is used to specify repeated execution, such as [j := 1,n]. An example of an iteration by putting an asterisk after the message sequence number is 3*.
  2. **[condition-clause].** A condition is specified in square brackets to indicate a branch condition. The optional condition clause is used for specifying branches – for example, [x < n] – meaning that the message is sent only if the condition is true. Examples of conditional message passing by showing a condition after the message sequence number are 4[x < n] and 5[Normal]. In each case, the message is sent only if the condition is true.
- **Message name.** The message name is specified.
- **Argument list.** The argument list of the message is optional and specifies any parameters sent as part of the message.

There can also be optional return values from the message sent. However, it is recommended to use only simple messages during the analysis phase, in which case there are no return values, and to postpone to the design phase the decision about which kind of message to use.

9.2.2 Message Sequence Numbering on Interaction Diagrams

On a communication diagram supporting a use case, the sequence in which the objects participate in each use case is described and depicted by message sequence numbers. A message sequence number for a use case takes the following form:

[first optional letter sequence] [numeric sequence] [second optional

letter sequence]

The first optional letter sequence is an optional use case ID and identifies a specific concrete use case or abstract use case. The first letter is an uppercase letter and might be followed by one or more upper- or lowercase letters if a more descriptive use case ID is desired.

The simplest form of message sequencing is to use a sequence of whole numbers, such as M1, M2, and M3. However, in an interactive system with several external inputs from the actor, it is often helpful to include a numeric sequence that includes decimal numbers – that is, to number the external events as whole numbers followed by decimal numbers for the ensuing internal events. For example, if the actor's inputs were designated as A1, A2, and A3, the full message sequence depicted on the communication diagram would be A1, A1.1, A1.2, A1.3,..., A2, A2.1, A2.2,..., and A3, A3.1, A3.2,....

An example is V1, where the letter V identifies the use case and the number identifies the message sequence within the communication diagram supporting the use case. The object sending the first message – V1 – is the initiator of the use case–based communication. Thus, in the communication and sequence diagram examples in Figures 9.2 and 9.3, respectively, the input from the actor is V1. Subsequent message numbers following this input message are V1.1, V1.2, and V1.3. If the dialog were to continue, the next input from the actor would be V2.

9.2.3 Concurrent and Alternative Message Sequences

The second optional letter sequence is used to depict special cases of branches – either concurrent or alternative – in the message sequence numbering.

Concurrent message sequences may also be depicted on a communication diagram. A lowercase letter represents a concurrent sequence; in other words, sequences designated as A3 and A3a would be concurrent sequences. For example, the arrival of message A2 at an object X might result in the sending of two messages from object X to two objects Y and Z, which could then execute in parallel. To indicate the concurrency in this case, the message sent to object Y would be designated as A3, and the one to object Z, as A3a. Subsequent messages in the A3 sequence would be A4, A5, A6,..., and subsequent messages in the independent A3a sequence would be A3a.1, A3a.2, A3a.3, and so on. Because the sequence numbering is more cumbersome for the A3a sequence, use A3 for the main message sequence and A3a and A3b for the supporting message sequences. An alternative way to show two concurrent sequences is to avoid A3 altogether and use the sequence numbers A3a and A3b; however, this can lead to a more cumbersome numbering scheme if A3a initiates another concurrent sequence, so the former approach is preferred.

Alternative message sequences are depicted with the condition indicated after the message. An uppercase letter is used to name the alternative branch. For example, the main branch may be labeled 1.4[Normal], and the other, less frequently used branch could be named 1.4A[Error]. The message sequence numbers for the normal branch would be 1.4[Normal], 1.5, 1.6, and so on. The message sequence numbers for the alternative branch would be 1.4A[Error], 1.4A.1, 1.4A.2, and so on.

9.2.4 Message Sequence Description

A **message sequence description** is supplementary documentation, which is useful to provide with an interaction diagram. It is developed as part of the dynamic model and describes how the analysis model objects participate in each use case as depicted on an interaction diagram. The message sequence description is a narrative description, describing what happens when each message arrives at a destination object depicted on a communication diagram or sequence diagram. The message sequence description uses the message sequence numbers that appear on the communication diagram. It describes the sequence of messages sent from source objects to destination objects and describes what each destination object does with a message it receives. The message sequence description usually provides additional information that is not depicted on the object interaction diagram. For example, every time an entity object is accessed, the message sequence description can provide additional information, such as which attributes of the object are referenced.

Examples of message sequence descriptions are given in Section 9.5.

9.3 DYNAMIC INTERACTION MODELING

Dynamic interaction modeling is an iterative strategy to help determine how the analysis model objects interact with each other to support the use cases. Dynamic interaction modeling is carried out for each use case. A first attempt is made to determine the objects that participate in a use case, using the object structuring criteria described in Chapter 8. Then the way in which these objects collaborate to execute the use case is analyzed. This analysis might show a need for additional objects and/or additional interactions to be defined.

Dynamic interaction modeling can be either state-dependent or stateless, depending on whether the object communication is state-dependent. This chapter describes stateless dynamic interaction modeling. State-dependent dynamic interaction modeling is described in Chapter 11.

9.4 STATELESS DYNAMIC INTERACTION MODELING

The main steps in the **stateless dynamic interaction modeling approach** are as follows, starting with the use case. Next consider the objects needed to realize the use case, then determine the sequence of message communication among the objects.

1. **Develop use case model.** This step is described in Chapter 6. For dynamic modeling, consider each interaction between the primary actor and the system. Remember that the actor starts the interaction with the system through an external input. The system responds to this input with some internal execution and then typically provides a system output. The sequence of actor inputs and system responses is described in the use case. Start by developing the communication sequence for the scenario described in the main path of the use case. Consider each interaction in sequence between the actor and the system.

2. **Determine objects needed to realize use case.** This step requires applying the object structuring criteria (see Chaper 8) to determine the software objects needed to realize the use case, both boundary objects (2a below) and internal software objects (2b below).

2a. **Determine boundary object(s).** Consider the actor (or actors) that participates in the use case; determine the external objects (external to the system) through which the actor communicates with the system, and the software objects that receive the actor's inputs.

Start by considering the inputs from the external objects to the system. For each external input event, consider the software objects required to process the event. A software boundary object (such as an input object or user interaction object) is needed to receive the input from the external object. On receipt of the external input, the boundary object does some processing and typically sends a message to an internal object.

2b. **Determine internal software objects.** Consider the main sequence of the use case. Using the object structuring criteria, make a first attempt at determining the internal software objects that participate in the use case, such as control or entity objects.

3. **Determine message communication sequence.** For each input event from the external object, consider the communication required between the boundary object that receives the input event and the subsequent objects – entity or control objects – that cooperate in processing this event. Draw a communication diagram or sequence diagram showing the objects participating in the use case and the sequence of messages passing between them. This sequence typically starts with an external input from the actor (external object), followed by a sequence of internal message between the participating software objects, through to an external output to the actor (external object). Repeat this process for each subsequent interaction between the actor(s) and the system. As a result, additional objects may be required to participate, and additional message communication, along with message sequence numbering, will need to be specified.

4. **Determine alternative sequences.** Consider the different alternatives, such as error handling, which are described in the Alternatives section of the use case. Then consider what objects need to participate in executing the alternative branches and the sequence of message communication among them.

9.5 EXAMPLES OF STATELESS DYNAMIC INTERACTION MODELING

Two examples are given of stateless dynamic interaction modeling. The first example starts with the use case for View Alarms, and the second example starts with the use case for Process Delivery Order.

9.5.1 View Alarms Example

As an example of stateless dynamic interaction modeling, consider View Alarms use case from the Emergency Monitoring System case study. This example follows the four steps for dynamic modeling described in Section 9.4, although because it is a simple example, there are no alternative sequences.

1. Develop Use Case Model

There is one actor in the View Alarms use case, the monitoring operator, who can request to view the status of alarms, as shown in Figure 9.1. The use case description is briefly described as follows:

Use case name: View Alarms
Actor: Monitoring Operator
Summary: The monitoring operator views outstanding alarms and acknowledges that the cause of an alarm is being addressed.
Precondition: The monitoring operator is logged in.
Main sequence:
1. The Monitoring Operator requests to view the outstanding alarms.
2. The system displays the outstanding alarms. For each alarm, the system displays the name of the alarm, alarm description, location of alarm, and severity of alarm (high, medium, low).

Postcondition: Outstanding alarms have been displayed.

2. Determine Objects Needed to Realize Use Case

Because View Alarms is a simple use case, only two objects participate in the use case, as shown in Figure 9.2. The required objects can be determined by a careful reading of the use case. These are a user interaction object called Operator Interaction, which receives inputs from and sends outputs to the actor, and a service object called Alarm Service, which provides access to the alarm repository and responds to alarm requests.

3. Determine Message Communication Sequence

The communication diagram for this use case depicts the user interaction object, the Operator Interaction object, making a request to the service object, Alarm Service, which responds with the desired information (see Figure 9.2). The message sequence corresponds to the interaction sequence between the actor and the system described in the use case, and is described as follows:

A1: The Monitoring Operator requests an alarm handling service – for example, to view alarms or to subscribe to receive alarm messages of a specific type. The request is sent to Operator Interaction.
A1.1: Operator Interaction sends the alarm request to Alarm Service.
A1.2: Alarm Service performs the request – for example, reads the list of current alarms or adds the name of this user interaction object to the subscription list – and sends a response to the Operator Interaction object.
A1.3: Operator Interaction displays the response – for example, alarm information – to the operator.

9.5.2 Make Order Request Example

The second example of stateless dynamic interaction modeling is from the online shopping service-oriented system. This example follows the four steps for dynamic modeling described in Section 9.4.

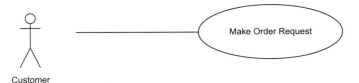

Figure 9.4. Use case diagram for the Make Order Request use case

1. Develop Use Case Model

In the Make Order Request use case, a customer actor enters the order request information; the system then gets the account information and requests credit card authorization. If the credit card is authorized, the system creates a new delivery order and displays the order. The use case diagram is depicted in Figure 9.4 and the use case description is as follows:

Use case name: Make Order Request
Summary: Customer enters an order request to purchase items from the online shopping system. The customer's credit card is checked for validity and sufficient credit to pay for the requested catalog items.
Actor: Customer
Precondition: Customer has selected one or more catalog items.
Main sequence:
1. **Customer** provides order request and customer account Id to pay for purchase.
2. System retrieves **customer account information**, including the customer's credit card details.
3. System checks the customer's **credit card** for the purchase amount and, if approved, creates a credit card purchase authorization number.
4. System creates a **delivery order** containing order details, customer Id, and credit card authorization number.
5. System confirms approval of purchase and displays order information to customer.
6. System sends **email** confirmation to customer.

Alternative sequences:

Step 2: If customer does not have account, the system prompts the customer to provide information in order to create a new account. The customer can either enter the account information or cancel the order.
Step 3: If authorization of the customer's credit card is denied (e.g., invalid credit card or insufficient funds in the customer's credit card account), the system prompts the customer to enter a different credit card number. The customer can either enter a different credit card number or cancel the order.

Postcondition: System has created a delivery order for the customer.

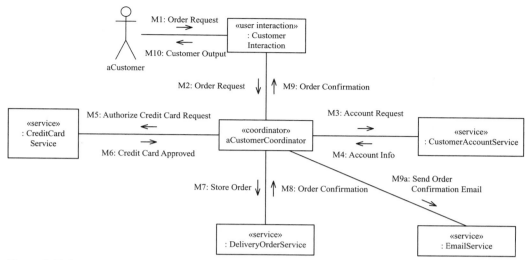

Figure 9.5. Communication diagram for the Make Order Request use case: main sequence

2. Determine Objects Needed to Realize Use Case

As before, the objects needed to realize this use case can be determined by a careful reading of the use case, as shown in bold type. Given the customer actor, there will need to be a user interaction object, Customer Interaction. Service objects are needed for the four services needed to realize this use case, Customer Account Service, Credit Card Service, Delivery Order Service, and Email Service. There will also need to be a coordinator object, Customer Coordinator, to coordinate the interactions between Customer Interaction and the four service objects.

3. Determine Message Communication Sequence

Next consider the sequence of interactions among these objects, as depicted in Figure 9.5. The interaction sequence among the objects needs to reflect the interaction sequence between the actor and the system, as described in the use case. The use case description (step 1) indicates that the customer requests to create an order. To realize this use case step, Customer Interaction makes an order request to Customer Coordinator (messages M1 and M2 in the communication diagram). In step 2 of the use case, the system retrieves the account information. To realize this use case step, Customer Coordinator needs to request account information from Customer Account Service (messages M3 and M4 in the communication diagram). In step 3 of the use case, the system checks the customer's credit card. To realize this use case step, Customer Coordinator needs to request credit card authorization from Credit Card Service (message M5 in the communication diagram). In the main sequence of the use case, the credit card authorization request is approved, as given by message M6 on the communication diagram. In step 4 of the use case, the system creates a delivery order. To realize this use case step, Customer Coordinator needs to store the order at Delivery Order Service (messages M7 and M8 in the communication diagram). Next in the use case, the system confirms the order to the user (messages M9 and M10), and sends a confirmation email via the email service (concurrent message M9a).

The communication diagram for the Make Order Request use case is depicted in Figure 9.5. The message descriptions are as follows:

M1: The customer provides order request to Customer Interaction.

M2: Customer Interaction sends the order request to Customer Coordinator.

M3, M4: Customer Coordinator sends the account request to Customer Account Service and receives the account information, including the customer's credit card details.

M5: Customer Coordinator sends the customer's credit card information to Credit Card Service.

M6: Credit Card Service sends a credit card approval to Customer Coordinator.

M7, M8: Customer Coordinator sends order request to Delivery Order Service.

M9, M9a: Customer Coordinator sends the order confirmation to Customer Interaction and sends an email of the order confirmation to the customer via the Email Service.

M10: Customer Interaction outputs the order confirmation to the customer.

The sequence diagram for the same scenario, namely, the main sequence of the Make Order Request use case, is depicted in Figure 9.6, which shows the message sequence from top to bottom of the page.

4. Determine Alternative Sequences

Alternative scenarios for this use case are that the customer does not have an account, in which case a new account will be created, or that the credit card authorization is denied, in which case the customer has the option of selecting a different card. Both of these alternative scenarios are analyzed.

The new account alternative scenario is depicted in Figure 9.7. This scenario diverges from the main scenario at step M4A. The alternative response to the account request of step M3 is M4A [no account]: Account does not exist. M4A is a conditional message, which is only sent if the Boolean condition [no account] condition is true. The message sequence for this alternative scenario is M4A through M4A.8, which is described as follows:

M4A: Customer Account Service returns message to Customer Coordinator indicating customer has no account.

M4A.1, M4A.2: Customer Coordinator sends a new account request to customer via Customer Interaction.

M4A.3, M4A.4: Customer inputs account information to Customer Interaction, which forwards the message to Customer Coordinator.

M4A.5: Customer Coordinator requests Customer Account Service to create a new account.

M4A.6, M4A.7, M4A.8: Customer Account Service confirms new account, which is returned to the customer via Customer Coordinator and Customer Interaction.

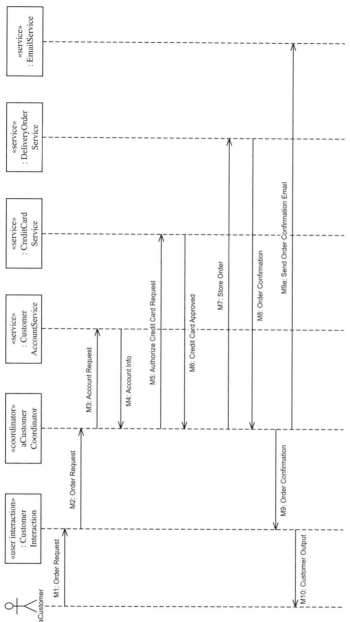

Figure 9.6. Sequence diagram for the Make Order Request use case: main sequence

145

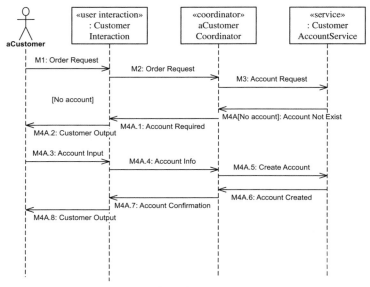

Figure 9.7. Sequence diagram for the Make Order Request use case: alternative sequence for Create New Account

The credit card denied alternative scenario is depicted in Figure 9.8. This scenario diverges from the main scenario at step M6A. The alternative response to the authorize credit card request of step M5 is M6A [denied]: Credit card denied. M6A is a conditional message, which is only sent if the Boolean condition [denied] is true. The message sequence for this alternative scenario is M6A through M6A.2, which is described as follows:

M6A: Credit Card Service sends message to Customer Coordinator denying authorization of credit card.

M6A.1: Customer Coordinator notifies Customer Interaction of credit card denial.

M6A.2: Customer Interaction informs customer of denial and prompts for different credit card.

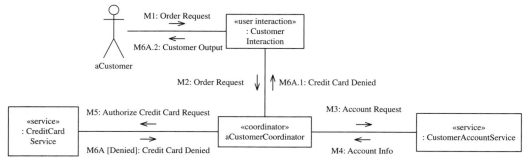

Figure 9.8. Communication diagram for the Make Order Request use case: alternative sequence for Credit Card Denied

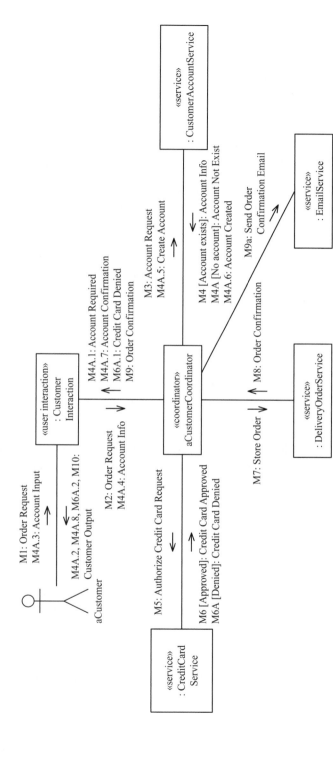

Figure 9.9. Generic communication diagram for the Make Order Request use case: main and alternative sequences

The sequence diagram in Figure 9.6 and the communication diagrams in Figures 9.5, 9.7, and 9.8 all depict individual scenarios (main or alternative) of the Make Order Request use case. It is possible to combine several scenarios onto a generic interaction diagram. Figure 9.9 depicts a generic communication diagram for the three scenarios depicted on Figure 9.5 (main sequence) and Figures 9.7 and 9.8 (alternative sequences). Note the use of alternative message sequence numbering for the different scenarios. The alternatives to the M3 account request message are the two alternatives given by M4 [account exists] and M4A [no account]. The alternatives to the M5 authorize credit card request message are the two alternatives given by M6 [approved] and M6A [denied].

The same three scenarios of the Make Order Request use case are depicted on the generic sequence diagram in Figure 9.10. The sequence diagram depicts the two alternative sequences for account creation and the other for credit card approval. The first *alt* segment depicts the two alternatives of [account exists] and [no account]. The second *alt* segment depicts the two alternatives of [approved] and [denied]. In each case, a dashed line is the separator between the alternatives. The message sequence numbering is optional on the sequence diagram; however, it is explicitly depicted to illustrate the correspondence with the communication diagram.

9.6 SUMMARY

This chapter discussed dynamic modeling, in which the objects that participate in each use case are determined, as well as the sequence of their interactions. This chapter first described **communication diagrams** and **sequence diagrams** before explaining how they are used in dynamic modeling. It then described the details of the **dynamic interaction modeling** approach for determining how objects collaborate with each other. **State-dependent dynamic interaction modeling** involves a state-dependent communication controlled by a statechart (as described in Chapter 11), and **stateless dynamic interaction modeling** does not.

During design, the communication diagrams corresponding to each use case are synthesized into an integrated communication diagram, which represents the first step in developing the software architecture of the system, as described in Chapter 13. During analysis, all message interactions are depicted as simple messages, because no decision has yet been made about the characteristics of the messages. During design, the message interfaces are defined as described in Chapters 12 and 13.

EXERCISES

Multiple-choice questions: For each question, choose one of the answers.

1. What does an interaction diagram depict?
(a) The state and transitions inside a control object
(b) Classes and their relationships
(c) Software objects and the sequence of their interactions
(d) The external objects communicating with the system

2. How is an actor depicted on an interaction diagram?
(a) An actor has an association with the interaction diagram.

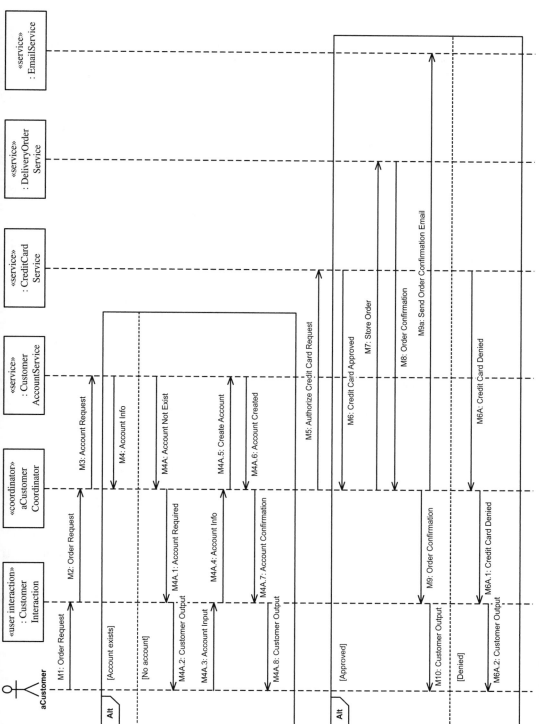

Figure 9.10. Generic sequence diagram for the Make Order Request use case: main and alternative sequences

149

(b) An actor can provide input to or receive output from a boundary object.

(c) An actor can provide input to or receive output from a boundary class.

(d) An instance of an actor can provide input to or receive output from a boundary object.

3. What does a sequence diagram depict?
   (a) The sequence of external objects communicating with each other
   (b) Classes and their relationships
   (c) Software objects and the sequence of their interactions
   (d) The external objects communicating with the system

4. What does a communication diagram depict?
   (a) The sequence of external objects communicating with each other
   (b) Classes and their relationships
   (c) Software objects and the sequence of their interactions
   (d) The external objects communicating with the system

5. What is the instance form of an interaction diagram?
   (a) Depicts several object instances interacting with each other
   (b) Depicts one possible sequence of interactions among object instances
   (c) Depicts all possible interactions among object instances
   (d) Depicts all object instances and their links to each other

6. What is the generic form of an interaction diagram?
   (a) Depicts several objects interacting with each other
   (b) Depicts one possible sequence of interactions among objects
   (c) Depicts all possible interactions among objects

(d) Depicts all classes and their associations with each other

7. During dynamic interaction modeling, use cases are realized as follows:
   (a) Determine objects that participate in each use case and the sequence of interactions among them.
   (b) Determine external objects and the sequence in which they provide inputs to and receive outputs from each use case.
   (c) Determine sequence of interactions among use cases.
   (d) Determine how a use case is depicted through internal states and transitions between them.

8. Which of the following interactions could happen on an interaction diagram?
   (a) An external user sends a message to a user interaction object.
   (b) An external user sends a message to an entity object.
   (c) An external user sends a message to an I/O object.
   (d) An external user sends a message to a printer object.

9. Which of the following interactions is NOT likely to happen on an interaction diagram?
   (a) A user interaction object sends a message to an entity object.
   (b) An input object sends a message to a state-dependent control object.
   (c) An input object sends a message to a printer object.
   (d) A user interaction object sends a message to a proxy object.

10. What kind of object would be the first object to receive an input from an external object?
    (a) A user interaction object
    (b) A proxy object
    (c) An entity object
    (d) A boundary object

Finite State Machines

Finite state machines are used for modeling the control and sequencing view of a system or object. Many systems, such as real-time systems, are highly state-dependent; that is, their actions depend not only on their inputs but also on what has previously happened in the system. Notations used to define finite state machines are the state transition diagram, statechart, and state transition table. In highly state-dependent systems, these notations can help greatly by providing insight into understanding the complexity of these systems.

In the UML notation, a state transition diagram is referred to as a *state machine diagram*. The UML state machine diagram notation is based on Harel's statechart notation (Harel 1988; Harel and Politi 1998). In this book, the terms **statechart** and *state machine diagram* are used interchangeably. We refer to a traditional state transition diagram, which is not hierarchical, as a *flat statechart* and use the term *hierarchical statechart* to refer to the concept of hierarchical state decomposition. A brief overview of the statechart notation is given in Chapter 2 (Section 2.6).

This chapter starts by considering the characteristics of flat statecharts and then describes hierarchical statecharts. To show the benefits of hierarchical statecharts, this chapter starts with the simplest form of flat statechart and gradually shows how it can be improved upon to achieve the full modeling power of hierarchical statecharts. Several examples are given throughout the chapter from two case studies, the Automated Teller Machine and Microwave Oven finite state machines.

Section 10.1 describes events and states in finite state machines. Section 10.2 introduces the statechart examples. Section 10.3 describes events and guard conditions, and Section 10.4 describes statechart actions. Section 10.5 describes hierarchical statecharts. Section 10.6 provides guidelines for developing statecharts. The process of developing statecharts from use cases is then described in Section 10.7.

10.1 FINITE STATE MACHINES AND STATE TRANSITIONS

A **finite state machine** (also referred to as *state machine*) is a conceptual machine with a finite number of states. The state machine can be in only one state at any one time. A **state transition** is a change in state that is caused by an input event. In response to an input event, the finite state machine might transition to a different state. Alternatively, the event might have no effect, in which case the finite state machine remains in the same state. The next state depends on the current state, as well as on the input event. Optionally, an output action might result from the state transition.

Although a whole system can be modeled by means of a finite state machine, in object-oriented analysis and design, a finite state machine is encapsulated inside one object. In other words, the object is state-dependent and is always in one of the states of the finite state machine. The object's finite state machine is depicted by means of a statechart. In an object-oriented model, the state-dependent view of a system is defined by means of one or more finite state machines, in which each finite state machine is encapsulated inside its own object. This section describes the basic concepts of events and states before giving some examples of statecharts.

10.1.1 Events

An **event** is an occurrence at a point in time; it is also known as a discrete event, discrete signal, or stimulus. An event is an atomic occurrence (not interruptible) and conceptually has zero duration. Examples of events are Card Inserted, Pin Entered, and Door Opened.

Events can depend on each other. For example, the event Card Inserted always precedes Pin Entered for a given sequence of events. In this situation, the first event (Card Inserted) causes a transition into the state (Waiting for PIN), whereas the next event (Pin Entered) causes the transition out of that state; the precedence of the two events is reflected in the state that connects them, as shown in Figure 10.1.

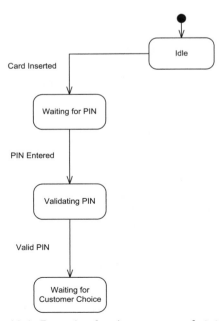

Figure 10.1. Example of main sequence of statechart

An event can originate from an external source, such as Card Inserted (which is the result of the user inserting the card into the card reader), or can be internally generated by the system, such as Valid PIN.

10.1.2 States

A **state** represents a recognizable situation that exists over an interval of time. Whereas an event occurs at a point in time, a finite state machine is in a given state over an interval of time. The arrival of an event at the finite state machine usually causes a transition from one state to another. Alternatively, an event can have a null effect, in which case the finite state machine remains in the same state. In theory, a state transition is meant to take zero time to occur. In practice, the time for a state transition to occur is negligible compared to the time spent in the state.

Some states represent the state machine waiting for an event from the external environment; for example, the state Waiting for PIN is the state in which the state machine is waiting for the customer to enter the PIN, as shown in Figure 10.1. Other states represent situations in which the state machine is waiting for a response from another part of the system. For example, Validating PIN is the state in which the customer PIN is being checked by the system; the next event will indicate whether the validation succeeded or not.

The initial state of a state machine is the state that is entered when the state machine is activated. For example, the initial state in the ATM statechart is the Idle state, as identified in UML by the arc originating from the small black circle in Figure 10.1.

10.2 EXAMPLES OF STATECHARTS

The use of flat statecharts is illustrated by means of two examples, an ATM statechart and a Microwave Oven statechart.

10.2.1 Example of ATM Statechart

Consider an example, shown in Figure 10.1, of a partial statechart for an automated teller machine. The initial state of the ATM statechart is Idle. Consider the scenario consisting of the customer inserting the card into the ATM, entering the PIN, and then selecting cash withdrawal. When the Card Inserted event arrives, the ATM statechart transitions from the Idle state to the Waiting for PIN state, during which time the ATM is waiting for the customer to input the PIN. When the PIN Entered event arrives, the ATM transitions to the Validating PIN state. In this state the bank system determines whether the customer-entered PIN matches the stored PIN for this card, and whether the ATM card has been reported lost or stolen. Assuming that the card and PIN validation is successful (event Valid PIN), the ATM transitions into Waiting for Customer Choice state.

It is possible to have more than one transition out of a state, with each transition caused by a different event. Consider the alternative transitions that could result from PIN validation. Figure 10.2 shows three possible state transitions out of the Validating PIN state. If the two PIN numbers match, the ATM makes the Valid PIN

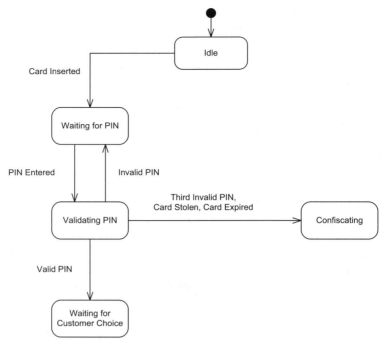

Figure 10.2. Example of alternative events on statechart

transition to the Waiting for Customer Choice state. If the PIN numbers do not match, the ATM makes the Invalid PIN transition to re-enter the Waiting for PIN state and prompts the customer to enter a different PIN number. If the customer-entered PIN is invalid after the third attempt, the ATM makes the Third Invalid PIN transition to the Confiscating state, which results in the card being confiscated. The ATM also transitions to the same state if the ATM card is reported lost or stolen during card validation, or if the card has expired.

In some cases, it is also possible for the same event to occur in different states and have the same effect; an example is given in Figure 10.3. The customer may decide to enter Cancel in any of the three states Waiting for PIN, Validating PIN, or Waiting for Customer Choice, which results in the statechart entering the Ejecting state, the ATM card being ejected, and the transaction terminated.

It is also possible for the same event to occur in a different state and have a different effect. For example, if the PIN Entered event arrives in Idle state, it is ignored.

Next consider the case in which, after successful PIN validation, the customer decides to withdraw cash from the ATM, as shown in Figure 10.4. From the Waiting for Customer Choice state, the customer makes a selection – for example, the customer selects withdrawal. The statechart then receives a Withdrawal Selected event, upon which the Processing Withdrawal state is entered. If the withdrawal is approved, the statechart goes into the Dispensing state, where the cash is dispensed. When the Cash Dispensed event arrives, the ATM transitions to the Printing state to print the receipt. When the receipt is printed, the Ejecting state is entered. When the card has been ejected, as indicated by the Card Ejected event, the Terminating state is entered.

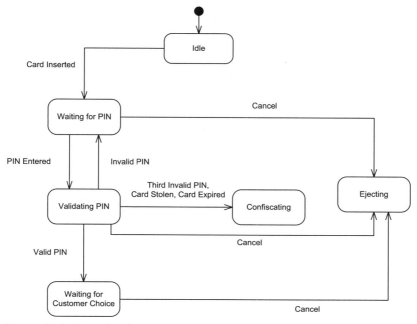

Figure 10.3. Example of same event occurring in different states

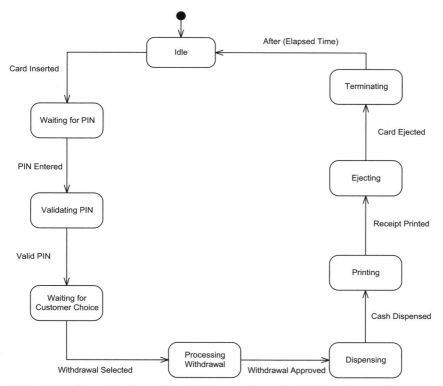

Figure 10.4. Example of complete ATM scenario: cash withdrawal scenario

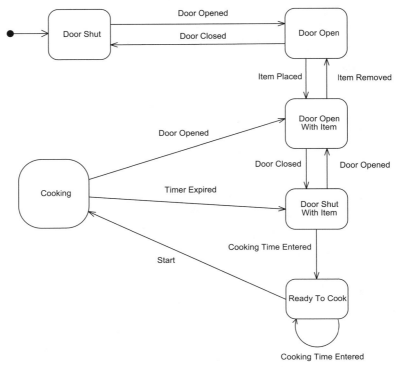

Figure 10.5. Simplified statechart for Microwave Oven Control

From the Terminating state, a timer event causes a transition back to the Idle state. The timer event is depicted by after (Elapsed Time), where Elapsed Time is the time spent in the Terminating state (from entry into the state until exit from the state caused by the timer event).

10.2.2 Example of Microwave Oven Statechart

As a second example of a statechart, consider a simplified version of the Microwave Oven Control statechart, which is shown in Figure 10.5. The statechart shows the different states for cooking food. The initial state is Door Shut. Consider a scenario that starts when the user opens the door. As a result, the statechart transitions into the Door Open state. The user then places an item in the oven, causing the statechart to transition into the Door Open with Item state. When the user closes the door, the statechart then transitions into the Door Shut with Item state. After the user inputs the cooking time, the Ready to Cook state is entered. Next the user presses the Start button, which causes the statechart to transition into the Cooking state. When the timer expires, the statechart leaves the Cooking state and reenters the Door Shut with Item state. If instead the door were opened during cooking, the statechart would enter the Door Open with Item state.

10.3 EVENTS AND GUARD CONDITIONS

It is possible to make a state transition conditional through the use of a guard condition. This can be achieved by combining events and guard conditions in defining a state transition. The notation used is *Event [Condition].* A condition is a Boolean expression with a value of True or False, which holds for some time. When the event arrives, it causes a state transition, provided that the guard condition given in square brackets is True. Conditions are optional.

In some cases, an event does not cause an immediate state transition, but its impact needs to be remembered because it will affect a future state transition. The fact that an event has occurred can be stored as a condition that can be checked later.

Examples of guard conditions in Figure 10.6 are Zero Time and Time Remaining in the microwave statechart. The two transitions out of the Door Open with Item state are Door Closed [Zero Time] and Door Closed [Time Remaining]. Thus the transition taken depends on whether the user has previously entered the time or not (or whether timer previously expired). If the condition Zero Time is true, the statechart transitions to Door Shut with Item, waiting for the user to enter the time. If the condition Time Remaining is true, the statechart transitions to the Ready to Cook state.

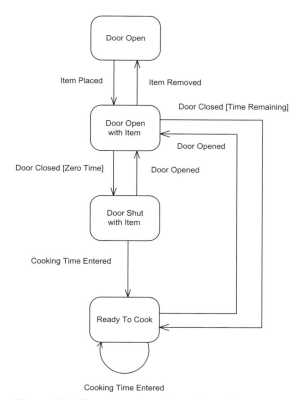

Figure 10.6. Example of events and conditions

10.4 ACTIONS

Associated with a state transition is an optional output **action**. An action is a computation that executes as a result of a state transition. Whereas an event is the cause of a state transition, an action is the effect of the transition. An action is triggered at a state transition. It executes and then terminates itself. The action executes instantaneously at the state transition; thus conceptually an action is of zero duration. In practice, the duration of an action is very small compared to the duration of a state.

Actions can be depicted on state transitions, as described in Section 10.4.1. Certain actions can be depicted more concisely as being associated with the state rather than with the transition into or out of the state. These are entry and exit actions. Entry actions are triggered when the state is entered, as described in Section 10.4.2, and exit actions are triggered on leaving the state, as described in Section 10.4.3.

10.4.1 Actions on State Transitions

A transition action is an action that is a result of a transition from one state to another – it could also happen if the state transitions to itself. To depict a transition action on a statechart, the state transition is labeled *Event/Action* or *Event [Condition]/Action*.

As an example of actions, consider the ATM statechart. When the Card Inserted event arrives, the ATM statechart transitions from the Idle state to the Waiting for PIN state (Figure 10.2). The action that takes place at the transition into this state is Get PIN, which is a prompt the state machine outputs to the customer to enter the

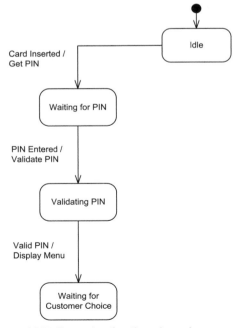

Figure 10.7. Example of actions in main sequence

PIN. This example is shown in Figure 10.7, which shows the partial statechart for the ATM (originally shown in Figure 10.1) with the actions added. In the Waiting for PIN state, the ATM is waiting for the customer to input the PIN. When the PIN Entered event arrives, the ATM transitions to the Validating PIN state and the action Validate PIN is executed. This state transition is labeled PIN entered / Validate PIN. In the Validating PIN state, the system determines whether the customer-entered PIN matches the stored PIN for this card, and whether the ATM card has been reported lost or stolen. Assuming that the card and PIN validation is successful (event Valid PIN), the ATM transitions into Waiting for Customer Choice state.

More than one action can be associated with a transition. Because the actions all execute simultaneously, there must not be any interdependencies between the actions. For example, it is not correct to have two simultaneous actions such as Compute Change and Display Change. Because there is a sequential dependency between the two actions, the change cannot be displayed before it has been computed. To avoid this problem, introduce an intermediate state called Computing Change. The Compute Change action is executed on entry to this state, and the Display Change action is executed on exit from this state.

An example of a statechart with alternative actions is shown in Figure 10.8. Many actions are possible as a result of PIN validation. If the PIN is valid, the statechart transitions to the Waiting for Customer Choice state and the action is to display the selection menu. If the PIN is invalid, the statechart transitions back to the Waiting for PIN state and the action is the Invalid PIN Prompt. If the PIN is invalid for the third time, or the card is stolen or has expired, then the statechart transitions to the Confiscating state and the action is to confiscate the card. Another situation is that

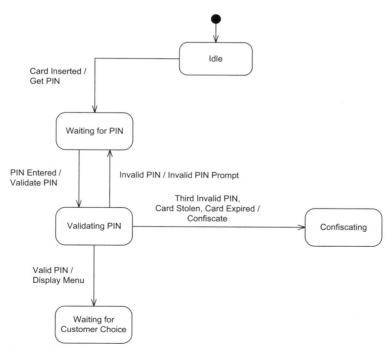

Figure 10.8. Example of alternative state transitions and actions

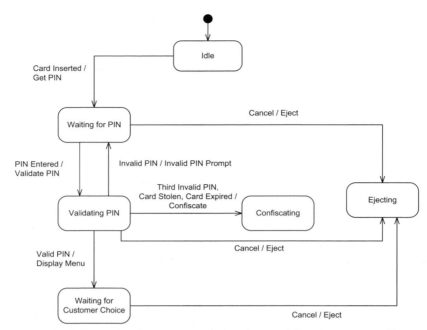

Figure 10.9. Example of same event and action on different state transitions

the same event can cause transitions out of several states, with the same action in each case. An example of this is given in Figure 10.9. In any of the three states, Waiting for PIN, Validating PIN, and Waiting for Customer Choice, the customer may decide to enter Cancel, which results in the system ejecting the ATM card and entering Ejecting state.

10.4.2 Entry Actions

An **entry action** is an instantaneous action that is performed on transition into the state. An entry action is represented by the reserved word *entry* and is depicted as *entry/Action* inside the state box. Whereas transition actions (actions explicitly depicted on state transitions) can always be used, entry actions should only be used in certain situations. The best time to use an entry action is when the following occur:

- There is more than one transition into a state.
- The same action needs to be performed on every transition into this state.
- The action is performed on entry into this state and not on exit from the previous state.

In this situation, the action is only depicted once inside the state box, instead of on each transition into the state. On the other hand, if an action is only performed on some transitions into the state and not others, then the entry action should not be used. Instead, transition actions should be used on the relevant state transitions.

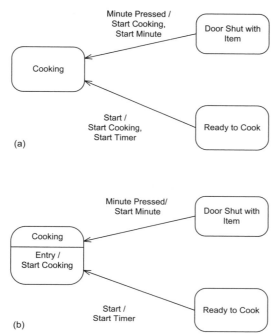

Figure 10.10. Example of entry action: *(a)* Actions on state transitions *(b)* Entry actions.

An example of an entry action is given in Figure 10.10. In Figure 10.10*a*, actions are shown on the state transitions. If the Start button is pressed (resulting in the Start event) while the microwave oven is in the Ready to Cook state, the statechart transitions to the Cooking state. There are two actions – Start Cooking and Start Timer. On the other hand, if the user presses the Minute Plus button (to cook the food for one minute) while in Door Shut with Item state, the statechart will also transition to the Cooking state. In this case, however, the actions are Start Cooking and Start Minute. Thus, in the two transitions into Cooking state, one action is the same (Start Cooking) but the second is different. An alternative decision is to use an entry action for Start Cooking as shown in Figure 10.10*b*. On entry into Cooking state, the entry action Start Cooking is executed because this action is executed on every transition into the state. However, the Start Timer action is shown as an action on the state transition from Ready to Cook state into Cooking state. This is because the Start Timer action is only executed on that specific transition into Cooking state and not on the other transition. Thus, on the transition from Door Shut with Item state into Cooking state, the transition action is Start Minute. Figures 10.10a and 10.10b are semantically equivalent to each other but Figure 10.10b is more concise.

10.4.3 Exit Actions

An **exit action** is an instantaneous action that is performed on transition out of the state. An exit action is represented by the reserved word *exit* and is depicted

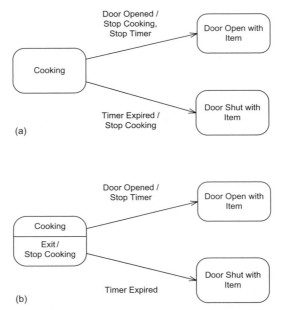

Figure 10.11. Example of exit action. *(a)* Actions on state transitions. *(b)* Exit actions

as *exit/Action* inside the state box. Whereas transition actions (actions explicitly depicted on state transitions) can always be used, exit actions should only be used in certain situations. The best time to use an exit action is when the following occur:

■ There is more than one transition out of a state.
■ The same action needs to be performed on every transition out of the state.
■ The action is performed on exit from this state and not on entry into the next state.

In this situation, the action is only depicted once inside the state box, instead of on each transition out of the state. On the other hand, if an action is only performed on some transitions out of the state and not others, then the exit action should not be used. Instead, transition actions should be used on the relevant state transitions.

An example of an **exit action** is given in Figure 10.11. In Figure 10.11a, actions are shown on the state transitions out of Cooking state. Consider the action Stop Cooking. If the timer expires, the microwave oven transitions from the Cooking state to the Door Shut with Item state and the action Stop Cooking is executed (Figure 10.11a). If the door is opened, the oven transitions out of the Cooking state into Door Open with Item state. In this transition, two actions are executed – Stop Cooking and Stop Timer. Thus, in both transitions out of Cooking state (Figure 10.11a), the action Stop Cooking is executed. However, when the door is opened and the transition is to Door Open with Item state, there is an additional Stop Timer action. An alternative design is shown in Figure 10.11b, in which an exit action Stop Cooking is depicted. This means that whenever there is a transition out of Cooking state, the exit action Stop Cooking is executed. In addition, in the transition to Door Open with Item state, the transition action Stop Timer will also be executed. Having the Stop Cooking action as an exit action instead of an action on the state transition is more concise, as shown in Figure 10.11b. The alternative of having transition actions, as shown in Figure 10.11a, would require the Stop Cooking action to be explicitly depicted on each of the state transitions out of the Cooking state. Figures 10.11a and 10.11b are semantically equivalent to each other but Figure 10.11b is more concise.

10.5 HIERARCHICAL STATECHARTS

One of the potential problems of flat statecharts is the proliferation of states and transitions, which makes the statechart very cluttered and difficult to read. A very important way of simplifying statecharts and increasing their modeling power is to introduce *composite* states, which are also known as superstates, and the hierarchical decomposition of statecharts. With this approach, a *composite* state at one level of a statechart is decomposed into two or more *substates* on a lower-level statechart.

The objective of hierarchical statecharts is to exploit the basic concepts and visual advantages of state transition diagrams, while overcoming the disadvantages of overly complex and cluttered diagrams, through hierarchical structuring. Note that any hierarchical statechart can be mapped to a flat statechart, so for every hierarchical statechart there is a semantically equivalent flat statechart.

10.5.1 Hierarchical State Decomposition

Statecharts can often be significantly simplified by the hierarchical decomposition of states, in which a composite state is decomposed into two or more interconnected sequential substates. This kind of decomposition is referred to as *sequential state decomposition*. The notation for state decomposition also allows both the composite state and the substates to be shown on the same diagram or, alternatively, on separate diagrams, depending on the complexity of the decomposition.

An example of hierarchical state decomposition is given in Figure 10.12a, where the Processing Customer Input composite state consists of the Waiting for PIN, Validating PIN, and Waiting for Customer Choice substates. (On the hierarchical statechart, the composite state is shown as the outer rounded box, with the name of the composite state shown at the top left of the box. The substates are shown as inner rounded boxes.) When the system is in Processing Customer Input composite state, it is in one (and only one) of the Waiting for PIN, Validating PIN, and Waiting for Customer Choice substates. Because the substates are executed sequentially, this kind of hierarchical state decomposition is referred to as resulting in a *sequential statechart*.

10.5.2 Composite States

Composite states can be depicted in two ways on statecharts, as described next. A composite state can be depicted with its internal substates, as shown for the Processing Customer Input composite state in Figure 10.12a. Alternatively, a composite state can be depicted as a black box without revealing its internal substates, as shown in Figure 10.12b. It should be pointed out that when a composite state is decomposed into substates, the transitions into and out of the composite state must be preserved.

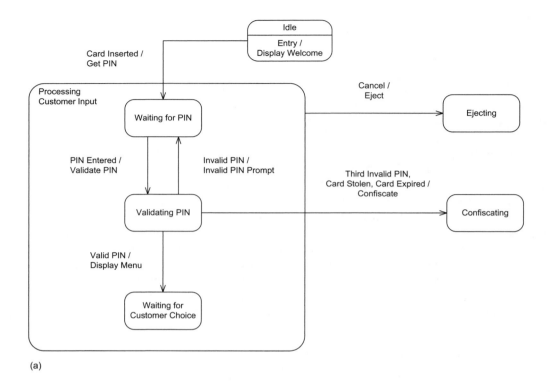

(a)

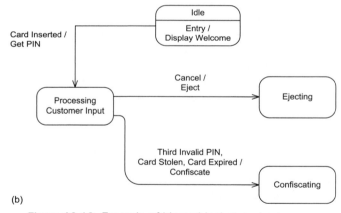

(b)

Figure 10.12. Example of hierarchical statechart

Thus, there is one state transition into the Processing Customer Input composite state and two transitions out of it, as shown in Figures 10.12*a* and 10.12b.

Each transition into the composite state Processing Customer Input is, in fact, a transition into one (and only one) of the substates on the lower-level statechart. Each individual transition out of the composite state has to actually originate from one (and only one) of the substates on the lower-level statechart. Thus. the input event Card Inserted causes a transition to the Waiting for PIN substate within the

Processing Customer Input composite state, as shown in Figure 10.12a. The transition out of the Processing Customer Input composite state into the Confiscating state actually originates from the Validating PIN substate, as shown in Figure 10.12a. The case of the Cancel transition into Ejecting state is described in the next section.

10.5.3 Aggregation of State Transitions

The hierarchical statechart notation also allows a transition out of every one of the substates on a statechart to be aggregated into a transition out of the composite state. Careful use of this feature can significantly reduce the number of state transitions on a statechart.

Consider the following example in which aggregation of state transitions would be useful. In the flat statechart shown in Figure 10.9, it is possible for the customer to press the Cancel button on the ATM machine in any of the three states Waiting for PIN, Validating PIN, and Waiting for Customer Choice. In each case, the Cancel event transitions the ATM to Ejecting state. This is depicted by a Cancel arc leaving each of these states and entering the Ejecting state.

This can be expressed more concisely on a hierarchical statechart. From each of the three substates of the Processing Customer Input composite state, the input event Cancel causes a transition to the Ejecting state. Because the Cancel event can take place in any of the three Processing Customer Input substates, a Cancel transition could be shown leaving each substate. However, it is more concise to show one Cancel transition leaving the Processing Customer Input composite state, as shown in Figure 10.12*a*. The transitions out of the substates are not shown (even though an individual transition would actually originate from one of the substates). This kind of state transition, in which the same event causes a transition out of several states to another state, usually results in a plethora of arcs on flat statecharts and state transition diagrams.

In contrast, because the Third Invalid event only occurs in Validating PIN state (Figure 10.12*a*), it is shown leaving this substate only and not from the composite state.

10.5.4 Orthogonal Statecharts

Another kind of hierarchical state decomposition is orthogonal state decomposition, which is used to model different views of the same object's state. With this approach, a high-level state on one statechart is decomposed into two (or more) orthogonal statecharts. The two orthogonal statecharts are shown separated by a dashed line. When the higher-level statechart is in the composite state, it is simultaneously in one of the substates on the first lower-level orthogonal statechart *and* in one of the substates on the second lower-level orthogonal statechart.

Although orthogonal statecharts can be used to depict concurrent activity within the object containing the statechart, it is better to use this kind of decomposition to show different parts of the same object that are not concurrent. Designing objects with only one thread of control is much simpler and is strongly recommended. When true concurrency is required, use separate objects and define each object with its own statechart.

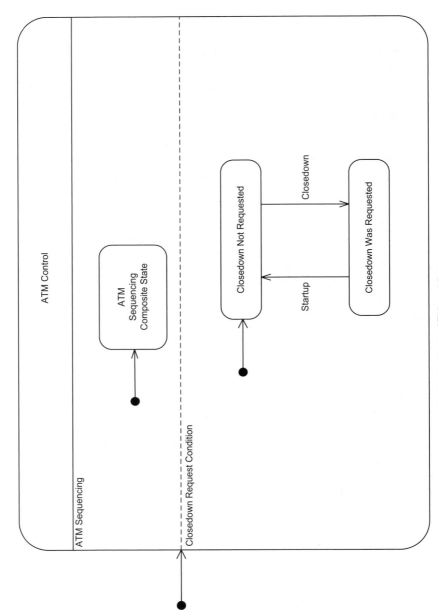

Figure 10.13. Example of orthogonal statecharts in the ATM problem

The use of orthogonal statecharts to depict conditions can be seen in the ATM example. This case is illustrated in Figure 10.13, where the statechart for the ATM Machine, ATM Control, is now decomposed into two orthogonal statecharts, one for ATM Sequencing and one for Closedown Request Condition. The two statecharts are depicted on a high-level statechart, with a dashed line separating them. The ATM Sequencing statechart is in fact the main statechart of the ATM, which depicts the states the ATM goes through while processing a customer request.

Note that, at any one time, the ATM Control composite state is in one of the substates of the ATM Sequencing statechart and one of the substates of the Closedown Request Condition statechart. Closedown Request Condition is a simple statechart with two states reflecting whether closedown has been requested or not, with Closedown Not Requested as the initial state. The Closedown event causes a transition to the state Closedown Was Requested, and the Startup event causes a transition back to Closedown Not Requested. The ATM Control statechart is the union of the Closedown Request Condition and the ATM Sequencing statecharts. The Closedown Was Requested and Closedown Not Requested states of the Closedown Request Condition statechart (see Figure 10.13) are the conditions checked on the ATM Sequencing statechart, when the after (Elapsed Time) event is received in Terminating state (Figure 10.17). Note that the Closed Down state is actually a state on the ATM Sequencing statechart.

10.6 GUIDELINES FOR DEVELOPING STATECHARTS

The following guidelines apply to developing either flat or hierarchical statecharts, unless otherwise explicitly stated:

- A state name must reflect an identifiable situation or an interval of time when something is *happening* in the system. Thus, a state name is often an adjective (e.g., Idle), a phrase with an adjective (e.g., ATM Idle), a gerund (e.g., Dispensing), or a phrase with a gerund (e.g., Waiting for PIN). The state name should not reflect an event or action such as ATM Dispenses or Dispense Cash, respectively.
- On a given statechart, each state must have a unique name. It is usually ambiguous to have two states with the same name. In theory, a substate within one composite state could have the same name as a substate of a different composite state; however, this is confusing and should therefore be avoided.
- It must be possible to exit from every state. It is not necessary for a statechart to have a terminating state, because the statechart might exist for the duration of the system or object.
- On a sequential statechart, the statechart is in only one state at a time. Two states cannot be active simultaneously (e.g., Waiting for PIN and Dispensing). One state must follow sequentially from the other.
- Do not confuse events and actions. An event is the *cause* of the state transition, and the action is the *effect* of the state transition.
- An event happens at a moment in time. The event name indicates that something has just happened (e.g., Card Inserted, Door Closed) or the result of an action such as Valid PIN or Third Invalid.
- An action is a command – for example, Dispense Cash, Start Cooking, Eject.
- An action executes instantaneously. It is possible to have more than one action associated with a state transition. All these actions conceptually execute simultaneously; hence, no assumptions can be made about the order in which the

actions are executed. Consequently, no interdependencies must exist between the actions. If a dependency does exist, it is necessary to introduce an intermediate state.

- A condition is a Boolean value. If a state transition is labeled **event [condition]**, a state transition takes place only if, at the moment the event happens, the condition is *true*. A condition is *true* for some interval of time. The state transition Door Closed [Time Remaining] is only taken if there is a finite time remaining when the door is closed. The state transition will not take place if there is no time left when the door is closed.
- Actions and conditions are optional. They should only be used when necessary.

10.7 DEVELOPING STATECHARTS FROM USE CASES

To develop a statechart from a use case, start with a typical scenario given by the use case – that is, one particular path through the use case. Ideally, this scenario should be the main sequence through the use case, involving the most usual sequence of interactions between the actor(s) and the system. Now consider the sequence of external events given in the scenario. Usually, an input event from the external environment causes a transition to a new state, which is given a name corresponding to what happens in that state. If an action is associated with the transition, the action occurs in the transition from one state to the other. Actions are determined by considering the response of the system to the input event, as given in the use case description.

Initially, a flat statechart is developed that follows the event sequence given in the main scenario. The states depicted on the statechart should all be externally visible states – that is, the actor should be aware of each of these states. In fact, the states represent consequences of actions taken by the actor, either directly or indirectly. This is illustrated in the detailed example given in the next section.

To complete the statechart, determine all the possible external events that could be input to the statechart. You do this by considering the description of alternative paths given in the use case. Several alternatives describe the reaction of the system to alternative inputs from the actor. Determine the effect of the arrival of these events on each state of the initial statechart; in many cases, an event could not occur in a given state or will have no impact. In other states, however, the arrival of an event will cause a transition to an existing state or some new state that needs to be added to the statechart. The actions resulting from each alternative state transition also need to be considered. These actions should already be documented in the use case description as the system reaction to an alternative input event.

In some applications, one statechart can participate in more than one use case. In such situations, there will be one partial statechart for each use case. The partial statecharts will need to be integrated to form a complete statechart. The implication is that there is some precedence in the execution of (at least some of) the use cases and their corresponding statecharts. To integrate two partial statecharts, it is necessary to find one or more common states. A common state might be the last state of one statechart and the first state of the next statechart. However, other situations are possible. The integration approach is to integrate the partial statecharts at the common state, in effect superimposing the common state of the second statechart on top of the same state on the first statechart. This can be repeated as necessary, depending on how many partial statecharts need to be integrated.

Given the complete flat statechart, the next step is to develop hierarchical state-charts where possible. There are actually two main approaches to developing hier-archical statecharts. The first approach is a top-down approach to determine major high-level states, sometimes referred to as *modes of operation*. For example, in an airplane control statechart, the modes might be Taking Off, In Flight, and Landing. Within each mode, there are several states, some of which might in turn be com-posite states. This approach is more likely to be used in complex real-time systems, which are frequently highly state-dependent. The second approach is to first develop a flat statechart and then identify states that can be aggregated into composite states, as described in Section 10.8.4.

10.8 EXAMPLE OF DEVELOPING A STATECHART FROM A USE CASE

To illustrate how to develop a statechart from a use case, consider the ATM Control statechart from the Banking System case study.

10.8.1 Develop Statechart for Each Use Case

The use cases for the Banking System are given in Chapter 21. In this example, we will consider the use cases for Validate PIN and Withdraw Cash. Both use cases describe the sequence of interactions between the actor – the ATM Customer – and the system, in which PIN validation precedes withdrawing cash. For each use case, a statechart is constructed as illustrated in Figures 10.14 and 10.15. Figure 10.14

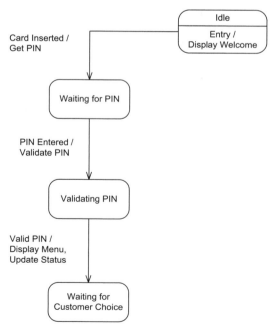

Figure 10.14. Statechart for ATM Control: Validate PIN use case

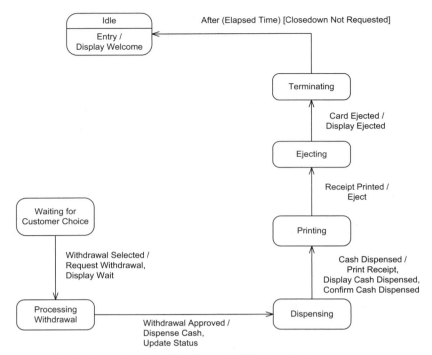

Figure 10.15. Statechart for ATM Control: Withdraw Funds use case

shows the statechart for the main sequence of the Validate PIN use case depicting the scenario in which the PIN is valid, as described in Section 10.4.1. This statechart starts in Idle state and ends in Waiting for Customer Choice state.

Figure 10.15 shows the statechart for the Withdraw Funds use case corresponding to the main scenario of the use case. This statechart starts in Waiting for Customer Choice state. In the main scenario, withdrawal is selected (resulting in transition into Processing Withdrawal state), withdrawal is approved (resulting in transition to Dispensing state), cash is dispensed (resulting in transition to Printing state), a receipt is printed (resulting in transition to Ejecting state), the card is ejected, transition into Terminating state for a fixed period, and finally return to Idle state, when the period elapses.

In this example, the states of the ATM statechart are all externally visible; that is, the actor is aware of each of these states. In fact, the states depict consequences of actions taken by the actor, either directly or indirectly.

10.8.2 Consider Alternative Sequences

After the first version of the statechart is completed, further refinements can be made. To complete the statechart, it is necessary to consider the effect of each alternative sequence described in the Alternatives section of the use cases. Figure 10.9 shows the Validate PIN statechart with the alternative sequences added to the main sequence, as described in Section 10.4.1. Figure 10.16 shows the Withdraw Funds statechart with the alternative sequences added to the main sequence. Thus, in

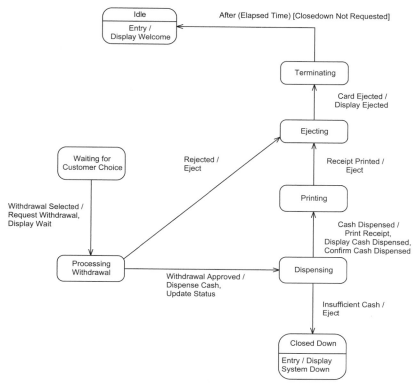

Figure 10.16. Statechart for ATM Control: Withdraw Funds use case with alternatives

addition to the main sequence for the scenario in which cash is dispensed, there are two additional scenarios: withdrawal transaction rejected (transition directly from Processing Withdrawal state to Ejecting State) and insufficient cash in ATM (transition from Dispensing state to Closed Down State).

10.8.3 Develop Integrated Statechart

The integrated statechart consists of the integration of the use case–based statecharts, after consideration of alternatives. Thus, the statecharts depicted in Figures 10.9 (Validate PIN use case with alternatives) and 10.16 (Withdraw Cash use case with alternatives) are combined with the statecharts for the other use cases. This statechart would represent the main sequence through each use case together with the alternatives.

Figure 10.17 shows the integrated statechart from the Validate PIN and Withdraw Cash statecharts, with main and alternatives sequences. The main statechart integration point is Waiting for Customer Choice state, the end state for Validate PIN statechart, and the initial state for Withdraw Funds (and also Transfer Funds and Query Account) statechart. However, other statechart integration points are the Ejecting and Confiscating states for the alternative scenarios of Validate PIN.

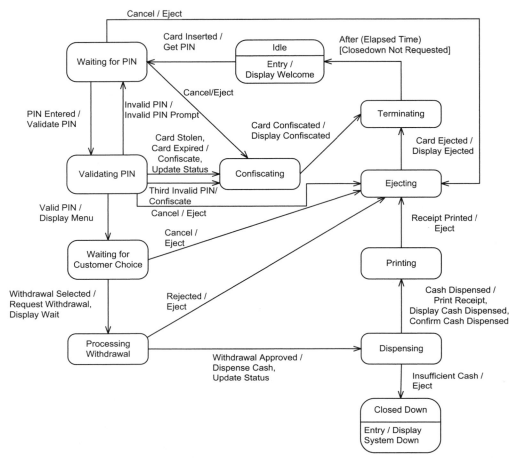

Figure 10.17. Statechart for ATM Control: integrated statechart for Validate PIN and Withdraw Funds use case with alternatives

10.8.4 Develop Hierarchical Statechart

It is usually easier to initially develop a flat statechart. After enhancing the flat statechart by considering alternative events, look for ways to simplify the statechart by developing a hierarchical statechart. Look for states that can be aggregated because they constitute a natural composite state. In particular, look for situations in which the aggregation of state transitions simplifies the statechart.

The hierarchical statechart for ATM Control is shown in Figures 10.18 through 10.21. Three states on Figure 10.18 are composite states: Processing Customer Input (decomposed into three substates on Figure 10.19), Processing Transaction (decomposed into three substates on Figure 10.20), and Terminating Transaction (decomposed into five substates on Figure 10.21). Aggregation of state transitions is the main reason for the Processing Customer Input composite state (Figure 10.18). In particular, the Cancel event is aggregated into a transition out of the composite state instead of the three substates. Aggregation of state transitions is also used for the Processing Transaction composite state (Figure 10.19), with the Rejected event

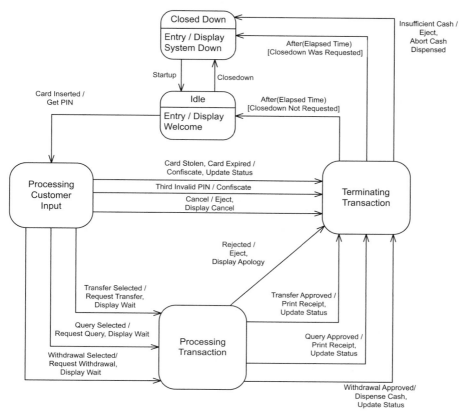

Figure 10.18. Top-level statechart for ATM Control

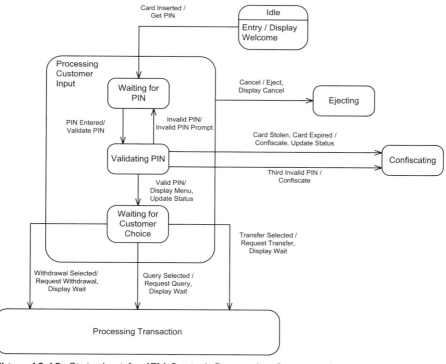

Figure 10.19. Statechart for ATM Control: Processing Customer Input composite state

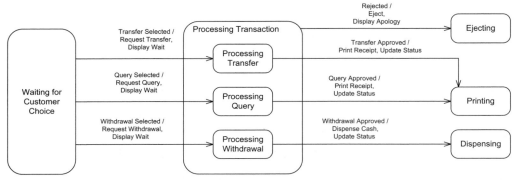

Figure 10.20. Statechart for ATM Control: Processing Transaction composite state

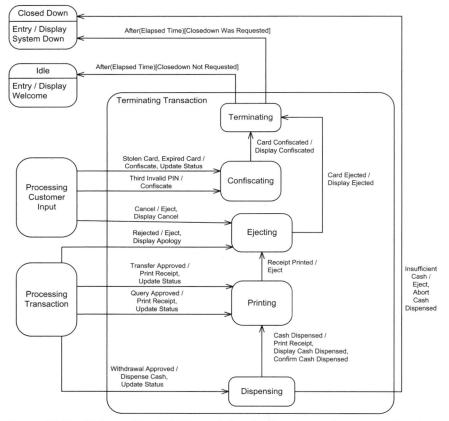

Figure 10.21. Statechart for ATM Control: Terminating Transaction composite state

aggregated from a transition out of each substate to a transition out of the composite state. In the case of the Terminating Transaction composite state, it contains substates that deal with finishing the transaction, such as dispensing cash, printing the receipt, and ejecting the ATM card. It also has substates for canceling the transaction and terminating the transaction. This statechart is described in more detail in Section 21.6.

10.9 SUMMARY

This chapter described the characteristics of flat statecharts and hierarchical statecharts. Guidelines for developing statecharts were given. The process of developing a statechart from a use case was then described in detail. It is possible for a statechart to support several use cases, with each use case contributing to some subset of the statechart. Such cases can also be addressed by considering the statechart in conjunction with the object interaction model, in which a state-dependent control object executes the statechart, as described in Chapter 11. Examples of statecharts are also given in the Banking System and Automated Guided Vehicle System case studies.

EXERCISES

Multiple-choice questions: For each question, choose one of the answers.

1. What is a state in a state machine?
   (a) A recognizable situation that exists over an interval of time
   (b) A condition that is True or False
   (c) An input from the external environment
   (d) An output from the system

2. What is an event in a state machine?
   (a) A discrete signal that causes a change of state
   (b) An input from the external environment
   (c) An input that is True or False
   (d) The result of a state transition

3. What is an action in a state machine?
   (a) An occurrence at a point in time
   (b) A cause of a state transition
   (c) An interval between two successive events
   (d) A computation that executes as a result of a state transition

4. What is an entry action in a state machine?
   (a) An action that is performed when the state is entered
   (b) An action that is performed when the state is left

   (c) An action that starts executing when the state is entered and completes executing when the state is left
   (d) An action that executes as a result of a state transition

5. What is an exit action in a state machine?
   (a) An action that is performed when the state is entered
   (b) An action that is performed when the state is left
   (c) An action that starts executing when the state is entered and completes executing when the state is left
   (d) An action that executes as a result of a state transition

6. What is a condition used for in a state machine?
   (a) A conditional action
   (b) A conditional state
   (c) A conditional state transition
   (d) A conditional event

7. What is a state transition into a composite state equivalent to?
   (a) A transition into only one of the substates
   (b) A transition into each of the substates

(c) A transition into none of the sub-states

(d) A transition into any one of the substates

8. What is a state transition out of a composite state equivalent to?

   (a) A transition out of only one of the substates

   (b) A transition out of each of the sub-states

   (c) A transition out of none of the sub-states

   (d) A transition out of any one of the substates

9. How does a composite state relate to a substate?

   (a) A composite state is decomposed into substates.

(b) Composite states are composed into substates.

(c) A composite state transitions to a substate.

(d) A substate transitions to a composite state.

10. If two actions are shown on a given state transition, which of the following is true?

    (a) The two actions are dependent on each other.

    (b) The two actions are independent of each other.

    (c) One action provides an input to the other action.

    (d) The second action executes when the first action completes execution.

11

State-Dependent Dynamic Interaction Modeling

State-dependent dynamic interaction modeling deals with situations in which object interactions are state-dependent. State-dependent interactions involve at least one state-dependent control object that, by executing a statechart (as described in Chapter 10), provides the overall control and sequencing of its interactions with other objects.

Chapter 9 describes basic dynamic interaction modeling, which is stateless and, hence, does not involve any state-dependent interactions. During object structuring, the objects that participate in the realization of a use case are determined. If at least one of the objects is a state-dependent control object, then the interaction is defined as state-dependent and the term **state-dependent dynamic interaction modeling** should be used, as described in this chapter. State-dependent dynamic interaction modeling is a strategy to help determine how objects interact with each other in dynamic interactions involving at least one state-dependent control object. In more complex interactions, it is possible to have more than one state-dependent control object. Each state-dependent control object is defined by means of a statechart.

Section 11.1 describes the steps in state-dependent dynamic interaction modeling. Section 11.2 describes how to model interaction scenarios on interaction (both communication and sequence) diagrams and statecharts. Section 11.3 gives a detailed example of state-dependent dynamic interaction modeling from the Banking System.

11.1 STEPS IN STATE-DEPENDENT DYNAMIC INTERACTION MODELING

In state-dependent dynamic interaction modeling, the objective is to determine the interactions among the following objects:

- The state-dependent control object, which executes the state machine
- The objects, usually software boundary objects, which send events to the control object. These events cause state transitions in the control object's internal state machine.

■ The objects that provide the actions and activities, which are triggered by the control object as a result of the state transitions
■ Any other objects that participate in realizing the use case

The interaction among these objects is depicted on a communication diagram or sequence diagram.

The main steps in the state-dependent dynamic interaction modeling strategy are presented in the following list. The sequence of interactions needs to reflect the main sequence of interactions described in the use case.

1. **Determine the boundary object(s).** Consider the objects that receive the inputs sent by the external objects in the external environment.
2. **Determine the state-dependent control object.** There is at least one control object, which executes the statechart. Others might also be required.
3. **Determine the other software objects.** These are *software* objects that interact with the control object or boundary objects.
4. **Determine object interactions in the main sequence scenario.** Carry out this step in conjunction with step 5 because the interaction between the state-dependent control object and the statechart it executes needs to be determined in detail.
5. **Determine the execution of the statechart**.
6. **Consider alternative sequence scenarios.** Perform the state-dependent dynamic analysis on scenarios described by the alternative sequences of the use case.

11.2 MODELING INTERACTION SCENARIOS USING INTERACTION DIAGRAMS AND STATECHARTS

This section describes how interaction diagrams – in particular, communication diagrams and sequence diagrams – can be used with statecharts to model state-dependent interaction scenarios (steps 4 and 5 above).

A message on an interaction diagram consists of an event and the data that accompany the event. Consider the relationship between messages and events in the case of a state-dependent control object that executes a statechart. When a message arrives at the control object on a communication diagram, the event part of the message causes the state transition on the statechart. The action on the statechart is the result of the state transition and corresponds to the output message depicted on the communication diagram. In general, a *message* on an interaction diagram (communication or sequence diagram) is referred to as an *event* on a statechart; in descriptions of state-dependent dynamic scenarios, however, for conciseness only the term *event* is used.

A source object sends an event to the state-dependent control object. The arrival of this input event causes a state transition on the statechart. The effect of the state transition is one or more output events. The state-dependent control object sends each output event to a destination object. An *output event* is depicted on the statechart as an *action*, which can be a state transition action, an entry action, or an exit action.

To ensure that the communication diagram and statechart are consistent with each other, the equivalent communication diagram *message* and statechart *event* must be given the same name. Furthermore, for a given state-dependent scenario it is necessary to use the same message-numbering sequence on both diagrams. Using the same sequence ensures that the scenario is represented accurately on both diagrams and can be reviewed for consistency. These issues are illustrated in the following section.

11.3 EXAMPLE OF STATE-DEPENDENT DYNAMIC INTERACTION MODELING: BANKING SYSTEM

As an example of state-dependent dynamic interaction modeling, consider the following example from the Banking System, the Validate PIN use case. The objects that participate in the realization of this use case are determined by using the object structuring criteria (described in Chapter 8). First, the main sequence is considered, followed by the alternative sequences.

11.3.1 Determine Main Sequence

Consider the main sequence of the Validate PIN use case. It describes the customer inserting the ATM card into the card reader, the system prompting for the PIN, and the system checking whether the customer-entered PIN matches the PIN maintained by the system for that ATM card number. In the main sequence, the PIN number is valid.

Consider the objects needed to realize this use case. We first determine the need for the Card Reader Interface object to read the ATM card. The information read off the ATM card needs to be stored temporarily, so we identify the need for an entity object to store the ATM Card information. The Customer Interaction object is used for interacting with the customer via the keyboard/display – in this case, to prompt for the PIN. The information to be sent to the Banking Service subsystem for PIN validation is stored in an ATM Transaction. For PIN validation, the transaction information needs to contain the PIN number and the ATM card number. To control the sequence in which actions take place, we identify the need for a control object, ATM Control. Because the actions of this control object vary depending on what happened previously, the control object needs to be state-dependent and, therefore, execute a statechart.

This use case starts when the customer inserts the ATM card into the card reader. The message sequence number starts at 1, which is the first external event initiated by the Customer Actor, as described in the Validate PIN use case. Subsequent numbering in sequence, representing the objects in the system reacting to the actor, is 1.1, 1.2, 1.3, ending with 1.4, which is the system's response displayed to the actor. The next input from the actor is the external event, numbered 2, and so on. The scenario for a valid ATM card and PIN card is shown as a communication diagram in Figure 11.1 and as a sequence diagram in Figure 11.2.

The message sequencing on the object interaction diagrams is faithful to the use case description for the main sequence of the use case. The message sequence from 1 to 1.4 starts with the card being read by the Card Reader Interface (message 1),

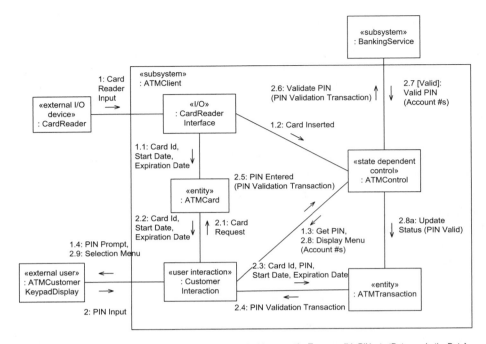

PIN Validation Transaction = {transactionId, transactionType, cardId, PIN, startDate, expirationDate}

Figure 11.1. Communication diagram for Validate PIN use case: Valid PIN scenario

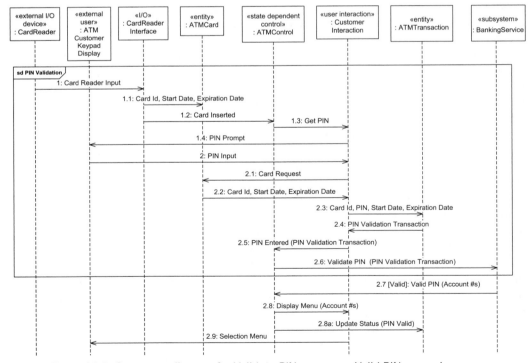

Figure 11.2. Sequence diagram for Validate PIN use case: Valid PIN scenario

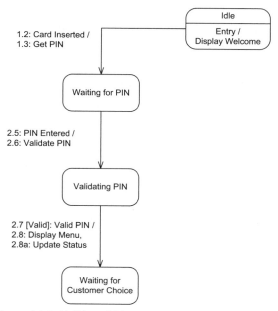

Figure 11.3. Validate PIN statechart: Valid PIN scenario

followed by card data stored (1.1), sending the card inserted event to the ATM Control object (1.2), which results in the state change and the Get PIN action (1.3) sent to Customer Interaction, which outputs the PIN prompt to the customer display (1.4). The message sequence from 2 to 2.9 starts with the user entering the PIN (message 2) to Customer Interaction, followed by retrieving card data (2.1, 2.2), preparing PIN Validation transaction (2.3, 2.4), and sending the transaction to ATM Control (2.5) and from there to Banking Service (2.6). The message sequence from 1 through 2.6 is grouped into a *PIN Validation* segment on the sequence diagram (shown in the box entitled *sd PIN Validation*) in Figure 11.2 for future reference. In this scenario, the Banking Service sends a Valid PIN response (message 2.7) to ATM Control, which eventually leads to Customer Interaction displaying the selection menu to the customer (2.8 and 2.9).

A message arriving at the ATM Control object causes a state transition on the ATM Control statechart (Figure 11.3). For example, Card Reader Interface sends the Card Inserted message (message 1.2 in Figures 11.1 and 11.2) to ATM Control. As a result of this Card Inserted event (event 1.2 corresponds to message 1.2 in Figures 11.1 and 11.2, with the number 1.2 emphasizing the correspondence between the message and the event), the ATM Control statechart transitions from Idle state (the initial state) to Waiting for PIN state. The output event associated with this transition is Get PIN (event 1.3). This output event corresponds to message 1.3, Get PIN, sent by ATM Control to Customer Interaction.

A concurrent sequence is shown in Figure 11.1 with messages 2.8 and 2.8a. ATM Control sends these two messages at the same state transition, so the two message sequences may execute concurrently, one to Customer Interaction and the other to ATM Transaction.

The message sequence description, which describes the messages on the communication diagram (see Figure 11.1) and the messages on the sequence diagram (see Figure 11.2), is described in the Banking System case study in Section 21.5.

11.3.2 Determine Alternative Sequences

Next, consider the alternative sequences of the Validate PIN use case. The main sequence, as described in the previous section, assumes that the ATM card and PIN are valid. Consider the various alternatives of the Validate PIN use case in dealing with invalid cards and incorrect PIN numbers. These can be determined from the Alternatives section of the use case (given in full in Chapter 21).

Consider the Validate Pin message sent to the Banking Service (message 2.6). Several alternative responses are possible from the Banking Service. At the stage in the message sequencing where alternative sequences are possible, each alternative sequence is shown with a different uppercase letter. Thus, the alternative messages to message 2.7 Valid PIN are messages 2.7A, 2.7B, 2.7C. Each of these alternative scenarios can be depicted on a separate interaction diagram. Consider the main and alternative scenarios as described in the following sections.

11.3.3 Main Sequence: Valid PIN

A valid card and PIN were entered. This case, which corresponds to the main sequence, is given the condition [Valid]:

2.7 [Valid]: Valid PIN

In this case, the Banking Service sends the Valid PIN message. The main scenario is depicted on the interaction diagrams (see Figures 11.1 and 11.2) and statechart (see Figure 11.3).

11.3.4 Alternative Sequence: Invalid PIN

An incorrect PIN was entered. This alternative is given the condition [Invalid]:

2.7A* [Invalid]: Invalid PIN

In this case, the Banking Service sends the Invalid PIN message.

Figure 11.4 depicts on a sequence diagram the alternative scenario of an invalid PIN entered. Messages in the message sequence 1 through 2.6 (originally shown in Figure 11.2) are unchanged and are inside the *PIN Validation* segment in Figure 11.4. In the Invalid PIN scenario, the guard condition [Invalid] is true, indicating that message 2.7A: Invalid PIN is sent from the Banking Service. The use of the * indicates that the Invalid PIN message may be sent more than once (in this scenario, it can be sent twice). The iteration of messages, namely, the sequence 2.7A through 2.7A.11 (Invalid PIN through to resend Validate PIN message), is inside the loop segment on Figure 11.4. If an Invalid PIN message is sent a second time, the sequence of messages from 2.7A through 2.7A.11 is repeated.

The scenario shown in Figure 11.4 is for the user to enter the correct PIN number on the second or third attempt. In this case, the response from the Banking Service

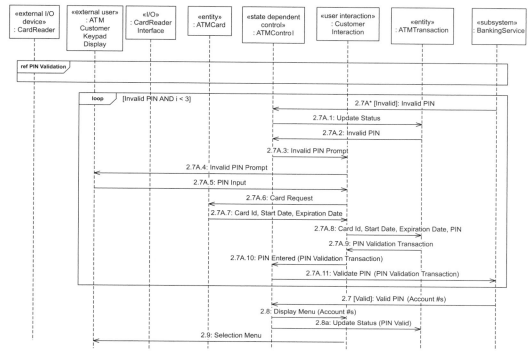

Figure 11.4. Sequence diagram for Validate PIN use case: Invalid PIN scenario

is Pin Valid and the guard condition [Valid] is true. The message sequence from 2.7 to 2.9 at the bottom of Figure 11.4 is the same as that shown in Figure 11.2.

11.3.5 Alternative Sequence: Third Invalid PIN

An incorrect PIN was entered three times. This alternative sequence is also given the condition [Invalid]. However, it is then determined at the ATM Client, which maintains the invalid PIN count in the ATM Transaction entity object, that the count has reached three; consequently, this is the Third Invalid PIN scenario.

2.7B [Third Invalid]: Third Invalid PIN

In this scenario, the Banking Service sends the Invalid PIN message to ATM Control three times.

The Third Invalid PIN scenario starts on the sequence diagram (Figure 11.5) with the message sequence for the *PIN validation* segment followed by looping twice in the loop segment, which starts with the Invalid PIN message (2.7A) from Banking Service. The Update Status message (2.7A.1) to ATM Transaction is followed by a response that indicates the PIN Status is Invalid PIN (2.7A.2), looping twice. This is followed by an exit from the loop and then a third 2.7A: Invalid PIN message from Banking Service. This time the response to the Update Status message (2.7A.1) is 2.7B [Third Invalid]: Third Invalid PIN, because the Third Invalid condition is True, in which case the card is confiscated (message sequence 2.7B–2.7B.2).

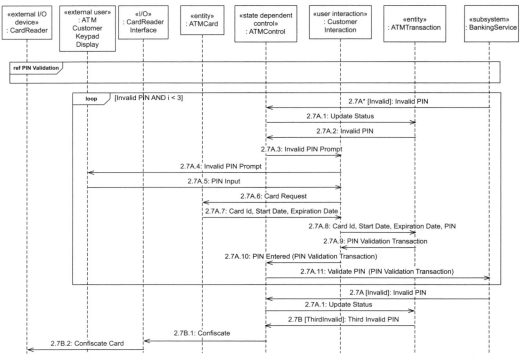

Figure 11.5. Sequence diagram for Validate PIN use case: Third invalid PIN scenario

11.3.6 **Alternative Sequence: Stolen or Expired Card**

The card was stolen or the card has expired.

2.7C [Stolen OR expired]: Card stolen, Card expired

In the case of either a stolen card or an expired card, the message sequence is the same, resulting in confiscation of the card.

This alternative sequence is depicted on the sequence diagram in Figure 11.6. It depicts when the ATM card has expired or been reported as stolen (message sequence 2.7C–2.7C.2). These two scenarios are handled in the same way: Banking

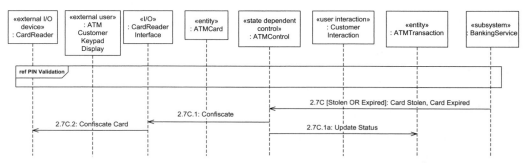

Figure 11.6. Sequence diagram for Validate PIN use case: Stolen or expired card scenario

Service sends the Card stolen or Card expired message (2.7C) to ATM Control, which in turn sends a Confiscate message (2.7C.1) to Card Reader Interface, which results in the confiscation of the ATM card.

11.3.7 Generic Interaction Diagram with all Scenarios

It is possible to show all these alternatives on a generic interaction diagram, either on a generic communication diagram (Figure 11.7) or generic sequence diagram. The generic communication diagram for the use case covers the main sequence as well as all the alternative sequences. Although all the alternatives are shown on the same diagram, resulting in a compact depiction of the object interactions, the generic diagram is more difficult to read than single scenario diagrams, which depict each scenario (main or alternative) separately. A generic communication or sequence diagram (depicting all the alternatives) should be used only if the alternatives can be clearly depicted. If the generic communication or sequence diagram is too cluttered, use a separate communication diagram or sequence diagram for each alternative.

11.3.8 Sequencing on Control Object and Statechart

The control object ATM Control, shown in Figures 11.1 through 11.7, executes the statecharts depicted in Figure 11.8 and Figure 11.9 (which depicts the substates of the Validating PIN composite state). The statechart shows the various states during the execution of the main and alternative sequences of the Validate PIN use case. Thus, when the PIN Entered event (event 2.5) is received from Customer Interaction, ATM Control transitions to Validating PIN composite state (Validating PIN and Card substate) and sends the Validate PIN message to the Banking Service. The possible responses from the Banking Service are shown in Figure 11.7. The resulting states and actions are shown in Figures 11.8 and 11.9, and the resulting interactions with the controlled objects are shown in Figure 11.7. The Valid PIN response (event 2.7) results in a transition to Waiting for Customer Choice. The Invalid PIN response (event 2.7A) results in transitioning of the statechart to the Checking PIN Status substate (Figure 11.9). A second Invalid PIN response (event 2.7A.1) results in the transition back to the Waiting for PIN state and triggering of the Invalid PIN Prompt action (event 2.7A.3) in the Customer Interaction object. The Third Invalid PIN (2.7B) response results in transitioning of the statechart to the Confiscating state and triggering of the Confiscate action (event 2.7B.1) in the Card Reader Interface object. A Card Stolen response (event 2.7C) is treated in the same way. Finally, if the customer decides to Cancel (event 2A.1) instead of re-entering the PIN, the statechart transitions to Ejecting state and triggers the Eject action (event 2A.2) in the Card Reader Interface object. Because the customer can Cancel while ATM Control is in any of the substates Waiting for PIN, Validating PIN, or Waiting for Customer Choice, the state transition is shown out of the composite state Processing Customer Input (Figure 11.8.)

The statechart also initiates concurrent action sequences, which are triggered at the same state transition. Thus, all actions that occur at a given transition are executed in an unconstrained, nondeterministic order. For example, the actions 2.8:

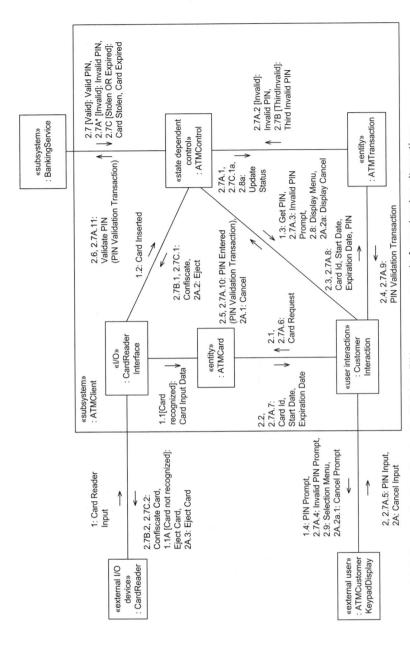

Figure 11.7. Communication diagram for Validate PIN use case: generic form showing alternatives

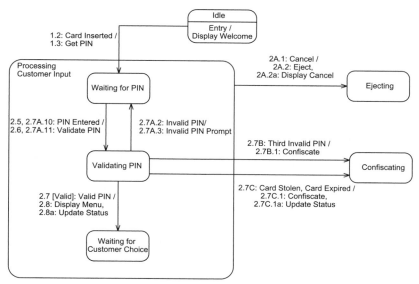

Figure 11.8. Statechart for ATM Control for Validate PIN use case, showing alternatives

Display Menu and 2.8a: Update Status, which result from the Valid Pin state transition (see Figure 11.8), execute concurrently, as also depicted in Figure 11.7.

11.4 SUMMARY

This chapter described state-dependent interaction modeling, in which object inter- actions are state-dependent. A state-dependent interaction involves at least one

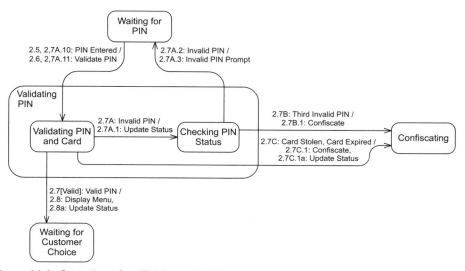

Figure 11.9. Statechart for ATM Control Validating PIN composite state

state-dependent control object, which executes a statechart (as described in Chapter 10) that provides the overall control and sequencing of the interactions. This chapter built on the stateless dynamic interaction modeling, described in Chapter 9, which does not involve any state-dependent interactions.

EXERCISES

Multiple-choice questions: For each question, choose one of the answers.

1. What does a state-dependent interaction involve?
   (a) A control object
   (b) A state-dependent entity object
   (c) A state-dependent control object
   (d) A state-dependent user interaction object

2. Which kind of object executes a state machine
   (a) Any software object
   (b) An entity object
   (c) A state-dependent control object
   (d) A statechart

3. An input message to a state-dependent control object corresponds to:
   (a) An event on the internal state machine
   (b) An action on the internal state machine
   (c) A condition on the internal state machine
   (d) A state on the internal state machine

4. An output message from a state-dependent control object corresponds to:
   (a) An event on the internal state machine
   (b) An action on the internal state machine
   (c) A condition on the internal state machine
   (d) A state on the internal state machine

5. An interaction diagram should be developed for:
   (a) Only the main sequence of the use case
   (b) The main sequence and every alternative sequence of the use case
   (c) The main sequence and a representative alternative sequence of the use case
   (d) The alternative sequences of the use case

6. Which of the following could happen on an interaction diagram?
   (a) A state-dependent control object sends a message to an entity object.
   (b) A state-dependent control object sends a message to a coordinator object.
   (c) A state-dependent control object sends a message to a printer object.
   (d) All of the above

7. If the same state machine is used in more than one use case, how is this modeled on interaction diagrams?
   (a) Develop one state-dependent control object for each use case.
   (b) Develop one state-dependent control object containing states from each use case.
   (c) Develop a hierarchical state machine.
   (d) Develop a coordinator object.

8. How would two state-dependent control objects communicate with each other?
   (a) By sending messages to each other
   (b) By transitioning to the same state
   (c) Through an entity object
   (d) Through a proxy object

9. An object can send alternative messages a or b to a state-dependent control object. How is this handled in the state machine?
   (a) One state with a different transition out of it for each incoming message
   (b) One state for each of the alternative messages
   (c) A composite state to handle the alternative messages
   (d) A substate for each alternative message

10. In a system in which a client object executes a state machine and communicates with a service, which of the following is true?

(a) The client has a state-dependent control object but the service does not.

(b) The service has a state-dependent control object but the client does not.

(c) Both the client and the service have state-dependent control objects.

(d) Neither the client nor the service has a state-dependent control object.

PART III

Architectural Design

12

Overview of Software Architecture

The software architecture separates the overall structure of the system, in terms of subsystems and their interfaces, from the internal details of the individual subsystems. A software architecture is structured into subsystems, in which each subsystem should be relatively independent of other subsystems. This chapter presents an overview of software architecture, which is also referred to as a high- level design. The concepts of software architecture and multiple views of a software architecture were first introduced in Chapter 1. The concepts of design patterns, components, and interfaces were introduced in Chapter 4.

In this chapter, Section 12.1 describes the concepts of software architecture and component-based software architecture. Section 12.2 then describes how having multiple views of a software architecture helps with both its design and understanding. Section 12.3 introduces the concept of software architectural patterns as a basis for developing software architectures, whereas Section 12.4 describes how to document such patterns. Section 12.5 describes the concept of software components and interfaces. Finally, Section 12.6 provides an overview of designing software architectures, as described in Chapters 14 through 20.

12.1 SOFTWARE ARCHITECTURE AND COMPONENT-BASED SOFTWARE ARCHITECTURE

A software architecture is defined by Bass, Clements, and Kazman (2003) as follows:

> "The software architecture of a program or computing system is the structure or structures of the system, which comprise software elements, the externally visible properties of those elements, and the relationships among them."

Thus, a software architecture is considered primarily from a structural perspective. In order to fully understand a software architecture, however, it is also necessary to study it from several perspectives, including both static and dynamic perspectives, as described in Section 12.2. It is also necessary to address the architecture from functional (functionality provided by the architecture) and nonfunctional perspectives (quality of the functionality provided). The software quality attributes of an architecture are described in Chapter 20.

12.1.1 Component-Based Software Architecture

A structural perspective on software architecture is given by the widely held concept of component-based software architecture. A component-based software architecture consists of multiple components in which each component is self-contained and encapsulates certain information. A component is either a composite object composed of other objects or a simple object. A component provides an interface through which it communicates with other components. All information that is needed by one component to communicate with another component is contained in the interface, which is separate from the implementation. Thus, a component can be considered a black box, because its implementation is hidden from other components. Components communicate with each other in different ways using predefined communication patterns.

A sequential design is a program in which the components are classes and component instances are objects (instances of the classes); the components are passive classes without a thread of control. A component is self-contained; therefore, it can be compiled separately, stored in a library, and then subsequently instantiated and linked into an application. In a sequential design, the only communication pattern is call/return, as described in Section 12.3.2.

In a concurrent or distributed design, the components are active (concurrent) and capable of being deployed to different nodes in a distributed environment. In this design, concurrent components can communicate with each other using several different communication patterns (see Section 12.3), such as synchronous, asynchronous, brokered, or group communication. An underlying middleware framework is typically provided to allow components to communicate.

12.1.2 Architecture Stereotypes

In UML 2, a modeling element can be described with more than one stereotype. During analysis modeling, one stereotype was used to represent the *role* characteristic of a modeling element (class or object), During design modeling, a different stereotype can be used to represent the architectural characteristic of a modeling element. This capability is very useful, and the COMET method takes full advantage of it. In particular, one stereotype is used to describe the role played by the modeling element, such as whether it is a boundary or entity class. A second stereotype can be used in design modeling to represent the architectural structuring element such as subsystem (Chapter 12), component (Chapter 17), service (Chapter 16), or concurrent task (Chapter 18). It is important to realize that for a given class, the role stereotype and the architectural structuring stereotype are orthogonal – that is, independent of each other.

12.2 MULTIPLE VIEWS OF A SOFTWARE ARCHITECTURE

The design of the software architecture can be depicted from different perspectives, referred to as different views. The structural view of the software architecture is depicted on class diagrams, as described in Section 12.2.1. The dynamic view of the software architecture is depicted on communication diagrams, as described in Section 12.2.2. The deployment view of the software architecture is depicted on deployment diagrams, as described in Section 12.2.3. Another architectural view, the component-based software architecture view, is described in Chapter 17.

12.2.1 Structural View of a Software Architecture

The structural view of a software architecture is a static view, which does not change with time. At the highest level, subsystems are depicted on a class diagram. In particular, a *subsystem class diagram* depicts the static structural relationship between the subsystems, which are represented as composite or aggregate classes, and multiplicity of associations among them.

As an example of the structural view of a software architecture, consider the design of a client/server software architecture, in which there are multiple clients and a single service. An example of such an architecture is the Banking System, in which there are multiple instances of the ATM Client subsystem and a single instance of the Banking Service subsystem. In Figure 12.1, the client and service subsystems are depicted on a class diagram, which provides a static view of the architecture. Figure 12.1 depicts the static relationship between the Banking Service and the ATM Client for the Banking System, particularly the name and direction of the association ATM Client *Requests Service From* Banking Service, as well as the multiplicity of the association, namely, the one-to-many association between the service and the clients. Furthermore, both the client and service subsystems (depicted as aggregate classes in Figure 12.1) are depicted with two stereotypes, the first is the role

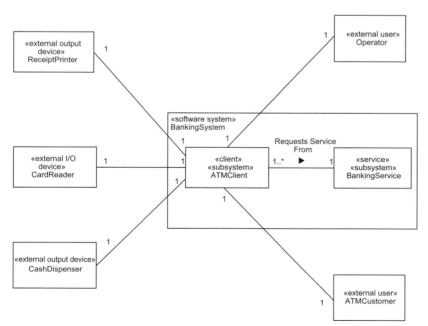

Figure 12.1. Structural view of client/server software architecture: high-level class diagram for Banking System

stereotype, client or service, and the second is the architectural structuring stereotype, which, in this example, is subsystem for both.

12.2.2 Dynamic View of a Software Architecture

The dynamic view of a software architecture is a behavioral view, which is depicted on a communication diagram. A *subsystem communication diagram* shows the subsystems (depicted as aggregate or composite objects) and the message communication between them. As the subsystems can be deployed to different nodes, they are depicted as concurrent components, because they execute in parallel and communicate with each other over a network.

An example of the dynamic view of the architecture is given for the Banking System client/server software architecture, which is depicted on a subsystem communication diagram in Figure 12.2. Figure 12.2 depicts two subsystems of the Banking System: ATM Client, of which there are many instances, and Banking Service, of which there is one instance. Each ATM Client sends transactions to and receives responses from the Banking Service. The ATM Client and Banking Service are depicted as concurrent components, because each executes in parallel with the other, although at times they need to communicate with each other. Thus, while one client is preparing to make a request to the service, the Banking Service can be servicing a different client. While the service is processing the request of a given client, the client typically waits for the response. This form of communication, synchronous message communication with reply, is described in more detail in Section 12.3.4. On UML communication diagrams such as Figure 12.2, the synchronous message (ATMTransaction) is depicted with a black arrowhead and the reply (bankResponse) is depicted as a dashed arrow with a stick arrowhead. An alternative notation for synchronous communication is described in Section 12.3.4 and depicted in Figure 12.11.

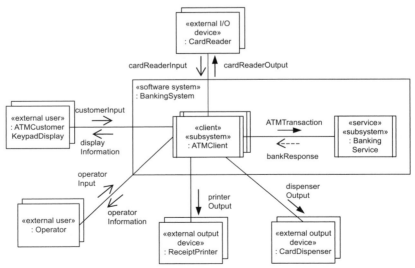

Figure 12.2. Dynamic view of client/server software architecture: high-level communication diagram for Banking System

A subsystem communication diagram is a *generic* communication diagram, because it depicts all possible interactions between objects (see Section 9.1.5). Because it depicts all possible scenarios, message sequence numbers are not used. Furthermore, because generic communication diagrams depict generic instances (which means that they depict potential instances rather than actual instances), they use the UML 2 convention of not underlining the object names.

In addition to being *generic,* a subsystem communication diagram is also *concurrent* because it depicts objects executing concurrently (see Section 2.8 for description of UML notation). Thus, Figure 12.2 depicts two concurrent subsystems, the ATM Client and Banking Service, which are geographically distributed.

12.2.3 Deployment View of a Software Architecture

The deployment view of the software architecture depicts the physical configuration of the software architecture, in particular how the subsystems of the architecture are allocated to physical nodes in a distributed configuration. A deployment diagram can depict a specific deployment with a fixed number of nodes. Alternatively, it can depict the overall structure of the deployment – for example, identifying that a subsystem can have many instances, each deployable to a separate node, but not depicting the specific number of instances. An example of this view is given in Figure 12.3 for the Banking System client/server software architecture. In this deployment, each ATM Client instance is allocated to its own physical node, whereas the centralized Banking Service is allocated to a single node. In addition, the nodes are connected by means of a wide area network.

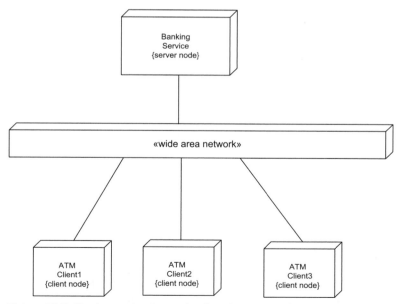

Figure 12.3. Deployment view of client/server software architecture: deployment diagram

12.3 SOFTWARE ARCHITECTURAL PATTERNS

Chapter 4 introduced the concept of software patterns and the different kinds of patterns, including software architectural patterns and software design patterns. Software **architectural patterns** provide the skeleton or template for the overall software architecture or high-level design of an application. Shaw and Garlan (1996) referred to *architectural styles* or patterns of software architecture, which are recurring architectures used in a variety of software applications (see also Bass, Clements, and Kazman 2003). These include such widely used architectures as client/server and layered architectures.

Software architectural patterns can be grouped into two main categories: architectural structure patterns, which address the static structure of the architecture, and architectural communication patterns, which address the dynamic communication among distributed components of the architecture. This chapter introduces the concept of software architectural patterns and describes one architectural structure pattern, the Layers of Abstraction pattern (Section 12.3.1). It also describes three architectural communication patterns – the Call/Return pattern (Section 12.3.2), the Asynchronous Message Communication pattern (Section 12.3.3), and the Synchronous Message Communication with Reply pattern (Section 12.3.4). Other patterns are described in later chapters. Tables 12.1, 12.2, and 12.3 summarize where the patterns are described.

12.3.1 Layers of Abstraction Architectural Pattern

The **Layers of Abstraction** pattern (also known as the *Hierarchical Layers* or *Levels of Abstraction* pattern) is a common architectural pattern that is applied in many different software domains (Buschmann et al. 1996). Operating systems, database management systems, and network communication software are examples of software systems that are often structured as hierarchies.

As Parnas (1979) pointed out in his seminal paper on designing software for ease of extension and contraction (see also Hoffman and Weiss 2001), if software is designed in the form of layers, it can be extended by the addition of upper layers that use services provided by lower layers and contracted by the removal of upper layers.

With a *strict hierarchy*, each layer uses services in the layer immediately below it (e.g., layer 3 can only invoke services provided by layer 2). With a *flexible hierarchy*, a layer does not have to invoke a service at the layer immediately below it, but it

Table 12.1. Software architectural structure patterns

Software architectural structure patterns	Chapter
Centralized Control Pattern	Chapter 18, Section 18.3.1
Distributed Control Pattern	Chapter 18, Section 18.3.2
Hierarchical Control Pattern	Chapter 18, Section 18.3.3
Layers of Abstraction Pattern	Chapter 12, Section 12. 3.1
Multiple Client/Multiple Service Pattern	Chapter 15, Section 15.2.2
Multiple Client/Single Service Pattern	Chapter 15, Section 15.2.1
Multi-tier Client/Service Pattern	Chapter 15, Section 15.2.3

Table 12.2. Software architectural communication patterns

Software architectural communication patterns	Chapter
Asynchronous Message Communication Pattern	Chapter 12, Section 12.3.3
Asynchronous Message Communication with Callback Pattern	Chapter 15, Section 15.3.2
Bidirectional Asynchronous Message Communication	Chapter 12, Section 12.3.3
Broadcast Pattern	Chapter 17, Section 17.6.1
Broker Forwarding Pattern	Chapter 16, Section 16.2.2
Broker Handle Pattern	Chapter 16, Section 16.2.3
Call/Return	Chapter 12, Section 12.3.2
Negotiation Pattern	Chapter 16, Section 16.5
Service Discovery Pattern	Chapter 16, Section 16.2.4
Service Registration	Chapter 16, Section 16.2.1
Subscription/Notification Pattern	Chapter 17, Section 17.6.2
Synchronous Message Communication with Reply Pattern	Chapter 12, Section 12.3.4; Chapter 15, Section 15.3.1
Synchronous Message Communication without Reply Pattern	Chapter 18, Section 18.8.3

can invoke services at more than one layer below (e.g., layer 3 could directly invoke services provided by layer 1).

The Layers of Abstraction architectural pattern is used in the TCP/IP, which is the most widely used protocol on the Internet (Comer 2008). Each layer deals with a specific characteristic of network communication and provides an interface, as a set of operations, to the layer above it. For each layer on the sender node, there is an equivalent layer on the receiver node. TCP/IP is organized into five conceptual layers, as shown in Figure 12.4 and enumerated here:

Layer 1: Physical layer. Corresponds to the basic network hardware, including electrical and mechanical interfaces, and the physical transmission medium.

Layer 2: Network interface layer. Specifies how data are organized into frames and how frames are transmitted over the network.

Layer 3: Internet layer, also referred to as the Internet Protocol (IP) layer. Specifies the format of packets sent over the Internet and the mechanisms for forwarding packets through one or more routers from a source to a destination (Figure 12.5). The router node in Figure 12.5 is a gateway that interconnects a local area network to a wide area network.

Layer 4: Transport layer (TCP). Assembles packets into messages in the order they were originally sent. The Transmission Control Protocol, or TCP, uses the IP network protocol to carry messages. It provides a virtual connection

Table 12.3. Software architectural transaction patterns

Software architectural transaction patterns	Chapter
Compound Transaction Pattern	Chapter 16, Section 16.4.2
Long-Living Transaction Pattern	Chapter 16, Section 16.4.3
Two-Phase Commit Protocol Pattern	Chapter 16, Section 16.4.1

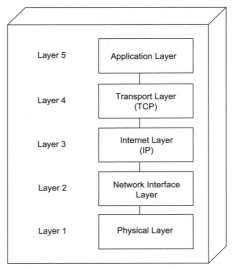

Figure 12.4. Layers of Abstraction architectural pattern: example of the Internet (TCP/IP) reference model

from an application on one node to an application on a remote node, hence providing what is termed an *end-to-end protocol* (see Figure 12.5).

Layer 5: Application layer. Supports various network applications, such as file transfer (FTP), electronic mail, and the World Wide Web.

An interesting characteristic of the layered architecture is that it is straightforward to replace the upper layers of the architecture with different layers that use

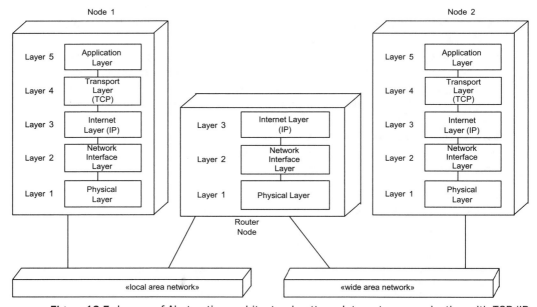

Figure 12.5. Layers of Abstraction architectural pattern: Internet communication with TCP/IP

the unchanged services provided by the lower layers. Another interesting characteristic of the layered architecture is shown in Figure 12.5. The router node uses the lower three layers of the TCP/IP protocol, whereas the application nodes use all five layers.

An example of a strict layered software architecture from one of the case studies in the book is the Online Shopping System described in Chapter 22 and depicted in Figure 12.6. At the lowest layer is the Service Layer, which provides services that are used by higher layers. The top layer is a User Layer consisting of user interaction objects. The middle layer is a Coordination Layer that coordinates user requests to the services.

12.3.2 Call/Return Pattern

The simplest form of communication between objects uses the **Call/Return** pattern. A sequential design consists of passive classes, which are instantiated as passive objects. The only possible form of communication between objects in a sequential design is operation (also known as method) invocation, which is also referred to as the Call/Return pattern. In this pattern, a calling operation in the calling object invokes a called operation in the called object, as depicted in Figure 12.7a. Control is passed from the calling operation to the called operation at the time of operation invocation. Any input parameters are passed from the calling operation to the called operation at the same time that control is passed. When the called operation finishes executing, it returns control and any output parameters to the calling operation. On UML communication diagrams such as Figure 12.7a, the Call/Return pattern uses the UML notation for synchronous communication (arrow with black arrowhead).

As an example of the Call/Return pattern, consider the example of a sequential design with instance of the checking account and savings account classes (Figure 12.7b). Each object provides credit and debit operations, which can be invoked by the Withdrawal Transaction Manager or Transfer Transaction Manager objects. The Withdrawal Transaction Manager invokes the debit operation of either account object with input parameters consisting of the account# and the withdrawal amount. When called, another operation, readBalance, returns the account balance after withdrawal. To process a transfer request, the Transfer Transaction Manager invokes the debit operation of one account (with account# and debit amount as parameters) and the credit operation of the other account (with account# and credit amount as parameters).

12.3.3 Asynchronous Message Communication Pattern

In concurrent and distributed designs, other forms of communication are possible. With the **Asynchronous** (also referred to as *Loosely Coupled*) **Message Communication** pattern, the producer component sends a message to the consumer component (Figure 12.8) and does not wait for a reply. The producer continues because it either does not need a response or has other functions to perform before receiving a response. The consumer receives the message; if the consumer is busy when the message arrives, the message is queued. Because the producer and consumer components proceed asynchronously (i.e., at different speeds), a first-in, first-out (FIFO) message queue can build up between producer and consumer. If no

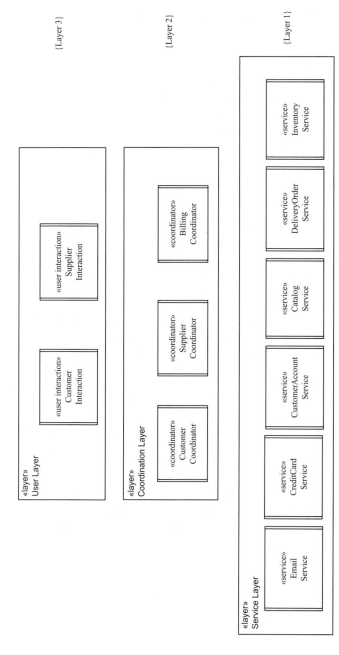

Figure 12.6. Example of layered architecture: Online Shopping System

202

(a) Call/Return pattern

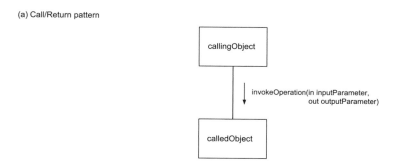

(b) Example of Call/Return pattern

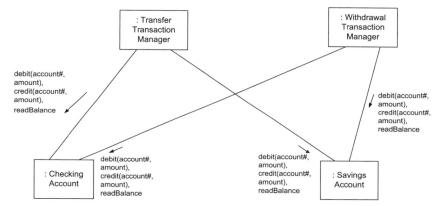

Figure 12.7. Call/return pattern

message is available when the consumer requests one, the consumer is suspended. The consumer is then reawakened when a message arrives. In distributed environments, the Asynchronous Message Communication pattern is used wherever possible for greater flexibility. This approach can be used if the sender does not need a response from the receiver.

Figure 12.8 is a UML instance communication diagram because it shows a particular scenario consisting of a producer sending an asynchronous message to a consumer. On UML communication diagrams such as Figure 12.8, the Asynchronous Message Communication pattern uses the UML notation for asynchronous communication (arrow with stick arrowhead).

An example of the Asynchronous Message Communication pattern in a distributed environment is given on the generic communication diagram depicted in Figure 12.9 for the Automated Guided Vehicle System, in which all communication

Figure 12.8. Asynchronous Message Communication pattern

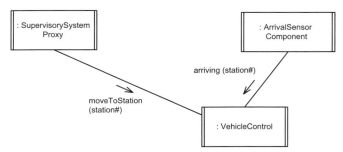

Figure 12.9. Example of the Asynchronous Message Communication pattern: Automated Guided Vehicle System

between the components is asynchronous. Both the Supervisory System Proxy and the Arrival Sensor Component send asynchronous messages to Vehicle Control, which are queued first-in-first-out. Vehicle Control has one input message queue from which it receives whichever message arrives first, move message or arriving message.

It is also possible to have peer-to-peer communication between two components, which send asynchronous messages to each other. This kind of communication is referred to as **bidirectional asynchronous communication** and is depicted in Figure 12.10. Examples of bidirectional asynchronous communication are given in Chapters 16 and 18.

12.3.4 **Synchronous Message Communication with Reply Pattern**

With the **Synchronous** (also referred to as *Tightly Coupled*) **Message Communication with Reply** pattern, the client component sends a message to the service component and then waits for a reply from the service (Figure 12.11). When the message arrives, the service accepts it, processes it, generates a reply, and then sends the reply. The client and service then both continue. The service is suspended if no message is available. Although there might only be one client and one service, it is more likely that synchronous message communication involves multiple clients and one service. Because this pattern is fundamental to client/server architectures, it is described in more detail in Chapter 15.

Figure 12.11 is a UML instance communication diagram because it shows a particular scenario consisting of a producer sending a synchronous message to a consumer and receiving a response. On UML communication diagrams such as Figure 12.11, the Synchronous Message Communication pattern uses the UML notation for synchronous message communication with reply (arrow with black arrowhead), the outgoing request is the input parameter message, and the reply is the output parameter response.

Figure 12.10. Bidirectional Asynchronous Message Communication pattern

Figure 12.11. Synchronous Message Communication with Reply pattern

12.4 DOCUMENTING SOFTWARE ARCHITECTURAL PATTERNS

Whatever the category of pattern, it is very useful to have a standard way of describing and documenting a pattern so that it can be easily referenced, compared with other patterns, and reused. Three important aspects of a pattern that need to be captured (Buschmann et al. 1996) are the context, problem, and solution. The *context* is the situation that gives rise to a problem. The *problem* refers to a recurring problem that arises in this context. The *solution* is a proven resolution to the problem. A template for describing a pattern usually also addresses its strengths, weaknesses, and related patterns. A typical template looks like this:

- **Pattern name**
- **Aliases.** Other names by which this pattern is known.
- **Context.** The situation that gives rise to this problem.
- **Problem.** Brief description of the problem.
- **Summary of solution.** Brief description of the solution.
- **Strengths of solution**
- **Weaknesses of solution**
- **Applicability.** When you can use the pattern.
- **Related patterns**
- **Reference.** Where you can find more information about the pattern.

An example of documenting a pattern is given next for the Layered Pattern. The complete set of patterns described in this book are documented with this standard template in Appendix A.

Pattern name	Layers of Abstraction
Aliases	Hierarchical Layers, Levels of Abstraction
Context	Software architectural design
Problem	A software architecture that encourages design for ease of extension and contraction is needed.
Summary of solution	Components at lower layers provide services for components at higher layers. Components may use only services provided by components at lower layers.
Strengths of solution	Promotes extension and contraction of software design
Weaknesses of solution	Could lead to inefficiency if too many layers need to be traversed
Applicability	Operating systems, communication protocols, software product lines
Related patterns	Kernel can be lowest layer of Layers of Abstraction architecture. Variations of this pattern include Flexible Layers of Abstraction.
Reference	Chapter 12, Section 12.3.1; Hoffman and Weiss 2001; Parnas 1979.

12.5 INTERFACE DESIGN

An important goal of both object-oriented design and component-based software architecture is the separation of the interface from the implementation. An **interface** specifies the externally visible operations of a class, service, or component without revealing the internal structure (implementation) of the operations. The interface can be considered a *contract* between the designer of the external view of the class and the implementer of the class internals. It is also a *contract* between a class that requires (uses) the interface (i.e., invokes the operations provided by the interface) and the class that provides the interface.

Following the concept of information hiding (Section 4.2), class attributes are private and the public operations provided by a class constitute the interface. In static modeling using class diagram notation, the interface (class operations) is depicted in the third compartment of the class. An example of this is in Figure 12.12, which shows the class Account, with two private attributes depicted in the second compartment of the class ("minus" sign depicts private in UML) and the interface consisting of the five public operations depicted in the third compartment of the class ("plus" sign depicts public in UML).

Because the same interface can be implemented in different ways, it is useful to depict the design of the interface separately from the component that realizes (i.e., implements) the interface. Furthermore, interfaces can be realized in wider contexts than classes. Thus, interfaces for subsystems, distributed components, and passive classes can all be depicted using the same interface notation.

An interface can be depicted with a different name from the class or component that realizes the interface. By convention, the name starts with the letter "I." In UML, an interface can be modeled separately from a component that realizes the interface. An interface can be depicted in two ways: simple and expanded. In the simple case, the interface is depicted as a little circle with the interface name next to it. The class or component that provides the interface is connected to the small circle, as shown in Figure 12.13a. In the expanded case, the interface is depicted in a rectangular box with the static modeling notation, as shown in Figure 12.13b, with the stereotype «interface» and the interface name in the first compartment. The operations of the interface are depicted in the third compartment. The second compartment is left blank (note that in other texts, interfaces are sometimes depicted with the middle compartment omitted).

An example of an interface is IBasicAlarmService, which provides two operations, one to read alarm data and one to post new alarms, as follows:

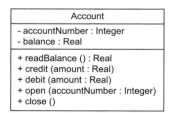

Figure 12.12. Example of class with public interface and private attributes

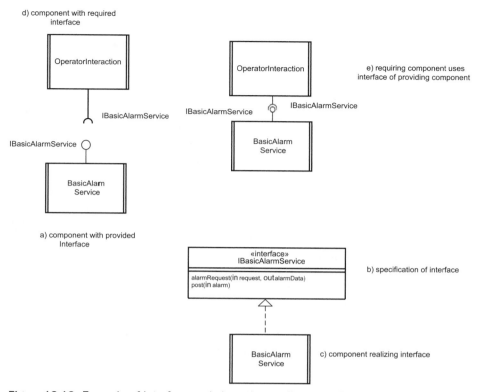

Figure 12.13. Example of interface and class that realizes interface

Interface: IBasicAlarmService
Operations provided:
- alarmRequest (**in** request, **out** alarmData)
- post (**in** alarm)

The component that realizes the interface is called BasicAlarmService, which provides the implementation of the interface. In UML, the realization relationship is depicted as shown in Figure 12.13c (dashed arrow with a triangular arrowhead), which shows the component BasicAlarmService realizing the IBasicAlarmService interface. A required interface is depicted with a small semicircle notation with the interface name next to it. The class or component that requires the interface is connected to the semicircle, as shown in Figure 12.13d. To show that a component with a required interface uses a component with a provided interface, the semicircle (sometimes referred to as a socket) with the required interface is drawn around the circle (sometimes referred to as a ball) with the provided interface, as shown in Figure 12.13e.

12.6 DESIGNING SOFTWARE ARCHITECTURES

During software design modeling, design decisions are made relating to the characteristics of the software architecture. The following chapters describe the design of different kinds of software architectures:

- **Object-oriented software architectures.** Chapter 14 describes object-oriented design using the concepts of information hiding, classes, and inheritance. This results in the design of a sequential object-oriented software architecture, which would be implemented as a sequential program with one thread of control. This chapter describes the design of object-oriented software architectures, to clearly distinguish how object-oriented concepts are applied, before considering other important concepts that are usually needed in designing software architectures.

- **Client/server software architectures.** Chapter 15 describes the design of client/server software architectures. A typical design consists of one service and multiple clients. Decisions need to be made about the design of both the client and server architectures: whether they should be designed as sequential or concurrent subsystems, and what patterns to use for the design of the individual subsystems. Client/server software architectures and architecture patterns are so widespread in software systems that it is worthwhile understanding the fundamental concepts and issues in designing these systems.

- **Service-oriented architectures.** Chapter 16 describes the design of service-oriented architectures, which typically consist of multiple distributed autonomous services that can be composed into distributed software applications. This chapter describes how to design service-oriented architectures, including how to design services, how to coordinate different services, and how to reuse services. Service-oriented architectures, which are increasingly being used, incorporate concepts from client/server and distributed component-based systems. The architectural issues dealing with service-oriented architecture are addressed in this chapter.

- **Distributed component-based software architectures.** Chapter 17 describes the design of component-based software architectures. It describes the component structuring criteria for designing components that can be deployed to execute on distributed platforms in a distributed configuration. The design of component interfaces is described, with component ports that have provided and required interfaces and connectors that join compatible ports. The component-based software architecture is depicted with the UML 2 notation for composite structure diagrams. Distributed applications are usually component-based, in which the exact nature of the systems depends on the component technology used. However, there are important architectural concepts for developing these systems, which are addressed in this chapter.

- **Concurrent and real-time software architectures.** Chapter 18 describes the design of real-time software architectures, which are concurrent architectures usually having to deal with multiple streams of input events. They are typically state-dependent, with either centralized or decentralized control. For these systems, a concurrent software architecture is developed in which the system is structured into concurrent tasks, and the interfaces and interconnections between the concurrent tasks are defined. Real-time embedded software systems are an important domain of software applications. Many of the concepts described for the other types of software architectures, such as information hiding and concurrency, can also be applied in real-time design. This chapter addresses other important issues in designing real-time software architectures.

- **Software product line architectures.** Chapter 19 describes the design of software product line architectures, which are architectures for families of products that need to capture both the commonality and variability in the family. The problems of developing individual software architectures are scaled upwards when developing software product line architectures because of the increased complexity due to variability management. Software product line concepts can be applied to all the different architectures described in previous chapters, because they address issues of commonality and variability in software families. They are also a natural way to explicitly model evolving systems, in which each version can be considered a member of the software family.

Chapter 20 describes the quality attributes of software architectures that address nonfunctional requirements of software, which can have a profound effect on the quality of a software product. Many of these attributes can be addressed and evaluated at the time the software architecture is developed. Software quality attributes include maintainability, modifiability, testability, traceability, scalability, reusability, performance, availability, and security.

12.7 SUMMARY

This chapter presented an overview of software architecture. It described the multiple views of a software architecture, particularly the static, dynamic, and deployment views. In designing the overall software architecture, it helps to consider applying the software architectural patterns, both architectural structure patterns and architectural communication patterns. Architectural structure patterns are applied to the design of the overall structure of the software architecture, which addresses how the system is structured into subsystems. One architectural structure pattern, the Layers of Abstraction pattern, was described. Architectural communication patterns address the ways in which subsystems communicate with each other. Three architectural communication patterns, the Call/Return pattern, the Asynchronous Message Communication pattern, and the Synchronous Message Communication with Reply pattern, were described. Each subsystem is designed such that its interface is explicitly defined in terms of the operations it provides, as well as the operations it uses. Communication between distributed subsystems can be synchronous or asynchronous.

During software design modeling, design decisions are made relating to the characteristics of the software architecture. Chapter 13 describes the transition from analysis to design and the structuring of the system into subsystems. Chapter 14 describes object-oriented design using the concepts of information hiding, classes, and inheritance. Chapter 15 describes the design of client/server software architectures, in which a typical design consists of one server and multiple clients. Chapter 16 describes the design of service-oriented architectures, which typically consist of multiple distributed autonomous services that can be composed into distributed software applications. Chapter 17 describes the design of component-based software architectures, including the design of component interfaces, with component ports that have provided and required interfaces, and connectors that join compatible ports. Chapter 18 describes the design of real-time software architectures, which are concurrent architectures usually having to deal with multiple streams of input events. Chapter 19 describes the design of software product line architectures, which are architectures for families of products that need to capture both the commonality and variability in the family.

Chapter 20 describes the software quality attributes of a software architecture and how they are used to evaluate the quality of the software architecture. Chapters 21 to 24 provide case study examples of applying COMET/UML to the modeling and design of different software architectures.

EXERCISES

Multiple-choice questions: For each question, choose one of the answers.

1. What does the software architecture describe?
   (a) The software inside a building
   (b) The structure of a client/server system
   (c) The overall structure of a software system
   (d) The software classes and their relationships

2. Which of the following statements is NOT true for a component?
   (a) A composite object composed of other objects
   (b) An operation
   (c) A simple object
   (d) Provides an interface

3. What is a structural view of a software architecture?
   (a) A view in terms of a module hierarchy
   (b) A view in terms of components and connectors
   (c) A view of the physical configuration in terms of nodes and interconnections
   (d) A view in terms of objects and messages

4. What is a dynamic view of a software architecture?
   (a) A view in terms of a module hierarchy
   (b) A view in terms of components and connectors
   (c) A view of the physical configuration in terms of nodes and interconnections
   (d) A view in terms of objects and messages

5. What is a deployment view of a software architecture?
   (a) A static view in terms of a module hierarchy
   (b) A static view in terms of components and connectors
   (c) A view of the physical configuration in terms of nodes and interconnections
   (d) A dynamic interaction view in terms of objects and messages

6. What is a software architectural pattern?
   (a) The structure of the major subsystems of a system
   (b) The components and connectors in a software architecture
   (c) A small group of collaborating objects
   (d) A recurring architecture used in a variety of systems

7. What happens in a Layers of Abstraction pattern?
   (a) Each layer uses services in the layer immediately below it.
   (b) Each layer uses services in the layer immediately above it.
   (c) Each layer uses services in the layers immediately above it and below it.
   (d) Each layer is independent of the other layers.

8. What happens in a Call/Return pattern?
   (a) A calling operation in the calling object sends a message to an operation (a.k.a. method) in the called object.

(b) A calling operation in the calling object invokes an operation (a.k.a. method) in the called object.

(c) The calling object waits for a response from the called object.

(d) The calling object does not wait for a response from the called object.

9. A producer sends a message to a consumer. Which one of the following is asynchronous message communication?

(a) The producer waits for a response from the consumer.

(b) The producer does not wait for a response from the consumer.

(c) The producer goes to sleep.

(d) The producer waits for a timeout.

10. A producer sends a message to a consumer. Which one of the following is synchronous message communication with reply?

(a) The producer waits for a response from the consumer.

(b) The producer does not wait for a response from the consumer.

(c) The producer goes to sleep.

(d) The producer waits for a timeout.

13

Software Subsystem Architectural Design

During analysis modeling, the problem is analyzed by breaking it down and studying it on a use case–by–use case basis. During design modeling, the solution is synthesized by designing a software architecture that defines the structural and behavioral properties of the software system. To successfully manage the inherent complexity of a large-scale software system, it is necessary to provide an approach for decomposing the system into subsystems and developing the overall software architecture of the system. After performing this decomposition, each subsystem can then be designed independently, as described in subsequent chapters.

Section 13.1 describes issues in software architectural design. To design the software architecture, it is necessary to start with the analysis model. Several decisions need to be made in designing the software architecture:

- Integrate the use case–based interaction models into an initial software architecture, as described in Section 13.2.
- Determine the subsystems using separation of concerns and subsystem structuring criteria, as described in Sections 13.3 and 13.4, respectively.
- Determine the precise type of message communication among the subsystems, as described in Section 13.5.

13.1 ISSUES IN SOFTWARE ARCHITECTURAL DESIGN

In the analysis of the problem domain and structuring a system into subsystems, the emphasis is on functional decomposition, such that each subsystem addresses a distinctly separate part of the system (as discussed in Section 13.3). The design goal is for each subsystem to perform a major function that is relatively independent of the functionality provided by other subsystems. A subsystem can be structured further into smaller subsystems, consisting of a subset of the functionality provided by the parent subsystem. After the interface between subsystems has been defined, subsystem design can proceed independently.

Some subsystems can be determined relatively easily because of geographical distribution or server responsibility. One of the most common forms of geographical

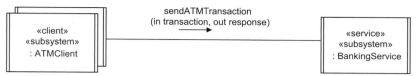

Figure 13.1. High-level software architecture: Banking System

distribution involves clients and services, which are allocated to different subsystems: a client subsystem and a service subsystem. Thus, the software architecture of the Banking System illustrated in Figure 13.1 consists of a client subsystem called ATM Client, which is located at each ATM machine, and a service subsystem called Bank Service. This is an example of geographical subsystem structuring, in which the geographical distribution of the system is given in the problem description. In such cases, subsystem structuring can be done early in the design process.

In other applications, it is not so obvious how to structure the system into subsystems. Because one of the goals of subsystem structuring is to have objects that are functionally related and highly coupled in the same subsystem, a good place to start is with the use cases. Objects that participate in the same use case are candidates to be grouped into the same subsystem. Because of this, subsystem structuring is often done after the interaction among the constituent objects of each use case has been determined during dynamic modeling (see Chapter 9). In particular, it can be carried out early in the design phase, as described in this chapter.

A subsystem provides a larger-grained information hiding solution than an object. To structure the system into subsystems, start with the use cases. Objects that realize the same use case have higher coupling because they communicate with each other (as depicted on the use case–based interaction diagram) and have lower (or no) coupling with objects in other use cases. Whereas an object can participate in more than one use case, it can only be part of one subsystem; thus, an object that participates in more than one use case needs to be allocated to a single subsystem, usually the subsystem with which it is most highly coupled. In some cases, a subsystem might incorporate the objects from more than one use case, most probably when the use cases share common objects because they are functionally related. However, there are also situations in which objects that participate in the same use case need to be assigned to different subsystems (e.g., because they are located in separate geographical locations). These issues are addressed further in Section 13.3.

13.2 INTEGRATED COMMUNICATION DIAGRAMS

To transition from analysis to design and to determine the subsystems, it is necessary to synthesize an initial software design from the analysis carried out so far. This is done by integrating the use case–based interaction diagrams developed as part of the dynamic model. Although dynamic interaction between objects can be depicted on either sequence diagrams or communication diagrams, this integration uses communication diagrams because they visually depict the interconnection between objects, as well as the messages passed between them.

In the analysis model, at least one communication diagram is developed for each use case. The **integrated communication diagram** is a synthesis of all the communication diagrams developed to support the use cases. The integrated communication diagram is, in effect, a merger of the communication diagrams, and its development is described next.

Frequently, there is a precedence order in which use cases are executed. The order of the synthesis of the communication diagrams should correspond to the order in which the use cases are executed. From a visual perspective, the integration is done in the following manner. Start with the communication diagram for the first use case and superimpose the communication diagram for the second use case on top of the first to form a integrated diagram. Next, superimpose the third diagram on top of the integrated diagram of the first two, and so on. In each case, add new objects and new message interactions from each subsequent diagram onto the integrated diagram, which gradually gets bigger as more objects and message interactions are added. Objects and message interactions that appear on more than one communication diagram are only shown once.

It is important to realize that the integrated communication diagram must show all message communication derived from the individual use case–based communication diagrams. Communication diagrams often show the main sequence through a use case, but not all the alternative sequences. In the integrated communication diagram, it is necessary to show the messages that are sent as a result of executing the alternative sequences in addition to the main sequence through each use case. An example was given in Chapter 11 of interaction diagrams supporting the main sequence and several alternative sequences for the Validate PIN use case in the Banking System. All these additional messages need to appear on the integrated communication diagram, which is intended to be a complete description of all message communication among objects.

The integrated communication diagram is a synthesis of all relevant use case–based communication diagrams showing all objects and their interactions. The integrated communication diagram is represented as a generic UML communication diagram (see Section 12.2.2), which means that it depicts all possible interactions between the objects. On the integrated communication diagram, objects and messages are shown, but the message sequence numbering does not need to be shown because this would only add clutter. As with the use case–based communication diagrams, messages on the integrated communication diagram are depicted as simple messages, before the decision on type of message communication (synchronous or asynchronous) is made, as described in Section 13.5.

An example of an integrated communication diagram for the ATM Client subsystem of the Banking System is given in Figure 13.2. This consists of the integration of the communication diagrams that realize the seven use cases of the Banking System, including the main and alternative sequences for each use case. The integrated communication diagram is a generic diagram, so the object names are not underlined.

The integrated communication diagram can get very complicated for a large system; therefore, it is necessary to have ways to reduce the amount of information. One way to reduce the amount of information on the diagram is to aggregate the messages – that is, if one object sends several individual messages to another,

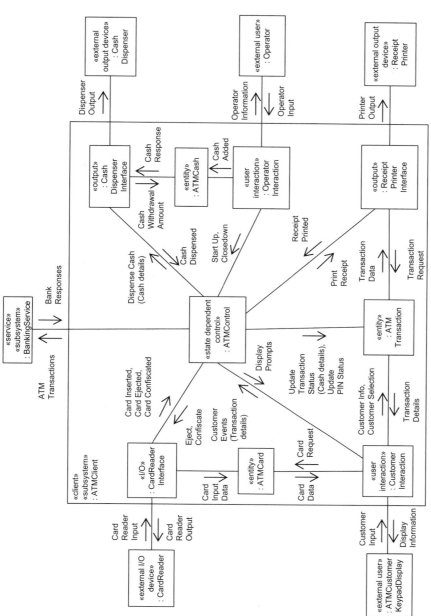

Figure 13.2. Integrated communication diagram for ATM Client subsystem

Table 13.1. Aggregate message composed of simple messages	
Aggregate message	**Consists of simple messages**
Display Prompts	Get PIN, Invalid PIN Prompt, Display Menu, Display Cancel, Display Menu, Display Confiscate, Display Eject

instead of showing all these messages on the diagram, use one aggregate message. The aggregate message is a useful way of grouping messages to reduce clutter on the diagram. It does not represent an actual message sent from one object to another; rather, it represents messages sent at different times between the same pair of objects. For example, the messages sent by the ATM Control object to the Customer Interaction object in Figure 13.2 can be aggregated into an aggregate message called Display Prompts. A message dictionary is then used to define the contents of Display Prompts, as shown in Table 13.1. Other examples of aggregate message names in Figure 13.2 are ATM Transactions, Bank Responses, and Customer Events. This example of the integrated communication diagram is described in more detail in the Banking System case study in Chapter 21.

Furthermore, showing all the objects on one diagram might not be practical. A solution to this problem is to develop integrated communication diagrams for each subsystem and develop a higher-level subsystem communication diagram to show the interaction between the subsystems, as described next.

The dynamic interactions between subsystems can be depicted on a **subsystem communication diagram**, which is a high-level integrated communication diagram, as shown in Figure 13.1 for the Banking System. The structure of an individual subsystem can be depicted on an integrated communication diagram, which shows all the objects in the subsystem and their interconnections, as depicted in Figure 13.2.

13.3 SEPARATION OF CONCERNS IN SUBSYSTEM DESIGN

Some important structuring decisions need to be made when designing subsystems. The following design considerations, which address separation of concerns, should be made when structuring the system into subsystems. The goal is to make subsystems more self-contained, so that different concerns are addressed by different subsystems.

13.3.1 Composite Object

Objects that are part of the same composite object should be in the same subsystem and separate from objects that are not part of the same composite object. As described in Chapter 7, both aggregation and composition are whole/part relationships; however, composition is a stronger form of aggregation. With composition, the composite object (the whole) and its constituent objects (the parts) are created together, live together, and die together. Thus, a subsystem consisting of a composite object and its constituent objects is more strongly coupled than one consisting of an aggregate object and its constituent objects.

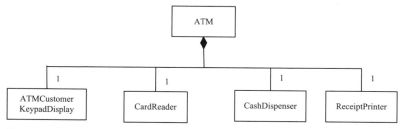

Figure 13.3. Example of composite class: ATM

A subsystem supports information hiding at a higher level of abstraction than an individual object does. A software object can be used to model a real-world object in the problem domain. A composite object models a composite real-world object in the problem domain. A composite object is typically composed of a group of related objects that work together in a coordinated fashion. This arrangement is analogous to the assembly structure in manufacturing. Often, multiple instances of a composite object (and hence, multiple instances of each of its constituent objects) are needed in an application. The relationship between a composite class and its constituent classes is best depicted in the static model because the class diagram depicts the multiplicity of the association between each constituent class and the composite class.

An example of a composite class is the ATM class (Figure 13.3). The ATM is a composite class that consists of an ATM card reader, a cash dispenser, a receipt printer, and an ATM Customer keypad/display. There are several instances of the ATM composite class in the Banking System – one for each ATM.

It is possible for an aggregate subsystem to be a higher-level subsystem that contains composite subsystems (components). An **aggregate subsystem** contains objects grouped by functional similarity, which might span geographical boundaries. These aggregate objects are grouped together because they are functionally similar or because they interact with each other in the same use case(s). Aggregate subsystems can be used as a convenient higher-level abstraction than composite subsystems, particularly when there are many components in a highly distributed application. In a software architecture that spans multiple organizations, it can be useful to depict each organization as an aggregate subsystem. A layered architecture can also be structured, with each layer designed as an aggregate subsystem. Each layer might itself consist of multiple **composite subsystems** (designed as components or services) that are geographically distributed. The Emergency Monitoring System case study is an example of a software architecture with each layer (user, monitoring, service) designed as an aggregate subsystem, as depicted in Figure 13.4 and described in Chapter 23. Each layer contains one or more composite subsystems (components or services). Thus, the Monitoring Layer has two components, Monitoring Sensor Component and Remote System Proxy, and the Service Layer has two services, Alarm Service and Monitoring Data Service.

13.3.2 Geographical Location

If two objects could potentially be physically separated in different geographical locations, they should be in different subsystems. In a distributed environment,

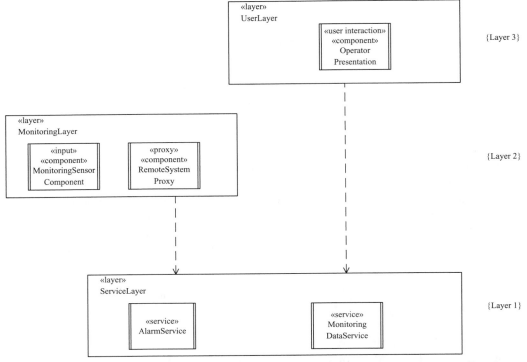

Figure 13.4. Layered architecture with aggregate and composite subsystems: Emergency Monitoring System

component-based subsystems communicate only by means of messages that can be sent from one subsystem to another. In the Emergency Monitoring System shown on the deployment diagram in Figure 13.5, there are several instances of the Monitoring Sensor component, several instances of the Remote System Proxy, and several instances of the Operator Presentation component. In addition, there are two service components, Alarm Service and Monitoring Data Service. Each instance of these components could physically reside on a separate microcomputer node located in a different geographical location, connected by a wide area network.

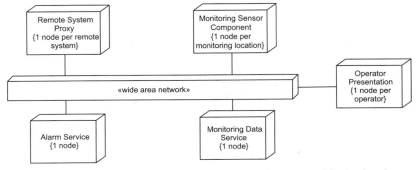

Figure 13.5. Example of geographical distribution: Emergency Monitoring System

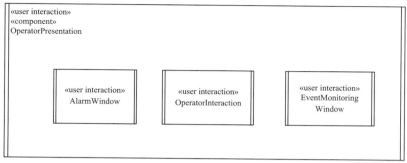

Figure 13.6. Example of user interaction subsystem

13.3.3 **Clients and Services**

Clients and services should be in separate subsystems. This guideline can be viewed as a special case of the geographical location rule because clients and services are usually at different locations. For example, the Banking System shown in Figures 13.1 has many ATM Client subsystems of the same type, which reside at physical ATMs distributed around the country. Bank Service is located at a centralized location, perhaps in New York City. In the Emergency Monitoring System shown in Figure 13.4, there are two services, Alarm Service and Monitoring Data Service, which are in separate subsystems from their clients.

13.3.4 **User Interaction**

Users often use their own PCs as part of a larger distributed configuration, so the most flexible option is to keep user interaction objects in separate subsystems. Because user interaction objects are usually clients, this guideline can be viewed as a special case of the client/service guideline. Furthermore, a user interaction object may be a composite graphical user interaction object composed of several simpler user interaction objects. The Operator Presentation component in Figure 13.6 is an example composite graphical user interaction object, which contains three simple graphical user interaction objects, an Operator Interaction object, an Alarm Window, and an Event Monitoring Window, as described in more detail in Chapter 17.

13.3.5 **Interface to External Objects**

A subsystem deals with a subset of the actors shown in the use case model and a subset of the external real-world objects shown on the context diagram. An external real-world object should interface to only one subsystem. An example is given for the ATM Client subsystem in Figure 13.7, in which the ATM Client interfaces to several external real-world classes, including the Card Reader, Cash Dispenser, and Receipt Printer, which in turn only interface to the ATM Client.

13.3.6 **Scope of Control**

A control object and all the entity and I/O objects it directly controls should all be part of one subsystem and not split among subsystems. An example is the ATM

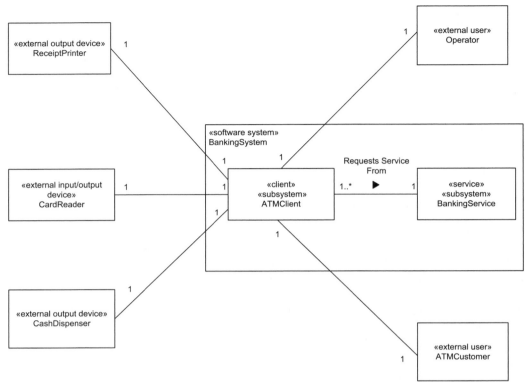

Figure 13.7. Example of interfacing to external classes

Control object within the ATM Client Subsystem, shown in Figures 13.2, which provides the overall control of the objects in the ATM Client subsystem, including several internal I/O objects (such as Card Reader Interface and Cash Dispenser Interface), user interaction objects (such as Customer Interaction), and entity objects (such as ATM Transaction).

13.4 SUBSYSTEM STRUCTURING CRITERIA

The design considerations described in the previous section can be formalized as subsystem structuring criteria, which help ensure that subsystems are designed effectively. The subsystem structuring criteria are described in this section with examples. A subsystem can satisfy more than one of the structuring criteria. Subsystems are generally depicted with the stereotype «subsystem». For certain software architectures consisting of distributed component-based subsystems, the stereotype «component» is used for such a subsystem, and in service-oriented architecture consisting of service subsystems, the stereotype «service» is used for a service subsystem.

13.4.1 Client Subsystem

A client subsystem is a requester of one or more services. There are many different types of clients; some may be wholly dependent on a given service, and some may be only partially dependent. The former only communicate with one service, whereas the latter might communicate with more than one service. Client subsystems include user interaction subsystems, control subsystems, and I/O subsystems, which are described in more detail in Sections 13.4.2, 13.4.4, and 13.4.6, respectively. In some applications, a client subsystem combines more than one role. For example, the ATM Client subsystem depicted in Figures 13.1, which is a client of Bank Service, has both user interaction and control characteristics.

In the Emergency Monitoring System shown in Figure 13.4, there are two service subsystems, Alarm Service and Monitoring Data Service. The Monitoring Sensor Component, Remote System Proxy, and Operator Presentation components are clients of Alarm Service and Monitoring Data Service.

13.4.2 User Interaction Subsystem

A user interaction subsystem provides the user interface and performs the role of a client in a client/server system, providing user access to services. There may be more than one user interaction subsystem – one for each type of user. A user interaction subsystem is usually a composite object that is composed of several simpler user interaction objects. It may also contain one or more entity objects for local storage and/or caching, as well as control objects for overall sequencing of user input and output.

With the proliferation of graphical workstations and personal computers, a subsystem providing a user interaction role might run on a separate node and interact with subsystems on other nodes. A user interaction subsystem can provide rapid responses to simple requests supported completely by the node, and relatively slower responses to requests requiring the cooperation of other nodes. This kind of subsystem usually needs to interface to specific user I/O devices, such as graphical displays and keyboards. The ATM Client subsystem in Figure 13.1 satisfies this criterion.

A user interaction client subsystem could support a simple user interface, consisting of a command line interface or a graphical user interface that contains multiple objects. A simple user interaction client subsystem would have a single thread of control.

A more complex user interaction subsystem would typically involve multiple windows and multiple threads of control. For example, a Windows client consists of multiple windows that operate independently, with each window supported by a concurrent object with its own separate thread of control. The concurrent objects might access some shared data.

Figure 13.8 shows an example of a user interaction subsystem from a basic Emergency Monitoring System. Basic Operator Presentation is a user interaction subsystem, which has several instances. Each instance sends requests to the Alarm Service and the Monitoring Data Service subsystems. The Basic Operator Presentation

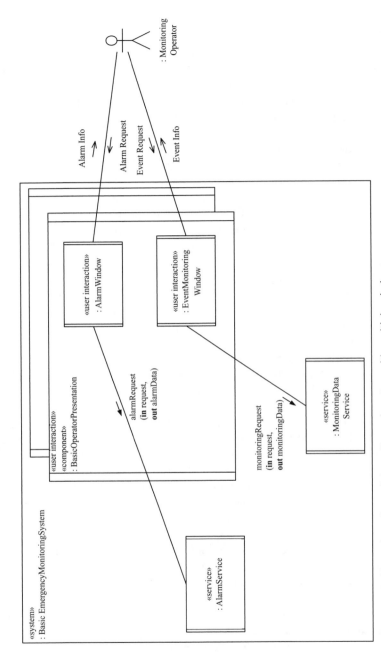

Figure 13.8. Examples of user interaction subsystem with multiple windows

subsystem has one internal user interaction object to display alarms in an Alarm Window and a second internal user interaction object to display monitoring status in an Event Monitoring Window.

13.4.3 Service Subsystem

A service subsystem provides a service for client subsystems. It responds to requests from client subsystems, although it does not initiate any requests. A service subsystem is any subsystem that provides a service, servicing client requests. Service subsystems are usually composite objects that are composed of two or more objects. These include entity objects, coordinator objects that service client requests and determine what object should be assigned to handle them, and business logic objects that encapsulate application logic. Frequently, a service is associated with a data repository or a set of related data repositories, or it might provide access to a database. Alternatively, the service might be associated with an I/O device or a set of related I/O devices, such as a file service or line printer service.

A service subsystem is often allocated its own node. A data service supports remote access to a centralized database or file store. An I/O service processes requests for a physical resource that resides at that node. Examples of data service subsystems are the Alarm Service and the Monitoring Data Service subsystem shown in Figures 13.8 and 13.9, which store current and historical alarm and sensor data,

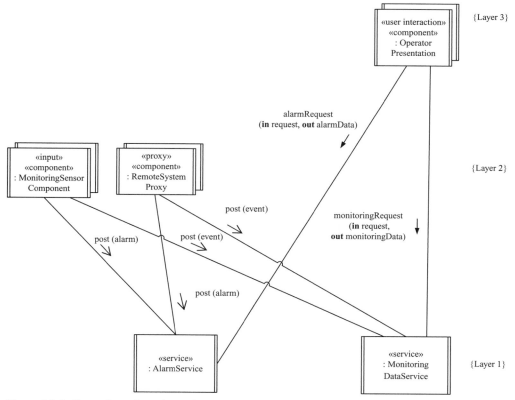

Figure 13.9. Examples of service subsystems

respectively. Monitoring Data Service receives new sensor data from the Monitoring Sensor and Remote System Proxy subsystems. Sensor data are requested by other subsystems, such as the Operator Presentation subsystem, which displays the data.

13.4.4 Control Subsystem

A control subsystem controls a given part of the system. The subsystem receives its inputs from the external environment and generates outputs to the external environment, usually without any human intervention. A control subsystem is often state-dependent, in which case it includes at least one state-dependent control object. In some cases, some input data might be gathered by some other subsystem(s) and used by this subsystem. Alternatively, this subsystem might provide some data for use by other subsystems.

A control subsystem might receive some high-level commands from another subsystem that gives it overall direction, after which it provides the lower-level control, sending status information to other nodes, either on an ongoing basis or on demand.

An example of a control subsystem is ATM Client subsystem in Figure 13.1, which combines the roles of control and user interaction. There are multiple instances of the ATM Client, one for each ATM; however, each instance is independent of the others and only communicates with the Banking Service subsystem. The control role of the ATM Client is to sequence the interactions with the ATM customer, communicating with the Banking Service subsystem, and controlling the I/O devices that dispense cash, print the receipt, and read and eject (or confiscate) the ATM card. The control role is explicitly depicted in the ATM statechart, in which the statechart actions trigger actions in the controlled objects.

Another example of a control subsystem is from the Automated Guided Vehicle System and is given in Figure 13.10, in which the control is provided by an internal state-dependent control object, Vehicle Control (not shown), which receives move

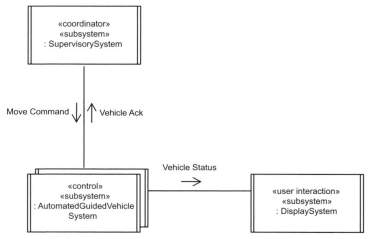

Figure 13.10. Example of control and coordinator subsystems in Factory Automation System

commands from a Supervisory System and controls the motor component (to start and stop moving along the track) and the arm component (to load and unload parts), as described in more detail in Chapter 24. Automated Guided Vehicle System sends vehicle acknowledgements to the Supervisory System and vehicle status to the Display System.

13.4.5 Coordinator Subsystem

Coordinator subsystems coordinate the execution of other subsystems, such as control subsystems or service subsystems. Both kinds of coordination are described next.

In software architectures with multiple control subsystems, it is sometimes necessary to have a coordinator subsystem that coordinates the control subsystems. If the multiple control subsystems are completely independent of each other, as with the ATM Clients in Figure 13.1, no coordination is required. In other situations, control subsystems can coordinate activities among themselves. Such distributed coordination is usually possible if the coordination is relatively simple. If the coordination activity is relatively complex, however, it is usually more advantageous to have a hierarchical control system with a separate coordinator subsystem overseeing the control subsystems. For example, the coordinator subsystem might decide what item of work a control subsystem should do next. An example of a coordinator subsystem assigning jobs to control subsystems is given for the Factory Automation System, in which the Supervisory System (Figure 13.10) is a coordinator that assigns jobs to the individual Automated Guided Vehicle Systems to move to a factory station, pick up a part, and transport it to a different station.

Another kind of coordinator subsystem decides the execution sequence (also known as *workflow*) of multiple service subsystems, which is described in more detail in Chapter 16. An example of coordination in service-oriented architectures is given for the Customer Coordinator in the online shopping system. The Customer Coordinator receives shopping requests from the Customer Interaction component. It then interacts with several service subsystems, including Catalog Service, Customer Account Service, Credit Card Service, and Email Service, as shown in Figure 13.11.

13.4.6 Input/Output Subsystem

An input, output, or input/output subsystem is a subsystem that performs input and/or output operations on behalf of other subsystems. It can be designed to be relatively autonomous. In particular, "smart" devices are given greater local autonomy and consist of the hardware plus the software that interfaces to and controls the device. An I/O subsystem typically consists of one or more device interface objects, and it may also contain control objects to provide localized control and entity objects to store local data.

An example of an input subsystem is the Monitoring Sensor Component in the Emergency Monitoring System in Figure 13.9, which receives sensor inputs from external sensors. It is a client of two services, posting alarms to Alarm Service and events to Monitoring Data Service.

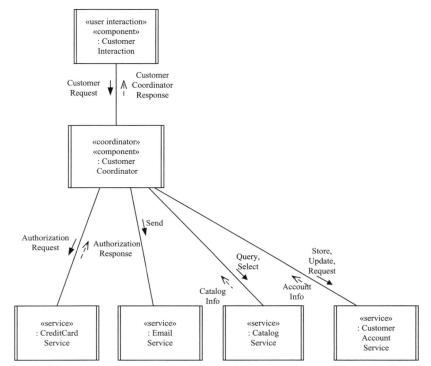

Figure 13.11. Example of coordinator subsystem in service-oriented architectures

13.5 DECISIONS ABOUT MESSAGE COMMUNICATION BETWEEN SUBSYSTEMS

In the transition from the analysis model to the design model, one of the most important decisions relates to what type of message communication is needed between the subsystems. A second related decision is to determine more precisely the name and parameters of each message (i.e., the interface specification). In the analysis model, no decisions are made about the type of message communication. In addition, the emphasis is on the information passed between objects, rather than on precise message names and parameters. In design modeling, after the subsystem structure is determined (as described in Section 13.4), a decision has to be made about the precise semantics of message communication, such as whether message communication will be synchronous or asynchronous (see Chapters 4 and 12).

Message communication between two subsystems can be unidirectional or bidirectional. Figure 13.12*a* depicts an analysis model example of unidirectional message communication between a producer and a consumer, as well as an example of bidirectional message communication between a client and a service. All messages in the analysis model are depicted with one notation (the stick arrowhead) because no decision has yet been made about the type of message communication. This decision is made during design, so the designer now needs to decide what type of message communication is required in both of these examples. (For an overview of the UML notation for message communication, see Chapter 2, Section 2.8.1.)

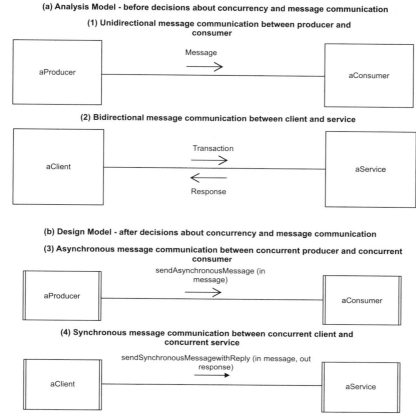

(a) Analysis Model - before decisions about concurrency and message communication

(1) Unidirectional message communication between producer and consumer

aProducer — Message → aConsumer

(2) Bidirectional message communication between client and service

aClient — Transaction → ← Response — aService

(b) Design Model - after decisions about concurrency and message communication

(3) Asynchronous message communication between concurrent producer and concurrent consumer

aProducer — sendAsynchronousMessage (in message) → aConsumer

(4) Synchronous message communication between concurrent client and concurrent service

aClient — sendSynchronousMessagewithReply (in message, out response) → aService

Figure 13.12. Transition from analysis to design: decisions about concurrency and message communication

Figure 13.12*b* shows the result of two design decisions. First, the four analysis model objects in Figure 13.12*a* are designed as concurrent subsystems in Figure 13.12*b*. Second, the design decision is made about the type of message communication between the subsystems. Figure 13.12*b* depicts the decision to use asynchronous message communication between the producer and consumer, and synchronous message communication between the client and service. In addition, the precise name and parameters of each message are determined. The asynchronous message (in UML 2, the stick arrowhead means asynchronous communication) has the name send Asynchronous Message and content called message. The synchronous message (in UML 2, the black arrowhead means synchronous communication) has the name send Asynchronous Message With Reply, with the input content called message and the service's reply called response.

The aforementioned decisions concerning asynchronous and synchronous communication are formalized into architectural communication patterns, as described in Chapter 12. Thus, the Asynchronous Message Communication pattern is applied to the unidirectional message between the producer and consumer and the Synchronous Message Communication with Reply pattern is applied to the message and response between the client and service.

13.6 SUMMARY

This chapter described software architectural design. The overall design of the software architecture was described, including the design decisions that need to be made when in the transition from analysis modeling to design modeling. Subsystems are categorized according to the roles they play in the software architecture. Several examples of such architectures will be given in the case studies described in Chapters 21 through 24.

In designing the overall software architecture, it helps to consider applying the software architectural patterns, both architectural structure patterns and architectural communication patterns. Architectural structure patterns are applied to design of the overall structure of the software architecture, which addresses how the system is structured into subsystems. Architectural communication patterns address the ways in which subsystems communicate with each other. Each subsystem is designed such that its interface is explicitly defined in terms of the operations it provides, as well as the operations it uses. Communication between distributed subsystems can be synchronous or asynchronous.

During software design modeling, design decisions are made relating to the characteristics of the software architecture. Chapter 14 describes object-oriented design using the concepts of information hiding, classes, and inheritance. Chapter 15 describes the design of client/server software architectures, in which a typical design consists of one service and multiple clients. Chapter 16 describes the design of service-oriented architectures, which typically consist of multiple distributed autonomous services that can be composed into distributed software applications. Chapter 17 describes the design of component-based software architectures, including the design of component interfaces, with component ports that have provided and required interfaces, and connectors that join compatible ports. Chapter 18 describes the design of real-time software architectures, which are concurrent architectures usually having to deal with multiple streams of input events. Chapter 19 describes the design of software product line architectures, which are architectures for families of products that need to capture both the commonality and variability in the family.

EXERCISES

Multiple-choice questions: For each question, choose one of the answers.

1. What is an integrated communication diagram?
   (a) A communication diagram formed by combining objects
   (b) A synthesis of all the communication diagrams developed to support the use cases
   (c) A communication diagram depicting the objects that realize a use case
   (d) A communication diagram that integrates the entity objects from the static model

2. Which of the following objects should be assigned to the same subsystem?
   (a) Objects that are part of the same composite object
   (b) Client and server objects
   (c) User interface and entity objects
   (d) Objects that are associated with each other

3. Objects that are in geographically different locations should be:
   (a) In the same subsystem

(b) In different subsystems

(c) In a composite subsystem

(d) In layered subsystems

4. If scope of control is used in subsystem structuring, then:

(a) A user interface object is placed in the same subsystem as an entity object it updates.

(b) A state-dependent control object is placed in the same subsystem as the objects it controls.

(c) A state-dependent control object is placed in a different subsystem from the objects it controls.

(d) A user interface object is placed in a different subsystem from an entity object it updates.

5. How should an external object be designed to interface to the system?

(a) It should interface to one subsystem.

(b) It should interface to several subsystems.

(c) It should interface to every subsystem.

(d) It should interface to none of the subsystems.

6. A user interface subsystem is a type of:

(a) Control subsystem

(b) Service subsystem

(c) Client subsystem

(d) I/O subsystem

7. Which of the following objects are NOT likely to be in the same subsystem?

(a) User interface object and entity object

(b) State-dependent control object and coordinator object

(c) Business logic object and entity object

(d) I/O object and state-dependent control object

8. Which of the following subsystems is NOT likely to be a client subsystem?

(a) Control subsystem

(b) User interaction subsystem

(c) Service subsystem

(d) I/O subsystem

9. When is a coordinator subsystem required?

(a) If the subsystem needs to coordinate several internal objects

(b) If the subsystem needs to coordinate multiple I/O devices

(c) If the subsystem receives messages from multiple client subsystems

(d) If the subsystem needs to coordinate the execution of other subsystems

10. When is a control subsystem required?

(a) If the subsystem needs to control several internal objects

(b) If the subsystem needs to control multiple I/O devices

(c) If the subsystem needs to control multiple client subsystems

(d) If the subsystem needs to control the execution of other subsystems

14

Designing Object-Oriented Software Architectures

Object-oriented concepts are fundamental to software design. Object-oriented design refers to software systems that are designed using the concepts of information hiding, classes, and inheritance. Objects are instantiated from classes and are accessed through operations, which are also referred to as methods.

A class is designed using the **information hiding** concept to encapsulate different kinds of information, such as details of a data structure or state machine. These classes are originally determined during the object and class structuring phase of analysis modeling, as described in Chapter 8. In particular, this chapter describes the design of class interfaces and the operations provided by each class. This chapter also describes the use of **inheritance** in software design. An introduction to information hiding, classes, and inheritance was given in Chapter 4. As pointed out in Chapter 4, the term *operation* refers to both the specification and the implementation of a function performed by an object.

Section 14.1 gives an overview of the concepts, architectures, and patterns used in designing sequential object-oriented architectures. Section 14.2 describes important issues in the design of information hiding classes. Section 14.3 describes the design of the class interface and operations, as well as how they are determined from the dynamic model. The following sections describe the design of different kinds of information hiding classes: Section 14.4 describes the design of data abstraction classes, which encapsulate data structures; Section 14.5 describes the design of state machine classes, which encapsulate finite state machines; Section 14.6 describes the design of graphical user interaction classes, which hide details of the user interface; and Section 14.7 describes the design of business logic classes, which encapsulate business rules. Section 14.8 describes inheritance in object-oriented design, including the design of class hierarchies, abstract classes, and subclasses. Section 14.9 describes the design of class interface specifications, which includes the specification of class operations. Section 14.10 describes the detailed design of information hiding classes. Section 14.11 describes polymorphism and dynamic binding. Section 14.12 describes the implementation of classes with an example of class implementation in Java.

14.1 CONCEPTS, ARCHITECTURES, AND PATTERNS

Information hiding is a fundamental design concept in which a class encapsulates some information, such as a data structure, that is hidden from the rest of the system. The designer of the class needs to decide what information should be hidden inside the class and what information should be revealed in the class interface. Another important concept is the separation of the interface from the implementation, such that the interface forms a *contract* between the provider of the interface and the user of the interface. See Chapter 4 for more details about information hiding concepts.

This chapter describes the design of sequential object-oriented software architectures, which are typically implemented as a sequential program with one thread of control. Object-oriented concepts have also been applied and extended in the design of distributed and component-based software architectures, concurrent and real-time software architectures, service-oriented architectures, and software product line architectures, as described in future chapters. For communication between objects, the *Call/Return* pattern is the only pattern of communication in a sequential architecture, as described in Chapter 12.

14.2 DESIGNING INFORMATION HIDING CLASSES

In design modeling, information hiding classes are categorized by stereotype. Classes determined from the analysis model (Chapter 8) – that is, those determined from the problem domain – are categorized as entity classes, boundary classes, control classes, and application logic classes. Because some of these classes are more likely to be designed as active (concurrent) classes, as described in future chapters, this chapter concentrates on those classes that are more likely to be designed as passive classes.

- **Entity classes.** Classes determined in the analysis model that encapsulate data. On class diagrams, they are depicted with the stereotype «entity». Entity objects, which are instances of entity classes, are usually long-lasting objects that store information. For database-intensive applications, it is likely that, in some cases, the encapsulated data will need to be stored in a database. In this situation, the entity class will actually provide an interface to the database rather than encapsulating the data. Thus, during class design, entity classes are further categorized as **data abstraction classes**, which encapsulate data structures, and **wrapper classes**. A wrapper class hides the details of how to interface to an existing system or legacy system, which might be to access data stored in a file management system or a database management system. A **database wrapper class** hides how data is accessed if it is stored in a database, usually a relational database. A wrapper class can also hide the details of how to interface to a legacy system. Wrapper classes are described in Chapter 15.
- **Boundary classes.** Communicate with and interface to the external environment. Boundary classes, such as device I/O classes and proxy classes, are often active (concurrent) classes and are therefore described in Chapter 18. One passive boundary class described in this section is the **graphical user interaction class**, which interfaces to human users and presents information to them.

- **Control classes.** Provide the overall coordination for a collection of objects. Control classes are often active (concurrent) classes and are therefore also described in Chapter 18. One passive control class described in this chapter is the **state-machine class**, which encapsulates a finite state machine. Coordinator classes and timer classes are assumed to be active classes (tasks) and so are not discussed in this section.

- **Application logic classes.** Encapsulate application-specific logic and algorithms. Categorized as **business logic classes, service classes**, or **algorithm classes.** Business logic classes are described in this chapter. Service classes are described in Chapter 16 on service-oriented architectures. Algorithm classes are often active and are described in Chapter 18.

14.3 DESIGNING CLASS INTERFACE AND OPERATIONS

As described in Chapter 13, the class interface consists of the operations provided by each class. Each operation can have input parameters, output parameters, and (if it is a function) a return value. The operations of a class can be determined from either the static model or the dynamic model. Although the static model is intended to show each class's operations, it is usually easier to determine operations from the dynamic model, particularly the communication diagrams or sequence diagrams. This is because the dynamic model shows the message interaction between objects, and, hence, operations being invoked at the destination object receiving the message. Message passing between passive objects consists of an operation in one object invoking an operation provided by another object. Several examples of class design are given in this chapter.

14.3.1 Designing Class Operations from the Interaction Model

This section describes how to use the object interaction model to help determine each class's operations. Either sequence diagrams or communication diagrams may be used for this purpose. Thus, a class's operations are determined by considering how an object instantiated from the class interacts with other objects. In particular, when two objects interact, one object provides an operation that is used by the other object. This section describes the design of class operations, starting from interaction diagrams, and then depicts the operation designs on a class diagram.

If two objects interact, it is necessary to know which of the two objects invokes an operation on the other object. This information cannot usually be determined from a class diagram in the static model because it only shows the static relationships between classes. On the other hand, the dynamic interaction model does show the direction in which one object sends a message to the other. If the objects are mapped to a sequential program, the sender object invokes an operation on the receiver object. In this situation, the message is mapped to an operation call. The name of the message is mapped to the name of the operation and the parameters of the message are mapped to the parameters of the operation.

An object's operations can be determined directly from the interaction diagrams on which it appears. In the analysis model, the emphasis is on capturing the information passed between objects and not on the precise syntax of the operation;

therefore, the message shown on the communication diagram may be either a noun, reflecting the data that are passed, or a verb, reflecting an operation to be executed.

In the design model, the class's operations are specified. If the message is shown as a noun, it is now necessary to define the operation of the object that will receive this information. If the message is shown as a verb, the verb represents the name of the operation. It is important that the name given to the operation in the design model reflect a service provided by the class.

It is also necessary to consider whether the operation has any input and/or output parameters. In the analysis model, messages on the communication diagrams are usually depicted as simple messages sent by sender objects to receiver objects. In some cases, a simple message represents a response to a previous message. All messages that invoke operations are depicted as synchronous messages on the design model communication diagrams. Simple messages depicted in the analysis model that actually represent responses – that is, data returned by an operation – are mapped to a return parameter of the operation.

In addition to passing a variable as a parameter of an operation, it is also possible to pass an object as a parameter. Once an object has been created, it can be passed as the parameter of an operation call to another object. An example of this is in the Banking System, which has an ATM Transaction entity class. Once a transaction has been created, such as the PIN Validation Transaction, it is a passed from the ATM Client to the Banking Service as a parameter of the ATM Transaction.

14.3.2 Example of Designing Class Operations from the Interaction Model

As an example of designing class operations from the object interaction model, consider the ATM Card class (a data abstraction class as described in Section 14.4), which encapsulates the information read off an ATM card. By examining the analysis model communication diagram in Figure 14.1a, it can be seen that the Card Reader Interface object sends three data items: Card Id, Start Date, and Expiration Date (previously read off the ATM Card) to be stored in the ATM Card entity object. The Customer Interaction object later sends a Card Request message to ATM Card, which returns these same three data items. During design, the precise class interface is designed. Because these three data items are written to ATM Card, in the design model (see Figure 14.1b), an operation of the ATM Card data abstraction object called write is designed, which has three input parameters (cardId, startDate, and expirationDate). The Card Request message sent by Customer Interaction is designed as a read operation provided by ATM Card. The three data items returned by ATM Card are designed to be output parameters (cardId, startDate, and expirationDate) returned by the read operation. The operation calls are depicted, using the UML synchronous message notation.

After the object's operations have been determined from the communication diagram, the operation is specified in the static model, together with the class that provides the operation. Thus, proceeding in tandem with determining the class operations from the communication diagrams and depicting them on the class diagrams is beneficial. This approach is used throughout this chapter.

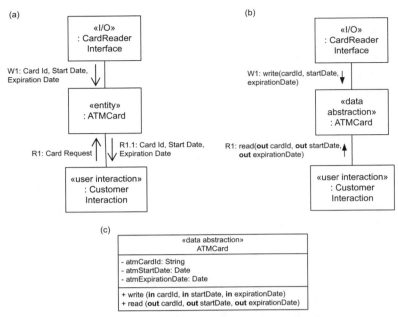

Figure 14.1. Example of data abstraction class: (*a*) Analysis model: communication diagram. (*b*) Design model: communication diagram. (*c*) Design model: class diagram

Thus, Figure 14.1*c* depicts the ATM Card data abstraction class. The attributes are encapsulated in the ATM Card class. They are depicted as private attributes; therefore, they are not visible outside the class. These attributes are stored by the write operation and accessed by the read operation. The class interface is defined in terms of the public read and write operations and the parameters of each operation.

14.3.3 Designing Class Operations from the Static Model

Determining a class's operations from the class diagrams of the static model is possible, particularly for the entity classes. Standard operations are create, read, update, delete. However, it is often possible to tailor operations to more specific needs of the specific data abstraction class by defining the services provided by the class. This will be illustrated by several examples of the design of class operations in the following sections.

14.4 DATA ABSTRACTION CLASSES

Each entity class in the analysis model that encapsulates data is designed as a **data abstraction class**. An entity class stores some data and provides operations to access the data and to read or write to the data. The data abstraction class is used to encapsulate the data structure, thereby hiding the internal details of how the data structure is represented. The operations are designed as access procedures or functions whose internals, which define how the data structure is manipulated, are also hidden.

The information on the attributes encapsulated by the data abstraction class should be available from the static model of the problem domain (discussed in Chapter 7). The operations of the data abstraction class are determined by considering the needs of the client objects that use the data abstraction object in order to indirectly access the data structure. This can be determined by analyzing how the data abstraction object is accessed by other objects, as given in the communication model. This is best illustrated by means of an example, which is presented in the next section.

14.4.1 Example of Data Abstraction Class

As an example of a data abstraction class, consider the analysis model communication diagram shown in Figure 14.2a, which consists of two objects that need to access the ATM Cash data abstraction object. The attributes of ATM Cash are given in the static model. ATM Cash stores the amount of cash maintained by the ATM cash dispenser, in twenty-, ten-, and five-dollar bills; therefore, it has internal variables to maintain the number of five-dollar bills, the number of ten-dollar bills, and the number of twenty-dollar bills. Based on this, an ATM Cash class is designed that encapsulates four variables – cashAvailable, fives, tens, and twenties – whose initial values are all set to zero.

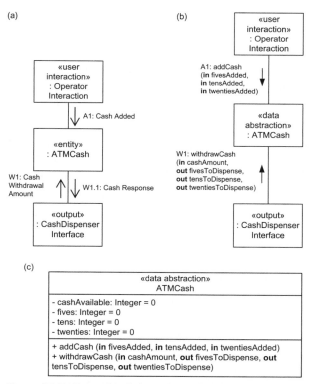

Figure 14.2. Example of data abstraction class: (a) Analysis model: communication diagram. (b) Design model: communication diagram. (c) Design model: class diagram.

In addition to knowing what messages are sent to ATM Cash, it is also important to know the sequence in which the messages are sent. Thus, in the analysis model, when ATM Cash receives a Cash Withdrawal Amount message from the Cash Dispenser Interface object, containing the amount in dollars to be dispensed, it needs to compute how many bills of each denomination need to be dispensed to satisfy the request. In the analysis model, ATM Cash sends this information in a response message, Cash Response.

ATM Cash receives another kind of message from the Operator Interaction object. The real-world ATM operator replenishes the ATM cash dispenser with new dollar bills of each denomination. This information needs to be stored in ATM Cash. After adding the cash to the dispenser, the operator confirms this to the Operator Interaction object, which then sends a Cash Added message to the ATM Cash object, as shown in Figure 14.2a.

From the previous discussion, the operations of the ATM Cash class can be specified, as depicted in the Design Model communication diagram shown in Figure 14.2b. Two operations are needed to addCash and withdrawCash. The operation withdrawCash has one input parameter, cashAmount, and three output parameters to identify the number of bills of each denomination: fivesToDispense, tensToDispense, and twentiesToDispense. Correspondingly, the addCash operation has three input parameters to indentify the number of bills of each denomination added: fivesAdded, tensAdded, and twentiesAdded. The class interface (depicted in Figure 14.2c) consists of the public operations, addCash and withdrawCash,and the parameters of the operations:

withdrawCash (**in** cashAmount, **out** fivesToDispense, **out** tensToDispense, **out** twentiesToDispense)
addCash (**in** fivesAdded, **in** tensAdded, **in** twentiesAdded)

An invariant maintained by objects of this class is that the total cash available for dispensing is equal to the sum of the value of the number of five dollar bills, the number of ten dollar bills, and the number of twenty dollar bills:

cashAvailable $= 5$ * fives $+ 10$ * tens $+ 20$ * twenties

Insufficient cash is an error case that needs to be detected. Such error situations are usually handled as exceptions.

14.5 STATE-MACHINE CLASSES

A **state-machine class** encapsulates the information contained on a statechart. During class design, the state-machine class determined in the analysis model is designed. The statechart executed by the state-machine object is encapsulated in a state transition table. Thus the state-machine class hides the contents of the state transition table and maintains the current state of the object.

The state-machine class provides the operations that access the state transition table and change the state of the object. In particular, one or more operations are designed to process the incoming events that cause state changes. One way of

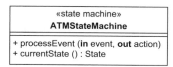

Figure 14.3. Example of state-machine control class

designing the operations of a state-machine class is to have one operation for each incoming event. This means that each state-machine class is designed explicitly for a particular statechart. However, it is desirable to make a state-machine class more reusable.

A reusable state-machine class hides the contents of the state transition table as before; however, it provides two reusable operations that are not application-specific, processEvent and currentState. The processEvent operation is called when there is a new event to process, with the new event passed in as an input parameter. The currentState operation is optional; it returns the ATM control state and is only needed in applications in which the current state needs to be known by clients of the state-machine class. The two operations are

```
processEvent (in event, out action)
currentState (): State
```

When called to process a new event, the processEvent operation looks up the state transition table to determine the impact of this event, given the current state of the state machine and any specified conditions that must hold. The table identifies what the new state is (if any) and whether any actions are to be performed. The processEvent operation then changes the state of the object and returns the actions to be performed as an output parameter.

A state-machine class is a reusable class in that it can be used to encapsulate any state transition table. The contents of the table are application-dependent and are defined at the time the state-machine class is instantiated and/or initialized. The initial value of the current state of the state machine (which is set to the ATM initial state) is also defined at initialization time.

An example of a state-machine class from the Banking System is the ATM State Machine state-machine class, shown in Figure 14.3. The class encapsulates the ATM state transition table (which is mapped from the ATM statechart, as depicted in Chapters 10 and 21) and provides the processEvent and currentState operations.

14.6 GRAPHICAL USER INTERACTION CLASSES

A graphical user interaction (GUI) class hides from other classes the details of the interface to the user. In a given application, the user interface might be a simple command line interface or a sophisticated graphical user interface. A command line interface is typically handled by one user interaction class. However, the design of a graphical user interface typically necessitates the design of several GUI classes. Low-level GUI classes, such as windows, menus, buttons, and dialog boxes, are

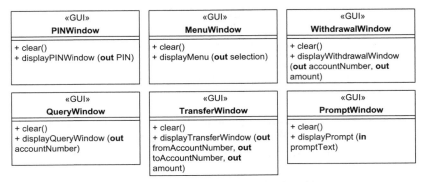

Figure 14.4. Example of graphical user interaction (GUI) classes

typically stored in a user interface component library. Higher-level composite user interaction classes (passive or active classes, as described in Chapter 18) are often created that contain these lower-level GUI classes.

In the analysis model, the emphasis should be on identifying the composite user interaction classes and capturing the information that needs to be entered by the user and the information that needs to be displayed to the user. Individual GUI screens can also be designed as part of the analysis model. In the design model for a GUI-based application, the GUI classes required for each of the individual screens are designed.

Examples of user interaction classes from a banking application are classes used in designing the GUI. These GUI classes are designed for each of the windows used for interacting with the customer (Figure 14.4): the main Menu Window, the PIN Window, the Withdrawal Window, the Transfer Window, the Query Window, and the Prompt Window classes. A GUI class has operations for the window it displays and through which it interacts with the customer. Each class has a clear operation to make the screen blank (clear) and at least one operation related to the output function it provides (displayPINWindow for the PIN Window class, displayWithdrawalWindow for the Withdrawal Window class, displayTransferWindow for the Transfer Window class, and displayQueryWindow for the Query Window class), as well as displayMenu for the main menu. For each display window, the display operation outputs a prompt to the user, and then receives the user's input, which it returns as the output parameter(s) of the operation. For example, Figure 14.4 depicts the Menu Window GUI class, which provides the operation displayMenu (**out** selection). When called, displayMenu outputs a prompt with the menu selections for the customer: withdraw, query, or transfer. The customer selects an option (e.g., withdraw), which displayMenu returns as the selection output parameter. In the case of the Withdrawal Window class, the displayWithdrawalWindow (**out** accountNumber, **out** amount) operation prompts the user for the account number and withdrawal amount. After the user enters this data, the account number and withdrawal amount are returned as the output parameters of the operation.

There is also an operation for a smaller window used to display prompts and information messages to the customer, where no customer input is expected. The input parameter of this operation identifies the specific prompt or message that should be displayed. Figure 14.4 depicts the Prompt Window class, which has an operation to clear the prompt window and an operation to displayPrompt (**in** promptText).

14.7 BUSINESS LOGIC CLASSES

A **business logic class** defines the decision-making, business-specific application logic for processing a client's request. The goal is to encapsulate business rules that could change independently of each other into separate business logic classes. Usually a business logic object accesses various entity objects during its execution.

An example of a business logic class is the Withdrawal Transaction Manager class (shown in Figure 14.5), which encapsulates the rules for processing an ATM withdrawal request. It has operations to initialize, withdraw, confirm, and abort. The operation initialize is called at initialization time; withdraw is called to withdraw funds from a customer account; confirm is called to confirm that the withdrawal transaction was successfully completed; and abort is called if the transaction was not successfully completed (e.g., if the cash was not dispensed at the ATM). The operations are determined by careful study of the Banking Service analysis model communication diagram, as shown in Figure 14.5*a*, and the message sequence descriptions that identify the contents of the messages (see Chapter 19). From this, the design model communication diagram shown in Figure 14.5*b* and the class diagram shown in Figure 14.5*c* are determined.

14.8 INHERITANCE IN DESIGN

Inheritance can be used when designing two similar, but not identical, classes – in other words, classes that share many, but not all, characteristics. During architectural design, the classes need to be designed with inheritance in mind so that code sharing and adaptation can be exploited in detailed design and coding. Inheritance can also be used when adapting a design for either maintenance or reuse purposes. Used in this way, the biggest benefit is from using inheritance as an incremental modification mechanism.

14.8.1 Class Hierarchies

Class hierarchies (also referred to as generalization/specialization hierarchies and inheritance hierarchies) can be developed either top-down, bottom-up, or by some combination of the two approaches. Using a top-down approach, a class is designed that captures the overall characteristics of a set of classes. Specializing the class to form variant subclasses separates the differences among the classes. Alternatively, it can be recognized that an initial design contains classes that have some common properties (operations and/or attributes) as well as some variant properties. In this case, the common properties can be generalized into a superclass; these attributes and/or operations are inherited by the variant subclasses.

It should be noted that when designing with inheritance, the internals of the parent classes are visible to the subclasses. For this reason, design and reuse by subclasses is referred to as *white box reuse*. Thus, inheritance breaks the encapsulation (i.e., information hiding) concept. The implementation of the child class is

240

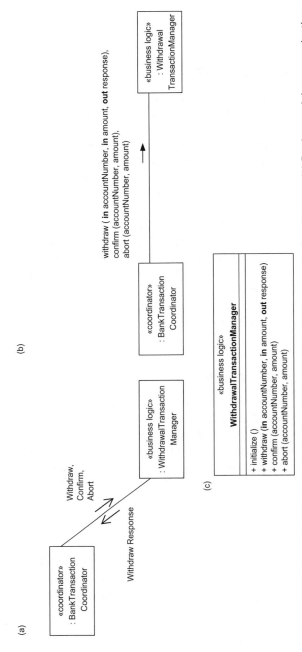

(a)

(b)

(c)

Figure 14.5. Example of business logic class: (a) Analysis model: communication diagram. (b) Design model: communication diagram. (c) Design model: class diagram

bound up with the implementation of the parent class, which can lead to ripple-effect problems with deep inheritance hierarchies. Thus, an error made to a class high up in the inheritance hierarchy will be inherited by its descendent classes at all lower levels in the hierarchy. For this reason, it is advisable to limit the depth of class hierarchies.

14.8.2 Abstract Classes

An **abstract class** is a class with no instances. Because an abstract class has no instances, it is used as a template for creating subclasses instead of as a template for creating objects. Thus, it is used only as a superclass and defines a common interface for its subclasses. An **abstract operation** is an operation that is declared in an abstract class but not implemented. An abstract class must have at least one abstract operation.

An abstract class defers all or some of its operation implementations to operations defined in subclasses. Given the interface provided by the abstract operation, a subclass can define the implementation of the operation. Different subclasses of the same abstract class can define different implementations of the same abstract operation. An abstract class can thus define an interface in the form of abstract operations. The subclasses define the implementation of the abstract operations and may extend the interface by adding other operations.

Some of the operations may be implemented in the abstract class, especially in cases in which some or all of the subclasses need to use the same implementation. Alternatively, the abstract class may define a default implementation of an operation. A subclass may choose to override an operation defined by a parent class by providing a different implementation for the same operation. This approach can be used when a particular subclass has to deal with a special case that requires a different implementation of the operation.

14.8.3 Example of Abstract Classes and Subclasses

This example of abstract classes and subclasses is for a Banking System, which provides different kinds of accounts. Initially, checking accounts and saving accounts are provided, although later other types of accounts, such as money market accounts, could be added. The starting point for the design is the generalization/specialization class diagram (Figure 14.6) developed during static modeling, as

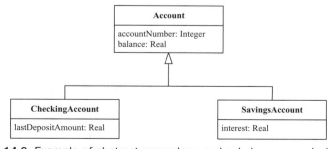

Figure 14.6. Example of abstract superclass and subclasses: analysis model

described in Chapter 7, which depicts the Account superclass and the two subclasses, Checking Account and Savings Account. The next step is to design the class operations.

An abstract class is designed called Account, which encapsulates the two generalized attributes that are needed by all accounts: accountNumber and balance. Because it is necessary to be able to open and close accounts, read the account balance, and credit and debit the account, the following generalized operations are specified for the Account class:

- open (accountNumber : Integer)
- close ()
- readBalance () : Real
- credit (amount : Real)
- debit (amount : Real)

Initially, the Banking System handles two types of accounts: checking accounts and savings accounts. Account is a good candidate for using inheritance, with a generalized account superclass and specialized subclasses for checking account and savings account. At this stage, we need to ask these questions: What should be the generalized operations and attributes of the account superclass? What are the specialized operations and attributes of the checking account and savings account subclasses? Should the account class be an abstract class; that is, which of the operations should be abstract, if any?

Before we can answer these questions, we need to understand in what ways checking and savings accounts are similar and in what ways they differ. First consider the attributes. It is clear that both checking and saving accounts need account-Number and balance attributes, so these attributes can be generalized and made attributes of the Account class, to be inherited by both the Checking Account and Savings Account subclasses. One requirement for checking accounts is that it is desirable to know the last amount deposited in the account. Checking Account thus needs a specialized attribute called lastDepositAmount. On the other hand, in this bank, savings accounts accrue interest but checking accounts do not. We need to know the accumulated interest on a savings account, so the attribute cumulativeInterest is declared as an attribute of the Savings Account subclass. In addition, only three debits are allowed per month from a savings account without a bank charge, so the attribute debitCount is also declared as an attribute of the Savings Account subclass.

Two additional static class attributes are declared for Savings Account; these are attributes for which only one value exists for the whole class, which is accessible to all objects of the class. The static attributes are maxFreeDebits (the maximum number of free debits, which is initialized to 3) and bankCharge (the amount the bank charges for every debit over the maximum number of free debits, which is initialized to $2.50).

Both Checking Account and Savings Account will need the same operations as the Account class – namely, open, close, readBalance, credit, and debit. The interface of these operations is defined in the Account superclass, so the two subclasses will inherit the same interface from Account. The open and close operations are done in the same way on checking and savings accounts, so the implementation of these operations can also be defined in Account and then inherited. The credit and debit operations are handled differently for checking and savings accounts. For this reason, the credit and debit operations are designed as abstract operations with the interface for the operations specified in the superclass but the implementations of the operations deferred to the subclasses.

In the case of the Checking Account subclass, the implementation of the debit operation needs to deduct amount from balance. The implementation of the credit operation needs to increment balance by amount and then set lastDepositAmount equal to amount. For Savings Account, the implementation of the credit operation needs to increment balance by amount. The implementation of the debit operation must, in addition to debiting the balance of the savings account, increment debitCount and deduct bankCharge for every debit in excess of maxFreeDebits. There is also a need for an additional clearDebitCount operation, which reinitializes debitCount to zero at the end of each month.

At first glance, the read operations for checking and savings accounts appear to be identical; however, a more careful examination reveals that this is not the case. When we read a checking account, we wish to read the balance and the last deposit amount. When we read a savings account, we wish to read the balance and the accumulated interest. The solution is to have more than one read operation. The generalized read operation is the readBalance operation, which is inherited by both Checking Account and Savings Account. A specialized read operation, readCumulativeInterest, is then added in the Savings Account subclass; and a specialized read operation, readLastDepositAmount, is added to the Checking Account subclass.

The design of the Account generalization/specialization hierarchy is depicted in Figure 14.7 and described next. This figure uses the UML convention of depicting abstract class names in italics.

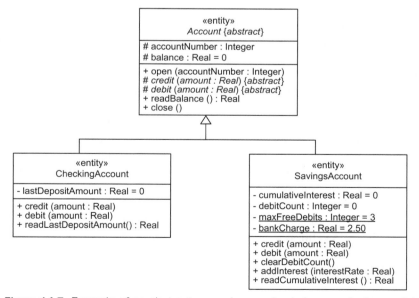

Figure 14.7. Example of an abstract superclass and subclasses: design model

14.8.4 Abstract Superclass and Subclass Design

Design of the Account Abstract Superclass

■ Attributes:
  - Specifies the attributes accountNumber and balance. Both attributes are declared as protected in the Account superclass; hence, they are visible to the subclasses.
■ Operations:
  - Defines the specification and implementation of the operations open, close, and readBalance.
  - Defines the specification of the abstract operations credit and debit.

Design of the Checking Account Subclass

■ Attributes:
  - Inherits the attributes accountNumber and balance.
  - Adds the attribute lastDepositAmount.
■ Operations:
  - Inherits the specification and implementation of the operations open, close, and readBalance.
  - Inherits the specification of the abstract operation credit; defines the implementation to add amount to balance as well as to set lastDepositAmount equal to amount.
  - Inherits the specification of the abstract operation debit; defines the implementation to deduct amount from balance.
  - Adds the operation readLastDepositAmount (): Real.

Design of the Savings Account Subclass

■ Attributes:
  - Inherits the attributes accountNumber and balance.
  - Adds the attributes cumulativeInterest and debitCount.
  - Adds the static class attributes maxFreeDebits and bankCharge. Static attributes are underlined in UML, as shown in Figure 13.9.
■ Operations:
  - Inherits both the specification and implementation of the operations open, close, and readBalance.
  - Inherits the specification of the abstract operation debit; defines the implementation to deduct amount from balance, increment debitCount, and deduct bankCharge from balance if maxFreeDebits is greater than debitCount.
  - Inherits the specification of the abstract operation credit; defines the implementation to add amount to balance.
  - Adds the following operations:
    - addInterest (interestRate : Real), which adds interest on a daily basis
    - readCumulativeInterest () : Real, which returns the cumulative interest of a savings account.
    - clearDebitCount (), which reinitializes debitCount to zero at the end of each month.

14.9 CLASS INTERFACE SPECIFICATIONS

A **class interface specification** defines the interface of the information hiding class, including the specification of the operations provided by the class. It defines the following:

- Information hidden by information hiding class: for example, data structure(s) encapsulated, in the case of a data abstraction class.
- Class structuring criteria used to design this class
- Assumptions made in specifying the class: for example, whether one operation needs to be called before another.
- Anticipated changes. This is to encourage consideration of design for change.
- Superclass (if applicable)
- Inherited operations (if applicable)
- Operations provided by the class. For each operation, define
  - Function performed
  - Precondition (a condition that must be true when the operation is invoked)
  - Postcondition (a condition that must be true at the completion of the operation)
  - Invariant (a condition that must be true at all times: before, during, and after execution of the operation)
  - Input parameters
  - Output parameters
  - Operations used from other classes

14.9.1 Example of Class Interface Specification

An example of a class interface specification for an information hiding class is now given for the Checking Account class depicted in Figure 14.9 and described in Section 14.8.

> **Information Hiding Class:** CheckingAccount
> **Information Hidden:** Encapsulates checking account attributes and their current values.
> **Class structuring criterion:** Data abstraction class
> **Assumptions:** Checking accounts do not have interest.
> **Anticipated changes:** Checking accounts may be allowed to earn interest.
> **Superclass:** Account
> **Inherited operations:** open, credit, debit, readBalance, close
> **Operations provided:**
>   1. credit (**in** amount : Real)
>
>> **Function:** Adds the amount credited to the current balance and stores it as the amount last deposited.
>> **Precondition:** Account has been created.
>> **Postcondition:** Checking account has been credited.
>> **Input parameters:** amount – funds to be added to account
>> **Operations used:** None

2. debit (**in** amount : Real)

>   **Function:** Deducts amount from balance.
>   **Precondition:** Account has been created.
>   **Postcondition:** Checking account has been debited.
>   **Input parameters:** amount – funds to be deducted from account
>   **Output parameters:** None
>   **Operations used:** None

3. readLastDepositAmount (): Real

>   **Function:** Returns the amount last deposited into the account.
>   **Precondition:** Account exists.
>   **Invariant:** Values of account attributes remain unchanged.
>   **Postcondition:** Amount last deposited into the account has been read.
>   **Input parameter:** None
>   **Output parameters:** Amount last deposited into the account
>   **Operations used:** None

14.10 DETAILED DESIGN OF INFORMATION HIDING CLASSES

During detailed design of the information hiding classes, the internal algorithmic design of each operation is determined. The operation internals are documented in pseudocode, which is also known as Structured English. The concept is that the algorithmic design is programming language–independent but can be readily mapped to the implementation language. The pseudocode uses structured programming constructs for decision statements (such as If-Then-Else, loops, and case statements) and English language for sequential statements. An example of an algorithmic design using pseudocode is given next for the Account class.

14.10.1 Detailed Design of the Account Abstract Superclass

■ Attributes:

   accountNumber, balance

■ Operations:
   • open (**in** accountNumber : Integer)

      begin;

            create new account;
            assign accountNumber;
            set balance to zero;

      end.

   • close ()

      begin; close the account; **end.**

■ readBalance () : Real

begin; return value of balance; **end**.

- credit (**in** amount : Real)

    Defer implementation to subclass.

- debit (**in** amount : Real)

    Defer implementation to subclass.

14.10.2 Detailed Design of the Checking Account Subclass

- Attributes:
  - Inherit: accountNumber, balance
  - Declare: lastDepositAmount
- Operations:
  - Inherit specification and implementation: open, close, readBalance
  - Inherit specification and define implementation:

        credit(**in** amount : Real);

            begin;

                Add amount to balance;
                Set lastDepositAmount equal to amount;

            end.

  - Inherit specification and define implementation of:

        debit (**in** amount : Real);

            begin;

                Deduct amount from balance;

            end.

  - Add operation:

        readLastDepositAmount () : Real

            begin;

                return value of lastDepositAmount;

            end.

14.10.3 Detailed Design of the Savings Account Subclass

- Attributes:
  - Inherit: accountNumber, balance
  - Declare: cumulativeInterest, debitCount
  - Declare static class attributes: maxFreeDebits, bankCharge
- Operations:
  - Inherit specification and implementation: open, close, and readBalance.

- Inherit specification and redefine implementation:

  debit (**in** amount : Real);

      begin

          Deduct amount from balance;
          Increment debitCount;
          if maxFreeDebits > debitCount
            then deduct bankCharge from balance;

      end.

- Inherit specification and redefine implementation:

  credit(**in** amount : Real);
      begin; add amount to balance; **end**.

- Declared operations:

  addInterest (interestRate : Real)

      begin

          Compute dailyInterest = balance * interestRate;
          Add dailyInterest to cumulativeInterest and to balance;

      end.

- readCumulativeInterest () : Real

      begin; return value of cumulativeInterest; **end**.

- clearDebitCount (),

      begin; Reset debitCount to zero; **end**.

14.11 POLYMORPHISM AND DYNAMIC BINDING

Polymorphism is Greek for "many forms." In object-oriented design, polymorphism is used to mean that different classes may have the same operation name. The specification of the operation is identical for each class; however, classes can implement the operation differently. This allows objects with identical interfaces to be substituted for each other at run-time.

Dynamic binding is used in conjunction with polymorphism and is the run-time association of a request to an object and one of its operations. With compile-time binding, the typical form of binding used with a procedural language, association of a request to an operation is done at compile time and cannot be changed at run-time. Dynamic binding means that the association of a request to an object's operation is done at run-time and can thus change from one invocation to the next. Looking at it from the requestor's point of view, a variable may reference objects of different classes at different times and invoke an operation of the same name on these different objects.

14.11.1 Example of Polymorphism and Dynamic Binding

Now consider the instantiation of objects from these classes, as well as an example of the use of polymorphism and dynamic binding:

```
begin
private anAccount: Account;
Prompt customer for account type and withdrawal amount
if customer responds checking
    then – assign customer's checking account to anAccount
        . . .
        anAccount := customerCheckingAccount;
        . . .
    elseif customer responds savings
        then – assign customer's savings account to anAccount
        . . .
        anAccount := customerSavingsAccount;
        . . .
    endif;
    . . .
    – debit an Account, which is a checking or savings account
    anAccount.debit (amount);
    . . .
end;
```

In this example, if the account type is a checking account, anAccount is assigned a Checking Account object. Executing anAccount.debit will invoke the debit operation of the Checking Account object. If, on the other hand, the account is a savings account, executing anAccount.debit will invoke the debit operation of a Savings Account object. A different variant of the debit operation is executed for savings accounts than for checking accounts, because the specialized variant operation for savings accounts has an additional bank charge if the maximum number of free debits has been exceeded.

It should be noted that an object of type Checking Account or type Savings Account can be assigned to an object of type Account but not vice versa. This is because every Checking Account subclass **is a**(n) Account superclass and every Savings Account subclass **is a**(n) Account superclass. However, the reverse is not possible, because not every account is a checking account – it might be a savings account!

14.12 IMPLEMENTATION OF CLASSES IN JAVA

This section describes the implementation of classes with an example of how classes are implemented in Java. The class operations are implemented as Java methods. Consider the ATMCash class depicted in Figure 14.2 and described in Section

14.4.1. As shown below, after the declaration of the public class name comes the declaration of the private variables, the amount of cash available, the number of five-, ten-, and twenty-dollar bills, all of which are initialized to zero. This is followed by the declaration of the public methods, addCash and withdrawCash.

The addCash method has three integer input parameters – the number five-, ten-, and twenty-dollar bills to be added. In the implementation, the count of new bills of each denomination is added to the bill counts already stored in the ATM. The value of the cashAvailable variable is then computed by adding the total cash value of the bills of each denomination.

In the withdrawCash method, the amount desired to withdraw is the first parameter cashAmount. The second parameter is the integer array in which are returned the number of five-, ten-, and twenty-dollar bills to dispense.

```
public class ATMCash {
    private int cashAvailable = 0;
        int fives = 0;
        int tens = 0;
        int twenties = 0;
    public void addCash(int fivesAdded, int tensAdded, int twentiesAdded) {
        // increment the number of bills of each denomination
        fives = fives + fivesAdded;
        tens = tens + tensAdded;
        twenties = twenties + twentiesAdded;
        // set the total cash in the ATM
        cashAvailable = 5 * fives + 10 * tens + 20 * twenties;
    }
    public int withdrawCash(int cashAmount, int [] bills) {}
    // given the cash amount to withdraw, return the number of bills of
    each denomination
```

14.13 SUMMARY

This chapter described the design of object-oriented software architectures using the concepts of information hiding, classes, and inheritance. This chapter described the design of information hiding classes, from which the passive objects are instantiated. These classes were originally determined during the object and class structuring step in analysis modeling, as described in Chapter 8. This chapter also described the design of the operations of each class and the design of the class interfaces, as well as the use of inheritance in software design. For more information on the design of classes and inheritance and on the use of preconditions, postconditions, and invariants in software construction, an excellent reference is Meyer (2000). Another informative reference that describes these topics from a UML perspective is Page-Jones (2000).

The object-oriented design concepts described in this chapter result in the design of a sequential object-oriented software architecture, which would be implemented as a sequential program with one thread of control. An example of the design of a sequential object-oriented software architecture is the Banking Service subsystem in the Banking System case study described in Chapter 21.

Object-oriented concepts are also applied and extended in the design of more advanced software architectures, including client-server software architectures (Chapter 15), service-oriented architectures (Chapter 16), component-based software architectures (Chapter 17), concurrent and real-time software architectures (Chapter 18), and software product line architectures (Chapter 19).

EXERCISES

Multiple-choice questions: For each question, choose one of the answers.

1. What is an information hiding object?
   (a) An active object that encapsulates data
   (b) A passive object that encapsulates data
   (c) A class that encapsulates data
   (d) A task that encapsulates data

2. What is a class interface?
   (a) Specifies the internals of the operations of a class
   (b) Specifies the externally visible operations of a class
   (c) Specifies the parameters of a class operation.
   (d) Specifies the signature of a class operation

3. Which of the following is NOT an object-oriented concept?
   (a) Information hiding
   (b) Class
   (c) Subclass
   (d) Subroutine

4. Which of the following is a class that realizes an interface?
   (a) The class calls the interface.
   (b) The class implements the interface.
   (c) The class is called by the interface.
   (d) The class is independent of the interface.

5. Which of the following is an entity class?
   (a) An information hiding class
   (b) A subclass
   (c) A control class
   (d) A data abstraction class

6. What does a state machine class encapsulate?
   (a) A state transition table

   (b) A statechart
   (c) The current state of the machine
   (d) A state transition table and the current state of the machine

7. Which of the following is unlikely to be a graphical user interface class?
   (a) A menu
   (b) A window
   (c) A button
   (d) A pin

8. Which of the following is unlikely to be encapsulated in a business logic class?
   (a) A business rule
   (b) Calls to operations of an entity class
   (c) Deny cash withdrawal if balance of account is less than $10
   (d) A dialog box

9. Which of the following is NOT allowed through inheritance?
   (a) Subclass inherits attributes from superclass.
   (b) Subclass inherits operations from superclass.
   (c) Subclass redefines attributes inherited from superclass.
   (d) Subclass redefines operations inherited from superclass.

10. Which of the following is true for an abstract class?
    (a) It is used as a template for creating objects.
    (b) It is used as a template for creating subclasses.
    (c) It is used as a template for creating classes.
    (d) It is used as a template for creating superclasses.

11. In object-oriented design, polymorphism means that:
    (a) Different classes may have the same name.

(b) Different classes may have the same interface name.

(c) Different classes may have the same superclass name.

(d) Different classes may have the same operation name.

12. With polymorphism and dynamic binding, an object can:

(a) Invoke operation of different names on the same objects.

(b) Invoke operations of different names on different objects.

(c) Invoke an operation of the same name on the same object.

(d) Invoke an operation of the same name on different objects.

15

Designing Client/Server Software Architectures

This chapter describes the design of software architectures for client/server systems. In these systems, a **client** is a requester of services and a **server** is a provider of services. Typical servers are file servers, database servers, and line printer servers. **Client/server** architectures are based on client/service architectural patterns, the simplest of which consists of one service and multiple clients. This pattern has several variations, which will be described in this chapter. In addition, certain decisions need to be considered about the design of client/server architectures, such as whether the server should be designed as a sequential or concurrent subsystem, what architectural structure patterns to use for the design of the client/server architecture, and what architectural communication patterns to use for interaction between the clients and the services.

This chapter differentiates between a *server* and a *service*. A *server* is a hardware/software system that provides one or more services for multiple clients. A *service* in a client/server system is an application software component that fulfills the needs of multiple clients. Because services execute on servers, there is sometimes confusion between the two terms, and the two terms are sometimes used interchangeably. Sometimes, a server will support just one service or perhaps more than one; on the other hand, a large service might span more than one server node. In client/server systems, the service executes on a fixed server node(s) and the client has a fixed connection to the server.

Section 15.1 describes concepts, architectures, and patterns for client/server architectures. Sections 15.2 and 15.3 describe client/service software architectural patterns, and Section 15.4 provides an overview of middleware technology in client/server systems. Section 15.5 describes the design of sequential service subsystems and concurrent service subsystems. Because servers are frequently database-intensive, Section 15.6 describes wrapper classes, which leads into the discussion of the database wrapper classes. This is followed by a description of the logical database design for client/server systems in Section 15.7.

15.1 CONCEPTS, ARCHITECTURES, AND PATTERNS FOR CLIENT/SERVER ARCHITECTURES

This chapter describes client/server software architectures in which there are multiple clients and one or more services, and addresses the characteristics of both sequential and concurrent services. Chapter 16 describes service-oriented software architectures, which builds on the concept of loosely coupled services that can be discovered and linked to by clients with the assistance of service brokers. Chapter 17 describes a more general component-based software architecture in which all classes are designed as components.

The simplest client/server architecture has one service and many clients. More complex client/server systems might have multiple services. Section 15.2 describes a variety of client/service architectural structure patterns, including Multiple Client/Single Service pattern and Multiple Client/Multiple Service pattern. Section 15.3 describes architectural communication patterns for client/server architectures, including Synchronous Message Communication with Reply and Asynchronous Message Communication with Callback.

15.2 CLIENT/SERVICE SOFTWARE ARCHITECTURAL STRUCTURE PATTERNS

This section describes a variety of client/service software architectural structure patterns ranging from multiple clients with a single service to multiple clients with multiple services and multi-tier client/server architectures.

15.2.1 Multiple Client/Single Service Architectural Pattern

The **Multiple Client/Single Service** architectural pattern consists of several clients that request a service and a service that fulfills client requests. The simplest and most common client/server architecture has one service and many clients, and for this reason the Multiple Client/Single Service architectural pattern is also known as the *Client/Server* or *Client/Service* pattern. The Multiple Client/Single Service architectural pattern can be depicted on a deployment diagram, as in Figure 15.1, which shows multiple clients connected to a service that executes on a server node via a local area network.

An example of this pattern comes from the Banking System, as depicted on the class diagram in Figure 15.2. This system contains multiple ATMs and one banking service. For each ATM there is one ATM Client Subsystem, which handles customer requests by reading the ATM card and prompting for transaction details at the keyboard/display. For an approved withdrawal request, the ATM dispenses cash, prints a receipt, and ejects the ATM card. The Banking Service maintains a database of customer accounts and customer ATM cards. It validates ATM transactions and either approves or rejects customer requests, depending on the status of the customer accounts.

The Multiple Client/Single Service architectural pattern can also be depicted on a communication diagram, as shown in Figure 15.3 for the Banking System and described in more detail in Chapter 19. The clients are ATM Client components,

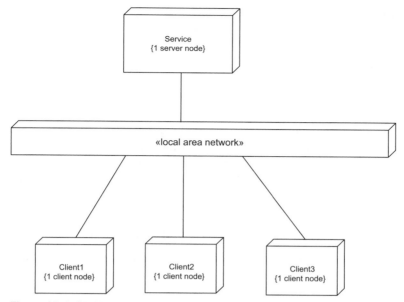

Figure 15.1. Multiple Client/Single Service architectural pattern

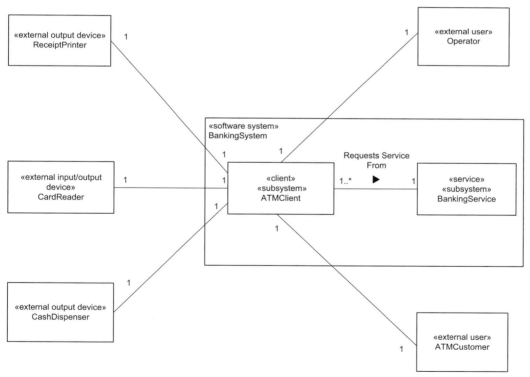

Figure 15.2. Example of Multiple Client/Single Service architectural pattern: Banking System

Figure 15.3. Example of Multiple Client/Single Service architectural pattern: Banking System communication diagram

which send synchronous messages to the Banking Service. Each client is tightly coupled with the service, because it sends a message and then waits for a response. After receiving the message, the service processes the message, prepares a reply, and sends the reply to the client. After receiving the response, the client resumes execution.

15.2.2 Multiple Client/Multiple Service Architectural Pattern

More complex client/server systems might support multiple services. In the **Multiple Client/Multiple Service** pattern, in addition to clients requesting a service, a client might communicate with several services, and services might communicate with each other. The Multiple Client/Multiple Service pattern is depicted on the deployment diagram in Figure 15.4, in which each service resides on a separate server node, and both services can be invoked by the same client. With this pattern, a client could communicate with each service sequentially or could communicate with multiple services concurrently.

An example of the Multiple Client/Multiple Service architectural pattern is a banking consortium consisting of multiple interconnected banks, such as the

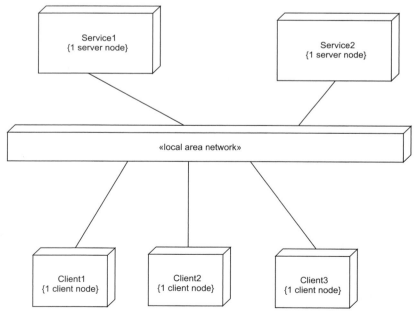

Figure 15.4. Multiple Client/Multiple Service architectural pattern

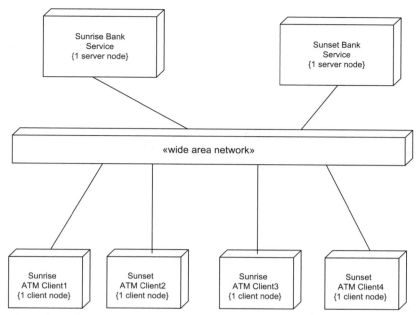

Figure 15.5. Example of Multiple Client/Multiple Service architectural pattern: Banking Federation System

Banking Federation System shown in Figure 15.5. Continuing with the ATM example, besides several ATM clients accessing the same bank service, it is possible for one ATM client to access multiple bank services. This feature allows customers to access their own bank service from a different bank's ATM client. In this example, ATM customers from Sunrise bank can withdraw funds from Sunset bank in addition to their own Sunrise bank, and vice versa. Figure 15.5 depicts the two bank services, Sunrise Bank Service and Sunset Bank Service, as well as two instances of each of the clients, Sunrise ATM Client and Sunset ATM Client.

15.2.3 Multi-tier Client/Service Architectural Pattern

The **Multi-tier Client/Service** pattern has an intermediate tier (i.e., layer) that provides both a client and a service role. An intermediate tier is a client of its service tier and also provides a service for its clients. It is possible to have more than one intermediate tier. When viewed as a layered architecture, the client is considered to be at a higher layer than the service because the client depends on and uses the service.

Figure 15.6. Example of the Multi-tier Client/Service architectural pattern: a three-tier Banking System

An example of a three-tier client/service pattern for the banking system is given in Figure 15.5. The Banking Service tier provides a service to the ATM Client tier but is itself a client of the Database Service tier. Because the third tier is provided by a COTS database management system, it is not part of the application software and so is not explicitly depicted in the application-level communication diagram shown in Figure 15.3. Furthermore, the Bank Service and Database Service might execute on the same server node.

15.3 ARCHITECTURAL COMMUNICATION PATTERNS FOR CLIENT/SERVER ARCHITECTURES

In client/server communication, there is usually a request from a client to a service, and a response from the service. In some cases, there might not be a service response, for example, when data are being updated instead of requested. The nature of the communication between the client and service affects the communication patterns used. However, several software architectural communication patterns can be used, as summarized below:

- Synchronous Message Communication with Reply, as described in Section 15.3.1
- Asynchronous Message Communication, as described in Chapter 12
- Asynchronous Message Communication with Callback, as described in Section 15.3.2
- Synchronous Communication without Reply, as described in Chapter 18
- Broker patterns, as described in Chapter 16
- Group communication patterns, as described in Chapter 17

15.3.1 Synchronous Message Communication with Reply Pattern

The most common form of software architectural communication pattern for client/server communication is **Synchronous Message Communication with Reply**, also known as the request/response pattern.

Synchronous Message Communication with Reply (Figure 15.7) can involve a single client sending a message to a service and then waiting for a reply, in which case no message queue develops between the client and the service. However, it is more likely to involve multiple clients interacting with a single service, as described next. In the typical client/server situation, each client sends a request message to a service and waits for a response from it. In this pattern, because there are several clients sending service requests, a message queue can build up at the service. The client uses synchronous message communication and waits for a response from the service.

Figure 15.7. Synchronous Message Communication with Reply pattern

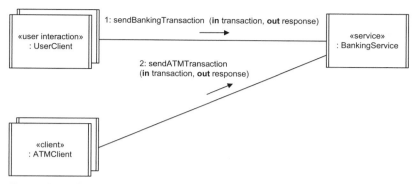

Figure 15.8. Examples of the Synchronous Message Communication with Reply pattern: Banking application

Whether the client uses synchronous or asynchronous message communication with the service depends on the application and does not affect the design of the service. Indeed, some of a service's clients may communicate with it via synchronous message communication and others via asynchronous message communication. An example of Multiple Client/Single Service message communication using synchronous message communication with reply is shown in Figure 15.8, in which the Banking Service responds to service requests from multiple clients, both user clients and ATM clients. Banking Service has a message queue of incoming synchronous requests from the multiple clients. Each ATM Client component sends a synchronous message to Banking Service and then waits for the response. The service processes each incoming transaction message on a FIFO basis and then sends a synchronous response message to the client.

If the client and server are to have a dialog that involves several messages and responses, a connection can be established between them. Messages are then sent and received over the connection.

15.3.2 Asynchronous Message Communication with Callback Pattern

The **Asynchronous Message Communication with Callback** pattern is used between a client and a service when the client sends a request to the service and can continue executing without needing to wait for the service response; however, it does need the service response later (Figure 15.9). The callback is an asynchronous response to a client request message sent previously. This pattern allows the client to execute asynchronously but still follows the client/service paradigm in which a client sends only one message at a time to the service and receives a response from the service.

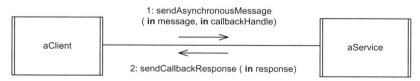

Figure 15.9. Asynchronous Message Communication with Callback pattern

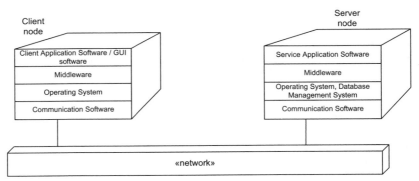

Figure 15.10. Example of middleware in client and server nodes

With the callback pattern, the client sends a remote reference or handle, which is then used by the service to respond to the client. A variation on the callback pattern is for the service to delegate the response to another component by forwarding to it the callback handle.

15.4 MIDDLEWARE IN CLIENT/SERVER SYSTEMS

Middleware is a layer of software that sits above the heterogeneous operating system to provide a uniform platform above which distributed applications, such as client/server systems, can run (Bacon 1997). An early form of middleware was the remote procedure call (RPC). Other examples of middleware technology (Szyperski 2003) are Distributed Computing Environment (DCE), which uses RPC technology; Java remote method invocation (RMI); Component Object Model (COM); Jini Java 2 Platform Enterprise Edition (J2EE); and Common Object Request Broker Architecture (CORBA) .

An example of middleware in a client/server configuration is shown in Figure 15.10. On the client node is the client application, which uses a graphical user interface (GUI). There is a standard operating system, such as Windows, and network communication software, such as TCP/IP (Transmission Control Protocol/Internet Protocol), which is the most widely used protocol on the Internet. A middleware layer sits above the operating system and the network communication software. On the server node is the service application software, which makes use of the middleware services that reside on top of the operating system (e.g., UNIX, Linux, or Windows), and the network communication software. A file or database management system, usually relational, is used for long-term information storage.

15.4.1 Platforms for Client/Server Systems

Communication in the client/server architecture is frequently synchronous communication, which is typically provided by middleware technology such as the remote procedure call (RPC) or remote method invocation (RMI). With RPC, procedures are located in the address space of the servers and are invoked by remote procedure calls from clients. The server receives a request from a client, invokes the appropriate procedure, and returns a reply to the client.

15.4.2 Java Remote Method Invocation

The Java programming environment supports a middleware technology called Java remote method invocation (RMI) to allow distributed Java objects to communicate with each other. With RMI, instead of sending a message to a specific procedure (as with RPC), the client object sends the message to a specific service object and invokes the object's method (procedure or function).

A client object on the client node makes a remote method invocation to a service object on the server node. A remote method invocation is similar to a local method invocation, so the fact that the service object is on a remote server node is hidden from the client.

A client proxy provides the same interface to the client object as the service object and hides all the details of the communication from the client. On the server side, a service proxy hides all the details of the communication from the service object. The service proxy invokes the service object's method. If the service object is not present, the service proxy instantiates the service object.

The local method called by the client is provided by the client proxy. The client proxy takes the local request and any parameters, packs them into a message (this process is often referred to as *marshalling*), and sends the message to the server node. At the server node, the service proxy unpacks the message (referred to as *unmarshalling*) and calls the appropriate service method (which represents the remote method invocation), passing it any parameters. When the service method finishes processing the request, it returns any results to the service proxy. The service proxy packs the results into a response message, which it sends to the client proxy. The client proxy extracts the results from the message and returns them as output parameters to the client object.

Thus, the role of the client and service proxies is to make the remote method invocation appear like a local method invocation to both the client and service, as illustrated in Figure 15.11. Figure 15.11a depicts one object making a local method invocation to another object. Figure 15.11b depicts a communication diagram showing the message sequence for the distributed solution to the same problem, in which an object on the client node makes a remote method invocation to a service object on the server node. The local method invocation is to the client proxy (1), which *marshals* the method name and parameters into the message, and then sends the message over the network (2). The service proxy on the remote node receives the message, *unmarshals* the message, and calls the remote method of the service object (3). For the service response (4), the service proxy *marshals* the response and sends it over the network (5). The client proxy *unmarshals* the response and passes it back to the client object (6).

15.5 DESIGN OF SERVICE SUBSYSTEMS

A service subsystem provides a service for multiple clients. As pointed out in Section 15.2.3, it is very common for services to need access to a database in which

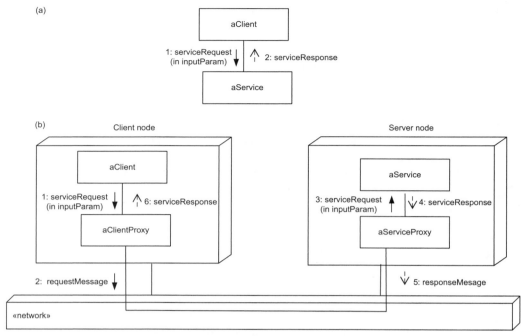

Figure 15.11. Remote method invocation (RMI)

persistent data are stored. Section 15.7 describes the design of relational databases, and Section 15.6 describes the design of wrapper classes to provide an object-oriented interface to the database.

A simple service does not initiate any requests for services but responds to requests from clients. There are two kinds of service components: sequential and concurrent.

15.5.1 Sequential Service Design

A sequential service processes client requests sequentially; that is, it completes one request before it starts servicing the next. A **sequential service** is designed as one concurrent object (thread of control) that responds to requests from clients to access the service. For example, a simple sequential service responds to requests from clients to update or read data from a passive data abstraction object. When the service receives a message from a client, it invokes the appropriate operation provided by the passive data abstraction object – for example, to credit or debit an account object in a banking application.

The service typically has a message queue of incoming service requests. There is one message type for each operation provided by the service. The service coordinator unpacks the client's message and, depending on the message type, invokes the appropriate operation provided by a service object. The parameters of the message are used as the parameters of the operation. The service object processes the client's request and returns the appropriate response to the service coordinator, which then prepares a service response message and sends it to the client.

15.5.2 Example of Sequential Service Design

An example of a sequential service is given for the Banking Service of the Banking System. The integrated communication diagram for the Banking Service, consisting of the integration of the use case–based communication diagrams (see Chapter 13), shows all the objects contained in the service and their interactions. Because all communication between objects is by means of operation invocation, the object interfaces are designed to show the synchronous operation invocation as well as the input and output parameters for each operation (using the guidelines given in Chapter 14), as shown in Figure 15.12.

In Figure 15.12, the Banking Service sequentially services ATM transactions from clients requesting PIN validation, withdrawals from accounts, transfers between accounts, and account queries. Banking Service services the transaction, invokes the service operation, returns a bankResponse message to the client, and then services the next transaction. Each transaction is executed to completion before the next transaction is started. The sequential service design should only be used if the server node can adequately handle the transaction rate.

The service is designed using the layers of abstraction pattern. Because the service data are stored in a relational database, at the lowest level of the architecture are database wrapper objects (see Section 15.6), which encapsulate how the data are accessed from the database. At the next layer are the business logic objects, which encapsulate the business rules for processing client requests. At the highest layer is the coordinator object, which uses the **façade** pattern to provide a uniform interface for clients. The façade is provided by a coordinator object that presents a common interface to clients. During execution, the coordinator (the object providing the façade) delegates each incoming client request to the appropriate business logic object, which in turn interacts with the database wrapper objects that access the database, where the account and debit card data are stored.

Thus, when an ATM Client sends a PIN validation request to the Banking Service, the request is received by the Bank Transaction Coordinator, which delegates it to the PIN Validation Transaction Manager. This business logic object will then access both the Debit Card and Card Account database wrapper objects to carry out the validation and return the validation response to the coordinator, which in turn sends a synchronous response to the client request. This example is described in more detail in the Client/Server Banking System design described in Chapter 21.

15.5.3 Concurrent Service Design

In a concurrent service design, the service functionality is shared among several concurrent objects. If the client demand for services is high enough that the sequential service could potentially become a bottleneck in the system, an alternative approach is for the services to be provided by a concurrent service consisting of several concurrent objects. This approach assumes that improved throughput can be obtained by objects providing concurrent access to the data – for example, if the data are stored on secondary storage.

An example of a concurrent service design is given in Figure 15.13. This shows an alternative design for the Banking Service, in which the Bank Transaction Coordinator

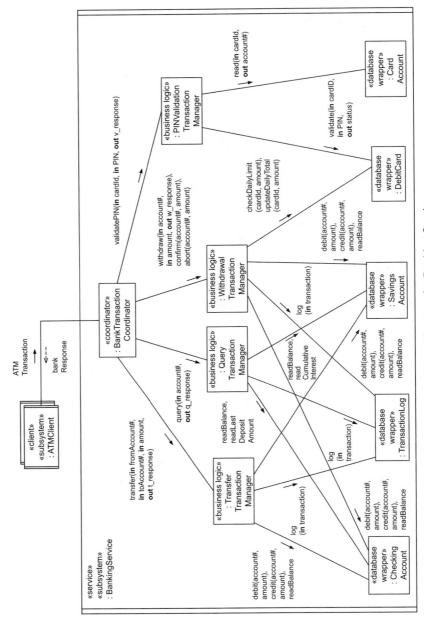

Figure 15.12. Example of object-oriented software architecture for Banking Service

264

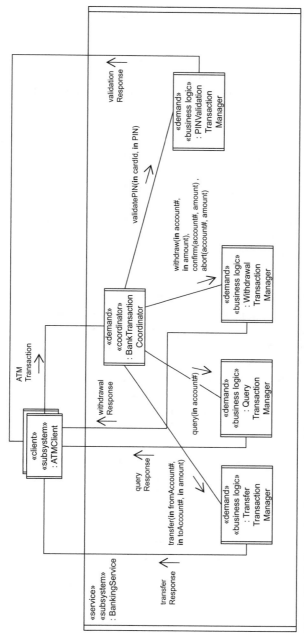

Figure 15.13. Example of concurrent object-oriented software architecture for Banking Service

and each transaction manager is designed as a separate concurrent object. The Bank Transaction Coordinator delegates individual transactions to the individual transaction managers to allow concurrent processing of transactions. More than one instance of each transaction manager could also be executed. Access to the database wrapper objects (not shown) also needs to be synchronized.

In this example, the clients communicate with the service by using the Asynchronous Message Communication with Callback pattern (see Section 15.2.1). This means that the clients do not wait and can do other things before receiving the service response. In this case, the service response is handled as a **callback**. With the callback approach, the client sends an operation handle with the original request. The service uses the handle to remotely call the client operation (the callback) when it finishes servicing the client request. In the example illustrated in Figure 15.13, Bank Transaction Coordinator passes the ATM Client's callback handle to the appropriate transaction manager. On completion, the transaction manager concurrent object remotely invokes the callback, which is depicted as the appropriate service response message sent to the ATM client.

15.6 DESIGN OF WRAPPER CLASSES

Although many legacy applications cannot be easily integrated into a new application, one approach is to develop wrapper classes. A **wrapper class** is a server class that handles the communication and management of client requests to legacy applications (Tanenbaum and Van Steen 2006).

Most legacy applications were developed as stand-alone applications. In some cases, the legacy code is modified so that the wrapper class can access it. However, such modification is often impractical because there is often little or no documentation and the original developers are no longer present. Consequently, wrapper classes often interface to legacy code through crude mechanisms such as files, which might be purely sequential or indexed sequential files. The wrapper class reads or updates files maintained by the legacy application. If the legacy application uses a database, the database could be accessed directly through the use of database wrapper classes that would hide the details of how to access the database. For example, with a relational database, the database wrapper would use Structured Query Language (SQL) statements to access the database.

Developers can integrate legacy code into a client/server application by placing a wrapper around the legacy code and providing an interface to it. The wrapper converts external requests from clients into calls to the legacy code. The wrapper also converts outputs from the legacy code into responses to the client.

15.6.1 Design of Database Wrapper Classes

In the analysis model, an entity class is designed that encapsulates data. During design, a decision has to be made whether the encapsulated data are to be managed directly by the entity class or whether the data are actually to be stored in a database. The former case is handled by **data abstraction classes**, which encapsulate data structures, as described in Section 14.4. The latter case is handled by **database**

wrapper classes, which hide how the data are accessed if stored in a database, and they are described in this section. In client/server systems, data abstraction classes are more likely to be designed on the client side, but they might also be needed on the server side. However database wrapper classes are much more likely to be designed on the server side, because that is where the database support is provided.

Most databases in use today are relational databases, so the database wrapper class provides an object-oriented interface to the database. If a relational database is being used, any entity class defined in the static model that is to be mapped to a relational database needs to be determined and designed as a database wrapper class. Sometimes, data retrieved from a database via a database wrapper class are stored temporarily in a data abstraction class.

The attributes of the analysis model entity class are mapped to a database relational table (as described in Section 15.7), and the operations to access the attributes are mapped to a database wrapper class.

The database wrapper class hides the details of how to access the data maintained in the relational table, so it hides all the SQL statements. A database wrapper class usually hides the details of access to one relational table. However, a database wrapper class might also hide a database view; that is, a SQL *join* of two or more relations (Silberschatz, Korth, and Sudarshan 2010).

15.6.2 Example of Database Wrapper Class

An example of a database wrapper class is given in Figure 15.14. In the Banking System example, all persistent data are stored in a relational database. Hence, each entity class maintained at the bank server is mapped to both a database relational

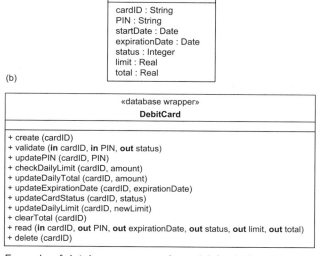

(a)

```
          «entity»
          DebitCard

cardID : String
PIN : String
startDate : Date
expirationDate : Date
status : Integer
limit : Real
total : Real
```

(b)

```
               «database wrapper»
               DebitCard

+ create (cardID)
+ validate (in cardID, in PIN, out status)
+ updatePIN (cardID, PIN)
+ checkDailyLimit (cardID, amount)
+ updateDailyTotal (cardID, amount)
+ updateExpirationDate (cardID, expirationDate)
+ updateCardStatus (cardID, status)
+ updateDailyLimit (cardID, newLimit)
+ clearTotal (cardID)
+ read (in cardID, out PIN, out expirationDate, out status, out limit, out total)
+ delete (cardID)
```

Figure 15.14. Example of database wrapper class: (*a*) Analysis model. (*b*) Design model

table and a database wrapper class. For example, consider the Debit Card entity class as depicted in the analysis model in Figure 15.14*a*. As the debit card data will actually be stored in a relational database, from a database perspective, the entity class is mapped to a relational table. The attributes of the entity class are mapped to the attributes of the relation.

It is also necessary to design the Debit Card database wrapper class (Figure 15.14*b*), which has the following operations: create, validate, checkDailyLimit, clearTotal, update, read, and delete. These operations encapsulate the SQL statements for accessing the Debit Card relational table. Note that because the class attributes can be updated separately, different update operations are provided for each of the attributes that are updated, such as the daily limit and the card status. A call to each of the operations results in execution of a SQL statement.

15.7 FROM STATIC MODELS TO RELATIONAL DATABASE DESIGN

This section describes how the data contained in the entity classes of a static model are mapped to a database. Most databases are relational databases; the objective is therefore to carry out the logical design of the relational database from the conceptual static model, particularly for those entity classes that need to be persistent. For other information on relational database design, such as normalization, the reader should refer to a standard database textbook such as that by Silberschatz, Korth, and Sudarshan (2010).

It is useful to refer to Chapter 7 for the details of entity class modeling, which is the starting point for relational database design. The relational database design involves the design of the relational tables and primary keys, design of foreign keys to represent associations, design of association tables to represent association classes, design of whole/part (aggregation) relationships, and design of generalization/specialization relationships.

15.7.1 Relational Database Concepts

A relational database consists of several relational tables, each with a unique name. In the simplest case, an entity class is designed as a relational table with the entity class name corresponding to the name of the table. Each attribute of the entity class maps to a column of the table. Each object instance maps to a row of the table.

For example, the entity class Account (Figure 15.15*a*) is designed as a relational table of the same name. The attributes, accountNumber and balance, become the columns of the table. Each instance of an account becomes a row of the table, as shown in Table 15.1, which depicts an Account table with three individual accounts.

Table 15.1. Account relational table

accountNumber	balance
1234	398.07
5678	439.72
1287	851.65

15.7.2 Identifying Primary Keys

Each relational table in a relational database must have a primary key. In its simplest form, the primary key is an attribute that is used to uniquely locate a row in a table. For example, the account number is the primary key of the Account table, because it uniquely identifies an individual account. The relational table can be expressed using the following notation:

Account (<u>accountNumber</u>, balance)

With this notation, Account is the name of the table, and accountNumber and balance are the attributes. The <u>primary key</u> is underlined. Thus, in the Account table, <u>accountNumber</u> is the primary key.

In some tables, it is necessary to have a primary key that is a combination of more than one attribute. For example, if the Account table stores both checking accounts and savings accounts (with overlapping account numbers), a second attribute (the account type) would also be needed as part of the primary key, to uniquely locate an individual account. In this example, the primary key is a concatenated key consisting of the attributes <u>accountNumber</u> and <u>accountType</u>.

Account (<u>accountNumber</u>, <u>accountType</u>, balance)

15.7.3 Mapping Associations to Foreign Keys

Associations in relational databases can be represented in different ways. The simplest way is used for one-to-one and one-to-many associations, in which the association is represented by a foreign key. A foreign key is a primary key of one table that is embedded in another table and is used to represent the mapping of an association between classes into a table. A foreign key allows navigation between tables.

For example, to depict the relationship between Customer and Account (as shown in the class diagram in Figure 15.15), which is Customer *Owns* Account, the primary key of the Customer table customerId is added as a foreign key to the

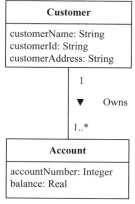

Figure 15.15. Identifying primary and secondary keys (one-to-many association)

Table 15.2. Navigation between relational tables

Navigation from *customerId* (foreign key) in Account table . . .

accountNumber	Balance	customerId
1234	398.07	24193
5678	439.72	26537
1287	851.65	21849

. . . to customerId (primary key) in Customer Table

customerName	customerId	customerAddress
Smith	21849	New York
Patel	26537	Chicago
Chang	24193	Washington

Account table. The Account table is then depicted as follows with the primary key underlined and the *foreign key* in italics.

Account (accountNumber, balance, *customerId*)

In this way, it is possible to navigate from a row in the Account table (e.g., where the *customerId* foreign key is 26537) to the row in the Customer table where the same customerId is the primary key, in order to retrieve more data about the customer, as shown in Table 15.2.

15.7.3.1 Mapping One-to-One and Zero-or-One Associations to Foreign Keys

In a one-to-one association between two classes, there is a choice of foreign key. The primary key of either relational table can be designed as a foreign key in the other relational table. In the case of a zero-or-one association between two classes, the foreign key must be in the "optional" relational table to avoid null references, which are considered undesirable by database designers.

For example, consider the zero-or-one association in the relationship Customer *Owns* Debit Card, which is depicted in the static model (Figure 15.16). In the relational database design, customerId is chosen as the primary key of the Customer table and cardId is chosen as the primary key of the Debit Card table.

Customer (customerName, customerId, customerAddress)

Because it is possible for a customer not to have a debit card (optional relationship), making *cardId* a foreign key in the Customer table would result in some customers having a null value for card id. On the other hand, because each debit card is always owned by a customer (one-to-one relationship), making *customerId* a foreign key in the Debit Card table is a better solution because it would never have a null value. *customerId* is therefore chosen as foreign key in Debit Card, as it represents the association between **Customer** and **Debit Card** tables:

Debit Card (cardId, PIN, expirationDate, status, *customerId*)
(underline = primary key, italic = *foreign key*)

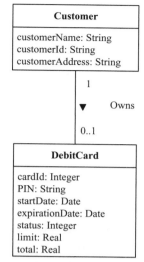

Figure 15.16. Identifying primary and secondary keys (zero-or-one association)

15.7.3.2 Mapping One-to-Many Associations to Foreign Keys

A one-to-many association is designed as a relational structure such that the foreign key is in the "many" relational table. Consider the one-to-many association Customer <u>Owns</u> Account, as depicted on the class diagram in Figure 15.15. In the relational database design, the primary key of the "one" relational table (Customer) is chosen as the foreign key in the "many" relational table (Account).

In this example, the <u>customerId</u> is chosen as primary key of the Customer table:

Customer (customerName, <u>customerId</u>, customerAddress)

The accountNumber is chosen as the primary key of the Account table. *customerId* is also chosen to be the foreign key in the Account table:

Account (<u>accountNumber</u>, balance, *customerId*)

In this example, because every account has one customer (one-to-one relationship), there will always be one value for the foreign key *customerId*. If the foreign key was *accountNumber* in the Customer table, the foreign key would need to be a list, because each customer can have many accounts (one-to-many relationship). An attribute array within a relational table is not allowed, because it would necessitate a hierarchy, which would violate the flat (nonhierarchical) table rule for relational databases.

15.7.4 Mapping Association Classes to Association Tables

An association class models an association between two or more classes and is typically used to represent a many-to-many association. An association class is mapped to an association table. An association table represents the association between two or more relations. The primary key of an association table is the concatenated key

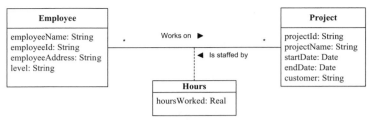

Figure 15.17. Mapping association class to association table

formed from the primary key of each relational table that participates in the association.

For example, in the static model in Figure 15.17, the Hours association class represents the association between the Project and Employee classes. The Hours class has one attribute, hoursWorked, which is an attribute of the association, because it represents the time worked by an individual employee on a specific project.

Each entity class is mapped to a relational table, including the Hours association class, which is designed as the association table called Hours. In the relational database design, projectId is selected as the primary key of the Project table and employeeId is selected as the primary key of the Employee table. These two primary keys form a concatenated primary key (projectId, employeeId) of the Hours association table. Each of these two attributes is also a foreign key: *projectId* allows navigation from the Hours table to the Project table, whereas *employeeId* allows navigation from the Hours table to the Employee table. The tables are designed as follows:

Project (projectId, projectName)
Employee (employeeId, employeeName, employeeAddress)
Hours (*projectId*, *employeeId*, hoursWorked)

15.7.5 Mapping Whole/Part Relationship to Relational Database

A whole/part relationship is either a composite or aggregate relationship. It consists of one entity class representing the composite or aggregate class, and two or more entity classes representing the part classes. When mapping a whole/part relationship to a relational database, the aggregate or composite (the whole) class is designed as a relational table and each part class is also designed as a relational table.

The primary key of the whole (composite or aggregate) relational table is made one of the following in the part relational table:

- **The primary key of the part table**, in the case of a one-to-one association between the whole class and the part class
- **Part of a concatenated primary key of the part table**, in the case of a one-to-many association between the whole class and the part class
- **A foreign key in the part table**, if a concatenated primary key is not needed to uniquely identify a row in the part table, in the case of a one-to-many association between the whole class and the part class

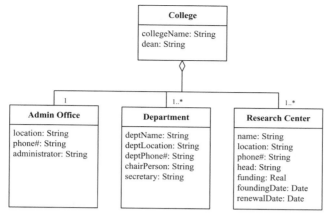

Figure 15.18. Mapping whole/part relationship to relational tables

As an example, consider the aggregate relationship shown in the static model (Figure 15.18), which consists of a Department aggregate (whole) class and three part classes – Department, Admin Office, and Research Center. In the relational database design, the primary key of the aggregate table is collegeName. For the Admin Office part table, which has a one-to-one association with College, the primary key is also <u>collegeName</u>. For the Department part table, which has a one-to-many association with College, it is assumed that <u>departmentName</u> uniquely identifies the department, so collegeName is not needed as an attribute of a concatenated primary key. Instead, *collegeName* is added to become a foreign key, because it allows navigation from the part table Department to the aggregate table College:

> College (<u>collegeName</u>)
> Admin Office (<u>collegeName</u>, location)
> Department (<u>departmentName</u>, *collegeName*, location)

15.7.6 Mapping Generalization/Specialization Relationship to Relational Database

There are three different ways of mapping a generalization/specialization hierarchy to a relational database:

- The superclass and subclasses are each mapped to a relational table.
- Only the subclasses are mapped to relational tables.
- Only the superclass is mapped to a relational table.

15.7.6.1 Mapping Superclass and Subclasses to Relational Tables

The superclass is mapped to a relational table. Each subclass is also mapped to a relational table. There is a shared attribute for the primary key; in other words, the same primary key is used in the superclass and the subclass tables.

The main advantage of this approach is that it is clean and extensible, because each class is mapped to a table. However, the main disadvantage is that superclass/subclass navigation could be slow. In particular, every time the superclass table

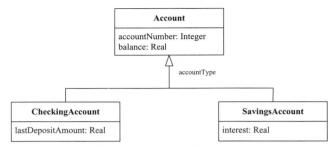

Figure 15.19. Mapping generalization/specialization relationship to relational tables

is accessed, one of the subclass tables will also need to be accessed (to access the subclass attributes), thereby doubling the number of accesses to the database.

In addition, the discriminator, which is an attribute that identifies which property is abstracted in the generalization relationship, is made an explicit attribute of the superclass table. Although the static model does not explicitly use the discriminator as an attribute, it is needed in the superclass table to determine which subclass table to navigate to.

Consider the example of an Account superclass with Checking Account and Savings Account subclasses, as shown in the Static Model (Figure 15.19). In the relational database design, the attributes of the Account superclass become attributes of the Account table, with the primary key of the Account table chosen to be accountNumber. In addition, discriminator attribute accountType becomes an attribute of the Account table. The primary key attribute of the superclass table is also added to each subclass table and becomes the primary key of these tables. Thus, both the Checking Account and Savings Account tables have the same primary key attribute, accountNumber, as the Account table. Note that this solution assumes that the account number is unique.

> Account (accountNumber, accountType, balance)
> Checking Account (accountNumber, lastDepositAmount)
> Savings Account (accountNumber, interest)

15.7.6.2 Mapping Subclasses Only to Relational Tables

In the second case, subclasses only are mapped to relational tables. With this approach, each subclass is designed as a table. However, there is no superclass table. Instead, the superclass attributes are replicated in each subclass table. This approach works particularly well if the subclass has many attributes and the superclass has few attributes. In addition, the application would need to know which subclass to search.

Consider an example of subclasses only mapped to the relational database using the Account Generalization/Specialization Hierarchy, as shown in the Static Model (Figure 15.19). In the relational database design, there are two subclass tables, Checking Account and Savings Account, but no superclass table. The two attributes of the superclass, accountNumber and balance, are replicated in each of the subclass tables and accountNumber is made the primary key of both subclass tables. Thus Checking Account table consists of the two inherited Account attributes (accountNumber and balance) plus the attribute specific to checking accounts, lastDepositAmount. The Savings Account table consists of the two inherited Account attributes plus the attribute specific to savings accounts, interest.

Checking Account (accountNumber, balance, lastDepositAmount)
Savings Account (accountNumber, balance, interest)

The approach of only mapping subclasses to a relational database is most often used to speed up database performance, since it avoids having to navigate between superclass and subclass tables as described in the previous subsection.

15.7.6.3 Mapping Superclass Only to Relational Tables

In the third case, only the superclass is mapped to a relational table and not the subclasses. In this approach, there is one superclass table but no subclass tables. Instead, all the subclass attributes are brought up to the superclass table. The discriminator (accountType) is added as an attribute of the superclass table. Each row in the superclass table uses the attributes relevant to the one subclass it represents with the other attribute values set to null. This approach can be used if the superclass has many attributes, each subclass has only a few attributes, and there are a small number (two or three) of subclasses.

Consider an example of the superclass only mapped to a relational table, using the Account Generalization / Specialization Hierarchy as shown in the Static Model (see Figure 15.19). In the relational database design, there is only one table, an Account table, and no separate subclass tables. The attributes of the two subclasses Checking Account and Savings Account are integrated with the attributes of the Account table. There is one primary key, accountNumber, for the Account table. The balance attribute is also an attribute of this table. In addition, a new attribute representing the discriminator, accountType, is added to differentiate between accounts. The attribute from Checking Account subclass, lastDepositAmount, is integrated into the single Account table. The attribute from Savings Account subclass, interest, is also integrated into the single Account table.

Account (accountNumber, accountType, balance, lastDepositAmount, interest)

15.8 SUMMARY

This chapter described the design of client/server software architectures. These architectures are based on client/service architectural patterns, the simplest of which consists of one service and multiple clients. There are several variations of this pattern, which have been described in this chapter. In addition, there are design decisions to be considered about the design of the client/server architecture, such as whether a service should be designed as a sequential or concurrent subsystem, and what communication patterns to use between the client and service subsystems. Client/server architectures have been incorporated into service-oriented architectures, as described in Chapter 16, and component-based software architectures, as described in Chapter 17. A case study of the design of a client/server software architecture, namely, the Banking System, is presented in Chapter 21. This chapter has also described how static models are mapped to database wrapper classes and relational databases. Mapping a static model to a relational database is described in more detail in Rumbaugh et al. (1991, 2005) and Blaha and Premerlani (1998). More information on relational database design is given in standard database textbooks such as the text by Silberschatz, Korth, and Sudarshan (2010).

EXERCISES

Multiple-choice questions: For each question, choose one of the answers.

1. What is a server?
   (a) A hardware/software system that serves customers
   (b) A subsystem that makes requests and waits for the responses
   (c) A subsystem that responds to requests from clients
   (d) A hardware/software system that provides one or more services for multiple clients

2. The basic client/single service architectural pattern states that:
   (a) Multiple clients request services, and multiple services fulfill client requests.
   (b) Multiple clients request services, and a service fulfills client requests.
   (c) A client requests services, and a service fulfills client requests.
   (d) A client requests services, and multiple services fulfill client requests.

3. In a Multi-tier Client/Service architectural pattern, which of the following is true about an intermediate tier?
   (a) An intermediate tier is a client tier.
   (b) An intermediate tier is a service tier.
   (c) An intermediate tier is both a control tier and a service tier.
   (d) An intermediate tier is both a client tier and a service tier.

4. How is Multiple Client/Multiple Service architectural pattern different from a Multiple Client/Single Service architectural pattern?
   (a) A service can receive requests from multiple clients.
   (b) A client can send requests to multiple services.
   (c) A client can send requests to other clients.
   (d) A service can respond to requests from multiple clients.

5. How is a sequential service designed?
   (a) One object that responds to requests from clients
   (b) Multiple objects that respond to requests from clients
   (c) One subsystem that responds to requests from clients
   (d) Multiple subsystems that respond to requests from clients

6. How is a concurrent service designed?
   (a) One object that responds to requests from clients
   (b) Multiple objects that respond to requests from clients
   (c) One subsystem that responds to requests from clients
   (d) Multiple subsystems that respond to requests from clients

7. What is a database wrapper class?
   (a) A class that encapsulates a data structure
   (b) A class that encapsulates a database
   (c) A class that encapsulates the details of how to access data in a database
   (d) A class that encapsulates a relational table

8. When designing an entity class as a relational table, which of the following is NOT true?
   (a) The relational table has multiple primary keys.
   (b) The relational table has multiple foreign keys.
   (c) The relational table has a primary key.
   (d) The relational table has a concatenated primary key.

9. When mapping an aggregation hierarchy to a relational table, which of the following is NOT true?
   (a) The aggregate and part tables have different primary keys.
   (b) The aggregate and part tables have the same primary key.

(c) The primary key of the aggregate table is a foreign key of the part table.

(d) The primary key of the part table is a foreign key of the aggregate table.

10. When mapping a generalization/specialization relationship to a relational database, which of the following is NOT possible?

(a) The superclass and each subclass are designed as relational tables.

(b) Only subclasses are designed as relational tables.

(c) The aggregate and part classes are designed as relational tables.

(d) Only the superclass is designed as a relational table.

16

Designing Service-Oriented Architectures

A service-oriented architecture (SOA) is a distributed software architecture that consists of multiple autonomous services. The services are distributed such that they can execute on different nodes with different service providers. With a SOA, the goal is to develop software applications that are composed of distributed services, such that individual services can execute on different platforms and be implemented in different languages. Standard protocols are provided to allow services to communicate with each other and to exchange information. In order to allow applications to discover and communicate with services, each service has a service description, The service description defines the name of the service, the location of the service, and its data exchange requirements (Erl 2006, 2009).

A service provider supports services used by multiple clients. Usually, a client will sign up for a service provided by a service provider, such as an Internet, email, or Voice over Internet Protocol (VoIP) service. Unlike client/server architectures, in which a client communicates with a specific service provided on a fixed server configuration, this chapter describes SOAs, which build on the concept of loosely coupled services that can be discovered and linked to by clients (also referred to as service consumers or service requesters) with the assistance of service brokers.

This chapter describes how to design SOAs, how to design services, and how to reuse services. This chapter briefly describes technology support for SOA. However, as the technology is changing rapidly and concepts are longer lasting, this chapter concentrates on architectural concepts, methods, and patterns for designing SOA. This chapter describes software architectural patterns to support SOA, service design, and service reuse.

Section 16.1 describes concepts, architectures, and patterns for SOA. Section 16.2 describes software architectural broker patterns, and Section 16.3 describes technology support for SOAs, which are implemented as web services. Section 16.4 describes software architectural transaction patterns. Section 16.5 describes negotiation patterns. Section 16.6 describes service interface design, Section 16.7 describes service coordination, and Section 16.8 describes designing SOAs. Finally, Section 16.9 describes service reuse.

16.1 CONCEPTS, ARCHITECTURES, AND PATTERNS FOR SERVICE-ORIENTED ARCHITECTURE

An important goal of SOA is to design services as autonomous reusable components. Services are intended to be self-contained and loosely coupled, meaning that dependencies between services are kept to a minimum. Instead of one service depending on another, coordination services are provided in situations in which multiple services need to be accessed and access to them needs to be sequenced. Several software architectural patterns are described for service-oriented applications: Broker patterns, including Service Registration, Service Brokering, and Service Discovery (Section 16.2); Transaction patterns, including Two-Phase Commit, Compound, and Long-Living Transaction patterns (Section 16.4); and Negotiation patterns (Section 16.5).

16.1.1 Design Principles for Services

Services need to be designed according to certain key principles (Erl 2006, 2009). Many of these concepts are good software engineering and design principles, which have been incorporated into SOA design.

- **Loose coupling.** Services should be relatively independent of each other. Thus, a service should hold a minimum amount of information about other services and ideally should not depend on other services.
- **Service contract.** A service provides a contract, which a SOA application can rely on. The contract is typically defined in the service interface in the form of a set of operations. Each operation usually has input and output parameters, but it can also include quality of service parameters such as response time and availability. This principle builds on the object-oriented design concept of separating the interface and the implementation, and establishing the interface as the contract between the provider of the service and the user of the service.
- **Autonomy.** Each service is self-contained, such that it can operate independently without the need of other services. This concept can be achieved by separating services from coordination, so that services do not directly communicate with each other.
- **Abstraction.** As with object-oriented design, the details of a service are hidden, A service only reveals its interface in terms of the operations it provides, and for each operation, the inputs it needs, and the outputs it returns.
- **Reusability.** A key goal of SOA is to design services that are reusable. The preceding design goals of services are intended to facilitate reuse.
- **Composability.** Services are designed to be capable of being assembled into larger composite services. In some cases, a composite service also needs to provide coordination of the individual services.
- **Statelessness.** Where possible, services maintain little or no information about specific client activities.
- **Discoverability.** A service provides an external description to help allow it to be discovered by a discovery mechanism.

16.2 SOFTWARE ARCHITECTURAL BROKER PATTERNS

In a SOA, object brokers act as intermediaries between clients and services. The broker frees clients from having to maintain information about where a particular service is provided and how to obtain that service. Sophisticated brokers provide white pages (naming services) and yellow pages (trader services) so that clients can locate services more easily.

In the **Broker** pattern (which is also known as the *Object Broker* or *Object Request Broker* pattern), the **broker** acts as an intermediary between the clients and services. Services register with the broker. Clients locate services through the broker. After the broker has brokered the connection between client and service, communication between client and service can be direct or via the broker.

The broker provides both location transparency and platform transparency. **Location transparency** means that if the service is moved to a different location, clients are unaware of the move and only the broker needs to be notified. **Platform transparency** means that each service can execute on a different hardware/software platform and does not need to maintain information about the platforms that other services execute on.

With brokered communication, instead of a client having to know the location of a given service, the client queries the broker for services provided. First, the service has to register with a broker as described by the Service Registration pattern in Section 16.2.1. The pattern of communication, in which the client knows the service required but not the location, is referred to as **white page brokering**, analogous to the white pages of the telephone directory, and is described by the Broker Forwarding pattern in Section 16.2.2 and the Broker Handle pattern in Section 16.2.3. Yellow page brokering, in which the specific service is not known and has to be discovered, is described in Section 16.2.4.

16.2.1 Service Registration Pattern

In the **Service Registration** pattern, the service needs to register service information with the broker, including the service name, a description of the service, and the location at which the service is provided. Service registration is carried out the first time the service joins the brokering exchange (analogous to the stock exchange). On subsequent occasions, if the service relocates, it needs to re-register with the broker by providing its new location. The Service Registration pattern is illustrated in Figure 16.1, which depicts the service registering (or re-registering after a relocation) a service with the broker in the following message sequence:

R1: The service sends a register Service request to the broker.
R2: The broker registers the service in the service registry and sends a registration acknowledgment to the service.

16.2.2 Broker Forwarding Pattern

There is more than one way for a broker to handle a client request. With the **Broker Forwarding** pattern, a client sends a message identifying the service

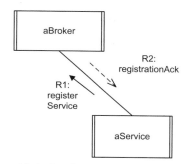

Figure 16.1. Service registration with Broker

required – for example, to withdraw cash from a given bank. The broker receives the client request, determines the location of the service (the ID of the node the service resides on), and forwards the message to the service at the specific location. The message arrives at the service, and the requested service is invoked. The broker receives the service response and forwards it back to the client. The pattern is depicted in Figure 16.2 and consists of the following message sequence:

1. The client (service requester) sends a service request to the broker.
2. The broker looks up the location of the service and forwards the request to the appropriate service.
3. The service executes the request and sends the reply to the broker.
4. The broker forwards the reply to the client.

The Broker Forwarding pattern provides an intermediary for every message sent between a client and a service. This pattern potentially provides a high level of security because each message can be vetted. However, this security comes at the cost of performance compared with the basic Client/Service pattern (see Section 15.1) because the message traffic is doubled, with four messages required for communication from the client to the service via the broker, compared to two messages for direct communication between the client and the service.

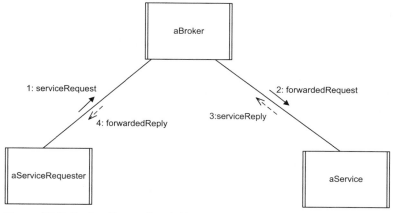

Figure 16.2. Broker Forwarding (white pages) pattern

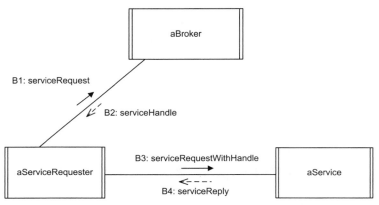

Figure 16.3. Broker Handle (white pages) pattern

16.2.3 Broker Handle Pattern

The **Broker Handle** pattern keeps the benefit of location transparency while adding the advantage of reducing message traffic. Instead of forwarding each client message to the service, the broker returns a service handle to the client, which is then used for direct communication between client and service. This pattern is particularly useful when the client and service are likely to have a dialog and exchange several messages between them. The pattern is depicted in Figure 16.3 and consists of the following message sequence:

B1: The client (service requester) sends a service request to the broker.

B2: The broker looks up the location of the service and returns a service handle to the client.

B3: The client uses the service handle to make the request to the appropriate service.

B4: The service executes the request and sends the reply directly to the client.

This approach is more efficient than Broker Forwarding if the client and service are likely to have a dialog that results in the exchange of several messages. The reason is that with Broker Handle, the interaction with the broker is only done once at the start of the dialog instead of every time, as with Broker Forwarding. Most commercial object brokers use a Broker Handle design. With this approach, it is the responsibility of the client to discard the handle after the dialog is over. Using an old handle is liable to fail because the service might have moved in the interval. If the service does move, it needs to inform the broker so that the broker can update the name table.

16.2.4 Service Discovery Pattern

The brokered patterns of communication described in the preceding sections, in which the client knows the service required but not the location, are referred to as

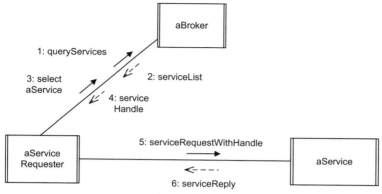

Figure 16.4. Service Discovery (yellow pages) pattern

white page brokering. A different brokering pattern is **yellow page brokering**, analogous to the yellow pages of the telephone directory, in which the client knows the type of service required but not the specific service. This pattern, which is shown in Figure 16.4, is also known as the **Service Discovery** pattern because it allows the client to discover new services. The client sends a query request to the broker, requesting all services of a given type. The broker responds with a list of all services that match the client's request. The client, possibly after consultation with the user, selects a specific service. The broker returns the service handle, which the client uses for communicating directly with the service. The pattern interactions, in which a yellow pages request is followed by a white pages request, are described in more detail as follows:

1. The client (service requester) sends a *yellow pages* request to the broker requesting information about all services of a given type.
2. The broker looks up this information and returns a list of all services that satisfy the query criteria.
3. The client selects one of the services and sends a *white pages* request to the broker.
4. The broker looks up the location of the service and returns a service handle to the client.
5. The client uses the service handle to request the appropriate service.
6. The service executes the request and sends the response directly to the client.

16.3 TECHNOLOGY SUPPORT FOR SERVICE-ORIENTED ARCHITECTURE

Although SOAs are conceptually platform-independent, they are currently provided very successfully on Web service technology platforms. A web service is a service that is accessed using standard Internet and XML-based protocols. This section provides a brief description of technology support for SOA implemented as Web services.

16.3.1 Web Service Protocols

Application clients and services need to have a communication protocol for inter-component communication. Extensible Markup Language (XML) is a technology that allows different systems to interoperate through exchange of data and text. The Simple Object Access Protocol (SOAP), which is a lightweight protocol developed by the World Wide Web Consortium (W3C), builds on XML and HTTP to permit exchange of information in a distributed environment. SOAP defines a unified approach for sending XML-encoded data and consists of three parts: an envelope that defines a framework for describing what is in a message and how to process it, a set of encoding rules for expressing instances of application-defined data types, and a convention for representing remote procedure calls and responses.

16.3.2 Web Services

Applications provide services for clients. One example of application services is **Web services**, which use the World Wide Web for application-to-application communication. From a software perspective, Web services are the application programming interfaces (APIs) that provide a standard means of communication among different software applications on the World Wide Web. From a business application perspective, a Web service is business functionality provided by a company in the form of an explicit service over the Internet for other companies or programs to use. A Web service is provided by a service provider and may be composed of other services to form new services and applications. An example of a Web client invoking a Web service is given in Figure 16.5.

Several component technologies exist to support the building of applications by means of component technology and Web services, including.NET, J2EE, WebSphere, and WebLogic.

16.3.3 Registration Services

A registration service is provided for services to make their services available to clients. Services register their services with a registration service – a process referred

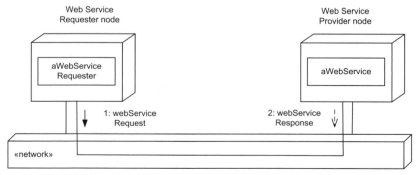

Figure 16.5. Web client and Web service in a World Wide Web services application

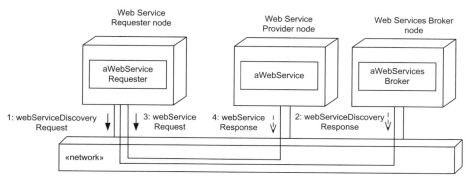

Figure 16.6. Example of a Web services broker

to as *publishing* or *registering* the service. Most brokers, such as CORBA and Web service brokers, provide a registration service. For Web services, a **service registry** is provided to allow services to be published and located via the World Wide Web. Service providers register their services together with service descriptions in a service registry. Clients searching for a service can look up the service registry to find a suitable service. The Web Services Description Language (WSDL) is an XML-based language used to describe what a service does, where it resides, and how to invoke it.

16.3.4 Brokering and Discovery Services

In a distributed environment, an **object broker** is an intermediary in interactions between clients and services. An example of brokering technology is a Web services broker. Information about a Web service can be defined by the Universal Description, Discovery, and Integration (UDDI) framework for Web services integration. A UDDI specification consists of several related documents and an XML schema that defines a SOAP-based protocol for registering and discovering Web services. A Web services broker can use the UDDI framework to provide a mechanism for clients to dynamically find services on the Web.

Figure 16.6 shows an example of a Web client making a Web services discovery request to a Web services broker, which uses the Broker Handle pattern (1). The broker responds by identifying a particular Web service that matches the client's needs (2). The Web client then sends a request to the Web service for the discovered service (3).

16.4 SOFTWARE ARCHITECTURAL TRANSACTION PATTERNS

A service often encapsulates data or provides access to data that need to be read or updated by clients. Many services need to provide coordinated update operations. This section describes how transactions and transaction patterns are used for this purpose.

A **transaction** is a request from a client to a service that consists of two or more operations that perform a single logical function and that must be completed in its entirety or not at all. Transactions are generated at the client and sent to the service for processing. For transactions that need to be atomic (i.e., indivisible), services are needed to begin the transaction, commit the transaction, or abort the transaction. Transactions are typically used for updates to a distributed database that needs to be atomic – for example, transferring funds from an account at one bank to an account at a different bank. With this approach, updates to the distributed database are coordinated such that they are either all performed (commit) or all rolled back (abort).

A transaction must be completed in its entirety or not at all. Consider an inter-bank electronic funds transfer. For a transaction to be considered complete, all its operations must be performed successfully. If any operation of the transaction cannot be performed, the transaction must be aborted. This means that individual operations that have been completed need to be undone, so the effect of an aborted transaction is as if it never occurred.

Transactions have the following properties, sometimes referred to as ACID properties:

- **Atomicity (A).** A transaction is an indivisible unit of work. It is either entirely completed (committed) or aborted (rolled back).
- **Consistency (C).** After the transaction executes, the system must be in a consistent state.
- **Isolation (I).** A transaction's behavior must not be affected by other transactions.
- **Durability (D).** Changes are permanent after a transaction completes. These changes must survive system failures. This is also referred to as *persistence*.

16.4.1 Two-Phase Commit Protocol Pattern

The **Two-Phase Commit Protocol** pattern addresses the problem of managing atomic transactions in distributed systems. Consider two examples of banking transactions:

1. **Withdrawal transaction.** A withdrawal transaction can be handled in one operation. A semaphore is needed for synchronization to ensure that access to the customer account record is mutually exclusive. The transaction processor locks the account record for this customer, performs the update, and then unlocks the record.
2. **Transfer transaction.** Consider a transfer transaction between two accounts – for example, from a savings account to a checking account – in which the accounts are maintained at two separate banks (services). In this case, it is necessary to debit the savings account and credit the checking account. Therefore, the transfer transaction consists of two operations that must be atomic – a debit operation and a credit operation – and the transfer transaction must be either committed or aborted:
   - **Committed.** Both credit and debit operations occur.
   - **Aborted.** Neither the credit nor the debit operation occurs.

One way to achieve this result is to use the Two-Phase Commit Protocol, which synchronizes updates on different nodes in distributed applications. The result of the Two-Phase Commit Protocol is that either the transaction is committed (in which

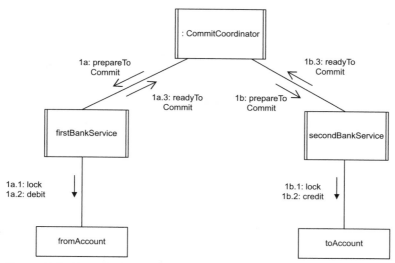

Figure 16.7. Example of the first phase of the Two-Phase Commit Protocol: bank transfer

case all updates succeed) or the transaction is aborted (in which case all updates fail).

Coordination of the transaction is provided by the Commit Coordinator. There is one participant service for each node. There are two participants in the bank transfer transaction: first Bank Service, which maintains the account *from* which money is being transferred (from Account), and second Bank Service, which maintains the account *to* which money is being transferred (to Account). In the first phase of the Two-Phase Commit Protocol (Figure 16.7), Commit Coordinator sends a prepare To Commit message (1a, 1b) to each participant service. Each participant service locks the record (1a.1, 1b.1), performs the debit or credit update (1a.2, 1b.2), and then sends a ready To Commit message (1a.3, 1b.3) to Commit Coordinator. If a participant service is unable to perform the update, it sends a refuse To Commit message. Commit Coordinator waits to receive responses from all participants.

When all participant services have responded, Commit Coordinator proceeds to the second phase of the Two-Phase Commit Protocol (Figure 16.8). If all participants have sent ready To Commit messages, Commit Coordinator sends the commit message (2a, 2b) to each participant service. Each participant service makes the update permanent (2a.1, 2b.1), unlocks the record (2a.2, 2b.2), and sends a commit Completed message (2a.3, 2b.3), to Commit Coordinator. Commit Coordinator waits for all commit Completed messages.

If a participant service responds to the prepare To Commit message with a ready To Commit message, it is committed to completing the transaction. The participant service must then complete the transaction even if a delay occurs (e.g., even if it goes down after it has sent the ready To Commit message). If, on the other hand, any participant service responds to the prepare To Commit message with a refuse To Commit message, the Commit Coordinator sends an abort message to all participants. The participants then roll back the update.

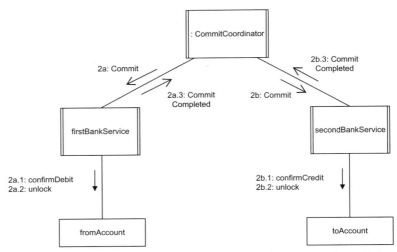

Figure 16.8. Example of the second phase of the Two-Phase Commit Protocol: bank transfer

16.4.2 Compound Transaction Pattern

The previous bank transfer transaction is an example of a flat transaction, which has an "all-or-nothing" characteristic. A compound transaction, in contrast, might need only a partial rollback. The **Compound Transaction** pattern can be used when the client's transaction requirement can be broken down into smaller flat atomic transactions, in which each atomic transaction can be performed separately and rolled back separately. For example, if a travel agent makes an airplane reservation, followed by a hotel reservation and a rental car reservation, it is more flexible to treat this reservation as consisting of three flat transactions. Treating the transaction as a compound transaction allows part of a reservation to be changed or canceled without the other parts of the reservation being affected.

The example of the travel agent, which is depicted in Figure 16.9, illustrates the Compound Transaction pattern. The travel agent plans a trip for a client consisting of separate reservations for an airline (1, 2), a hotel (3, 4), and a rental car (5, 6). If the three parts of the trip are treated as separate flat transactions, each transaction can be handled independently. Thus, the hotel reservation could be changed from one hotel to another independently of the airline and car rental reservations. In certain cases, of course – for example, if the trip is postponed or canceled – all three reservations have to be changed.

16.4.3 Long-Living Transaction Pattern

A long-living transaction is a transaction that has a human in the loop and that could take a long and possibly indefinite time to execute, because individual human behavior is unpredictable. With transactions involving human interaction, it is undesirable to keep records locked for a relatively long time while the human is considering various options. For example, in an airline reservation using a flat transaction, the record would be locked for the duration of the transaction. With human involvement in the transaction, the record could be locked for several minutes. In this case, it is better

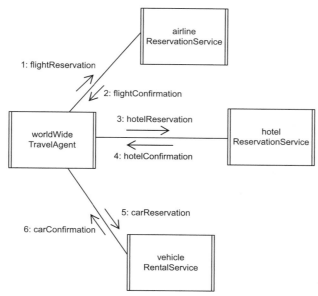

Figure 16.9. Example of the Compound Transaction pattern

to use the **Long-Living Transaction** pattern, which splits a long-living transaction into two or more separate transactions (usually two) so that human decision making takes place between the successive pairs (such as first and second) of transactions.

For the airline reservation example, first a query transaction displays the available seats. The query transaction is followed by a reserve transaction. With this approach, it is necessary to recheck seat availability before the reservation is made. A seat available at query time might no longer be available at reservation time because several agents might be querying the same flight at the same time. If only one seat is available, the first agent will get the seat but not the others. Note that this problem still applies even if the airline allows seat overbooking, although the upper limit would then be the number of actual seats on the aircraft plus the number of seats allowed to be overbooked on the flight.

This approach is illustrated in the travel agent example depicted in Figure 16.10. The travel agent first queries the airline reservation services (1a, 1b, 1c) to determine available flights. The three reservation services all respond positively with seat availability (1a.1, 1b.1, 1c.1). After considering the options and consulting the client, the travel agent makes a reserve request (2) to the Unified Airlines reservation service. Because no lock was placed on the record, however, the reservation is no longer available, so the reservation service responds with a reject response (3). The travel agent then reserves a flight with the second choice, Britannic Airways (4). This time the reservation service responds with a confirmation that the reservation was accepted (5).

16.5 NEGOTIATION PATTERN

In some SOAs, the coordination between services involves negotiations between software agents so that they can cooperatively make decisions. In the **Negotiation**

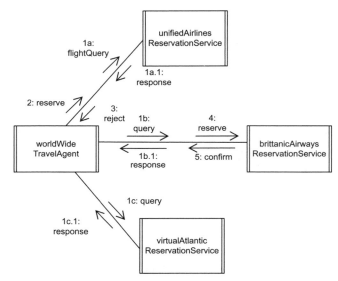

Figure 16.10. Example of the Long-Living Transaction pattern

pattern (also known as the *Agent-Based Negotiation* or *Multi-Agent Negotiation* pattern), a client agent acts on behalf of the user and makes a proposal to a service agent. The service agent attempts to satisfy the client's proposal, which might involve communication with other services. Having determined the available options, the service agent then offers the client agent one or more options that come closest to matching the original client agent proposal. The client agent may then request one of the options, propose further options, or reject the offer. If the service agent can satisfy the client agent request, it accepts the request; otherwise, it rejects the request.

To allow software agents to negotiate with each other, the following communication services are provided (Pitt et al. 1996):

The client agent, who acts on behalf of the client, may do any of the following:

- **Propose a service.** The client agent proposes a service to the service agent. This proposed service is *negotiable*, meaning that the client agent is willing to consider counteroffers.
- **Request a service.** The client agent requests a service from the service agent. This requested service is *nonnegotiable*, meaning that the client agent is not willing to consider counteroffers.
- **Reject a service offer.** The client agent rejects an offer made by the service agent.

The service agent, who acts on behalf of the service, may do any of the following:

- **Offer a service.** In response to a client proposal, a service agent offers a counter-proposal.
- **Reject a client request/proposal.** The service agent rejects the client agent's proposed or requested service.
- **Accept a client request/proposal.** The service agent accepts the client agent's proposed or requested service.

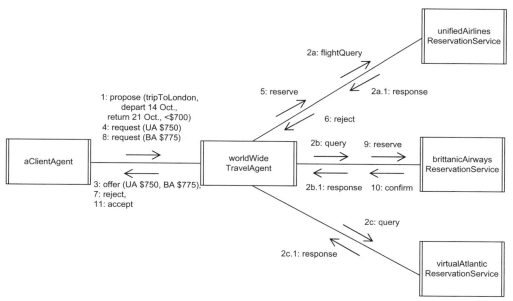

Figure 16.11. Example of Negotiation pattern

16.5.1 Example of Negotiation Pattern

Consider the following example involving negotiation between a client agent and a software travel agent that follows a scenario similar to that between a human client and a human travel agent. This example used the Negotiation pattern and the Long-Living Transaction pattern. In this travel agency example, the client agent discovers an appropriate service travel agent – for our purposes, the world Wide Travel Agent – via the object broker's yellow pages (Figure 16.4). The client agent then initiates the negotiation on behalf of a user who wishes to take an airplane trip from Washington, D.C., to London, departing on October 14 and returning on October 21, for a price of less than $700. The negotiation process is depicted on a communication diagram (see Figure 16.11) and described next:

1. The Client Agent uses the propose service to propose the trip to London with the stipulated constraints.
2. The world Wide Travel Agent determines that three airlines, Britannic Airways (BA), Unified Airlines (UA), and Virtual Atlantic (VA), service the Washington D.C.-to-London route. It sends a flight Query to the three respective services – UA Service (2a), BA Service (2b), and VA Service (2c) – for flights on those dates. It receives responses from all three services with the times and prices of the flights.
3. The world Wide Travel Agent sends an offer message to the Client Agent consisting of the available flights at the proposed price. If only more expensive flights are available, the world Wide Travel Agent offers the cheapest it can find. In this case, it determines that the two best offers for the proposed dates are from UA for $750 and BA for $775. There is no flight below $700, so it

offers the available flight that come closest to the proposed price. It therefore sends the offer message for the UA flight at $750 to the Client Agent.

4. The Client Agent displays the choice to the user. The Client Agent may then request a service (i.e., request one of the choices offered by the service agent). Alternatively, the Client Agent may reject the service offer if the user does not like any of the options and propose a service on a different date. In this case, the user selects the UA offer and the Client Agent sends the request UA flight message to the world Wide Travel Agent.
5. The world Wide Travel Agent makes a reserve request to the UA Service.
6. Assuming the flight is no longer available, the UA Service rejects the reservation.
7. Since the flight is no longer available, the world Wide Travel Agent responds to the Client Agent's request with a reject message.
8. The Client Agent makes a request for the next best offer, the BA flight at $775, and sends the request BA flight message to the world Wide Travel Agent.
9. The world Wide Travel Agent makes a reserve request to the BA Service.
10. Assuming the flight is still available, the BA Service confirms the reservation.
11. The world Wide Travel Agent responds to the Client Agent's request with an accept message.

In this example, note that the world Wide Travel Agent plays a service role when communicating with the Client Agent and a client role when communicating with the airline services.

16.6 SERVICE INTERFACE DESIGN IN SERVICE-ORIENTED ARCHITECTURE

New services are designed by applying the COMET method, initially by using the object structuring criteria described in Chapter 8. During dynamic interaction modeling, the interaction between client objects and service objects is determined. The approach taken for designing service operations is similar to that used in class interface design, as described in Chapter 14. The messages arriving at a service form the basis for designing the service operations. The messages are analyzed to determine the name of the operation, as well as to determine the input and output parameters.

As an example, consider the online shopping system SOA case study described in Chapter 22. Figure 16.12 shows an example in which customers purchase items from suppliers. In the figure, which depicts a communication diagram for the realization of the Process Delivery Order use case, two services are involved, a Delivery Order Service and an Inventory Service.

The operations of each service are determined by analyzing the message requests made to each service. In the object interactions depicted in Figure 16.12 for the Process Delivery Order communication diagram, there is message sent (D5) to the Inventory Service to check the inventory to determine that the items in the delivery order are available. This request is designed as a checkInventory operation with the itemId as an input parameter and inventoryStatus as output parameter, corresponding to message D6. A second request to the Inventory Service is made to

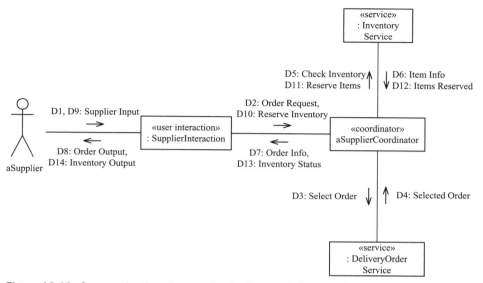

Figure 16.12. Communication diagram for the Process Delivery Order use case

reserve inventory (message D11). This request is designed as a reserveInventory operation with itemId and amount as input parameters. This reservation operation is equivalent to prepare to commit inventory, which is the first phase of a two-phase commit protocol. The partial communication diagram in Figure 16.13 depicts some of the objects for the subsequent Confirm Shipment and Bill Customer use case. There is a message to commit inventory (message S9), which leads to updating the inventory to confirm that the items were removed, packed, and shipped. This request is designed as a commitInventory operation with itemId and amount as input parameters, and it corresponds to the second phase of the two-phase commit protocol. Inventory Service also needs additional operations to abort the inventory (if the order is cancelled and inventory released prior to shipment) and update the inventory (to replenish inventory). Figure 16.14 depicts the interface for Inventory Service (called IInventoryService), which consists of the checkInventory, reserveInventory, and commitInventory operations, in addition to the update and abortInventory operations. Inventory Service, as depicted in Figure 16.14, has a provided port

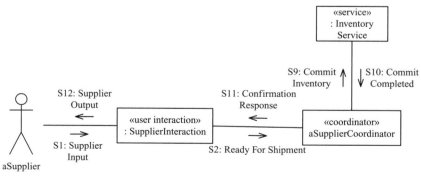

Figure 16.13. Partial communication diagram for the Confirm Shipment and Bill Customer use case

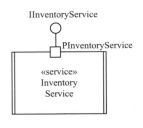

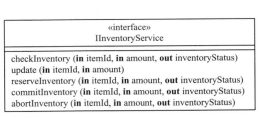

checkInventory (**in** itemId, **in** amount, **out** inventoryStatus)
update (**in** itemId, **in** amount)
reserveInventory (**in** itemId, **in** amount, **out** inventoryStatus)
commitInventory (**in** itemId, **in** amount, **out** inventoryStatus)
abortInventory (**in** itemId, **in** amount, **out** inventoryStatus)

Figure 16.14. Service interface for Inventory Service

(see Chapter 17) called PInventoryService, which supports the provided interface called IInventoryService. A similar analysis would be used to determine the operations of the other services. The full case study description is given in Chapter 22.

16.7 SERVICE COORDINATION IN SERVICE-ORIENTED ARCHITECTURE

In SOA applications that involve multiple services, coordination of these services is usually required. To ensure loose coupling among the services, it is often better to separate the details of the coordination from the functionality of the individual services. In any complex activity involving multiple services, coordination is usually needed to sequence the access to the individual services. In SOA, different types of coordination are provided, including orchestration and choreography. **Orchestration** consists of centrally controlled workflow coordination logic for coordinating multiple participant services. This allows the reuse of existing services by incorporating them into new service applications. **Choreography** provides distributed coordination among services, and it can be used when coordination is needed between different business organizations. Thus, choreography can be used for collaboration between services from different service providers provided by different business organizations. Whereas orchestration is centrally controlled, choreography involves distributed control.

Because the terms *orchestration* and *choreography* are often used interchangeably, this chapter will use the more general term **coordination** to describe the control and sequencing of different services as needed by a SOA application, whether they are centrally controlled or involve distributed control. Transaction patterns, as described in Section 16.4 can also be used for service coordination.

The goal is for services to be stateless so that they can be more reusable. In some cases, when state information is needed (e.g., the status of the delivery order), this state information is saved in the delivery order record and stored in a database. When the delivery order status is needed, it is read (and updated, if necessary) from the delivery order record. The sequencing of multiple service invocations, whether it is sequential or concurrent, and whether or not it is state-dependent, is encapsulated inside the coordinator.

An example of a coordinator object is given in Figures 16.12 and 16.13, in which the Supplier Coordinator object coordinates the interactions of the Supplier Interaction object with the Delivery Order Service and Inventory Service objects. Supplier

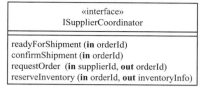

Figure 16.15. Coordinator interface for Supplier Coordinator

Coordinator provides the overall control and sequencing, which is also referred to as the workflow.

Supplier Coordinator receives supplier requests from Supplier Interaction via the provided interface called ISupplierCoordinator. Supplier Coordinator is a client of the Inventory Service and thus has a required interface IInventoryService (Figure 16.14), and a client of Delivery Order Service. The requests Supplier Coordinator receives from Supplier Interaction are to:

1. Request a new delivery order to process (message D2 in Figure 16.12), which is mapped to the requestOrder operation,
2. Reserve order items from inventory (message D10 in Figure 16.12), which is mapped to the reserveInventory operation,
3. Identify that order is ready for shipment (message S2 in Figure 16.13), which is mapped to the readyForShipment operation, and
4. Order has been shipped (message S14 in Figure 16.13), which is mapped to the confirmShipment operation.

The interface ISupplierCoordinator consists of the four operations just described, which are the requestOrder, reserveInventory, readyForShipment, and confirmShipment operations, as depicted in Figure 16.15.

16.8 DESIGNING SERVICE-ORIENTED ARCHITECTURES

After determining the service and coordinator interfaces as described in the previous two sections, the integrated communication diagram can be developed. For SOA, this diagram is both concurrent and distributed. The concurrent communication diagrams show the dynamic message sequencing in which the services participate, and the interaction between services and coordinator components and user interaction components. A concurrent communication diagram is developed by integrating the use case–based communication diagrams (as described in Chapter 13) and then defining the message communication interfaces between the components and services. For communication with a service, synchronous communication is most common, because the service needs a request/response communication. However, it is also possible to use Asynchronous Message Communication with Callback (Chapter 15). For peer-to-peer communication, such as between two coordinators, asynchronous communication can be used.

A concurrent communication diagram for the online shopping system is given in Figure 16.16, which shows the dynamic message communication between each user interaction component (Customer Interaction and Supplier Interaction) with the

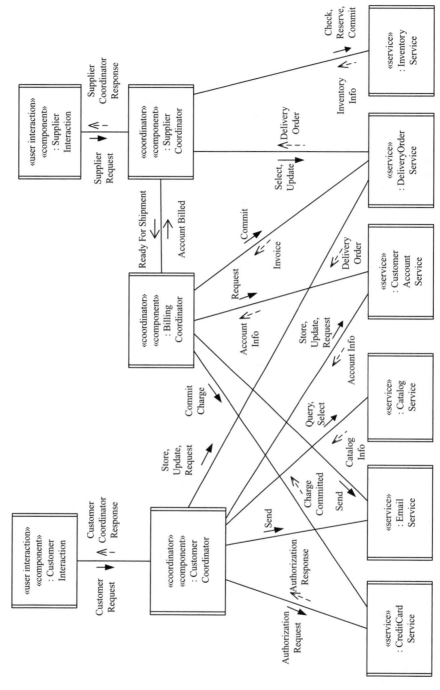

Figure 16.16. Concurrent communication diagram for the Online Shopping System

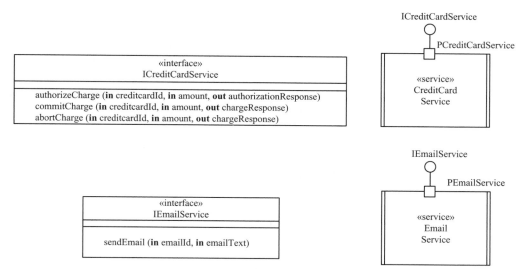

Figure 16.17. Service interfaces for Credit Card Service and Email Service

appropriate coordinator components (Customer Coordinator, Supplier Coordinator, and Billing Coordinator), and then with the six services. The online shopping case study is described in Chapter 22. Most of the communication between the components and the services is Synchronous Message Communication with Reply, the communication pattern most commonly used in SOA because for each request a response is needed. This pattern is used particularly between user interaction components and coordinators (e.g., between Customer Interaction and Customer Coordinator), and between coordinators and services (e.g., between Customer Coordinator and Catalog Service). However, between the coordinators (Supplier Coordinator and Billing Coordinator), peer-to-peer asynchronous message communication is used, so that the coordinator does not have to wait for a response; if a response is needed, it is also asynchronous.

16.9 SERVICE REUSE

Once services have been designed, they can be reused. Although a service could invoke an operation on a different service, this can make the service less reusable, because it is now dependent on another service. To encourage software reuse, it is recommended that services only have provided interfaces and not have any required interfaces (unless asynchronous communication with callback is used). This makes the service more self-contained. All the services depicted in Figure 16.16 follow this guideline by only having provided interfaces and no required interfaces.

Each of the services described could be used in different applications. In each case, new coordinator objects would be created to control and sequence the desired application workflow, taking full advantage of the provided services. If a service is reused, then the interface is already known and it is up to the component invoking the service, be it client or coordinator, to ensure that it invokes the service correctly, using the operations as defined, including the appropriate input and output parameters. It may also be necessary to follow any specified constraints on calling the operations; for example, if one operation needs to be called before another.

In the online shopping system, two external services are reused, namely, the Credit Card Service and the Email Service. The Email Service is the simpler of the two, with only one operation invoked to send an email. The operation invoked is sendEmail (recipient, message). In the case of the Credit Card Service, two operations need to be invoked and follow a predefined sequence, first to authorize the transaction (authorizeCharge) and second to charge the transaction (commitCharge). There is a third operation to abort the transaction, abortCharge.

16.10 SUMMARY

This chapter described how to design SOAs, including how to design services and then how to reuse services. This chapter also briefly described technology support for SOA but concentrated on architectural concepts, methods, and patterns for designing SOA – the technology is changing rapidly, but the concepts last longer. Services can also be designed to be part of a distributed component-based software architecture, as described in the next chapter. A case study of designing a SOA, the online shopping system, is given in Chapter 22.

EXERCISES

Multiple-choice questions: For each question, choose one of the answers.

1. What is a service-oriented architecture (SOA)?
   (a) A distributed software architecture consisting of multiple related services
   (b) A distributed software architecture consisting of multiple autonomous services
   (c) A distributed client/service architecture
   (d) A distributed software architecture

2. Which of the following properties DOES NOT apply to a service?
   (a) Reusable
   (b) Discoverable
   (c) Fixed
   (d) Autonomous

3. In a SOA, which of the following is NOT true?
   (a) A client communicates with a specific service provided on a fixed server configuration.
   (b) A client discovers and links to a service.
   (c) Multiple clients communicate with a service.
   (d) Standard protocols are provided to allow clients to communicate with services.

4. What is an object broker?
   (a) An object that breaks into a system
   (b) An object that sends requests to other objects
   (c) An object that handles requests sent by other objects
   (d) An object that mediates interactions between clients and services

5. Why does a service register with a broker?
   (a) So that service requesters can discover it
   (b) So that a service can interrogate the broker
   (c) So that the registry is up to date
   (d) So that the service can relocate

6. When is it particularly useful to use the Broker Handle pattern in place of the Broker Forwarding pattern?
   (a) If the client only communicates with the service once
   (b) If the client needs to have a dialog with the service
   (c) If the client knows the type of service required but not the specific service
   (d) If the client needs to provide the broker with a handle

7. Yellow pages brokering is useful when a service requester:
   (a) Needs to discover the location of the service
   (b) Knows the type of service required but not the specific service
   (c) Knows the specific service required but not the type of service
   (d) Needs to discover the broker
8. What is a transaction?
   (a) Consists of two or more operations
   (b) Consists of one operation
   (c) Consists of two or more operations that are indivisible
   (d) Consists of two or more operations that are divisible
9. What is a compound transaction?
   (a) The compound transaction is indivisible.
   (b) The compound transaction is atomic.
   (c) The compound transaction is decomposed into atomic transactions.
   (d) The compound transaction is decomposed into subatomic transactions.
10. With a Negotiation pattern, which of the following is NOT true?
   (a) The client agent can propose a service.
   (b) The service agent can offer a service in response to a client agent proposal.
   (c) The client agent can request a service.
   (d) The service agent can offer a service in response to a client agent request.

17

Designing Component-Based Software Architectures

In distributed component-based software design, the component-based software architecture for the distributed application is developed. The software application is structured into components, and the interfaces between the components are defined. To assist with this process, guidelines are provided for determining the components. Components are designed to be configurable so that each component instance can be deployed to a different node in a geographically distributed environment.

Components are initially designed using the subsystem structuring criteria described in Chapter 12. Additional component configuration criteria are used to ensure that components are indeed configurable – in other words, that they can be effectively deployed to distributed physical nodes in a distributed environment.

Section 17.1 describes concepts, architectures, and patterns for distributed component-based software architectures. Section 17.2 describes the steps in designing distributed component-based software architectures. Section 17.3 describes the concepts and design of composite subsystems and components. Section 17.4 describes how components can be modeled and designed with UML. Section 17.5 describes component structuring criteria for structuring a distributed application into configurable distributed components. Section 17.6 describes group communication patterns, including Broadcast Message Communication and Subscription/Notification Message Communication patterns. Finally, Section 17.7 describes application deployment.

17.1 CONCEPTS, ARCHITECTURES, AND PATTERNS FOR COMPONENT-BASED SOFTWARE ARCHITECTURES

In Chapter 12, the term *component* was introduced in a general way. This chapter describes the design of distributed components as used in distributed component-based software architectures. It describes the component structuring criteria for designing components that can be deployed to execute on distributed platforms in a distributed configuration. The design of component interfaces is described, with component ports that have provided and required interfaces, and connectors that join compatible ports. The component-based software architectures are depicted with the UML notation for composite structure diagrams.

Architectural communication patterns described previously can be used for these architectures, including Synchronous, Asynchronous, and Broker patterns. In addition, group communication patterns can be used as described in Section 17.6.

An important goal of a component-based software architecture is to provide a concurrent message-based design that is highly configurable. In other words, the objective is that the same software architecture should be capable of being deployed to many different distributed configurations. Thus, a given software application could be configured to have each component-based subsystem allocated to its own separate physical node, or, alternatively, to have all or some of its components allocated to the same physical node. To achieve this flexibility, it is necessary to design the software architecture in such a way that the decision about how components will be mapped to physical nodes is not made at design time but is made later, at system deployment time.

A component-based development approach, in which each subsystem is designed as a distributed self-contained component, helps achieve the goal of a distributed, highly configurable, message-based design. A **distributed component** is a concurrent object with a well-defined interface, which is a logical unit of distribution and deployment. A well-designed component is capable of being reused in applications other than the one for which it was originally developed. A component can be either a composite component or a simple component. A **composite component** is composed of other part components. A **simple component** has no part components within it.

Services can be integrated into distributed component-based software architectures. Services are designed with provided interfaces that can be discovered by components using the Service Discovery pattern and then communicated with using a Broker pattern, such as the Broker Handle pattern, as described in Chapter 16.

Because components can be allocated to different nodes in a geographically distributed environment, all communication between components must be restricted to message communication. Thus, a source component on one node sends a message over the network to a destination component on a different node.

17.2 DESIGNING DISTRIBUTED COMPONENT-BASED SOFTWARE ARCHITECTURES

A **distributed application** consists of distributed components that can be configured to execute on distributed physical nodes. To successfully manage the inherent complexity of large-scale distributed applications, it is necessary to provide an approach for structuring the application into components in which each component can potentially execute on its own node. After this design is performed and the interfaces between the components are carefully defined, each component can be designed independently.

The three main steps in designing a component-based software architecture for a distributed application are:

1. **Design distributed software architecture.** Structure the distributed application into constituent components that potentially could execute on separate

nodes in a distributed environment. Because components can reside on separate nodes, all communication between components must be restricted to message communication. The interfaces between components are defined. The subsystem structuring criteria, as described in Section 13.8, are used to initially determine the components. Additional component structuring criteria are used to ensure that the components are designed as configurable components that can be effectively mapped to physical nodes, as described in Section 17.5.

2. **Design constituent components.** Because, by definition, a simple component can execute on only one node, the internals of each simple component can be designed by means of a design method for sequential object-oriented software architectures, as described in Chapter 14.

3. **Deploy the application.** After a distributed application has been designed, instances of it can be defined and deployed. During this stage, the component instances of the application are defined, interconnected, and mapped onto a hardware configuration consisting of distributed physical nodes.

17.3 COMPOSITE SUBSYSTEMS AND COMPONENTS

A composite subsystem is a component and adheres to the principle of geographical distribution. Thus, objects that are part of a composite subsystem must reside at the same location, but objects in different geographical locations are never in the same composite subsystem. As described in Chapter 13, however, objects in different composite subsystems can be combined into an aggregate subsystem – for example, in a layered architecture, in which each layer is designed as an aggregate subsystem consisting of one or more composite subsystems.

A **composite subsystem** is a component that encapsulates the internal components (objects) it contains. The component is both a logical and a physical container, but it adds no further functionality; thus, a component's functionality is provided entirely by the part components it contains. An example of a composite component with internal components is depicted in Figure 17.1, in which the composite Operator Presentation user interaction component contains three internal simple components, Operator Interaction, Alarm Window, and Event Monitoring Window. Components are usually concurrent, so they are depicted with the UML active class notation.

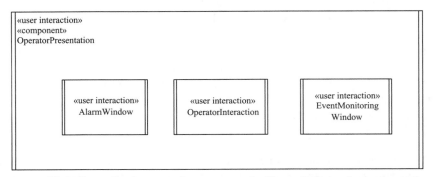

Figure 17.1. Example of composite component with nested simple components

Incoming messages to a component are passed through to the appropriate internal destination component, and outgoing messages from an internal component are passed through to the appropriate external destination component. The exact pass-through mechanisms are implementation-dependent. This is a view of whole/part relationships (Buschmann et al. 1996) that is shared by many component-based systems (Bass, Clements, and Kazman 2003; Magee, Kramer, and Sloman 2006; Selic, Gullekson, and Ward 1994; Shaw and Garlan 1996; Szyperski 2003). An example of a software architecture with composite components is the Emergency Monitoring System, as described in Chapter 23.

17.4 MODELING COMPONENTS WITH UML

This section describes the design of component interfaces, an important issue in software architecture, which was first introduced in Chapter 12. It describes how interfaces are specified before describing provided and required interfaces, ports (and how they are specified in terms of provided and required interfaces), connectors that interconnect components, and guidelines on designing components for component-based software architectures.

Components can be effectively modeled in UML with structured classes and depicted on composite structure diagrams. Structured classes have ports with provided and required interfaces. Structured classes can be interconnected through their ports via connectors that join the ports of communicating classes. This section describes how component-based software architectures are designed with the UML notation.

17.4.1 Design of Component Interfaces

An **interface** specifies the externally visible operations of a class or component without revealing the internal structure (implementation) of the operations, as described in Chapter 12. Although many components are designed with one interface, it is possible for a component to provide more than one interface. If different components use a component differently, it is possible to design a separate interface for each component that requires a different interface.

An example of a component that provides more than one interface is Alarm Service. Two interfaces from the Emergency Monitoring System will be used in the examples that follow. Each interface consists of one or more operations, as follows:

1. **Interface:** IAlarmService
   Operations provided:
   - alarmRequest (**in** request, **out** alarmData)
   - alarmSubscribe (**in** request, **in** notificationHandle, **out** ack)
2. **Interface:** IAlarmStatus
   Operation provided: post (**in** alarm)
3. **Interface:** IAlarmNotification
   Operation provided: alarmNotify (**in** alarm)

The interface of a component can be depicted with the static modeling notation (see Chapter 12), as shown in Figure 17.2 for the preceding example, with the stereotype «interface».

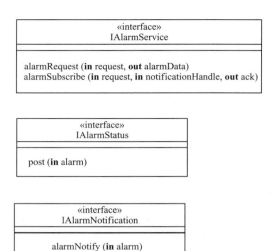

Figure 17.2. Example of component interfaces

17.4.2 Provided and Required Interfaces

To provide a complete definition of the component-based software architecture for a software application, it is necessary to specify the interface(s) provided by each component and the interface(s) required by each component. A **provided interface** specifies the operations that a component must fulfill. A **required interface** describes the operations that other components provide for this component to operate properly in a particular environment.

A component has one or more ports through which it interacts with other components. Each component port is defined in terms of provided and/or required interfaces. A *provided* interface of a port specifies the requests that other components can make of this component. A *required* interface of a port specifies the requests that this component can make of other components. A provided port supports a provided interface. A required port supports a required interface. A complex port supports both a provided interface and a required interface. A component can have more than one port. In particular, if a component communicates with more than one component, it can use a different port for each component with which it communicates. Figure 17.3 shows an example of components with ports, as well as provided and required interfaces.

By convention, the name of a component's required port starts with the letter *R* to emphasize that the component has a *required* port. The name of a component's provided port starts with the letter *P* to emphasize that the component has a *provided* port. In Figure 17.3, the Monitoring Sensor Component has one required port, called RAlarmStatus, which supports a required interface called IAlarmStatus, as defined in Figure 17.2. The Operator Alarm Presentation component is a client component, which has a required port with a required interface (IAlarmService) and a provided port with a provided interface IAlarmNotification. Alarm Service has two provided ports called PAlarmStatus and PAlarmService, and one required port RAlarmNotification. The port PAlarmStatus provides an interface called IAlarmStatus,

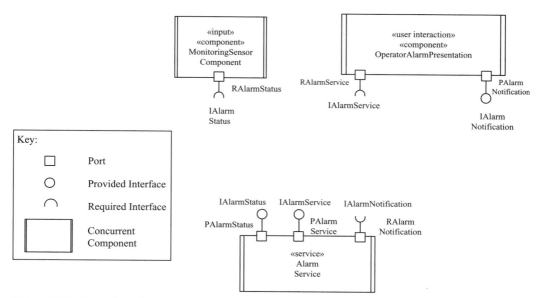

Figure 17.3. Examples of component ports, with provided and required interfaces

through which alarm status messages are sent. The port PAlarmService provides the main interface through which clients request alarm services (provided interface IAlarmService). Alarm Service sends alarm notifications through its RAlarmNotification port.

17.4.3 Connectors and Interconnecting Components

A connector joins the required port of one component to the provided port of another component. The connected ports must be compatible with each other. This means that if two ports are connected, the required interface of one port must be compatible with the provided interface of the other port; that is, the operations required in one component's required interface must be the same as the operations provided in the other component's provided interface. In the case of a connector joining two complex ports (each with one provided interface and one required interface), the required interface of the first port must be compatible with the provided interface of the second port, and the required interface of the second port must be compatible with the provided interface of the first port.

Figure 17.4 shows how the three components (Monitoring Sensor Component, Operator Alarm Presentation, and Alarm Service) are interconnected. The first connector is unidirectional (as shown by the direction of the arrow representing the connector) and joins Monitoring Sensor Component's RAlarmStatus required port to Alarm Service's PAlarmStatus provided port. Figure 17.3 shows that these ports are compatible because it results in the IAlarmStatus required interface being connected to the IAlarmStatus provided interface. The second connector is also unidirectional and joins Operator Alarm Presentation's required port RAlarmService to Alarm Service's provided port PAlarmService. Examination of the port design in Figure 17.3 shows that these ports are also compatible, with the required IAlarmService

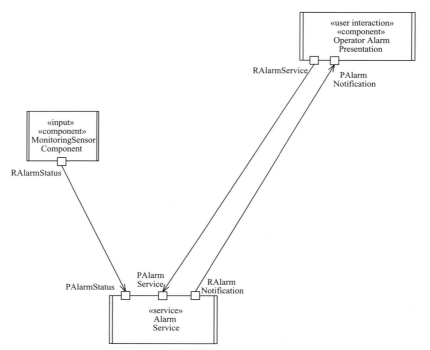

Figure 17.4. Example of components, ports, and connectors in a software architecture

interface connected to the provided interface of the same name. The third connector is also unidirectional and joins Alarm Service's RAlarmNotification required port to Operator Alarm Presentation's PAlarmNotification provided port and is through which alarm notifications are sent via the IAlarmNotification interface.

17.4.4 Designing Composite Components

A composite component is structured into part components, which are also depicted as UML structured classes. A component with no internal components is referred to as a *simple component*. The part components within a composite component are depicted as instances because it is possible to have more than one instance of the same part within the composite component.

Figure 17.5 shows an example of a composite component, the Display component, which contains two simple components: a concurrent component called Display Interface and a passive component called Display Prompts. The provided port of the composite Display component is connected directly to the provided port of the internal Display Interface component. The connector joining the two ports is called a **delegation connector**, which means that the outer delegating port provided by Display forwards each message it receives from Display Producer to the inner port provided by Display Interface. The two ports are given the same name, PDisplay, because they provide the same interface.

Only distributed components can be deployed to the physical nodes of a distributed configuration. Passive components cannot be independently deployed, nor

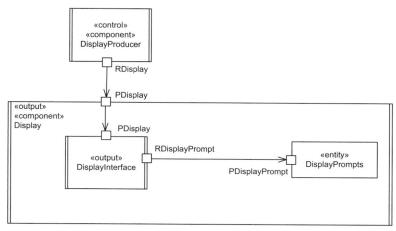

Figure 17.5. Design of composite component

can any component that directly invokes the operations of a passive component; in that situation, only the composite component (which contains the passive component) can be deployed. Thus, in Figure 17.5, only the Display composite component can be deployed. By a COMET convention, only the deployable components are depicted with the component stereotype.

17.5 COMPONENT STRUCTURING CRITERIA

A distributed application needs to be designed with an understanding of the distributed environments in which it is likely to operate. The component structuring criteria provide guidelines on how to structure a distributed application into configurable distributed components, which can be mapped to geographically distributed nodes in a distributed environment. The actual mapping of components to physical nodes is done later, when an individual target system is instantiated and deployed. However, it is necessary to design the components as configurable components, which are indeed capable of later being effectively mapped to distributed physical nodes. Consequently, the component structuring criteria need to consider the characteristics of distributed environments.

In a distributed environment, a component might be associated with a particular physical location or constrained to execute on a given hardware resource. In such a case, a component is constrained to execute on the node at that location or on the given hardware.

17.5.1 Proximity to the Source of Physical Data

In a distributed environment, the sources of data might be physically distant from each other. Designing the component so that it is close to the source of physical data ensures fast access to the data, which is particularly important if data access rates are high. An example of a component designed to be in close proximity to the source of physical data is the Remote System Proxy component in the Emergency Monitoring System, as shown in Figure 17.6.

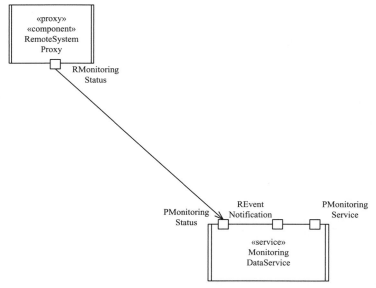

Figure 17.6. Example of component proximity to the source of physical data

17.5.2 Localized Autonomy

A distributed component often performs a specific site-related service, where the same service is performed at multiple sites. Each instance of the component resides on a separate node, thereby providing greater local autonomy. Assuming that a component on a given node operates relatively independently of other nodes, it can be operational even if the other nodes are temporarily unavailable. An example of an autonomous local component is the Automated Guided Vehicle System component of the Factory Automation System in Figure 17.7.

The example of localized autonomy from the Automated Guided Vehicle System is depicted in more detail in Figure 17.8. Control is provided by a control

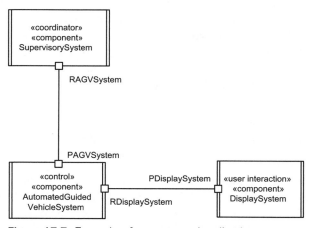

Figure 17.7. Example of component localized autonomy

component, Vehicle Control, which receives move commands from a Supervisory System Proxy component, and controls the Motor Component, to start and stop moving along the track, and Arm Component, to load and unload parts. It also receives inputs from an Arrival Sensor Component, to indicate arrival at a station.

17.5.3 Performance

If a time-critical function is provided within a node, better and more-predictable component performance can often be achieved. In a given distributed application, a real-time component can perform a time-critical service at a given node, with non–real-time or less time-critical services performed elsewhere. An example of a component that satisfies this criterion is the Automated Guided Vehicle System component in Figure 17.7.

17.5.4 Specialized Hardware

A component might need to reside on a particular node because it supports special-purpose hardware, such as a vector processor, or because it has to interface to special-purpose peripherals, sensors, or actuators that are connected to a specific node. Instances of the Monitoring Sensor Component (Figure 17.4) interface to special-purpose sensors. Both the Arm Component and Motor Component (Figure 17.8) interface to special-purpose actuators.

17.5.5 I/O Component

An I/O component can be designed to be relatively autonomous and in close proximity to the source of physical data. In particular, "smart" devices are given greater

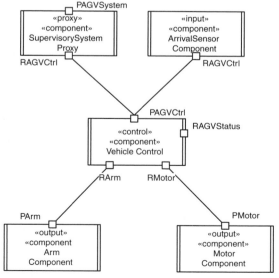

Figure 17.8. Example of control and I/O components

local autonomy and consist of the hardware plus the software that interfaces to and controls the device. An I/O component typically consists of one or more device interface objects, and it may also contain control objects to provide localized control and entity objects to store local data.

I/O component is a general name given to components that interact with the external environment; they include input components, output components, I/O components (which provide both input and output), network interface components, and system interface components.

In the Automated Guided Vehicle example illustrated in Figure 17.8, Arrival Sensor Component is an example of an input component; and Arm Component and Motor Component are examples of output components.

17.6 GROUP MESSAGE COMMUNICATION PATTERNS

The message communication patterns described so far have involved one source component and one destination component. A desirable property in some distributed applications is group communication. This is a form of one-to-many message communication in which a sender sends one message to many recipients. Two kinds of group message communication (sometimes referred to as *groupcast communication*) supported in distributed applications are broadcast and multicast communication.

17.6.1 Broadcast Message Communication Pattern

With the **Broadcast** (or *Broadcast Communication*) pattern, an unsolicited message is sent to all recipients, perhaps informing them of a pending shutdown. Each recipient must then decide whether it wishes to process the message or discard it. An example of the Broadcast pattern is given in Figure 17.9. Alarm Handling

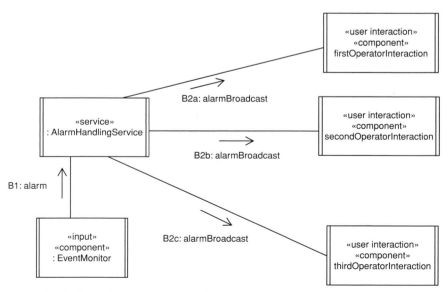

Figure 17.9. Example of Broadcast pattern

Service sends alarm Broadcast messages to all instances of the Operator Interaction component. Each recipient must decide whether it wishes to take action in response to the alarm or to ignore the message. The pattern interactions are described in more detail as follows:

B1: Event Monitor sends an alarm message to Alarm Handling Service.

B2a, B2b, B2c: Alarm Handling Service broadcasts the alarm as an alarm Broadcast message to all the Operator Interaction components. Each recipient decides whether to take action or discard the message.

17.6.2 Subscription/Notification Message Communication Pattern

Multicast communication provides a more selective form of group communication, in which the same message is sent to all members of a group. The **Subscription/ Notification** pattern uses a form of multicast communication in which components subscribe to a group and receive messages destined for all members of the group. A component can subscribe to (request to join) or unsubscribe from (leave) a group and can be a member of more than one group. A sender, also referred to as a *publisher*, sends a message to the group without having to know who all the individual members are. The message is then sent to all members of the group. Sending the same message to all members of a group is referred to as *multicast communication*. A message sent to a subscriber is also referred to as an *event notification*. While on a subscription list, a member can receive several event notification messages. The Subscription/Notification pattern is popular on the Internet.

An example of the Subscription/Notification pattern is shown in Figure 17.10. First, three instances of the Operator Interaction component send a subscribe message to Alarm Handling Service to request to receive alarms of a certain type. Every time

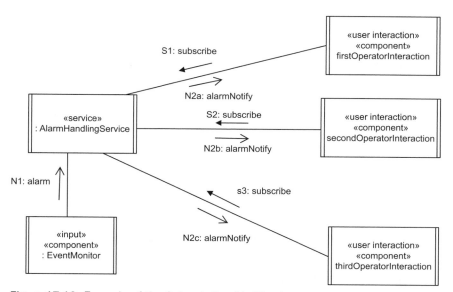

Figure 17.10. Example of the Subscription/Notification pattern

the Alarm Handling Service receives a new alarm message of this type, it multicasts the alarm Notification message to all subscriber Operator Interaction components. The pattern interactions are described in more detail as follows:

S1, S2, S3: Operator Interaction components subscribe to receive alarm notifications.

N1: Event Monitor sends an alarm message to Alarm Handling Service.

N2a, N2b, N2c: Alarm Handling Service looks up the list of subscribers who have requested to be notified of alarms of this type. It multicasts the alarm Notification message to the appropriate subscriber Operator Interaction components. Each recipient takes appropriate action in response to the alarm notification.

A variation on the Subscription/Notification pattern is to have only one subscriber. This arrangement is useful in peer-to-peer situations in which the producer does not know who the consumer is and the consumer might be optional. The consumer can subscribe to the producer, sending it a handle, which the producer then uses for sending messages to the consumer. This is useful for reversing a dependency, because, by virtue of the subscription, the consumer is dependent on the producer rather than vice versa.

17.6.3 Concurrent Service Design with Subscription and Notification

An example of a concurrent service design is shown in Figure 17.11, which consists of a news archive service that supports the Subscription/Notification pattern (see Section 17.6.2). This concurrent service consists of a news archive, multiple

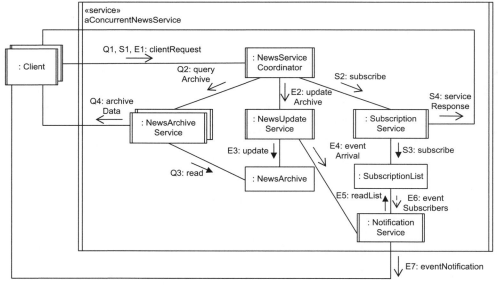

Figure 17.11. Example of a concurrent service: subscription/notification

instances of services, including News Archive Service and News Update Service, and provides a subscription/notification service to its clients. Subscription Service maintains a subscription list of clients that wish to be notified of news events. When a Correspondent posts a news event, News Update Service updates a news archive and informs Notification Service of the event arrival. Notification Service queries the Subscription List to determine the clients who have subscribed to receive events of this type, and then notifies those clients of the news event.

The concurrent communication diagram in Figure 17.11 shows three separate interactions: a simple query interaction, a news event subscription interaction, and a news event notification interaction. In the query interaction (which does not involve a subscription),a client makes a request to News Service Coordinator, which in turn sends a news archive query to News Archive Service. The latter queries the News Archive and sends the response directly to Client. Because multiple services could be accessing the news archive and subscription list concurrently, access synchronization would need to be provided, either through the underlying database or by the services that access the data.

The three event sequences are given different prefixes to differentiate them:

Query interaction (*Q* prefix):

Q1: A client sends a query to News Service Coordinator – for example, requesting news events over the past 24 hours.

Q2: News Service Coordinator forwards the query to an instance of News Archive Service.

Q3: News Archive Service sends the appropriate archive data – for example, news events over the past 24 hours – to the client.

Event subscription interaction (*S* prefix):

S1: News Service Coordinator receives a subscription request from a client.

S2: News Service Coordinator sends a subscribe message to Subscription Service.

S3: Subscription Service adds this client to the Subscription List.

S4: Subscription Service confirms the subscription by sending a subscription service Response message to the client.

Event notification interaction (*E* prefix):

E1: A news correspondent client sends a news update request to News Service Coordinator.

E2: News Service Coordinator forwards the update request to News Update Service.

E3, E4: News Update Service updates the News Archive and sends an event Arrival message to Notification Service.

> **E5, E6:** Notification Service queries Subscription List to get the list of event subscribers (i.e., clients that have subscribed to receive events of this type).
>
> **E7:** Notification Service multicasts an event Notification message to all clients that have subscribed for this event.

17.7 APPLICATION DEPLOYMENT

After a distributed application has been designed and implemented, instances of it can be defined and deployed. During system deployment, an instance of the distributed application – referred to as a *target application* – is defined and mapped to a distributed configuration consisting of multiple geographically distributed physical nodes connected by a network.

17.7.1 Application Deployment Issues

During application deployment, a decision is made about what component instances are required. In addition, it is necessary to determine how the component instances should be interconnected and how the component instances should be allocated to nodes. Specifically, the following activities need to be performed:

- **Define instances of the component.** For each component that can have multiple instances, it is necessary to define the instances desired. For example, in a distributed Emergency Monitoring System, it is necessary to define the number of instances of components required in the target application. It is also necessary to define one Monitoring Sensor Component instance for each sensor, one Remote System Proxy instance for each remote system, and one instance of the Operator Interaction component for each operator. Each component instance must have a unique name so that it can be uniquely identified. For components that are parameterized, the parameters for each instance need to be defined. Examples of component parameters are instance name (such as remote proxy Id or operator Id), sensor names, sensor limits, and alarm names.
- **Interconnect component instances.** The application architecture defines how components communicate with one another. At this stage, the component instances are connected. In the distributed Emergency Monitoring System in Figure 17.12, for example, each instance of the Monitoring Sensor Component is connected to the Alarm Service and the Monitoring Data Service. When Alarm Service sends an alarm notification message to Operator Presentation, it must identify to which operator it is sending the message.
- **Map the component instances to physical nodes.** For example, two components could be deployed such that each one could run on a separate physical node. Alternatively, they could both run on the same physical node. The physical configuration of the target application is depicted on a deployment diagram.

17.7.2 Example of Application Deployment

As an example of application deployment, consider the distributed Emergency Monitoring System. The application configuration is depicted on a deployment

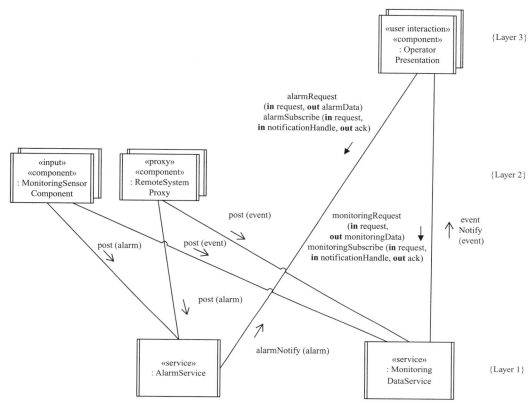

Figure 17.12. Example of a distributed Emergency Monitoring System

diagram as shown in Figure 17.13. Each instance of Monitoring Sensor Component (one per sensor) is deployed to a separate node to achieve localized autonomy and adequate performance. Thus, the failure of one sensor node will not affect other nodes. Each instance of Remote System Proxy (one per remote system) is deployed to a separate node because of proximity to the source of physical data. Loss of a remote system node means that the specific remote system will not be serviced, but other nodes will not be affected. Alarm Service and Monitoring Data Service are each deployed to a separate node for performance reasons, so that they can be responsive

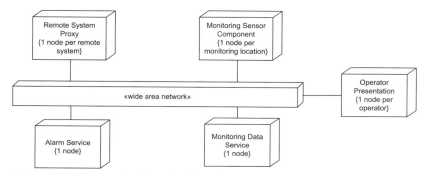

Figure 17.13. Example of a distributed application deployment: Emergency Monitoring System

to service requests. Finally, each instance of the Operator Presentation component is deployed to a separate operator node because of localized autonomy.

17.8 SUMMARY

This chapter described the design of component-based software architectures. It described the component structuring criteria for designing components that can be deployed to execute on distributed platforms in a distributed configuration. Also discussed was the design of component interfaces, with component ports that have provided and required interfaces, and connectors that join compatible ports. The component-based software architecture was depicted with the UML 2 notation for composite structure diagrams. Considerations and tradeoffs in component design were also discussed. A case study of designing a component-based software architecture, the Emergency Monitoring System, is given in Chapter 23. Distributed components can also be integrated into service-oriented architectures, as described in the Online Shopping System case study in Chapter 22.

EXERCISES

Multiple-choice questions: For each question, choose one of the answers.

1. In a distributed component-based software architecture, which of the following statements is the most complete description of component deployment?
   (a) Component instances can be deployed to different nodes in a geographically distributed environment.
   (b) Component instances can be deployed to different nodes in a geographically distributed environment before design.
   (c) Component instances can be deployed to different nodes in a geographically distributed environment before implementation.
   (d) Component instances can be deployed to different nodes in a geographically distributed environment after design and implementation.

2. What does a component interface consist of?
   (a) The externally visible operations of a component
   (b) The operations provided by a component
   (c) The operations required by a component

   (d) The operations that a component supports

3. What does a component's provided interface consist of?
   (a) The operations that a component must fulfill
   (b) The operations inside a component
   (c) The operations that a component uses
   (d) The operations of a component

4. What does a component's required interface consist of?
   (a) The operations that a component must fulfill
   (b) The operations inside a component
   (c) The operations that a component uses
   (d) The visible operations of a component

5. What does a connector join?
   (a) The provided port of one component to the required port of another component
   (b) The provided port of one component to the provided port of another component
   (c) The required port of one component to the provided port of another component
   (d) The required port of one component to the required port of another component

6. What does a delegation connector join?
   - (a) An outer provided port to an inner provided port
   - (b) An outer provided port to an inner required port
   - (c) An outer required port to an inner provided port
   - (d) An outer provided port to an outer required port
7. What is broadcast message communication?
   - (a) A message sent to several recipients
   - (b) A message sent to a specific recipient
   - (c) A message sent to all recipients
   - (d) A message sent to recipients who are members of a group
8. What are the communication characteristics of subscription/notification?
   - (a) A message sent to several recipients
   - (b) A message sent to a specific recipient
   - (c) A message sent to all recipients
   - (d) A message sent to recipients who have joined a group
9. During application deployment:
   - (a) The application is executed.
   - (b) Component instances are executed.
   - (c) Component instances are assigned to hardware nodes.
   - (d) Component instances are instantiated.
10. What is an advantage of localized autonomy in component-based design?
    - (a) If a component goes down, other components can continue to execute.
    - (b) Components execute concurrently.
    - (c) Components are distributed.
    - (d) Components communicate using messages.

18

Designing Concurrent and Real-Time Software Architectures

This chapter describes the design of concurrent and real-time software architectures. Real-time software architectures are concurrent architectures that usually have to deal with multiple streams of input events. They are typically state-dependent, with either centralized or decentralized control. Thus, the design of finite state machines, as described in Chapter 10, state-dependent interaction modeling, as described in Chapter 11, and the control patterns, as described in this chapter, are very important in the design of real-time software architectures.

Section 18.1 describes concepts, architectures, and patterns for designing concurrent and real-time software architectures. Section 18.2 describes the characteristics of real-time systems. Section 18.3 describes control patterns for real-time software architectures. Section 18.4 describes the concurrent task structuring criteria. Section 18.5 describes the I/O task structuring criteria, and Section 18.6 describes the internal task structuring criteria. Section 18.7 describes the steps in developing the concurrent task architecture. Section 18.8 describes designing the task interfaces using task communication and synchronization. Section 18.9 describes documenting task interface and behavior specifications. Section 18.10 describes concurrent task implementation in Java using threads.

18.1 CONCEPTS, ARCHITECTURES, AND PATTERNS FOR CONCURRENT AND REAL-TIME SOFTWARE ARCHITECTURES

An important activity in designing real-time software architectures is to design concurrent objects, which are referred to as concurrent tasks in this chapter. Chapter 14 described the design of passive objects, which do not have threads of control. Concurrency concepts were introduced in Chapter 4. The design of concurrent and real-time software architectures consists of designing the concurrent tasks, as described in this chapter, and designing the information hiding classes from which passive objects are instantiated, as described in Chapter 14. Real-time software architectures can also be distributed; for this reason they can be considered a special case of component-based software architectures. In this context, a *task* is equivalent to a *simple component*, as described in Chapter 17, and the two terms are used inter-changeably in this chapter.

During concurrent software design, a **concurrent software architecture** is developed in which the system is structured into concurrent tasks, and the interfaces and interconnections between the concurrent tasks are defined. To help determine the concurrent tasks, concurrent task structuring criteria are provided to assist in mapping an object-oriented analysis model of the system to a concurrent software architecture. These criteria are a set of heuristics, also referred to as guidelines, that capture expert designer knowledge in the software design of concurrent and real-time systems. Concurrent tasks also participate in software architectural patterns; thus, they can participate in patterns already described, such as Layered patterns (Chapter 12) and Client/Service patterns (Chapter 15), in which both the client and service could be designed as concurrent software architectures. In addition, it is possible for concurrent tasks to participate in various control patterns, as described in Section 18.3.

18.2 CHARACTERISTICS OF REAL-TIME SYSTEMS

Real-time systems (Figure 18.1) are concurrent systems with timing constraints. They have widespread use in industrial, commercial, and military applications. The term *real-time system* usually refers to the whole system, including the real-time application, real-time operating system, and the real-time I/O subsystem, with special-purpose device drivers to interface to the various sensors and actuators. Because the emphasis in this chapter is on designing applications, we use the term *real-time application* and not *real-time system*. However, this section describes real-time applications in the broader context of real-time systems.

Real-time systems are often complex because they have to deal with multiple independent streams of input events and produce multiple independent outputs. These events have arrival rates that are often unpredictable, although they must be subject to timing constraints specified in the system requirements. Frequently,

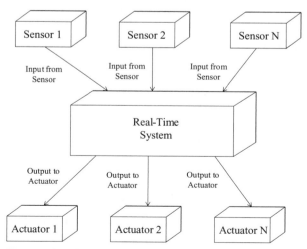

Figure 18.1. Real-time system

the order of incoming events is not predictable. Also, the input load might vary significantly and unpredictably with time.

Real-time systems are frequently classified as hard real-time systems or soft real-time systems. A hard real-time system has time-critical deadlines that must be met to prevent a catastrophic system failure. In a soft real-time system, missing deadlines occasionally is considered undesirable but not catastrophic, so it can be tolerated.

18.3 CONTROL PATTERNS FOR REAL-TIME SOFTWARE ARCHITECTURES

Many real-time systems have a control function. This section describes the different kinds of control patterns that could be used for this purpose: centralized control patterns, distributed control patterns, and hierarchical control patterns. To make the patterns applicable to component-based software architectures as well as real-time software architectures, the «component» stereotype is used in these patterns.

18.3.1 Centralized Control Architectural Pattern

In the **Centralized Control** architectural pattern, there is one control component, which conceptually executes a statechart and provides the overall control and sequencing of the system. The control component receives events from other components with which it interacts. These include events from various input components and user interface components that interact with the external environment – for example, through sensors that detect changes in the environment. An input event to a control component usually causes a state transition on its statechart, which results in one or more state-dependent actions. The control component uses these actions to control other components, such as output components, which output to the external environment – for example, to switch actuators on and off. Entity objects are also used to store any temporary data needed by the other objects.

Examples of this pattern can be found in the Cruise Control System (Gomaa 2000) and the Microwave Oven Control System case study (Gomaa 2005). Figure 18.2 gives an example of the Centralized Control architectural pattern from the latter case study, in which the concurrent components are depicted on a generic communication diagram. The Microwave Control component is a centralized control component, which executes the statechart that provides the overall control and sequencing for the microwave oven. Microwave Control receives messages from three input components – Door Component, Weight Component, and Keypad Component – when they detect inputs from the external environment. Microwave Control actions are sent to two output components, Heating Element Component (to switch the heating element on or off) and Microwave Display (to display information and prompts to the user).

18.3.2 Distributed Control Architectural Pattern

The **Distributed Control** pattern contains several control components. Each of these components controls a given part of the system by conceptually executing a statechart. Control is distributed among the various control components, with no single

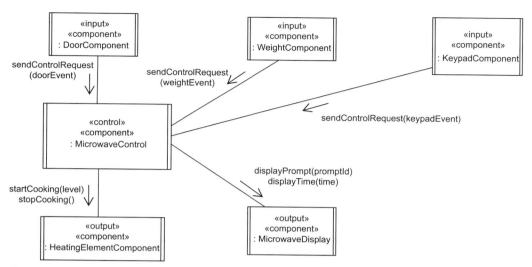

Figure 18.2. Example of the Centralized Control architectural pattern

component in overall control. To notify each other of important events, the control components communicate through peer-to-peer communication. They also interact with the external environment as in the Centralized Control pattern (see Section 12.2.6).

An example of the Distributed Control pattern is given in Figure 18.3, in which the control is distributed among the several distributed controller components. Each distributed controller executes a state machine, receiving inputs from the external environment through sensor components and controlling the external environment by sending outputs to actuator components. Each distributed controller communicates with the other distributed controller components by means of messages containing events.

18.3.3 Hierarchical Control Architectural Pattern

The **Hierarchical Control** pattern (also known as the *Multilevel Control* pattern) contains several control components. Each component controls a given part of a system by conceptually executing a state machine. In addition, a coordinator component provides the overall system control by coordinating several control components. The coordinator provides high-level control by deciding the next job

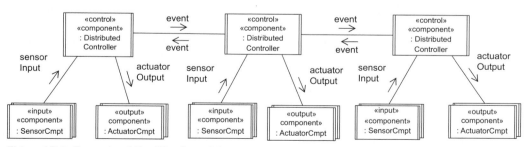

Figure 18.3. Example of the Distributed Control architectural pattern

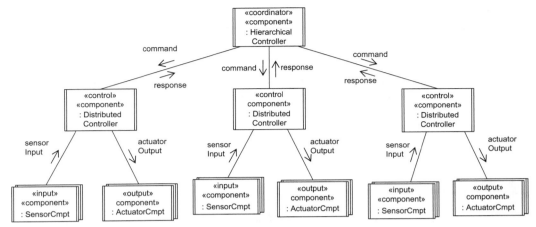

Figure 18.4. Example of the Hierarchical Control architectural pattern

for each control component and communicating that information directly to the control component. The coordinator also receives status information from the control components.

One example of the Hierarchical Control pattern is given in Figure 18.4, in which the Hierarchical Controller sends high-level commands to each of the distributed controllers. The distributed controllers provide the low-level control, interacting with sensor and actuator components, and respond to the Hierarchical Controller when they have finished. They may also send progress reports to the Hierarchical Controller.

18.4 CONCURRENT TASK STRUCTURING

A **concurrent task** is an active object, also referred to as a process or thread. In this chapter, the term *concurrent task* is used to refer to an active object with one thread of control. In some systems, a concurrent task would be implemented as a single-threaded process; in other systems, it might be implemented as a thread (lightweight process) within a heavyweight process (Gomaa 2000).

The concurrent structure of a system is best understood by considering the dynamic aspects of the system. In the analysis model, the system is represented as a collection of collaborating objects that communicate by means of messages. During the concurrent task structuring phase, the concurrent nature of the system is formalized by defining the concurrent tasks and the communication/synchronization interfaces between them.

The objects in the analysis model are analyzed to determine which of these may execute concurrently and which need to execute sequentially. Hence, the determination is made as to which of the analysis model objects should be active and which should be passive. In addition, a composite concurrent task can contain passive objects, whose operations are executed sequentially within the thread of control of the composite task.

Following the approach used in Chapter 8 for object structuring, stereotypes are used to depict the different kinds of concurrent tasks. Each task is depicted with two stereotypes: the first is the object role criterion, which is determined during object structuring, as described in Chapter 8; and the second stereotype is used to depict the type of concurrency. During concurrent task structuring, if an object in the analysis model is determined to be active, it is categorized further to show its concurrent task characteristics. For example, an active «I/O» object is concurrent and is categorized further using a second stereotype as one of the following: an «event driven» task, a «periodic» task, or a task activated on «demand». Stereotypes are also used to depict the kinds of devices to which the concurrent tasks interface. Thus, an «external input device» is further classified, depending on its characteristics, into an «event-driven» external input device or a «passive» external input device.

18.5 I/O TASK STRUCTURING CRITERIA

This section describes the various I/O task structuring criteria. An important factor in deciding on the characteristics of an I/O task is to determine the characteristics of the I/O device to which it has to interface.

18.5.1 Event Driven I/O Tasks

An event driven I/O task is needed when there is an event driven (also referred to as interrupt driven) I/O device to which the system has to interface. The event driven I/O task (referred to as asynchronous I/O task in [Gomaa 2000]) is activated by an interrupt from the event driven device. During task structuring, each device I/O object in the analysis model that interfaces to an event driven I/O device is designed as an event driven I/O task.

An event driven I/O task is constrained to execute at the speed of the I/O device with which it is interacting. Thus an input task might be suspended indefinitely awaiting an input. However, when activated by an interrupt, the input task often has to respond to a subsequent interrupt within a few milliseconds to avoid any loss of data. After the input data is read, the input task processes the data and then passes it on, e.g., it sends the data to be processed by another task. This frees the input task to respond to another interrupt that might closely follow the first.

Another kind of event driven I/O task is the *event driven proxy* task, which interfaces to an external system instead of an I/O device. An event driven *proxy* task usually interacts with an external system by using messages.

As an example of an event driven I/O task, consider the Door Sensor Interface input object shown on the analysis model communication diagram in Figure 18.5a. The Door Sensor Interface object receives door inputs from the real-world door, which is depicted as an external input device. The Door Sensor Interface object then converts the input to an internal format and sends the door request to the Microwave Control object. For task structuring, it is given that the door is an event driven input device, depicted on the design model concurrent communication diagram (Figure 18.5b) with the stereotypes «event driven» «external input device», which generates an interrupt when the door is opened or closed. The Door Sensor Interface object is designed as an event driven input task of the same name, depicted on the concurrent communication diagram with the stereotype «event driven» «input». When the task is activated by the Door Interrupt, it reads the Door Input, converts the input to

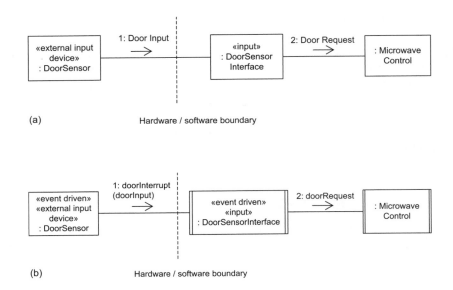

(Note: the dashed line for the hardware/software boundary is for illustrative purposes only and does not conform to the UML notation.)

Figure 18.5. Example of event driven I/O task: *(a)* Analysis model: communication diagram. *(b)* Design model: concurrent communication diagram

an internal format, and sends it as a Door Request message to the Microwave Control task. In the design model, the interrupt is depicted as an asynchronous event.

18.5.2 Periodic I/O Tasks

Unlike an event driven I/O task, which deals with an event driven I/O device, a periodic I/O task deals with a passive I/O device, in which the device is polled on a regular basis. In this situation, the activation of the task is periodic but its function is I/O-related. The periodic I/O task is activated by a timer event sent by an external timer, performs an I/O action, and then waits for the next timer event. The task's period is the time between successive activations.

Periodic I/O tasks are often used for simple I/O devices that, unlike event driven I/O devices, do not generate interrupts when I/O is available. Thus, they are often used for passive sensor devices that need to be sampled periodically. The concept of a periodic I/O task is used in many sensor-based industrial systems. Such systems often have a large number of digital and analog sensors. A periodic I/O task is activated on a regular basis, scans the sensors, and reads their values.

Consider a passive digital input device – for example, the engine sensor. This is handled by a **periodic I/O task**. The task is activated by a timer event and then reads the status of the device. If the value of the digital sensor has changed since the previous time it was sampled, the task indicates the change in status. In the case of an analog sensor – a temperature sensor, for example – the device is sampled periodically and the current value of the sensor is read.

As an example of a periodic I/O task, consider the Temperature Sensor Interface object shown in Figure 18.6*a*. In the analysis model depicted on the

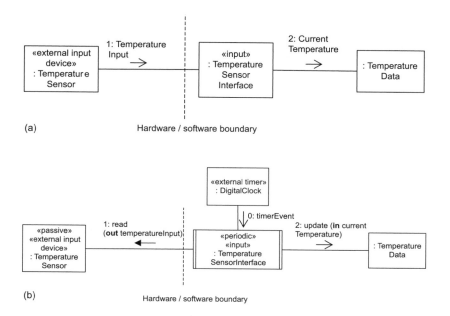

(Note: the dashed line for the hardware/software boundary is for illustrative purposes only and does not conform to the UML notation.)

Figure 18.6. Example of a periodic I/O task: *(a)* Analysis model: communication diagram. *(b)* Design model: concurrent communication diagram

communication diagram, the Temperature Sensor Interface object is an «input» object that receives temperature inputs from the real-world Temperature Sensor, depicted with the stereotype «external input device». Because the Temperature Sensor is a passive device, it is depicted on the concurrent communication diagram with the stereotypes «passive» «external input device» (see Figure 18.6*b*). Because a passive device does not generate an interrupt, an event driven input task cannot be used. Instead, this case is handled by a periodic input task, the Temperature Sensor Interface task, which is activated periodically by an external timer to sample the value of the temperature sensor. Thus, the Temperature Sensor Interface object is designed as the Temperature Sensor Interface «periodic» «input» task, as depicted on the concurrent communication diagram. To activate the Temperature Sensor Interface task periodically, it is necessary to add an «external timer» object, the Digital Clock, as depicted in Figure 18.6b. When activated, the Temperature Sensor Interface task samples the temperature sensor, updates the Temperature Data entity object with the current value of temperature, and then waits for the next timer event. The timer event is depicted as an asynchronous event in the design model.

18.5.3 Demand Driven I/O Tasks

Demand driven I/O tasks (referred to as passive I/O task in Gomaa [2000]) are used when dealing with passive I/O devices that do not need to be polled and, hence, do not need periodic I/O tasks. In particular, they are used when it is considered

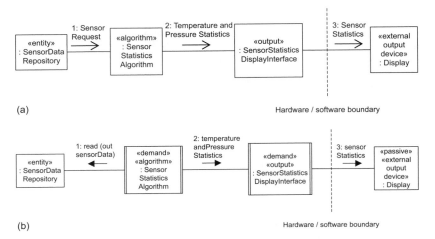

(Note: the dashed line for the hardware/software boundary is for illustrative purposes only and does not conform to the UML notation.)

Figure 18.7. Example of a demand driven output task: *(a)* Analysis model: communication diagram. *(b)* Design model: concurrent communication diagram

desirable to overlap computation with I/O. A demand driven I/O task is used in such a situation to interface to the passive I/O device. Consider the following cases:

- In the case of input, overlap the input from the passive device with the computational task that receives and consumes the data. This is achieved by using a demand driven input task to read the data from the input device when requested to do so.
- In the case of output, overlap the output to the device with the computational task that produces the data. This is achieved by using a demand driven output task to output to the device when requested to do so, usually via a message.

Demand driven I/O tasks are used more often with output devices than with input devices, because the output can be overlapped with the computation more often, as shown in the following example. Usually, if the I/O and computation are to be overlapped for a passive input device, a periodic input task is used.

Consider a demand driven output task that receives a message from a producer task. A demand driven task is depicted with the stereotype «demand». Overlapping computation and output is achieved as follows: the consumer task outputs the data contained in the message to the passive output device, the display, while the producer is preparing the next message. This case is shown in Figure 18.7. The Sensor Statistics Display Interface is a demand driven output task. It accepts a message to display from the Sensor Statistics Algorithm task, and it displays the sensor statistics while the Sensor Statistics Algorithm task is computing the next set of values to display; thus, the computation is overlapped with the output. The Sensor Statistics Display Interface task is depicted on the concurrent communication diagram with the stereotypes «demand» «output» task.

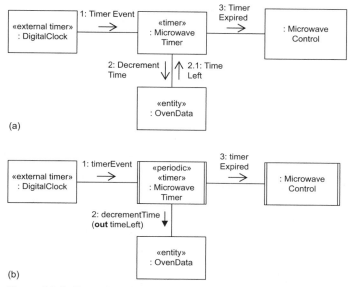

(a)

(b)

Figure 18.8. Example of a periodic task: *(a)* Analysis model: communication diagram. *(b)* Design model: concurrent communication diagram

18.6 INTERNAL TASK STRUCTURING CRITERIA

Whereas the I/O task structuring criteria are used to determine I/O tasks, the internal task structuring criteria are used to determine internal (i.e., non I/O) tasks.

18.6.1 Periodic Tasks

Many real-time and concurrent systems have activities that need to be executed on a periodic basis – for example, computing the distance traveled by the car or the current speed of the car. These periodic activities are typically handled by periodic tasks. Although periodic I/O activities are structured as periodic I/O tasks, periodic internal activities are structured as **periodic tasks**. Internal periodic tasks include *periodic algorithm* tasks.

An activity that needs to be executed periodically (i.e., at regular, equally spaced intervals of time) is structured as a separate periodic task. The task is activated by a timer event, performs the periodic activity, and then waits for the next timer event. The task's period is the time between successive activations.

As an example of a periodic task, consider the Microwave Timer object shown in Figure 18.8a. The Microwave Timer object is activated by a timer event every second. It then requests the Oven Data object to decrement the cooking time by one second and return the time left. If the cooking time has expired, then the Microwave Timer object sends a Timer Expired message to Microwave Control. The Microwave Timer object is designed as a periodic task (Figure 18.8b) that, when activated periodically, requests the Oven Data object to decrement the cooking time. The Microwave

Timer task is depicted on the concurrent communication diagram with the stereo-type «periodic» task. Oven Data is a passive object. The timer event is depicted as an asynchronous event.

18.6.2 Demand Driven Tasks

Many real-time and concurrent systems have activities that need to be executed on demand. These demand-driven activities are typically handled by means of demand driven tasks. Whereas event driven I/O tasks are activated by the arrival of external interrupts, demand driven internal tasks (also referred to as *aperiodic tasks*) are activated on demand by the arrival of internal messages or events.

An object that is activated on demand (i.e., when it receives an internal message or event sent by a different task) is structured as a separate **demand driven task**. The task is activated on demand by the arrival of the message or event sent by the requesting task, performs the demanded request, and then waits for the next message or event. Internal demand driven tasks include *demand driven algorithm* and tasks. A demand driven task is depicted with the stereotype «demand».

An example of a demand driven task is given in Figure 18.9. In the analysis model, the Gas Flow Algorithm object is activated on demand by the arrival of a Pump Command message from the Pump Control object. It then executes an algorithm

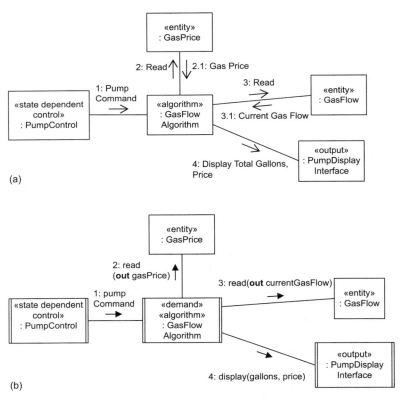

Figure 18.9. Example of a demand driven task: *(a)* Analysis model: communication diagram. *(b)* Design model: concurrent communication diagram

to read the current gas flow and the gas price and compute the total gallons pumped and total price, which are then sent to the Pump Display Interface object (Figure 18.9a). In the design model, the Gas Flow Algorithm object is structured as a demand driven algorithm task with the same name, which is activated by the arrival of a Pump Command message. The Gas Flow Algorithm task is depicted on the concurrent communication diagram with the stereotypes «demand» «algorithm» task (Figure 18.9b). The Pump Control and Pump Display Interface objects are also structured as tasks. The Gas Flow and Gas Price entity objects are passive objects.

18.6.3 Control Tasks

In the analysis model, a state-dependent control object executes a statechart. Using the restricted form of statecharts whereby concurrency within an object is not permitted, it follows that the execution of a statechart is strictly sequential. Hence, a task, whose execution is also strictly sequential, can perform the control activity. A task that executes a sequential statechart (typically implemented as a state transition table) is referred to as a state-dependent control task. A control task is usually a demand driven task that is activated on demand by a message sent by another task. A state-dependent control task is depicted with the stereotype «state-dependent control».

An example of a control task is shown in Figure 18.10. The state-dependent control object Microwave Control (Figure 18.10a), which executes the Microwave Control statechart, is structured as the Microwave Control task (Figure 18.10b) because execution of the statechart is strictly sequential. The task is depicted on the concurrent communication diagram with the stereotypes «demand» «state-dependent control» task.

It is possible to have many objects of the same type. Each object is designed as a task, in which all the tasks are instances of the same task type. In the case of a state-dependent control object, each object executes an instance of the same sequential statechart, although each object is likely to be in a different state. This is addressed by having one state-dependent control task for each control object, in which the task executes the statechart.

An example of multiple control tasks of the same type comes from the Elevator Control System, as shown in Figure 18.11. The control aspects of a real-world

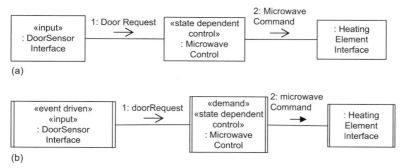

Figure 18.10. Example of a control task: *(a)* Analysis model: communication diagram. *(b)* Design model: concurrent communication diagram

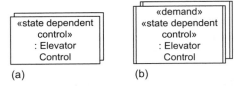

Figure 18.11. Example of multiple control tasks of same type: *(a)* Analysis model: control object (multiple instances). *(b)* Design model: one task for each elevator

elevator are modeled by means of a state-dependent control object, Elevator Control, and defined by means of a sequential statechart. During task structuring, the Elevator Control object is designed as an Elevator state-dependent Control task. In a multiple-elevator system, there is one elevator task for each Elevator Control object. The tasks are identical, and each task executes an instance of the same statechart. However, each elevator is likely to be in a different state on its statechart. In both Figures 18.11a and 18.11b the multiple instances of the Elevator Control object and Elevator Control task are depicted using the UML multiple instance notation.

In addition to state-dependent control objects, coordinator objects from the analysis model are designed as *coordinator tasks*. In this case, the job of the task is to control other tasks, although it is not state-dependent.

18.6.4 User Interaction Tasks

A user typically performs a set of sequential actions. Because the user's interaction with the system is a sequential activity, this can be handled by a **user interaction task**. The speed of this task is frequently constrained by the speed of user interaction. As its name implies, a **user interaction object** in the analysis model is designed as a user interaction task. User interaction tasks are usually event driven because they are awakened by inputs from the external user.

A user interaction task usually interfaces with various standard I/O devices, such as the input keyboard, output display, and mouse, that are typically handled by the operating system. Because the operating system provides a standard interface to these devices, it is usually not necessary to develop special-purpose I/O tasks to handle them.

The concept of one task per user is typical in many multiuser operating systems. For example, in the UNIX operating system, there is one task (process) per user. If, on the other hand, the user engages in several activities concurrently, one user interaction task is allocated for each sequential activity. Thus, in the UNIX operating system, users can spawn background tasks. All the user interaction tasks that belong to the same user execute concurrently.

The concept of one task per sequential activity is also used on modern workstations with multiple windows. Each window executes a sequential activity, so there is one task for each window. In the Windows operating system, it is possible for the user to have Word executing in one window and PowerPoint executing in another window. There is one user interaction task for each window, and each of these tasks can spawn other tasks (e.g., to overlap printing with editing).

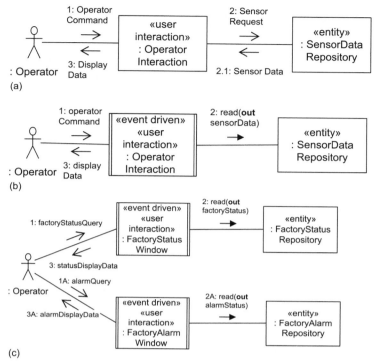

Figure 18.12. Example of a user interaction task: *(a)* Analysis model: communication diagram. *(b)* Design model: concurrent communication diagram with one task. *(c)* Design model: concurrent communication diagram with two tasks.

An example of a user interaction task is given in Figure 18.12. The object Operator Interface accepts operator commands, reads from the Sensor Data Repository entity object, and displays data to the operator (Figure 18.12*a*). Because all operator interactions are sequential in this example, the Operator Interface object is structured as a user interaction task (Figure 18.12*b*). The task is depicted on the concurrent communication diagram with the stereotypes «event driven» «user interaction» task. It is activated by an input from the user.

In a multiple-window workstation environment, a factory operator might view factory status in one window (supported by one user interaction task) and acknowledge alarms in another window (supported by a different user interaction task). An example of this is given in Figure 18.12*c*. Two user interaction tasks, Factory Status Window and Factory Alarm Window, are active concurrently. The Factory Status Window task interacts with the passive Factory Status Repository object while the Factory Alarm Window task interacts with the passive Factory Alarm Repository object.

18.7 DEVELOPING THE CONCURRENT TASK ARCHITECTURE

The task structuring criteria may be applied to the analysis model in the following order. In each case, one must first decide whether the analysis model object should be designed as an active object (task) or a passive object in the design model. It is possible to have multiple tasks of the same type.

Table 18.1. Mapping from analysis model objects to design model tasks

Analysis model (Object)	Design model (Task)
User interaction	Event driven user interaction
Input/Output (input, output, I/O)	Event driven I/O (input, output, I/O)
	Periodic I/O (input, output, I/O)
	Demand driven I/O (usually output)
Proxy	Event driven proxy
Timer	Periodic timer
State-dependent control	Demand driven state-dependent control
Coordinator	Demand driven coordinator
Algorithm	Demand driven algorithm
	Periodic algorithm

1. **I/O tasks.** Start with the device I/O objects that interact with the outside world. Determine whether the object should be structured as an event driven I/O task, a periodic I/O task, or a demand driven I/O task.
2. **Control tasks.** Analyze each state-dependent control object and coordinator object. Structure this object as a (usually demand driven) state-dependent control or coordinator task.
3. **Periodic tasks.** Analyze the internal periodic activities, which are structured as periodic tasks.
4. **Other internal tasks.** For each internal task activated by an internal event, structure this task as a demand driven task.

The guidelines for mapping analysis model objects to design model tasks are summarized in Table 18.1.

18.7.1 Initial Concurrent Communication Diagram

After structuring the system into concurrent tasks, an initial concurrent communication diagram is drawn, showing all the tasks in the system. On this initial concurrent communication diagram, the interfaces between the tasks are still simple messages as depicted on the analysis model communication diagrams. An example of an initial concurrent communication diagram is given in Figure 18.13 for the ATM Client subsystem of the Banking System case study. The design of the ATM Client is described in detail in Chapter 21. Designing task interfaces is described next.

18.8 TASK COMMUNICATION AND SYNCHRONIZATION

After structuring the system into concurrent tasks, the next step is to design the task interfaces. At this stage, the interfaces between tasks are still simple messages as depicted on the analysis model communication diagrams. It is necessary to map these interfaces to task interfaces in the form of message communication, event synchronization, or access to information hiding objects.

The UML notation for message communication is described in Chapter 2. Message communication patterns for concurrent components are described in Chapters 12 and 15. In the communication diagrams developed for the analysis model and in

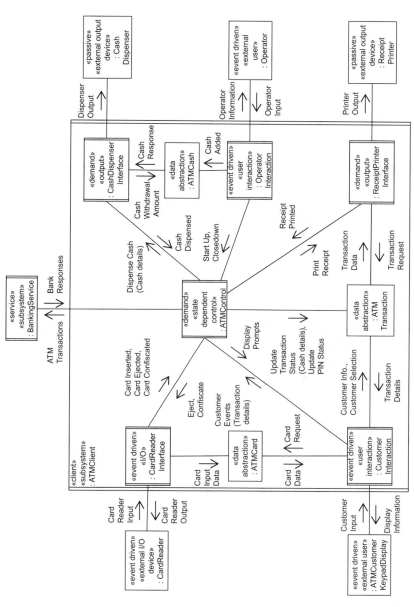

Figure 18.13. Task architecture: example of initial concurrent communication diagram for ATM Client subsystem

333

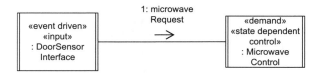

Figure 18.14. Example of Asynchronous Message Communication

the preliminary concurrent communication diagram for the design model, all communication is shown using simple messages. In this step of the design modeling, the task interfaces are defined and depicted on revised concurrent communication diagrams.

Message interfaces between tasks are either asynchronous (loosely coupled) or synchronous (tightly coupled), as introduced in Chapter 4 and described in more detail in Chapter 12. For synchronous message communication, two possibilities exist: synchronous message communication with reply and synchronous message communication without reply.

18.8.1 Asynchronous (Loosely Coupled) Message Communication

Asynchronous message communication, also referred to as **loosely coupled message communication**, between concurrent tasks is based on the Asynchronous Message Communication pattern described in Section 12.3.3. The producer sends a message to the consumer and continues without waiting for a response.

Consider the concurrent communication diagram (Figure 18.14), which depicts the Door Sensor Interface task sending a message to the Microwave Control task. It is desirable to design this message interface as using asynchronous message communication. The Door Sensor Interface task sends the message and does not wait for it to be accepted by the Microwave Control task. This allows the Door Sensor Interface task to quickly service any new external input that might arrive. Asynchronous message communication also provides the greatest flexibility for the Microwave Control task, because it can wait on a queue of messages that arrive from multiple sources. It then accepts the first message that arrives, whatever the source.

18.8.2 Synchronous (Tightly Coupled) Message Communication with Reply

Synchronous message communication with reply, also referred to as **tightly coupled message communication with reply**, between concurrent tasks is based on the Synchronous Message Communication with Reply pattern described in Section 12.3.4. The producer sends a message to the consumer and then waits for a reply.

Although used in client/server systems (Chapter 15), Synchronous Message Communication with Reply can also involve a single producer sending a message to a consumer and then waiting for a reply, in which case no message queue develops between the producer and the consumer. An example of Synchronous Message Communication with Reply involving a producer and consumer is from the Automated Guided Vehicle System, in which the producer task, Vehicle Control, sends start and stop messages to the consumer task, Motor Interface, and waits for a reply,

Figure 18.15. Example of Synchronous Message Communication with Reply

as depicted on the concurrent communication diagram (Figure 18.15). The producer needs to be tightly coupled with the consumer, because it sends a message and then waits for a response. After receiving the message, the consumer processes the message, prepares a reply, and sends the reply to the producer. The notation for Synchronous Message Communication with Reply on the concurrent communication diagram (Figure 18.15) shows a synchronous message sent from the producer to the consumer with a dashed message, representing the response, sent by the consumer back to the producer.

18.8.3 Synchronous (Tightly Coupled) Message Communication without Reply

Synchronous message communication without reply, also referred to as **tightly coupled message communication without reply**, between concurrent tasks is based on the Synchronous Message Communication without Reply pattern. The producer sends a message to the consumer and then waits for acceptance of the message by the consumer. When the message arrives, the consumer accepts the message, thereby releasing the producer. The producer and consumer then both continue. The consumer is suspended if no message is available.

An example of Synchronous Message Communication without Reply is shown in Figure 18.16. The Sensor Statistics Display Interface is a demand output task. It accepts a message to display from the Sensor Statistics Algorithm task, as depicted on the concurrent communication diagram (Figure 18.16). It displays the sensor statistics while the Sensor Statistics Algorithm task is computing the next set of values to display. Thus, the computation is overlapped with the output.

The producer task, the Sensor Statistics Algorithm task, sends temperature and pressure statistics to the consumer task, the Sensor Statistics Display Interface, which then displays the information. In this example, the decision made is that there is no point in having the Sensor Statistics Algorithm task compute temperature and pressure statistics if the Sensor Statistics Display Interface cannot keep up with displaying them. Consequently, the interface between the two tasks is designed as a Synchronous Message Communication without Reply interface, as depicted on

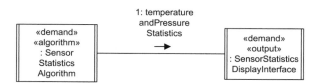

Figure 18.16. Example of Synchronous Message Communication without Reply

the revised concurrent communication diagram (Figure 18.16). The Sensor Statistics Algorithm computes the statistics, sends the message, and then waits for the acceptance of the message by the Sensor Statistics Display Interface before resuming execution. The Sensor Statistics Algorithm is held up until the Sensor Statistics Display Interface finishes displaying the previous message. As soon as the Sensor Statistics Display Interface accepts the new message, the Sensor Statistics Algorithm is released from its wait and computes the next set of statistics while the Sensor Statistics Display Interface displays the previous set. By this means, computation of the statistics (a compute-bound activity) can be overlapped with displaying of the statistics (an I/O bound activity), while preventing an unnecessary message queue build-up of statistics at the display task. Thus, the synchronous interface between the two tasks acts as a brake on the producer task.

18.8.4 Event Synchronization

Three types of event synchronization are possible: an external event, a timer event, and an internal event. An external event is an event from an external object, typically an interrupt from an external I/O device. An internal event represents internal synchronization between a source task and a destination task. A timer event represents a periodic activation of a task. Events are depicted in UML, using the asynchronous message notation to depict an event signal.

An example of an external event, typically a hardware interrupt from an input device, is given in Figure 18.17. The Door Sensor «event driven» «external input device» generates an interrupt when it has door Input. The interrupt activates the Door Sensor Interface «event driven» «input» task, which then reads the doorInput. This interaction could be depicted as an event signal input from the device, followed by a read by the task. However, it is more concise to depict the interaction as an asynchronous event signal sent by the device, with the input data as a parameter, as depicted on the concurrent communication diagram (Figure 18.17).

An example of a timer event is given in Figure 18.18. The digital clock, which is an external timer device, generates a timer event to awaken the Microwave Timer «periodic» task. The Microwave Timer task then performs a periodic activity – in this case, decrementing the cooking time by one second and checking whether the cooking time has expired (see Figure 18.8). The timer event is generated at fixed intervals of time.

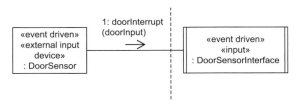

Hardware / software boundary

(Note: the dashed line for the hardware/software boundary is for illustrative purposes only and does not conform to the UML notation.)

Figure 18.17. Example of external event

Figure 18.18. Example of timer event

Internal event synchronization is used when two tasks need to synchronize their actions without communicating data between the tasks. The source task signals the event. The destination task waits for the event and is suspended until the event is signaled. It is not suspended if the event has previously been signaled. The event signal is depicted in UML by an asynchronous message that does not contain any data. An example of this is shown in Figure 18.19, in which the pick-and-place robot task signals the event partReady. This awakens the drilling robot, which operates on the part and then signals the event partCompleted, which the pick-and-place robot is waiting to receive.

18.8.5 Task Interaction via Information Hiding Object

It is also possible for tasks to exchange information by means of a passive information hiding object. Access to information hiding objects was previously described in Chapter 14. An example of task access to a passive information hiding object is given in Figure 18.20, in which the Sensor Statistics Algorithm task reads from the Sensor Data Repository entity object, and the Sensor Interface task updates the entity object. On the initial concurrent communication diagram, the Sensor Statistics Algorithm task sends a simple message, Read, to the entity object and receives a Sensor Data response, which is also depicted as a simple message (Figure 18.20a). Because the task is reading from a passive information hiding object, this interface corresponds to an operation call. The entity object provides a read operation, which is called by the Sensor Statistics Algorithm task. The sensorData response is an output parameter of the call. The read operation is executed in the thread of control of the task. On the revised concurrent communication diagram (Figure 18.20b), the call to the read operation is depicted by using the synchronous message notation. The sensor Data response is depicted as the output parameter of the read synchronous message. The Sensor Interface task calls a write operation provided by the Sensor Data Repository entity object, with the sensorData as an input parameter.

It is important to realize how the synchronous message notation used between two concurrent tasks differs from that used between a task and a passive object. The notation looks the same in the UML: an arrow with a filled-in arrowhead. The semantics are different, however. The synchronous message notation between two concurrent tasks represents a producer task waiting for a consumer task to either

Figure 18.19. Example of internal events

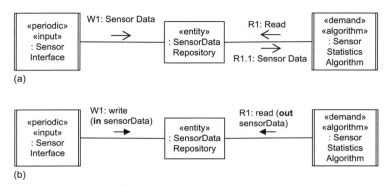

Figure 18.20. Example of tasks invoking operations of passive object: *(a)* Initial concurrent communication diagram with simple messages. *(b)* Revised concurrent communication diagram with tasks invoking operations of passive object

respond to or accept the producer's message, as shown in Figures 18.15 and 18.16. The synchronous message notation between a task and a passive object represents an operation call, as shown in Figures 18.20.

18.8.6 Revised Concurrent Communication Diagram

After having determined the task interfaces, the initial concurrent communication diagram is revised to depict the various types of task interface. An example of the revised concurrent communication diagram is given for the ATM Client subsystem of the Banking System case study, as shown in Figure 18.21, in which the initial concurrent communication diagram of Figure 18.13 is updated to show all the task interfaces. The design of the ATM Client is described in detail in Chapter 21.

18.9 TASK INTERFACE AND TASK BEHAVIOR SPECIFICATIONS

A **task interface specification (TIS)** describes a concurrent task's interface. It is an extension of the class interface specification with additional information specific to a task, including task structure, timing characteristics, relative priority, and errors detected. A **task behavior specification (TBS)** describes the task's event sequencing logic. The task's interface defines how it interfaces to other tasks. The task's structure describes how its structure is derived, using the task structuring criteria. The task's timing characteristics address frequency of activation and estimated execution time. This information is used for real-time scheduling purposes and is not discussed further in this textbook.

The TIS is introduced with the **task architecture** to specify the characteristics of each task. The TBS is defined later, during detailed software design, and describes the **task event sequencing logic**, which is how the task responds to the input events it receives.

A task (active class) differs from a passive class in that it should be designed with only one operation (in Java, this can be implemented as the *run* method). For this reason, the TIS only has a specification of one operation, instead of several for a

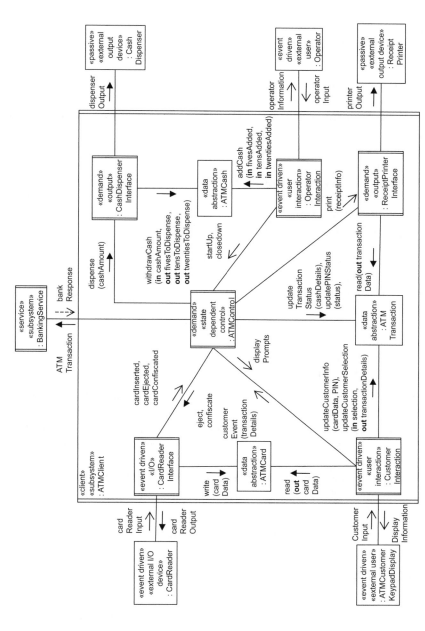

Figure 18.21. Task architecture: example of revised concurrent communication diagram for ATM Client subsystem

339

typical passive class. The TIS is defined as follows, with the first five items identical to the class interface specification:

- **Name**
- **Information hidden**
- **Structuring criteria:** For class structuring criteria, only the role criterion (e.g., input) is used; for concurrent tasks, the concurrency criterion (e.g., event driven) needs to be added.
- **Assumptions**
- **Anticipated changes**
- **Task interface:** The task interface should include a definition of
  - **Messages inputs and outputs.** For each message interface (input or output) there should be a description of
    - **Type of interface:** asynchronous, synchronous with reply, or synchronous without reply
    - For each message type supported by this interface: message name and message parameters
  - **Events signaled** (input and output), name of event, type of event: external, internal, timer
  - **External inputs or outputs.** Define the inputs from and outputs to the external environment.
  - **Passive objects referenced**
- **Errors detected by this task**

This section describes the possible errors that could be detected during execution of this task.

The TBS describes the task's **event sequencing logic**, which is how the task responds to each of its message or event inputs, in particular, what output is generated as a result of each input. The event sequencing logic is defined during the detailed software design step. Examples of task event sequencing logic are given in the Banking System case study in Chapter 21.

18.9.1 Example of TIS for Banking Service Task

The TIS for the Banking Service task (described in Chapter 21 and illustrated in Figure 18.21) is described here:

Name: BankingService
Information hidden: Details of how BankingService processes ATM transactions
Structuring criteria: role criterion: service; concurrency criterion: demand driven
Assumptions: Transactions are processed sequentially.
Anticipated changes: Possible addition of further transactions; possible change from sequential service to concurrent service processing
Task interface:

  Task inputs:

  Synchronous message communication with reply:

Messages:
- validatePIN

     Input parameters: cardId, PIN
     Reply: PINValidationResponse

- withdraw

     Input parameters: cardId, account#, amount
     Reply: withdrawalResponse

- query

     Input parameters: cardId, account#
     Reply: queryResponse

- transfer

     Input parameters: cardId, fromAccount#,
     toAccount#, amount
     Reply: transferResponse

Task outputs:

   Message replies as described previously.
   Errors detected: Unrecognized message

18.9.2 Example of TIS for Card Reader Interface Task

The task interface specification for the Card Reader Interface task (Chapter 21 and Figure 18.21) is described here:

Name: CardReaderInterface
Information hidden: Details of processing input from and output to card reader
Structuring criteria: role criterion: input/output; concurrency criterion: event driven
Assumptions: only one ATM card input and output is handled at one time.
Anticipated Changes: Possible additional information will need to be read from ATM card.
Task interface:

   Task inputs:
   Event input: Card reader external interrupt to indicate that a card has been input.
   External input: cardReaderInput.
   Synchronous message communication without reply:
   - eject
   - confiscate
   Task outputs:
   External output: cardReaderOutput

Asynchronous message communication:
- cardInserted
- cardEjected
- cardConfiscated

Passive objects accessed: ATMCard

Errors detected: Unrecognized card, Card reader malfunction.

18.10 IMPLEMENTATION OF CONCURRENT TASKS IN JAVA

As an example of task implementation, consider implementation in Java, in which tasks are implemented as threads. The simplest way to design a thread class in Java is to inherit from the Java Thread class, which has one method called *run*. The new thread class must then implement the *run* method, which, when invoked, will execute independently with its own thread of control. In the example below, the ATM Control class is designed to be a thread. The body of the thread is contained in the *run* method. Typically, the body of the task is a loop, in which the task would either wait for an external event (from an external device or timer) or wait for a message from a producer task.

```
public class ATMControl extends Thread{}
public void run (){
while (true)
//task body
}
```

18.11 SUMMARY

During the task structuring phase, the system is structured into concurrent tasks and the task interfaces are defined. To help determine the concurrent tasks, task structuring criteria are provided to assist in mapping an object-oriented analysis model of the system to a concurrent tasking architecture. The task communication and synchronization interfaces are also defined. Each task is determined by using the task structuring criteria. A case study of designing a real-time software architecture is given for the Automated Guided Vehicle System described in Chapter 24. In addition, an example of concurrent software design is the design of the ATM Client subsystem in the Banking System case study in Chapter 21.

More information on UML modeling for real-time and embedded systems is given in MARTE, the UML profile for Modeling and Analysis of Real-Time and Embedded Systems (Espinoza et al 2009). More information about designing real-software architectures is given in Gomaa (2000). To make concurrent task design more efficient (i.e., less demanding of resources), a group of related tasks can be combined into one clustered task by applying task clustering criteria, such as sequential, temporal, or control clustering (Gomaa 2000).

EXERCISES

Multiple-choice questions: For each question, choose one of the answers.

1. What is the difference between an active object and a passive object?
   (a) An active object controls a passive object.
   (b) An active object does not have a thread of control; a passive object has a thread of control.
   (c) An active object executes in a distributed system; a passive object executes in a centralized system.
   (d) An active object has a thread of control; a passive object does not have a thread of control.

2. What is an event-driven input task?
   (a) A task that executes every few seconds
   (b) A task that controls other tasks
   (c) A task that receives inputs from an external device when it generates interrupts
   (d) A task that checks whether there is new input from an external device

3. What is a periodic task?
   (a) A task that responds to each message it receives
   (b) A task that is activated by a timer event
   (c) A task that is activated by an external event
   (d) A task that is activated by an input event

4. What is a demand-driven task?
   (a) A task that responds to each message it receives
   (b) A task that is activated by an internal message or event from another task
   (c) A task that is activated by an external event
   (d) A task that is activated by an input event

5. What is a control task?
   (a) A task that control other tasks
   (b) A task that executes a statechart
   (c) A task that executes on demand
   (d) A task that controls I/O devices

6. What is a user interaction task?
   (a) A task that interacts with I/O devices
   (b) A task that interacts with users
   (c) A task that interacts with a user sequentially
   (d) A task that interacts with a user concurrently

7. Which of the following is true for a Centralized Control architectural pattern?
   (a) Control is divided among various control components.
   (b) It provides the overall control and sequencing of the system.
   (c) It provides overall control by coordinating several control components.
   (d) It provides overall control over various I/O objects.

8. Which of the following is true for a Distributed Control architectural pattern?
   (a) Control is divided among various control components.
   (b) It responds to multiple requests from client subsystems.
   (c) It provides overall control by coordinating several control components.
   (d) It provides distributed control over various I/O objects.

9. Which of the following is true for a Hierarchical Control architectural pattern?
   (a) Control is divided among various control components.
   (b) It provides overall control over several client subsystems.
   (c) It provides overall control by coordinating several control components.
   (d) It provides overall control over various I/O objects.

10. Which of the following is NOT a case of event synchronization?
   (a) External event
   (b) Internal event
   (c) Timer event
   (d) User event

19

Designing Software Product Line Architectures

A software product line (SPL) consists of a family of software systems that have some common functionality and some variable functionality (Clements and Northop 2002; Parnas 1979; Weiss and Lai 1999). Software product line engineering involves developing the requirements, architecture, and component implementations for a family of systems, from which products (family members) are derived and configured. The problems of developing individual software systems are scaled upwards when developing SPLs because of the increased complexity due to variability management.

As with single systems, a better understanding of a SPL can be obtained by considering the multiple views, such as requirements models, static models, and dynamic models of the product line. A graphical modeling language such as UML helps in developing, understanding, and communicating the different views. A key view in the multiple views of a SPL is the feature modeling view. The feature model is crucial for managing variability and product derivation because it describes the product line requirements in terms of commonality and variability, and defines the product line dependencies. Furthermore, it is desirable to have a development approach that promotes software evolution, such that original development and subsequent maintenance are both treated using feature-driven evolution.

This chapter gives an overview of designing SPL architectures using the Product Line UML-based Software) engineering (PLUS) method. PLUS builds on the COMET method by considering the added dimension of variability in each of the modeling views. Designing SPLs is covered in considerable detail in the author's book on this topic (Gomaa 2005a). Section 19.1 describes the evolutionary software process model for SPL Engineering. Section 19.2 describes use case modeling and feature modeling for SPLs. Section 19.3 describes static and dynamic modeling for SPLs. Section 19.4 describes how variability is handled in statecharts. Section 19.5 describes variability management in design models.

19.1 EVOLUTIONARY SOFTWARE PRODUCT LINE ENGINEERING

The software process model for SPL engineering is a highly iterative software process that eliminates the traditional distinction between software development and

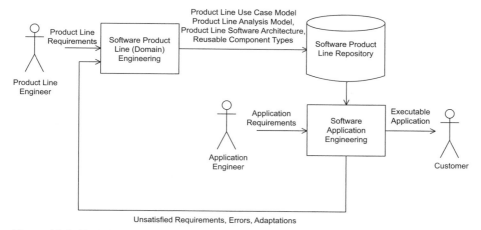

Figure 19.1. Evolutionary software process model for software product lines

maintenance. Furthermore, because new software systems are outgrowths of existing ones, the process takes a SPL perspective; it consists of two main processes (Figure 19.1):

1. **SPL Engineering** (also referred to as *domain engineering*). A product line
   multiple-view model that addresses the multiple views of a SPL is developed.
   The product line multiple-view model, product line architecture, and reusable
   components (referred to as *core assets* in Clements and Northrop [2002]) are
   developed and stored in the product line repository.
2. **Software Application Engineering.** A software application multiple-view
   model is an individual product line member derived from the SPL multiple-
   view model. The user selects the required features for the individual product
   line member. Given the features, the product line model and architecture are
   adapted and tailored to derive the application architecture. The architecture
   determines which of the reusable components are needed for deriving and
   configuring the executable application.

19.2 REQUIREMENTS MODELING FOR SOFTWARE PRODUCT LINES

For single systems, use case modeling is the primary vehicle for describing software
functional requirements. For SPLs, feature modeling is an additional important part
of requirements modeling. The strength of feature modeling is in differentiating
between the functionality provided by the different family members of the product line in terms of common functionality, optional functionality, and alternative
functionality.

19.2.1 Use Case Modeling for Software Product Lines

The functional requirements of a system are defined in terms of use cases and actors
(see Chapter 6). For a single system, all use cases are required. In a SPL, only some
of the use cases, which are referred to as kernel use cases, are required by all members of the family. Other use cases are optional, in that they are required by some
but not all members of the family. Some use cases might be alternatives to each other

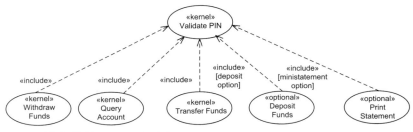

Figure 19.2. Software product line use cases

(i.e., different versions of the use case are required by different members of the family). In UML, the use cases are labeled with the stereotype «kernel», «optional» or «alternative» (Gomaa 2005a). In addition, variability can be inserted into a use case through variation points, which specify locations in the use case where variability can be introduced (Gomaa 2005a; Jacobson, Griss, and Jonsson 1997; Webber and Gomaa 2004).

Examples of kernel and optional product line use cases for a Banking SPL are given in Figure 19.2. The kernel of this SPL consists of the use cases that allow a customer to validate PIN, withdraw funds, query balance of account, and transfer funds between accounts (as described in Chapters 6 and 21). Optional use cases are provided for printing a statement (Print Statement) and cash deposit (Deposit Funds). Additional optional use cases are the ATM operator maintenance use cases to Startup, Shutdown, and Add Cash to the ATM (although not shown in Figure 19.2, these use cases are described in the case study in Chapter 21).

Variation points are provided for both the kernel and optional use cases. One variation point concerns the display prompt language. Since the Banking System family members will be deployed in different countries, a given bank can choose the prompt language. The default language is English, with alternative languages being French, Spanish, and German. An example of a variation point is for all steps that involve displaying information to the customer in the Validate PIN use case. This variation point is of type *mandatory alternative,* which means that a selection among the alternative choices must be made.

Variation point in Validate PIN use case:
Name: Display Language.
Type of functionality: Mandatory alternative.
Step number(s): 3, 8.
Description of functionality: There is a choice of language for displaying messages. The default is English. Alternative mutually exclusive languages are French, Spanish, and German.

19.2.2 Feature Modeling

Feature modeling is an important modeling view for product line engineering (Kang et al. 1990), because it addresses SPL variability. Features are analyzed and categorized as common features (must be supported in all product line members), optional features (only required in some product line members), alternative features (a choice of feature is available), and prerequisite features (dependent upon other features). The emphasis in feature modeling is capturing the product line variability, as given by optional and alternative features, because these features differentiate one member of the product family from the others.

Features are used widely in product line engineering but are not typically used in UML. In order to effectively model product lines, it is necessary to incorporate feature modeling concepts into UML. Features are incorporated into UML in the PLUS method using the meta-class concept, in which features are modeled using the UML static modeling notation and given stereotypes to differentiate between «common feature», «optional feature», and «alternative feature» (Gomaa 2005a). Feature dependencies are depicted as associations with the name *requires* (e.g., the Greeting feature *requires* the Language feature). Furthermore, feature groups, which place a constraint on how certain features can be selected for a product line member, such as mutually exclusive features, are also modeled using meta-classes and given stereotypes (e.g., «zero-or-one-of feature group» or «exactly-one-of feature group») (Gomaa 2005a). A feature group is modeled as an aggregation of features, because a feature *is part of* a feature group.

The feature model for the Banking SPL is shown in Figure 19.3. The common feature is the Banking System Kernel, which provides the core functionality of the ATM corresponding to the four kernel use cases in Figure 19.2. The Deposit feature, which corresponds to the optional Deposit Funds use case in Figure 19.2, is an optional feature that requires the kernel feature. Similarly, Statement is also an optional feature that corresponds to the optional Print Statement use case. Language is an exactly-one-of feature group, which corresponds to the Language variation point in the use case model. This feature group consists of the default feature English and the alternative features of Spanish, French, or German. There is a parameterized feature for Max PIN Attempts, which sets the maximum number of invalid

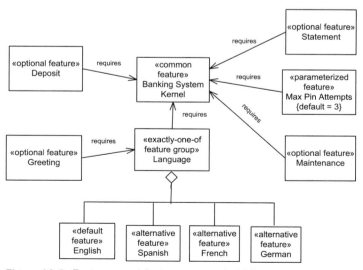

Figure 19.3. Features and feature groups in UML

PIN attempts at an ATM and has a default value of 3. Another optional feature is the Greeting feature, which depends on the Language feature and corresponds to the Greeting variation point. The ATM can output an optional greeting message to customers that needs to be displayed in the appropriate language.

In single systems, use cases are used to determine the functional requirements of a system; they can also serve this purpose in product families. Griss (Griss, Favaro, and d'Alessandro 1998) has pointed out that the goal of the use case analysis is to get a good understanding of the functional requirements, whereas the goal of feature analysis is to enable reuse. Use cases and features complement each other; thus, optional and alternative use cases are mapped to optional and alternative features, respectively, whereas use case variation points are also mapped to features (Gomaa 2005a).

The relationship between use cases and features can be explicitly depicted in a feature/use case relationship table, as shown in Table 19.1. For each feature, the use case it relates to is depicted. In the case of a feature derived from a variation point, the variation point name is listed. The Banking System Kernel feature is related to the Validate PIN, Query Account, Transfer Funds, and Withdraw Funds kernel use cases. The Deposit and Statement optional features correspond to the Deposit Funds and Print Statement optional use cases, respectively. The Maintenance feature corresponds to the ATM operator maintenance use cases to Startup, Shutdown, and Add Cash to the ATM. The optional Greeting feature and the parameterized Max PIN Attempts feature correspond to variation points in the Validate PIN use case. The English, French, German, and Spanish alternative language features are associated with the Language variation point in all use cases of the Banking System SPL. This variation point affects all display prompts of an ATM.

Table 19.1 Feature/use case relationship table

Feature name	Feature Category	Use case name	Use case / variation point (vp)	Variation point name
Banking System Kernel	Common	Validate PIN	Kernel	
		Query Account	Kernel	
		Transfer Funds	Kernel	
		Withdraw Funds	Kernel	
Deposit	Optional	Deposit Funds	Optional	
Statement	Optional	Print Statement	Optional	
Maintenance	Optional	Startup	Optional	
		Shutdown	Optional	
		Add Cash	Optional	
English	Default	All use cases	vp	Display Language
Spanish	Alternative	All use cases	vp	Display Language
French	Alternative	All use cases	vp	Display Language
German	Alternative	All use cases	vp	Display Language
Greeting	Optional	Validate PIN	vp	Greeting
Max PIN Attempts	Parameterized	Validate PIN	vp	PIN Attempts

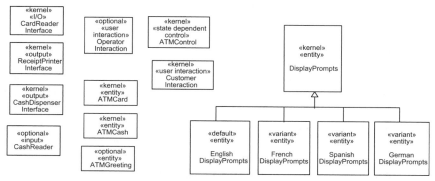

Figure 19.4. Role and reuse stereotypes in product line classes

19.3 ANALYSIS MODELING FOR SOFTWARE PRODUCT LINES

As with single systems, analysis modeling consists of both static and dynamic modeling. However, both modeling approaches need to address modeling SPL variability.

19.3.1 Static Modeling for Software Product Lines

In single systems, a class is categorized by the role it plays. Application classes are classified according to their role in the application using stereotypes (see Chapter 8), such as «entity class», «control class», or «boundary class». In modeling SPLs, each class can also be categorized according to its reuse characteristic using the stereotypes «kernel», «optional», and «variant». In UML, a modeling element can be described with more than one stereotype. Thus, one stereotype can be used to represent the reuse characteristic, whereas a different stereotype is used to represent the role played by the modeling element (Gomaa 2005a). The role a class plays in the application and the reuse characteristic are orthogonal.

Examples of kernel, optional, and variant entity classes are given in Figure 19.4. ATM Card and ATM Cash are kernel entity classes because they are needed in every SPL member. The ATM Greeting entity class is optional because it corresponds to the optional Greeting feature. For the Language feature group, there is an abstract kernel superclass Display Prompts, with variant subclasses, which contain the language-specific prompts corresponding to each Language feature. Each class is depicted with two stereotypes: the role stereotype, which is entity for the classes, and the reuse stereotype, which is kernel, optional, or variant.

19.3.2 Dynamic Interaction Modeling for Software Product Lines

Dynamic modeling for SPLs uses an iterative strategy called **evolutionary dynamic analysis** to help determine the dynamic impact of each feature on the software architecture. This results in new components being added or existing components having to be adapted. The **kernel system** is a minimal member of the product line. In some product lines, the kernel system consists of only the kernel objects; for other product lines, some default objects may be needed in addition to the kernel objects. The kernel system is developed by considering the kernel use cases, which are required by every member for the product line. For each kernel use case, a communication diagram is developed depicting the objects needed to realize the use case (using the approach described in Chapters 9 and 11). The kernel system is determined by integrating the kernel use case–based communication diagrams (using the approach described in Chapter 13) to depict all the objects in the kernel system and the message communication between them. The next step is to determine the classes from which these objects are instantiated.

The **software product line evolution approach** starts with the kernel system and considers the impact of optional and/or alternative features (Gomaa 2005a). This results in the addition of optional or variant objects to the product line architecture. This analysis is done by considering the variable (optional and alternative) use cases, as well as any variation points in the kernel or variable use cases. For each optional or alternative use case, an interaction diagram is developed consisting of new optional or variant objects. The variant objects are kernel or optional objects that are impacted by the variable scenarios and therefore need to be adapted.

An example of evolutionary dynamic analysis for the ATM client side of the Banking SPL is given in Figure 19.5. Figure 19.5a depicts two of the software objects that realize the Validate PIN use case (ATM Control and Customer Interaction). Consider the impact of the Greeting and Language features on the use case–based communication diagram for Validate PIN (Figure 19.5b). The optional ATM Greeting entity object is added, as is the appropriate variant Display Prompts entity object (e.g., French Display Prompts). Both of these objects are accessed by the Customer Interaction object. ATM Control sends Customer Interaction the prompt name. Customer

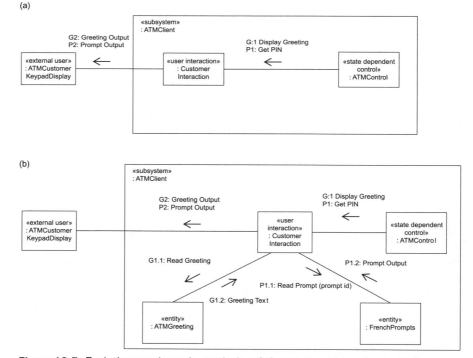

Figure 19.5. Evolutionary dynamic analysis of Greeting and Language features on Validate PIN communication diagram

Table 19.2. Feature/class dependency table for Banking SPL

Feature name	Feature category	Class name	Class reuse category	Class parameter
Banking System Kernel	Common	Card Reader Interface	Kernel	
		ATM Card	Kernel	
		ATM Control	Kernel, parameterized	
		Customer Interaction	Kernel, parameterized	
		Display Prompts	Kernel abstract	
		ATM Transaction	Kernel abstract	
		ATM Cash	Kernel	
		Receipt Printer Interface	Kernel	
		Cash Dispenser Interface	Kernel	
Deposit	Optional	ATM Control	Kernel, parameterized	Deposit condition
		Cash Reader Interface	Optional	
		Deposit Transaction	Optional	
Statement	Optional	ATM Control	Kernel, parameterized	Statement condition
		Statement Transaction	Optional	
Maintenance	Optional	ATM Control	Kernel, parameterized	Maintenance condition
		Operator Interaction	Optional	
English	Default	English Display Prompts	Default	
Spanish	Alternative	Spanish Display Prompts	Variant	
French	Alternative	French Display Prompts	Variant	
German	Alternative	German Display Prompts	Variant	
Greeting	Optional	ATM Greeting	Optional	
		Customer Interaction	Kernel, parameterized	Greeting condition
Max PIN Attempts	Parameterized	ATM Transaction	Kernel, parameterized	PIN attempts

Interaction then requests the prompt text from the Display Prompts object, which it then displays to the customer. For the prompt greeting, Customer Interaction will request the greeting text from the ATM Greeting object and display the greeting when the ATM is idle.

The relationship between features and the classes can be depicted on a feature/class dependency table, which shows for each feature the classes that realize the feature, as well as the class reuse category (kernel, optional, or variant), and, in the case of a parameterized class, the class parameter. This table is developed after the dynamic impact analysis has been carried out using evolutionary dynamic analysis.

19.4 DYNAMIC STATE MACHINE MODELING
FOR SOFTWARE PRODUCT LINES

When variable classes are developed, there are two main approaches to consider, specialization or parameterization. Specialization is effective when there are a relatively small number of changes to be made, so that the number of specialized classes is manageable. In product line development, however, there can be a large degree of variability. Consider the issue of variability in state-dependent control classes, which are modeling using state machines and depicted on statecharts as described in Chapter 10. This variability can be handled by using either parameterized state machines or specialized state machines. Depending on whether the product line uses a centralized or decentralized approach, it is likely that there will be several different state-dependent control classes, each modeled by its own state machine. The following discussion relates to the variability within a given state-dependent class.

To capture state machine variability and evolution, it is necessary to specify optional states, events and state transitions, and actions. A further decision that needs to be made is whether to use state machine inheritance or parameterization. The problem with using inheritance is that a different state machine is needed to model each alternative or optional feature, or feature combination, which rapidly leads to a combinatorial explosion of inherited state machines. For example, with only three features that could impact the state machine, there would be eight possible feature combinations, resulting in eight variant state machines. With 10 features, there would be over 1000 variant state machines. However, 10 features can be easily modeled on a parameterized state machine as 10 feature-dependent state transitions, states, or actions.

It is often more effective to design a parameterized state machine, in which there are feature-dependent states, events, and transitions. Optional state transitions are specified by having an event qualified by a Boolean feature condition, which guards entry into the state. Optional actions are also guarded by a Boolean feature condition, which is set to True if the feature is selected and False if the feature is not selected for a given SPL member.

Examples of feature-dependent state transitions and actions are given for an extract from a Microwave Oven product line. Figure 19.6 depicts three states (Cooking, Ready to Cook, and Door Shut with Item) from the Microwave Oven statechart. (The kernel statechart for this example is the same as that described in Chapter 10, Section 10.2.2.) Minute Plus is an optional microwave oven feature that cooks food for a minute. In the statechart, Minute Pressed is a feature-dependent state transition from Door Shut with Item state to Cooking state. This state transition is guarded by the feature condition minuteplus in Figure 19.6, which is True if the feature is selected. There are also feature-dependent actions, such as Switch On (entry action in Cooking state) and Switch Off (transition action out of Cooking state) in Figure 19.6, which are only enabled if the light feature condition is True, and the Beep action (exit action in Cooking state), which is only enabled if the beeper feature condition is True. Thus, the feature condition is True if the optional feature is selected for a given product line member (meaning that the transition or action is enabled), and False if the feature is not selected (meaning that the transition or action is disabled). The impact of feature interactions can be modeled very precisely

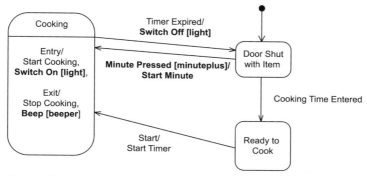

Figure 19.6. Feature-dependent state transitions and actions

using state machines through the introduction of alternative states or transitions. Designing parameterized statecharts is often more manageable than designing specialized statecharts.

19.5 DESIGN MODELING FOR SOFTWARE PRODUCT LINES

In design modeling, variability is handled by developing variant and parameterized components. Certain software architectural patterns are particularly appropriate for SPLs because they encourage variability and evolution.

19.5.1 Modeling Component-Based Software Architectures

A software component's interface is specified separately from its implementation, and, unlike a class, the component's required interface is designed explicitly in addition to the provided interface. This is particularly important for architecture-centric evolution, because it is necessary to know the impact of the change to a component on all components that interface to it.

This capability for modeling component-based software architectures is particularly valuable in product line engineering, to allow the development of kernel, optional and variant components, "plug-compatible" components, and component interface inheritance. There are various ways to design components. It is highly desirable, where possible, to design components that are **plug-compatible**, so that the required port of one component is compatible with the provided ports of other components to which it needs to connect (Gomaa 2005a). Consider the case in which a producer component needs to be able to connect to different alternative consumer components in different product line members, as shown in Figure 19.7. The most desirable approach, if possible, is to design all the consumer components with the same provided interface, so that the producer can be connected to any consumer without changing its required interface. In Figure 19.7, Customer Interaction can be connected to any variant version of the Display Prompts component, such as English Display Prompts and French Display Prompts (which correspond, respectively, to the default English and alternative French features in Figure 19.3). The component interface is shown in Figure 19.7, which specifies three operations, to initialize the component, read prompt text given the prompt Id, and add new prompt.

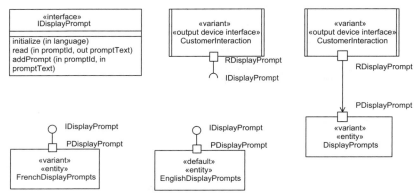

Figure 19.7. Design of plug-compatible variant components

Each default or variant component, such as English Display Prompts or French Display Prompts, that realizes the interface inherits the component interface from the abstract Display Prompts component and provides the language specific implementation.

It is possible for a component to connect to different components and have different interconnections such that in one case it communicates with one component and in a different case it communicates with two different components. This flexibility helps in evolving the software architecture. When plug-compatible components are not practical, an alternative component design approach is **component interface inheritance**. Consider a component architecture that evolves in such a way that the interface through which the two components communicate needs to be specialized to allow for additional functionality. In this case, both the component that provides the interface and the component that requires the interface have to be modified – the former to realize the new functionality, and the latter to request it. The above approaches can be used to complement compositional approaches for developing component-based software architectures.

19.5.2 Software Architectural Patterns

Software architectural patterns (see Chapter 12) provide the skeleton or template for the overall software architecture or high-level design of an application. These include such widely used architectures as client/server and layered architectures. Basing the software architecture of a product line on one or more software architectural patterns helps in designing the original architecture as well as evolving the architecture.

Most software systems and product lines can be based on well-understood overall software architectures; for example, the client/server software architecture is prevalent in many software applications. There is the basic client/service architectural pattern (see Chapter 15), with one service and many clients, but there are also many variations on this theme, such as the Multiple Client/Multiple Service architectural patterns and Broker patterns (see Chapter 16). Furthermore, with a client/service pattern, services can evolve with the addition of new services that are discovered and invoked by clients. New clients can be added that discover services provided by one or more service providers.

An architectural pattern that is worth considering because of its desirable properties for SPLs is the Layered architectural pattern (see Chapter 12). A layered architectural pattern allows for ease of extension and contraction because components can be added to or removed from higher layers, which use the services provided by components at lower layers of the architecture.

In addition to the aforementioned architectural structure patterns, certain architectural communication patterns also encourage evolution. In SPLs, it is often desirable to decouple components. The Broker, Discovery, and Subscription/Notification patterns encourage such decoupling. With the Broker patterns (see Chapter 16), services register with brokers, and clients can then discover new services; thus, a product line can evolve with the addition of new clients and services. A new version of a service can replace an older version and register itself with the broker. Clients communicating via the broker would automatically be connected to the new version of the service. The Subscription/Notification pattern (see Chapter 17) also decouples the original sender of the message from the recipients of the message.

19.6 SUMMARY

This chapter presented an overview of designing SPL architectures. It described how use case modeling, static modeling, dynamic interaction modeling, dynamic state machine modeling, and design modeling can be extended and applied to modeling SPLs. It was also noted that feature modeling is the unifying model for relating variability in requirements to variability in the SPL architecture. For more information on this topic, considerable detail is provided in the author's book on designing SPLs with UML (Gomaa 2005a).

EXERCISES

Multiple-choice questions: For each question, choose one of the answers.
1. What is a software product line (SPL)?
   (a) A family of systems with some common components and some variable components
   (b) An assembly line
   (c) A family of identical systems
   (d) The software products marketed by a company
2. What is an optional use case?
   (a) A use case with some optional steps
   (b) A use case that does not need to be developed
   (c) A use case that is required by some product line members but not others

(d) A use case that can be chosen in place of a different use case in a SPL member
3. What is a use case variation point?
   (a) A variable use case
   (b) A location in the use case at which change can occur
   (c) An alternative use case
   (d) A location in the use case where an alternative path can start
4. What is a SPL feature?
   (a) A requirement or characteristic that is provided by one or more SPL members
   (b) A marketing need
   (c) A class provided by the SPL
   (d) A SPL use case
5. What is a SPL feature group?
   (a) A collection of features

(b) A group of features with a particular constraint on their usage in a SPL member

(c) A group of mutually exclusive features

(d) A group of optional features with a particular constraint on their usage in a SPL member

6. What is a kernel class in a SPL?
   (a) An entity class in the SPL
   (b) A SPL class that stores essential data
   (c) A class that is required by all members of the SPL
   (d) An external class to the SPL

7. What two categories of stereotypes are used in modeling SPL classes?
   (a) Kernel and optional stereotypes
   (b) Optional and variant stereotypes
   (c) Common and variant stereotypes
   (d) Reuse and application role stereotypes

8. How are feature conditions used in a SPL state machine?
   (a) A guard condition
   (b) A condition that is True or False

(c) To identify if a feature is selected or not in the state machine

(d) To allow state machine inheritance

9. What is a kernel system in a SPL?
   (a) A member of the SPL only composed of kernel classes
   (b) A member of the SPL composed of kernel classes and possibly some default classes
   (c) A member of the SPL composed of kernel classes and possibly some optional classes
   (d) A member of the SPL composed of kernel classes and possibly some entity classes

10. What does the SPL software architecture describe?
    (a) The software inside a family of buildings
    (b) The structure of a client/server product family
    (c) The overall structure of the software product line
    (d) The software product line classes and their relationships

20

Software Quality Attributes

Software quality attributes (Bass, Clements, and Kazman 2003) refer to the non-functional requirements of software, which can have a profound effect on the quality of a software product. Many of these attributes can be addressed and evaluated at the time the software architecture is developed. Software quality attributes include maintainability, modifiability, testability, traceability, scalability, reusability, performance, availability, and security. An introduction to software quality attributes is given in Section 4.6. This section describes each of these attributes and discusses how they are supported by the COMET design method.

Some software quality attributes are also system quality attributes because they need both the hardware and software to achieve high quality. Examples of these quality attributes are performance, availability, and security. Other software quality attributes are purely software in nature because they rely entirely on the quality of the software. Examples of these quality attributes are maintainability, modifiability, testability, and traceability.

20.1 MAINTAINABILITY

Maintainability is the extent to which software is capable of being changed after deployment. Software may need to be modified for the following reasons:

- **Fix remaining errors.** These are errors that were not detected during testing of the software prior to deployment.
- **Address performance issues.** Performance problems may not become apparent until after the software application has been deployed and is operational in the field.
- **Changes in software requirements.** The biggest reason for software change is changes in software requirements.

In many cases, software maintenance is actually a misnomer for software evolution. In particular, unanticipated changes in software requirements necessitate modifications to the software that could be extensive. To cope with future evolution, software should be designed for change and adaptability. Quality must be built into the original product to make it maintainable, which means using a good software development process and providing comprehensive documentation of the product. The documentation should be kept up to date as the software is modified. Design rationale should be provided to explain the design decisions that were made. Otherwise, maintainers will have no option but to work with undocumented code, which might well be poorly structured.

COMET supports maintainability by providing comprehensive documentation of the design. Design decisions are actually captured in the design through the use of stereotypes, which allow design structuring decisions to be included in the design. With the use case–based development approach, the effect of a change to a requirement can be traced from use case to software design and implementation. In addition, the COMET support for modifiability and testability greatly assists in the maintainability of the product.

As an example of how maintainability is provided in COMET, consider a change in requirements that necessitates that the Banking System become available in South America, Europe, and Africa. In particular, this requires that prompts be displayed in different languages. Every use case that provides prompts to the customer is potentially affected by this change. An analysis of the design reveals that the only object that interfaces to the customer is Customer Interaction. A good design solution would attempt to limit the design change to a minimum. A change to achieve this goal is that all prompts sent by the ATM Control object to the Customer Interaction object have a prompt Id instead of the prompt text. If Customer Interaction already has the prompt messages hardcoded, the prompts would need to be removed and placed in a prompt table. The prompt table would have one column for prompt Ids and a second column for the corresponding prompt text. A simple table lookup would, given the prompt Id, return the prompt text. At system initialization time, the prompt table for the desired language would be loaded. The default prompt table would be in English. For the South American market (apart from Brazil) and for the Spanish market, the Spanish prompt table would be loaded. For France, Quebec, and large parts of West Africa, the French prompt table would be loaded at initialization time. An example of a prompt table with English prompts is given in Table 20.1.

20.2 MODIFIABILITY

Modifiability is the extent to which software is capable of being modified during and after initial development. A modular design consisting of modules with well-defined

---

Table 20.1. Example of maintainability in worldwide system: Prompt table with language-specific prompts

Prompt Id	Prompt text
Get-PIN	Please enter your PIN:
Invalid-PIN-Prompt	The PIN is invalid. Please re-enter your PIN:
Display-Confiscate	There is a problem with your request. Your card has been confiscated. Please contact your bank.

interfaces is essential. Parnas advocated *design for change* based on the information hiding concept, in which change is anticipated and managed by each information hiding module hiding a *secret* that could change independently of other parts of the software. Information hiding is a fundamental design concept (see Chapter 4) and forms the basis of object-oriented design (see Chapter 14).

COMET supports modifiability by providing support for information hiding at the class and component levels, and providing support for separation of concerns at the subsystem level. Decisions such as encapsulating (a) each finite state machine within a separate state machine class, (b) each interface to a separate external device, system, or user within a separate boundary class, and (c) each separate data structure within a separate data abstraction class, assist with modifiability. At the architecture level, the COMET component-based software architectural design approach leads to the design of components that can be deployed to different distributed nodes at software deployment time, so that the same architecture can be deployed to many different configurations in support of different instances of the application.

To continue with the prompt table example, using COMET, the design of the prompt table would affect the static and dynamic models. For a start, the prompt table would be encapsulated in a prompt class. Because support for different languages is required, a good approach is to design a superclass called Display Prompts and design subclasses for each language. The initial requirement is for English (default), French, Italian, Spanish, and German language prompts (Figure 20.1); however, the design should allow for extension to other languages. The solution is to design the Display Prompts class as an abstract class with a common interface consisting of a read operation to read prompts from the prompt table and an update operation, in order to update the prompt table and add a new prompt. The language-specific prompt subclasses would inherit the interface unchanged and then provide the language-specific implementation. An alternative solution to this problem using software product line concepts is described in Chapter 19.

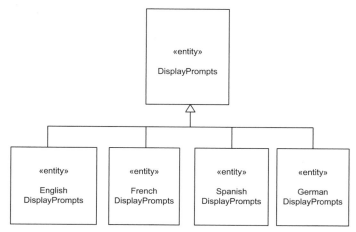

Figure 20.1. Example of modifiability: abstract Display Prompts superclass and language-specific subclasses

20.3 TESTABILITY

Testability is the extent to which software is capable of being tested. It is important to develop a software test plan early in the software life cycle and to plan on developing test cases in parallel with software development. The following paragraphs describe how the different stages of software testing can be integrated with the COMET method. A comprehensive description of software testing is given by Ammann and Offutt (2008).

During the requirements phase, it is necessary to develop functional (black box) test cases. These test cases can be developed from the use case model, particularly the use case descriptions. Because the use case descriptions describe the sequence of user interactions with the system, they describe the user inputs that need to be captured for the test cases and the expected system output. A test case needs to be developed for each use case scenario, one for the main sequence and one for each alternative sequence of the use case. Using this approach, a test suite can be developed to test the functional requirements of the system.

During software architectural design, it is necessary to develop integration test cases, which test the interfaces between the components that communicate with each other. A testing approach called scenario-based testing can be used to test the software using a sequence of scenarios that correspond to the realization of the use case scenarios on interaction models (diagrams), which show the sequence of objects communicating with each other and messages passed between the objects. Thus, an integration test case(s) would be developed for each object interaction scenario.

During detailed design and coding, in which the internal algorithms for each component are developed, white box test cases can be developed that test the component internals using well-known coverage criteria such as executing every line of code and the outcome of every decision. By this means, it is possible to develop unit test cases to test the individual units, such as components.

An example of a black box test case based on the Validate PIN use case in the Banking System would consist of inserting the card, prompting for the PIN, and validating the card Id/PIN combination. Initially, a test stub object could be developed that simulates the card reader and provides the inputs read off the simulated card: card Id, start date, and expiration date. The system then prompts for the PIN (another test stub simulating the user provides the PIN Id), and then sends the card and PIN information to the Banking Service subsystem (or server stub during development). A test environment could be set up with the Debit Card entity class implemented as a relational table. This would allow the main sequence of the use case (valid PIN) as well as all the alternative sequences to be tested (invalid PIN, third invalid PIN, card lost or stolen, etc.).

20.4 TRACEABILITY

Traceability is the extent to which products of each phase can be traced back to products of previous phases. Requirements traceability is used to ensure that each software requirement has been designed and implemented. Each requirement is traced to the software architecture and to the implemented code modules. Requirements traceability tables are a useful tool during software architecture reviews for

analyzing whether the software architecture has addressed all the software requirements.

It is possible to build traceability into the software development method, as is the
case with the COMET method. COMET is a use case–based development approach
that starts with use cases and then determines the objects required to realize each
use case. Each use case described in the software requirements is elaborated into
a use case–based interaction diagram, which describes the sequence of object communication resulting from an external input, as described in the use case, through
to system output. These interaction diagrams are integrated into the software architecture. This means that each requirement can be traced from use case to software
design and implementation. The impact of a change to a requirement can therefore
be determined by following the trace from requirement through to design.

As an example of traceability, consider the Validate PIN use case from the Banking System. This is realized in the dynamic model by the Validate PIN communication
diagram. The change required by the addition of the prompt language requirement
(see section 20.1) can be determined by an impact analysis, which reveals that the
prompt object would need to be accessed by the Customer Interaction object prior
to displaying the prompt, as shown in Figure 20.2. Figure 20.2a shows the original
design with Customer Interaction outputting directly to the display, whereas Figure
20.2b shows the modified design with Customer Interaction reading the prompt text
from the Display Prompts object before outputting to the display. An alternative solution to this problem using software product line concepts is described in Chapter 19.

20.5 SCALABILITY

Scalability is the extent to which the system is capable of growing after its initial
deployment. There are system and software factors to consider in scalability. From
a system perspective, there are issues of adding hardware to increase the capacity
of the system. In a centralized system, the scope for scalability is limited, such as
adding more memory, disk, or an additional CPU. A distributed system offers much
more scope for scalability, by adding more nodes to the configuration.

From a software perspective, the application needs to be designed in such a way
that it is capable of growth. A distributed component-based software architecture is
much more capable of scaling upwards than a centralized design. Components are
designed such that multiple instances of each component can be deployed to different nodes in a distributed configuration. An elevator control system that supports
multiple elevators and multiple floor can have an elevator component and a floor
component, such that there is one instance for each elevator and one instance for
each floor. Such a software architecture can be deployed to execute in a small building, in a large hotel, or in a skyscraper. A service-oriented architecture can scaled
up by adding more services or additional instances of existing services. New clients
can be added to the system as needed. Clients can discover new services and take
advantage of their offerings.

COMET addresses scalability by providing the capability of designing distributed component-based software architectures and service-oriented architectures
that can be scaled up after deployment. For example, the Emergency Monitoring
System can be expanded by adding more remote sensors, in the form of additional

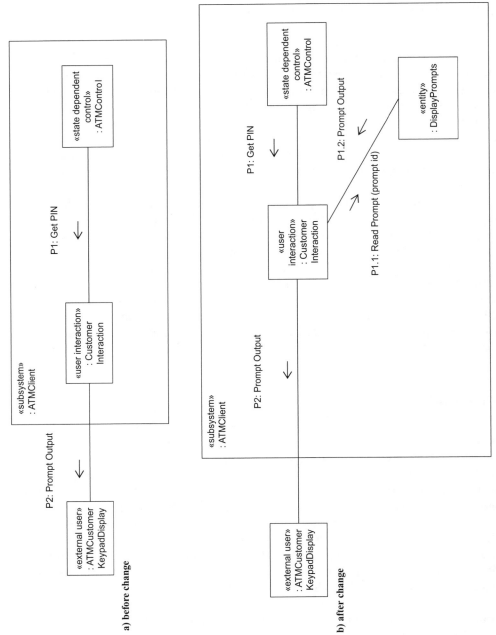

a) before change

b) after change

Figure 20.2. Traceability analysis before and after change to introduce Display Prompts object

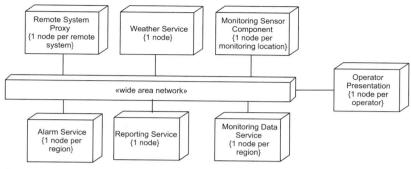

Figure 20.3. Scale-up in Emergency Monitoring System

sensors or additional external systems, as well as more instances of the services
Monitoring Data Service and the Alarm Service. It would also be possible to add more
services, such as Reporting Service and Weather Service, as well as more instances
of these services. The deployment diagram for the Emergency Monitoring System
(Figure 20.3) shows how the component-based software architecture could be scaled
up.

The Online Shopping System could be expanded by adding more services. The
catalog service could be extended to support multiple vendors (suppliers). These
different suppliers would then be added to the system. Each supplier could operate
quite differently but would need to conform to the interface specified by the service-
oriented architecture.

20.6 REUSABILITY

Software reusability is the extent to which software is capable of being reused. In
traditional software reuse, a library of reusable code components is developed – for
example, a statistical subroutine library. This approach requires the establishment
of a library of reusable components and of an approach for indexing, locating, and
distinguishing between similar components (Prieto-Diaz and Freeman 1987). Problems with this approach include managing the large number of components that
such a reuse library is likely to contain and distinguishing among similar, though not
identical, components.

When a new design is being developed, the designer is responsible for designing the software architecture – that is, the overall structure of the program and the
overall flow of control. Having located and selected a reusable component from
the library, the designer must then determine how this component fits into the new
architecture.

Instead of reusing an individual component, it is much more advantageous to
reuse a whole design or subsystem that consists of the components and their interconnections. This means reuse of the control structure of the application. Architecture reuse has much greater potential than component reuse because it is large-
grained reuse, which focuses on reuse of requirements and design.

The most promising approach for architecture reuse is to develop a software
product line architecture (Gomaa 2005a) which explicitly captures the commonality and variability in the family of systems that constitutes the product line. The

architecture for a software product line, which is the architecture for a family of products, needs to describe both the commonality and variability in the family. Depending on the development approach used (functional or object-oriented), the product line **commonality** is described in terms of common modules, classes, or components, and the product line **variability** is described in terms of optional or variant modules, classes, or components.

The term **application engineering** refers to the process of tailoring and configuring the product family architecture and components to create a specific application, which is a member of the product family.

PLUS is an extension of COMET to design software product line architectures. An overview of PLUS is given in Chapter 19, with a complete and detailed description given in Gomaa (2005a). The example of how the Display Prompts superclass and language-specific subclasses could be designed using a software product line approach is described in Chapter 19.

20.7 PERFORMANCE

Performance is also an important consideration in many systems. Performance modeling of a system at design time is important to determine whether the system will meet its performance goals, such as throughput and response times. Performance modeling methods include queuing modeling (Gomaa and Menasce 2001; Menasce and Gomaa 2000) and simulation modeling. Performance modeling is particularly important in real-time systems, in which failing to meet a deadline could be catastrophic. Real-time scheduling in conjunction with event sequence modeling is an approach for modeling real-time designs that are executing on given hardware configurations.

In COMET/RT, performance analysis of software designs is achieved by applying real-time scheduling theory. **Real-time scheduling** is an approach that is particularly appropriate for hard real-time systems that have deadlines that must be met (Gomaa 2000). With this approach, the real-time design is analyzed to determine whether it can meet its deadlines. A second approach for analyzing the performance of a design is to use **event sequence analysis** and to integrate this with the real-time scheduling theory. Event sequence analysis is used to analyze scenarios of communicating tasks and annotate them with the timing parameters for each of the participating tasks, in addition to considering system overhead for interobject communication and context switching (Gomaa 2000).

Consider the Banking System described in Chapter 21 and depicted on the deployment diagram in Figure 20.4, which has the Banking Service executing on a server node. Performance measurements for a banking service would include response time to ATM Client requests and the transaction-processing rate in transactions per second. A queuing model could be developed to estimate the performance of the Banking System under different ATM transaction workloads and, hence, to plan for the capacity required for the server, in terms of CPU, main memory, and secondary storage, as well as the network bandwidth required. Estimates can also be made for the amount of disk space required based on estimates of the number and size of customer and account records. Performance comparisons

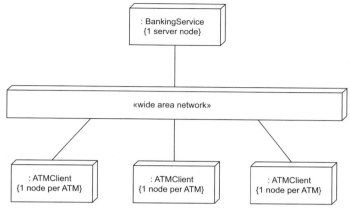

Figure 20.4. Experiments with different hardware configurations for Banking System

could be made with different hardware configurations, including single-processor and dual-processor configurations. Performance comparisons could be made with alternative software designs and hardware configurations – for example, a sequential Banking Service on one node and a concurrent Banking Service on two nodes.

20.8 SECURITY

Security is an important consideration in many systems. There are many potential threats to distributed application systems, such as electronic commerce and banking systems. There are several textbooks that address computer, information, and network security, including Bishop (2004) and Pfleeger (2006). Some of the potential threats are as follows:

- **System penetration.** An unauthorized person tries to gain access to an application system and execute unauthorized transactions.
- **Authorization violation**. A person authorized to use an application system misuses or abuses it.
- **Confidentiality disclosure.** Secret information such as card numbers and bank accounts are disclosed to an unauthorized person.
- **Integrity compromise.** An unauthorized person changes application data in database or communication data.
- **Repudiation.** A person who performs some transaction or communication activity later falsely denies that the transaction or activity occurred.
- **Denial of service.** Legitimate access to application systems is deliberately disturbed.

COMET extends the use case descriptions to allow the description of nonfunctional requirements, which include security requirements. An example of the extension of use cases to allow nonfunctional requirements is given in Chapter 6.

The following list describes how these potential threats can be addressed for the Banking System (note that not all of these threats can be addressed solely by software means):

- **System penetration.** The solution to this problem is to encrypt the messages at source, particularly transactions originating at the ATM Client and the responses sent by the Banking Service, and then to decrypt the messages at the destination.
- **Authorization violation.** A person authorized to use an application system misuses or abuses it. A log of all access to the system needs to be maintained, so that cases of misuse or abuse can be tracked down, so that any abuse can be corrected.
- **Confidentiality disclosure.** Secret information, such as card numbers and bank accounts, needs to be protected by an access control method that only allows users with the appropriate privileges to access the data.
- **Integrity compromise.** An access control method needs to be enforced to ensure that unauthorized persons are prevented from making changes to application data in the database or communication data.
- **Repudiation.** A log needs to be maintained of all transactions so that a claim that the transaction or activity did not occur can be verified by analyzing the log.
- **Denial of service.** An intrusion detection capability is required so that the system can detect unauthorized intrusions and act to reject them.

20.9 AVAILABILITY

Availability addresses system failure and its impact on users or other systems. There are times when the system is not available to users for scheduled system maintenance; this planned unavailability is not usually counted in measures of availability. However, unplanned system maintenance necessary as a result of system failure is always counted. Some systems need to be operational at all times; thus, the effect of a system failure on a system controlling an airplane or spacecraft could be catastrophic.

Fault-tolerant systems have recovery built into them so that the system can recover from failure automatically. However, such systems are typically very expensive, requiring such capabilities as triple redundancy and voting systems. Other less expensive solutions are possible, such as a hot standby, which is a machine ready for usage very soon after the failure of the system. The hot standby could be for a server in a client/server system. It is possible to design a distributed system without a single point of failure, such that the failure of one node results in reduced service, with the system operational in a degraded mode. This is usually preferable to having no service whatsoever.

From a software design perspective, support for availability necessitates the design of systems without single points of failure. COMET supports availability by providing an approach for designing distributed component-based software architectures that can be deployed to multiple nodes with distributed control, data, and services, so that the system does not fail if a single node goes down but can operate in a degraded mode.

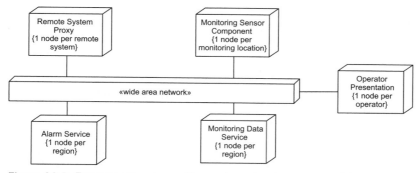

Figure 20.5. Example of system with no single hardware point of failure

For the case study examples, the hot standby could be used for the Banking System, which is a centralized client/server system in which the Bank Server is a single point of failure (Figure 20.4). A hot standby is a backup server that can be rapidly deployed if the main server goes down. An example of a distributed system without a single hardware point of failure is the Emergency Monitoring System, in which the user I/O components, the monitoring and alarm services, and the operator interaction components can all be replicated. There are several instances of each of the client components, so if a component goes down, the system can still operate. The services can be replicated so that there are multiple instances of Monitoring Data Service and Alarm Service. This is illustrated in the deployment diagram in Figure 20.5. It is assumed that the network used is the Internet, in which there might be local failures but not a global failure, so that individual nodes or even regional subnets might be unavailable at times but other regions would still be operational.

20.10 SUMMARY

This chapter described the software quality attributes of a software architecture and how they are used to evaluate the quality of the software architecture. The software quality attributes described in this chapter include maintainability, modifiability, testability, traceability, scalability, reusability, performance, availability, and security. Software quality attributes are described in more detail in Bass, Clements, and Kazman (2003) and Taylor, Medvidovic, and Dashofy (2009).

EXERCISES

Multiple-choice questions: For each question, choose one of the answers.

1. What do software quality attributes address?
   (a) Software functional requirements
   (b) Software nonfunctional requirements
   (c) Software performance requirements
   (d) Software availability requirements

2. What is maintainability?
   (a) The extent to which software is capable of being changed before deployment
   (b) The extent to which software is capable of being changed after deployment
   (c) The extent to which software is capable of being changed during development
   (d) The extent to which software is capable of being changed after development

3. What is modifiability?
   (a) The extent to which software is capable of being modified after deployment
   (b) The extent to which software is capable of being modified after initial development
   (c) The extent to which software is capable of being modified during and after initial development
   (d) The extent to which software is capable of being changed before deployment

4. What is testability?
   (a) The extent to which software is capable of being developed
   (b) The extent to which software is capable of being tested before deployment
   (c) The extent to which software is capable of being tested after deployment
   (d) The extent which the software is understood

5. Traceability is the extent to which a product:
   (a) Can be traced back to products of previous phases
   (b) Traced back to the requirements
   (c) Traced forward to implementation
   (d) Deployed to a hardware configuration

6. What is scalability?
   (a) The extent to which an application can grow

   (b) The extent to which the system is capable of growing after its initial deployment
   (c) The extent to which the system is capable of growing during development
   (d) The extent to which the system is capable of being scaled

7. What is reusability?
   (a) The extent to which software implementation is reusable
   (b) The extent to which software is capable of being reused
   (c) The extent to which SPL technology can be introduced
   (d) The extent to which the software is common among a program family

8. Which of the following is not performance-related?
   (a) System response time
   (b) System throughput
   (c) System availability
   (d) System capacity

9. Which of the following is not addressed by a secure system?
   (a) System penetration
   (b) Denial of service
   (c) System scalability
   (d) System authorization

10. Which of the following system problems does availability address?
    (a) Denial of service
    (b) Single point of failure
    (c) System throughput
    (d) System penetration

PART IV

Case Studies

21

Client/Server Software Architecture Case Study

Banking System

This chapter describes how the COMET/UML software modeling and design method is applied to the design of a client/server software architecture (see Chapter 15): a Banking System. In addition, the design of the ATM Client is an example of concurrent software design (see Chapter 18), and the design of the Banking Service is an example of sequential object-oriented software design (see Chapter 14).

The problem description is given in Section 21.1. Section 21.2 describes the use case model for the Banking System. Section 21.3 describes the static model, covering static modeling of both the system context and entity classes. Section 21.4 describes how to structure the system into objects. Section 21.5 describes dynamic modeling, in which interaction diagrams are developed for each of the use cases. Section 21.6 describes the ATM statechart. Sections 21.7 through 21.14 describe the design model for the Banking System.

21.1 PROBLEM DESCRIPTION

A bank has several automated teller machines (ATMs) that are geographically distributed and connected via a wide area network to a central server. Each ATM machine has a card reader, a cash dispenser, a keyboard/display, and a receipt printer. By using the ATM machine, a customer can withdraw cash from either a checking or savings account, query the balance of an account, or transfer funds from one account to another. A transaction is initiated when a customer inserts an ATM card into the card reader. Encoded on the magnetic strip on the back of the ATM card are the card number, the start date, and the expiration date. Assuming the card is recognized, the system validates the ATM card to determine that the expiration date has not passed, that the user-entered personal identification number, or PIN, matches the PIN maintained by the system, and that the card is not lost or stolen. The customer is allowed three attempts to enter the correct PIN; the card is confiscated if the third attempt fails. Cards that have been reported lost or stolen are also confiscated.

If the PIN is validated satisfactorily, the customer is prompted for a withdrawal, query, or transfer transaction. Before a withdrawal transaction can be approved, the system determines that sufficient funds exist in the requested account, that the maximum daily limit will not be exceeded, and that there are sufficient funds at the local cash dispenser. If the transaction is approved, the requested amount of cash is dispensed, a receipt is printed that contains information about the transaction, and the card is ejected. Before a transfer transaction can be approved, the system determines that the customer has at least two accounts and that there are sufficient funds in the account to be debited. For approved query and transfer requests, a receipt is printed and the card ejected. A customer may cancel a transaction at any time; the transaction is terminated, and the card is ejected. Customer records, account records, and debit card records are all maintained at the server.

An ATM operator may start up and close down the ATM to replenish the ATM cash dispenser and for routine maintenance. It is assumed that functionality to open and close accounts and to create, update, and delete customer and debit card records is provided by an existing system and is not part of this problem.

21.2 USE CASE MODEL

The use cases are described in the **use case model**. There are two actors, namely, the ATM Customer and the Operator, who are the users of the system. The customer can withdraw funds from a checking or savings account, query the balance of the account, and transfer funds from one account to another.

The customer interacts with the system via the ATM card reader and the keyboard. It is the customer who is the actor, not the card reader and keyboard; these input devices provide the means for the customer to initiate the use case and respond to prompts from the system. The printer and cash dispenser are output devices; they are not actors, because it is the customer who benefits from the use cases.

The ATM operator can shut down the ATM, replenish the ATM cash dispenser, and start the ATM. Because an actor represents a role played by a user, there can be multiple customers and operators.

Consider the ATM operator use cases. One option is to have one operator use case in which the operator shuts down the ATM, adds cash, and then starts up the ATM. However, because it is possible to shut down the machine for a hardware problem without adding cash, and to start up the machine after it goes down unexpectedly, it is more flexible to have three separate use cases instead of one. These use cases are to Add Cash (in order to replenish the ATM cash locally), Startup, and Shutdown, as shown in Figure 21.1.

Consider the use cases initiated by the ATM Customer. One possibility is to have one use case for all customer interactions. However, there are three separate, quite distinct transaction types for withdrawal, query, and transfer that can be initiated by a customer.

We therefore start by considering three separate use cases: Withdraw Funds, Query Account, and Transfer Funds, one for each transaction type. Consider the Withdraw Funds use case. In this use case, the main sequence assumes a successful cash withdrawal by the customer. This involves reading the ATM card, validating the customer's PIN, checking that the customer has enough funds in the requested account, and then – providing the validation is successful – dispensing cash, printing a receipt, and ejecting the card.

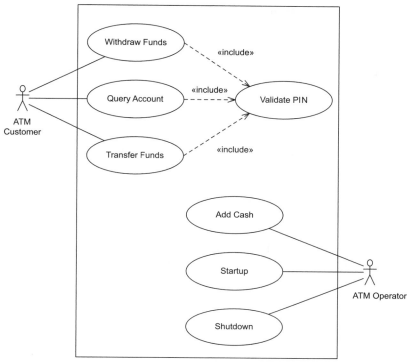

Figure 21.1. Banking System use case model

However, by comparing the three use cases, it can be seen that the first part of each use case – namely, reading the ATM card and validating the customer's PIN – is common to all three use cases. This common part of the three use cases is factored out as an inclusion use case called Validate PIN.

The Withdraw Funds, Query Account, and Transfer Funds use cases can then each be rewritten more concisely as concrete use cases that include the Validate PIN inclusion use case. The relationship between the use cases is shown in Figure 21.1. The concrete Withdraw Funds use case starts by including the description of the Validate PIN inclusion use case and then continues with the Withdraw Funds description. The concrete Transfer Funds use case also starts with the description of the Validate PIN inclusion use case, but then continues with the Transfer Funds description. The revised concrete Query Account use case is similarly organized. The inclusion use case and concrete use cases are described next.

The main sequence of the Validate PIN use case deals with reading the ATM card, validating the customer's PIN and card. If validation is successful, the system prompts the customer to select a transaction: withdrawal, query, or transfer. The alternative branches deal with all the possible error conditions, such as the customer enters the wrong PIN and must be re-prompted, or an ATM card is not recognized or has been reported stolen, and so on. Because these can be described quite simply in the alternative sequences, splitting them off into separate extension use cases is not necessary.

21.2.1 Validate PIN Use Case

Use case name: Validate PIN
Summary: System validates customer PIN
Actor: ATM Customer
Precondition: ATM is idle, displaying a Welcome message.
Main sequence:
1. Customer inserts the ATM card into the card reader.
2. If system recognizes the card, it reads the card number.
3. System prompts customer for PIN.
4. Customer enters PIN.
5. System checks the card's expiration date and whether the card has been reported as lost or stolen.
6. If card is valid, system then checks whether the user-entered PIN matches the card PIN maintained by the system.
7. If PIN numbers match, system checks what accounts are accessible with the ATM card.
8. System displays customer accounts and prompts customer for transaction type: withdrawal, query, or transfer.

Alternative sequences:
Step 2: If the system does not recognize the card, the system ejects the card.
Step 5: If the system determines that the card date has expired, the system confiscates the card.
Step 5: If the system determines that the card has been reported lost or stolen, the system confiscates the card.
Step 7: If the customer-entered PIN does not match the PIN number for this card, the system re-prompts for the PIN.
Step 7: If the customer enters the incorrect PIN three times, the system confiscates the card.
Steps 4–8: If the customer enters Cancel, the system cancels the transaction and ejects the card.
Postcondition: Customer PIN has been validated.

21.2.2 Withdraw Funds Concrete Use Case

Use case name: Withdraw Funds
Summary: Customer withdraws a specific amount of funds from a valid bank account.
Actor: ATM Customer
Dependency: Include Validate PIN use case.
Precondition: ATM is idle, displaying a Welcome message.

Main sequence:
1. Include Validate PIN use case.
2. Customer selects Withdrawal, enters the amount, and selects the account number.
3. System checks whether customer has enough funds in the account and whether the daily limit will not be exceeded.
4. If all checks are successful, system authorizes dispensing of cash.
5. System dispenses the cash amount.
6. System prints a receipt showing transaction number, transaction type, amount withdrawn, and account balance.
7. System ejects card.
8. System displays Welcome message.

Alternative sequences:
Step 3: If the system determines that the account number is invalid, then it displays an error message and ejects the card.
Step 3: If the system determines that there are insufficient funds in the customer's account, then it displays an apology and ejects the card.
Step 3: If the system determines that the maximum allowable daily withdrawal amount has been exceeded, it displays an apology and ejects the card.
Step 5: If the ATM is out of funds, the system displays an apology, ejects the card, and shuts down the ATM.
Postcondition: Customer funds have been withdrawn.

21.2.3 Query Account Concrete Use Case

Use case name: Query Account
Summary: Customer receives the balance of a valid bank account.
Actor: ATM Customer
Dependency: Include Validate PIN use case.
Precondition: ATM is idle, displaying a Welcome message.
Main sequence:
1. Include Validate PIN use case.
2. Customer selects Query, enters account number.
3. System reads account balance.
4. System prints a receipt that shows transaction number, transaction type, and account balance.
5. System ejects card.
6. System displays Welcome message.

Alternative sequence:
Step 3: If the system determines that the account number is invalid, it displays an error message and ejects the card.
Postcondition: Customer account has been queried.

21.2.4 Transfer Funds Concrete Use Case

Use case name: Transfer Funds
Summary: Customer transfers funds from one valid bank account to another.
Actor: ATM Customer
Dependency: Include Validate PIN use case.
Precondition: ATM is idle, displaying a Welcome message.
Main sequence:
1. Include Validate PIN use case.
2. Customer selects Transfer and enters amount, from account, and to account.
3. If the system determines the customer has enough funds in the from account, it performs the transfer.
4. System prints a receipt that shows transaction number, transaction type, amount transferred, and account balance.
5. System ejects card.
6. System displays Welcome message.

Alternative sequences:
Step 3: If the system determines that the from account number is invalid, it displays an error message and ejects the card.
Step 3: If the system determines that the to account number is invalid, it displays an error message and ejects the card.
Step 3: If the system determines that there are insufficient funds in the customer's from account, it displays an apology and ejects the card.
Postcondition: Customer funds have been transferred.

21.3 STATIC MODELING

This section begins by considering the problem domain and the system context, and then continues with a discussion of static modeling of the entity classes. Refer also to Chapter 7, which describes static modeling in detail with some examples from the Banking System.

21.3.1 Static Modeling of the Problem Domain

The conceptual static model of the problem domain is given in the class diagram depicted in Figure 21.2. A bank has several ATMs. Each ATM is modeled as a composite class consisting of a Card Reader, a Cash Dispenser, a Receipt Printer, and a keyboard/display through which the user interacts, the ATM Customer Keyboard Display. The ATM Customer actor inserts the card into the Card Reader and responds to system prompts though the ATM Customer Keyboard Display. The Cash Dispenser dispenses cash to the ATM Customer actor. The Receipt Printer prints a receipt for the ATM Customer actor. In addition, the Operator actor is a user whose job is to maintain the ATM.

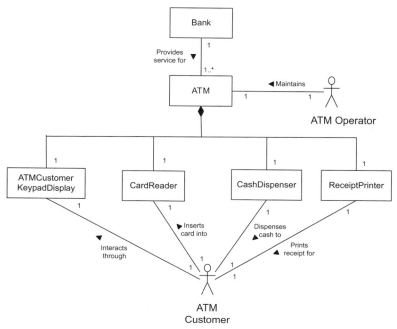

Figure 21.2. Conceptual static model for problem domain

21.3.2 Static Modeling of the System Context

The software system context class diagram, which uses the static modeling notation, is developed to show the external classes to which the Banking System, shown
as one aggregate class, has to interface. We develop the context class diagram by
considering the physical classes determined during static modeling of the problem
domain, as described in detail in Chapter 7.

From the total system perspective – that is, both hardware and software – the
ATM Customer and ATM Operator actors are external to the system, as shown in Figure
7.19. The ATM Operator interacts with the system via a keypad and display. The ATM
Customer actor interacts with the system via four I/O devices, which are the card
reader, cash dispenser, receipt printer, and ATM Customer keypad/display. From a
total hardware/software system perspective, these I/O devices are part of the system.
From a software perspective, the I/O devices are external to the software system. On
the software system context class diagram, the I/O devices are modeled as external
classes, as shown on Figure 21.3.

The four external classes used by the ATM Customer actor are the Card Reader,
the Cash Dispenser, the Receipt Printer, and the ATM Customer Keypad/Display; the
Operator interacts with the system via a keyboard/display. Both Customer Keypad/
Display and Operator are modeled as external users, as described in Chapter 7. There
is one instance of each of these external classes for each ATM. The software system
context class diagram for the Banking System (see Figure 21.3) depicts the software
system as one aggregate class that receives input from and provides output to the
external classes.

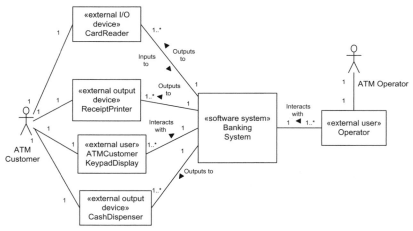

Figure 21.3. Banking System software context class diagram

21.3.3 Static Modeling of the Entity Classes

The static model of the entity classes, referred to as the entity class model, is shown in Figure 21.4. The attributes of each entity class are given in Figures 21.5, 21.6, and 21.7.

Figure 21.4 shows the Bank entity class, which has a one-to-many relationship with the Customer class and the Debit Card class. The Bank class is unusual in that it will only have one instance; its attributes are the bank Name, bank Address, and bank Id. The Customer has a many-to-many relationship with Account. Because there are both checking accounts and savings accounts, which have some common attributes, the Account class is specialized to be either a Checking Account or a Savings Account. Thus, some attributes are common to all accounts, namely, the account Number, account Type, and balance. Other attributes are specific to Checking Account (e.g., last Deposit Amount) and Savings Account (e.g., the accumulated interest).

An Account is modified by an ATM Transaction, which is specialized to depict the different types of transactions as a Withdrawal Transaction, Query Transaction, Transfer Transaction, or PIN Validation Transaction. The common attributes of a transaction are in the superclass ATM Transaction and consist of transaction Id (which actually consists of four concatenated attributes – bank Id, ATM Id, date, and time), transaction Type, card Id, PIN, and status. Other attributes are specific to the particular type of transaction. Thus, for the Withdrawal Transaction, the specific attributes maintained by the subclass are account Number, amount, and balance. For a Transfer Transaction, the attributes maintained by the subclass are from Account Number (checking or savings), to Account Number (savings or checking), and amount.

There is also a Card Account association class. Association classes are needed in cases in which the attributes are of the association, rather than of the classes connected by the association. Thus, in the many-to-many association between Debit Card and Account, the individual accounts that can be accessed by a given debit card are attributes of the Card Account association class and not of either Debit Card or

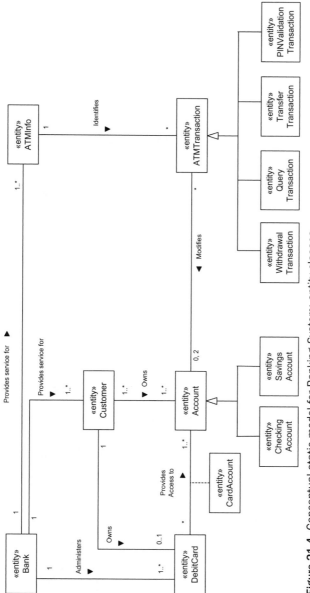

Figure 21.4. Conceptual static model for Banking System: entity classes

379

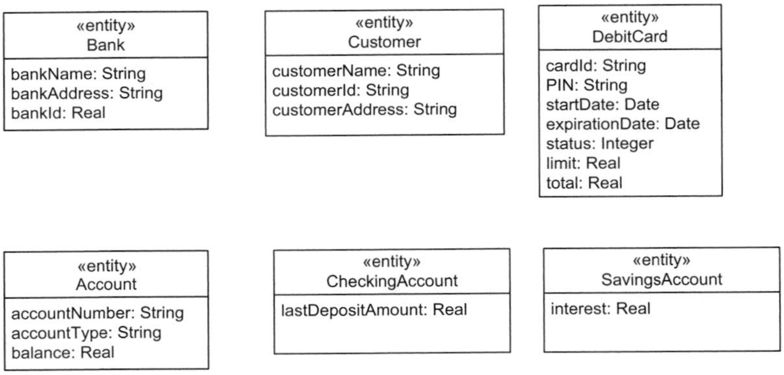

«entity» Bank
bankName: String bankAddress: String bankId: Real

«entity» Customer
customerName: String customerId: String customerAddress: String

«entity» DebitCard
cardId: String PIN: String startDate: Date expirationDate: Date status: Integer limit: Real total: Real

«entity» Account
accountNumber: String accountType: String balance: Real

«entity» CheckingAccount
lastDepositAmount: Real

«entity» SavingsAccount
interest: Real

Figure 21.5. Conceptual static model for Banking System: class attributes

«entity» ATMTransaction
bankId: String ATMId: String date: Date time: Time transactionType: String cardId: String PIN: String status: Integer

«entity» WithdrawalTransaction
accountNumber: String amount: Real balance: Real

«entity» QueryTransaction
accountNumber: String balance: Real lastDepositAmount: Real

«entity» TransferTransaction
fromAccountNumber: String toAccountNumber: String amount: Real

«entity» PINValidationTransaction
startDate: Date expirationDate: Date

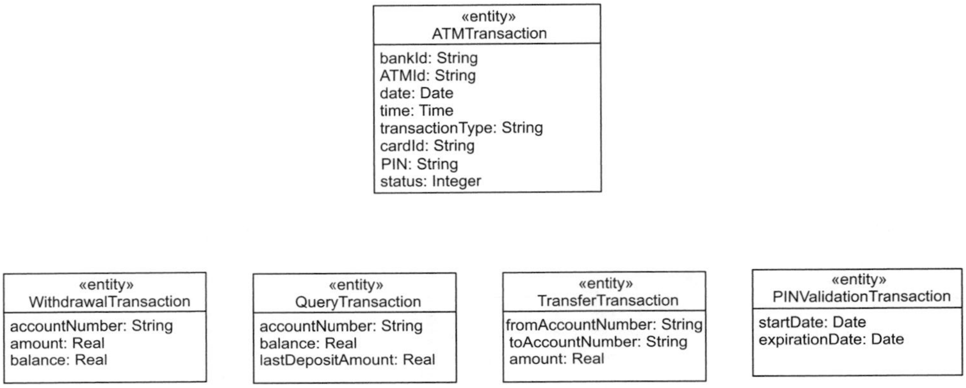

Figure 21.6. Conceptual static model for Banking System: class attributes (continued)

«entity» CardAccount
cardId: String accountNumber: String accountType: String

«entity» ATMInfo
bankId: String ATMId: String ATMLocation: String ATMAddress: String

«entity» ATMCash
cashAvailable: Integer fives: Integer tens: Integer twenties: Integer

«entity» ATMCard
cardId: String startDate: Date expirationDate: Date

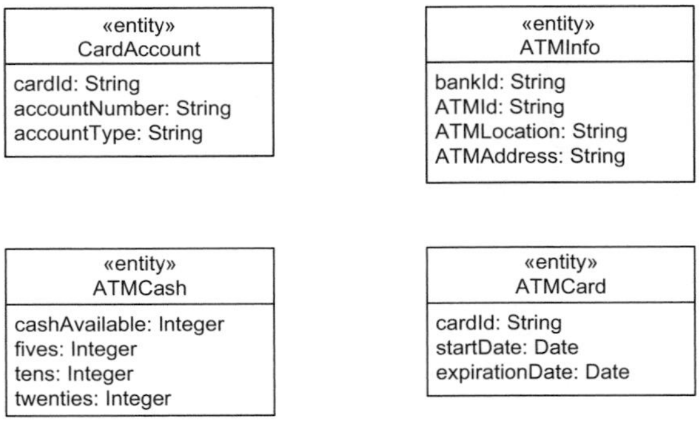

Figure 21.7. Conceptual static model for Banking System: class attributes (continued)

Account. The attributes of Card Account are Card Id, account Number, and account Type.

Entity classes are also required to model other information described in Section 21.2. These include ATM Card, which represents the information read off the magnetic strip on the plastic card. ATM Cash holds the amount of cash maintained at an ATM, in five-, ten-, and twenty-dollar bills. The Receipt holds information about a transaction, and because it holds similar information to the Transaction class described earlier, a separate entity class is unnecessary.

21.4 OBJECT STRUCTURING

We next consider structuring the system into objects in preparation for defining the dynamic model. The object structuring criteria help determine the objects in the system. After the objects and classes have been determined, a communication diagram or sequence diagram is developed for each use case to show the objects that participate in the use case and the dynamic sequence of interactions between them.

21.4.1 Client/Server Subsystem Structuring

Because the Banking System is a client/server application, some of the objects are part of the ATM client and some objects are part of the banking service, so we start by identifying subsystems, which are aggregate or composite objects. In client/server systems, the subsystems are often easily identifiable. Thus, in the Banking System, there is a client subsystem called ATM Client Subsystem, of which one instance is located at each ATM machine. There is also a service subsystem, the Banking Service Subsystem, of which there is one instance (Figure 21.8). This is an example of geographical subsystem structuring, in which the geographical distribution of the

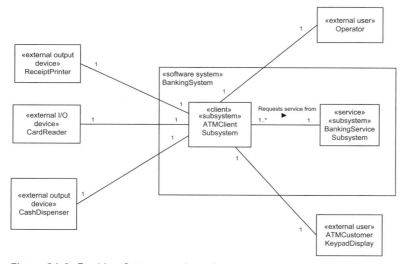

Figure 21.8. Banking System: major subsystems

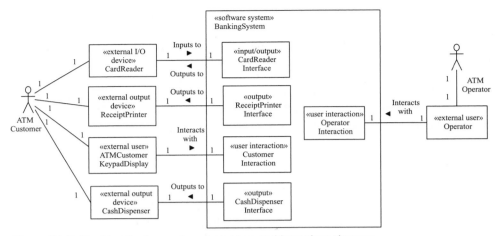

Figure 21.9. Banking System external classes and boundary classes

system is given in the problem description. Both subsystems are depicted as aggregate classes, with a one-to-many association between the Banking Service Subsystem and the ATM Client Subsystem. All the external classes interface to and communicate with the ATM Client Subsystem.

21.4.2 ATM Client Object and Class Structuring: Boundary Objects

The next step is to determine the software objects and classes at the ATM Client. First, consider the boundary objects and classes. The boundary classes are determined from the software system context diagram, as shown in Figure 21.9, which shows the Banking System as an aggregate class.

We design one boundary class for each external class. The device I/O classes are the Card Reader Interface, through which ATM cards are read, the Cash Dispenser Interface, which dispenses cash, and the Receipt Printer Interface, which prints receipts. There is also Customer Interaction, which is the user interaction class that interacts with the customer via the keyboard/display, displaying textual messages, prompting the customer, and receiving the customer's inputs. The Operator Interaction class is a user interaction class that interacts with the ATM operator, who replenishes the ATM machine with cash. There is one instance of each of these boundary classes for each ATM.

21.4.3 ATM Client Object and Class Structuring: Objects Participating in Use Cases

Next, consider the individual use cases and determine the objects that participate in them. First, consider the Validate PIN inclusion use case, which describes the customer inserting the ATM Card into the card reader, the system prompting for the PIN, and the system checking whether the customer-entered PIN matches the PIN maintained by the system for that ATM card number. From this use case, we first determine the need for the Card Reader Interface object to read the ATM card. The information read off the ATM card needs to be stored, so we identify the need for an entity object to store the ATM Card information. The Customer Interaction object is used for interacting with the customer via the keyboard/display, in this case to prompt for the PIN. The information to be sent to the Banking Service Subsystem for PIN validation is stored in an ATM Transaction. For PIN validation, the transaction information needs to contain the PIN number and the ATM Card number. To control the sequence in which actions at the ATM take place, we identify the need for a control object, ATM Control.

Next consider the objects in the Withdraw Funds use case, which is entered if the PIN is valid and the customer selects withdrawal. In this use case, the customer enters the amount to be withdrawn and the account to be debited, the system checks whether the withdrawal should be authorized, and if positive, dispenses the cash, prints the receipt, and ejects the card. For this use case, additional objects are needed. The information about the customer withdrawal, including the account number and withdrawal amount, needs to be stored in the ATM Transaction object. To dispense the cash, a Cash Dispenser Interface object is needed. We also need to maintain the amount of cash in the ATM, so we identify the need for an entity object called ATM Cash, which is decremented every time there is a cash withdrawal. Finally, we need a Receipt Printer Interface object to print the receipt. As before, the ATM Control object controls the sequencing of the use case.

Inspecting the other use cases reveals that one additional object is needed, namely, the Operator Interaction object, which participates in all use cases initiated by the Operator actor. The Operator Interaction object needs to send startup and shutdown events to ATM Control, because operator maintenance and ATM customer activities are mutually exclusive.

Given the preceding analysis, Figure 21.10 shows the classes in the ATM Client Subsystem, which is depicted as an aggregate class. In addition to the three device

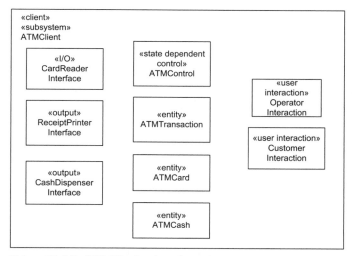

Figure 21.10. ATM Client subsystem classes

I/O classes and two user interaction classes depicted in Figure 21.9, there are also three entity classes and one state-dependent control class.

21.4.4 Object Structuring in Service Subsystem

Several entity objects are bank-wide and need to be accessible from any ATM. Consequently, these objects must be stored in the Banking Service subsystem at the server. These objects include Customer objects that hold information about bank customers, Account objects (both checking and saving) that hold information about individual bank accounts, and Debit Card objects that hold information about all the debit cards maintained at the bank. The classes from which these objects are instantiated all appear on the static model of the entity classes depicted in Figure 21.4.

In the Banking Service Subsystem, the entity classes are Customer, the Account superclass, Checking Account and Savings Account subclasses, and Debit Card. There is also the ATM Transaction object, which migrates from the client to the server. The client sends the transaction request to the Banking Service, which sends a response to the client. The transaction is also stored at the server as an entity object in the form of a Transaction Log, so that a transaction history is maintained. The transient data sent as part of the ATM Transaction message might differ from the persistent transaction data; for example, transaction status is known at the end of the transaction but not during it.

Business logic objects are also needed at the server to define the business-specific application logic for processing client requests. In particular, each ATM transaction type needs a transaction manager to specify the business rules for handling the transaction. The business logic objects are the PIN Validation Transaction Manager, the Withdrawal Transaction Manager, the Query Transaction Manager, and the Transfer Transaction Manager. For example, the business rules maintained by the Withdrawal Transaction Manager are that (1) the account must always have a balance greater or equal to zero after each withdrawal, and that (2) there is a maximum amount that can be withdrawn each day, which is given by the attribute limit in the entity class Debit Card.

21.5 DYNAMIC MODELING

The dynamic model depicts the interaction among the objects that participate in each use case. The starting point for developing the dynamic model is the use cases and the objects determined during object structuring. The sequence of interobject message communication to satisfy the needs of a use case is depicted on either a sequence diagram or a communication diagram. Usually one or the other of the diagrams suffices. In this example, both diagrams are developed for the client subsystem to allow a comparison of the two approaches.

Because the Banking System is a client/server system, the decision was made earlier to structure the system into client and service subsystems, as shown in Figure 21.8. The communication diagrams are structured for client and service subsystems.

The communication diagrams depicted in Figures 21.11 and 21.16 are for the realizations of the Validate PIN and Withdraw Funds use cases on the ATM client. Communication diagrams are also needed to realize the Transfer Funds and Query

Account use cases on the ATM client, as well as for the use cases initiated by the operator.

The Validate PIN and Withdraw Funds communication diagrams for the ATM client are state-dependent. The state-dependent parts of the interactions are defined by the ATM Control object, which executes the ATM statechart. The state-dependent dynamic analysis approach is used to determine how the objects interact with each other. Statecharts are shown for the two use cases in Figures 21.13 and 21.18, respectively. The dynamic analysis for these two client-side use cases is described in Sections 21.5.1 and 21.5.3, respectively.

The Banking Service processes transactions from multiple ATMs in the order it receives them. The processing of each transaction is self-contained; thus, the banking service part of the use cases is not state-dependent. Consequently, a stateless dynamic analysis is needed for these use cases. The communication diagrams for the server side Validate PIN and Withdraw Funds use cases are given in Figures 21.14 and 21.19. The dynamic analysis for these two server-side use cases is given in Sections 21.5.2 and 21.5.4, respectively.

Consider how the objects interact with each other. A detailed example is given for the Validate PIN and Withdraw Funds use cases. On the client side, both communication diagram and sequence diagrams are shown. The same message sequence numbering and message sequence description applies to both the sequence diagram and the communication diagram.

21.5.1 Message Sequence Description for Client-Side Validate PIN Interaction Diagram

The client-side Validate PIN interaction diagram starts with the customer inserting the ATM card into the card reader. The message sequence number starts at 1, which is the first external event initiated by the actor. Subsequent numbering in sequence, representing the messages arriving at software objects in the system, is 1.1, 1.2, 1.3 and ends with 1.4, the system's response displayed to the actor. The next input from the actor is the external event numbered 2, followed by the internal events 2.1, 2.2, and so on. The following message sequence description corresponds to the communication diagram shown in Figure 21.11 and the sequence diagram in Figure 21.12.

Because the Validate PIN interaction diagram is state-dependent, it is also necessary to consider the ATM statechart, which is executed by the ATM Control object. In particular, the interaction between the statechart (shown in Figure 21.13) and ATM Control (depicted on the communication diagram) needs to be considered. The following message sequence description also addresses the states and transitions on the statechart that correspond to the events on the communication diagram in Figure 21.11 and the events on the sequence diagram in Figure 21.12. The message sequence description is as follows:

1: The ATM Customer actor inserts the ATM card into the Card Reader. The Card Reader Interface object reads the card input.

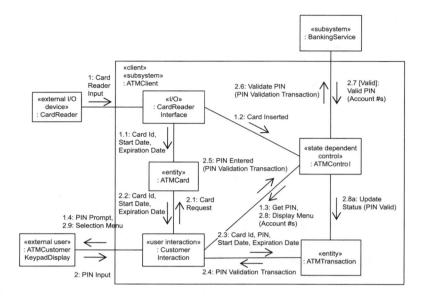

PIN Validation Transaction = {transactionId, transactionType, cardId, PIN, starDate, expirationDate}

Figure 21.11. Communication diagram: ATM client Validate PIN use case

1.1: The Card Reader Interface object sends the card input data, containing Card Id, Start Date, Expiration Date to the entity object ATM Card.

1.2: Card Reader Interface sends the Card Inserted message to ATM Control. The equivalent Card Inserted event causes the ATM Control statechart to transition from Idle state (the initial state) to Waiting for PIN state. The output event associated with this transition is Get PIN.

1.3: ATM Control sends the Get PIN message to Customer Interaction.

1.4: Customer Interaction displays the PIN Prompt to the ATM Customer actor.

2: ATM Customer inputs the PIN number to the Customer Interaction object.

2.1: Customer Interaction requests card data from ATM Card.

2.2: ATM Card provides the card data to the Customer Interaction.

2.3: Customer Interaction sends Card Id, PIN, Start Date, Expiration Date, to the ATM Transaction entity object.

2.4: ATM Transaction entity object sends the PIN Validation Transaction to Customer Interaction.

2.5: Customer Interaction sends the PIN Entered (PIN Validation Transaction) message to ATM Control. The PIN Entered event causes the ATM Control statechart to transition from Waiting for PIN state to Validating PIN state. The output event associated with this transition is Validate PIN.

2.6: ATM control sends a Validate PIN (PIN Validation Transaction) request to the Banking Service.

2.7: Banking Service validates the PIN and sends a Valid PIN response to ATM Control. As a result of this event, ATM Control transitions to Waiting for

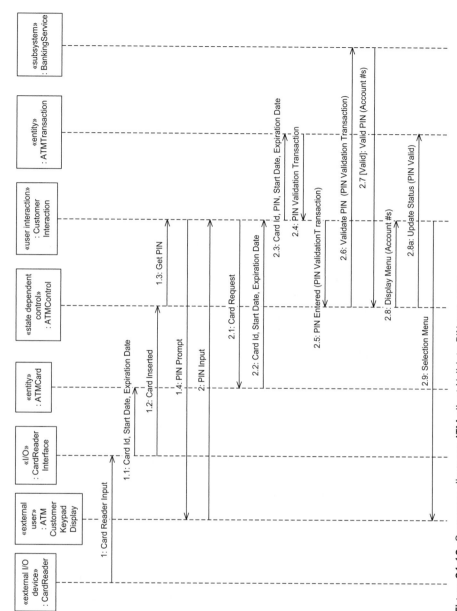

Figure 21.12. Sequence diagram: ATM client Validate PIN use case

387

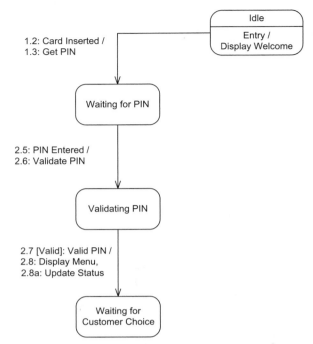

Figure 21.13. Statechart for ATM Control: Validate PIN use case

Customer Choice state. The output events for this transition are Display Menu and Update Status, which correspond to the output messages sent by ATM Control.

2.8: ATM Control sends the Display Menu message to Customer Interaction.

2.8a: ATM Control sends an Update Status message to the ATM Transaction.

2.9: Customer Interaction displays a menu showing the Withdraw, Query, and Transfer options to the ATM Customer.

The dynamic modeling of the alternative scenarios, corresponding to the alternative sequences through the Validate PIN use case, is described in Chapter 11. The alternative scenarios are depicted on interaction diagrams and statecharts.

21.5.2 Message Sequence Description for Server-Side Validate PIN Interaction Diagram

Consider the interaction diagram for the server side Validate PIN inclusion use case. To validate the PIN at the server, the Debit card entity object, which contains all the information pertinent to all debit cards that belong to the bank, needs to be accessed. If PIN validation is successful, the Card Account entity object needs to be accessed to retrieve the account numbers of the accounts that can be accessed by this debit card.

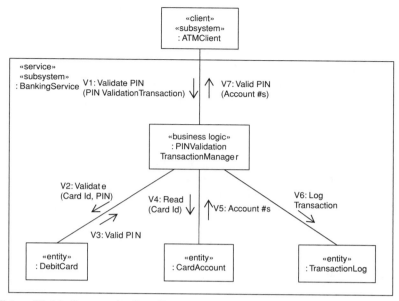

Figure 21.14. Communication diagram: Banking Service Validate PIN use case

In addition, each transaction has a **business logic object** that encapsulates the business application logic to manage the execution of the transaction. The business logic object receives the transaction request from the ATM Control object at the client and then interacts with the entity objects to determine what response to return to ATM Control. For example, the business logic object for the PIN Validation transaction is the PIN Validation Transaction Manager.

The following message sequence description for the server side Validate PIN interaction diagram corresponds to the communication diagram shown in Figure 21.14 and the sequence diagram shown in Figure 21.15.

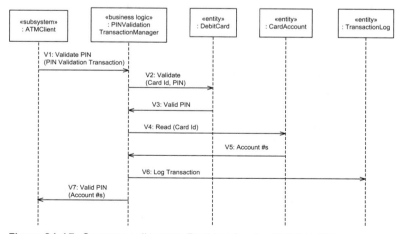

Figure 21.15. Sequence diagram: Banking Service Validate PIN use case

V1: ATM Client sends the incoming Validate PIN request to the PIN Validation Transaction Manager. The PIN Validation Transaction Manager contains the business logic to determine whether the customer-entered PIN matches the PIN stored in the Banking Service database.

V2: PIN Validation Transaction Manager sends a Validate (Card Id, PIN) message to the Debit Card entity object, requesting it to validate this customer's debit card, given the card Id and customer-entered PIN.

V3: Debit Card checks that customer-entered PIN matches the Debit Card record PIN, that card Status is okay (not reported missing or stolen), and that Expiration Date has not passed. If card passes all checks, Debit Card sends PIN Validation Transaction Manager a Valid PIN response.

V4: If validation is positive, PIN Validation Transaction Manager sends a message to the Card Account entity object requesting it to return the account numbers that may be accessed for this card Id.

V5: Card Account responds with the valid account numbers.

V6: PIN Validation Transaction Manager logs the transaction with the Transaction Log.

V7: PIN Validation Transaction Manager sends a Valid PIN response to the ATM Client. If the PIN validation checks are satisfactory, the account numbers are also sent.

21.5.3 Message Sequence Description for Client-Side Withdraw Funds Interaction Diagram

The message sequence description for the client-side Withdraw Funds interaction diagram addresses the messages on the communication diagram (Figure 21.16) and the sequence diagram (Figure 21.17). It also describes the relevant states and transitions on the ATM statechart (Figure 21.18). The message numbering is a continuation of that described for the client-side Validate PIN interaction diagram in Section 21.5.1.

3: ATM Customer actor inputs Withdrawal selection to Customer Interaction, together with the account number for checking or savings account and withdrawal amount.

3.1: Customer Interaction sends the customer selection to ATM Transaction.

3.2: ATM Transaction responds to Customer Interaction with the Withdrawal Transaction details. Withdrawal Transaction contains transaction Id, transaction Type, card Id, PIN, account number, and amount.

3.3: Customer Interaction sends the Withdrawal Selected (Withdrawal Transaction) request to ATM Control. ATM Control transitions to Processing Withdrawal state. Two output events are associated with this transition, Request Withdrawal and Display Wait.

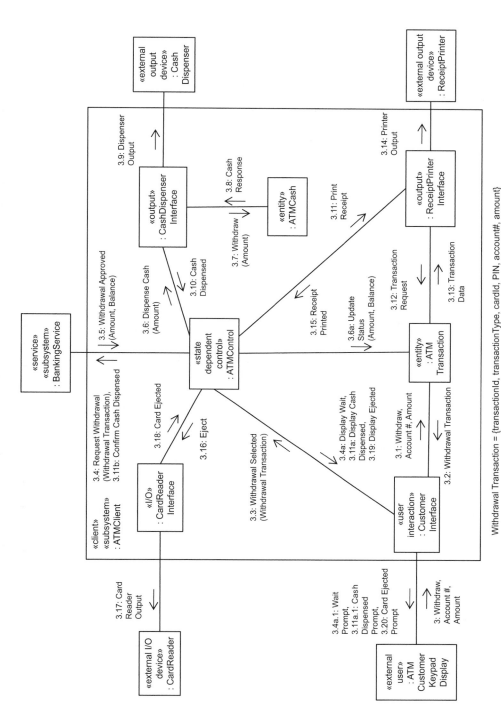

Withdrawal Transaction = {transactionId, transactionType, cardId, PIN, account#, amount}

Figure 21.16. Communication diagram: ATM client Withdraw Funds use case

391

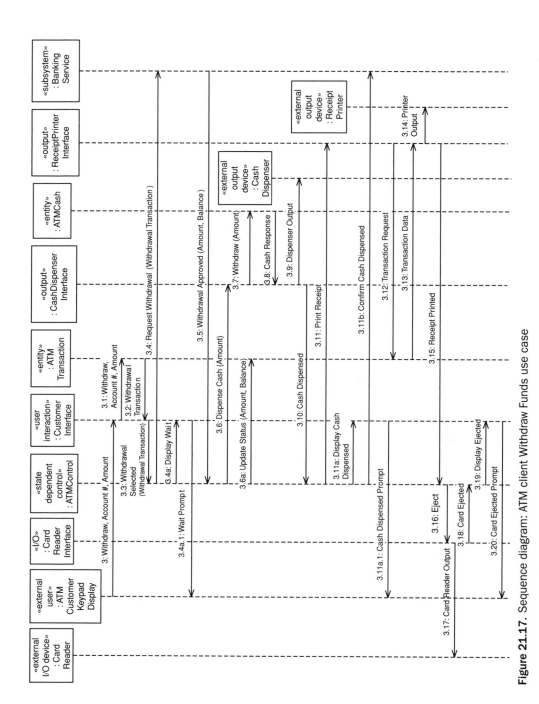

Figure 21.17. Sequence diagram: ATM client Withdraw Funds use case

392

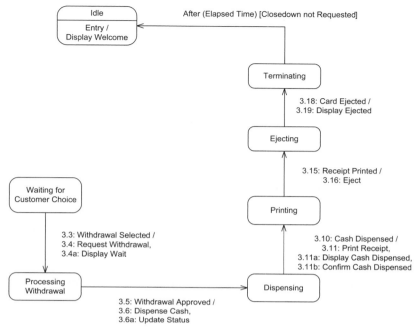

Figure 21.18. Statechart for ATM Control: Withdraw Funds use case

3.4: ATM Control sends a Request Withdrawal transaction containing the Withdrawal Transaction to the Banking Service.

3.4a: ATM Control sends a Display Wait message to Customer Interaction.

3.4a.1: Customer Interaction displays the Wait Prompt to the ATM Customer.

3.5: Banking Service sends a Withdrawal Approved (Amount, Balance) response to ATM Control. This event causes ATM Control to transition to Dispensing state. The output events are Dispense Cash and Update Status.

3.6: ATM Control sends a Dispense Cash (Amount) message to Cash Dispenser Interface.

3.6a: ATM Control sends an Update Status (Amount, Balance) message to ATM Transaction.

3.7: Cash Dispenser Interface sends the Withdraw (Amount) to ATM Cash.

3.8: ATM Cash sends a positive Cash Response to the Cash Dispenser Interface, identifying the number of bills of each denomination to be dispensed.

3.9: Cash Dispenser Interface sends the Dispenser Output command to the Cash Dispenser external output device to dispense cash to the customer.

3.10: Cash Dispenser Interface sends the Cash Dispensed message to ATM Control. The equivalent Cash Dispensed event causes ATM Control to transition to Printing state. The three output events associated with this transition are Print Receipt, Display Cash Dispensed, and Confirm Cash Dispensed.

3.11: ATM Control sends Print Receipt message to Receipt Printer Interface.

3.11a: ATM Control sends Customer Interaction the Display Cash Dispensed message.

3.11a.1: Customer Interaction displays Cash Dispensed prompt to ATM Customer.

3.11b: ATM Control sends a Confirm Cash Dispensed message to the Banking Service.

3.12: Receipt Printer Interface requests transaction data from ATM Transaction.

3.13: ATM Transaction sends the transaction data to the Receipt Printer Interface.

3.14: Receipt Printer Interface sends the Printer Output to the Receipt Printer external output device.

3.15: Receipt Printer Interface sends the Receipt Printed message to ATM Control. As a result, ATM Control transitions to Ejecting state. The output event is Eject.

3.16: ATM Control sends the Eject message to Card Reader Interface.

3.17: Card Reader Interface sends the Card Reader Output to the Card Reader external I/O device.

3.18: Card Reader Interface sends the Card Ejected message to ATM Control. ATM Control transitions to Terminated state. The output event is Display Ejected.

3.19: ATM Control sends the Display Ejected message to the Customer Interaction.

3.20: Customer Interaction displays the Card Ejected prompt to the ATM Customer.

21.5.4 Message Sequence Description for Server-Side Withdraw Funds Interaction Diagram

The **business logic object** that participates in the server-side Withdraw Funds use case is the Withdrawal Transaction Manager, which encapsulates the logic for determining whether the customer is allowed to withdraw funds from the selected account. The other business logic objects that participate in the server use cases are the Transfer Transaction Manager, which encapsulates the logic for determining whether the customer can transfer funds from one account to another, and the Query Transaction Manager. The latter is sufficiently simple that a separate business logic object is not strictly necessary; the functionality could be handled by the read operation of the Account object. However, to be consistent with the other business logic objects, it is kept as a separate object.

A detailed analysis is given for the server-side Withdraw Funds use case. A similar approach is needed for the server-side Transfer Funds and server-side Query Account use cases. The following message sequence description corresponds to the communication diagram shown in Figure 21.19 for the server-side Withdraw Funds use case and sequence shown in Figure 21.20.

W1: ATM Client sends the Request Withdrawal request to the Withdrawal Transaction Manager, which contains the business logic for determining whether a withdrawal can be allowed. The incoming withdrawal

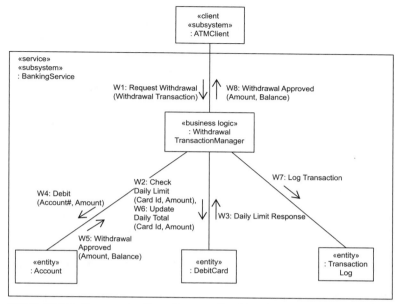

Figure 21.19. Communication diagram: Banking Service Withdraw Funds use case

transaction consists of transaction Id, transaction Type, card Id, PIN, account Number, and amount.

W2: Withdrawal Transaction Manager sends a Check Daily Limit (Card Id, Amount) message to Debit Card, with the card Id and amount requested. Debit Card checks whether the daily limit for cash withdrawal has been

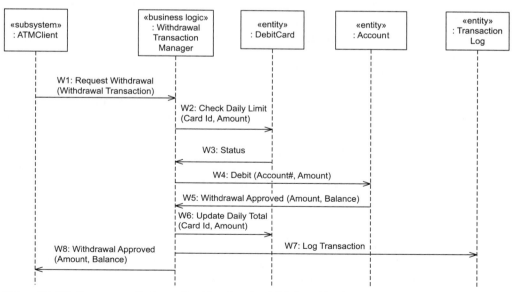

Figure 21.20. Sequence diagram: Banking Service Withdraw Funds use case

exceeded for this card Id. Debit Card determines if: Total Withdrawn Today + Amount Requested ≤ Daily Limit

W3: Debit Card responds to Withdrawal Transaction Manager with a positive or negative Daily Limit Response.

W4: If the response is positive, Withdrawal Transaction Manager sends a message to Account (which is an instance of either Checking Account or Savings Account), requesting it to debit the customer's account if there are sufficient funds in the account. Account determines whether there are sufficient funds in the account:

$$\text{Account Balance} - \text{Amount Requested} \geq 0$$

If there are sufficient funds, Account decrements the balance by the Amount Requested.

W5: Account responds to Withdrawal Transaction Manager with either Withdrawal Approved (Amount, Balance) or Withdrawal Denied.

W6: If the account was debited satisfactorily, the Withdrawal Transaction Manager sends an Update Daily Total (Card Id, Amount) to Debit Card so it increments the total withdrawn today by the amount requested.

W7: Withdrawal Transaction Manager logs the transaction with the Transaction Log.

W8: Withdrawal Transaction Manager returns Withdrawal Approved (Amount, Balance) or Withdrawal Denied to the ATM Client.

21.6 ATM STATECHART

Because there is one control object, ATM Control, a statechart needs to be defined for it. Partial statecharts are shown corresponding to the Validate PIN and Withdraw Funds use cases in Figures 21.14 and 21.18, respectively. It is necessary to develop similar statecharts for the other use cases, and to develop states and transitions for the alternative paths of the use cases, which in this application address error situations. Flat statecharts are used initially for the use cases. Integration of the statecharts for the individual use cases and design of the hierarchical ATM Control statechart are described in Chapter 10. One of the advantages of a hierarchical statechart is that it can be presented in stages, as is shown for the ATM statechart in Figures 21.21 through 21.24. The event sequence numbers shown on these figures correspond to the object interactions previously described.

Five states are shown on the top-level statechart in Figure 21.21: Closed Down (which is the initial state), Idle, and three composite states, Processing Customer Input, Processing Transaction, and Terminating Transaction. Each composite state is decomposed into its own statechart, as shown on Figures 21.22, 21.23, and 21.24, respectively.

At system initialization time, given by the event Startup, the ATM transitions from the initial Closed Down state to Idle state. The event Display Welcome is triggered on entry into Idle state. In Idle state, the ATM is waiting for a customer-initiated event.

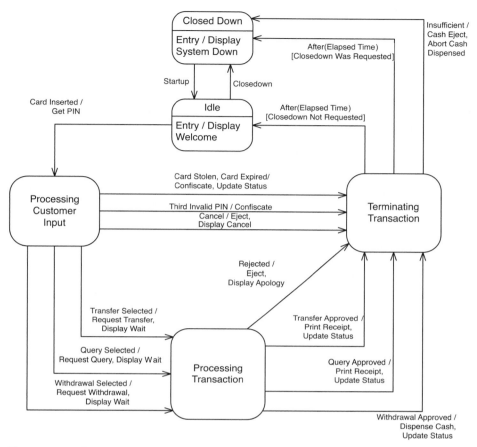

Figure 21.21. Top-level statechart for ATM Control

21.6.1 Processing Customer Input Composite State

The Processing Customer Input composite state (Figure 21.22) is decomposed into three substates – Waiting for PIN, Validating PIN, and Waiting for Customer Choice:

1. **Waiting for PIN.** This substate is entered from Idle state when the customer inserts the card in the ATM, resulting in the Card Inserted event. In this state, the ATM waits for the customer to enter the PIN.
2. **Validating PIN.** This substate is entered when the customer enters the PIN. In this substate, the Banking Service validates the PIN.
3. **Waiting for Customer Choice.** This substate is entered as a result of a Valid PIN event, indicating a valid PIN was entered. In this state, the customer enters a selection: Withdraw, Transfer, or Query.

The statechart is developed by considering the different states of the ATM as the customer actor proceeds through each of the use cases, starting with the Validate PIN use case. When a customer inserts an ATM card, the event Card Inserted causes the ATM to transition to the Waiting for PIN substate of the Processing Customer Input composite state (see Figure 21.22a). During this time, the ATM is waiting for the customer to input the PIN. The output event, Get PIN, results in a display prompt

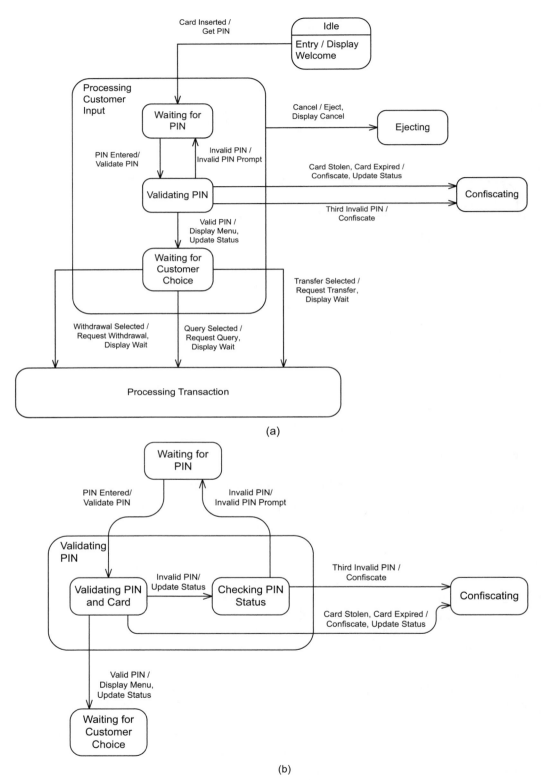

Figure 21.22. Statechart for ATM Control: Processing Customer Input composite state

to the customer. When the customer enters the PIN number, the PIN Entered event causes a transition to the Validating PIN substate, during which the Banking Service determines whether the customer-entered PIN matches the PIN stored by the Banking System for this particular card. There are three possible state transitions out of the Validating PIN state. If the two PIN numbers match, the Valid PIN transition is taken to the Waiting for Customer Choice state. If the PIN numbers do not match, the Invalid PIN transition is taken to re-enter the Waiting for PIN state and allow the customer to enter a different PIN number. If the customer-entered PIN is still invalid after the third attempt, the Third Invalid transition is taken to the Confiscating substate of the Terminating Transaction composite state.

The Validating PIN substate is itself a composite state consisting of two substates: Validating PIN and Card as well as Checking PIN Status (see Figure 21.22b). In the first substate, the card Id (read off card) and PIN (entered by customer) combination are validated by comparing them with the card Id/PIN combination stored in the Card Account entity object. In addition, the card Id is checked to ensure that the card is not lost or stolen. If the validation is successful, the ATM transitions to Waiting for Customer Choice. If the card is lost or stolen, the ATM transitions to Confiscating state. However, if the PIN is invalid, an additional check needs to be made to determine whether this is the third time that the PIN is incorrect. It is better to store the Invalid PIN count at the client rather than the server, because this is a local ATM concern. An invalid PIN count is therefore stored in ATM Transaction. This count is updated and checked after each invalid PIN response from the server – if the count is less than three, then the ATM transitions back to Waiting for PIN. If the count is Third Invalid PIN, then the ATM transitions to Confiscating state.

The customer can also press the Cancel button on the ATM machine in any of the three Processing Customer Input substates. The Cancel event transitions the ATM to the Ejecting substate of the Terminating Transaction composite state. Because the Cancel event can occur in any of the three substates of the Processing Customer Input composite state, it is more concise to show the Cancel transition leaving the composite state.

21.6.2 Processing Transaction Composite State

The Processing Transaction composite state (Figure 21.23) is also decomposed into three substates, one for each transaction: Processing Withdrawal, Processing Transfer,

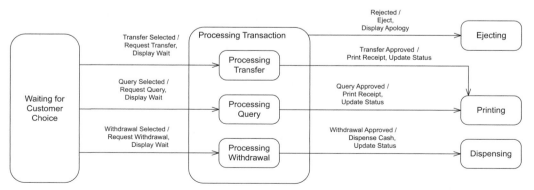

Figure 21.23. Statechart for ATM: Processing Transaction composite state

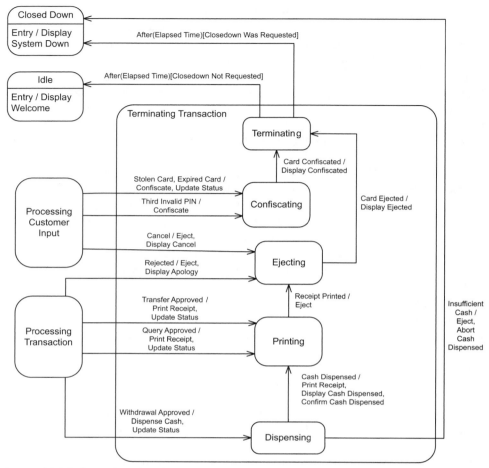

Figure 21.24. Statechart for ATM Control: Terminating Transaction composite state

and Processing Query. Depending on the customer's selection – for example, withdrawal – the appropriate substate within Processing Transaction – for example, Processing Withdrawal – is entered, during which the customer's request is processed.

From Waiting for Customer Choice state, the customer may select Withdraw, Query, or Transfer and enter the appropriate substate within the Processing Transaction composite state (see Figure 21.23) – for example, Processing Withdrawal. When a Withdrawal transaction is completed, the event Withdrawal Approved is issued if the customer has enough funds, and the Dispensing substate of the Terminating Transaction composite state is entered (Figure 21.24). Alternatively, if the customer has insufficient funds or has exceeded the daily withdrawal limit, a Rejected event is issued.

21.6.3 Terminating Transaction Composite State

The Terminating Transaction composite state (see Figure 21.24) has substates for Dispensing, Printing, Ejecting, Confiscating, and Terminating.

The actions associated with the transition to Dispensing state are to Dispense Cash and Update Status. After the Cash Dispensed event has taken place, the ATM transitions to Printing state to print the receipt. The action Print Receipt is executed at the transition. When the receipt is printed, the state Ejecting is entered and the Eject action is executed. When the card has been ejected (event Card Ejected), the Terminating state is entered.

For the Query and Transfer transactions, the sequence of states following approval of the transaction is similar, except that no cash is dispensed, as can be seen on the ATM statecharts.

21.7 DESIGN OF BANKING SYSTEM

Next, the analysis model of the Banking System is mapped to a design model. The steps in this process are as follows:

1. Integrate the communication model. Develop integrated communication diagrams.
2. Structure the Banking System into subsystems. Define the interfaces of the subsystems.
3. For each subsystem, structure the system into concurrent tasks.
4. For each subsystem, design the information hiding classes.
5. Develop the detailed software design.

21.8 INTEGRATING THE COMMUNICATION MODEL

Because the Banking System is a client/server system (Section 21.4), a decision was made earlier to structure the system into client and service subsystems, as shown in Figure 21.8. The communication diagrams are also structured for client and service subsystems.

The communication diagrams for the client-side Validate PIN and Withdraw Funds use cases are depicted in Figures 21.11 and 21.16. Communication diagrams are also needed for the client-side Transfer Funds and Query Account use cases, as well as for the use cases initiated by the operator. The integrated communication diagram for the ATM Client Subsystem (Figure 21.25) is the result of the merger of all these use case–based communication diagrams, as described in Chapter 13. To be complete, the integration must consist of communication scenarios for the main and alternative sequences through each use case.

Some objects participate in all the client-side communications, such as ATM Control, but others participate in as few as one, such as the Cash Dispenser Interface. Some of the messages depicted on the integrated communication diagram are aggregate messages, such as Customer Events and Display Prompts. The integrated diagram must also include messages from all the alternative sequences, as described in Chapter 13. Thus, the Confiscate and Card Confiscated messages originate from alternative sequences in which the customer transaction is unsuccessful. Similarly, the aggregate Display Prompts messages include messages dealing with incorrect PIN entry, insufficient cash in the customer account, and so on.

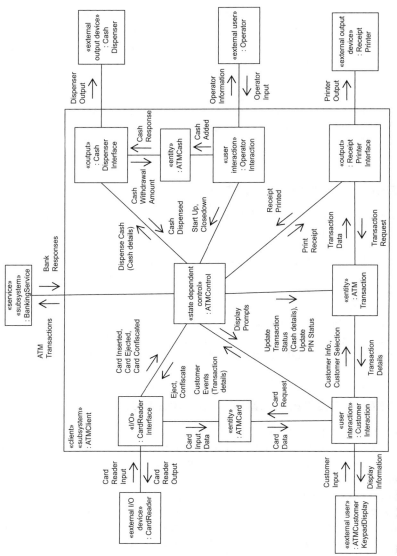

Figure 21.25. Integrated communication diagram for ATM client subsystem

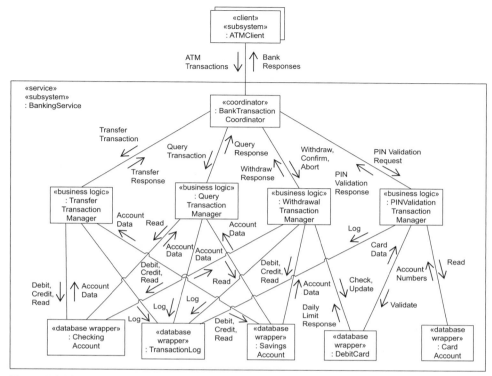

Figure 21.26. Integrated communication diagram for Banking Service subsystem

Now consider the Banking Service Subsystem. Figures 21.14 and 21.19 are the communication diagrams for the server-side Validate PIN and Withdraw Funds use cases. Additional communication diagrams are needed for the server-side Transfer Funds and Query Account use cases. The integrated communication diagram for the Banking Service Subsystem is shown in Figure 21.26. For each transaction, there is a transaction manager object that encapsulates the business logic for the transaction. These are the PIN Validation Transaction Manager, Withdrawal Transaction Manager, Query Transaction Manager, and Transfer Transaction Manager objects. In addition, it is decided at design time that there is a need for a coordinator object, the Bank Transaction Coordinator, which receives client requests and delegates them to the appropriate transaction manager, as described in Chapter 15.

21.9 STRUCTURING THE SYSTEM INTO SUBSYSTEMS

In the case of the Banking System, the step of structuring the system into subsystems is straightforward. The Banking System is a classic client/server architecture that is based around the multiple client/single service architectural pattern. There are two subsystems, the multiple instances of the ATM Client Subsystem and the Banking Service Subsystem, as initially depicted in Figure 21.8. The two subsystems might also be depicted on a high-level communication diagram, as shown in Figure 21.27.

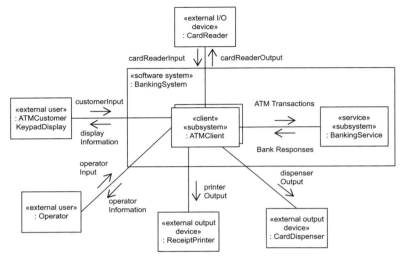

Figure 21.27. Subsystem design: high-level communication diagram for Banking System

Figure 21.27 is an analysis-level communication diagram showing the two subsystems and simple messages passed between them. The ATM Client Subsystem sends ATM Transactions to the Banking Service Subsystem, which responds with Bank Responses. ATM Transactions is an aggregate message consisting of the PIN Validation, Withdraw, Query, Transfer, Confirm, and Abort messages. The Bank Responses are responses to these messages.

The next step is to consider the distributed nature of the application and define the distributed message interfaces. Because this is a client/server subsystem, there are multiple instances of the client subsystem and one instance of the service subsystem. Each subsystem instance executes on its own node. In the design model, each of these subsystems is a concurrent subsystem, consisting of at least one task. The message interface is **synchronous message communication with reply**. Each ATM client sends a message to the Banking Service and then waits for a response. Because the Banking Service can receive messages from several ATM clients, a message queue can build up at the Banking Service, which processes incoming messages on a FIFO basis. The design model communication diagram is depicted in Figure 21.28.

The next step is to structure each subsystem into concurrent tasks. In the following sections, the design of the ATM Client Subsystem and then the design of the Banking Service Subsystem are considered.

21.10 DESIGN OF ATM CLIENT SUBSYSTEM

To determine the tasks in a system, it is necessary to understand how the objects in the application interact with each other. This is best depicted on the analysis model communication diagram, which shows the sequence of messages passed between objects in support of a given use case. For the ATM Client Subsystem, consider the communication diagrams for the Client Validate PIN and Client Withdraw Funds use cases in addition to the integrated communication diagram for this subsystem. The

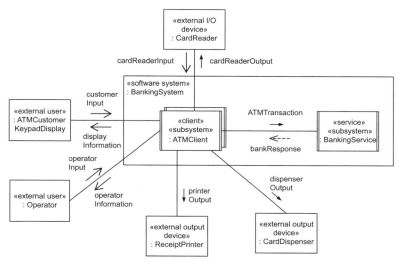

Figure 21.28. Subsystem interfaces: high-level concurrent communication diagram for Banking System

task design described in this section leads to the concurrent communication diagram shown in Figure 21.29.

21.10.1 Design the ATM Subsystem Concurrent Task Architecture

Consider the communication diagram supporting the Validate PIN use case (see Figure 21.11). The first object to participate in the communication is the Card Reader Interface object, which is an I/O object that interfaces to the real-world card reader. The characteristics of the Card Reader external I/O device are that it is an event driven I/O device that generates an interrupt when some input is available. The Card Reader Interface object is structured as an event driven I/O task, as shown in Figure 21.29. Initially, the task is dormant. It is activated by an interrupt, reads the card reader input, and converts it into an internal format. It then writes the contents of the card to the ATM Card entity object. ATM Card is a passive object and thus does not need a separate thread of control. It is further categorized as a data abstraction object.

The Card Reader Interface task then sends a Card Inserted message to ATM Control, which is a state-dependent control object that executes the ATM Control statechart. ATM Control is structured as a demand driven state-dependent control task because it needs to have a separate thread of control to allow it to react to incoming messages from a variety of sources. Initially, it is idle until it is activated on demand by the arrival of a control request message. On receiving the Card Inserted message, ATM Control executes the statechart and transitions to Waiting for PIN substate (see Figures 21.21 and 21.22). The action associated with the state transition is to send a Get PIN message to Customer Interaction, which is a user interaction object that interacts with the user, providing outputs to the display and receiving inputs from the keypad. Customer Interaction is structured as an event driven user interaction task with its own separate thread of control. It prompts the customer for the PIN,

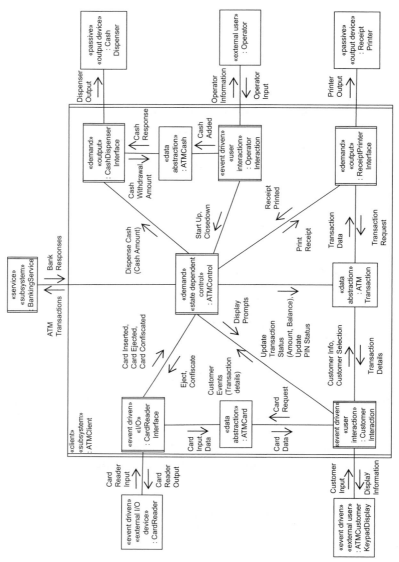

Figure 21.29. Task architecture: initial concurrent communication diagram for ATM client subsystem

406

receives the PIN, reads the card information from ATM Card, and then writes the card and PIN information to ATM Transaction, which is also a passive data abstraction object. Because the ATM Card and ATM Transaction data abstraction objects are each accessed by more than one task, they are both placed outside any task.

Next, consider the communication diagram supporting the Withdraw Funds use case, which has many of the same objects as the Validate PIN communication diagram. The additional objects are Receipt Printer Interface, Cash Dispenser Interface, and ATM Cash.

The external Cash Dispenser is a passive output device, so it does not need an event driven output task. Instead, the Cash Dispenser Interface object is structured as a demand driven output task, which is activated on demand by message arrival from ATM Control. Similarly, the Receipt Printer Interface object is structured as a demand driven output task, which is activated by message arrival from the ATM Control task.

The Operator Interaction user interaction object (see Figure 21.24), which participates in the three operator-initiated use cases, is also mapped to an event driven user interaction task (see Figure 21.29). The ATM Cash entity object is a passive data abstraction object and thus does not need a separate thread of control, which is accessed by both the Cash Dispenser Interface and Operator Interaction tasks.

To summarize, there is one event driven I/O task, Card Reader Interface, one demand driven state-dependent control task, ATM Control, two demand driven output tasks, Cash Dispenser Interface and Receipt Printer Interface, and two event driven user interaction tasks, Customer Interaction and Operator Interaction. There are three passive entity objects, ATM Card, ATM Transaction, and ATM Cash, which are all categorized further as data abstraction objects.

21.10.2 Define the ATM Subsystem Task Interfaces

To determine the task interfaces, it is necessary to analyze the way the objects (active or passive) interact with each other. First, consider the interaction of the tasks just determined with the passive data abstraction objects. In each case, the task calls an operation provided by the passive object. This has to be a synchronous call, because the operation executes in the thread of control of the task. Similarly, all other operations of the data abstraction objects are invoked as synchronous calls. Because each of these passive objects is invoked by more than one task, it is necessary for the operations to synchronize the access to the data. The operations provided by these passive objects are described in the next section.

Next consider the message interaction between the tasks. Consider the interface between the Card Reader Interface and ATM Control tasks. It is desirable for Card Reader Interface task to be able to send a message to ATM Control and not have to wait for it to be accepted. For this to be the case, an asynchronous message interface is needed, as shown in Figure 21.30. This means that there is also a message interface in the opposite direction because ATM Control sends Eject and Confiscate messages to the Card Reader Interface task. This is designed as a synchronous message interface without reply because, after sending a message to ATM Control, the Card Reader Interface waits for an Eject or Confiscate return message. This means that ATM Control can send a synchronous message and not have to wait for Card Reader Interface to accept the message. The latter task's responses are asynchronous, providing the greatest flexibility in the interface between the Card Reader Interface and ATM Control tasks.

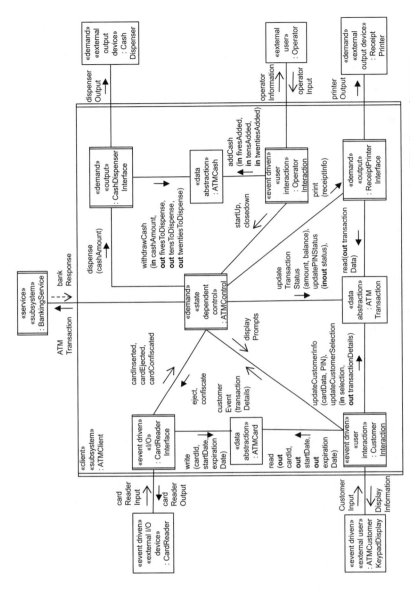

Figure 21.30. Task architecture: revised concurrent communication diagram for ATM client subsystem

Consider the interface between Customer Interaction and ATM Control. Should it be asynchronous or synchronous? First, consider a synchronous with response scenario. Customer Interaction sends a Withdrawal request to ATM Control, which then sends the transaction to the Banking Service. After receiving the Server's response, ATM Control sends a display prompt to Customer Interaction. In the meantime, it is not possible for Customer Interaction to have any interaction with the customer, because it is suspended, waiting for the response from the ATM Control. This is undesirable from the customer's viewpoint. Consider, instead, an asynchronous interface, as shown in Figure 21.30. With this approach, Customer Interaction sends the Withdrawal request to ATM Control and does not wait for a response. In this case, Customer Interaction can respond to customer inputs such as a Cancel request before a response is received from the server. Customer Interaction receives responses from ATM Control as a separate asynchronous message interface. Customer Interaction is designed to be capable of receiving inputs from either the customer or ATM Control. It processes whichever input comes first.

The Operator Interaction task's interface is also asynchronous. The operator actor's requests are independent of the customer's requests, so messages from the customer and the operator could arrive in any order at ATM Control. To allow for this, ATM Control receives all incoming messages on a message queue and processes them on a FIFO basis.

The two output tasks, Cash Dispenser Interface and Receipt Printer Interface, are activated by messages arriving from ATM Control on demand. In each case, the output task is idle prior to the arrival of the message, so a synchronous interface is acceptable because it will not hold up ATM Control. In Figure 21.30, the concurrent communication diagram is updated to show the task interfaces.

21.10.3 Design the ATM Client Information Hiding Classes

The objects and classes for the Banking System are initially determined in the analysis model. Further categorization of passive classes is possible during design; for example, entity classes are categorized further as data abstraction classes or database wrapper classes. During class design, the class interfaces are designed, as described in Chapter 14. To determine the class interfaces, it is necessary to consider how the objects on the communication diagrams interact with each other.

First, consider the design of the entity classes in the ATM Client Subsystem. Because there is no database in the ATM Client Subsystem, all the entity classes encapsulate their own data and are therefore categorized further as data abstraction classes. The ATM Client Subsystem has three data abstraction classes: ATM Card, ATM Transaction, and ATM Cash. The attributes of data abstraction classes are determined during the conceptual static modeling of the entity classes, as described in Section 21.3. The operations of these classes are determined by analyzing the way they are used on the communication diagrams.

The designs of the ATM Cash and ATM Card classes are described in Chapter 14. For the ATM Transaction class, the attributes are also determined from the static model, but its operations are determined from the way it is accessed by other objects, as given on the communication diagrams. The operations are update Customer Information, update Customer Selection, update PIN Status, update Transaction Status, and read. The first two operations are invoked by the Customer Interaction task. The next two operations are invoked by the ATM Control task. The read operation is invoked by the Receipt Printer Interface task prior to printing the receipt.

There is one state-machine class, namely, ATM State Machine, which is internal to the ATM Control task and encapsulates the ATM statechart, which is implemented as a state transition table. The operations are process Event and current State, which are standard operations for a state-machine class.

The design of the classes is shown in more detail in Figure 21.31, which shows the attributes and operations of the classes.

21.11 DESIGN OF BANKING SERVICE SUBSYSTEM

Because the bank server holds the centralized database for the Banking System, we start the design of the Banking Service Subsystem by considering some important design decisions concerning the static model. The conceptual static model of the entity classes (see Figures 21.4–21.7) contains several entity classes that actually reside at the bank server. A design decision is made that the entity classes at the server, which were originally depicted in the static model of the problem domain (see Figure 21.4), are to be stored as relational tables in a relational database. Thus, during design we determine that the entity classes at the server do not actually encapsulate any data but rather encapsulate the interface to the relational database and are actually database wrapper classes. The design of the database wrapper classes and the mapping of the entity class model to the relational database are described later in this section.

21.11.1 Design the Banking Service Subsystem Concurrent Task Architecture

Now consider the Banking Service Subsystem design. A decision is made to use a sequential service. As long as the throughput of the server is fast enough, this is not a problem. In a sequential service, the service is designed as one task; thus, it is designed as one program with one thread of control. Each transaction is received on a FIFO message queue and is processed to completion before the next transaction is started.

The Banking Service Subsystem is designed as one sequential service task, which is activated on demand. Inside the task are the coordinator object (the Bank Transaction Coordinator), the business logic objects (PIN Validation Transaction Manager, Withdrawal Transaction Manager, Query Transaction Manager, and Transfer Transaction Manager), and the entity classes, now categorized further as database wrapper classes. The initial task design for the service subsystem, consisting of one task, is shown in Figure 21.32.

The Bank Transaction Coordinator task receives the incoming transaction messages and replies with the bank responses. It delegates the transaction processing to the transaction managers, which in turn access the database wrapper objects. All communication internal to the Banking Service Subsystem is synchronous, corresponding to operation calls, as described next.

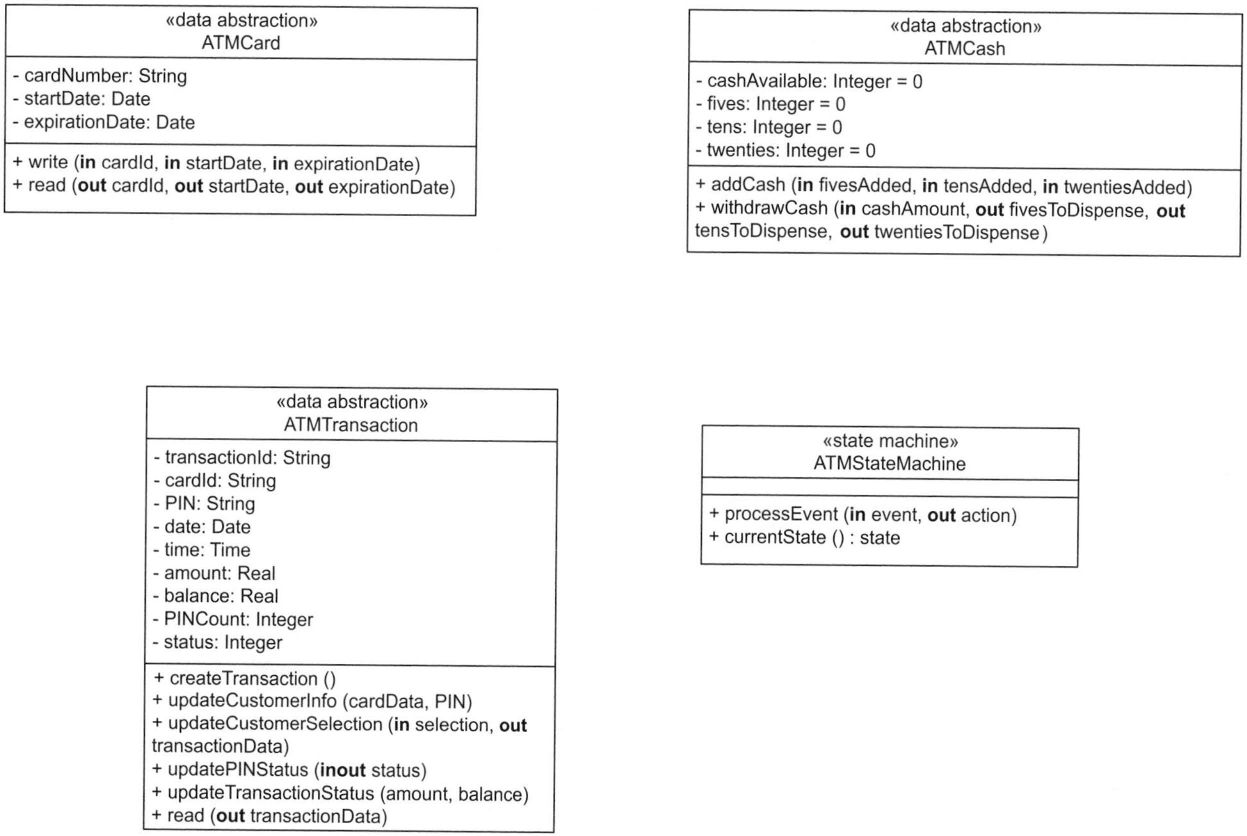

«data abstraction»
ATMCard

- cardNumber: String
- startDate: Date
- expirationDate: Date

+ write (**in** cardId, **in** startDate, **in** expirationDate)
+ read (**out** cardId, **out** startDate, **out** expirationDate)

«data abstraction»
ATMCash

- cashAvailable: Integer = 0
- fives: Integer = 0
- tens: Integer = 0
- twenties: Integer = 0

+ addCash (**in** fivesAdded, **in** tensAdded, **in** twentiesAdded)
+ withdrawCash (**in** cashAmount, **out** fivesToDispense, **out** tensToDispense, **out** twentiesToDispense)

«state machine»
ATMStateMachine

+ processEvent (**in** event, **out** action)
+ currentState () : state

«data abstraction»
ATMTransaction

- transactionId: String
- cardId: String
- PIN: String
- date: Date
- time: Time
- amount: Real
- balance: Real
- PINCount: Integer
- status: Integer

+ createTransaction ()
+ updateCustomerInfo (cardData, PIN)
+ updateCustomerSelection (**in** selection, **out** transactionData)
+ updatePINStatus (**inout** status)
+ update TransactionStatus (amount, balance)
+ read (**out** transactionData)

Figure 21.31. ATM client information hiding classes

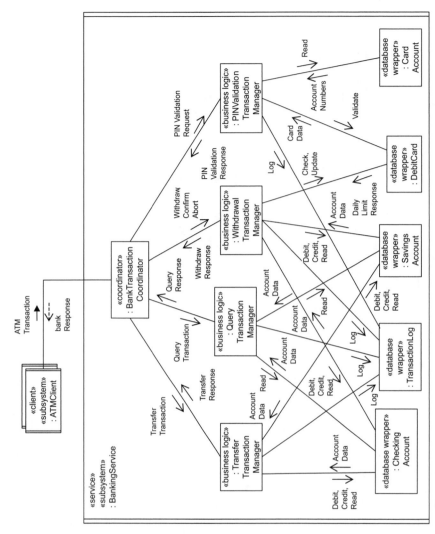

Figure 21.32. Initial concurrent communication diagram for Banking Service subsystem

412

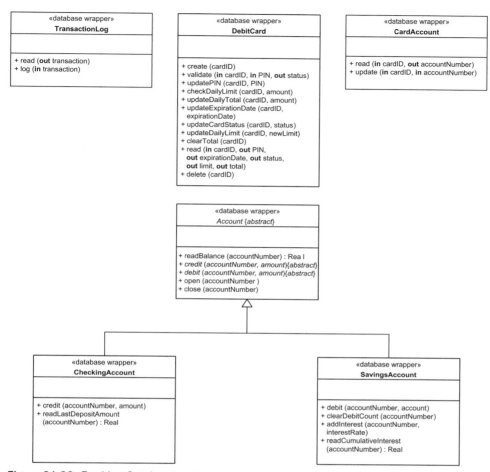

Figure 21.33. Banking Service database wrapper classes

21.11.2 Design the Banking Service Information Hiding Classes

Chapter 15 describes the design of database wrapper classes as well as the mapping of analysis model entity classes to design model database wrapper classes and relational tables (flat files) for a relational database. At the Banking Service, the database wrapper classes are Account, Checking Account, Savings Account, Debit Card, Card Account, and Transaction Log, as shown in Figure 21.33. Each of these classes encapsulates an interface to a database relation. Because a relational database consists of flat files and does not support class hierarchies, from a database perspective, the Account generalization/specialization hierarchy is flattened so that the attributes of the Account superclass are assigned to the Checking Account and Savings Account relations (as described in Chapter 15). However, in the Banking Service class design of the database wrappers, the Account generalization/specialization hierarchy is preserved so that the Checking Account and Savings Account database wrapper classes inherit generalized operations from the abstract Account superclass.

There are also four business logic classes whose interfaces need to be designed. These are the PIN Validation Transaction Manager, the Withdrawal Transaction

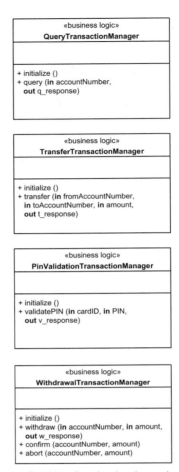

Figure 21.34. Banking Service business logic classes

Manager, the Query Transaction Manager, and the Transfer Transaction Manager, as shown in Figure 21.34. Each transaction manager handles an atomic transaction. For example, the Withdrawal Transaction Manager provides a withdraw operation, which is called to handle a customer request to withdraw funds, as well as two other operations. The confirm operation is called when an ATM Client confirms that the cash was dispensed to the client. The abort operation is called when an ATM Client aborts the transaction, for example, because the cash dispenser failed to dispense the cash or the customer cancelled the transaction.

21.11.3 Design the Banking Service Interfaces

The Banking Service is a sequential service subsystem with one thread of control. In particular, the design of the Banking Service task needs to be considered at this stage. The task is a composite task composed of passive objects. The Bank Transaction Coordinator receives incoming transactions and delegates them to the business logic objects, namely, the PIN Validation Transaction Manager, the Withdrawal Transaction Manager, the Query Transaction Manager, and the Transfer Transaction Manager.

The Bank Transaction Coordinator actually receives the messages FIFO from the ATM Clients. For each message, it determines the type of the transaction and then delegates the transaction processing to the appropriate transaction manager. Each transaction is processed to completion, with the response returned to the Bank Transaction Coordinator, which in turn sends the response to the appropriate ATM Client. The Bank Transaction Coordinator then processes the next transaction message.

Figure 21.32 shows the initial design of the Banking Service Subsystem In the initial concurrent communication diagram for the Banking Service, all interfaces are simple messages. Figure 21.35 shows the final version of the Banking Service Subsystem concurrent communication diagram. Communication between the multiple instances of the ATM Client and the Banking Service is synchronous with reply. All internal interaction within the Banking Service is between passive objects; hence, all internal interfaces are defined in terms of operation calls (depicted by using the synchronous message notation).

21.12 RELATIONAL DATABASE DESIGN

This section describes the logical design of the bank's relational database, starting from the conceptual entity class model described in Section 21.3.3 and depicted in Figures 21.4 through 21.7. All the entity classes depicted on the class diagram (Figure 21.4) reside on the bank server. The data held by these entity classes need to be persistent and therefore need to be stored in a database. As described in Section 21.12, the entity classes are designed as database wrapper classes, whereas the contents of the entity classes (as defined by the attributes of the entity classes) need to be stored in relational tables in the database. In the following description, primary keys are underlined and foreign keys are shown in italics: (underline = primary key, italic = *foreign key*).

The guidelines for designing a relational database from a static model are described in Section 15.5. Consider the entity classes in Figure 21.4. Each of the Bank, ATM Info, Customer, and Debit Card entity classes is mapped to a relational table. In each case, an attribute that uniquely locates a row of the respective table is made the primary key, such as the primary key customerId for the Customer table. Foreign keys are chosen to allow navigation between the tables.

For the Account generalization/specialization hierarchy, the decision is made to flatten the hierarchy by replicating the attributes of the superclass in the subclass tables Checking Account and Savings Account. Although account type (savings or checking) is an attribute of the Account classes, it is assumed that the account type can be determined from the Account Number; therefore, the primary key for both Checking Account and Savings Account tables is accountNumber. The association class Card Account (explicitly depicted in Figure 21.4) is designed as an association table, which represents the many-many relationship between Card and Account. Customer Account is also designed as an association table, representing the many-many relationship between Customer and Account. Even though a Customer Account association class is not explicitly modeled in the static mode (it is not needed by the ATM transactions), it is necessary in the relational database.

For the ATM Transaction generalization/specialization hierarchy, the same decision is made to flatten the hierarchy and only provide relational tables for the transaction subclasses. The primary key for an ATM transaction is the transaction

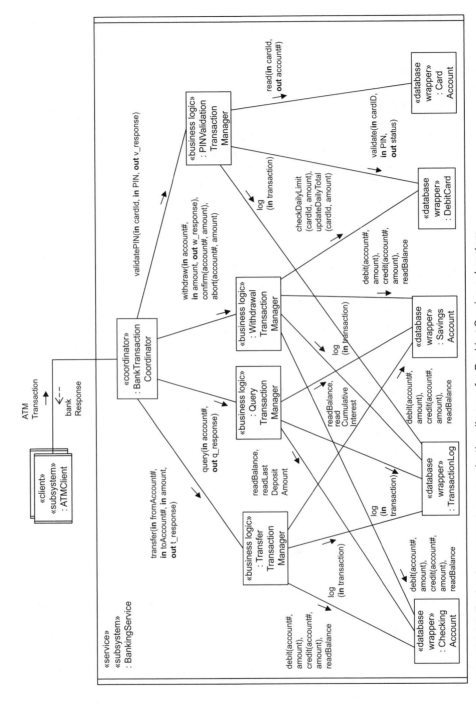

Figure 21.35. Revised concurrent communication diagram for Banking Service subsystem

416

Id, which consists of a concatenated key: <u>bankId</u>, <u>ATMId</u>, <u>date</u>, <u>time</u>. *bankId* and *ATMId* are also foreign keys because they allow navigation to the Bank and ATMInfo tables. ATMInfo has a concatenated primary key consisting of <u>bankId</u>, <u>ATMId</u>, with *bankId* also a foreign key. The attributes date and time provide a time stamp to uniquely identify a transaction.

Bank (bankName, bankAddress, <u>bankId</u>)

Customer (customerName, <u>customer Id</u>, customerAddress)

Debit Card (<u>cardId</u>, PIN, startDate, expirationDate, status, limit, total, *customerId*)

Checking   Account   (<u>accountNumber</u>,   accountType,   balance, lastDepositAmount)

Savings Account (<u>accountNumber</u>, accountType, balance, interest)

Card Account (<u>cardId</u>, <u>accountNumber</u>)

Customer Account (<u>customerId</u>, <u>accountNumber</u>)

ATM Info (<u>*bankId*</u>, <u>ATMId</u>, ATMLocation, ATMAddress)

Withdrawal Transaction (<u>*bankId*</u>, <u>*ATMId*</u>, <u>date</u>, <u>time</u>, transactionType, cardId, PIN, accountNumber, amount, balance)

Query Transaction (<u>*bankId*</u>, <u>*ATMId*</u>, <u>date</u>, <u>time</u>, transactionType, cardId, PIN, accountNumber, balance)

Transfer Transaction (<u>*bankId*</u>, <u>*ATMId*</u>, <u>date</u>, <u>time</u>, transactionType, cardId, PIN, fromAccountNumber, toAccountNumber, amount)

PIN Validation Transaction (<u>*bankId*</u>, <u>*ATMId*</u>, <u>date</u>, <u>time</u>, transactionType, cardId, PIN, startDate, expirationDate)

21.13 DEPLOYMENT OF BANKING SYSTEM

Because this is a client/server system, there are multiple instances of the client subsystem and one instance of the service subsystem. Each subsystem instance executes on its own node, as depicted in the deployment diagram in Figure 21.36. Thus, each instance of the ATM Client executes on an ATM node, and the one instance of the Banking Service executes on the server node.

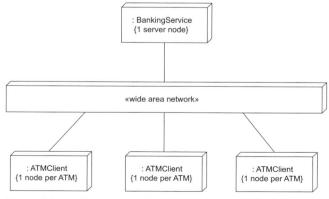

Figure 21.36. Deployment diagram for Banking System

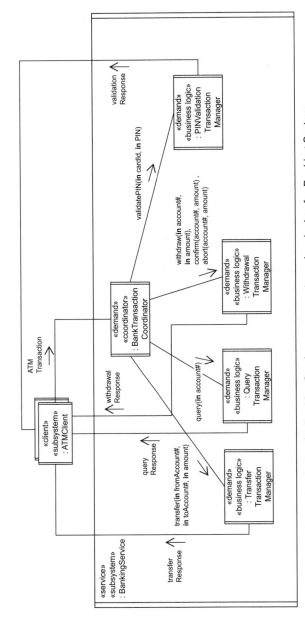

Figure 21.37. Alternative design for Banking Service: concurrent service design for Banking System

21.14 ALTERNATIVE DESIGN CONSIDERATIONS

An alternative design decision is to design the Banking Service as a concurrent service, in which the Bank Transaction Coordinator and each of the business logic objects are designed as separate demand driven tasks that are activated on demand. With this concurrent service design, the Bank Transaction Coordinator delegates a transaction to a business logic object and then immediately accepts the next transaction; thus, multiple transactions would be processed concurrently at the server. This solution should be adopted if the sequential service design is inadequate for handling the transaction load. For more information on the design of concurrent services, refer to Chapter 15.

21.15 DETAILED DESIGN

The detailed design of the Banking System is described in terms of the task event sequencing logic. Examples of task behavior specifications for the Card Reader Interface and ATM Control tasks in the ATM Client Subsystem and for the Banking Service task in the Banking Service Subsystem are given in Chapter 18. This section describes the event sequencing logic for these tasks.

21.15.1 Example of Event Sequencing Logic for Card Reader Interface Task

The Card Reader Interface task (see Figure 21.30) is awakened by a card reader external event, reads the ATM card input, writes the card contents to the ATM Card object, sends a cardInserted message to the ATM Control, and then waits for a message. If the message sent by the ATM Controller is eject, the card is ejected, and if it is confiscate, the card is confiscated. The passive data abstraction object, ATM Card, is outside the task and is used to store the contents of the card.

All message communication in the Banking System is through calls to the operating system. Thus, the message queue, ATMControlMessageQ, between the Card Reader Interface task (producer) and ATM Control (consumer) is provided by the operating system, as is the synchronous communication between ATM Control and the Card Reader Interface task (see Figure 21.32). A synchronous message from ATM Control is received in a message buffer called cardReaderMessageBuffer.

```
Initialize card reader;
loop
-- Wait for external interrupt from card reader
wait (cardReaderEvent);
Read card data held on card's magnetic strip;
if card is recognized
then -- Write card data to ATM Card object;
    ATMCard.write (cardID, startDate, expirationDate);
-- send card Inserted message to ATM Control;
send (ATMControlMessageQ, cardInserted);
-- Wait for message from ATM Control;
```

```
receive (cardReaderMessageBuffer, message);
if message = eject
then
    Eject card;
    -- Send card Ejected message to ATM Control;
    send (ATMControlMessageQ, cardEjected);
  elseif message = confiscate
    then
    Confiscate card;
    -- Send card Confiscated message to ATM Control;
    send (ATMControlMessageQ, cardConfiscated);
    else error condition;
  end if;
else -- card was not recognized so eject;
  Eject card;
end if;
end loop;
```

21.15.2 Example of Event Sequencing Logic for ATM Control Task

The ATM Control task is at the heart of the ATM Client subsystem (see Figure 21.30) and interacts with several tasks. ATM Control has an input message queue called ATM-ControlMessageQ, from which it receives messages from its three producers – Card Reader Interface, Customer Interaction, and Operator Interaction. ATM Control sends messages to several tasks. It sends synchronous messages without reply to the Card Reader Interface. It sends synchronous messages with reply to the Cash Dispenser Interface and Receipt Printer Interface tasks. It sends asynchronous messages to the Customer Interaction task on the promptMessageQueue message queue. It sends synchronous messages with reply to the Banking Service.

Because it is state-dependent, the ATM Control task does not process incoming events but rather the state-dependent actions as given by the statechart. The implementation of the statechart is encapsulated in the ATM State Machine state-machine object, which is nested inside ATM Control. Given the new event, the process Event operation returns the action(s) to be performed. Most events are received on the ATM Control input message queue, although there are three exceptions to this. Because the communication with the Banking Service is synchronous, the response is received as the output parameter of the send message. Because of the synchronous communication with the Cash Dispenser Interface and the Receipt Printer Interface tasks, the dispense Cash and print Receipt actions are synchronous messages with reply, which return whether the respective dispensing and printing actions were successful.

When an event is generated internally as a result of a response to a synchronous message, the variable newEvent is set to the value of this event and the Boolean variable outstandingEvent is set to True. Examples of such internal events are withdrawalResponse (several synchronous bank responses are possible, as described in the next section in the event sequencing logic for the Banking Service) or cash

Dispensed. The event sequencing logic is given below, which describes most of the actions executed by ATM Control. After the execution of each action case, the next execution step is a transfer to the end of the pseudocode case block (for brevity, the transfer is not explicitly shown below). The pseudocode for the ATM Control task follows:

```
loop
    -- Messages from all senders are received on Message Queue
    Receive (ATMControlMessageQ, message);
    -- Extract the event name and any message parameters
    -- Given the incoming event, lookup state transition table;
    -- change state if required; return action to be performed;
    newEvent = message.event
    outstandingEvent = true;
while outstandingEvent do
    ATMStateMachine.processEvent (in newEvent, out action);
    outstandingEvent = false;
    -- Execute action(s) as given on ATM Control statechart
case action of
    Get PIN: -- Prompt for PIN;
        send (promptMessageQueue, displayPINPrompt);
    Validate PIN: --Validate customer entered PIN at Banking Service;
        send (Banking Service, in validatePIN, out
            validationResponse);
        newEvent = validationResponse; outstandingEvent = true;
    Display Menu: -- Display selection menu to customer;
        send (promptMessageQueue,displayMenu);
        ATMTransaction.updatePINStatus (valid);
    Invalid PIN Action: -- Display Invalid PIN prompt;
        send (promptMessageQueue, displayInvalidPINPrompt);
        ATMTransaction.updatePINStatus (invalid);
    Request Withdrawal: -- Send withdraw request to Banking
            Service;
        send (promptMessageQueue, displayWait);
        send (Banking Service, in withdrawalRequest, out
            withdrawalResponse);
        newEvent = withdrawalResponse; outstandingEvent = true;
    Request Query: -- Send query request to Banking Service;
        send (promptMessageQueue, displayWait);
        send (Banking Service, in queryRequest, out queryResponse);
        newEvent = queryResponse; outstandingEvent = true;
    Request Transfer: -- Send transfer request to Banking Service;
        send (promptMessageQueue, displayWait);
        send (Banking Service, in transferRequest, out
            transferResponse);
        newEvent = transferResponse; outstandingEvent = true;
```

```
Dispense: -- Dispense cash and update transaction status;
    ATMTransaction.updateTransactionStatus (withdrawalOK);
    send (cashDispenserInterface, in cashAmount, out dispenseStatus);
newEvent = cashDispensed; outstandingEvent = true;
Print: -- Print receipt and send confirmation to Banking
        Service;
    send (promptMessageQueue, displayCashDispensed);
    send (Banking Service, in confirmRequest);
    send (receiptPrinterInterface, in receiptInfo, out
      printStatus);
    newEvent = receiptPrinted; outstandingEvent = true;
Eject: -- Eject ATM card;
    send (cardReaderInterface, eject);
Confiscate: -- Confiscate ATM card;
    send (cardReaderMessageBuffer, confiscate);
    ATMTransaction.updatePINStatus (status);
Display Ejected: -- Display Card Ejected prompt;
    send (promptMessageQueue, displayEjected);
Display Confiscated: -- Display Card Confiscated prompt;
    send (promptMessageQueue, displayConfiscated);

    . . .
  end case;
end while;
end loop;
```

21.15.3 Example of Event Sequencing Logic for Banking Service Task

The Banking Service receives messages from all the ATM Clients (see Figure 21.36). Although the communication is synchronous with reply, a message queue can build up at the Banking Service as it receives messages from multiple ATM clients. In this sequential solution, the Banking Service is a sequential service task, which processes each request to completion before starting the next.

```
loop
receive (ATMClientMessageQ, message) from Banking Service Message Queue;
Extract message name and message parameters from message;
case Message of
Validate PIN:
    -- Check that ATM Card is valid and that PIN entered by
    -- customer matches PIN maintained by Server;
PINValidationTransactionManager.ValidatePIN
      (in CardId, in PIN, out validationResponse);
    -- If successful, validation Response is valid and return
    -- Account Numbers accessible by this debit card;
```

```
            -- otherwise validation Response is invalid,
            -- third Invalid, or stolen;
            reply (ATMClient, validationResponse);
Withdrawal:
            -- Check that daily limit has not been exceeded and that
            -- customer has enough funds in account to satisfy request.
            -- If all checks are successful, then debit account.
            WithdrawalTransactionManager.withdraw
                (in AccountNumber, in Amount, out withdrawalResponse);
            -- If approved, then withdrawal Response is
            -- {successful, amount, currentBalance};
            -- otherwise withdrawalResponse is {unsuccessful};
            reply (client, withdrawalResponse);
Query:
            -- Read account balance
            queryTransactionManager.query
            (in accountNumber, out queryresponse);
            -- Query Response = Current Balance and either Last Deposit
            -- Amount (checking account) or Interest (savings acount);
            reply (client, queryResponse);
Transfer:
            -- Check that customer has enough funds in From Account to
            -- satisfy request. If approved, then debit From Account
            -- and credit To Account;
            transferTransactionManager.transfer (in fromAccount#,
                in toAccount#, in amount, out transferResponse);
            -- If approved, then transfer Response is
            -- {successful, amount, Current Balance of From Account};
            -- otherwise Transfer Response is {unsuccessful};
            reply (client, transferResponse);
Confirm:
            -- Confirm withdrawal transaction was completed successfully
            withdrawalTransactionManager.confirm (in accountNumber, in amount);
Abort:
            -- Abort withdrawal transaction
            withdrawalTransactionManager.abort (in accountNumber, in amount);
end case;
end loop;
```

Service-Oriented Architecture Case Study

Online Shopping System

The Online Shopping System case study is a highly distributed World Wide Web–based system that provides services for purchasing items such as books or clothes. The solution uses a service-oriented architecture with multiple services; coordinator objects are used to facilitate the integration of the services. In addition, object brokers are used to provide service registration, brokering, and discovery. Services include a catalog service, an inventory service, a customer account service, a delivery order service, an email service, and a credit card authorization service.

The problem is described in Section 22.1. Section 22.2 describes the use case model for the Online Shopping System. Section 22.3 describes the static model, which includes the system context model that depicts the boundary between the system and the external environment. This section also describes the use of broker technology in this system before going on to describe static modeling of the entity classes. Section 22.4 describes how to structure the system into objects. Section 22.5 describes dynamic modeling, in which communication diagrams are developed for each of the use cases. Section 22.6 describes the design model for the system, which is designed as a layered architecture based on the Layers of Abstraction pattern consisting of services and components.

22.1 PROBLEM DESCRIPTION

In the Web-based Online Shopping System, customers can request to purchase one or more items from the supplier. The customer provides personal details, such as address and credit card information. This information is stored in a customer account. If the credit card is valid, then a delivery order is created and sent to the supplier. The supplier checks the available inventory, confirms the order, and enters a planned shipping date. When the order is shipped, the customer is notified and the customer's credit card account is charged.

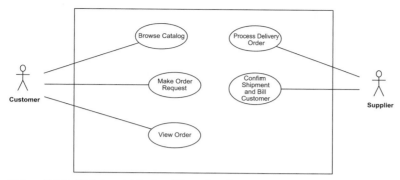

Figure 22.1. Web-based Online Shopping System: use cases

22.2 USE CASE MODELING

The use case model for Web-based Online Shopping System is depicted in Figure 22.1. There are two actors: Customer, who browses a catalog and requests to purchase items, and Supplier, who provides the catalog and services customer purchase requests. The customer initiates three use cases, which are Browse Catalog, to browse the catalog and select items; Make Order Request, to make a purchase request; and View Order. The supplier initiates two use cases, namely, Process Delivery Order, to service the customer's order, and Confirm Shipment and Bill Customer, to finalize the purchase.

In the Browse Catalog use case, the customer browses a World Wide Web catalog, views various catalog items from a given supplier's catalog, and selects items from the catalog. In the Make Purchase Request use case, the customer enters personal details. The system creates a customer account if one does not already exist. The customer's credit card is checked for validity and sufficient credit to pay for the requested catalog items. If the credit card check shows that the credit card is valid and has sufficient credit, then the customer purchase is approved and the system sends the purchase request to the supplier. In View Order, the customer requests to view the details of the delivery order.

The supplier-initiated use cases are Process Delivery Order and Confirm Shipment and Bill Customer. In the Process Delivery Order use case, the supplier requests a delivery order, determines that the inventory is available to fulfill the order, and displays the order.

In the Confirm Shipment and Bill Customer use case, the supplier prepares the shipment manually and confirms that the shipment is ready for shipment. The system then retrieves the customer's credit card details from the customer account and bills the customer's credit card.

The use cases are described in detail, except for the very simple View Order use case. Each use case is described textually and is depicted using an activity diagram. Activity diagrams are popular in business process modeling. They can be integrated into the analysis and design of service-oriented applications to model the sequence of use case activities. In particular, they describe more precisely the main and alternative sequences of the use case, depicting exactly how they diverge from each other.

22.2.1 Use Case Description for Browse Catalog

Use case name: Browse Catalog
Summary: Customer browses World Wide Web catalog, views various catalog items from the supplier's catalog, and selects items from the catalog.
Actor: Customer
Precondition: Customer browser is linked to supplier catalog Web site.
Main sequence:
1. Customer requests to browse catalog.
2. System displays catalog information to customer.
3. Customer selects items from catalog
4. System displays an itemized list containing each item description and price, as well as the total price.

Alternative sequence: Step 3: Customer does not select item and exits.
Postcondition: System has displayed list of selected catalog items.

The activity diagram describing the sequence of use case activities for Browse Catalog, which corresponds to the preceding description of the main sequence of the use case, is depicted in Figure 22.2.

22.2.2 Use Case Description for Make Order Request

Use case name: Make Order Request
Summary: Customer enters an order request to purchase catalog items. The customer's credit card is checked for validity and sufficient credit to pay for the requested catalog items.
Actor: Customer
Precondition: Customer has selected one or more catalog items
Main sequence:
1. Customer provides order request and customer account Id to pay for purchase.
2. System retrieves customer account information, including the customer's credit card details.
3. System checks the customer's credit card for the purchase amount and, if approved, creates a credit card purchase authorization number.
4. System creates a delivery order containing order details, customer Id, and credit card authorization number.

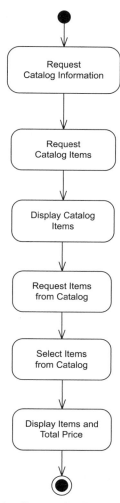

Figure 22.2. Activity diagram for Browse Catalog use case

5. System confirms approval of purchase and displays order information to customer.

Alternative sequences:

Step 2: If customer does not have an account, the system prompts the customer to provide information in order to create a new account. The customer can either enter the account information or cancel the order.

Step 3: If authorization of the customer's credit card is denied (e.g., invalid credit card or insufficient funds in the customer's credit card account), the system prompts the customer to enter a different credit card number. The customer can either enter a different credit card number or cancel the order.

Postcondition: System has created a delivery order for the customer.

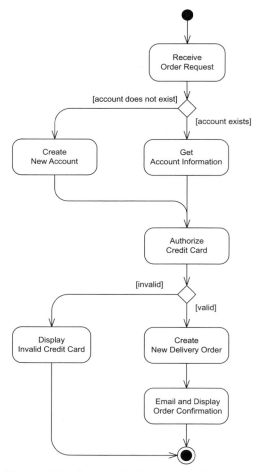

Figure 22.3. Activity diagram for Make Order Request use case

The activity diagram for Make Order Request (Figure 22.3) depicts the activities that correspond to the main sequence of the use case, for making an order and authorizing the credit card, as well as the two alternatives that deal with creating a new account and denying credit card authorization.

22.2.3 Use Case Description for Process Delivery Order

Summary: Supplier requests a delivery order; system determines that the inventory is available to fulfill the order, and displays the order.
Actor: Supplier
Precondition: Supplier needs to process a delivery order and a delivery order exists.

Main sequence:
1. Supplier requests next delivery order.
2. System retrieves and displays delivery order.
3. Supplier requests inventory check on items for delivery order.
4. System determines that items are available in inventory to satisfy delivery order and reserves items.
5. System displays inventory information to Supplier and confirms that items are reserved.

Alternative sequence: Step 4: If item is out of stock, system displays warning message.

Postcondition: System has reserved inventory items for delivery order.

The activity diagram for Process Delivery Order (Figure 22.4) depicts the activities corresponding to the main sequence of the use case, for viewing and reserving inventory items, as well the alternative sequence dealing with inventory item(s) out of stock.

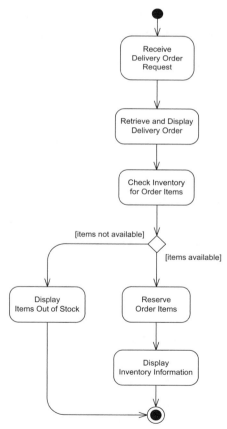

Figure 22.4. Activity diagram for Process Delivery Order use case

22.2.4 Use Case Description for Confirm Shipment and Bill Customer

Summary: Supplier prepares the shipment manually and then confirms that the delivery order is ready for shipment. System notifies customer that order is being shipped. System charges customer's credit card for purchase and commits inventory items removal.

Actor: Supplier

Precondition: Inventory items have been reserved for customer delivery order.

Main sequence:
1. Supplier prepares shipment manually and identifies that delivery order is ready to ship.
2. System retrieves customer account information, including the invoice and customer's credit card details.
3. System updates inventory to confirm purchase.
4. System charges customer's credit card for purchase and creates a credit card charge confirmation number.
5. System updates delivery order information with credit card charge confirmation.
6. System sends email confirmation to customer.
7. System displays confirmation to the supplier to complete shipment of the delivery order.

Postcondition: System has committed inventory, charged customer, and sent confirmation.

The activity diagram for Confirm Shipment and Bill Customer (Figure 22.5) depicts the activities corresponding to the main sequence of the use case.

22.2.5 Activity Diagram for View Order Use Case

In this simple use case, the customer requests to view an order. The activity diagram for the View Order use case is depicted in Figure 22.6.

22.3 STATIC MODELING

This section describes the static model, which consists of the system context model and the entity class model. This section also discusses the use of brokering technology in online shopping service-oriented architectures.

22.3.1 Software System Context Modeling

The software system context model depicts two external user classes that are depicted as actors: the Customer and Supplier classes. The context diagram (Figure 22.7)

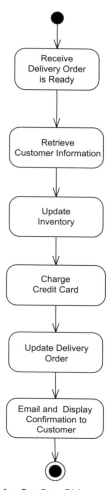

Figure 22.5. Activity diagram for Confirm Shipment and Bill Customer use case

is very similar to the use case diagram because the external classes correspond to the actors on the use case diagram.

22.3.2 Static Entity Class Modeling of the Problem Domain

A static model of the problem domain is developed and depicted on a class diagram (Figure 22.8). Because this is a data-intensive application, the emphasis is on the entity classes. The static entity class model shows the entity classes and the relationships among these classes. The classes include customer classes (Customer and Customer Account), supplier classes (Supplier, Inventory, and Catalog), and classes that deal with the customer's order such as Delivery Order, which is an aggregation of Item. The attributes for the classes are shown in Figure 22.9. This example is also described in more detail in Chapter 7.

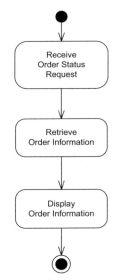

Figure 22.6. Activity diagram for View Order use case

Figure 22.7. Online Shopping System Software System Context class diagram

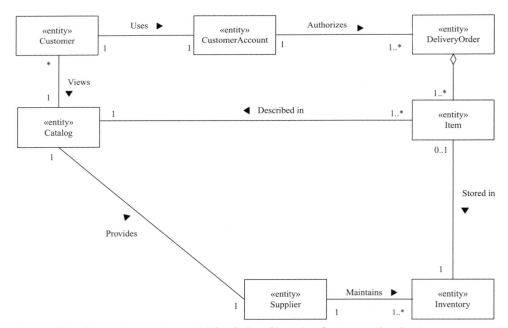

Figure 22.8. Conceptual static model for Online Shopping System entity classes

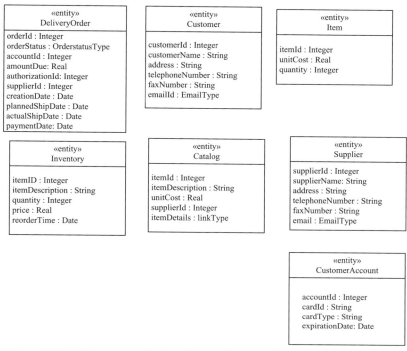

Figure 22.9. Entity classes for the Online Shopping System

22.4 OBJECT AND CLASS STRUCTURING

The entity classes determined in the previous section are integrated into a service-oriented architecture by means of service classes. Catalog Service, Customer Account Service, Delivery Order Service, and Inventory Service are service classes that provide access to the entity classes (Figure 22.10). Catalog Service uses the Catalog and Supplier entity classes. Customer Account Service uses the Customer

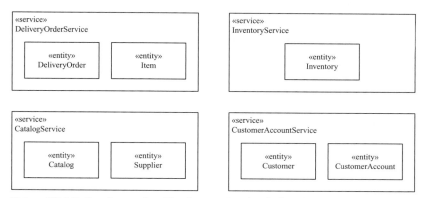

Figure 22.10. Service and entity classes for the Online Shopping System

Account and Customer entity classes. Delivery Order Service uses the Delivery Order and Item entity classes. The Inventory Service uses the Inventory entity class.

There is also a service class, Credit Card Service, which deals with credit card authorization and charging. In this way, the credit card billing is integrated with the customer purchasing and supplier delivery. Another service class is Email Service, which enables the Online Shopping System to send email messages to customers.

User interaction classes are needed to interact with the external users – in particular, Customer Interaction and Supplier Interaction, which correspond to the actors in the use cases. In addition, to coordinate and sequence the customer and supplier access to the online shopping services, two coordinator objects, Customer Coordinator and Supplier Coordinator, are provided,. A third autonomous coordinator, Billing Coordinator, is needed to deal with billing customers. The classes in the Online Shopping System are depicted in Figure 22.11.

22.5 DYNAMIC MODELING

For each use case, a communication diagram is developed that depicts the objects that participate in the use case and the sequence of messages passed between them.

22.5.1 Dynamic Modeling for Browse Catalog

In the communication diagram for the Browse Catalog use case (Figure 22.12), Customer Interaction interacts with Customer Coordinator, which in turn communicates with Catalog Service. The message descriptions are as follows:

B1: The customer makes a catalog request via Customer Interaction.

B2: Customer Coordinator is instantiated to assist the customer. On the basis of the customer's request, Customer Coordinator selects a catalog for the customer to browse.

B3: Customer Coordinator requests information from Catalog Service.

B4: Catalog Service sends catalog information to Customer Coordinator.

B5: Customer Coordinator forwards the information to Customer Interaction.

B6: Customer Interaction displays the catalog information to the customer.

B7: The customer makes a catalog selection through Customer Interaction.

B8: Customer Interaction passes the request on to Customer Coordinator.

B9: Customer Coordinator requests the catalog selection from Catalog Service.

B10: Catalog Service confirms the availability of the catalog items and sends the item prices to Customer Coordinator.

B11: Customer Coordinator forwards the information to Customer Interaction.

B12: Customer Interaction displays the catalog information to the customer, including item prices and total.

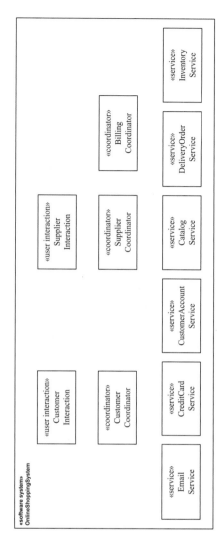

Figure 22.11. Class structuring for the Online Shopping System

435

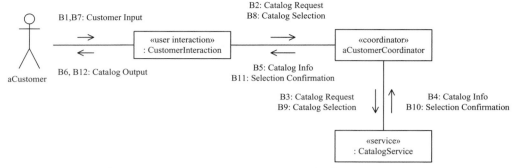

Figure 22.12. Communication diagram for the Browse Catalog use case

22.5.2 Dynamic Modeling for Make Order Request

In the communication diagram for the Make Order Request use case (Figure 22.13), a customer provides the account information, which is used to access the Customer Account Service. Credit card details are sent by Customer Coordinator to the Credit Card Service for approval. The Customer Coordinator then sends a new order request to Delivery Order Service and a confirmation email to the Email Service. The message descriptions are as follows:

M1: The customer provides order request to Customer Interaction.

M2: Customer Interaction sends the order request to Customer Coordinator.

M3, M4: Customer Coordinator sends the account request to Customer Account Service and receives the account information, including the customer's credit card details.

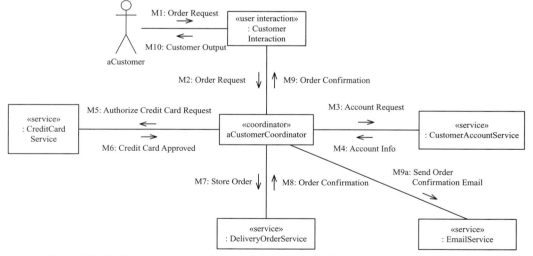

Figure 22.13. Communication diagram for the Make Order Request use case

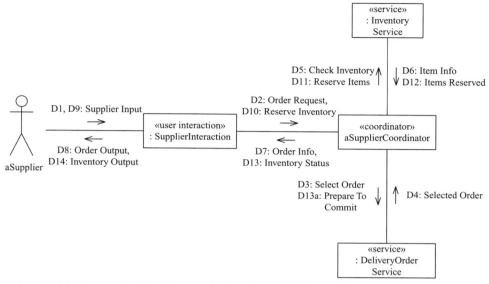

Figure 22.14. Communication diagram for the Process Delivery Order use case

M5: Customer Coordinator sends the customer's credit card information and charge authorization request to Credit Card Service (this is equivalent to a Prepare to Commit message).

M6: Credit Card Service sends a credit card approval to Customer Coordinator (this is equivalent to a Ready to Commit message).

M7, M8: Customer Coordinator sends order request to Delivery Order Service.

M9, M9a: Customer Coordinator sends the order confirmation to Customer Interaction and sends an email of the order confirmation to the customer via the Email Service.

M10: Customer Interaction outputs the order confirmation to the customer

Alternative scenarios for this use case are that the customer does not have an account, in which case a new account will be created, or that the credit card authorization is denied, in which case the customer has the option of selecting a different card. These alternative scenarios are described in Chapter 9.

22.5.3 Dynamic Modeling for Process Delivery Order

In the communication diagram for the next use case, Process Delivery Order (Figure 22.14), Supplier Coordinator requests Delivery Order Service for a new delivery order, and Delivery Order Service selects a delivery order. Supplier Coordinator requests Inventory Service to check the inventory and sends the order and inventory information to the supplier via the user interaction object. The message descriptions are as follows:

D1: The supplier requests a new delivery order.

D2: Supplier Interaction sends the supplier request to Supplier Coordinator.

D3: Supplier Coordinator requests Delivery Order Service to select a delivery order.

D4: Delivery Order Service sends the delivery order to Supplier Coordinator.

D5: Supplier Coordinator requests inventory item check.

D6: Inventory Service returns item information.

D7: Supplier Coordinator sends order status to Supplier Interaction.

D8: Supplier Interaction displays the delivery order information to the supplier.

D9: Supplier requests the system to reserve the items in inventory.

D10: Supplier Interaction sends the supplier request to reserve inventory to Supplier Coordinator.

D11: Supplier Coordinator requests Inventory Service to reserve the items in inventory (this is equivalent to a Prepare to Commit message)

D12: Inventory Service confirms reservation of items to Supplier Coordinator (this is equivalent to a Ready to Commit message).

D13: Supplier Coordinator sends the inventory status to Supplier Interaction.

D14: Supplier Interaction displays the inventory information to the supplier.

An alternative scenario for this use case (not shown in figure) is that the item is out of stock, in which case Inventory Service returns an Out of Stock message, which is then displayed to the supplier.

22.5.4 Dynamic Modeling for Confirm Shipment and Bill Customer

In the communication diagram for the Confirm Shipment and Bill Customer use case (Figure 22.15), the supplier prepares the shipment manually. The supplier then sends the Ready for Shipment message to the Supplier Coordinator, which requests Inventory Service to commit the inventory and send a Ready for Shipment message to Billing Coordinator. The Billing Coordinator retrieves the invoice from the Delivery Order Service, account information from Customer Account Service, and charges the customer through Credit Card Service. The updates to the credit card, delivery order, and inventory are coordinated using the two-phase commit protocol (see Chapter 16). The message descriptions are as follows:

S1: The supplier inputs the shipping information.

S2: Supplier Interaction sends the Ready for Shipment request to Supplier Coordinator.

S3: Supplier Coordinator sends the Order Ready for Shipment message to Billing Coordinator.

S4: Billing Coordinator sends Prepare to Commit order to Delivery Order Service.

S5: Delivery Order Service replies with Ready to Commit message and invoice containing order Id, account Id, and amount.

S6, S7: Billing Coordinator sends account request to Customer Account Service, which responds with account information.

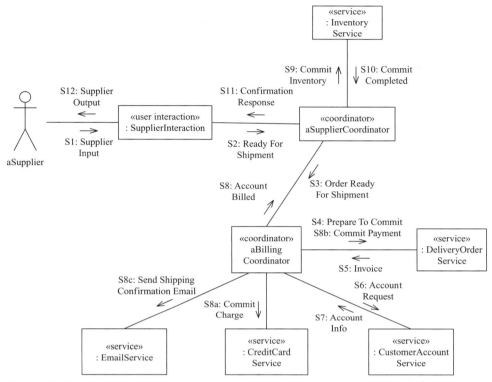

Figure 22.15. Communication diagram for the Confirm Shipment and Bill Customer use case

> **S8, S8a, S8b, S8c:** Billing Coordinator sends Commit Charge message to Credit
> Card Service, Commit Payment message to Delivery Order Service, confirma-
> tion email to customer through Email Service, and Account Billed message
> to Supplier Coordinator.
> **S9, S10:** Supplier Coordinator sends Commit Inventory message to Inventory
> Service, which responds that commit is completed.
> **S11, S12:** Supplier Coordinator sends confirmation response to Supplier
> Interaction, which in turn sends the shipping confirmation message to
> the supplier.

22.5.5 Dynamic Modeling for View Order

In the communication diagram for the View Order use case (Figure 22.16), Customer
Interaction interacts with Customer Coordinator, which in turn communicates with
Delivery Order Service. The message descriptions are as follows:

> **V1, V2:** The customer makes an order invoice request via Customer Inter-
> action.
> **V3:** Customer Coordinator makes an order request to Delivery Order Service.

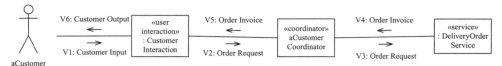

Figure 22.16. Communication diagram for the View Order use case

> **V4:** Delivery Order Service sends order invoice information to Customer Coordinator.
>
> **V5:** Customer Coordinator forwards the information to Customer Interaction.
>
> **V6:** Customer Interaction displays the order information to the customer.

22.6 BROKER AND WRAPPER TECHNOLOGY SUPPORT FOR SERVICE-ORIENTED ARCHITECTURE

Several legacy databases are used in the Online Shopping System. Many of the entity classes in the static model represent persistent data stored in legacy databases. Each legacy database is a stand-alone database that resides on a mainframe. These databases need to be integrated into the application, by means of a broker and wrapper technology. Chapter 15 provides information on database wrapper classes, and Chapter 16 provides information on Broker patterns.

Although different legacy databases exist, object broker and wrapper technology provide a systematic way of integrating the disparate legacy databases into a service-oriented architecture. The legacy databases in the supplier organization are the catalog database, the inventory database, the customer account service, and the delivery order database.

Database wrapper classes are designed to provide an object-oriented interface to the legacy databases that hides the details of how to read and update the individual databases. To integrate these databases into the online shopping application, service classes are designed that access the legacy databases through database wrapper classes.

22.7 DESIGN MODELING

This section describes the architectural structure and communication patterns used in the design, the concurrent software design, service and component interface design, and the design of the service-oriented architecture, which fully integrates services and components.

22.7.1 Overview of Service-Oriented Architecture

In service-oriented architectures, services register their service name and location with a broker. Clients can then discover new services by using the Service Discovery pattern (also known as yellow pages) to query the broker for services of a given type. The client can then choose a service and make a white pages request to the broker.

The Online Shopping System is designed as a layered architecture based on the Layers of Abstraction architecture pattern. The software architecture consists of three layers – a service layer, a coordinator layer, and a user interaction layer. Furthermore, because this system needs to be highly flexible and distributed, the decision is made to design a service-oriented architecture, in which distributed components can discover services and communicate with them.

Each component is depicted with the component stereotype (what kind of component it is, as specified by the component structuring criteria). The design of the component and service interfaces are determined by analysis of the communication diagrams for each use case.

22.7.2 Layered Software Architecture

The components are structured into the layered architecture such that each component is in a layer where it depends on components in the layers below but not the layers above. This layered architecture is based on the Layers of Abstraction pattern (Chapter 12). The layered architecture facilitates future adaptation of the online shopping software architecture. User interaction components at the user interaction layer communicate only with coordinator components. Coordinator components communicate with services. Applying the component structuring criteria, the following components and services, organized by layer, are determined, as depicted in Figure 22.17:

Layer 1: Service Layer. There are six services ; four are part of the application, and two are external services. The application services are Catalog Service, Delivery Order Service, Inventory Service, and Customer Account Service. The external services are Credit Card Service (one for each credit card company, such as Mastercard and Visa), which is used for charging customer purchases, and Email Service, for sending email messages to customers.

Layer 2: Coordination Layer. There are three coordinator components: Supplier Coordinator, Customer Coordinator, and Billing Coordinator.

Layer 3: User Layer. There are two user interaction components: Supplier Interaction and Customer Interaction.

22.7.3 Architectural Communication Patterns

To handle the variety of communication between the components in the software architecture, several communication patterns are applied:

- **Synchronous Message Communication with Reply.** This is the typical service-oriented architecture pattern of communication and is used when the client needs information from the service and cannot proceed before receiving the response. This pattern is used between user interaction clients and coordinators. It is also used between coordinators and various services.

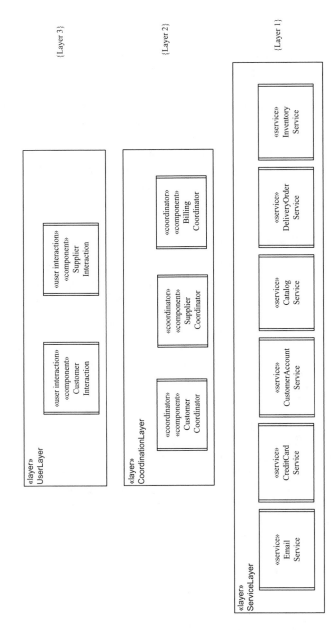

Figure 22.17. Layered architecture for Online Shopping System

- **Broker Handle.** Each service registers service information, including service name, service description and location with the broker. The Broker Handle pattern allows clients to query the broker to determine the services to which they should be connected.
- **Service Discovery.** Service Discovery patterns are used by service requesters to discover new services. They could be used to discover new catalogs to browse.
- **Bidirectional Asynchronous Message Communication.** This pattern is used for communication between the Supplier Coordinator and Billing Coordinator to asynchronously communicate with each other in both directions.
- **Two-Phase Commit.** This pattern is used to ensure that updates to inventory, credit card, and delivery order are atomic, so either all updates are committed or all are aborted.

22.7.4 Concurrent Software Design

The service-oriented architecture is designed by integrating the use case–based interaction diagrams described in Section 22.5, and then designing the message interfaces. The concurrent software design is depicted on the concurrent communication diagram for the Online Shopping System (Figure 22.18), which depicts the concurrent components and services. It represents the integrated communication diagram determined from the individual communication diagrams supporting the use cases. Furthermore, the design of the message interactions is also depicted.

To keep the design simple, the Synchronous Message Communication with Reply pattern has been widely used in this case study. As described in Chapter 12, however, this approach has the disadvantage of suspending the client while it awaits a response from the service. An alternative design to avoid suspending the client is to use the Asynchronous Message Communication with Callback pattern, as described in Chapter 15. The Bidirectional Asynchronous Communication pattern is used for Supplier Coordinator and Billing Coordinator to communicate with each other in both directions.

22.7.5 Service Interface Design

The service interfaces are designed as follows. Each service has one provided interface through which the service operations are accessed. Figure 22.19 depicts the service interfaces and ports. The clients of the service invoke the appropriate operations provided by the interface synchronously.

The service operations are designed by considering how each individual service is accessed on the use case–based interaction diagrams. Typically, each service is accessed in different ways corresponding to requests for different service operations. The interaction diagrams depict the messages arriving at the service (corresponding to service operation invocation and possible input parameters to the service) and the service response (corresponding to data returned by the service), which is either synchronous (as a synchronous message reply) or asynchronous (in a separate asynchronous message).

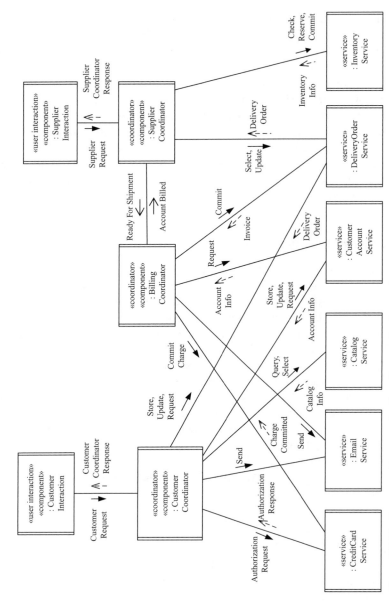

Figure 22.18. Concurrent communication diagram for Online Shopping System

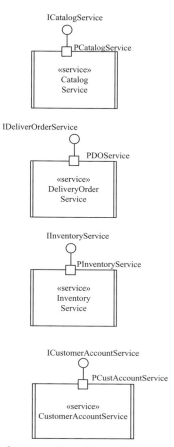

Figure 22.19. Component ports and interfaces for services

The Catalog Service has operations to request to view a catalog and to select catalog items (Figure 22.20). These operations access data maintained in the Catalog Info and Item Info entity classes. The access needs are determined from the Browse Catalog communication diagram (see Figure 22.7) and static model (see Figures 22.3 and 22.4). The requestCatalog operation returns catalog items of a given type and is determined from message B3 in Figure 22.12. The catalog information returned is given by the attributes of the Catalog entity class shown on Figures 22.9 and 22.20. The requestSelection operation is determined from message B9 in Figure 22.12, which returns (determined from message B10) the item information for the specific item.

The Customer Account Service has operations to create a new account, update the account, and read an account (Figure 22.21). These operations access data maintained in the Customer Account and Customer entity classes. The operations are determined from the Make Order Request communication diagram (see Figure 22.13). The requestAccount operation corresponds to message M3 in Figure 22.13 and message S6 in the Confirm Shipment and Bill Customer communication diagram (see Figure 22.15). The createAccount and updateAccount operations correspond

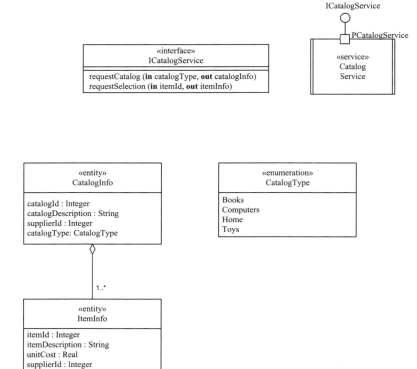

Figure 22.20. Service interface for Catalog Service

to alternatives to the main sequence of Make Order Request, as described in Section 22.5.2.

Confirm Shipment and Bill Customer (see Figure 22.8) also involves the Delivery Order Service (to commit the payment), the Credit Card Service (to authorize a charge), and the Email Service (to send a confirmation email).

The Make Order Request communication diagram also involves three other services: Delivery Order Service, Credit Card Service, and Email Service.

Delivery Order Service has several operations (Figure 22.22), which are determined as follows. The operations access data maintained in the Delivery Order and Item entity classes; the Invoice entity class contains data extracted from Delivery Order. Message M7 (on Figure 22.13) to store the delivery order corresponds to the store operation shown in Figure 22.22 for the Delivery Order Service. Message D3 to select the delivery order in the Process Delivery Order communication diagram (see Figure 22.14) corresponds to the select operation shown in Figure 22.22. Further operations are determined from the Confirm Shipment and Bill Customer (see Figure 22.15) communication diagram, particularly the Delivery Order Service messages to Prepare to Commit (message S4) the order and Commit the Payment (message S8b). The read operation is determined from message V3 on the View Order communication diagram (see Figure 22.16). The service interface for Delivery Order Service is depicted on Figure 22.22. The abort operation is invoked if the order is cancelled prior to shipment.

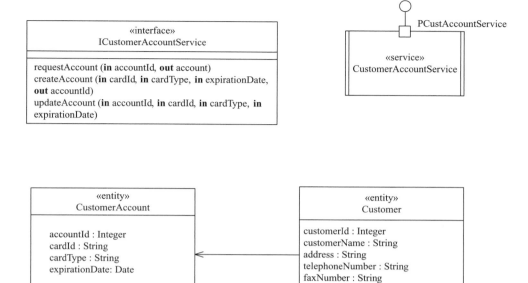

Figure 22.21. Service interface for Customer Account Service

Inventory Service needs operations to check inventory (determined from message D5 on Figure 22.14); reserve inventory (determined from message D11 on the same figure), which is equivalent to prepare to commit inventory; commit inventory (message S9 in Confirm Shipment and Bill Customer in Figure 22.15); and update

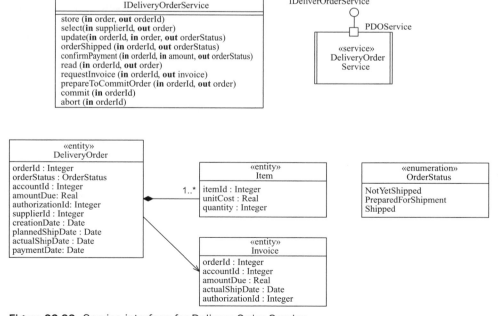

Figure 22.22. Service interface for Delivery Order Service

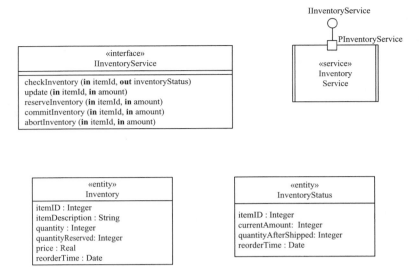

Figure 22.23. Service interface for Inventory Service

inventory. The abort operation is invoked if the order is cancelled and inventory released prior to shipment. The updateInventory service operation is needed when the inventory is replenished. This example is described in more detail in Chapter 16, Section 16.6.

Figure 22.15 shows the service interfaces for the external services: Credit Card Service and Email Service. Both external services have provided interfaces in the same way as the application services. The Credit Card Service supports one provided interface consisting of two operations – one for authorizing a credit card purchase (message M5 in Make Order Request) and the other for charging the credit card (message S8a in Confirm Shipment and Bill Customer). The Email Service has one provided interface with one operation to send an email message (message M9a in Make Order Request and message S8c in Confirm Shipment and Bill Customer).

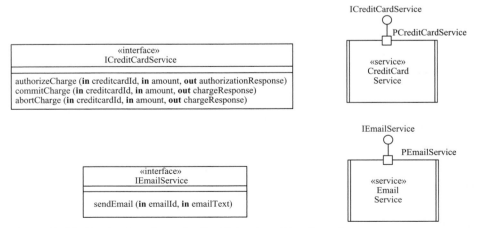

Figure 22.24. Service interfaces for Credit Card and Email services

22.7.6 Design of Service-Oriented Software Architecture

This section describes the design of the service-oriented architecture for the Online Shopping System, which is depicted on a composite structure diagram, as shown in Figure 22.25. The service interface design has already been described in the previous sections; the user interaction and coordinator objects are designed as components and are described in the next section.

Each service has one port with one provided interface, whereas each coordinator component has one or more ports, with provided interfaces, required interfaces, or both. In the three-layer architecture, each client-user interaction component has one required port, which supports a required interface. Each service has one provided port, which supports a provided interface. The coordinators have ports with both required and provided interfaces because they act as intermediaries between the clients and services and need to communicate with several services. The provided interfaces of the services and the required ports of the coordinators are explicitly depicted in order to identify that services are intended to be discovered; thus, the binding between the service provider and the service requester is dynamic.

For customer requests, Customer Interaction is a client and thus has only a required port. Customer Coordinator has both required and provided ports. Customer Interaction only communicates with the Customer Coordinator, whereas the Customer Coordinator communicates with five services, of which there are two external services (Credit Card Service and Email Service) and three application services (Catalog Service, Delivery Order Service, and Customer Account Service).

For supplier requests, Supplier Interaction has a required port, and the Supplier Coordinator component has both provided and required interfaces. Supplier Interaction only communicates with the Supplier Coordinator, whereas the Supplier Coordinator communicates with both Delivery Order Service and Inventory Service. Supplier Coordinator also communicates with the Billing Coordinator. Billing Coordinator communicates with four services, of which there are two external services (Credit Card Service and Email Service) and two application services (Delivery Order Service and Customer Account Service). Because all customer payment is made by credit card, this necessitates the Credit Card Service, of which there could be many service instances, one for each credit card company. Each service instance is designed and implemented differently but must conform to the SOA credit card interface.

22.7.7 Design of Component Ports and Interfaces

The ports and interfaces for the user interaction and coordination components are described next. The Customer Interaction user interaction component has a required port, which consists of a required interface, as does Supplier Interaction, as shown in Figures 22.25 and 22.26,

The component ports and interfaces for Customer Coordinator are depicted in Figure 22.27, which also depicts the component's provided and required interfaces. Customer Coordinator has five required ports and one provided port. The required ports support required interfaces to Catalog Service, Customer Account Service, Delivery Order Service, Email Service, and Credit Card Service. The required interfaces are

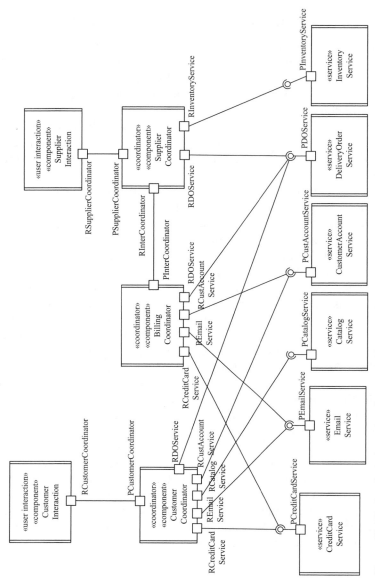

Figure 22.25. Service-oriented software architecture for the Online Shopping System

450

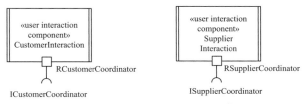

Figure 22.26. Component ports and interfaces for Customer Interaction and Supplier Interaction

because Customer Coordinator is a client when communicating with services. Each Customer Coordinator component has a provided port to communicate with Customer Interaction.

The component ports and interfaces for Supplier Coordinator are depicted in Figure 22.28. Supplier Coordinator receives supplier requests from Supplier Interaction via the PSupplierCoordinator port, which supports a provided interface called ISupplierCoordinator. Supplier Coordinator is a client of the Inventory Service and communicates with it via the required interface IInventoryService. It is also a client of and has the same required interface IDeliveryOrderService to Delivery Order Service as the Customer Coordinator. Supplier Coordinator also communicates with the Billing Coordinator, as depicted in Figure 22.15, sending it a message (S3) when an order is ready for shipment and billing. The interface for this communication is IShipment.

Billing Coordinator (see Figure 22.29) has required ports to communicate with two external services (Credit Card Service and Email Service) and two application services (Delivery Order Service and Customer Account Service). It also has a provided interface IShipment.

22.8 SERVICE REUSE

With the service-oriented architecture paradigm, once the services have been designed and their interfaces specified, the service interface information can be registered with a service broker. Services can be composed into new applications. This case study has described an Online Shopping System. However, other electronic commerce systems could be designed that would reuse the services provided by the

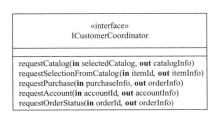

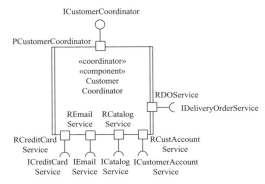

Figure 22.27. Component ports and interfaces for Customer Coordinator

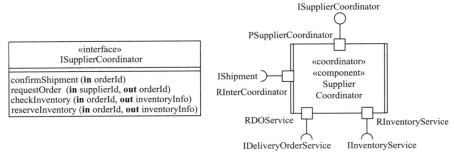

Figure 22.28. Component ports and interfaces for Supplier Coordinator

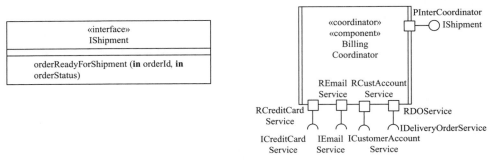

Figure 22.29. Component ports and interfaces for Billing Coordinator

Online Shopping System, such as Catalog Service, Delivery Order Service, and Inventory Service.

In a business to business (B2B) system, for example, instead of using customer accounts, contracts would be established between business customers and suppliers. Each contract would be between a specific business customer and a specific supplier, would be of a specified duration, and would have a maximum fiscal amount in a specified currency. A business customer would select items from the catalog, specify the contract that should be used, and then send the delivery order. Once the order shipment had been made, the payment to the supplier would be made through an electronic funds transfer from the business customer bank to the supplier bank.

The B2B system would necessitate the creation of additional services as well as different versions of the Customer and Supplier Coordinators. The Catalog, Delivery Order, and Inventory Services would be reused. However, new services would be required for Contract Service, Invoice Service, and Accounts Payable Service. A reusable service-oriented architecture for an Electronic Commerce software product line, consisting of kernel, optional, and variant components and services, is described in (Gomaa 2005a).

Component-Based Software Architecture Case Study

Emergency Monitoring System

This chapter describes how the COMET software modeling and architectural design method is applied to the design of a component-based software architecture: an Emergency Monitoring System.

The problem description is given in Section 23.1. Section 23.2 describes the use case model for the Emergency Monitoring System. Section 23.3 describes the Emergency Monitoring System static model, covering static modeling of both the system context and entity classes. Section 23.4 describes dynamic modeling, in which communication diagrams are developed for each of the use cases. Section 23.5 describes the design model for the Emergency Monitoring System, which is designed as a layered architecture based on the Layers of Abstraction pattern combined with the client/service pattern and several architectural communication patterns. Section 23.6 describes software component deployment.

23.1 PROBLEM DESCRIPTION

An Emergency Monitoring System consists of several remote monitoring systems and monitoring sensors that provide sensor input to the system. The status of the external environment is monitored with a variety of sensors. Some of these sensors are attached to remote monitoring systems, which send regular status input that is stored at a monitoring service. In addition, from the sensor information, alarms are generated concerning undesirable situations in the external environment that require human intervention. Alarms are stored at an alarm service. Monitoring operators view the status of the different sensors and view and update alarm conditions.

23.2 USE CASE MODELING

This section describes the use case model for the Emergency Monitoring System. From the problem description, three actors are determined. The system has one human actor, Monitoring Operator, which initiates use cases to view sensor data and alarms. There is an external input device actor, the Monitoring Sensor, and an

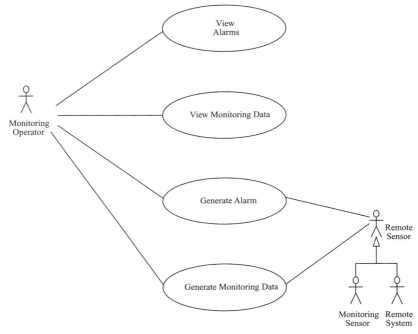

Figure 23.1. Emergency Monitoring System use cases and actors

external system actor, the Remote System. Both these actors behave in a similar way by monitoring remote sensors and sending sensor data and alarms to the system. This similar behavior can be modeled by a generalized actor, Remote Sensor, which represents the common role – that is, the behavior that is common to both the specialized actors, Monitoring Sensor and Remote System. The actors are depicted in Figure 23.1. Remote Sensor is the primary actor for two of the use cases.

All four use cases involve Monitoring Operator, as either primary or secondary actor, as depicted in Figure 23.1. An overview of the use cases is presented in the following list:

1. **View Alarms.** The Monitoring Operator actor views outstanding alarms and acknowledges that the cause of an alarm is being addressed. The operator may also subscribe or unsubscribe to receive notification of alarms of a given type.
2. **View Monitoring Data.** The Monitoring Operator actor requests to view the current status of one or more sensors. Operator requests are made on demand. The operator may also subscribe or unsubscribe to receive notification of changes in monitoring status.
3. **Generate Monitoring Data.** Monitoring data are generated on an ongoing basis by the generalized actor, Remote Sensor. Operators are notified of monitoring status events to which they have subscribed.
4. **Generate Alarm.** If an alarm condition is detected by the Remote Sensor, an alarm is generated. Operators are notified of alarms to which they have subscribed.

23.2.1 View Monitoring Data Use Case Description

Use case name: View Monitoring Data
Summary: The monitoring operator requests to view the current status of one or more locations.
Actor: Monitoring Operator
Precondition: The monitoring operator is logged in.
Main sequence:
1. The monitoring operator requests to view the status of a monitoring location.
2. The system displays the monitoring status as follows:
   Sensor status for each sensor (value, upper limit, lower limit, alarm status).

Alternative sequence:
Step 2: Emergency situation. System displays emergency warning message to operator.
Postcondition: Monitoring status has been displayed.

23.2.2 View Alarms Use Case Description

Use case name: View Alarms
Summary: The monitoring operator views outstanding alarms and acknowledges that the cause of an alarm is being addressed.
Actor: Monitoring Operator
Precondition: The monitoring operator is logged in.
Main sequence:
1. The monitoring operator requests to view the outstanding alarms.
2. The system displays the outstanding alarms. For each alarm, the system displays the name of the alarm, alarm description, location of alarm, and severity of alarm (high, medium, low).

Alternative sequence:
Step 2: Emergency situation. System displays emergency warning message to operator.
Postcondition: Outstanding alarms have been displayed.

23.2.3 Generate Monitoring Data Use Case Description

Use case name: Generate Monitoring Data
Summary: Monitoring data is generated on an ongoing basis. Operators are notified of new monitoring status to which they have subscribed
Actor: Remote Sensor (primary), Monitoring Operator (secondary)
Precondition: The remote system is operational.

> **Main sequence:**
>   1. The Remote Sensor sends new monitoring data to the system.
>   2. The system updates the monitoring status as follows: Sensor status for each sensor (value, upper limit, lower limit, alarm status).
>   3. The system sends new monitoring status to monitoring operators who have subscribed to receive status updates.
>
> **Alternative sequence:**
> **Step 2:** Emergency situation. System displays emergency warning message to operator.
> **Postcondition:** Monitoring status has been updated.

23.2.4 Generate Alarm Use Case Description

> **Use case name:** Generate Alarm
> **Summary:** If an alarm condition is detected, an alarm is generated. Operators are notified of new alarms to which they have subscribed.
> **Actor:** Remote Sensor (primary), Monitoring Operator (secondary)
> **Precondition:** The external sensor is operational.
> **Main sequence:**
>   1. The Remote Sensor sends an alarm to the system.
>   2. The system updates the alarm data. The system stores the name of the alarm, alarm description, location of alarm, and severity of alarm (high, medium, low).
>   3. The system sends the new alarm data to monitoring operators who have subscribed to receive alarm updates.
>
> **Alternative sequence:**
> **Step 2:** Emergency situation. System displays emergency warning message to operator.
> **Step 3:** If the alarm is severe, display flashing warning.
> **Postcondition:** Alarm data have been updated.

23.3 Static Modeling

The static model for the Emergency Monitoring System consists of the software system context class diagram. The external classes are determined from the use case actors, such that there is a one-to-one correspondence between the use case actors and the external classes.

23.3.1 Emergency Monitoring System Context Class Diagram

The context class diagram defines the boundary of the software system. For the Emergency Monitoring System (see Figure 23.2), the external classes consist of one external user (Monitoring Operator), one external system (Remote System), and one external input device, Monitoring Sensor. Since there are multiple instances of each

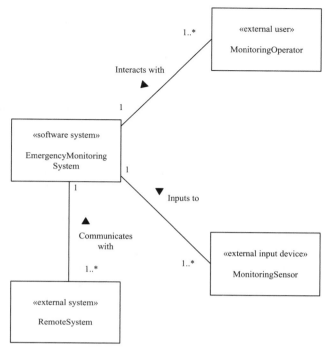

Figure 23.2. Software system context class diagram for Emergency Monitoring System

external class, each of the external classes has a one-to-many association with the Emergency Monitoring System in Figure 23.2. The common behavior of Remote System and Monitoring Sensor is captured by means of a generalized external class, Remote Sensor, although it is not necessary to explicitly depict this in Figure 23.2.

23.4 DYNAMIC MODELING

In order to understand how the use cases are realized by the system, it is necessary to analyze how the objects in the Emergency Monitoring System participate in the use cases. The dynamic model for the system is depicted on communication diagrams. There are four communication diagrams, one for each use case. Because object/class structuring and dynamic modeling are iterative activities, both are described in this section, the former in Section 23.4.1 and the latter in Sections 23.4.2 to 23.4.6. As the event monitoring is not state dependent, there are no state dependent control objects and consequently no state machine modeling.

23.4.1 Class and Object Structuring

During dynamic modeling, the objects that participate in each use case are determined, and then the sequence of interactions among the objects is analyzed. The first step is to analyze how the Emergency Monitoring System is structured into classes and objects.

Entity classes are usually persistent classes that store information. The entity classes for the Emergency Monitoring System are Alarm Data Repository and

Monitoring Data Repository, since there is a need to store both alarm data and monitoring data. However, the entity classes are encapsulated inside services that are accessed by various clients. For this reason, on the communication diagrams, the entity objects are within the services: Alarm Service, and Monitoring Data Service.

For each of the human actors there needs to be a user interaction class. For this system, there is one human actor, Monitoring Operator, and a corresponding user interaction class, Operator Interaction. Because the operator uses a multi-windowing interface, there are two supporting user interaction classes to display status and alarm information that is updated dynamically, Event Monitoring Window and Alarm Window, respectively (See section 23.5).

In addition, there is an input object, Monitoring Sensor Component, which receives sensor inputs from the external monitoring sensors and sends status data to the Monitoring Data Service object and alarms to the Alarm Service object. There is a proxy object, Remote System Proxy, which receives sensor data from the external remote systems and also sends status data to the Monitoring Data Service object and alarms to the Alarm Service object. Finally, there is a boundary superclass, Remote Sensor Component, which captures the common behavior of two boundary subclasses: Monitoring Sensor Component and Remote System Proxy. The class structuring for the Emergency Monitoring System is shown in Figure 23.3, which shows the classes from which the objects are instantiated.

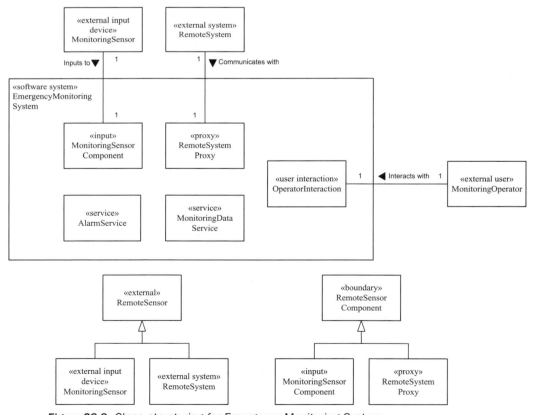

Figure 23.3. Class structuring for Emergency Monitoring System

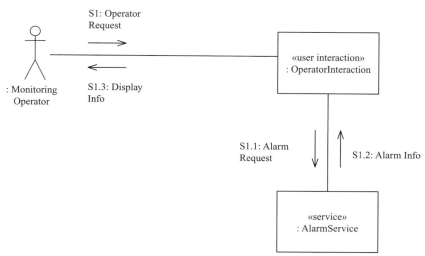

Figure 23.4. Communication diagram for the View Alarms use case

23.4.2 Communication Diagrams for Use Cases

After object structuring, dynamic modeling is carried out, such that a communication diagram is developed for each use case. In analyzing the object communication for each use case, various architectural patterns are recognized for future reference during design. Two of the communication diagrams apply the Multiple Client/Single Service pattern (see Chapter 15), in which multiple instances of a client interact with a single service. The two other communication diagrams also apply the Subscription/Notification pattern (see Chapter 17), in which a client is notified of new events previously subscribed to in one of the client/service use cases.

23.4.3 Communication Diagram for View Alarms Use Case

First consider the communication diagram for the View Alarms use case, depicted in Figure 23.4. In this scenario based on the Multiple Client/Single Service pattern, the client can request to view alarms or may subscribe to be notified of future alarm events. The client is the Operator Interaction object, and the service is provided by the Alarm Service object. The message sequence, which starts with input from the primary actor, the Monitoring Operator, is as follows:

> **S1:** The Monitoring Operator requests an alarm-handling service – for example, to view alarms or to subscribe to receive alarm messages of a specific type.
>
> **S1.1:** Operator Interaction sends the alarm request to Alarm Service.
>
> **S1.2:** Alarm Service performs the request – for example, reads the list of current alarms or adds the name of this client to the subscription list – and sends a response to the Operator Interaction object.
>
> **S1.3:** Operator Interaction displays the response – for example, alarm information – to the operator.

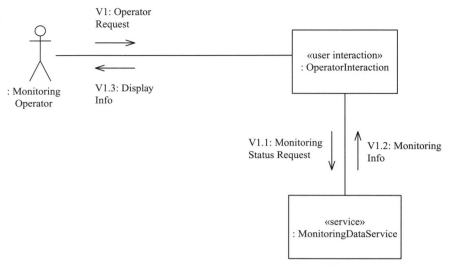

Figure 23.5. Communication diagram for the View Monitoring Data use case

23.4.4 Communication Diagram for View Monitoring Data Use Case

The communication diagram for the View Monitoring Data use case (Figure 23.5) also applies the Multiple Client/Single Service pattern and is very similar to the communication diagram for View Alarms (see Figure 20.4). The client is again the Operator Interaction object, and the service is provided by the Monitoring Data Service object. The client can request to view monitoring data or may subscribe to be notified of future status events. The message sequence, which starts with input from the primary actor, the Monitoring Operator, is as follows:

> **V1:** The Monitoring Operator requests a monitoring status service – for example, to view the current status of a monitoring station.
>
> **V1.1:** Operator Interaction sends a monitoring status request to Monitoring Data Service.
>
> **V1.2:** Monitoring Data Service responds – for example, with the requested monitoring status data.
>
> **V1.3:** Operator Interaction displays the monitoring status information to the operator.

23.4.5 Communication Diagram for Generate Alarm Use Cases

Consider the communication diagram for the Generate Alarm use case, shown in Figure 23.6. This scenario applies the Subscription/Notification pattern, in which the arrival of a new alarm results in subscribers being notified: Remote Sensor Component (representing the common behavior of both Monitoring Sensor Component and Remote System Proxy) sends alarms to the Alarm Service object, which then notifies

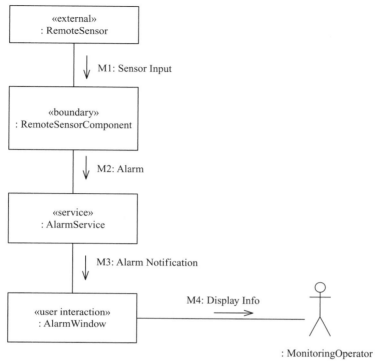

Figure 23.6. Communication diagram for the Generate Alarm use case

client objects (in this example, Alarm Window) of new events that they previously subscribed to receive. The message sequence is as follows:

M1: Remote Sensor Component receives sensor input from the external sensor, indicating an alarm condition.

M2: Remote Sensor Component sends an alarm to Alarm Service.

M3: Alarm Service sends a multicast message containing the alarm to all subscribers registered to receive messages of this type.

M4: Alarm Window receives the alarm notification and displays the information to the monitoring operator.

23.4.6 Communication Diagram for Generate Monitoring Status Use Case

The communication diagram for the Generate Monitoring Status use case also applies the Subscription/Notification pattern and is shown in Figure 23.7. In this scenario, as in the previous one, Remote Sensor Component (as before, representing the common behavior of both Monitoring Sensor Component and Remote System Proxy) sends monitoring status to the Monitoring Data Service object, which then notifies client

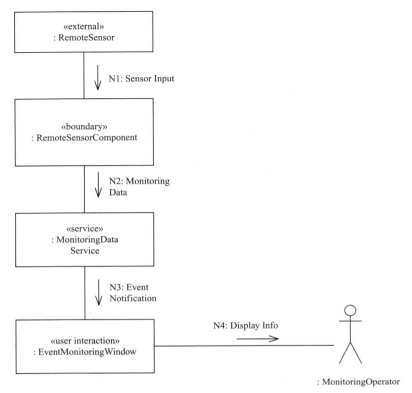

Figure 23.7. Communication diagram for the Generate Monitoring Status use case

objects (in this example, Event Monitoring Window) of new events that they previously subscribed to receive. The message sequence is as follows:

N1: Remote Sensor Component receives sensor input from the external remote system, indicating a change in monitoring status.

N2: Remote Sensor Component sends a monitoring data message to Monitoring Data Service.

N3: Monitoring Data Service sends a multicast message containing the new event notification to all subscribers registered to receive messages of this type.

N4: Event Monitoring Window receives the event notification message and displays the information to the monitoring operator.

23.5 DESIGN MODELING

The software architecture for the Emergency Monitoring System is designed as a distributed component-based software architecture that applies the software architectural patterns described in Chapters 12, 15, and 17. The Emergency Monitoring

System is designed as a layered architecture based on the Layers of Abstraction architectural pattern.

23.5.1 Integrated Communication Diagram

The first step in design modeling is to integrate the four use case–based communication diagrams to form the integrated communication diagram for the Emergency Monitoring System, which depicts all the software objects, as shown on Figure 23.8. The three user interaction objects are grouped into one composite user interaction object, Operator Presentation, which contains the Alarm Window, Event Monitoring Window, and Operator Interaction objects. Operator Interaction interacts with both Alarm Service and Monitoring Data Service; Alarm Window receives alarm notification from Alarm Service; and Event Monitoring Window receives event notification from Monitoring Data Service. The multiple instances of the specialized boundary classes, Monitoring Sensor Component and Remote System Proxy, are explicitly depicted. Both of these client objects communicate with Alarm Service and Monitoring Data Service to send alarms and monitoring data, respectively.

23.5.2 Layered Component-Based Architecture

Applying the subsystem structuring criteria to the integrated communication diagram, the following components and services are determined:

- **Services.** The services are Alarm Service and Monitoring Data Service.
- **User interaction components.** The user interaction components are Operator Interaction, Alarm Window, and Event Monitoring Window, which are grouped into one composite user interaction object, Operator Presentation.
- **Proxy component.** The proxy component is the Remote System Proxy.
- **Input component.** The input component is the Monitoring Sensor Component.

Each component is depicted with the component stereotype, which identifies what kind of component it is. The components are structured into the layered architecture such that each component is in a layer where it depends on components in the layers below but not the layers above. This layered architecture is based on the Flexible Layers of Abstraction pattern, which is a less restrictive variant of the Layers of Abstraction pattern, in which a layer can use the services of any of the layers below it, not just the layer immediately below it. The main advantage of applying this pattern is it allows for future software evolution by adding new components at upper layers (or modifying components at those layers) which use services at lower layers that are not affected by the change. Furthermore, additional services can be added at the lowest layer, which can then be discovered by requestor components at higher layers. This layered architecture, which is depicted in Figure 23.9, is described as follows::

> **Layer 1: Service Layer.** This layer consists of the services Alarm Service and Monitoring Data Service.
> **Layer 2: Monitoring Layer.** This layer consists of the Remote System Proxy and Monitoring Sensor Component. The components require the two services at the Service Layer.

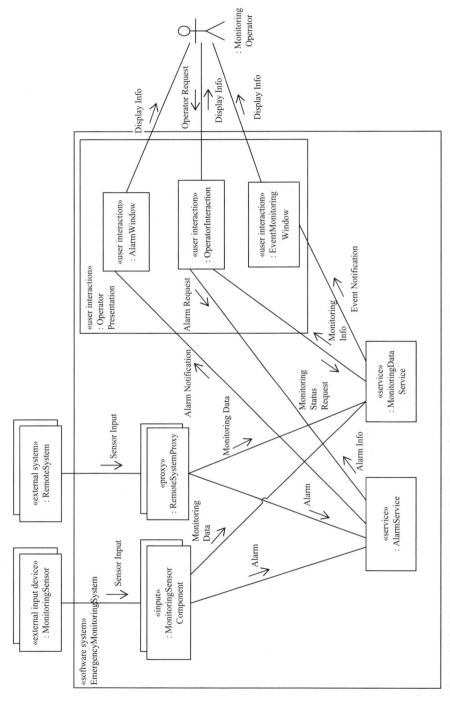

Figure 23.8. Integrated communication diagram for Emergency Monitoring System

464

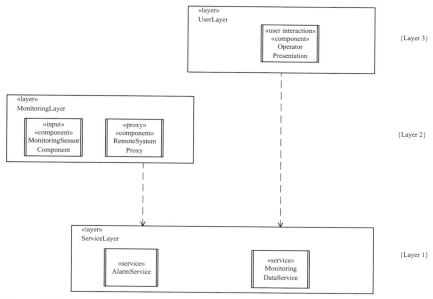

Figure 23.9. Layered architecture of the Emergency Monitoring System

Layer 3: User Layer. This layer consists of the user interaction component Operator Presentation and the components it contains.

If two layers do not depend on each other, such as layers 2 and 3 in the preceding list, the choice of which layer should be higher is a design decision. In addition to the Layers of Abstraction architectural patterns, one other architectural structure pattern is also used:

■ **Multiple Client/Multiple Service pattern.** There are several examples of the Multiple Client /Multiple Service pattern used in the architecture. Initially identified as the Multiple Client/Single Service pattern in the use case–based interactions diagrams in which each client only interacted with one service, the full picture given in the integrated communication diagram (see Figure 23.8) shows that each client (such as Remote System Proxy) actually interacts with two services (Alarm Service and Monitoring Data Service). In the Layers of Abstraction architecture, client components are designed to be at higher layers than the services that they require. With the Flexible Layers of Abstraction architecture, a client can be at any of the higher levels. For example, Operator Presentation, which is a client user interaction component, is at layer 3, whereas the services it uses (Alarm Service and Monitoring Data Service) are at layer 1.

23.5.3 Architectural Communication Patterns

The communication diagrams explicitly show the type of message communication – synchronous or asynchronous. Message communication between the components of the Emergency Monitoring System is shown on the concurrent communication diagram in Figure 23.10. The communication patterns (see Chapters 12, 15, and 17)

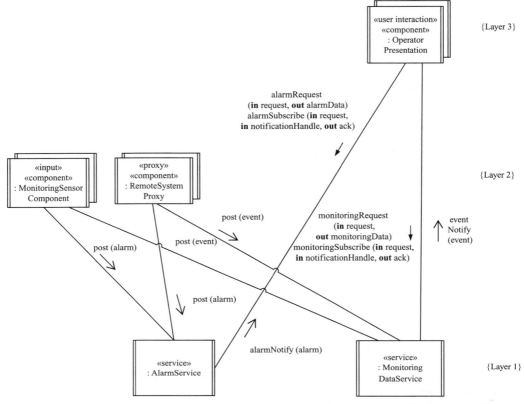

Figure 23.10. Concurrent communication diagram for the Emergency Monitoring System

used are Synchronous Message Communication with Reply, Asynchronous Message Communication, and Subscription/Notification. In addition, the Broker and Discovery patterns are also used.

To handle the variety of communication between the components in the software architecture, several communication patterns are applied, as depicted on the communication diagram in Figure 23.10:

- **Synchronous Message Communication with Reply.** This pattern is the typical client/service pattern of communication and is used when the client needs information from the service and cannot proceed before receiving the response. This pattern is used between the user interaction clients and services, because the clients need a response from the service before they can continue. Thus, it is used between Operator Presentation and Alarm Service, as well as between Operator Presentation and Monitoring Data Service (see Figure 23.10).

- **Asynchronous Message Communication.** The Monitoring Sensor Component and Remote System Proxy components send asynchronous messages to Alarm Service to post new alarms. The Monitoring Sensor Component and Remote System Proxy components also send asynchronous messages to Monitoring Data Service (as shown in Figure 23.10). The reason for asynchronous communication is that the Remote System Proxy and Monitoring Sensor Component components need to post alarms and monitoring status on a regular basis; they need to continue executing without delay, and they do not need a response.

- **Broker Handle.** Broker patterns are used during system initialization. Services register service information with the broker. The Broker Handle pattern allows clients to query the broker to determine the services to which they should be connected.
- **Service Discovery.** The Service Discovery pattern is used to allow clients to discover services, which would also permit the system to evolve after deployment.
- **Subscription/Notification (Multicast).** Operator Presentation has two patterns of communication with Alarm Service and Monitoring Data Service (see Figure 23.10). The first is the usual communication pattern in client/service situations, namely, Synchronous message Communication with Reply pattern, which is used to make alarm requests and receive responses. The second pattern is the Subscription/Notification pattern, in which Operator Presentation subscribes to receive alarms of a certain type (e.g., high-priority alarms). When the Monitoring Sensor Component or Remote System Proxy posts an alarm of that type to Alarm Service, the service notifies all subscriber Operator Presentation components of the new alarm. The same approach is used for communication with Monitoring Data Service, in which the client is notified of monitoring events.

23.5.4 Distributed Component-Based Software Architecture

The distributed component-based software architecture of the Emergency Monitoring System is depicted in Figure 23.11, in which services are fully integrated. All the concurrent components and services communicate through ports. The ports are provided ports that support provided interfaces or required ports that support required interfaces. There are no complex ports that support both provided and required interfaces. The interfaces are explicitly depicted in subsequent figures. By convention, the name of a port with a provided interface starts with the prefix P (e.g., PAlarmService), and the name of a port with a required interface starts with the prefix R (e.g., RAlarmService).

The software architecture of the Emergency Monitoring System (Figure 23.11) depicts two services that each support two provided ports with provided interfaces and one required port with a required interface. Two client components, Remote System Proxy and Monitoring Sensor Component, each support two required ports with required interfaces. The third client component, Operator Presentation, has two required ports, each with a required interface, and two provided ports, each with a provided interface.

23.5.5 Component and Service Interface Design

The interface designs for the individual components and services are depicted in Figures 23.12 through 23.15, in which each component/service is depicted with the ports and interfaces it provides and/or requires. Each interface is explicitly depicted in terms of the operations it provides. Each operation specifies its name, input parameters, and output parameters.

Consider first an example of a service with its ports, interfaces, and operations; consider also the clients that communicate with this service. The Alarm Service has

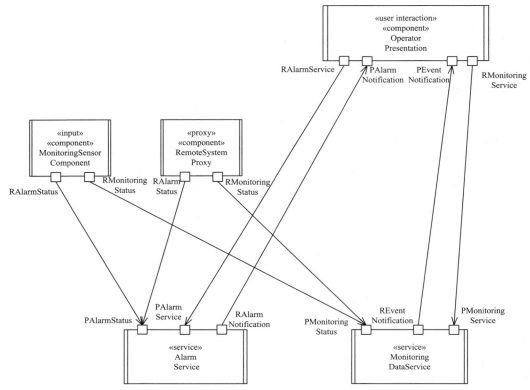

Figure 23.11. Distributed component-based software architecture for Emergency Monitoring System

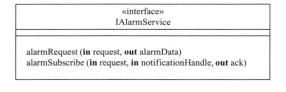

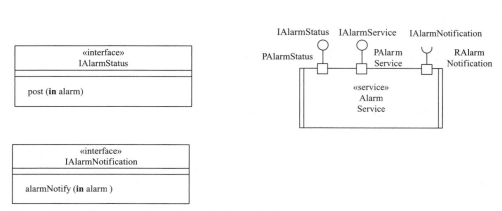

Figure 23.12. Component interfaces of Alarm Service

three ports: PAlarmStatus, PAlarmService, and RAlarmNotification (as shown in Figure 23.12). Alarm Service is designed with two provided ports because it has two different kinds of clients. There are clients, such as Operator Presentation, that make synchronous client/service requests to view data or make subscription requests. There are other clients, such as Monitoring Sensor Component, that post alarms asynchronously. Clients that post alarms use the PAlarmStatus port, which consists of one provided interface called IAlarmStatus, which in turn provides one operation called post (**in** Alarm). Clients making synchronous requests that need a response use the PAlarmService port, which has one provided interface (IAlarmService). The required port, RAlarmNotification port, consists of one required interface (IAlarmNotification), which is used to notify clients of new events as a result of an alarm being posted. The interfaces and operations are specified as follows:

- **Provided interface:** IAlarmService
  Operations:
  - alarmRequest (**in** request, **out** alarmData)
  - alarmSubscribe (**in** request, **in** notificationHandle **out** ack)
- **Provided interface:** IAlarmStatus
  Operation: post (**in** alarm)
- **Required interface:** IAlarmNotification
  Operation: alarmNotify (**in** alarm)

These interfaces are used as follows:

- The Operator Presentation component (see Figure 23.11) uses the IAlarmService required interface (see Figure 23.12) via the RAlarmService required port to send alarm requests and subscription requests to Alarm Service.
- Remote System Proxy and Monitoring Sensor Component (see Figure 23.11) use the IAlarmStatus required interface via the RAlarmStatus required port (e.g., see Figure 23.12) to post new alarms at Alarm Service.
- The Alarm Service (see Figures 23.11 and 23.12) sends alarm notifications to the Operator Presentation component by using its IAlarmNotification required interface via the RAlarmNotification required port (see Figure 23.12).

The Monitoring Data Service (Figure 23.13) is designed in a similar way to the Alarm Service. It has two provided interfaces, one of which is connected to the required interfaces of the client Monitoring Sensor Component and Remote System Proxy components to receive new events; the other is connected to the required interface of the Operator Presentation component to receive monitoring requests. It has one required interface, which is connected to the provided interface of the Operator Presentation component to send notification events.

Figure 23.14 depicts the three client components. Both Remote System Proxy and Monitoring Sensor Component have two required ports, each with a required interface, that are used to post events with the Monitoring Data Service and alarms with the Alarm Service. Operator Presentation has two provided ports and two required ports. The two required ports are used to communicate with the two services, Monitoring Data Service and Alarm Service. The two provided ports receive event and alarm notifications from Monitoring Data Service and Alarm Service, respectively.

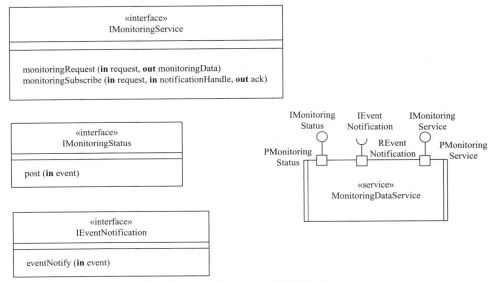

Figure 23.13. Component interfaces of Monitoring Data Service

Operator Presentation is a composite component that contains three simple user interaction components, as depicted in Figure 23.15. The three simple components are Operator Interaction, Alarm Window, and Event Monitoring Window. Consider the provided ports: the provided ports of the composite Operator Presentation component are connected directly to the provided ports of the internal Alarm Window and Event Monitoring Window components. Each connector that joins an outer provided port to an inner provided port is a **delegation connector**, through which the outer

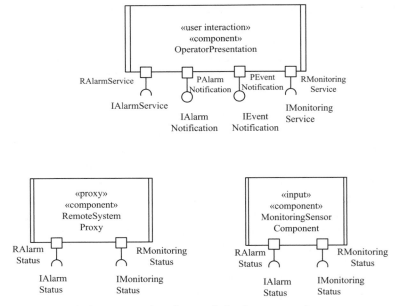

Figure 23.14. Component interfaces of client components

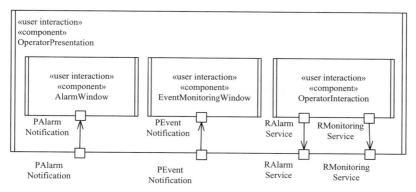

Figure 23.15. Component interfaces of user interaction components

delegating port provided by Operator Presentation forwards each message it receives to the inner port provided by the nested component, e.g., Alarm Window. By convention, the two ports are given the same name (e.g., PAlarmNotification for both Operator Presentation and Alarm Window), because they provide the same interface. Similarly, the inner required ports (RAlarmService and RMonitoringService) of the Operator Interaction component are connected directly to the similarly named outer required ports of Operator Presentation.

23.6 SOFTWARE COMPONENT DEPLOYMENT

A typical deployment of the software components for the Emergency Monitoring System is given in Figure 23.16. Each client component (of which there are multiple instances) and each service is assigned its own physical node, as shown in Figure 23.16. The client components are Monitoring Sensor Component (one node per monitoring location), Remote System Proxy (one node per remote system), and Operator Presentation (one node per operator). The services are Monitoring Data Service and Alarm Service (one node per service). The nodes are interconnected by means of the Internet.

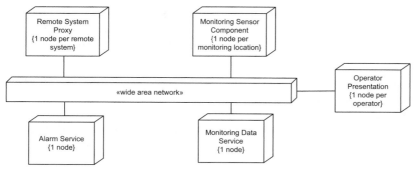

Figure 23.16. Deployment diagram for an Emergency Monitoring System

24

Real-Time Software Architecture Case Study

Automated Guided Vehicle System

The Automated Guided Vehicle (AGV) System case study is an example of a real-time system. Taken in conjunction with the other systems with which it interfaces, the Supervisory System and the Display System, it is also an example of a distributed *system of systems*. The Supervisory System and the Display System are existing systems to which the AGV System must interface.

The problem is described in Section 24.1. Section 24.2 describes the use case model for the AGV System. Section 24.3 describes the static model, which includes the system context model that depicts the boundary between the system and the external environment. Section 24.4 describes the object structuring for the AGV System. Section 24.5 describes dynamic state machine modeling, and Section 24.6 describes dynamic interaction modeling in which communication diagrams are developed for each of the use cases. Section 24.7 describes the design model for the AGV System, which involves the design of a component-based real-time software architecture.

24.1 PROBLEM DESCRIPTION

An AGV System has the following characteristics:

A computer-based AGV can move along a track in the factory in a clockwise direction, and start and stop at factory stations. The AGV has the following characteristics:

1. A motor, which is commanded to Start Moving and Stop Moving. The motor sends Started and Stopped responses.
2. An arrival sensor to detect when the AGV has arrived at a station, e.g., arrived at station *x*. If this is the destination station, the AGV should stop. If it is not the destination station, the AGV should continue moving past the station.
3. A robot arm for loading and unloading a part onto and off of the AGV.

The AGV system receives Move commands from an external Supervisory System. It sends vehicle Acknowledgements (Acks) to the Supervisory System

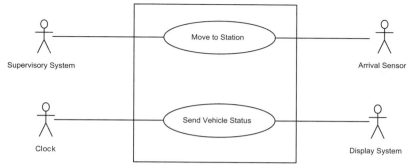

Figure 24.1. Automated Guided Vehicle System: use cases

indicating that is has started moving, passed a station, or stopped at a station. The AGV system also sends vehicle status to an external Display System every 30 seconds.

It is given that the arrival sensor is an event-driven input device and that the motor and arm are passive I/O devices. It is also given that the AGV system communicates with the Supervisory System and Display System by means of messages.

24.2 USE CASE MODELING

The use case model for the AGV System is depicted in Figure 24.1. From the problem description, it can be determined that there are two use cases, one dealing with the vehicle moving to a station and the second dealing with sending vehicle status to the display system. There are four actors: Supervisory System, Display System, Arrival Sensor, and Clock. From the perspective of the AGV System, the Supervisory System and Display System are external system actors. The Arrival Sensor is an input device actor, whereas the Clock is a timer actor. The use case descriptions are given next.

24.2.1 Move to Station Use Case

The Supervisory System is a primary actor that initiates the Move to Station use case, because it sends the move command to the AGV System. The Arrival Sensor is a secondary actor that participates in the use case as it notifies the vehicle when it has reached a station. The use case description is as follows:

> **Use case name:** Move to Station
> **Summary:** The AGV moves a part to a factory station
> **Actor:** Supervisory System (primary), Arrival Sensor (secondary)
> **Precondition:** The AGV is stationary.
> **Main sequence:**
> 1. The Supervisory System sends a message to the AGV system requesting it to move to a factory station and load a part.
> 2. The AGV System commands the motor to start moving.
> 3. The motor notifies the AGV System that the vehicle has started moving.
> 4. The AGV System sends a Departed message to the Supervisory System.

5. The arrival sensor notifies the AGV System that it has arrived at factory station (#).
6. The AGV System determines that this station is the destination station and commands the motor to stop moving.
7. The motor notifies the AGV System that the vehicle has stopped moving.
8. The AGV System commands the robot arm to load the part.
9. The arm notifies the AGV System that the part has been loaded.
10. The AGV System sends an Arrived message to the Supervisory System.

Alternative sequences:
Step 6: If the vehicle arrives at a different station from the destination station, the vehicle passes the station without stopping and sends a "Passed factory station (#) without stopping" message to the Supervisory System.
Steps 8, 9: If the Supervisory System requests the AGV to move to a factory station and unload a part, the AGV will unload the part after it arrives at the destination station.
Postcondition: AGV has completed its mission and is at the destination station.

24.2.2 Send Status Use Case

The Clock is a primary actor, which initiates the Send Vehicle Status use case, for which the Display System is a secondary actor. The use case description is as follows:

Use case name: Send Vehicle Status
Summary: The AGV sends status information about its location and idle/busy status to the display system.
Actor: Clock (primary), Display System (secondary)
Precondition: The AGV is operational.
Main sequence:
1. Clock notifies AGV System that the timer has expired.
2. AGV System reads the status information about AGV location and idle/busy status.
3. AGV System sends the AGV status information to the Display System.

Postcondition: AGV system has sent status information

24.3 STATIC MODELING

This section describes the static model, which consists of the system context model and the entity class model.

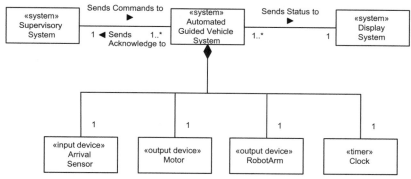

Figure 24.2. Conceptual static model for the Automated Guided Vehicle System

24.3.1 Conceptual Static Modeling

The conceptual static model is shown in Figure 24.2 using a class diagram. It depicts a system of systems, consisting of the Supervisory System, the AGV System, and the Display System. The AGV System is modeled as a composite class, which receives commands from and sends acknowledgments to the Supervisory System, and sends status to the Display System. The AGV System is composed of four classes: the Arrival Sensor, the Motor, the Robot Arm, and the Clock.

24.3.2 Software System Context Modeling

The software system context diagram (Figure 24.3) is modeled from the perspective of the software system to be developed, the AGV System. It therefore depicts two external system classes (the Supervisory System and the Display System) and the Clock external timer class, which were originally depicted as actors in the use case model.

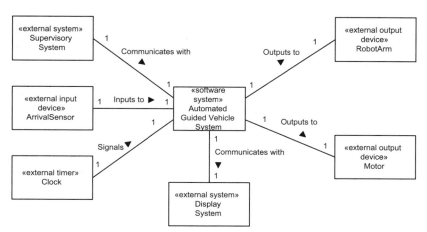

Figure 24.3. Software system context class diagram for Automated Guided Vehicle System

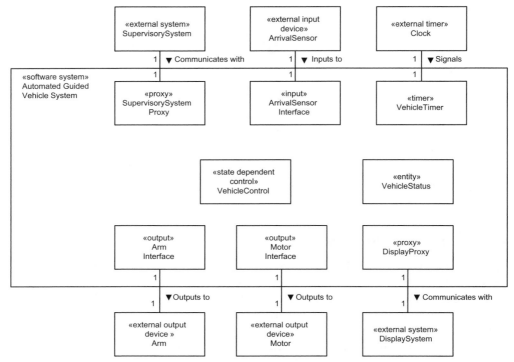

Figure 24.4. Object structuring for the Automated Guided Vehicle System

There is one external input device class, Arrival Sensor, and two external output device classes, Motor and Robot Arm.

24.4 OBJECT AND CLASS STRUCTURING

Object structuring for the AGV System is depicted in Figure 24.4. For each external class on the software system context diagram, there is a corresponding internal software class. Thus, there are two proxy classes, Supervisory System Proxy and Display Proxy, which communicate with the two external systems, Supervisory System and Display System, respectively. There is one input class, Arrival Sensor Interface, which communicates with the Arrival Sensor external input device, and two output classes, Motor Interface and Arm Interface, which communicate with the Motor and Arm external output devices, respectively. There are two additional classes, a state-dependent control class, Vehicle Control, which executes the vehicle state machine, and an entity class, Vehicle Status, which contains data about the vehicle destination and command. In addition, there is one timer class, Vehicle Timer.

24.5 DYNAMIC STATE MACHINE MODELING

Vehicle Control executes the vehicle state machine, which is depicted on the statechart in Figure 24.5. The state machine follows the states of the vehicle as it transitions from idle state to moving, arriving at destination, loading or unloading the

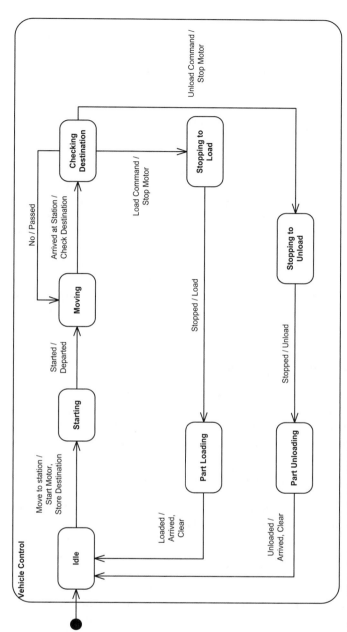

Figure 24.5. Automated Guided Vehicle statechart

part, and then restarting. The states are determined by following the main sequence textually described in the Move to Station use case, and are as follows:

- **Idle.** This is the initial state, in which the AGV is idle, waiting for a command from the Supervisory System.
- **Starting.** This state is entered when the AGV has received a Move to Station message from the Supervisory System and has sent a start command to the motor.
- **Moving.** The AGV is moving to the next station.
- **Checking Destination.** The AGV has arrived at a station and is checking to determine whether this is its destination.
- **Stopping to Load.** This station is the destination, and the AGV is to load a part. The AGV commands the motor to stop on entry to this state.
- **Part Loading.** This robot arm is loading the part onto the AGV.
- **Stopping to Unload.** This station is the destination, and the AGV is to unload a part. The AGV commands the motor to stop on entry to this state.
- **Part Unloading.** This robot arm is unloading the part off the AGV.

Note that the Stopping to Load and the Stopping to Unload states are kept separate because the actions leaving these states are different (Load and Unload, respectively).

24.6 DYNAMIC INTERACTION MODELING

For each use case, a communication diagram is developed that depicts the objects that participate in the use case and the sequence of messages passed between them. Several objects realize the main use case, Move to Station; however, only three software objects are needed to realize the supporting use case, Send Vehicle Status.

24.6.1 Dynamic Modeling for Move to Station

In the communication diagram for the Move to Station use case (Figure 24.6), the sequence of external inputs and external outputs on the communication diagram corresponds to the sequence described in the use case and starts with the command sent by the Supervisory System, which is the primary actor. The objects that realize this use case are Supervisory System Proxy, which receives the inputs from the Supervisory System; Vehicle Control, which controls the objects that participate in the use case; Vehicle Status, for storing and retrieving destination location information; Arm Interface and Motor Interface, for interfacing to the two external output devices; and Arrival Sensor Interface, for receiving input from the arrival sensor. The message sequence description is as follows for a scenario in which the vehicle goes past the first station and stops at the second station to load a part:

1: The external Supervisory System sends a Move command message to the AGV System requesting it to move to a factory station and load a part.
1.1: The Supervisory System Proxy, which receives the Move command, sends a Move to Station message to Vehicle Control.

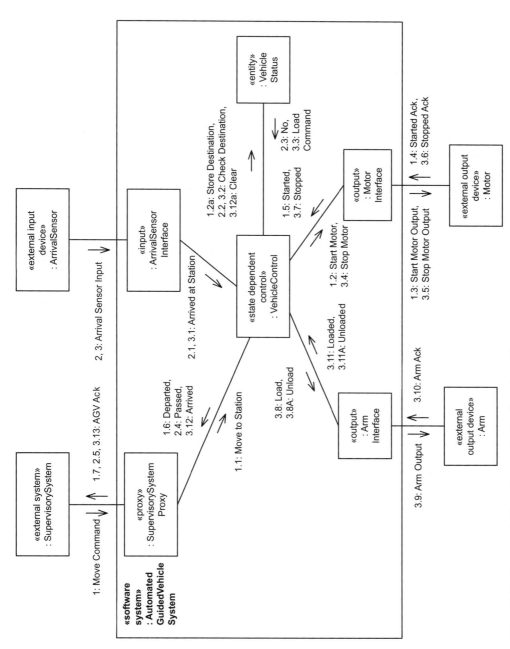

Figure 24.6. Communication diagram for the Move to Station use case

1.2: Vehicle Control sends a Start Motor command to Motor Interface to start moving.

1.2a: Vehicle Control stores destination and load/unload command in Vehicle Status.

1.3: Motor Interface sends Start Motor command to external Motor.

1.4: Motor sends Started acknowledge message to Motor Interface.

1.5: Motor Interface notifies the Vehicle Control that the vehicle has started moving.

1.6: Vehicle Control sends a Departed message to the Supervisory System Proxy

1.7: Supervisory System Proxy forwards Departed message to the Supervisory System.

2: The arrival sensor notifies the AGV system that it has arrived at factory station (#).

2.1: Arrival Sensor Interface sends Arrived at Station message to Vehicle Control.

2.2: Vehicle Control sends Check Destination message to Vehicle Status.

2.3: Vehicle Status indicates that this is not the destination.

2.4: Vehicle Control sends a Passed message to the Supervisory System Proxy

2.5: Supervisory System Proxy forwards Passed message to the Supervisory System.

3: The arrival sensor notifies the AGV System that it has arrived at factory station (#).

3.1: Arrival Sensor Interface sends Arrived at Station message to Vehicle Control.

3.2: Vehicle Control sends Check Destination message to Vehicle Status.

3.3: Vehicle Status indicates that this station is the destination station and that the command is to load a part.

3.4: Vehicle Control sends Stop Motor message to Motor Interface.

3.5: Motor Interface sends Stop Motor command to external Motor.

3.6: Motor sends Stopped acknowledge message to Motor Interface.

3.7: Motor Interface notifies the Vehicle Control that the vehicle has stopped moving.

3.8: Vehicle Control sends Load message to Arm Interface.

3.9: Arm Interface sends Load message to external Arm.

3.10: Arm sends acknowledgement message to Vehicle Control indicating that the arm has finished.

3.11: Arm Interface sends Loaded message to Vehicle Control.

3.12: Vehicle Control sends an Arrived message to the Supervisory System Proxy

3.13: Supervisory System Proxy forwards Arrived message to the Supervisory System.

The messages into and out of Vehicle Control correspond to the events and actions depicted on the statechart in Figure 24.7 and follow the same scenario given in the preceding message sequence description.

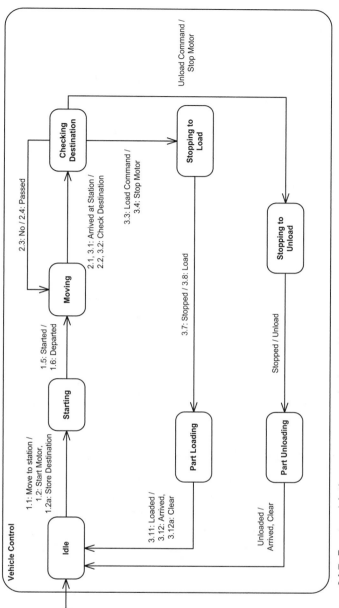

Figure 24.7. Event and Action sequence numbering on Vehicle Control statechart

481

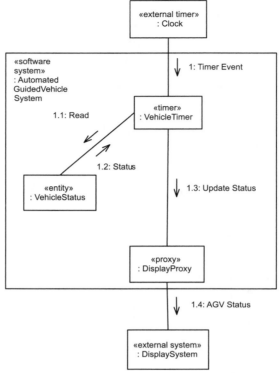

Figure 24.8. Communication diagram for the Send Vehicle Status use case

24.6.2 Dynamic Modeling for Send Vehicle Status

The communication diagram for the Send Vehicle Status use case is shown in Figure 24.8. The objects that realize this use case are the Vehicle Timer, which receives clock inputs, Vehicle Status, which stores status information, and Display Proxy, which sends vehicle status to the external Display System. The message sequence starts with the external timer event from the external Clock and the message numbering is as follows:

> **1:** Clock sends Timer Event to Vehicle Timer.
> **1.1, 1.2:** Vehicle Timer reads Vehicle Status.
> **1.3:** Vehicle Timer sends Update Status message to Display Proxy.
> **1.4:** Display Proxy sends Vehicle Status to external Display System.

24.7 DESIGN MODELING

The software architecture of the AGV System is designed around a centralized control pattern. Centralized control is provided by the Vehicle Control component receiving inputs from the Supervisory System and the Arrival Sensor, and controlling the external environment by means of the Motor and Arm. When viewed from the larger perspective of a factory automation system, the architecture is a based around a hierarchical control pattern, with several instances of the AGV System (each instance controlling an individual vehicle) operating under the overall direction of a Supervisory System, which provides hierarchical control of the individual AGVs by sending move commands to each vehicle.

24.7.1 Integrated Communication Diagram

The initial attempt at design modeling involves developing the integrated communication diagram for the AGV System, which requires the integration of the two use case–based communication diagrams shown in Figures 24.6 and 24.8. The integrated communication diagram is depicted in Figure 24.9. The integration is quite straightforward, because the only object that participates in both the use case–based communication diagrams is Vehicle Status. The integrated communication diagram is a generic communication diagram in that it depicts all possible communications between the objects.

24.7.2 Component-Based Software Architecture of Factory Automation System

The distributed software architecture for the Factory Automation System, which is a system of systems, is shown on the system communication diagram in Figure 24.10. It depicts the three interacting distributed systems (designed as components): the Supervisory System, the Automated Guided Vehicle (AGV) System, and the Display System. There is one instance of the Supervisory System, and multiple instances of the AGV System and the Display System. All communication between the distributed components is asynchronous, which allows the greatest flexibility in message communication. Communication between the Supervisory System and the AGV System is an example of bidirectional asynchronous communication.

The component-based software architecture for the Factory Automation System is shown in Figure 24.11, in which the three systems are designed as distributed components. The AGV System has a provided port for receiving messages from the Supervisory System and a required port for sending messages to the Display System. The provided port PAGVSystem is a complex port because it has both a provided interface, IAGVSystem, for receiving command messages and a required interface, ISupervisorySystem, for sending acknowledgement messages, as shown in Figure 24.12. The required port RDisplaySystem supports a required interface, IDisplaySystem, for sending AGV status messages to the Display System. The three component interfaces are also defined in Figure 24.12.

The configuration of the Factory Automation System is depicted on the deployment diagram of Figure 24.13. There is one node for each of the Supervisory System, one node per AGV System and one node for the Display System. The distributed nodes are connected by a local area network in the factory.

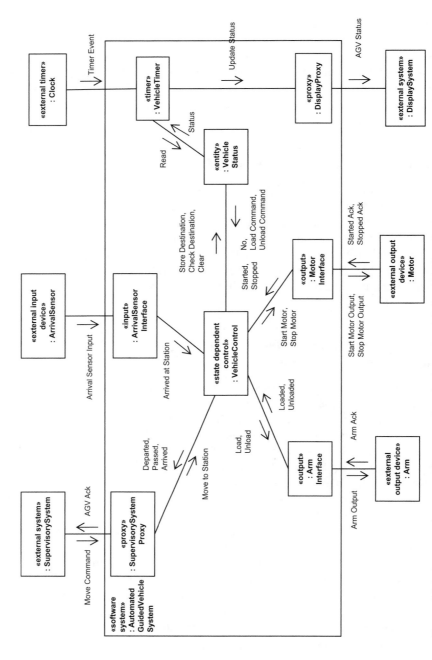

Figure 24.9. Integrated communication diagram for Automated Guided Vehicle System

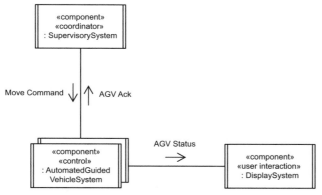

Figure 24.10. System communication diagram for Factory Automation System

24.7.3 Software Architecture of Automatic Guided Vehicle System

The AGV System is designed as a real-time component-based software architecture. A component-based design provides the advantages of a configurable design and follows the concepts described in Chapter 17. The real-time design is needed because of the characteristics of the application, and it follows the concurrent task structuring criteria and message-based task interface design described in Chapter 18.

The design of the AGV System is based on the centralized control pattern for real-time designs (see Chapter 18). One control component, Vehicle Control, provides the overall control of the system. In addition, the AGV System is designed as a distributed component-based software architecture, which allows the option for input and output components to reside on separate nodes that are connected by a

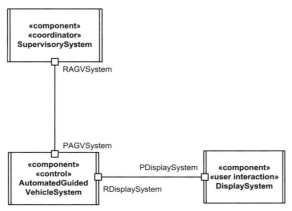

Figure 24.11. Component-based software architecture for Factory Automation System

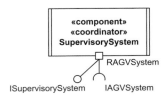

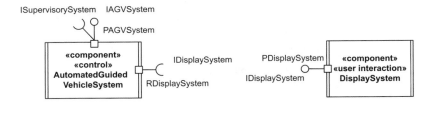

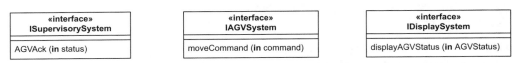

Figure 24.12. Composite component ports and interfaces for Factory Automation System

high-speed bus. At system deployment time, the type of configuration required – centralized or distributed – is determined.

The concurrent software architecture for the AGV System is developed from the integrated communication diagram by applying the task structuring criteria to design the concurrent tasks and architectural communication patterns to design the message communication between tasks. Next the component-based architecture is designed. Finally, the provided and required interfaces of each component are described. Each component port is defined in terms of its provided and/or required interfaces.

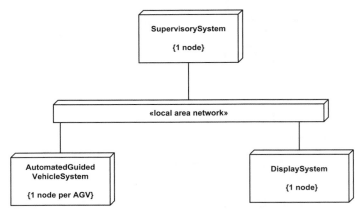

Figure 24.13. Distributed system deployment for Factory Automation System

24.7.4 Concurrent Software Architecture

In this concurrent real-time design, the concurrent task structuring criteria are applied to determine the tasks in the Automatic Guided Vehicle System. The concurrent task design (see Figure 22.14) is developed by starting from the integrated communication diagram in Figure 24.9, which depicts all the objects in the AGV System. All these objects are concurrent because they need to operate independently, except Vehicle Status, which is a passive data abstraction object. Because the goal is to design a concurrent component-based software architecture, the tasks are all designed as simple concurrent components, each with its own single thread of control. Thus, in this design, the terms *task* and *simple component* are synonymous. The concurrent tasks are described in the following list.

- **Input tasks.** Concurrent input tasks receive inputs from the external environment and send corresponding messages to the control task. Arrival Sensor Component (Figure 24.14) is designed as an event-driven input task, which is awakened by the arrival of an arrival sensor input. The input task consists of the individual input device interface object depicted in the analysis model (see Figure 24.9): Arrival Sensor Interface.
- **Proxy tasks.** Supervisory System Proxy acts on behalf of the Supervisory System, from which it receives Move commands that are forwarded to Vehicle Control, and it sends AGV acknowledgements to Supervisory System. Supervisory System Proxy is designed as an event-driven task, which is awakened by messages from either the external Supervisory System or the internal Vehicle Control. Note that if a task receives both external and internal messages, it is categorized as an event driven task and not a demand driven task. Display Proxy acts on behalf of the Display System, to which it forwards AGV status messages. Display Proxy is designed as a demand driven task, awakened on demand by the arrival of a message from Vehicle Timer.
- **Control task.** Vehicle Control is the centralized state dependent control task for the AGV system. It executes the Vehicle Control state machine and receives messages from other tasks that contain events, causing Vehicle Control to change state and send action messages to other tasks. Vehicle Control is designed as a demand driven task, which is awakened by arrival of a message from either Supervisory System Proxy or Arrival Sensor Component.
- **Output tasks.** The Arm Component interfaces to the external Arm. The Arm Interface object from the analysis model is mapped to this output task (see Figures 24.9 and 24.14). Similarly, the Motor Component interfaces to the external Motor and is designed from the analysis model Motor Interface object. Both of the output tasks are designed as demand driven tasks, which are awakened on demand by arrival of a message from Vehicle Control.

24.7.5 Architectural Communication Patterns

The concurrent communication diagram for the AGV System is shown in Figure 24.14, which depicts the concurrent tasks in the AGV software architecture. Next the task interfaces are designed.

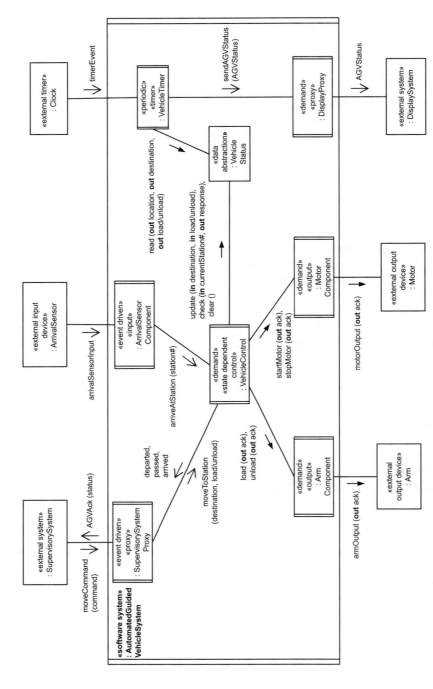

Figure 24.14. Concurrent communication diagram for Automated Guided Vehicle System

The messages to be sent between the tasks in the AGV system are determined from the integrated communication diagram in Figure 24.9. The actual type of message communication – synchronous or asynchronous – still needs to be determined. To handle the variety of communication between the tasks in the AGV System, four communication patterns are applied:

1. **Asynchronous Message Communication.** The Asynchronous Message Communication pattern is widely used in the AGV System because most communication is one-way, and this pattern has the advantage of not letting the consumers hold up the producers. The Vehicle Control task needs to be able to receive messages from either of its two producers, Supervisory System Proxy and Arrival Sensor Component, in any order. The best way to handle this requirement for flexibility is through asynchronous message communication, with one input message queue for the Vehicle Control task, so that Vehicle Control will receive whichever message arrives first, move command or station arrival. The Vehicle Timer task sends asynchronous AGV status messages to the Display Proxy task, which receives these messages on a message queue.

2. **Bidirectional Asynchronous Communication.** This communication pattern is used between the Supervisory System Proxy and Vehicle Control, because considerable time could elapse between Supervisory System Proxy sending the move command to Vehicle Control and Vehicle Control sending the acknowledge response to the Supervisory System Proxy (after the AGV has arrived at its destination). Thus, move and acknowledge messages are decoupled.

3. **Synchronous Message Communication without Reply**. This pattern is used when the producer needs to make sure that the consumer has accepted the message before the producer continues. This pattern is used between the Vehicle Control and Arm Component, as well as between Vehicle Control and Motor Component. In both cases, the consumer task is idle until it accepts the message, so the Vehicle Control producer is not held up after sending the message.

4. **Call/Return**. This pattern is used when AGV Control and Vehicle Timer invoke the operations of the passive Vehicle Status (see Figure 24.14) data abstraction object.

24.7.6 Component-Based Software Architecture

The component-based software architecture for the AGV System is given on Figure 24.15. Figure 24.15 depicts a UML composite structure diagram showing the AGV System component ports and connectors. All the components are concurrent except one and communicate with other components through ports. The overall architecture and connectivity among components is determined from the AGV System concurrent communication diagram. Thus, the composite structure of the component architecture depicted in Figure 24.15 is determined from the concurrent communication design shown in Figure 24.14.

The Automated Guided Vehicle System component is designed as a composite component that contains eight simple part components; seven of these are concurrent components (Supervisory System Proxy, Arrival Sensor Component, Vehicle Control, Vehicle Timer, Arm Component, Motor Component, and Display Proxy), and the

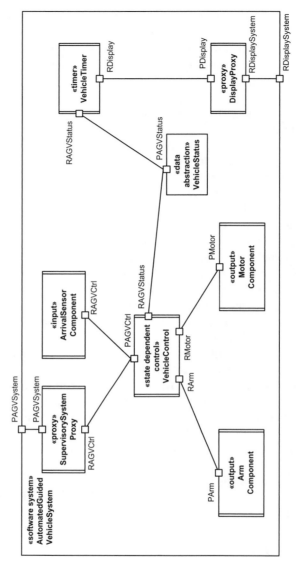

Figure 24.15. Automatic Guided Vehicle System component-based software architecture

other is a passive data abstraction object (Vehicle Status). The seven simple concurrent components correspond to the tasks determined in Section 24.7.4 and depicted on the concurrent communication diagram of Figure 24.14.

Figure 24.15 shows the decomposition of the Automatic Guided Vehicle System component into the seven simple concurrent components and the passive data abstraction object described in the previous paragraph. The provided port of the composite Automatic Guided Vehicle System component is connected directly to the provided port of the simple Supervisory System Proxy component, and both ports are given the same name (PAGV System) because they provide the same interface. The connector joining the two ports is actually a delegation connector, meaning that the outer port provided by Automatic Guided Vehicle System forwards each message it receives to the inner port provided by Supervisory System Proxy. The required ports of the Display Proxy component is also connected to the required port of the composite Automatic Guided Vehicle System component, via delegation connectors.

Vehicle Control, which executes the vehicle state machine, has one provided port, which supports a provided interface that receives all incoming messages from Supervisory System Proxy and Arrival Sensor Component. In this way, Vehicle Control receives all incoming messages on a FIFO basis. Vehicle Status also has one provided port and provided interface. Because Vehicle Status is passive, it provides operations, which are invoked by Vehicle Control and Vehicle Timer. Vehicle Control also has two required ports through which it communicates with Arm Component and Motor Component.

Because the two producer components (Supervisory System Proxy and Arrival Sensor Component) send messages to the Vehicle Control component in Figure 24.14, each producer component is designed to have an output port, referred to as a *required port*, which is joined by means of a connector to the control component's input port, referred to as a *provided port*, as shown in Figure 24.15. The name of the required port on each producer component is RAGVCtrl; by a COMET convention, the first letter of the port name is *R* to emphasize that the component has a *required* port. The name of the provided port for Vehicle Control is PAGVCtrl; the first letter of the port name is *P* to emphasize that the component has a provided port. Connectors join the required ports of the two producer components to the provided port of the control component.

24.7.7 Design of Component Interfaces

Each component port is defined in terms of its provided and/or required interfaces. Some producer components – in particular, the input component – do not provide a software interface, because they receive their inputs directly from the external hardware input device. However, they require an interface provided by the control component in order to send messages to the control component. Figure 24.16 depicts the port and required interface for the input component Arrival Sensor Component. This input component, as well as the Supervisory System Proxy component, has the same required interface – IAGVControl, which is provided by the Vehicle Control component.

The Vehicle Control component has three required ports from which it sends messages to the provided ports of the two output components depicted in Figure 24.14

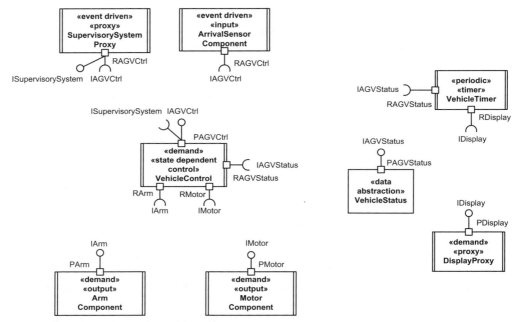

Figure 24.16. Automated Guided Vehicle System component ports and interfaces

(Arm Component and Motor Component), and it invokes operations on Vehicle Status data abstraction object through its provided port.

The output components do not require a software interface because their outputs go directly to external hardware output devices. However, they need to provide an interface to receive messages sent by the control component. Figure 24.16 depicts the ports and provided interfaces for the two output components of the AGV System. Figure 24.17 also shows the specifications of the interfaces in terms of the operations they provide. The Arm Component and Motor Component output components each have a provided port:

- PArm for Arm Component, which provides the interface IArm
- PMotor for Motor Component, which provides the interface IMotor

The Display Proxy component has a provided port called PDisplay, which in turn provides an interface called IDisplay, as shown in Figure 24.16. Figure 24.17 shows the specification of the interface.

Some components, such as control components, need to provide interfaces for the producer components to use and require interfaces that are provided by output components. The Vehicle Control component has several ports – one provided port and three required ports – as shown in Figure 24.16. Each required port is used to interface to a different consumer component and is given the prefix R – for example, RArm. The provided port, which is called PAGVControl, provides the interface IAGVControl, which is required by the producer components.

The Vehicle Control component (see Figures 24.14 and 24.15), which conceptually executes the AGV statechart, receives asynchronous control request messages from two producer components. The provided interface IAGVControl is specified in

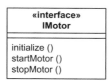

«interface»
IAGVControl

moveToStation (**in** destination, **in** load/Unload)
arrivingAtStation (**in** station#)

«interface»
IAGVStatus

update (**in** destination, **in** loadUnload)
check (**in** currentStation#, **out** response)
read (**out** AGVid, **out** location,
out destination, **out** loadUnload)
clear ()

«interface»
IArm

initialize ()
load ()
unload ()

«interface»
IMotor

initialize ()
startMotor ()
stopMotor ()

«interface»
IDisplay

displayAGVStatus (**in**
AGVStatus)

Figure 24.17. Automated Guided Vehicle System component interface specifications

Figure 24.17. It is kept simple by having only one operation, processControlRequest, which has an input parameter, controlRequest, that holds the name and contents of the individual message. Having each control request as a separate operation would make the interface more complicated when considering evolution of the system because it would need the addition or deletion of operations rather than changing a parameter.

The ports and interfaces of the periodic timer component are shown in Figures 24.16 and 24.17. The Vehicle Timer has two required ports with two required interfaces. The first required interface is IAGVStatus, which allows it to read AGV status information from the Vehicle Status data abstraction object. The second required interface is IDisplay, which allows Vehicle Timer to send AGV status messages to Display Proxy.

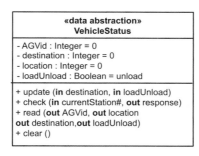

«data abstraction»
VehicleStatus

- AGVid : Integer = 0
- destination : Integer = 0
- location : Integer = 0
- loadUnload : Boolean = unload

+ update (**in** destination, **in** loadUnload)
+ check (**in** currentStation#, **out** response)
+ read (**out** AGVid, **out** location
out destination,**out** loadUnload)
+ clear ()

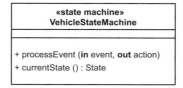

«state machine»
VehicleStateMachine

+ processEvent (**in** event, **out** action)
+ currentState () : State

Figure 24.18. Vehicle Status data abstraction class and Vehicle State Machine class

The port and interface of the passive data abstraction object (Vehicle Status) are shown in Figures 24.16 and 24.17. Vehicle Status provides one interface with three operations. The update operation stores the next AGV destination and the command to be executed there (load or unload). The check operation receives the current station number and returns whether this is the destination or not; if it is the destination, it also returns whether the station command is load or unload. The read operation returns the location, destination, and load/unload command. The attributes of the Vehicle Status data abstraction class are given in Figure 24.18. This figure also depicts the state machine class design for Vehicle State Machine, which is encapsulated inside the Vehicle Control component.

APPENDIX A

Catalog of Software Architectural Patterns

A template for describing a pattern typically addresses the following items from the perspective of the prospective user of the pattern:

- **Pattern name**
- **Aliases.** Other names by which this pattern is known.
- **Context.** The situation that gives rise to this problem.
- **Problem.** Brief description of the problem.
- **Summary of solution.** Brief description of the solution.
- **Strengths of solution.** Use to determine if the solution is right for your design problem.
- **Weaknesses of solution.** Use to determine if the solution is wrong for your design problem.
- **Applicability.** Situations in which you can use the pattern.
- **Related patterns.** Other patterns to consider for your solution.
- **Reference.** Where you can find more information about the pattern.

The architectural structure patterns, architectural communication patterns, and architectural transaction patterns are documented with this template in Sections A.1, A.2, and A.3, respectively. The patterns are summarized in the following tables:

Table A.1. Software architectural structure patterns

Software architectural structure patterns	Pattern description	Reference chapter
Broker Pattern	Section A.1.1	Chapter 16, Section 16.2
Centralized Control Pattern	Section A.1.2	Chapter 18, Section 18.3.1
Distributed Control Pattern	Section A.1.3	Chapter 18, Section 18.3.2
Hierarchical Control Pattern	Section A.1.4	Chapter 18, Section 18.3.3
Layers of Abstraction Pattern	Section A.1.5	Chapter 12, Section 12.3.1
Multiple Client/Multiple Service Pattern	Section A.1.6	Chapter 15, Section 15.2.2
Multiple Client/Single Service Pattern	Section A.1.7	Chapter 15, Section 15.2.1
Multi-tier Client/Service Pattern	Section A.1.8	Chapter 15, Section 15.2.3

Table A.2. Software architectural communication patterns

Software architectural communication patterns	Pattern description	Reference chapter
Asynchronous Message Communication Pattern	Section A.2.1	Chapter 12, Section 12.3.3
Asynchronous Message Communication with Callback Pattern	Section A.2.2	Chapter 15, Section 15.3.2
Bidirectional Asynchronous Message Communication	Section A.2.3	Chapter 12, Section 12.3.3
Broadcast Pattern	Section A.2.4	Chapter 17, Section 17.6.1
Broker Forwarding Pattern	Section A.2.5	Chapter 16, Section 16.2.2
Broker Handle Pattern	Section A.2.6	Chapter 16, Section 16.2.3
Call/Return	Section A.2.7	Chapter 12, Section 12.3.2
Negotiation Pattern	Section A.2.8	Chapter 16, Section 16.5
Service Discovery Pattern	Section A.2.9	Chapter 16, Section 16.2.4
Service Registration	Section A.2.10	Chapter 16, Section 16.2.1
Subscription/Notification Pattern	Section A.2.11	Chapter 17, Section 17.6.2
Synchronous Message Communication with Reply Pattern	Section A.2.12	Chapter 12, Section 12.3.4; Chapter 15, Section 15.3.1
Synchronous Message Communication without Reply Pattern	Section A.2.13	Chapter 18, Section 18.8.3

Table A.3. Software architectural transaction patterns

Software architectural transaction patterns	Pattern description	Reference chapter
Compound Transaction Pattern	Section A.3.1	Chapter 16, Section 16.4.2
Long-Living Transaction Pattern	Section A.3.2	Chapter 16, Section 16.4.3
Two-Phase Commit Protocol Pattern	Section A.3.3	Chapter 16, Section 16.4.1

A.1 SOFTWARE ARCHITECTURAL STRUCTURE PATTERNS

This section describes the architectural structure patterns, which address the static structure of the architecture, in alphabetical order, using the standard template.

A.1.1 Broker Pattern

Pattern name	Broker
Aliases	Object Broker, Object Request Broker
Context	Software architectural design, distributed systems
Problem	Distributed application in which multiple clients communicate with multiple services. Clients do not know locations of services.
Summary of solution	Services register with broker. Clients send service requests to broker. Broker acts as intermediary between client and service.
Strengths of solution	Location transparency: Services may relocate easily. Clients do not need to know locations of services.
Weaknesses of solution	Additional overhead because broker is involved in message communication. Broker can become a bottleneck if there is a heavy load at the broker. Client may keep outdated service handle instead of discarding.
Applicability	Distributed environments: client/service and distribution applications with multiple services
Related patterns	Broker Forwarding, Broker Handle
Reference	Chapter 16, Section 16.2

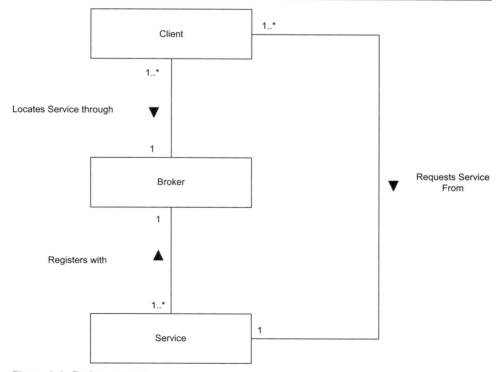

Figure A.1. Broker pattern

A.1.2 Centralized Control Pattern

Pattern name	Centralized Control
Aliases	Centralized Controller, System Controller
Context	Centralized application where overall control is needed
Problem	Several actions and activities are state-dependent and need to be controlled and sequenced.
Summary of solution	There is one control component, which conceptually executes a statechart and provides the overall control and sequencing of the system or subsystem.
Strengths of solution	Encapsulates all state-dependent control in one component
Weaknesses of solution	Could lead to overcentralized control, in which case decentralized control should be considered.
Applicability	Real-time control systems, state-dependent applications
Related patterns	Distributed Control, Hierarchical Control
Reference	Chapter 18, Section 18.3.1

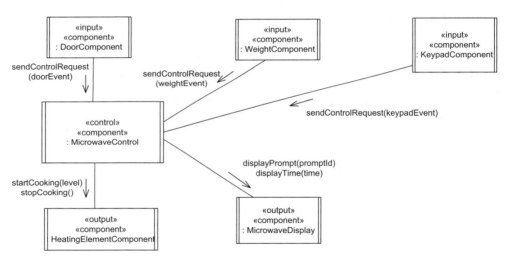

Figure A.2. Centralized Control pattern: Microwave Oven Control System example

A.1.3 Distributed Control Pattern

Pattern name	Distributed Control
Aliases	Distributed Controller
Context	Distributed application with real-time control requirement
Problem	Distributed application with multiple locations where real-time localized control is needed at several locations
Summary of solution	There are several control components, such that each component controls a given part of the system by conceptually executing a state machine. Control is distributed among the various control components; no single component has overall control.
Strengths of solution	Overcomes potential problem of overcentralized control.
Weaknesses of solution	Does not have an overall coordinator. If this is needed, consider using Hierarchical Control pattern.
Applicability	Distributed real-time control, distributed state-dependent applications
Related patterns	Hierarchical Control, Centralized Control
Reference	Chapter 18, Section 18.3.2

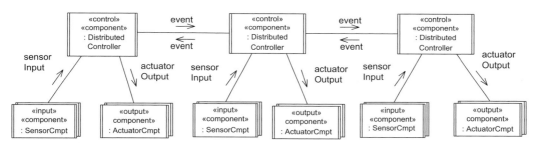

Figure A.3. Distributed Control pattern

A.1.4 Hierarchical Control Pattern

Pattern name	Hierarchical Control
Aliases	Multilevel Control
Context	Distributed application with real-time control requirement
Problem	Distributed application with multiple locations where both real-time localized control and overall control are needed
Summary of solution	There are several control components, each controlling a given part of a system by conceptually executing a statechart. There is also a coordinator component, which provides high-level control by deciding the next job for each control component and communicating that information directly to the control component.
Strengths of solution	Overcomes potential problem with Distributed Control pattern by providing high-level control and coordination
Weaknesses of solution	High-level coordinator may become a bottleneck when the load is high and is a single point of failure.
Applicability	Distributed real-time control, distributed state-dependent applications
Related patterns	Distributed Control, Centralized Control
Reference	Chapter 18, Section 18.3.3

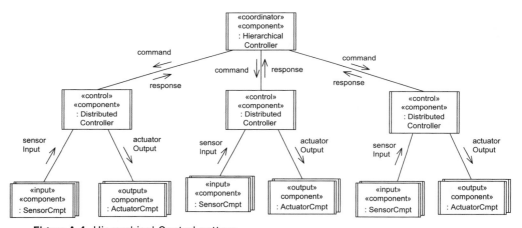

Figure A.4. Hierarchical Control pattern

A.1.5 Layers of Abstraction Pattern

Pattern name	Layers of Abstraction
Aliases	Hierarchical Layers, Levels of Abstraction
Context	Software architectural design
Problem	A software architecture that encourages design for ease of extension and contraction is needed.
Summary of solution	Components at lower layers provide services for components at higher layers. Components may use only services provided by components at lower layers.
Strengths of solution	Promotes extension and contraction of software design
Weaknesses of solution	Could lead to inefficiency if too many layers need to be traversed
Applicability	Operating systems, communication protocols, software product lines
Related patterns	Software kernel can be lowest layer of Layers of Abstraction architecture. Variations of this pattern include Flexible Layers of Abstraction.
Reference	Chapter 12, Section 12. 3.1; Hoffman and Weiss 2001; Parnas 1979

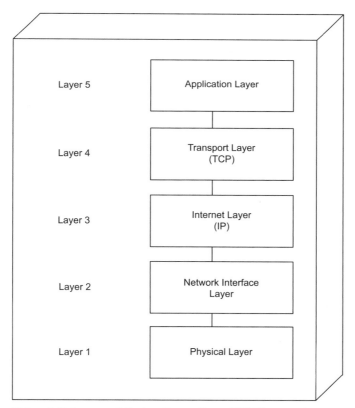

Figure A.5. Layers of Abstraction pattern: TCP/IP example

A.1.6 Multiple Client/Multiple Service Pattern

Pattern name	Multiple Client/Multiple Service
Aliases	Client/Service, Client/Server
Context	Software architectural design, distributed systems
Problem	Distributed application in which multiple clients require services from multiple services
Summary of solution	Client communicates with multiple services, usually sequentially but could also be in parallel. Each service responds to client requests. Each service handles multiple client requests. A service may delegate a client request to a different service.
Strengths of solution	Good way for client to communicate with multiple services when it needs different information from each service.
Weaknesses of solution	Client can be held up indefinitely if there is a heavy load at any server.
Applicability	Distributed processing: client/service and distribution applications with multiple services
Related patterns	Multiple Client/Single Service and Multi-tier Client/Service
Reference	Chapter 15, Section 15.2.2

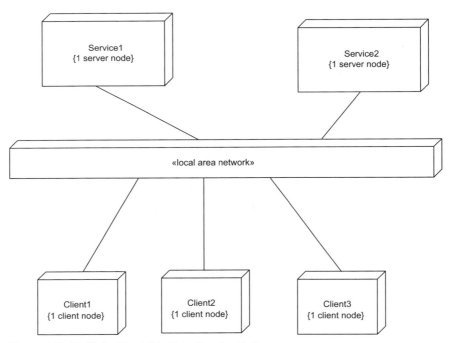

Figure A.6. Multiple Client/Multiple Service Pattern

A.1.7 Multiple Client/Single Service Pattern

Pattern name	Multiple Client/Single Service
Aliases	Client/Service, Client/Server
Context	Software architectural design, distributed systems
Problem	Distributed application in which multiple clients require services from a single service
Summary of solution	Client requests service. Service responds to client requests and does not initiate requests. Service handles multiple client requests.
Strengths of solution	Good way for client to communicate with service when it needs a reply from service. Very common form of communication in client/server applications.
Weaknesses of solution	Client can be held up indefinitely if there is a heavy load at the server.
Applicability	Distributed processing: client/service applications
Related patterns	Multiple Client/Multiple Service and Multi-tier Client/Service
Reference	Chapter 15, Section 15.2.1

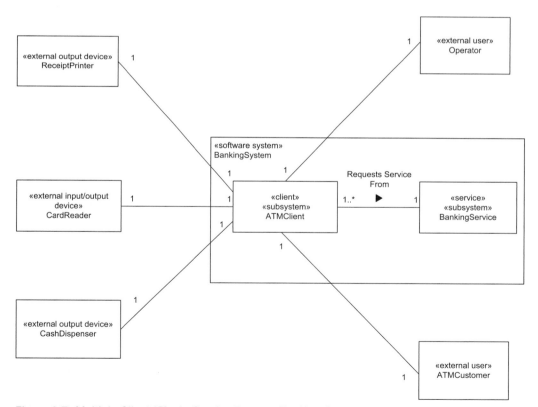

Figure A.7. Multiple Client/Single Service Pattern: Banking System example

A.1.8 Multi-tier Client/Service Pattern

Pattern name	Multi-tier Client/Service
Aliases	Client/Service, Client/Server
Context	Software architectural design, distributed systems
Problem	Distributed application in which there is more than one tier (layer) of service
Summary of solution	Client requests service. Solution consists of more than one tier of service. Intermediate tier provides both client and service role. There can be more than one intermediate tier.
Strengths of solution	Good way of layering services if multiple services are needed to handle an individual client's request and one service needs assistance of another service.
Weaknesses of solution	Client can be held up indefinitely if there is a heavy load at the server.
Applicability	Distributed processing: client/service and distribution applications with multiple services
Related patterns	Multiple Client/Single Service and Multiple Client/Multiple Service
Reference	Chapter 15, Section 15.2.3

Figure A.8. Multi-tier Client/Service Pattern: Banking System example

A.2 SOFTWARE ARCHITECTURAL COMMUNICATION PATTERNS

This section describes the architectural communication patterns, which address the dynamic communication among distributed components of the architecture, in alphabetical order, using the standard template.

A.2.1 Asynchronous Message Communication Pattern

Pattern name	Asynchronous Message Communication
Aliases	Loosely Coupled Message Communication
Context	Concurrent or distributed systems
Problem	Concurrent or distributed application has concurrent components that need to communicate with each other. Producer does not need to wait for consumer. Producer does not need a reply.
Summary of solution	Use message queue between producer component and consumer component. Producer sends message to consumer and continues. Consumer receives message. Messages are queued FIFO if consumer is busy. Consumer is suspended if no message is available. Producer needs timeout notification if consumer node is down.
Strengths of solution	Consumer does not hold up producer.
Weaknesses of solution	If producer produces messages more quickly than consumer can process them, the message queue will eventually overflow.
Applicability	Centralized and distributed environments: real-time systems, client/server and distribution applications
Related patterns	Asynchronous Message Communication with Callback
Reference	Chapter 12, Section 12.3.3

Figure A.9. Asynchronous Message Communication pattern

A.2.2 Asynchronous Message Communication with Callback Pattern

Pattern name	Asynchronous Message Communication with Callback
Aliases	Loosely Coupled Communication with Callback
Context	Concurrent or distributed systems
Problem	Concurrent or distributed application in which concurrent components need to communicate with each other. Client does not need to wait for service but does need to receive a reply later.
Summary of solution	Use synchronous communication between clients and service. Client sends request to service, which includes client operation (callback) handle. Client does not wait for reply. After service processes the client request, it uses the handle to call the client operation remotely (the callback).
Strengths of solution	Good way for client to communicate with service when it needs a reply but can continue executing and receive reply later
Weaknesses of solution	Suitable only if the client does not need to send multiple requests before receiving the first reply
Applicability	Distributed environments: client/server and distribution applications with multiple servers
Related patterns	Consider Bidirectional Asynchronous Message Communication as alternative pattern.
Reference	Chapter 15, Section 15.3.2

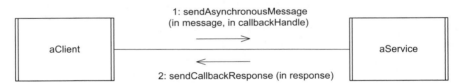

Figure A.10. Asynchronous Message Communication with Callback pattern

A.2.3 Bidirectional Asynchronous Message Communication Pattern

Pattern name	Bidirectional Asynchronous Message Communication
Aliases	Bidirectional Loosely Coupled Message Communication
Context	Concurrent or distributed systems
Problem	Concurrent or distributed application in which concurrent components need to communicate with each other. Producer does not need to wait for consumer, although it does need to receive replies later. Producer can send several requests before receiving first reply.
Summary of solution	Use two message queues between producer component and consumer component: one for messages from producer to consumer, and one for messages from consumer to producer. Producer sends message to consumer on P→C queue and continues. Consumer receives message. Messages are queued if consumer is busy. Consumer sends replies on C→P queue.
Strengths of solution	Producer does not get held up by consumer. Producer receives replies later, when it needs them.
Weaknesses of solution	If producer produces messages more quickly than consumer can process them, the message (P→C) queue will eventually overflow. If producer does not service replies quickly enough, the reply (C→P) queue will overflow.
Applicability	Centralized and distributed environments: real-time systems, client/server and distribution applications
Related patterns	Asynchronous Message Communication with Callback
Reference	Chapter 12, Section 12.3.3

Figure A.11. Bidirectional Asynchronous Message Communication pattern

A.2.4 Broadcast Pattern

Pattern name	Broadcast
Aliases	Broadcast Communication
Context	Distributed systems
Problem	Distributed application with multiple clients and services. At times, a service needs to send the same message to several clients.
Summary of solution	Crude form of group communication in which service sends a message to all clients, regardless of whether clients want the message or not. Client decides whether it wants to process the message or just discard the message.
Strengths of solution	Simple form of group communication
Weaknesses of solution	Places an additional load on the client, because the client may not want the message
Applicability	Distributed environments: client/server and distribution applications with multiple servers
Related patterns	Similar to Subscription/Notification, except that it is not selective
Reference	Chapter 17, Section 17.6.1

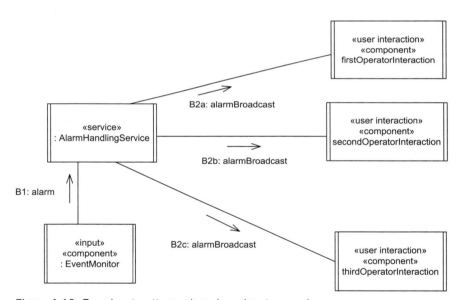

Figure A.12. Broadcast pattern: alarm broadcast example

A.2.5 Broker Forwarding Pattern

Pattern name	Broker Forwarding
Aliases	White Pages Broker Forwarding, Broker with Forwarding Design
Context	Distributed systems
Problem	Distributed application in which multiple clients communicate with multiple services. Clients do not know locations of services.
Summary of solution	Services register with broker. Client sends service request to broker. Broker forwards request to service. Service processes request and sends reply to broker. Broker forwards reply to client.
Strengths of solution	Location transparency: Services may relocate easily. Clients do not need to know locations of services.
Weaknesses of solution	Additional overhead because broker is involved in all message communication. Broker can become a bottleneck if there is a heavy load at the broker.
Applicability	Distributed environments: client/server and distribution applications with multiple servers
Related patterns	Similar to Broker Handle; more secure, but performance is not as good
Reference	Chapter 16, Section 16.2.2

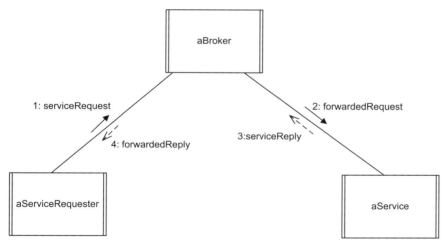

Figure A.13. Broker Forwarding pattern

A.2.6 Broker Handle Pattern

Pattern name	Broker Handle
Aliases	White Pages Broker Handle, Broker with Handle-Driven Design
Context	Distributed systems
Problem	Distributed application in which multiple clients communicate with multiple services. Clients do not know locations of services.
Summary of solution	Services register with broker. Client sends service request to broker. Broker returns service handle to client. Client uses service handle to make request to service. Service processes request and sends reply directly to client. Client can make multiple requests to service without broker involvement.
Strengths of solution	Location transparency: Services may relocate easily. Clients do not need to know locations of services.
Weaknesses of solution	Additional overhead because broker is involved in initial message communication. Broker can become a bottleneck if there is a heavy load at the broker. Client may keep outdated service handle instead of discarding.
Applicability	Distributed environments: client/server and distribution applications with multiple servers
Related patterns	Similar to Broker Forwarding, but with better performance
Reference	Chapter 16, Section 16.2.3

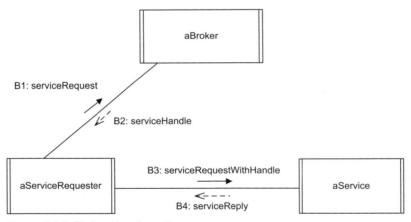

Figure A.14. Broker Handle pattern

A.2.7 Call/Return Pattern

Pattern name	Call/Return
Aliases	Operation invocation, method invocation
Context	Object-oriented programs and systems
Problem	An object needs to call an operation (also known as method) in a different object.
Summary of solution	A calling operation in a calling object invokes a called operation in a called object. Control is passed, together with any input parameters, from the calling operation to the called operation at the time of operation invocation. When the called operation finishes executing, it returns control and any output parameters to the calling operation.
Strengths of solution	This pattern is the only possible form of communication between objects in a sequential design.
Weaknesses of solution	If this pattern of communication is not suitable, then most likely a concurrent or distributed solution will be needed.
Applicability	Sequential object-oriented architectures, programs, and systems. A service designed as a sequential subsystem that communicates with internal objects using this pattern.
Related patterns	Software architectural communication patterns in which message passing is used instead of operation invocation.
Reference	Chapter 12, Section 12.3.2

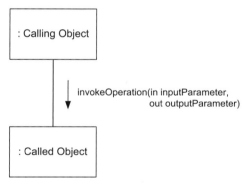

Figure A.15. Call/Return pattern

A.2.8 Negotiation Pattern

Pattern name	Negotiation
Aliases	Agent-Based Negotiation, Multi-Agent Negotiation
Context	Distributed multi-agent systems; service-oriented architectures
Problem	Client needs to negotiate with multiple services to find best available service.
Summary of solution	Client agent acts on behalf of client and makes a proposal to service agent, who acts on behalf of service. Service agent attempts to satisfy client's proposal, which might involve communication with other services. Having determined the available options, service agent then offers client agent one or more options that come closest to matching the original client agent proposal. Client agent may then request one of the options, propose further options, or reject the offer. If service agent can satisfy client agent request, client agent accepts the request; otherwise, it rejects the request.
Strengths of solution	Provides negotiation service to complement other services
Weaknesses of solution	Negotiation may be lengthy and inconclusive.
Applicability	Distributed environments: client/service and distribution applications with multiple services, service-oriented architectures
Related patterns	Often used in conjunction with broker patterns (Broker Forwarding, Broker Handle, Service Discovery)
Reference	Chapter 16, Section 16.5

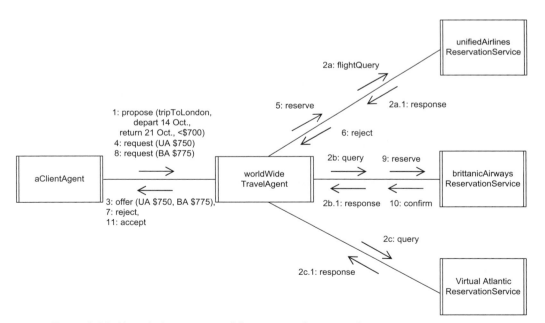

Figure A.16. Negotiation pattern: airline reservation example

A.2.9 Service Discovery Pattern

Pattern name	Service Discovery
Aliases	Yellow Pages Broker, Broker Trader, Discovery
Context	Distributed systems
Problem	Distributed application in which multiple clients communicate with multiple services. Client knows the type of service required but not the specific service.
Summary of solution	Use broker's discovery service. Services register with broker. Client sends discovery service request to broker. Broker returns names of all services that match discovery service request. Client selects a service and uses Broker Handle or Broker Forwarding pattern to communicate with service.
Strengths of solution	Location transparency: Services may relocate easily. Clients do not need to know specific service, only the service type.
Weaknesses of solution	Additional overhead because broker is involved in initial message communication. Broker can become a bottleneck if there is a heavy load at the broker.
Applicability	Distributed environments: client/service and distribution applications with multiple services
Related patterns	Other broker patterns (Broker Forwarding, Broker Handle)
Reference	Chapter 16, Section 16.2.4

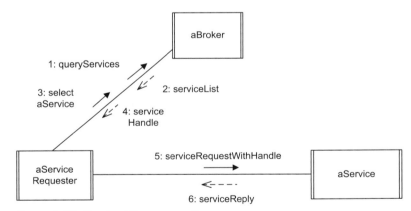

Figure A.17. Service Discovery pattern

A.2.10 Service Registration Pattern

Pattern name	Service Registration
Aliases	Broker Registration
Context	Software architectural design, distributed systems
Problem	Distributed application in which multiple clients communicate with multiple services. Clients do not know locations of services.
Summary of solution	Services register service information with broker, including service name, service description, and location. Clients send service requests to broker. Broker acts as intermediary between client and service.
Strengths of solution	Location transparency: Services may relocate easily. Clients do not need to know locations of services.
Weaknesses of solution	Additional overhead because broker is involved in message communication. Broker can become a bottleneck if there is a heavy load at the broker.
Applicability	Distributed environments: client/service and distribution applications with multiple services
Related patterns	Broker, Broker Forwarding, Broker Handle, Service Discovery
Reference	Chapter 16, Section 16.2.1

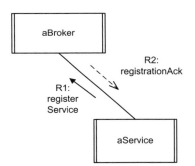

Figure A.18. Service Registration pattern

A.2.11 Subscription/Notification Pattern

Pattern name	Subscription/Notification
Aliases	Multicast
Context	Distributed systems
Problem	Distributed application with multiple clients and services. Clients want to receive messages of a given type.
Summary of solution	Selective form of group communication. Clients subscribe to receive messages of a given type. When service receives message of this type, it notifies all clients who have subscribed to it.
Strengths of solution	Selective form of group communication. Widely used on the Internet and in World Wide Web applications.
Weaknesses of solution	If client subscribes to too many services, it may unexpectedly receive a large number of messages.
Applicability	Distributed environments: client/service and distribution applications with multiple services
Related patterns	Similar to Broadcast, except that it is more selective
Reference	Chapter 17, Section 17.6.2

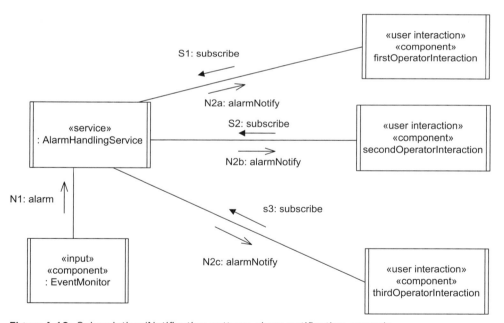

Figure A.19. Subscription/Notification pattern: alarm notification example

A.2.12 Synchronous Message Communication with Reply Pattern

Pattern name	Synchronous Message Communication with Reply
Aliases	Tightly Coupled Message Communication with Reply
Context	Concurrent or distributed systems
Problem	Concurrent or distributed application in which multiple clients communicate with a single service. Client needs to wait for reply from service.
Summary of solution	Use synchronous communication between clients and service. Client sends message to service and waits for reply. Use message queue at service because there are many clients. Service processes message FIFO. Service sends reply to client. Client is activated when it receives reply from service.
Strengths of solution	Good way for client to communicate with service when it needs a reply. Very common form of communication in client/server applications.
Weaknesses of solution	Client can be held up indefinitely if there is a heavy load at the server.
Applicability	Distributed environments: client/service and distribution applications with multiple services
Related patterns	Asynchronous Message Communication with Callback
Reference	Chapter 12, Section 12.3.4; Chapter 15, Section 15.3.1

Figure A.20. Synchronous Message Communication with Reply pattern

A.2.13 Synchronous Message Communication without Reply Pattern

Pattern name	Synchronous Message Communication without Reply
Aliases	Tightly Coupled Message Communication without Reply
Context	Concurrent or distributed systems
Problem	Concurrent or distributed application in which concurrent components need to communicate with each other. Producer needs to wait for consumer to accept message. Producer does not want to get ahead of consumer. There is no queue between producer and consumer.
Summary of solution	Use synchronous communication between producer and consumer. Producer sends message to consumer and waits for consumer to accept message. Consumer receives message. Consumer is suspended if no message is available. Consumer accepts message, thereby releasing producer.
Strengths of solution	Good way for producer to communicate with consumer when it wants confirmation that consumer received the message and producer does not want to get ahead of consumer.
Weaknesses of solution	Producer can be held up indefinitely if consumer is busy doing something else.
Applicability	Distributed environments: client/service and distribution applications with multiple services
Related patterns	Consider Synchronous Message Communication with Reply as alternative pattern.
Reference	Chapter 18, Section 18.8.3

Figure A.21. Synchronous Message Communication without Reply pattern

A.3 SOFTWARE ARCHITECTURAL TRANSACTION PATTERNS

This section describes the architectural transaction patterns, which address the transaction management in client/server architectures, in alphabetical order, using the standard template.

A.3.1 Compound Transaction Pattern

Pattern name	Compound Transaction
Aliases	
Context	Distributed systems, distributed databases
Problem	Client has a transaction requirement that can be broken down into smaller, separate flat transactions.
Summary of solution	Break down compound transaction into smaller atomic transactions, where each atomic transaction can be performed separately and rolled back separately.
Strengths of solution	Provides effective support for transactions that can be broken into two or more atomic transactions. Effective if a rollback or change is required to only one of the transactions.
Weaknesses of solution	More work is required to make sure that the individual atomic transactions are consistent with each other. More coordination is required if the whole compound transaction needs to be rolled back or modified.
Applicability	Transaction processing applications, distributed databases
Related patterns	Two-Phase Commit Protocol, Long-Living Transaction
Reference	Chapter 16, Section 16.4.2

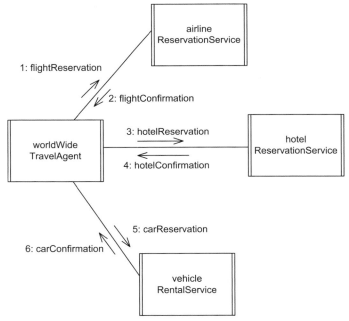

Figure A.22. Compound Transaction pattern: airline/hotel/car reservation example

A.3.2 Long-Living Transaction Pattern

Pattern name	Long-Living Transaction
Aliases	
Context	Distributed systems, distributed databases
Problem	Client has a long-living transaction requirement that has a human in the loop and that could take a long and possibly indefinite time to execute.
Summary of solution	Split a long-living transaction into two or more separate atomic transactions such that human decision making takes place between each successive pair of atomic transactions.
Strengths of solution	Provides effective support for long-living transactions that can be broken into two or more atomic transactions
Weaknesses of solution	Situations may change because of long delay between successive atomic transactions that constitute the long-living transaction, resulting in an unsuccessful long-living transaction.
Applicability	Transaction processing applications, distributed databases
Related patterns	Two-Phase Commit Protocol, Compound Transaction.
Reference	Chapter 16, Section 16.4.3

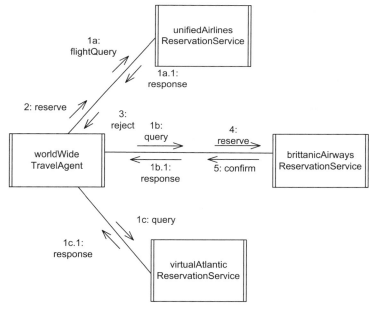

Figure A.23. Long-Living Transaction pattern: airline reservation example

A.3.3 Two-Phase Commit Protocol Pattern

Pattern name	Two-Phase Commit Protocol
Aliases	Atomic Transaction
Context	Distributed systems, distributed databases
Problem	Clients generate transactions and send them to the service for processing. A transaction is atomic (i.e., indivisible). It consists of two or more operations that perform a single logical function, and it must be completed in its entirety or not at all.
Summary of solution	For atomic transactions, services needed to commit or abort the transaction. The two-phase commit protocol is used to synchronize updates on different nodes in distributed applications. The result is that either the transaction is committed (in which case all updates succeed) or the transaction is aborted (in which case all updates fail).
Strengths of solution	Provides effective support for atomic transactions
Weaknesses of solution	Effective only for short transactions; that is, there are no long delays between the two phases of the transaction.
Applicability	Transaction processing applications, distributed databases
Related patterns	Compound Transaction, Long-Living Transaction
Reference	Chapter 16, Section 16.4.1

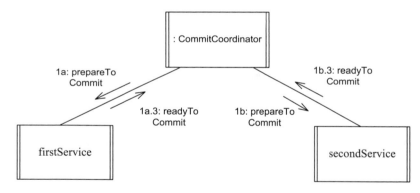

(a) First phase of Two-Phase Commit Protocol

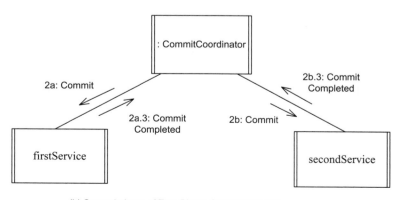

(b) Second phase of Two-Phase Commit Protocol

Figure A.24. Two-Phase Commit Protocol pattern

APPENDIX B

Teaching Considerations

B.1 OVERVIEW

The material in this book may be taught in different ways depending on the time available and the knowledge level of the students. This appendix describes possible academic and industrial courses that could be based on this book.

A prerequisite of these courses is an introductory course on software engineering that covers the software life cycle and the main activities in each phase of the life cycle. This prerequisite course would cover the material described in introductory books on software engineering, such as Pressman (Pressman 2009), or Sommerville (Sommerville 2010).

Each of these courses has three parts: description of the method, presentation of at least one case study using the method, and a hands-on design exercise for students to apply the method to a real-world problem.

B.2 SUGGESTED ACADEMIC COURSES

The following academic courses could be based on the material covered in this book:

1. A senior undergraduate or graduate level course on software modeling and design, with an overview of each of the architecture categories.
2. A variation on the preceding course is to concentrate on one of the architecture categories, such as service-oriented architectures or component-based software architectures, with a detailed case study and hands-on design exercise.
3. A design lab course is held as a follow-up course to the software modeling and design course (course 1) in which the students work in groups to develop a solution to a substantial software problem for one of the categories of software architecture. In this case, students could also implement all or part of the system.

B.3 SUGGESTED INDUSTRIAL COURSES

The following industrial courses could be based on the material covered in this book:

1. A course on software modeling and design. Concepts are presented briefly from Part I, and then the course would concentrate on Parts II and, depending on the length of the course, one or more of the architecture categories of Part III, together with a case study from Part IV in that category. For example, the course could concentrate on the design of service-oriented architectures and cover the Online Shopping System in detail. The hands-on design exercise would concentrate on the selected category of architecture. This course could be run at any length, from 2 to 5 days, depending on the level of detail covered.
2. A practical hands-on course in which each stage of the method is followed by a hands-on design lab. The design lab could be on a problem of the company's choice, assuming an in-house course. This course would focus on one architecture category, such as component-based software design. One option is to stage the course so that each phase of teaching the method is carried out in conjunction with that phase of an actual development project.

B.4 DESIGN EXERCISES

This discussion applies to both academic and industrial courses.

As part of the course, students should also work on one or more real-world problems, either individually or in groups. Whether one or more problems are tackled depends on the size of the problem and the length of the course. However, sufficient time should be allocated for students to work on the problems, because this is the best way for the students to really understand the method.

The following software problems may be used:

1. Microwave Oven System (real-time)
2. Supermarket Checkout System (client/server)
3. Factory Automation System (component-based software architecture)
4. Inventory Management System (service-oriented system)

Possible approaches are as follows:

1. Work on one problem throughout the course using one of the architecture categories, such as service-oriented architectures. This has the advantage that students get an in-depth appreciation of the method.
2. Divide the class up into groups. Each group solves a different kind of problem using a different category of architecture to solve the same problem. Time is allocated at the end of the course for each group to present its solution. A class discussion is held on the problems encountered while applying the method and how they were resolved.
3. A design lab course is held as a follow-up course to the course on software modeling and design, in which the students work in groups to develop a solution to a substantial software architecture for one of the architecture categories. In this case, students could also implement all or part of the system.

Glossary

abstract class   A *class* that cannot be directly instantiated (Booch, Rumbaugh, and Jacobson 2005). Compare *concrete class*.

abstract data type   A data type that is defined by the *operations* that manipulate it and thus has its representation details hidden.

abstract interface specification   A specification that defines the external view of the *information hiding class* – that is, all the information required by the user of the *class*.

abstract operation   An *operation* that is declared in an *abstract class* but not implemented.

action   A computation that executes as a result of a *state transition*.

active object   See *concurrent object*.

Activity diagram   A UML diagram depicting the flow of control and sequencing among activities.

actor   An outside user or related set of users who interact with the system (Rumbaugh, Booch, and Jacobson 2005).

aggregate class   A *class* that represents the whole in an *aggregation* relationship (Booch, Rumbaugh, and Jacobson 2005).

aggregate subsystem   A logical grouping of lower-level *subsystems* and/or *objects*.

aggregation   A weak form of *whole/part relationship*. Compare *composition*.

algorithm object   An object that encapsulates an algorithm used in the problem domain.

alternative feature   A *feature* that can be chosen in place of a different feature in the same *software product line*. Compare *common feature* and *optional feature*.

alternative use case   A *use case* that can be chosen in place of a different use case in the same *software product line*. Compare *kernel use case* and *optional use case*.

analog data   Continuous data that can, in principle, have an infinite number of values.

analysis modeling   A phase of the COMET use case–based software life cycle in which *static modeling* and *dynamic modeling* are performed. Compare *design modeling* and *requirements modeling*.

application deployment   A process for deciding which *component* instances are required, how component instances should be interconnected, and how the component instances should be allocated to physical *nodes* in a *distributed* environment.

application logic object   An *object* that hides the details of the application logic separately from the data being manipulated.

architectural pattern   See *software architectural pattern*.

association   A relationship between two or more *classes*.

asynchronous message communication   A form of communication in which a *concurrent* producer component (or task) sends a message to a concurrent consumer component (or task) and does not wait for a response; a message queue could potentially build up between the concurrent components (or tasks). Also referred to as *loosely coupled message communication*. Compare *synchronous message communication*.

at-least-one-of feature group   A *feature group* in which one or more *features* can be selected from the group, but at least one feature must be selected.

behavioral analysis   See *dynamic analysis*.

behavioral model   A model that describes the responses of the system to the inputs that the system receives from the external environment.

binary semaphore   A Boolean variable used to enforce *mutual exclusion*. Also referred to simply as *semaphore*.

black box specification   A specification that describes the externally visible characteristics of the system.

boundary object   A software *object* that interfaces to and communicates with the external environment.

broadcast communication   A form of group communication in which unsolicited messages are sent to all recipients.

broker   An intermediary in interactions between *clients* and *services*. Also referred to as *object broker* or *object request broker*.

brokered communication   Message communication in a *distributed* object environment in which *clients* and *services* interact via a *broker*.

business logic object   An *object* that encapsulates the business rules (business-specific application logic) for processing a *client* request.

callback   An *operation* handle sent by a *client* in an asynchronous request to a *service* and used by the *service* to respond to the client request.

CASE   See *Computer-Aided Software Engineering*.

category   A specifically defined division in a system of classification.

class   An *object* type; hence, a template for objects. An implementation of an *abstract data type*.

class diagram   A *UML* diagram that depicts a static view of a system in terms of *classes* and the relationships between classes. Compare *interaction diagram*.

class interface specification   A specification that defines the externally visible view of a *class*, including the specification of the *operations* provided by the class.

class structuring criteria   See *object structuring criteria*.

client   A requester of *services* in a *client/server system*. Compare *server*.

client/server system   A system that consists of *clients* that request *services* and one or more *servers* that provide *services*.

collaboration diagram   *UML* 1.x name for *communication diagram*.

Collaborative Object Modeling and Architectural Design Method (COMET)   An iterative use case driven and object-oriented method that addresses the requirements, analysis, and design modeling phases of the software development life cycle.

COMET   See *Collaborative Object Modeling and Architectural Design Method*.

commonality   The functionality that is common to all members of a *software product line*. Compare *variability*.

commonality/variability analysis   An approach for examining the functionality of a *software product line* to determine which functionality is common to all product line members and which is not.

common feature   A *feature* that must be provided by every member of the *software product line*. Compare *optional feature* and *alternative feature*.

Common Object Request Broker Architecture (CORBA)   An open systems standard for *middleware* technology, developed by the Object Management Group, that allows communication between *distributed* objects on heterogeneous platforms.

communication diagram   A *UML* 2 *interaction diagram* that depicts a dynamic view of a system in which *objects* interact by using messages. In *UML* 1.x, it is referred to as a *collaboration diagram*.

complex port   A *port* that supports both a *provided interface* and a *required interface*.

component   A *concurrent* self-contained *object* with a well-defined *interface*, capable of being used in different applications from that for which it was originally designed. Also referred to as *distributed component*.

component-based software architecture   A software architecture in which an infrastructure is provided that is specifically intended to accommodate preexisting *components*.

component-based system   A system in which an infrastructure is provided that is specifically intended to accommodate preexisting *components*.

component structuring criteria   A set of heuristics for assisting a designer in structuring a system into *components*.

composite component   A *component* that contains nested components. Also referred to as *composite subsystem*. Compare *simple component*.

composite object   An *object* that contains nested objects.

composite state   A *state* on a *statechart* that is decomposed into two or more *substates*. Also referred to as a *superstate*.

composite structure diagram   A *UML* 2 diagram that depicts the structure and interconnections of composite *classes*; often used to depict *components*, *ports*, and *connectors*.

composite subsystem   See *composite component*.

composition   A form of *whole/part relationship* that is stronger than an *aggregation*; the part *objects* are created, live, and die together with the composite (whole) object.

Computer-Aided Software Engineering (CASE) tool   A software tool that supports a software engineering method or notation.

concrete class   A *class* that can be directly instantiated (Booch, Rumbaugh, and Jacobson 2005). Compare *abstract class*.

concurrent   Referring to a problem, process, system, or application in which many activities happen in parallel, where the order of incoming *events* is not usually predictable and is often overlapping. A concurrent system or application has many threads of control. Compare *sequential*.

concurrent collaboration diagram   See *concurrent communication diagram*.

concurrent communication diagram   A *communication diagram* that depicts a network of *concurrent* objects and their interactions in the form of *asynchronous* and *synchronous message communication*. In *UML* 1.x, it is referred to as a *concurrent collaboration diagram*.

concurrent object   An autonomous *object* that has its own thread of control. Also referred to as an *active object, process, task, thread, concurrent process,* or *concurrent task*.

concurrent process   See *concurrent object*.

concurrent service   A *service* that services multiple *client* requests in parallel. Compare *sequential service*.

concurrent task   See *concurrent object*.

condition   The value of a Boolean variable that can be true or false over a finite interval of time.

connector   An *object* that encapsulates the interconnection protocol between two or more *components*.

constraint   A *condition* or restriction that must be true.

control object   An *object* that provides overall coordination for other objects.

coordinator object   An overall decision-making *object* that determines the overall sequencing for a collection of objects and is not *state-dependent*.

CORBA   See *Common Object Request Broker Architecture*.

critical section   The section of an *object*'s internal logic that is *mutually exclusive*.

data abstraction   An approach for defining a data structure or data type by the set of *operations* that manipulate it, thus separating and hiding the representation details.

data abstraction class   A *class* that encapsulates a data structure or data type, thereby hiding the representation details; *operations* provided by the class manipulate the hidden data.

database wrapper class   A *class* that hides how to access data stored in a database.

data replication   Duplication of data in more than one location in a *distributed application* to speed up access to the data.

deadlock   A situation in which two or more *concurrent objects* are suspended indefinitely because each concurrent object is waiting for a resource acquired by another concurrent object.

default feature   A *feature* out of a group of *alternative features* in the same *software product line* that is automatically chosen if no other feature is explicitly selected in its place.

delegation connector   A *connector* that joins the outer *port* of a *composite component* to the inner port of a *part component* such that messages arriving at the outer port are forwarded to the inner port.

demand driven task   A *task* that is activated on demand by the arrival of a message or internal event from another task.

deployment diagram   A *UML* diagram that shows the physical configuration of the system in terms of physical *nodes* and physical connections between the nodes, such as network connections.

design concept   A fundamental idea that can be applied to designing a system.

design method   A systematic approach for creating a design. The design method helps identify the design decisions to be made, the order in which to make them, and the criteria used in making them.

design modeling   A phase of the *COMET* use case–based software life cycle in which the *software architecture* of the system is designed. Compare *analysis modeling* and *requirements modeling*.

design notation   A graphical, symbolic, or textual means of describing a design.

design pattern   A description of a recurring design problem to be solved, a solution to the problem, and the context in which that solution works.

design strategy   An overall plan and direction for developing a design.

device interface object   An *information hiding object* that hides the characteristics of an I/O device and presents a virtual device *interface* to its users.

device I/O boundary object   A software *object* that receives input from and/or outputs to a hardware I/O device.

discrete data   Data that arrive at specific time intervals.

distributed   A system or application that is *concurrent* in nature and executes in an environment consisting of multiple *nodes*, which are in geographically different locations.

distributed application   An application that executes in a *distributed* environment.

distributed component   See *component*.

distributed kernel   The nucleus of an operating system that supports *distributed applications*.

distributed processing environment   A system configuration in which several geographically dispersed *nodes* are interconnected by means of a local area or wide area network.

distributed service   A *service* with functionality that is spread over several server *nodes*.

domain analysis   Analysis of a *software product line*.

domain engineering   See *software product line engineering*.

domain modeling   Modeling of a *software product line*.

domain-specific pattern   A software pattern that is specific to a given *software product line*.

domain-specific software architecture   See *software product line architecture*.

dynamic analysis   A strategy to help determine how the *objects* that participate in a *use case* interact. Also referred to as *behavioral analysis*.

dynamic model   A view of a problem or system in which control and sequencing are considered, either within an *object* by means of a *finite state machine*, or by consideration of the sequence of interaction among objects.

dynamic modeling   The process of developing the *dynamic model* of a system.

EJB   See *Enterprise JavaBeans*.

encapsulation   See *information hiding*.

Enterprise JavaBeans (EJB)   A Java-based component technology.

entity class   A class, in many cases persistent, whose instances are *objects* that encapsulate information.

entity object   A software *object*, in many cases persistent, which encapsulates information.

entry action   An *action* that is performed on entry into a *state*. Compare *exit action*.

event   (1) In *concurrent* processing, an external or internal stimulus used for synchronization purposes; it can be an external interrupt, a timer expiration, an internal signal, or an internal message. (2) On an *interaction diagram*, a stimulus that arrives at an *object* at a point in time. (3) On a *statechart*, the occurrence of a stimulus that can cause a *state transition* on a statechart.

event driven I/O device   An input/output device that generates an interrupt when it has produced some input or when it has finished processing an output operation.

event driven task   A *task* that is activated by an external event, such as an interrupt.

event sequencing logic   A description of how a task responds to each of its message or event inputs; in particular, what output is generated as a result of each input.

event synchronization   Control of *concurrent object* activation by means of signals. Three types of event synchronization are possible: external interrupts, timer expiration, and internal signals from other concurrent objects.

event trace   A time-ordered description of each external input and the time at which it occurred.

exactly-one-of feature group   A group of *features* from which one feature must always be selected for a given product line member. Also referred to as *one-and-only-one-of feature group*.

exit action   An *action* that is performed on exit from a *state*. Compare *entry action*.

Extensible Markup Language (XML)   A technology that allows different systems to interoperate through exchange of data and text.

external class   A *class* that is outside the system and part of the external environment.

external event   An *event* from an external object, typically an interrupt from an external I/O device. Compare *internal event*.

explicit feature   A *feature* that can be selected individually for a given application member of the *software product line*. Compare *implicit feature*.

family of systems   See *software product line*.

feature   A functional requirement; a reusable product line requirement or characteristic. A requirement or characteristic that is provided by one or more members of the *software product line*.

feature-based impact analysis   A means of assessing the impact of a *feature* on the *software product line*, usually through *dynamic modeling*.

feature/class dependency   The relationship in which one or more *classes* support a *feature* of a *software product line* (i.e., realize the functionality defined by the feature).

feature/class dependency analysis   A means of assessing *features* and *classes* in order to determine *feature/class dependency*.

feature group   A group of *features* with a particular *constraint* on their usage in a *software product line* member.

feature modeling The process of analyzing and specifying the *features* and *feature groups* of a *software product line*.

finite state machine A conceptual machine with a finite number of *states* and *state transitions* that are caused by input *events*. The notation used to represent a finite state machine is a *state transition diagram, statechart,* or *state transition table*. Also referred to simply as *state machine*.

formal method A software engineering method that uses a formal specification language – that is, a language with mathematically defined syntax and semantics.

generalization/specialization A relationship in which common attributes and *operations* are abstracted into a superclass (generalized class) and are then inherited by subclasses (specialized classes).

idiom A low-level pattern that describes an implementation solution specific to a given programming language.

implicit feature A *feature* that is not allowed to be selected individually. Compare *explicit feature*.

incremental software development See *iterative software development*.

information hiding The concept of encapsulating software design decisions in *objects* in such a way that the object's *interface* reveals only what its users need to know. Also referred to as *encapsulation*.

information hiding class A *class* that is structured according to the *information hiding* concept. The class hides a design decision that is considered likely to change.

information hiding class specification A specification of the external view of an information hiding class, including its operations.

information hiding object An instance of an *information hiding class*.

inheritance A mechanism for sharing and reusing code between *classes*.

input object A software device I/O boundary object that receives input from an external input device.

input/output (I/O) object A software device I/O boundary object that receives input from and sends output to an external I/O device.

integrated communication diagram A synthesis of several *communication diagrams* depicting all the *objects* and interactions shown on the individual diagrams. Also referred to as a consolidated collaboration diagram.

interaction diagram A *UML* diagram that depicts a dynamic view of a system in terms of *objects* and the sequence of messages passed between them. *Communication diagrams* and *sequence diagrams* are the two main types of interaction diagrams. Compare *class diagram*.

interface Specifies the externally visible *operations* of a *class, service,* or *component* without revealing the internal structure (implementation) of the operations.

internal event A means of synchronization between two *concurrent objects*. Compare *external event*.

I/O task structuring criteria A category of the *task structuring criteria* that addresses how device I/O objects are mapped to I/O tasks and when an I/O task is activated.

iterative software development An incremental approach to developing software in stages. Also referred to as *incremental software development*.

JavaBeans   A Java-based *component* technology.

Jini   A connection technology used in embedded systems and network-based computing applications for interconnecting computers and devices.

kernel   The core of a *software product line* or operating system.

kernel class   A *class* that is required by all members of the *software product line*. Compare *optional class* and *variant class*.

kernel component   A *component* that is required by all members of the *software product line*. Compare *optional component* and *variant component*.

kernel first approach   A *dynamic modeling* approach to determine the *objects* that realize the *kernel use cases* and how they interact.

kernel object   An *object* that is required by all members of the *software product line*; an instance of a *kernel class*. Compare *optional object* and *variant object*.

kernel system   A minimal member of the *software product line*, composed of the *kernel classes* and any required *default classes*.

kernel use case   A *use case* that is required by all members of the *software product line*. Compare *optional use case* and *alternative use case*.

loosely coupled message communication   See *asynchronous message communication*.

mathematical model   A mathematical representation of a system.

message dictionary   A collection of definitions of all aggregate messages depicted on *interaction diagrams* that consist of several individual messages.

message sequence description   A narrative description of the sequence of messages sent from source objects to destination objects, as depicted on a *communication diagram* or *sequence diagram*, describing what happens when each message arrives at a destination object.

middleware   A layer of software that sits above the heterogeneous operating system to provide a uniform platform above which *distributed applications* can run (Bacon 1997).

monitor   A data *object* that encapsulates data and has operations that are executed *mutually exclusively*.

multicast communication   See *subscription/notification*.

multiple readers and writers   An algorithm that allows multiple readers to access a shared data repository concurrently; however, writers must have mutually exclusive access to update the data repository. Compare *mutual exclusion*.

mutual exclusion   An algorithm that allows only one concurrent object to have access to shared data at a time, which can be enforced by means of *binary semaphores* or through the use of *monitors*. Compare *multiple readers and writers*.

mutually exclusive feature group   A *feature group* from which no more than one *feature* can be selected for any given *software product line* member. Compare *mutually inclusive feature*.

mutually inclusive feature   A *feature* that must be used together with another feature. Compare *mutually exclusive feature group*.

negotiation pattern   A communication approach used in multi-agent systems to allow software agents to negotiate with each other so that they can cooperatively make decisions.

node   In a *distributed* environment, a unit of deployment, usually consisting of one or more processors with shared memory.

object   An instance of a *class* that contains both hidden data and *operations* on that data.

object-based design   A software *design method* based on the concept of *information hiding*.

object broker   See *broker*.

object-oriented analysis   An analysis method that emphasizes identifying real-world objects in the problem domain and mapping them to software *objects*.

object-oriented design   A software *design method* based on the concept of *objects*, *classes*, and *inheritance*.

object request broker   See *broker*.

object structuring criteria   A set of heuristics for assisting a designer in structuring a system into *objects*. Also referred to as *class stucturing criteria*.

one-and-only-one-of feature group   See *exactly-one-of feature group*.

operation   A specification of a function performed by a *class*. An access procedure or function provided by a class.

optional class   A *class* that is required by some members of the *software product line*. Compare *kernel class* and *variant class*.

optional component   A *component* that is required by some members of the *software product line*. Compare *kernel component* and *variant component*.

optional feature   A *feature* that is required by some members of the *software product line*. Compare *common feature* and *alternative feature*.

optional object   An *object* that is required by some members of the *software product line*; an instance of an *optional class*. Compare *kernel object* and *variant object*.

optional use case   A *use case* that is required by some members of the *software product line*. Compare *kernel use case* and *alternative use case*.

output object   A software device I/O boundary object that sends output to an external output device

package   A grouping of *UML* model elements.

parameterized feature   A *feature* that defines a *software product line* parameter whose value needs to be defined for a given product line member.

part component   A *component* within a *composite component*.

passive I/O device   A device that does not generate an interrupt on completion of an input or output function. The input from a passive input device needs to be read either on a polled basis or on demand.

passive object   An *object* that has no thread of control; an object with *operations* that are invoked directly or indirectly by *concurrent objects*.

performance analysis   A quantitative analysis of a software design conceptually executing on a given hardware configuration with a given external workload applied to it.

performance model   An abstraction of the real computer system behavior, developed for the purpose of gaining greater insight into the performance of the system, whether or not the system actually exists.

periodic task   A *concurrent object* that is activated periodically (i.e., at regular, equally spaced intervals of time) by a *timer event*.

PLUS   See *Product Line UML-Based Software Engineering*.

port   A connection point through which a *component* communicates with other components.

prerequisite feature   A *feature* that another feature depends on.

primary actor   An *actor* that initiates a *use case*. Compare *secondary actor*.

priority message queue   A queue in which each message has an associated priority. The consumer always accepts higher-priority messages before lower-priority messages.

process   See *concurrent object*.

product family   See *software product line*.

product line   See *software product line*.

product line engineering   See *software product line engineering*.

Product Line UML-Based Software Engineering (PLUS)   A *design method* for *software product lines* that describes how to conduct *requirements modeling*, *analysis modeling*, and *design modeling* for software product lines in *UML*.

provided interface   Specifies the *operations* that a *component* (or *class*) must fulfill. Compare *required interface*.

provided port   A *port* that supports a *provided interface*. Compare *required port*.

proxy object   A software object that interfaces to and communicates with an external system or subsystem.

pseudocode   A form of structured English used to describe the algorithmic details of an *object* or *class*.

queuing model   A mathematical representation of a computer system that analyzes contention for limited resources.

Rational Unified Process (RUP)   See *Unified Software Development Process (USDP)*.

real-time   Referring to a problem, system, or application that is *concurrent* in nature and has timing *constraints* whereby incoming *events* must be processed within a given time frame.

remote method invocation (RMI)   A *middleware* technology that allows *distributed* Java *objects* to communicate with each other.

required interface   The operations that another *component* (or *class*) provides for a given component (or class) to operate properly in a particular environment. Compare *provided interface*.

required port   A *port* that supports a *required interface*. Compare *provided port*.

requirements modeling   A phase of the *COMET* use case–based software life cycle in which the functional requirements of the system are determined through the development of *use case models*. Compare *analysis modeling* and *design modeling*.

reuse category   A classification of a modeling element (*use case*, *feature*, *class*, etc.) in a *software product line* by its reuse properties, such as *kernel* or *optional*. Compare *role category*.

reuse stereotype   A *UML* notation for depicting the *reuse category* of a modeling element.

RMI   See *remote method invocation*.

role category   A classification of a modeling element (*class*, *object*, *component*) by the role it plays in an application, such as *control* or *entity*. Compare *reuse category*.

role stereotype   A *UML* notation for depicting the *role category* of a modeling element.

RUP   See *Rational Unified Process*.

scenario   A specific path through a *use case* or *object interaction diagram*.

secondary actor   An *actor* that participates in (but does not initiate) a *use case*. Compare *primary actor*.

semaphore   See *binary semaphore*.

sequence diagram   A *UML interaction diagram* that depicts a dynamic view of a system in which the objects participating in the interaction are depicted horizontally, time is represented by the vertical dimension, and the sequence of message interactions is depicted from top to bottom.

sequential   Referring to a problem, process, system, or application in which activities happen in strict sequence; a sequential system or application has only one thread of control. Compare *concurrent*.

sequential service   A *service* that completes one *client* request before it starts servicing the next. Compare *concurrent service*.

server   A system *node* that provides one or more services

service   In SOA, software functionality that is distributed, autonomous, heterogeneous, loosely coupled, discoverable, and reusable.

service object   A software object that provides a *service* for other objects.

service-oriented architecture (SOA)   A software architecture composed of services that are distributed, autonomous, heterogeneous, loosely coupled, discoverable, and reusable.

simple component   A *component* that has no components within it. Compare *composite component*.

simulation model   An algorithmic representation of a system, reflecting system structure and behavior, that explicitly recognizes the passage of time, hence providing a means of analyzing the behavior of the system over time.

SOA   See *service-oriented architecture*.

software application engineering   A process within *software product line engineering* in which the *software product line architecture* is adapted and configured to produce a given software application, which is a member of the *software product line*. Also referred to as *application engineering*.

software architectural pattern   A recurring architecture used in a variety of software applications. Also referred to simply as *architectural pattern*.

software architectural communication pattern   A *software architectural pattern* that addresses the dynamic communication among *distributed components* of the *software architecture*.

software architectural structure pattern   A *software architectural pattern* that addresses the static structure of the *software architecture*.

software architecture   A high-level design that describes the overall structure of a system in terms of *components* and their interconnections, separately from the internal details of the individual components.

software product family   See *software product line*.

software product family engineering   See *software product line engineering*.

software product line   A family of software systems that have some common functionality and some variable functionality; a set of software-intensive systems sharing a common, managed set of *features* that satisfy the specific needs of a particular market segment or mission and that are developed from a common set of core assets in a prescribed way (Clements and Northrop 2002). Also referred to as *family of systems*, *software product family*, *product family*, or *product line*.

software product line architecture   The architecture for a family of products, which describes the kernel, optional, and variable *components* in the *software product line*, and their interconnections. Also referred to as *domain-specific software architecture*.

software product line engineering   A process for analyzing the *commonality* and *variability* in a *software product line*, and developing a product line *use case model*, product line *analysis model*, *software product line architecture*, and reusable *components*. Also referred to as *software product family engineering*, *product family engineering*, or *product line engineering*.

software system context class diagram   A *class diagram* that depicts the relationships between the software system (depicted as one *aggregate class*) and the *external classes* outside the software system. Compare *system context class diagram*.

software system context model   A model of a software system boundary that is depicted on a *software system context class diagram*. Compare *system context model*.

spiral model   A risk-driven software process model.

state   A recognizable situation that exists over an interval of time.

statechart   A hierarchical *state transition diagram* in which the *nodes* represent *states* and the arcs represent *state transitions*.

statechart diagram   UML 1.x name for state machine diagram.

state-dependent control object   An *object* that hides the details of a *finite state machine*; that is, the object encapsulates a *statechart*, a *state transition diagram*, or the contents of a *state transition table*.

state machine   See *finite state machine*.

state machine diagram   A UML depiction of a *finite state machine or statechart*.

state transition   A change in *state* that is caused by an input *event*.

state transition diagram   A graphical representation of a *finite state machine* in which the *nodes* represent *states* and the arcs represent transitions between states.

state transition table   A tabular representation of a *finite state machine*.

static modeling   The process of developing a static, structural view of a problem, system, or *software product line*.

stereotype   A classification that defines a new building block that is derived from an existing *UML* modeling element but is tailored to the modeler's problem (Booch, Rumbaugh, and Jacobson 2005).

subscription/notification   A form of group communication in which subscribers receive *event* notifications. Also referred to as *multicast communication*.

substate   A *state* that is part of a *composite state*.

subsystem   A significant part of the whole system; a subsystem provides a subset of the overall system functionality.

subsystem communication diagram   A high-level *communication diagram* depicting the *subsystems* and their interactions.

superstate   A *composite state*.

synchronous message communication   A form of communication in which a producer *component* (or *concurrent task*) sends a message to a consumer component (or concurrent task) and then immediately waits for an acknowledgment. Also referred to as *tightly coupled message communication*. Compare *asynchronous message communication*.

synchronous message communication with reply   A form of communication in which a client *component* (or *producer task*) sends a message to a service component (or consumer task) and then waits for a reply. Also referred to as *tightly coupled message communication with reply*.

synchronous message communication without reply   A form of communication in which a producer *component* (or *task*) sends a message to a consumer component (or task) and then waits for acceptance of the message by the consumer. Also referred to as *tightly coupled message communication without reply*.

system context class diagram   A *class diagram* that depicts the relationships between the system (depicted as one *aggregate class*) and the *external classes* outside the system. Compare *software system context class diagram*.

system context model   A model of a system (hardware and software) boundary that is depicted on a *system context class diagram*. Compare *software system context model*.

system interface object   An *object* that hides the *interface* to an external system or *subsystem*.

task   See *concurrent object*.

task architecture   A description of the *concurrent objects* in a system or *subsystem* in terms of their *interfaces* and interconnections.

thread   See *concurrent object*.

tightly coupled message communication   See *synchronous message communication*.

tightly coupled message communication with reply   See *synchronous message communication with reply*.

tightly coupled message communication without reply   See *synchronous message communication without reply*.

timer event   A stimulus used for the periodic activation of a *concurrent object*.

timer object   A *control object* that is activated by an external timer.

timing diagram   A diagram that shows the time-ordered execution sequence of a group of *concurrent objects*.

transaction   A request from a *client* to a *service* consisting of two or more *operations* that must be completed in its entirety or not at all.

two-phase commit protocol   An algorithm used in *distributed applications* to synchronize updates to ensure that an atomic transaction is either committed or aborted.

UML   See *Unified Modeling Language*.

Unified Modeling Language (UML)   A language for visualizing, specifying, constructing, and documenting the artifacts of a software-intensive system (Booch, Rumbaugh, and Jacobson 2005).

Unified Software Development Process (USDP)   An iterative *use case* – driven software process that uses the *UML* notation. Also known as the *Rational Unified Process (RUP)*.

USDP   See *Unified Software Development Process*.

use case   A description of a sequence of interactions between one or more *actors* and the system.

use case diagram   A *UML* diagram that shows a set of *use cases* and *actors* and their relationships (Booch, Rumbaugh, and Jacobson 2005).

use case model   A description of the functional requirements of the system in terms of *actors* and *use cases.*

use case modeling   The process of developing the *use cases* of a system or *software product line.*

use case package   A group of related *use cases.*

user interaction object   A software *object* that interacts with and interfaces to a human user.

variability   The functionality that is provided by some, but not all, members of the *software product line.* Compare *commonality.*

variant class   A *class* that is similar to, but not identical to, another class; a subclass that is similar to, but not identical to, another subclass of the same superclass. Compare *kernel class* and *optional class.*

variant component   A *component* that is similar to, but not identical to, another component. Compare *kernel component* and *optional component.*

variant object   An *object* that is similar to, but not identical to, another object; an instance of a *variant class.* Compare *kernel object* and *optional object.*

variation point   A location at which change can occur in a *software product line* artifact (e.g., in a *use case* or *class*).

visibility   The characteristic that defines whether an element of a *class* is visible from outside the class.

Web service   Business functionality provided by a service provider over the Internet to users of the World Wide Web.

white page brokering   A pattern of communication between a *client* and a *broker* in which the client knows the service required but not the location. Compare *yellow page brokering.*

whole/part relationship   A *composition* or *aggregation* relationship in which a whole class is composed of part classes.

wrapper component   A *distributed component* that handles the communication and management of *client* requests to legacy applications (Mowbray and Ruh 1997).

XML   See *Extensible Markup Language.*

yellow page brokering   A pattern of communication between a *client* and a *broker* in which the client knows the type of service required but not the specific service. Compare *white page brokering.*

zero-or-more-of feature group   A *feature group* consisting of *optional features.*

zero-or-one-of feature group   A *feature group* in which all *features* are *mutually exclusive.*

Answers to Exercises

Bold numbers indicate questions and alphabets within parenthesis indicate answers.

CHAPTER 1: INTRODUCTION

1. (b) **2.** (d) **3.** (c) **4.** (b) **5.** (c) **6.** (d) **7.** (c) **8.** (a) **9.** (b) **10.** (c)

CHAPTER 2: OVERVIEW OF THE UML NOTATION

1. (b) **2.** (a) **3.** (c) **4.** (a) **5.** (a) **6.** (b) **7.** (c) **8.** (d) **9.** (d) **10.** (c)

CHAPTER 3: SOFTWARE LIFE CYCLE MODELS AND PROCESSES

1. (c) **2.** (b) **3.** (d) **4.** (b) **5.** (d) **6.** (c) **7.** (b) **8.** (c) **9.** (c) **10.** (d)

CHAPTER 4: SOFTWARE DESIGN AND ARCHITECTURE CONCEPTS

1. (c) **2.** (c) **3.** (c) **4.** (c) **5.** (c) **6.** (b) **7.** (c) **8.** (b) **9.** (b) **10.** (b)

CHAPTER 5: OVERVIEW OF SOFTWARE MODELING AND DESIGN METHOD

1. (b) **2.** (c) **3.** (d) **4.** (b) **5.** (c) **6.** (b)

CHAPTER 6: USE CASE MODELING

1. (c) **2.** (c) **3.** (b) **4.** (c) **5.** (b) **6.** (c) **7.** (d) **8.** (d) **9.** (a) **10.** (c)

CHAPTER 7: STATIC MODELING

1. (d) **2.** (c) **3.** (a) **4.** (d) **5.** (c) **6.** (b) **7.** (d) **8.** (c) **9.** (c) **10.** (b)

CHAPTER 8: OBJECT AND CLASS STRUCTURING

1. (c) **2.** (c) **3.** (d) **4.** (c) **5.** (c) **6.** (c) **7.** (a) **8.** (a) **9.** (a) **10.** (b)

CHAPTER 9: DYNAMIC INTERACTION MODELING

1. (c)   **2.** (d)   **3.** (c)   **4.** (c)   **5.** (b)   **6.** (c)   **7.** (a)   **8.** (a)   **9.** (c)   **10.** (d)

CHAPTER 10: FINITE STATE MACHINES

1. (a)   **2.** (a)   **3.** (d)   **4.** (a)   **5.** (b)   **6.** (c)   **7.** (a)   **8.** (b)   **9.** (a)   **10.** (b)

CHAPTER 11: STATE-DEPENDENT DYNAMIC INTERACTION MODELING

1. (c)   **2.** (c)   **3.** (a)   **4.** (b)   **5.** (b)   **6.** (d)   **7.** (b)   **8.** (a)   **9.** (a)   **10.** (a)

CHAPTER 12: OVERVIEW OF SOFTWARE ARCHITECTURE

1. (c)   **2.** (b)   **3.** (b)   **4.** (d)   **5.** (c)   **6.** (a)   **7.** (a)   **8.** (b)   **9.** (b)   **10.** (a)

CHAPTER 13: SOFTWARE SUBSYSTEM ARCHITECTURAL DESIGN

1. (b)   **2.** (a)   **3.** (b)   **4.** (b)   **5.** (a)   **6.** (c)   **7.** (b)   **8.** (c)   **9.** (d)   **10.** (a)

CHAPTER 14: DESIGNING OBJECT-ORIENTED SOFTWARE ARCHITECTURES

1. (b)   **2.** (b)   **3.** (d)   **4.** (c)   **5.** (d)   **6.** (d)   **7.** (d)   **8.** (d)   **9.** (c)   **10.** (b)
11. (d)   **12.** (d)

CHAPTER 15: DESIGNING CLIENT/SERVER SOFTWARE ARCHITECTURES

1. (d)   **2.** (b)   **3.** (d)   **4.** (b)   **5.** (a)   **6.** (b)   **7.** (c)   **8.** (a)   **9.** (d)   **10.** (c)

CHAPTER 16: DESIGNING SERVICE-ORIENTED ARCHITECTURES

1. (b)   **2.** (c)   **3.** (a)   **4.** (d)   **5.** (a)   **6.** (b)   **7.** (b)   **8.** (c)   **9.** (c)   **10.** (d)

CHAPTER 17: DESIGNING COMPONENT-BASED SOFTWARE ARCHITECTURES

1. (d)   **2.** (a)   **3.** (a)   **4.** (b)   **5.** (c)   **6.** (a)   **7.** (c)   **8.** (d)   **9.** (c)   **10.** (a)

CHAPTER 18: DESIGNING CONCURRENT AND REAL-TIME SOFTWARE ARCHITECTURES

1. (d)   **2.** (c)   **3.** (b)   **4.** (b)   **5.** (b)   **6.** (c)   **7.** (b)   **8.** (a)   **9.** (c)   **10.** (d)

CHAPTER 19: DESIGNING SOFTWARE PRODUCT LINE ARCHITECTURES

1. (a)   **2.** (c)   **3.** (b)   **4.** (a)   **5.** (b)   **6.** (c)   **7.** (d)   **8.** (c)   **9.** (b)   **10.** (c)

CHAPTER 20: SOFTWARE QUALITY ATTRIBUTES

1. (b)   **2.** (b)   **3.** (c)   **4.** (b)   **5.** (a)   **6.** (b)   **7.** (b)   **8.** (c)   **9.** (c)   **10.** (b)

Bibliography

Alexander, C. 1979. *The Timeless Way of Building*. New York: Oxford University Press.

Ammann, P., and J. Offutt. 2008. *Introduction to Software Testing*. New York: Cambridge University Press.

Ambler, S. 2005. *The Elements of UML 2.0 Style*. New York: Cambridge University Press.

Atkinson, C., J. Bayer, O. Laitenberger, et al. 2002. *Component-Based Product Line Engineering with UML*. Boston: Addison-Wesley.

Awad, M., J. Kuusela, and J. Ziegler. 1996. *Object-Oriented Technology for RealTime Systems: A Practical Approach Using OMT and Fusion*. Upper Saddle River, NJ: Prentice Hall.

Bacon, J. 2003. *Concurrent Systems: An Integrated Approach to Operating Systems, Database, and Distributed Systems*, 3rd ed. Reading, MA: Addison-Wesley.

Bass, L., P. Clements, and R. Kazman. 2003. *Software Architecture in Practice*, 2nd ed. Boston: Addison-Wesley.

Beizer, B., 1984. *Software System Testing and Quality Assurance*. New York: Van Nostrand.

Berners-Lee, T., R. Cailliau, A. Loutonen, et al. 1994. "The World-Wide Web." *Communications of the ACM* 37: 76–82.

Bjorkander, M., and C. Kobryn. 2003. "Architecting Systems with UML 2.0." *IEEE Software* 20(4): 57–61.

Blaha, J. M., and W. Premerlani. 1998. *"Object-Oriented Modeling and Design for Database Applications*. Upper Saddle River, NJ: Prentice Hall.

Blaha, J. M., and J. Rumbaugh. 2005. *"Object-Oriented Modeling and Design with UML*, 2nd ed. Upper Saddle River, NJ: Prentice Hall.

Boehm, B. 1981. *Software Engineering Economics*. Upper Saddle River, NJ: Prentice Hall.

Boehm, B. 1988. "A Spiral Model of Software Development and Enhancement." *IEEE Computer* 21(5): 61–72.

Boehm, B., and F. Belz. 1990. "Experiences with the Spiral Model as a Process Model Generator." In *Proceedings of the 5th International Software Process Workshop: Experience with Software Process Models, Kennebunkport, Maine, USA, October 10–13, 1989*, D. E. Perry (ed.), pp. 43–45. Los Alamitos, CA: IEEE Computer Society Press.

Boehm, B. 2006. "A view of 20th and 21st century software engineering." In *Proceedings of the International Conference on Software Engineering, May 20–26, 2006, Shanghai, China*, pp. 12–29. Los Alamitos, CA: IEEE Computer Society Press.

Booch, G., R. A. Maksimchuk, M. W. Engel, et al. 2007. *Object-Oriented Analysis and Design with Applications*, 3rd ed. Boston: Addison-Wesley.

Booch, G., J. Rumbaugh, and I. Jacobson. 2005. *The Unified Modeling Language User Guide*, 2nd ed. Boston: Addison-Wesley.

Bosch, J. 2000. *Design & Use of Software Architectures: Adopting and Evolving a Product-Line Approach*. Boston: Addison-Wesley.

Brooks, F. 1995. *The Mythical Man-Month: Essays on Software Engineering*, anniversary ed. Boston: Addison-Wesley.

Brown, A. 2000. *Large-Scale, Component-Based Development*. Upper Saddle River, NJ: Prentice Hall.

Budgen, D. 2003. *Software Design*, 2nd ed. Boston: Addison-Wesley.

Buhr, R. J. A., and R. S. Casselman. 1996. *Use Case Maps for Object-Oriented Systems*. Upper Saddle River, NJ: Prentice Hall.

Buschmann, F., R. Meunier, H. Rohnert, et al. 1996. *Pattern-Oriented Software Architecture: A System of Patterns*. New York: Wiley.

Cheesman, J., and J. Daniels. 2001. *UML Components*. Boston: Addison-Wesley.

Clements, P., and Northrop, L. 2002. *Software Product Lines: Practices and Patterns*. Boston: Addison-Wesley.

Coad, P., and E. Yourdon. 1991. *Object-Oriented Analysis*. Upper Saddle River, NJ: Prentice Hall.

Coad, P., and E. Yourdon. 1992. *Object-Oriented Design*. Upper Saddle River, NJ: Prentice Hall.

Coleman, D., P. Arnold, S. Bodoff, et al. 1993. *Object-Oriented Development: The Fusion Method*. Upper Saddle River, NJ: Prentice Hall.

Comer, D. E. 2008. *Computer Networks and Internets*, 5th ed. Upper Saddle River, NJ: Pearson/Prentice Hall.

Dollimore J., T. Kindberg, and G. Coulouris. 2005. *Distributed Systems: Concepts and Design*, 4th ed. Boston: Addison-Wesley.

Dahl, O., and C. A. R. Hoare. 1972. "Hierarchical Program Structures." In *Structured Programming*, O. Dahl, E. W. Dijkstra, and C. A. R. Hoare (eds.), pp. 175–220. London: Academic Press.

Davis, A. 1993. *Software Requirements: Objects, Functions, and States*, 2nd ed. Upper Saddle River, NJ: Prentice Hall.

Dijkstra, E. W. 1968. "The Structure of T. H. E. Multiprogramming System." *Communications of the ACM* 11: 341–346.

Douglass, B. P. 1999. *Doing Hard Time: Developing Real-Time Systems with UML, Objects, Frameworks, and Patterns*. Reading, MA: Addison-Wesley.

Douglass, B. P. 2002. *Real-Time Design Patterns: Robust Scalable Architecture for Real-Time Systems*. Boston: Addison-Wesley.

Douglass, B. P. 2004. *Real Time UML: Advances in the UML for Real-Time Systems*, 3rd ed. Boston: Addison-Wesley.

Eeles, P., K. Houston, and W. Kozaczynski. 2002. *Building J2EE Applications with the Rational Unified Process*. Boston: Addison-Wesley.

Eriksson, H. E., M. Penker, B. Lyons, et al. 2004. *UML 2 Toolkit*. Indianapolis, IN: Wiley.

Erl, T. 2006. *Service-Oriented Architecture (SOA): Concepts, Technology, and Design*. Upper Saddle River, NJ: Prentice Hall.

Erl, T. 2008. *SOA Principles of Service Design*. Upper Saddle River, NJ: Prentice Hall.

Erl, T. 2009. *SOA Design Patterns*. Upper Saddle River, NJ: Prentice Hall.

Espinoza H., D. Cancila, B. Selic and S. Gérard. 2009. "Challenges in Combining SysML and MARTE for Model-Based Design of Embedded Systems." Berlin: Springer LNCS 5562, pp. 98–113.

Fowler, M. 2002. *Patterns of Enterprise Application Architecture*. Boston: Addison-Wesley.

Fowler, M. 2004. *UML Distilled: Applying the Standard Object Modeling Language*, 3rd ed. Boston: Addison-Wesley.

Freeman, P. 1983a. "The Context of Design." In *Tutorial on Software Design Techniques*, 4th ed., P. Freeman and A. I. Wasserman (eds.), pp. 2–4. Silver Spring, MD: IEEE Computer Society Press.

Freeman, P. 1983b. "The Nature of Design." In *Tutorial on Software Design Techniques*, 4th ed., P. Freemanand A. I. Wasserman (eds.), pp. 46–53. Silver Spring, MD: IEEE Computer Society Press.

Freeman, P., and A. I. Wasserman (eds.). 1983. *Tutorial on Software Design Techniques*, 4th ed. Silver Spring, MD: IEEE Computer Society Press.

Friedenthal., A. Moore, and R. Steiner. 2009. A Practical Guide to SysML: The Systems Modeling Language. Burlington, MA: Morgan Kaufmann.

Gamma, E., R. Helm, R. Johnson, et al. 1995. *Design Patterns: Elements of Reusable Object-Oriented Software*. Reading, MA: Addison-Wesley.

Gomaa, H. 1984. "A Software Design Method for Real Time Systems." *Communications of the ACM* 27(9): 938–949.

Gomaa, H. 1986. "Software Development of Real Time Systems." *Communications of the ACM* 29(7): 657–668.

Gomaa, H. 1989a. "A Software Design Method for Distributed Real-Time Applications." *Journal of Systems and Software* 9: 81–94.

Gomaa, H. 1989b. "Structuring Criteria for Real Time System Design." In *Proceedings of the 11th International Conference on Software Engineering, May 15–18, 1989, Pittsburgh, PA, USA*, pp. 290–301. Los Alamitos, CA: IEEE Computer Society Press.

Gomaa, H. 1990. "The Impact of Prototyping on Software System Engineering." In *Systems and Software Requirements Engineering*, pp. 431–440. Los Alamitos, CA: IEEE Computer Society Press.

Gomaa, H. 1993. *Software Design Methods for Concurrent and Real-Time Systems*. Reading, MA: Addison-Wesley.

Gomaa, H. 1995. "Reusable Software Requirements and Architectures for Families of Systems." *Journal of Systems and Software* 28: 189–202.

Gomaa, H. 2001. "Use Cases for Distributed Real-Time Software Architectures." In *Engineering of Distributed Control Systems*, L. R. Welch and D. K. Hammer (eds.), pp. 1–18. Commack, NY: Nova Science.

Gomaa, H. 1999. "Inter-Agent Communication in Cooperative Information Agent-Based Systems." In *Proceedings of the Cooperative Information Agents III: Third International Workshop, CIA'99, Uppsala, Sweden, July 31–August 2, 1999*, pp. 137–148. Berlin: Springer.

Gomaa, H. 2000. *Designing Concurrent, Distributed, and Real-Time Applications with UML*. Boston: Addison-Wesley.

Gomaa, H. 2002. "Concurrent Systems Design." In *Encyclopedia of Software Engineering*, 2nd ed., J. Marciniak (ed.), pp. 172–179. New York: Wiley.

Gomaa, H. 2005a. *Designing Software Product Lines with UML*. Boston: Addison-Wesley.

Gomaa, H. 2005b. "Modern Software Design Methods for Concurrent and Real-Time Systems." In *Software Engineering*, vol. 1: *The Development Process*. 3rd ed. M. Dorfman and R. Thayer (eds.), pp. 221–234. Hoboken, NJ: Wiley Interscience.

Gomaa, H. 2006. "A Software Modeling Odyssey: Designing Evolutionary Architecture-centric Real-Time Systems and Product Lines." Keynote paper, *Proceedings of the ACM/IEEE 9th International Conference on Model-Driven Engineering, Languages and Systems, Genoa, Italy, October 2006,* pp. 1–15. Springer Verlag LNCS 4199.

Gomaa, H. 2008. "Model-based Software Design of Real-Time Embedded Systems." *International Journal of Software Engineering* 1(1): 19–41.

Gomaa, H. 2009. "Concurrent Programming." In *Encyclopedia of Computer Science and Engineering*, Benjamin Wah (ed.), pp. 648–655. Hoboken, NJ: Wiley.

Gomaa, H., and G. Farrukh. 1997. "Automated Configuration of Distributed Applications from Reusable Software Architectures." In *Proceedings of the IEEE International Conference on Automated Software Engineering, Lake Tahoe, November 1997,* pp. 193–200. Los Alamitos, CA: IEEE Computer Society Press.

Gomaa, H., and G. A. Farrukh. 1999. "Methods and Tools for the Automated Configuration of Distributed Applications from Reusable Software Architectures and Components." *IEEE Proceedings – Software* 146(6): 277–290.

Gomaa, H., and D. Menasce. 2001. "Performance Engineering of Component-Based Distributed Software Systems." In *Performance Engineering: State of the Art and Current Trends*, R. Dumke, C. Rautenstrauch, A. Schmietendorf, et al. (eds.), pp. 40–55. Berlin: Springer.

Gomaa, H., and E. O'Hara. 1998. "Dynamic Navigation in Multiple View Software Specifications and Designs." *Journal of Systems and Software* 41: 93–103.

Gomaa, H., and D. B. H. Scott. 1981. "Prototyping as a Tool in the Specification of User Requirements." In *Proceedings of the 5th International Conference on Software Engineering, San Diego, March 1981,* pp. 333–342. New York: ACM Press.

Gomaa, H., and M. E. Shin. 2002. "Multiple-View Meta-Modeling of Software Product Lines." In *Eighth International Conference on Engineering of Complex Computer Systems, December 2–4, 2002, Greenbelt, Maryland,* pp. 238–246. Los Alamitos, CA: IEEE Computer Society Press.

Gomaa, H., and D. Webber. 2004. "Modeling Adaptive and Evolvable Software Product Lines Using the Variation Point Model." In *Proceedings of the 37th Annual Hawaii International Conference on System Sciences, HICSS'04: January 5–8, 2004, Big Island, Hawaii,* pp. 1–10. Los Alamitos, CA: IEEE Computer Society Press.

Gomaa, H., L. Kerschberg, V. Sugumaran, et al. 1996. "A Knowledge-Based Software Engineering Environment for Reusable Software Requirements and Architectures." *Journal of Automated Software Engineering* 3(3/4): 285–307.

Gomaa, H., D. Menasce, and L. Kerschberg. 1996. "A Software Architectural Design Method for Large-Scale Distributed Information Systems." *Journal of Distributed Systems Engineering* 3(3): 162–172.

Griss, M., J. Favaro, and M. d'Alessandro. 1998. "Integrating Feature Modeling with the RSEB." In *Fifth International Conference on Software Reuse: Proceedings: June 2–5, 1998, Victoria, British Columbia, Canada*, P. Devanbu and J. Poulin (eds.), pp. 1–10. Los Alamitos, CA: IEEE Computer Society Press.

Harel, D. 1987. "Statecharts: A Visual Formalism for Complex Systems." *Science of Computer Programming* 8: 231–274.

Harel, D. 1988. "On Visual Formalisms." *Communications of the ACM* 31: 514–530.

Harel, D., and E. Gery. 1996. "Executable Object Modeling with Statecharts." In *Proceedings of the 18th International Conference on Software Engineering, Berlin, March 1996*, pp. 246–257. Los Alamitos, CA: IEEE Computer Society Press.

Harel, D., and M. Politi. 1998. *Modeling Reactive Systems with Statecharts: The Statemate Approach*. New York: McGraw-Hill.

Hoffman, D., and D. Weiss (eds.). 2001. *Software Fundamentals: Collected Papers by David L. Parnas*. Boston: Addison-Wesley.

Hofmeister, C., R. Nord, and D. Soni. 2000. *Applied Software Architecture*. Boston: Addison-Wesley.

IEEE Standard Glossary of Software Engineering Terminology, 1990, IEEE/Std 610.12-1990, Institute of Electrical and Electronic Engineers.

Jackson, M. 1983. *System Development*. Upper Saddle River, NJ: Prentice Hall.

Jacobson, I. 1992. *Object-Oriented Software Engineering: A Use Case Driven Approach*. Reading, MA: Addison-Wesley.

Jacobson, I., G. Booch, and J. Rumbaugh. 1999. *The Unified Software Development Process*. Reading, MA: Addison-Wesley.

Jacobson, I., M. Griss, and P. Jonsson. 1997. *Software Reuse: Architecture, Process and Organization for Business Success*. Reading, MA: Addison-Wesley.

Jacobson, I., and P. W. Ng. 2005. *Aspect-Oriented Software Development with Use Cases*. Boston, MA: Addison-Wesley.

Jazayeri, M., A. Ran, and P. Van Der Linden. 2000. *Software Architecture for Product Families: Principles and Practice*. Boston: Addison-Wesley.

Kang, K., S. Cohen, J. Hess, et al. 1990. *Feature-Oriented Domain Analysis (FODA) Feasibility Study* (Technical Report No. CMU/SEI-90-TR-021). Pittsburgh, PA: Software Engineering Institute.

Kobryn, C. 1999. "UML 2001: A Standardization Odyssey." *Communications of the ACM* 42(10): 29–37.

M. Kim, S. Kim, S. Park, et al. "Service Robot for the Elderly: Software Development with the COMET/UML Method." *IEEE Robotics and Automation Magazine*, March 2009.

Kramer, J., and J. Magee. 1985. "Dynamic Configuration for Distributed Systems." *IEEE Transactions on Software Engineering* 11(4): 424–436.

Kroll, P., and P. Kruchten. 2003. *The Rational Unified Process Made Easy: A Practitioner's Guide to the RUP*. Boston: Addison-Wesley.

Kruchten, P. 2003. *The Rational Unified Process: An Introduction*, 3rd ed. Boston: Addison-Wesley.

Larman, C. 2004. *Applying UML and Patterns*, 3rd ed. Boston: Prentice Hall.

Liskov, B., and J. Guttag. 2000. *Program Development in Java: Abstraction, Specification, and Object-Oriented Design*. Boston: Addison-Wesley.

Lea, D. 2000. *Concurrent Programming in Java: Design Principles and Patterns*, 2nd ed. Boston: Addison-Wesley.

Magee, J., and J. Kramer. 2006. *Concurrency: State Models & Java Programs*, 2nd ed. Chichester, England: Wiley.

Magee, J., N. Dulay, and J. Kramer. 1994. "Regis: A Constructive Development Environment for Parallel and Distributed Programs." *Journal of Distributed Systems Engineering* 1(5): 304–312.

Magee, J., J. Kramer, and M. Sloman. 1989. "Constructing Distributed Systems in Conic." *IEEE Transactions on Software Engineering* 15(6): 663–675.

Malek, S., N. Esfahani, D. A. Menascé, et al. 2009. "Self-Architecting Software Systems (SASSY) from QoS-Annotated Activity Models." In *Proceedings Workshop on Principles of Engineering Service-Oriented Systems (PESOS), Vancouver, Canada, May 2009.*

McComas, D., S. Leake, M. Stark, et al. 2000. "Addressing Variability in a Guidance, Navigation, and Control Flight Software Product Line." In *Software Product Lines: Experience and Research Directions: Proceedings of the First Software Product Lines Conference (SPLC1), August 28–31, 2000, Denver, Colorado*, P. Donohoe (ed.), pp. 1–11. Boston: Kluwer Academic.

Menascé, D. A., V. Almeida, and L. Dowdy. 2004. *Performance by Design: Computer Capacity Planning By Example.* Upper Saddle River, NJ: Prentice Hall.

Menascé, D. A., and H. Gomaa. 1998. "On a Language Based Method for Software Performance Engineering of Client/Server Systems." In *First International Workshop on Software Performance Engineering, Santa Fe, New Mexico, October 12–16, 1998*, pp. 63–69. New York: ACM Press.

Menascé, D. A., and H. Gomaa. 2000. "A Method for Design and Performance Modeling of Client/Server Systems." *IEEE Transactions on Software Engineering* 26: 1066–1085.

Menascé, D. A., H. Gomaa, and L. Kerschberg. 1995. "A Performance-Oriented Design Methodology for Large-Scale Distributed Data Intensive Information Systems." In *First IEEE International Conference on Engineering of Complex Computer Systems, Held Jointly with 5th CSESAW, 3rd IEEE RTAW, and 20th IFAC/IFIP WRTP: Proceedings, Ft. Lauderdale, Florida, USA, November 6–10, 1995*, pp. 72–79. Los Alamitos, CA: IEEE Computer Society Press.

Meyer, B. 1989. "Reusability: The Case for Object-Oriented Design." In *Software Reusability*, vol. 2: *Applications and Experience*, T. J. Biggerstaff and A. J. Perlis (eds.), pp. 1–33. New York: ACM Press.

Meyer, B. 2000. *Object-Oriented Software Construction*, 2nd ed. Upper Saddle River, NJ: Prentice Hall.

Mills, K., and H. Gomaa. 1996. "A Knowledge-Based Approach for Automating a Design Method for Concurrent and Real-Time Systems." In *Proceedings of the 8th International Conference on Software Engineering and Knowledge Engineering*, pp. 529–536. Skokie, IL: Knowledge Systems Institute.

Mills, K., and H. Gomaa. 2002. "Knowledge-Based Automation of a Design Method for Concurrent and Real-Time Systems." *IEEE Transactions on Software Engineering* 28(3): 228–255.

Morisio, M., G. H. Travassos, and M. E. Stark. 2000. "Extending UML to Support Domain Analysis." In *15th International Conference on Automated Software Engineering 2000*, pp. 321–324. Los Alamitos, CA: IEEE Computer Society Press.

Mowbray, T., and W. Ruh. 1997. *Inside CORBA: Distributed Object Standards and Applications.* Reading, MA: Addison-Wesley.

Olimpiew, E., and H. Homaa. 2009. "Reusable Model-Based Testing", In *Proceedings 11th International Conference on Software Reuse, Falls Church, VA, September 2009*, Berlin: Springer LNCS 5791, pp. 76–85.

Orfali, R., and D. Harkey. 1998. *Client/Server Survival Guide*, 2nd ed. New York: Wiley.

Orfali, R., D. Harkey, and J. Edwards. 1996. *Essential Distributed Objects Survival Guide.* New York: Wiley.

Orfali, R., D. Harkey, and J. Edwards. 1999. *Essential Client/Server Survival Guide*, 3rd ed. New York: Wiley.

Page-Jones, M. 2000. *Fundamentals of Object-Oriented Design in UML*. Boston: Addison-Wesley.

Parnas, D. 1972. "On the Criteria to Be Used in Decomposing a System into Modules." *Communications of the ACM* 15: 1053–1058.

Parnas, D. 1974. "On a 'Buzzword': Hierarchical Structure." In *Proceedings of IFIP Congress 74, Stockholm, Sweden*, pp. 336–339. Amsterdam: North Holland.

Parnas, D. 1979. "Designing Software for Ease of Extension and Contraction." *IEEE Transactions on Software Engineering* 5(2): 128–138.

Parnas, D., and D. Weiss. 1985. "Active Design Reviews: Principles and Practices." In *Proceedings, 8th International Conference on Software Engineering, August 28–30, 1985, London, UK*, pp. 132–136. Los Alamitos, CA: IEEE Computer Society Press.

Parnas, D., P. Clements, and D. Weiss. 1984. "The Modular Structure of Complex Systems." In *Proceedings of the 7th International Conference on Software Engineering, March 26–29, 1984, Orlando, Florida*, pp. 408–419. Los Alamitos, CA: IEEE Computer Society Press.

Pettit, R., and H. Gomaa. 2006. "Modeling Behavioral Design Patterns of Concurrent Objects." In *Proceedings of the IEEE International Conference on Software Engineering, May 2006, Shanghai, China*. Los Alamitos, CA: IEEE Computer Society Press.

Pettit, R., and H. Gomaa. 2007. "Analyzing Behavior of Concurrent Software Designs for Embedded Systems." In *Proceedings of the 10th IEEE International Symposium on Object and Component-Oriented Real-Time Distributed Computing, Santorini Island, Greece, May 2007*.

Pitt, J., M. Anderton, and R. J. Cunningham. 1996. "Normalized Interactions between Autonomous Agents: A Case Study in Inter-Organizational Project Management." *Computer Supported Cooperative Work: The Journal of Collaborative Computing* 5: 201–222.

Pree, W., and E. Gamma. 1995. *Design Patterns for Object-Oriented Software Development*. Reading, MA: Addison-Wesley.

Pressman, R. 2009. *Software Engineering: A Practitioner's Approach*, 7th ed. New York: McGraw-Hill.

Prieto-Diaz, R. 1987. "Domain Analysis for Reusability." In *Compsac '87: Eleventh International Computer Software and Applications Conference Proceedings*, pp. 23–29. Los Alamitos, CA: IEEE Computer Society Press.

Prieto-Diaz, R., and P. Freeman. 1987. "Classifying Software for Reusability." *IEEE Software* 4(1): 6–16.

Pyster, A. 1990. "The Synthesis Process for Software Development." In *Systems and Software Requirements Engineering*, R. J. Thayer and M. Dorfman (eds.), pp. 528–538. Los Alamitos, CA: IEEE Computer Society Press.

Quatrani, T. 2003. *Visual Modeling with Rational Rose 2002 and UML*. Boston: Addison-Wesley.

Rosenberg, D., and K. Scott. 1999. *Use Case Driven Object Modeling with UML: A Practical Approach*. Reading, MA: Addison-Wesley.

Rumbaugh, J., M. Blaha, W. Premerlani, et al. 1991. *Object-Oriented Modeling and Design*. Upper Saddle River, NJ: Prentice Hall.

Rumbaugh, J., G. Booch, and I. Jacobson. 2005. *The Unified Modeling Language Reference Manual*, 2nd ed. Boston: Addison-Wesley.

Schmidt, D., M. Stal, H. Rohnert, et al. 2000. *Pattern-Oriented Software Architecture*, vol. 2: *Patterns for Concurrent and Networked Objects*. Chichester, England: Wiley.

Schneider, G., and J. P. Winters. 2001. *Applying Use Cases: A Practical Guide*, 2nd ed. Boston: Addison-Wesley.

Selic, B. 1999. "Turning Clockwise: Using UML in the Real-Time Domain." *Communications of the ACM* 42(10): 46–54.

Selic, B., G. Gullekson, and P. Ward. 1994. *Real-Time Object-Oriented Modeling*. New York: Wiley.

Shan, Y. P., and R. H. Earle. 1998. *Enterprise Computing with Objects*. Reading, MA: Addison-Wesley.

Shaw, M., and D. Garlan. 1996. *Software Architecture: Perspectives on an Emerging Discipline*. Upper Saddle River, NJ: Prentice Hall.

Shlaer, S., and S. Mellor. 1988. *Object-Oriented Systems Analysis*. Upper Saddle River, NJ: Prentice Hall.

Shlaer, S., and S. Mellor. 1992. *Object Lifecycles: Modeling the World in States*. Upper Saddle River, NJ: Prentice Hall.

Silberschatz, A., P. Galvin, and G. Gagne. 2008. *Operating System Concepts*, 8th ed. New York: Wiley.

Silberschatz, A., H. F. Korth, and S. Sudarshan. 2010. *Database System Concepts*, 6th ed. Boston: McGraw Hill.

Smith, C. U. 1990. *Performance Engineering of Software Systems*. Reading, MA: Addison-Wesley.

Sommerville, I. 2010. *Software Engineering*, 9th ed. Boston: Addison-Wesley.

Stevens, P., and R. Pooley. 2000. *Using UML: Software Engineering with Objects and Components*, updated ed. New York: Addison-Wesley.

Street, J., and H. Gomaa, 2008. "Software Architectural Reuse Issues in Service-Oriented Architectures." In *Proceedings Hawaii International Conference on System Sciences, Hawaii, January 2008*.

Szyperski, C. 2003. *Component Software: Beyond Object-Oriented Programming*, 2nd ed. Boston: Addison-Wesley.

Tanenbaum, A. S. 2003. *Computer Networks*, 4th ed. Upper Saddle River, NJ: Prentice Hall.

Tanenbaum, A. S. 2008. *Modern Operating Systems*, 3rd ed. Upper Saddle River, NJ: Prentice Hall.

Tanenbaum, A. S., and M. Van Steen. 2006. *Distributed Systems: Principles and Paradigms*, 2nd ed. Upper Saddle River, NJ: Prentice Hall.

Taylor, R. N., N. Medvidovic, and E. M. Dashofy. 2009. *Software Architecture: Foundations, Theory, and Practice*. New York: Wiley.

Texel, P., and C. Williams. 1997. *Use Cases Combined with Booch/OMT/UML: Process and Products*. Upper Saddle River, NJ: Prentice Hall.

Warmer, J., and A. Kleppe. 1999. *The Object Constraint Language: Precise Modeling with UML*. Reading, MA: Addison-Wesley.

Webber, D., and H. Gomaa. 2004. "Modeling Variability in Software Product Lines with the Variation Point Model." *Journal of Science of Computer Programming* 53(3): 305–331.

Weiss, D., and C. T. R. Lai. 1999. *Software Product-Line Engineering: A Family-Based Software Development Process*. Reading, MA: Addison-Wesley.

Wirfs-Brock, R., B. Wilkerson, and L. Wiener. 1990. *Designing Object-Oriented Software*. Upper Saddle River, NJ: Prentice Hall.

Index

abstract
  class, 241
  data type, 46
  operation, 241
acceptance testing, 43
ACID transaction properties, 286
action, 20, 158
  entry, 160
  exit, 161
  transition, 158
active object, 21, 53
activity diagram, 89
actor, 76
  external system, 77
  human, 77
  input device, 77
  primary, 76
  secondary, 76
  timer, 77
aggregate subsystem, 217
aggregation
  hierarchy, 101
  relationship, 17, 101
algorithm
  class, 232
  object, 128
analysis modeling, 63, 349
application
  deployment, 314
  logic object, 118, 127
architectural
  communication patterns, 258
  design, 41
association, 16, 95
  class, 100, 271
  many-to-many, 97
  multiplicity of, 96
  numerically specified, 96
  one-to-many, 96
  one-to-one, 96
  optional, 96
  ternary, 99

  unary, 99
asynchronous message communication, 56, 227, 334
  Pattern, 201
  with Callback pattern, 259
atomic, 285
attribute, 47, 113
autonomy, 308
availability, 366

base use case, 82
black box testing, 64
boundary
  class, 118, 119
  object, 119
Broadcast Message Communication Pattern, 310
Broker
  Forwarding Pattern, 280
  Handle Pattern, 282
  pattern, 280
business logic
  class, 232, 239
  object, 127

Call/Return pattern, 201
callback, 266
categorization of classes, 107, 116
Centralized Control Architectural Pattern, 320
choreography, 294
class, 46
  design, 231–239
  diagram, 16, 95
  hierarchies, 52, 239
  interface specification, 245
  operations, 232–234
  structuring, 117
  structuring criteria, 116
client subsystem, 221
client/server
  architecture, 254
  configuration, 260
  systems, 253